PENGUIN BOOKS

FRIENDS DIVIDED

Gordon S. Wood is the Alva O. Way University Professor and Professor of History Emeritus at Brown University. His books have received the Pulitzer, Bancroft, and John H. Dunning prizes, as well as a National Book Award nomination and the New York Historical Society Prize in American History. They include *Empire of Liberty: A History of the Early Republic*, *Revolutionary Characters*, *The Purpose of the Past*, *The Americanization of Benjamin Franklin*, and *The Idea of America*. In 2010, he was awarded the National Humanities Medal by President Barack Obama.

———

Praise for *Friends Divided*

One of *The New York Times Book Review*'s Notable Books of 2017
One of *The Wall Street Journal*'s Best Books of 2017

"This is an engrossing story, which Wood tells with a mastery of detail and a modern plainness of expression that makes a refreshing contrast with the eighteenth-century locutions of his subjects."
—*The New York Times Book Review*

"Lucid and learned . . . Wood has become the leading historian of the 'Founding Fathers.' . . . Never has John Adams been more relevant than today."
—*The Wall Street Journal*

"Whenever I read Gordon Wood, the dean of eighteenth-century American historians, I feel as if I am absorbing wisdom at the feet of the master. *Friends Divided* is teeming with exceptionally acute and unvarnished insights into Thomas Jefferson and John Adams as they do battle for the nation's soul. Jefferson's sunny, almost Panglossian, optimism, juxtaposed with the dark, dyspeptic musings of Adams, presents readers with nothing less than a vivid composite portrait of the American mind."
—Ron Chernow, author of *Grant* and *Alexander Hamilton*

"This magisterial double biography recounts not only the lives of these two greatest founders but also the creation of the republic. It describes the world's first successful democratic revolution and the founding of the first non-monarchical republic. . . . It is a book about ideas as represented by two philosophical statesmen, and it makes political history and philosophy exciting. . . . In Wood's hands, Adams and Jefferson become Shakespearean in stature." —Edith B. Gelles, *The Washington Post*

"Excellent . . . *Friends Divided* is an engaging book that's sure to appeal to anyone with an abiding interest in Revolution-era America and the leaders who shaped the country. Beautifully written and with real insight into Jefferson and Adams, it's a worthy addition to the canon, and yet another compelling book from Wood." —*NPR*

"For decades now Gordon S. Wood, the Alva O. Way university professor of history at Brown and winner of the Pulitzer Prize, has been the go-to authority on everything related to the American Revolution. That Wood has written *Friends Divided*—a finely-crafted dual biography of Adams and Jefferson—is therefore a hearty cause for celebration. Every page sparkles with literary eloquence, flawless analysis, and dramatically plotted history that contains a lesson for a riven time." —Douglas Brinkley, *The Boston Globe*

"Gordon Wood is one of America's premier historians and a national treasure. Winner of the Pulitzer as well as the Bancroft Prize, he is a rare scholar who writes with a combination of insight, academic depth, and accessible prose. In his latest book, penned at the summit of his career, Wood now sets his sights on the relationship of two of America's most remarkable and fascinating statesmen, Thomas Jefferson and John Adams. The story is enthralling. . . . In this magnificent book, Gordon Wood has continued his invaluable work." —Jay Winik, *National Review*

"In *Friends Divided*, Gordon S. Wood, a professor at Brown University and our finest historian of eighteenth-century America, provides a splendid account of the improbable friendship, estrangement, and reconciliation between Adams, an irascible, ironic, hypersensitive middle-class New England lawyer, and Jefferson, a self-contained, diplomatic, slave-holding Virginia aristocrat." —*Minneapolis Star Tribune*

JOHN ADAMS

— and —

THOMAS JEFFERSON

FRIENDS DIVIDED

GORDON S. WOOD

PENGUIN BOOKS

To the editors of the *Papers of John Adams* and
The Papers of Thomas Jefferson

PENGUIN BOOKS
An imprint of Penguin Random House LLC
375 Hudson Street
New York, New York 10014
penguinrandomhouse.com

First published in the United States of America by Penguin Press,
an imprint of Penguin Random House LLC 2017
Published in Penguin Books 2018

Illustration credits
Insert page 1 (top): Massachusetts Historical Society, Boston, Mass., USA/Bridgeman Images;
6 (top): Print Collection, Miriam and Ira D. Wallach Division of Art, Prints, and Photographs,
The New York Public Library, Astor, Lenox, and Tilden Foundations;
6 (bottom): Martin Falbisoner / Wikimedia Commons / CC BY-SA 3.0;
9: Courtesy National Gallery of Art, Washington.

ISBN 9780735224735 (paperback)

THE LIBRARY OF CONGRESS HAS CATALOGED THE HARDCOVER EDITION AS FOLLOWS:
Name: Wood, Gordon S., author.
Title: Friends divided : John Adams and Thomas Jefferson / Gordon S. Wood.
Description: New York : Penguin Press, 2017.
Identifiers: LCCN 2017025116 (print) | LCCN 2017027494 (ebook) |
ISBN 9780735224728 (ebook) | ISBN 9780735224711 (hardback)
Subjects: LCSH: Jefferson, Thomas, 1743–1826—Friends and associates. |
Adams, John, 1735–1826—Friends and associates. | Presidents—United
States—Biography. | Founding Fathers of the United States—Biography. |
United States—Politics and government—1775–1783. | United States—Politics
and government—1783–1809. | BISAC: HISTORY / United States /
Revolutionary Period (1775–1800). | BIOGRAPHY & AUTOBIOGRAPHY /
Political. | POLITICAL SCIENCE / Government / General.
Classification: LCC E332.2 (ebook) | LCC E332.2 .W65 2017 (print) |
DDC 973.3092/2—dc23
LC record available at https://lccn.loc.gov/2017025116

Printed in the United States of America
1 3 5 7 9 10 8 6 4 2

Designed by Marysarah Quinn

CONTENTS

—

PROLOGUE: The Eulogies ✦ 1

ONE: Contrasts ✦ 7

TWO: Careers, Wives, and Other Women ✦ 38

THREE: The Imperial Crisis ✦ 69

FOUR: Independence ✦ 103

FIVE: Missions Abroad ✦ 137

SIX: Constitutions ✦ 167

SEVEN: The French Revolution ✦ 204

EIGHT: Federalists and Republicans ✦ 240

NINE: The President vs. the Vice President ✦ 279

TEN: The Jeffersonian Revolution of 1800 ✦ 320

ELEVEN: Reconciliation ✦ 356

TWELVE: The Great Reversal ✦ 389

EPILOGUE: The National Jubilee ✦ 426

ACKNOWLEDGMENTS ✦ 435

NOTES ✦ 437

INDEX ✦ 485

THE EULOGIES

T HEY DIED ON THE SAME DAY. And it was no ordinary day. It was the Fourth of July, 1826, exactly fifty years from the date the Continental Congress approved the Declaration of Independence. This, "our fiftieth anniversary," as Daniel Webster exclaimed, was "the great day of National Jubilee."[1]

Webster's two-hour eulogy, delivered in Boston on August 2, 1826, was only one of hundreds presented over the months following the deaths of John Adams and Thomas Jefferson. All the eulogies expressed awe and wonder at this "singular occurrence." "For one such man to die on such a day," said Caleb Cushing, a member of the Massachusetts legislature, at Newburyport on July 15, "would have been an event never to be forgotten." But for both these "glorious founders" to die on that same special day—that was beyond coincidence. "The mathematician was calculating the chance of such a death," declared the quirky writer and editor of the *Boston Commercial Gazette*, Samuel L. Knapp, "the superstitious viewed it as miraculous, and the judicious saw in the event the hand of that Providence, without whose notice *not a sparrow falls to the ground.*"[2] Up and down the continent people sought to draw "moral instruction" from the death of the two greatest surviving revolutionary leaders, these "twin sons of Liberty," as Maryland senator Samuel Smith called them in Baltimore, on such a memorable anniversary. In a lengthy and high-praised eulogy presented to Congress in October 1826, Attorney General William Wirt emphasized how the former political enemies had come together as friends in the last years of their lives. Their final friendship, he said, "reads a lesson of wisdom on the bitterness of party spirit, by which the wise and good will not fail to profit."[3]

Nearly all the eulogists compared the personalities and talents of the two men. Adams was praised for "his hearty frankness, his vivacity and the dignified simplicity of his deportment." He was "a man of robust intellect and of marked feelings." He possessed an "ardent temperament . . . marked by great fervor and great strength," which sometimes became "rapid almost to precipitancy," yet always "immovably fixed in its purposes."[4] By contrast, "Jefferson," said Samuel Knapp, "was shrewd, quick, philosophical and excursive in his views, and kept at all times such a command over his temper, that no one could discover the workings of his soul."[5]

The writings of each were different. Adams's compositions, declared the eulogies, were marked by dignity and energy and Roman power, Jefferson's by grace and refinement and Grecian elegance. Jefferson, said young Caleb Cushing, "wears something of the manner of one whose natural talents were assiduously cultivated in the closet, although still with a view to public usefulness; and therefore his writings indicated more originality, are of a more speculative cast, and more visibly traced with the footsteps of solitary investigation." By contrast, Adams "shows you in every sentence, that his understanding, although richly stored by retired study, was yet trained by the severe discipline of extensive practice at the bar, and active exertion in popular assemblies; and had thus acquired more the habit of prompt and vigorous action, of decisive practical views."[6]

Samuel Knapp claimed that the two men had different modes of thinking. "Adams grasped at facts drawn from practical life, and instantly reasoned upon them. Jefferson saw man and his nature through generalities, and formed his opinions from philosophical inductions of a more theoretical cast." Their compositions exuded different tones. "In the writings of Adams you sometimes find the abruptness and singularity of the language of prophecy; in those of Jefferson, the sweet wanderings of the descriptive, and the lovely creations of the inventive muse."[7]

Despite these differences, however, the careers of the two men, as many of the eulogists noted, were extraordinarily similar. Both were trained as lawyers. Both were leading politicians in their respective colonial assemblies. They represented the two oldest of the colonies, Virginia and Massachusetts, and both these colonies took the lead in opposing the actions of Great Britain. Both were ardent revolutionaries. Both served in the Continental Congress and on the committee that drafted the Declaration of Independence, "and one of them wrote what the other proposed and defended." Both became ministers abroad, one in France, the other in England. Both wrote important and influential works. Both became vice president and president of the United States. And most marvelous of all, although "they were rival leaders of the two great parties which divided the nation," in retirement the two patriarchs set aside their partisan differences and became reconciled in friendship. "What a train of curious coincidences," said Senator Smith of Maryland, "in the lives, the acts, and the deaths of these two great men."[8]

MOST OF THE EULOGISTS AGREED that the two patriots tended to complement each other and that both equally belonged in the American pantheon of heroes. Unlike traditional heroes, however, Adams and Jefferson were not military men. Both, said Caleb Cushing, were involved in "purer and nobler pursuits than the deadly trade of war." They were statesmen. "Theirs were the victories of mind," asserted Cushing; "their conquests were won by intellectual and moral energies alone." Neither man commanded armies, but more important, said William Wirt, they "commanded the master springs of the nation on which all its great political as well as military movements depended." They never fought battles, but they "formed and moved the great machinery of which battles were only a small, and, comparatively, trivial consequence."[9]

Lest this emphasis on the intellectual achievements of Adams and Jefferson detract from the glory of George Washington, several of the eulogists wanted it made clear that Washington remained "first in war, first in peace, and first in the hearts of his countrymen." Adams and Jefferson, said Cushing, were "second only to him in station, second only to him in the patriotic energies of souls created for the achievements of a nation's independence." Washington, declared Webster, "was in the clear upper sky," and "these two new stars have now joined the American constellation."[10]

DYING ON THE SAME DAY tended to give the two revolutionaries equal standing in the nation's consciousness, but this equality of eminence did not last. In fact, even some of the eulogists suggested that Jefferson possessed something that Adams lacked. Two of the southern speakers practically ignored Adams, revealing the sectional split that was already apparent. In Richmond the governor of Virginia and the future president, John Tyler, was fulsome in his adoration of Jefferson ("Who now shall set limits to his fame?"), but he mentioned Adams only briefly at the end of his oration. In Charleston, South Carolina, Associate Justice of the Supreme Court William Johnson, though he referred to the "two venerable Patriots" at the outset, actually invoked Adams's name only as one of the three diplomats in Europe negotiating commercial treaties. Instead, Johnson concentrated, rather ominously, on the "immortal JEFFERSON," the son of the South, whose spirit breathed "Beware" of all constitutional aggrandizement.[11]

Although most of the speakers tended to avoid Adams's controversial presidency, nearly everyone was happy to applaud Jefferson's presidency. Even the New England orators praised Jefferson's purchase of Louisiana, his defeat of the Barbary pirates, and his reelection in 1804 by a near unanimous vote. Indeed, the northerners were far more generous to Jefferson than the southerners were to Adams. Peleg Sprague, a member of the House of Representatives from Maine, extolled Jefferson for the ease of his manners and for a temperament that was always "constitutionally calm, circumspect, and philosophical." Jefferson impressed everyone. William Thornton, the architect of the U.S. Capitol, speaking in

Alexandria, said that the Virginian was endowed with "an extraordinary power of intense reflection—a spirit of profound and patient investigation—an acuteness in the discovery of truth, and a perspicuity in its development, of which the world has witnessed but few examples." Indeed, "nothing that was worth knowing, was indifferent to him."[12]

OVER THE PAST TWO CENTURIES or so, Jefferson's star has remained ascendant while Adams's seems to have virtually disappeared from the firmament. Despite being a slaveholder, Jefferson clearly and perhaps rightly has come to dominate America's historical memory. We are continually asking ourselves whether Jefferson still survives, or what is still living in the thought of Jefferson; and we quote him on every side of every major question in our history. No figure in our past has embodied so much of our heritage and so many of our hopes. Most Americans think of Jefferson much as America's first professional biographer, James Parton, did. "If Jefferson was wrong," wrote Parton in 1874, "America is wrong. If America is right, Jefferson was right."[13]

No one says that about Adams. Indeed, until recently few Americans paid much attention to Adams, and even now the two men command very different degrees of affection and attention as Founders. While Jefferson has hundreds if not thousands of books devoted to every aspect of his wide-ranging life, Adams has had relatively few works written about him, with many of these focused on his apparently archaic political theory. Jefferson's mountaintop home, Monticello, has become a World Heritage Site visited every year by hundreds of thousands of people from all over the world. By contrast, Adams's modest home in Quincy, Massachusetts, maintained by the National Park Service, is hard to get to and receives only a fraction of Monticello's visitors. Jefferson has a huge memorial dedicated to him located on the Tidal Basin just off the Mall in the nation's capital. Adams has no monument in Washington, and those who would like to erect one have struggled for nearly two decades without success.

In 1776 no American could have predicted that the reputations of Adams and Jefferson would so diverge. Indeed, at the time of independence Adams was the better known of the two. No one had contributed more to the movement for independence than he. Jefferson admired Adams and shared his passion for American rights and for American independence; and the two revolutionaries soon became good friends. During their missions abroad in the 1780s their friendship was enriched and deepened. Then the French Revolution and partisan politics of the 1790s strained their relationship. In 1796 Vice President Adams succeeded Washington as president, with Jefferson elected as vice president. Adams assumed that he, like Washington, would be reelected to a second term. When after a very bitter campaign in 1800 Jefferson defeated him for the presidency, Adams was humiliated, and the break between the former friends seemed irreparable.

But in 1812 as Adams's partisan passions faded, their earlier friendship was painstakingly restored, almost entirely through the efforts of Dr. Benjamin Rush. Rush admired both men and believed that the nation and posterity required the reconciliation of these two great patriot leaders. He considered Adams and Jefferson "as the North and South Poles of the American Revolution. Some talked, some wrote, and some fought to promote and establish it, but," he told Adams, "you and Mr. Jefferson *thought* for us all."[14] But alas, the two revolutionaries did not think alike.

Although the friendship was resumed in their retirement years, and the two friends exchanged dozens of warm and revealing letters with each other, the reconciliation was somewhat superficial. No doubt Adams and Jefferson had similar careers and no doubt they agreed on the rightness of resisting Great Britain and on the significance of the American Revolution. But despite all that the two patriot leaders shared and experienced together—and the many things they had in common are impressive—they remained divided in almost every fundamental way: in temperament, in their ideas of government, in their assumptions about human nature, in their notions of society, in their attitude toward religion, in their conception of America, indeed, in every single thing that mattered. Indeed, no two men who claimed to be friends were divided on so many crucial matters as Adams and Jefferson. What follows is the story of that divided friendship.

ONE

CONTRASTS

THE IRONIES AND PARADOXES expressed in the lives of these two Founders epitomize the strange and wondrous experience of the nation itself. Jefferson was an aristocratic Virginia planter, a well-connected slaveholder, a "patriarch," as he called himself, reared in a hierarchical slaveholding society. By contrast, Adams was middling-born in a Massachusetts society that was far more egalitarian than any society in the South. Adams had few connections outside of his town of Braintree, and his rise was due almost exclusively to merit. Yet Jefferson the slave-holding aristocrat emerged as the apostle of American democracy; he became the optimistic exponent of American equality and the promoter of the uniqueness of the nation and its special role in the world. Adams, on the other hand, became the representative of a crusty conservatism that emphasized the inequality and vice-ridden nature of American society, a man who believed that "Democracy will infallibly destroy all Civilization."[1] America, said Adams, was not unusual; it was not free from the sins of other societies. Jefferson told the American people what they wanted to hear—how exceptional they were. Adams told them what they needed to know—truths about themselves that were difficult to bear. Over the centuries Americans have tended to avoid Adams's message; they have much preferred to hear Jefferson's praise of their uniqueness.

The fundamental differences between the two men could often be subtle and slippery; other differences were more obvious and palpable. Jefferson was tall, perhaps six two or so, and lean, lanky, and gangling; he had a reddish freckled complexion, bright hazel eyes, and reddish blond hair, which he tended to wear unpowdered in a queue. He was careless of his dress and tended to wear what he wanted to wear, regardless of what was in style. He bowed to everyone he met and tended to talk with his arms folded, a sign of his reserved nature. In 1790 William Maclay, the caustic Scotch-Irish senator from western Pennsylvania, described the secretary of state in the new federal government as "a slender Man" whose "clothes seem too small for him" and whose "whole figure has a loose shackling Air." Jefferson tended to sit "in a lounging Manner on One hip, . . . with one of his shoulders elevated much above the other." To Maclay, who disliked anything that smacked of European court life, Jefferson affected a manner of "stiff Gentility, or lofty Gravity."[2]

In contrast to Jefferson, Adams was short, five seven or so, and stout; "by my Physical Constitution," he admitted, "I am but an ordinary Man." He had sharp blue eyes, and he often covered his thinning light brown hair with a wig. The acerbic Senator Maclay, who had few kind words for anyone in his journal, became increasingly contemptuous of Adams, the vice president in 1789 and thus president of the Senate. Adams, wrote Maclay, was a "Childish Man" with "a very silly Kind of laugh," who was usually wrapped up "in the Contemplation of his own importance." Whenever he looked at Adams presiding in his chair with his wig and small sword, Maclay said he could not "help thinking of a Monkey just put into Breeches."[3] There is no doubt that Adams could sometimes appear ridiculous in the eyes of others.

Although Jefferson was often hated and ridiculed in print by his political enemies, no one made fun of him in quite the way they did Adams. Jefferson possessed a dignity that Adams lacked; for many Jefferson was the model of an eighteenth-century gentleman—learned and genteel and possessing perfect self-control and serenity of spirit. His slave Madison Hemings recalled that Jefferson was the "quietist of men," who was "hardly ever known to get angry."[4]

Adams was certainly learned and could be genteel, but he lacked Jefferson's serenity of spirit. He was too excitable and too irascible for that. He never knew when to be reserved and silent, something Jefferson was skilled at. Indeed, Jefferson used his affability to keep people at a distance. Adams was just the opposite: familiarity bred his infectious amiability. In 1787 his Harvard classmate Jonathan Sewall, who had become a Loyalist, met Adams in London and was reminded of the appeal Adams had for him. "Adams," he told a judge back in Massachusetts, "has a heart formed for friendship, and susceptible of it's finest feelings; he is humane, generous, and open—warm to the friendly Attachments tho' perhaps rather implacable to those he thinks his enemies."[5]

Adams was high-strung and was never as relaxed and easygoing as Jefferson was in company. But once he felt at ease with someone he could be much more jovial and open than Jefferson, more familiar and more revealing of his feelings. As Sewall suggested, people who got to know him well found him utterly likable. His candor and his unvarnished honesty won their hearts. But these qualities of forthrightness did not work well in public. Adams never quite learned to tailor his remarks to his audience in the way Jefferson did. Consequently, he lacked Jefferson's suave and expert political skills.

BOTH MEN WERE CAUGHT UP in the currents of the Enlightenment. While Jefferson rode these currents and was exhilarated by the experience, Adams often resisted them and questioned their direction. Jefferson had few doubts about the future; indeed, perhaps more than any other American, Jefferson came to personify the eighteenth-century Enlightenment. He always dreamed of a new and better world to come; by contrast, Adams always had qualms and uncertainties about the future.

The difference came partly from their contrasting views of human nature. Jefferson was a moral idealist, a child of light. Humans, he believed, were basically good and good-hearted, guided by an instinctive moral sense. Only when people's good nature was perverted by outside forces, especially by the power and privilege of monarchical government, did they become bad. Adams also believed that people possessed an inner moral sense, which enabled them to distinguish between right and wrong, but he never had the confidence in it that Jefferson had. Adams may not have been a child of darkness, but he was not a child of light either. His conception of human nature was stained with a sense of sin inherited from his Puritan ancestors. But his bleak view of human nature and his irascibility were leavened by his often facetious joking, his droll stories, and his sense of the absurdity of things. By contrast, Jefferson was always much more serious about life. He never revealed much of a sense of humor, and when he did it was often so dry as to be barely felt.

Both Adams and Jefferson were extremely learned, and both were avid readers. As a teenager Adams "resolved never to be afraid to read any Book," however controversial, and that was true of Jefferson as well.[6] Although for both men the classics, law, and history dominated their reading, Adams seems to have enjoyed novels as well, especially in his retirement. He claimed to have "read all Sir Walter Scott's Novels as regularly as they appeared." He said that he had been "a Lover and a Reader of Romances all my Life. From Don Quixote and Gil Blas to the Scottish Chiefs and an hundred others."[7]

Jefferson was different. He admitted that fiction might occasionally be pleasurable, but he considered most novels to be "trash." He made some exceptions for moral tales, such as the didactic writings of Maria Edgeworth, but generally he believed the passion for novel reading was "a great obstacle to good education." It was a "poison" that "infects the mind, it destroys it's tone, and revolts it against wholesome reading." It resulted in "a bloated imagination, sickly judgment, and disgust toward all the real business of life."[8]

Learned as both men were, Adams never possessed Jefferson's breadth of knowledge. In fact, Jefferson had the most spacious and encyclopedic mind of any of his fellow Americans, including even Benjamin Franklin. He was interested in more things and knew more about more things than any other American. When he was abroad he traveled to more varied places in Europe than Adams ever did, and kept a detailed record of all that he had seen, especially of the many vineyards he visited. He amassed nearly seven thousand books and consulted them constantly; he wanted both his library and his mind to embrace virtually all of human knowledge, and he came as close to that embrace as an eighteenth-century American could. Every aspect of natural history and science fascinated him.

He knew about flowers, plants, birds, and animals, and had a passion for all facets of agriculture. He had a fascination for meteorology, archaeology, and the origins of the American Indians. He loved mathematics and sought to apply mathematical principles to almost everything, from coinage and weights and measures to the frequency of rebellions and the length of people's lives. He was an inveterate tinkerer and inventor and was constantly thinking of newer and better ways of doing things, whether it was plowing, the copying of handwriting, or measuring distances.

Machines and gadgets fascinated Jefferson. He was especially taken with the "orrery"—a working model of the universe—created by David Rittenhouse of Philadelphia. He concluded that Rittenhouse was one of America's three great geniuses, along with Washington and Franklin; he claimed that Rittenhouse "has exhibited as great a proof of mechanical genius as the world has ever produced."[9]

Jefferson also called himself "an enthusiast on the subject of the arts." He said music was "the favorite passion of my soul," and he became quite proficient playing the violin.[10] He loved to sing, even when he was alone, and apparently he had a fine clear voice. He was also passionate about architecture and became, according to one historian, "America's first great native-born architect."[11] As a young man he began making drawings of landscapes, gardens, and buildings, and over his lifetime he accumulated hundreds of these drawings. Nothing was more exciting to the young Virginian provincial than discovering the sixteenth-century Italian Andrea Palladio, whose *Four Books of Architecture* had long been familiar in Europe but was virtually unknown in America. Jefferson claimed that he would often stand for hours gazing at buildings that attracted him.

In the 1760s Jefferson pored through European art books and drew up ambitious lists of what experts considered the best paintings and sculptures in the world. When the earnest dilettante went abroad, he collected copies of some of these masterpieces and eventually installed a sizable collection of canvases, prints, medallions, and sculptures in his home.[12]

But even before he had gone to Europe he had developed an extraordinary reputation for the range of his knowledge and for the many talents he possessed. He was proud of his intellectual abilities. He claimed that he had learned Spanish by reading *Don Quixote* along with a grammar book on his nineteen-day voyage to Europe in 1784; "but," as John Quincy Adams commented on hearing Jefferson in 1804 describe this remarkable accomplishment, "Mr. Jefferson tells large stories." Indeed, said the young Adams, "you can never be an hour in this man's company without something of the marvelous."[13]

By the early 1780s Jefferson had become, as the French visitor the Marquis de Chastellux noted, "an American who, without having quitted his own country, is a Musician, Draftsman, Surveyor, Astronomer, Natural Philosopher, Jurist, and Statesman."[14]

ADAMS HAD LITTLE OF JEFFERSON'S fascination with gadgets and architecture, and he had none of Jefferson's interest in collecting paintings and sculptures and displaying them in his home. Late in life he told a French sculptor that he "would not give sixpence for a picture of Raphael or a statue of Phidias."[15] He had no interest in playing a musical instrument and never encouraged his children or grandchildren to have a taste for music. He advised one grandson to "renounce your Flute. If you must have Musick, get a fiddle."[16]

Yet Adams was far more sensuous than Jefferson, responding to works of art with more intensity. Indeed, Adams was the most sensuous of the Founders. He experienced the world with all his senses and reacted to it palpably. He felt everything directly and immediately, and he could express his feelings in the most vivid and powerful prose. Most impressive was his visual memory. He could recall objects he had seen—whether waxworks, gardens, or paintings—with incredible lucidity and accuracy. In 1779, while serving in Paris as one of the commissioners, he described to Henry Laurens in remarkably precise detail a painting by the Italian artist Francesco Casanova, *The Collapse of a Wooden Bridge*, which he had viewed in the gallery of the French foreign minister.[17] He even could call to mind paintings he had seen decades earlier, especially if the painting revealed a passion that obsessed him, as did a picture displaying jealousy among Jesus's disciples that he had seen in Antwerp during one of his missions abroad.[18]

Adams's sensuousness gave him an acute sense of the power of art. In fact, he said in 1777, insofar as America possessed the arts—"Painting, Sculpture, Statuary, and Poetry"—they ought to be enlisted on behalf of the American cause. Since people were not apt to be aroused by reason alone, Adams believed that the arts were needed to show to the world "the horrid deeds of our Enemies." "The public may be clearly convinced that a War is just, and yet, until their Passions are excited, will carry it languidly on."[19]

Yet at the same time, sensuous as he was, Adams was often alarmed by the effect of art on people. When he experienced the beauty of Paris—its gardens, its buildings, its statues, and its paintings—he was overwhelmed. But his Puritan sensibilities told him to beware of his own powerful feelings. Despite all the bewitching charms of Paris, he told his wife, Abigail, "it must be remembered there is every Thing here too, which can seduce, betray, deceive, deprave, corrupt and debauch." Adams was torn between the beauty of art and the corruption that he believed it represented. No wonder the Choice of Hercules, caught between a life of virtue and a life of sloth, became his favorite classical allegory.[20]

JEFFERSON HAD NONE OF ADAMS'S ambivalence in his approach to the arts. Although he recognized the role of the arts in promoting virtue, he seems to have had none of Adams's fears of their corrupting power. In fact, he regarded his countrymen as in such desperate need of refinement and cultivation that they could not have too much fine art; and consequently he became eager to introduce his fellow

Americans to the best and most enlightened aspects of European culture. His object, he said, was always "to improve the taste of my countrymen, to increase their reputation, to reconcile to them the respect of the
world, procure them it's praise."[21]

When Virginians in the 1780s realized that a statue of George Washington was needed for their state capitol, "there could be no question
raised," Jefferson wrote from Paris, "as to the Sculptor who should be
employed, the reputation of Monsr. [Jean-Antoine] Houdon of this city
being unrivalled in Europe." Washington was unwilling, as he told Jefferson, "to oppose my judgment to the taste of Connoisseurs," and thus
would accept having his statue done in whatever manner Jefferson
thought "decent and proper." He hoped, however, that instead of "the
garb of antiquity" there might be "some little deviation in favor" of a
modern costume. Fortunately, that turned out to be the case: Houdon
did the statue in Washington's military dress.

But two decades later tastes had changed. For a new commemorative
statue of Washington for the state capitol of North Carolina, Jefferson
now suggested "old [Antonio] Canove, of Rome," who, he claimed, "for
30 years, within my own knoledge, . . . had been considered by all Europe, as without a rival." The costume, however, was going to be different. Since Jefferson believed that "our boots & regimentals have a very
puny effect," he concluded that the modern dress that Houdon had once
favored was no longer fashionable. He was now "sure the artist and every
person of taste in Europe would be for the Roman" style—in a toga. In
everything—from scriptures to paintings, from gardening to poetry—
Jefferson wanted the latest in European taste.[22]

Despite all of his knowledge of the arts, there seems something forced
and affected about Jefferson's appreciation of them. Aside from music and
perhaps architecture, his response to the arts appears more intellectual,
more rational, more studied than sensuous. His knowledge came not from
experience but from books. And because he had more books than anyone
else, he took pride in knowing what others didn't know. Nothing pleased
him more than to draw up a list of books for a young person eager to learn
what was the best in the world. Even his fascination with the supposed

poet Ossian from the third century AD seems studied and strained. Although critics were accusing the presumed translator, James Macpherson, of fraud, of composing the poetry himself, Jefferson was convinced that "this rude bard of the North [was] the greatest poet that has ever existed." Maybe he reached this extraordinary judgment simply because Dr. William Small, Jefferson's beloved teacher in college and a classmate of Macpherson, had recommended Ossian to him. But despite the mounting evidence of Macpherson's duplicity, Jefferson continued to believe that Ossian was genuine.[23]

When Jefferson went to Europe, he was initially insecure about his taste for art and sought out advice about what paintings should be properly appreciated. When he returned to America, however, he had acquired enough confidence in his taste to see himself as a kind of impresario for the new nation, the connoisseur rescuing his countrymen from barbarism. Once he had acquired the best and finest of European culture, with his easy, genial manner he could graciously impress people with the extent of his knowledge and taste. Unlike Adams, however, he never bothered to describe his feelings about any of the masterpieces that he had had copied in Europe and had brought home to Virginia; it was enough to own them.[24]

ALTHOUGH ADAMS WAS VISUALLY SENSITIVE to works of art, they were never foremost in his thinking. As he explained to Abigail in 1780, it was "not indeed the fine Arts, which our Country requires." Since America was "a young Country, as yet simple and not far advanced in Luxury," it was "the mechanic Arts" that were most needed. Jefferson wanted the mechanic arts developed too, but he also believed that if America was to escape its barbarism, it had to acquire the arts and sciences without any delay whatsoever. By contrast, Adams thought it would take time—several generations at least. America first needed to defeat the British and get its governments in order before it could begin to acquire the arts and sciences. It was his duty to begin the process, "to study Politicks and War that my sons may have liberty to study Mathematicks and Philosophy . . . Geography, natural History, Naval

Architecture, navigation, Commerce, and Agriculture, in order to give their Children a right to study Painting, Poetry, Musick, Architecture, Statuary, Tapestry and Porcelaine."[25]

Because he saw the arts and sciences developing through several generations, Adams, unlike Jefferson, had little immediate interest in the natural sciences, mathematics, or meteorology; and he was not inclined to practice scientific agriculture on his farm in the way Jefferson tried to do.[26] In fact, the only science that truly fascinated Adams was the one he dedicated his life to—the "Divine Science of Politicks." He realized, as he told Benjamin Franklin, that this "Science of Government" was many centuries behind the other sciences; but since it was "the first in Importance," he hoped that eventually "it may overtake the rest, and that Mankind may find their Account in it."[27]

Perhaps because of their different sensibilities, the two men had different feelings about the role of religion in society. Jefferson was about as secular-minded on religious matters as eighteenth-century America allowed. Except for his many affirmations of religious freedom, he claimed that "I rarely permit myself to speak" on the subject of religion, and then "never but in a reasonable society," meaning only among friends who shared his derisive views of organized religion.[28] He had little or no emotional commitment to any religion and usually referred to the different religious faiths as "religious opinions," as if one could pick them up and discard them at will. Although both Jefferson and Adams denied the miracles of the Bible and the divinity of Christ, Adams always retained a respect for the religiosity of people that Jefferson never had; in fact, Jefferson tended in private company to mock religious feelings.

JEFFERSON AND ADAMS HAD DIFFERENT ranges of knowledge and different sensibilities, but what more than anything else distinguished the two patriots from each other were the backgrounds and environments in which they were raised. Both men knew this, and Jefferson actually voiced it when he told Adams that their differences of opinion about important matters were probably "produced by a difference of character in those among whom we live."[29]

The environments in which they were raised were profoundly different. Jefferson's Virginia was not only the oldest British colony in North America, but the largest in territory and the richest and most populous. In 1760 it had a population of 340,000. Most important, 40 percent of that population—136,000—constituted the labor force of black slaves.

Adams's Massachusetts was the second-oldest colony, and with a population on the eve of the Revolution of about 280,000, it was close to being the second most populous one, just behind Pennsylvania, with both far behind Virginia. Out of the Massachusetts population, fewer than 5,000 were African slaves. Nothing distinguished the societies of the two places from each other more than this fact.

Jefferson was raised and lived with slaves all around him. Slavery was woven into the fabric of Virginia life and could scarcely have been evaded. Jefferson's earliest memory, according to family lore, was being carried at age three or so on a pillow by a mounted slave from his father's home, Shadwell, in western Virginia to Tuckahoe, a Randolph plantation on the James River. Since the Randolphs were one of the most distinguished families in Virginia, by marrying Jane Randolph in 1742, Jefferson's father, Peter Jefferson, a surveyor and substantial planter, gained for his family extensive and influential connections that otherwise would not have been possible. Young Jefferson grew up in a privileged aristocratic world; and yet he tended to deny that he belonged to that world and indeed during the heady days of the Revolution he tried to change that world.

Virginia was largely rural, with very few towns. Its economy was dependent on production of a staple crop—tobacco—that had direct markets in Britain and that required a minimum of distribution and handling. This was why towns in Virginia were so few and far between. When on the eve of the Revolution some of the planters in the upper South turned to the production of wheat and other grains, which had diverse markets that required special handling and distribution centers, towns such as Norfolk and Baltimore suddenly emerged to market the grain. Still,

Virginia's society remained overwhelmingly rural and agricultural, dominated by slavery.

Although it was slavery more than anything else that separated Virginia from Massachusetts, Jefferson could at times be amazingly blind to that fact. He knew there were great differences between the people of the North and those in the South, but he attributed these differences mostly to differences of climate. In 1785 he outlined to a French friend his sense of the sectional differences. The northerners were "cool, sober, laborious, persevering, independent, jealous of their own liberties, and just to those of others, interested, chicaning, superstitious and hypocritical in their religion." By contrast, said Jefferson, the southerners were "fiery, voluptuary, indolent, unsteady, independent, zealous for their own liberties but trampling on those of others, generous, candid, [and] without attachment or pretensions to any religion but that of the heart." Jefferson implied that there was an intimate connection between the southerners' zeal for liberty and their capacity to trample on the liberty of others.[30]

By the end of their lives, the distinction between Adams's Massachusetts and Jefferson's Virginia had become ever more glaring. When Jefferson's granddaughter Ellen Randolph Coolidge moved north in 1825 with her husband, Joseph, she was immediately struck by the vast difference between New England and her native Virginia. She marveled at the "multitude of beautiful villages" in Adams's New England that stood in stark contrast to the depleted and unimproved rurality of her grandfather's Virginia, and she was amazed by the fecundity that the hardworking Yankee farmers had wrung from "the hard bosom of a stubborn and ungrateful land." For her the reason for the difference was obvious. The southern states, she told her grandfather, could not begin to match "the prosperity and the improvement" of the northern states "whilst the canker of slavery eats into their hearts, and diseases the whole body by this ulcer at the core."[31]

There were other contrasts between Virginia and Massachusetts. Virginia had no public school system resembling that of Massachusetts and its literacy rate was nowhere near that of Massachusetts, which had one of the most literate societies in the world. By the middle of the eighteenth century, 70 percent of males and 45 percent of females in Massachusetts were literate. Unlike colonial Virginia, the Massachusetts Bay Colony had no laws of primogeniture (by which the eldest son inherited the estate) and no laws of entail (by which the estate was kept in the stem line of the family). New Englanders prided themselves on the relative equality of their societies, which they believed flowed from their early abandonment of these aristocratic laws.

Although Massachusetts's economy, like Virginia's, was mainly agricultural, the colony had many more towns, especially on the seacoast and along the rivers. The bulk of the population was composed of middling farmers, most of whom traded with one another. Yet there was considerable overseas trade, both to Britain and elsewhere in Europe and to the other colonies and the West Indies. There was no single staple product; fish and rum probably came closest to playing that role. Artisans and mechanics existed everywhere and manufactured the tools and products that in Virginia were mainly made by slaves. Slavery was legal in colonial Massachusetts, but the province had relatively few slaves, perhaps comprising less than 2 percent of the population; and most of these were household servants in Boston and the other towns of the colony. However, many merchants in Massachusetts and in the other New England colonies were deeply involved in the slave trade, bringing blacks from Africa to the southern and Caribbean colonies.

Although slavery was not officially abolished in Massachusetts until 1784, well before independence it was already a dying institution in the colony; and the courts were reluctant to enforce it. Adams, recalling a case in 1766 in which an enslaved woman sued for her freedom and won, declared, "I never knew a Jury by a Verdict to determine a Negro to be a Slave—They always found them free."[32] Still, in the middle of the eighteenth century, one out of every five families in Boston owned at least one slave.[33] Although neither Adams nor his family ever owned any slaves, he later admitted that in colonial Massachusetts the owning of slaves "was not disgraceful," and "the best men in my Vicinity—thought it not inconsistent with their Characters."[34] His refusal to emulate them, he claimed, "cost me thousands of dollars for the Labour and

Subsistence of free men which I might have saved by the purchase of negroes in times when they were very Cheap."[35]

DIFFERENT AS THEY WERE, the colonial societies of Virginia and Massachusetts were still both hierarchies. Indeed, prior to the Revolution it was almost impossible to conceive of a civilized society not being a vertically organized hierarchy of some sort in which people were more aware of those above and below than of those alongside them. Everyone and everything could be located in the great chain of being and be made part of what Adams called the "regular and uniform Subordination of one Tribe to another down to the apparently insignificant animalcules in pepper Water."[36]

Jefferson certainly saw the society of colonial Virginia as a hierarchy. Later in his life William Wirt, who was writing a biography of Patrick Henry, asked Jefferson to describe the society he grew up in. In his response Jefferson emphasized the colonial society's insular and immobile character, the better to demonstrate the transformation that he believed he and the other revolutionaries had brought about. Colonial Virginia had been an utterly provincial society, he told Wirt, separated from both its sister colonies and the greater European world, and seldom visited by foreigners. It had experienced little social mobility. "Certain families had risen to splendor by wealth" and had preserved that wealth from generation to generation by the legal devices of primogeniture and entail. "Families in general had remained stationary on the grounds of their forefathers," because migration to the west had scarcely begun. Hostile Indians were still present on the other side of the mountains. In the mid-1760s parties of Indians attacked white settlements in the valley of Burke's Garden and wiped out entire households; as recently as 1768 the Cherokees and Shawnees had fought a ferocious two-day battle with each other near Rich Mountain in Tazewell County.[37] Prior to the Revolution, said Jefferson, only rough Scotch-Irish frontiersmen had moved into the valleys beyond the Blue Ridge, and few easterners had as yet chosen to settle among them.

This static hierarchical society, said Jefferson, was composed of "several strata, separated by no marked lines, but shading off imperceptibly, from top to bottom, nothing disturbing the order of their repose." At the top were the "aristocrats," whom Jefferson defined as "the great landholders who had seated themselves below the tide water on the main rivers." These would be the Randolphs, Lees, Carters, Byrds, and others—the families that came closest to emulating the English landed gentry. Only instead of tenants paying rents that supported the English landed gentry, the great Virginia planters possessed African slaves, hundreds of them on each of their plantations. Many of these great planters would lead the resistance against Great Britain. They were, as northern and British travelers often noted, "haughty and jealous of their liberties, impatient of restraint, and can scarcely bear the thought of being controlled by any superior power."[38]

Just below these great slaveholding planters, said Jefferson, were their descendants, their younger sons and daughters—"*half breeds*," Jefferson called them—who inherited the pride of their ancestors, without their wealth. Next came those whom Jefferson disdainfully labeled "the pretenders"—those "who from vanity, or the impulse of growing wealth, or from that enterprize which is natural to talents, sought to detach themselves from the plebeian ranks to which they properly belonged, and imitated, at some distance, the manners and habits of the great."

Jefferson's calling such men "pretenders" is surprising, since the republicanism of the Revolution presumably had justified such social mobility. Below the pretenders were those he always placed most trust in—the "solid and independent yeomanry" who, he said in his *Notes on the State of Virginia*, were free from the "casualties and caprice of customers." They were the stabilizing backbone of the society, "the chosen people of God, if ever he had a chosen people." They were more or less content with their middling status, "looking askance at those above them, yet not venturing to jostle them." At the bottom of this hierarchy, said Jefferson, were "a *feculum* of beings called Overseers, the most abject, degraded, unprincipled race, always cap in hand to the Dons who employed them, and furnishing materials for the exercise of their pride, insolence, and spirit of domination."[39]

Yet whom did these overseers oversee? In his description of Virginia's colonial society, Jefferson never mentioned the tens of thousands of black slaves who constituted nearly half of Virginia's population. He possessed hundreds of slaves himself; indeed, he became the second-largest slave-holder in Albemarle County and one of the largest slave owners in all of Virginia. In his eyes, however, it was as if the slaves were not part of Virginia's society at all.

But in some sense neither was he. In his social hierarchy he had no place for himself. Although he was in fact one of the "aristocrats," who, he said, "lived in a style of luxury and extravagance, insupportable by the other inhabitants," he did not want to be classed as such. But neither did he want to be a pretender or a half-breed. Although he sometimes saw himself as a western frontiersman with some of the qualities of an inde-pendent yeoman, he knew that given his wealth and status he could never really be that. And despite his admiration of the yeoman farmers, he himself had no natural affinity for farming, and later in his life he admit-ted as much, saying that he was "not fit to be a farmer with the kind of labour" that existed in Virginia. Tobacco was a major product of his plan-tations; nevertheless, he confessed in 1801 that he had never in his entire life seen a leaf of his tobacco packed in a hogshead.[40] By contrast, Adams may not have done much farming, but when he did he was much more hands-on than Jefferson—concerned, for example, with such matters as the proper mixture of constituents for the manure used for fertilizer.

In the 1790s, like other Virginia planters, Jefferson shifted from to-bacco production, which was depleting the land, to wheat. Since the production of wheat required only one-fifth the labor of tobacco, Jef-ferson was able to diversify and improve his plantation holdings. But his incompetence as a farmer hurt his transition to wheat production. His county had no mill large enough to handle all the wheat; by the time he built a mill complex on his Monticello plantation, it had taken years of hired labor and an enormous sum of money, and it never worked effi-ciently. Although corn was a staple of the diet of his slaves and livestock, he put all his land into wheat production and made no provision for growing corn; consequently, he ended up having to buy corn from his neighbors at high prices. Even his newly designed moldboard plow, which was supposed to save labor, cut the furrows in such a way as to aggravate the washing away of topsoil from the fields. His inadequacies as a farmer were graphically revealed when his grandson Thomas Jefferson Randolph took over management of the Monticello plantation in 1815 and tripled the yield of wheat.[41]

JEFFERSON MAY HAVE BEEN the patriarch of his self-contained extended family, both free and enslaved, but managing a successful and profitable plantation was never his greatest ambition. What he really wanted to be was the enlightened intellectual leader of his Virginia society, standing above it, superior to it, and reforming it.

Jefferson was born in 1743 at Shadwell on the wild edge of western settlement in Virginia. Although he became as cultivated as any eighteenth-century American, he always remained proud of his frontier origins. When Jefferson was only fourteen years old, his father died. Peter Jefferson's estate was not grand, but it was substantial—at least seventy-five hundred acres and over sixty slaves—of which his eldest son got his fair share. Jefferson was brought up by his mother's family, the socially prestigious Randolphs. Somehow or other, that Randolph experience made him question the benefits of inherited privilege. Jefferson scarcely mentions his mother in all his writings; by contrast, he tended to idolize his father as a hardy product of the wilderness.[42]

Both Jefferson and Adams wrote autobiographies, with Adams's being about four times longer than Jefferson's. Jefferson began his in 1821, at the age of seventy-seven. Although it is often perfunctory and not very revealing, beneath its placid surface one can detect Jefferson's restrained dislike of the dominant aristocracy of Virginia. He described his efforts in 1776 to bring down that "Patrician order, distinguished by the splendor and luxury of their establishments." No doubt he was thinking especially of the Randolphs. Perhaps his maternal grandmother had often corrected his teenage manners and blamed his uneducated father for the boy's rough edges. At any rate Jefferson came to value his frontier father—a man of "strong mind, sound judgment, and eager after information," a man who had "improved himself"—in a way that he did not value his refined Randolph mother, whose status was inherited. (Her death in 1776 produced the briefest of comments and that one was totally without sentiment.)[43] Jefferson came to believe that the privileges of this "aristocracy of wealth" needed to be destroyed in order "to make an opening for the aristocracy of virtue and talent," of which he considered himself a prime example.[44]

To us the wealthy slaveholding Jefferson does not seem all that different from the "Patrician order" he challenged, but he obviously saw a difference. In the opening pages of his autobiography, Jefferson tells us that the lineage of his Welsh father was lost in obscurity and he was able to find in the British records only a couple of references to his father's family. His mother, on the other hand, was a Randolph, one of the first families of Virginia. The Randolphs, he said with dry derision, "trace their pedigree far back in England & Scotland, to which let every one ascribe the faith & merit he chooses."[45]

ADAMS'S BACKGROUND WAS VERY DIFFERENT. He was born in 1735 in Braintree, Massachusetts, the eldest son of a substantial but nevertheless ungenteel farmer and shoemaker; in other words, despite his being a militia officer, a deacon in the local church, and a recently elected selectman of the town, his father remained one of what were called the "middling sort." Adams's mother, however, was a Boylston, a fairly distinguished family, which, like the Randolphs and Jefferson, gave Adams some social cachet. When he enrolled in Harvard in 1751, entering students were still ranked in accord with their "dignity of family." Because his mother was a Boylston and his father was a deacon in the Congregational Church, Adams was listed socially higher than he otherwise might have been—fourteenth out of twenty-five.

Like Jefferson, Adams admired his father more than his mother, not, as in Jefferson's case, for his rough manliness, but for his moral integrity and his selfless public virtue. "He was," said Adams, "the honestest Man I ever knew," and "in proportion to his Education and Sphere of Life, I have never seen his Superiour." Possessing a great "Admiration of Learning," his father was determined "to give his first son a liberal Education."[46]

As a boy Adams apparently had some doubts about attending college. In his autobiography, which he began writing in 1802 at age sixty-seven, he says that as a schoolboy he initially told his father to "lay aside the thoughts of sending me to Colledge." His father replied, "What would you do Child? Be a Farmer. A Farmer?" His father then proceeded to show exactly what it meant to be a farmer. He worked his son hard all one day at farming. That evening he asked young Adams what he thought of farming now. "Though the Labour had been very hard and very muddy I answered I like it very well Sir." His father responded, "Ay but I don't like it so well: so you shall go to School" and, as his eldest son, prepare for college. In 1751, the year he entered college, Adams began his personal library with a purchase of an edition of Cicero's orations.[47]

When Adams enrolled in Harvard, he also began keeping a diary. Keeping as full and honest a diary as he did was part of the inheritance passed on from his Puritan ancestors; but it was also an inevitable response to his acute self-awareness. None of his colleagues and in fact no American in the eighteenth century kept a diary like that of Adams. In it he poured out all his feelings—all his anxieties and ambitions, all his jealousies and resentments.

It is impossible to imagine Jefferson writing such a journal. Jefferson was always reserved and self-possessed and, unlike Adams, he scarcely ever revealed much of his inner self. Jefferson seemed to open up to no one, while Adams at times seemed to open up to everyone. He certainly opened up to his diary. "Honesty, Sincerity, and openness, I esteem essential marks of a good mind," he wrote, and once he got going his candid entries bore out that judgment.[48]

Adams used his diary to begin a lifelong struggle with what he often considered his unworthy pride and passions. "He is not a wise man and is unfit to fill any important Station in Society, that has left one Passion in his Soul unsubdued."[49] Like his seventeenth-century Puritan ancestors, he could not have success without guilt.

Although Adams was anything but an orthodox Puritan in his religious views, he often tormented himself in the early years of his diary as if he were one. And the kind of acute self-awareness that Adams had could lead to self-loathing. "Vanity, I am sensible, is my cardinal Vice and cardinal Folly," and he continually rebuked himself for it and sought to suppress it.[50] He confided in his diary all his feelings of self-conscious awkwardness. "I have not conversed enough with the World, to behave rightly," he confessed in January 1759, at age twenty-three. "I talk to [Robert Treat] Paine about Greek, that makes him laugh. I talk to Sam Quincy about Resolutions, and being a great Man, and study and improving Time, which makes him laugh. I talk to Ned [Quincy], about the Folly of affecting to a Heretick, which makes him mad. . . . Besides this I have insensibly fallen into a Habit of affecting Wit and Humour, of Shrugging my Shoulders, and moving [and] distorting the Muscles of my face. My Motions are stiff and uneasy, ungraceful, and my attention is unsteady and irregular." All these, he said, were "faults, Defects, Fopperies and follies, and Disadvantages. Can I mend these faults and supply these Defects?"[51]

Adams admonished himself for even the smallest expressions of vanity and self-conceit. "Oh," he said, "that I could wear out of my mind every mean and base affectation, conquer my natural Pride and Self Conceit, . . . acquire that meekness and humility, which are the sure marks and Characters of a great and generous Soul." Every social occasion called forth this self-conscious adolescent-like wincing and worrying, and he was in his midtwenties. Too often—in fact, "to a very heinous Degree"—he had tried to show off his learning, too often he had sought to make "a shining Figure in gay Company," and too often he had displayed "a childish Affectation of Wit and Gaiety." And all he ever did, he rued, was make a fool of himself. He reproached himself over and over and resolved to act more sensibly in the future—"Let it therefore be my constant endeavor to reform these great faults." Yet the self-criticism continued.[52]

. . .

JEFFERSON KEPT NO DIARY, and if he had, he would never have expressed any self-loathing in it. Instead of a diary, Jefferson kept records—records, it seems, of everything, with what he called "scrupulous fidelity."[53] He religiously recorded the weather, taking the temperature twice a day, once in the morning and again at four in the afternoon. He entered into memorandum books every financial transaction, every source of income and every expenditure, no matter how small or how large—seven pennies for chickens or thousands of dollars for a land sale. Unfortunately, he never added up his earnings and his expenses. Since his painstaking bookkeeping was not double entry, he never fully appreciated his overall financial situation. His daily and detailed record keeping gave him a false sense of control over his world that in the end played him false.[54]

He kept a variety of specialized books, including several commonplace books—a legal book, an equity book, and a literary book, in which he copied passages from his reading that he found important or interesting.[55] He also kept a case book and a fee book, for tracking work and income from his legal career as long as it lasted; a farm book, in which he entered, among other things, the births and sales of slaves as well as farm animals; and a garden book. In his garden book, he made such notations as how many peas he was planting would fill a pint measure, how much fodder a horse would eat in a night, and how many cucumbers fifty hills would yield in a season.

His habit of calculating everything even included the production of slaves. In a notorious letter in 1819 he told his steward to restrain the overseers from overworking the female slaves who were breeding children. "A child raised every 2 years is of more profit than the crop of the best laboring man." Although the labor of female slaves was important, it was, he said, "their increase which is the first consideration with us."[56]

WHEN ADAMS WENT OFF TO HARVARD, his father expected him to become a minister, which was what Deacon Adams believed an education at Harvard was all about. But young Adams knew that the liberal education he would receive at Harvard would do more than prepare him for a career. It would give the right to call himself a gentleman—a very important and distinctive status in the eighteenth century.

Both the societies of colonial Virginia and of colonial Massachusetts were vertically organized in hierarchies. There was, however, a horizontal division running through those hierarchical societies that was often more meaningful to people in the eighteenth century than the separation between free and slave that is so horrible to us today: that was the distinction between gentlemen and commoners.

In Virginia the distinction was there practically from birth. "Before a boy knows his right hand from his left, can discern black from white, or good from evil, who knows who made him, or how he exists, he is," declared one sardonic observer, "a Gentleman." And as a gentleman, "it would derogate greatly from his character, to learn a trade; or to put his hand to any servile employment."[57] Work, after all, was mean and despicable, as Aristotle and all of antiquity had said, and fit only for the lowly, which to the Virginian gentry meant African slaves.

In Virginia the great leisured gentry were few in numbers, constituting perhaps only 2 or 3 percent of the population. If there should be any doubt who the Virginia squires were, they had ways of displaying their presence among the common people. Only after their families and the ordinary people had been seated in the church on Sunday did the Virginia gentry enter as a body and tramp booted down the aisle to take their seats in their pews at the front; they exited the church in the same way, with women and ordinary folk waiting in their seats until the gentlemen had left.[58]

TO A NEW ENGLANDER LIKE ADAMS the South always seemed aristocratic, even though he had never been there. When he initially met the southern leaders in the Continental Congress, his prejudices were confirmed. The large slaveholding planters possessed an arrogant and patrician notion of themselves. Their separation from the common people, who were "very ignorant and very poor," was much greater than in New England.[59] Indeed, the southern aristocrats, claimed Adams, came close to thinking that the common people had distinct natures from themselves.

Adams actually feared that the South was so different from New England that unifying the sections in the cause of resisting British tyranny was going to be very difficult. But when Virginia and the other southern colonies began to draw up their new state constitutions in 1776, Adams expressed relief in seeing "the Pride of the Haughty" brought down "a little" by the revolutionary movement.[60]

COLONIAL NEW ENGLAND was obviously much more egalitarian than Virginia. The distinction between gentry and commoners was certainly less clear there, but it did exist, with perhaps 12 percent of the population designated as gentlemen.[61] Arthur Browne, an Anglican clergyman who lived in Newport, Boston, and Portsmouth, was sure that inequality had to exist everywhere, even in New England, which liked to pride itself on its lack of a nobility. The bigger New England towns, said Browne, were actually breeding grounds for gentlemen. Their inhabitants, by possessing "more information, better polish and greater intercourse with strangers, insensibly acquired an ascendency over the farmer of the country; the richer merchants of these towns, together with the clergy, lawyers, physicians and officers of the English navy who had occasionally settled there, were considered as gentry."[62]

Still, as Browne admitted, there was enough leveling and equality-mindedness in New England that the country folk sometimes mocked the gentry's pretensions to superiority. When General George Washington came to Massachusetts in the summer of 1775 to take command of the Continental Army, as a good Virginian militia officer he expected to find the soldiers paying due respect to their superiors. Instead, he found the opposite. The New Englanders—"an exceedingly dirty & nasty people," he called them—lacked all sense of discipline, order, and subordination. The problem, Washington realized, was that these New

Englanders had "from their Infancy imbibed Ideas of the most contrary Kind."[63] The "lower class of these people" was ignorant, and its members were full of themselves, which was not surprising since they even elected their militia officers. But the officers themselves were little better. They were, complained Washington, "nearly of the same Kidney with the Privates," often artisans and tradesmen and certainly not gentlemen. It was difficult if not impossible, he said, to get "Officers of this stamp to exert themselves in carrying orders into execution." Instead, they sought "to curry favour with the men (by whom they were chosen, & on whose Smiles possibly they may think they may again rely)." Most of the New England officers, he concluded, were "the most indifferent kind of People I ever saw."[64]

Although the division between gentleman and commoner may have been more difficult to sustain in New England, Adams always felt that he knew the difference. The distinction between "Yeoman and Gentleman," he said in 1761, was the "most ancient and universal of all Divisions of the People."[65] It persisted even in law. The colony's courts, for example, scrupulously sought to determine whether or not plaintiffs and defendants were properly identified as gentlemen. Adams especially knew when someone was not a gentleman. A person who springs "from ordinary Parents," who "can scarcely write his Name," whose "Business is Boating," who "never had any Commissions"—to call such a person a gentleman, he said in 1761, was "an arrant Prostitution of the Title."[66]

In fact, this distinction between gentlemen and ordinary folk was far more meaningful for Adams than it ever was for Jefferson, who took his gentry status for granted. Adams was always more self-conscious about this social cleavage, and he thought and talked about it all the time; indeed, this division between patricians and plebeians undergirded the political theory that he worked out over the course of his life.

Adams knew that ordinary individuals could become gentlemen, mainly by gaining enough wealth so they didn't have to work for a living. Adams noted, for example, that Philip Livingston of New York had once been "in Trade," but he became "rich, and now lives upon his Income."[67] But for Adams himself, who lacked that degree of wealth, it was his

Harvard degree that mattered. In his mind gentlemen were "all those who have received a liberal education, an ordinary degree of erudition in liberal arts and sciences."[68]

ALTHOUGH ADAMS ALWAYS divided society into two unequal parts—gentry-aristocrats and commoners—in the way most Virginians did, what really characterized his society of Massachusetts was the growing number of those who were called the "middling sort." These middling sorts, like Adams's farmer-shoemaker father, were middling because they could not easily be classified either as gentlemen or as out-and-out commoners. Yet because Adams's ideas of political science required that society be divided into two parts, he always classified the middling people as commoners.

In Adams's eyes and in the eyes of many others, these middling types could not be gentlemen, because they had occupations and worked for a living with their hands. Even artisans or mechanics who employed dozens of journeymen were regarded as something less than gentlemen. At the same time, however, these middling artisans, such as the successful Boston silversmith Paul Revere, were often too well off or too distinguished and knowledgeable to be placed among "the lower sort" or "the meaner sort." Indeed, many of these middling sorts were becoming quite well-to-do. Of the three thousand adult males in Boston in 1790, eighteen hundred, or 60 percent, made up this middling sort. Yet these artisans were not poor; they held 36 percent of the taxable wealth of the city and constituted the majority of its property holders. Although Revere the silversmith was wealthy and often moved in the highest circles of Massachusetts society, he remained an artisan; and despite his desperate desire to improve his status, he was never able to get the Massachusetts gentry to recognize him as one of them.[69]

From the beginning of the eighteenth century, thinkers like Daniel Defoe had tried to explain and justify these emerging middling people, including the "working trades, who labour hard but feel no want."[70] These well-to-do working people with property, like Benjamin Franklin as a young printer, increasingly had prided themselves on their separation from the idleness and dissipation shared by both the gentry above them and the propertyless poor beneath them. The middling sort combined work with the owning of a decent amount of property. This distinguished them, on the one hand, from the gentry who owned a good deal of property but did not engage in productive labor, at least not with their hands, and, on the other hand, from the wage earners who labored but owned very little if any property. These artisans, petty merchants, clerks, traders, and commercial farmers, who tended to dominate the towns of Massachusetts, were the beginnings of what would become the middle class of the nineteenth century.[71]

Although most yeoman farmers in Virginia were not big slaveholders or even slaveholders at all, most of them did not have the kind of middling consciousness that marked the commercial farmers and artisans of Massachusetts. They saw themselves as potential slaveholding planters, not as some middling stratum caught between the gentry and the slaves. Since slaves performed many of the tasks that artisans and craftsmen in Massachusetts did, a middling population and middling consciousness were slow to develop in the South. Although Jefferson often hired white supervisors on his plantation, most of the skilled workers—blacksmiths, coopers, carpenters, painters, nail- and textile-makers, charcoal burners, and other craftsmen—were black slaves. Compared with New England, the colonial South had virtually little or no middle class. In the end this made all the difference.

PRECISELY BECAUSE OF his middling origins, Adams was always keenly aware of the aristocrats of Massachusetts. Just as Virginia had its first families of Carters, Lees, Byrds, and Randolphs, so too did colonial Massachusetts, as Adams noted, have its grand families of Winslows, Hutchinsons, Saltonstals, Leonards, and others.[72] But Adams's reaction to these families and their pretensions was different from Jefferson's response to the great families of Virginia. Although both men saw themselves as outsiders in their respective societies, their positions were very different. Jefferson was thoroughly one of the Virginia aristocrats and confidently criticized his peers from a position of intellectual and cultural superiority. Adams, by contrast, never felt himself to be fully part of the Massachusetts aristocracy and thus came to criticize it ambivalently from a position of social inferiority.

Moving originally on the edges of the genteel Boston world, he was awed by the wealth, sophistication, and elegance that he witnessed. When he dined in 1766 at the home of the wealthy merchant and future Loyalist Nicholas Boylston, his distant relative, he was overwhelmed. Such a dinner! Such a house! Such furniture, "which alone cost a thousand Pounds sterling." Boylston's home, Adams told his diary, was a seat "for a noble Man, a Prince. The Turkey Carpets, the painted Hangings, the Marble Tables, the rich Beds with crimson Damask Curtains and Counterpins, the beautiful Chimney Clock, the spacious Garden, are the most magnificent of any Thing I have ever seen."[73]

For Adams the world was always larger and more impressive than he expected, and he was constantly taken aback by displays of wealth and refinement. After a day in court in 1758, where he "felt Shy, under Awe and concern," he attended a "Consort" where he "saw the most Spacious and elegant Room, the gayest Company of Gentlemen and the finest Row of Ladies, that I ever saw." In 1774 at the house of wealthy New Yorker Jeremiah Platt, he was shown "into as elegant a Chamber as I ever saw—the furniture as rich and splendid as any of Mr. Boylstones." In the home of John Morin Scott, another rich New Yorker, "a more elegant Breakfast, I never saw—rich plate—a very large Silver Coffee Pot, a very large Silver Tea Pott—Napkins of the very finest Materials, and toast and bread and butter to near Perfection."[74]

But Adams despised this world of affluence and elegance even as he envied it. Although he told his diary in 1772 that he was "wearied to death, with gazing wherever I go, at a Profusion of unmeaning Wealth and Magnificence," he couldn't help being fascinated. The very rich, he said, feel their fortunes. "They feel the Strength and Importance, which their Riches give them in the World . . . their imaginations are inflated by them."[75] Because he had personally felt "the Pride and Vanity" of the "great ones" of Massachusetts, he could not help but denounce them for their "certain Airs of Wisdom and Superiority" and their "Scorn and Contempt and turning up of the Nose."[76]

BY CONTRAST, Jefferson never felt snubbed in his life, or if he had, he would never have admitted it. And except perhaps when he went to France, he was never overawed by wealth and elegance in the way Adams was. Jefferson was certainly impressed by French culture, especially in the fine arts, but he never expressed such wide-eyed wonder at the world as Adams did. He was too self-confident and felt too cosmopolitan for that.

Even as a young man, Jefferson was the connoisseur informing his college friends what was to be considered fine in the world and what was to be dismissed as "indifferent," one of his favorite words of derision. Jefferson told his friends in 1766 that he planned to visit England, but instead at age twenty-three he took a grand tour up the Atlantic seaboard as far north as New York. In Philadelphia he had an introduction from his friend John Page to visit Dr. John Morgan and get inoculated for smallpox. Morgan had an excellent collection of copies of artworks that much impressed young Jefferson.[77]

When he toured Maryland, he was quick to condemn the parochialism and backwardness of his fellow colonials. On his visit to Annapolis, which he sarcastically called "this Metropolis," he described to Page the crude behavior of the colony's assembly. The old courthouse in which the colonial assembly met, "judging from it's form and appearance, was built in the year one." Its members made "as great a noise and hubbub as you will usually observe at a publick meeting of the planters in Virginia. . . . The mob (for such was their appearance) . . . were divided into little clubs amusing themselves in the common chit chat way." The speaker was "a little old man dressed but indifferently" who had "very little the air of a speaker." The clerk of the assembly read "a bill then before the houses with a schoolboy tone and an abrupt pause at every half dozen words." The assemblymen addressed the speaker without rising, spoke "three, four, and five at a time without being checked," shouted out their votes chaotically, and, in short, seemed unaware of the proper or usual forms of conducting a legislature. Doing things properly and in the right manner was important to Jefferson.[78]

MORE THAN OTHER LEADERS of his generation, Jefferson became fascinated with politeness, the ways in which men and women treated one another. In an important sense politeness, broadly conceived, was central to the Enlightenment, at least in the English-speaking world. The Enlightenment represented not just the spread of science, liberty, or self-government—important as those were—but also the spread of civility or what came to be called civilization.

Everywhere in the Western world people were making tiny, piecemeal assaults on the crudity and barbarism of the past. Everywhere in small, seemingly insignificant, ways, life was being made sociable, more refined, more comfortable, more enjoyable. Sometimes the contributions to civilization of improvements were quite palpable and material—with the addition of "conveniences," "decencies," or "comforts," as they were called. Did people eat with knives and forks instead of with their hands? Did they sleep on feather mattresses instead of straw? Did they drink out of china cups instead of wooden vessels? These were signs of prosperity, of happiness, of civilization. Jefferson believed that to know the real state of a society's enlightenment one "must ferret the people out of their hovels, . . . look into their kettle, eat their bread, loll on their beds under pretence of resting yourself, but in fact to find out if they are soft."[79]

But most important to Jefferson was the spread of civility, the social and moral behavior of people. People were more benevolent, conversations were more polite, manners were more gracious, than they had been in the past. Everywhere there were more courtesies, amenities, civilities—all designed to add to the sum of human happiness. Not talking loudly in company, not interrupting others' conversation, not cleaning one's teeth at the table, were small matters perhaps, but in the aggregate they seemed to be what made human sociability and civility possible. "Human Felicity," wrote Benjamin Franklin in his *Autobiography*, "is produc'd not so much by great Pieces of good Fortune that seldom happen, as by little Advantages that occur every Day."[80] People realized that all those seemingly trivial improvements in social behavior were contributions to civilization, and hence to enlightenment.

In 1808, after nearly a lifetime of experience, Jefferson knew how to get along with people, even people who were irascible and unfriendly. He advised his grandson that being good-humored was one of the most important sources of sociability. When combined with politeness, it became invaluable. "In truth," he said, "politeness is artificial good humor, it covers the natural want of it, and ends by rendering habitual a substitute nearly equivalent to the real virtue." Politeness meant "sacrificing to those we meet in society all the little conveniences and preferences which will gratify them." It meant "giving a pleasure and flattering turn to our expressions which will conciliate others, and make them pleased with us as well as themselves." It also meant "never entering into dispute or argument with another." He told his grandson, "Be a listener only, keep within yourself, and endeavor to establish with yourself the habit of silence, especially in politics."[81]

Such politeness—such an acute sensitivity to the feelings of others and a keen desire not to offend—was the secret of much of Jefferson's success in life. But since his polite words and his artificial good-humored behavior to people could never be an accurate expression of his real feelings, he was always open to accusations of duplicity and deceit. His politeness was a double-edged sword: it cut both ways.

JEFFERSON'S ADVICE ON how to win friends and influence people did not have much appeal for a pugnacious John Adams. He had become a gentleman, to be sure, and he tried to behave properly, and when he got to know someone well and felt secure with him, he could be extremely amiable; but, as he often lamented, he knew he had some rough edges and he knew he lacked the gift of silence. He had none of Jefferson's sophistication, self-confidence, and sense of restraint. He was, as his physician friend Dr. Benjamin Rush described him, "fearless of men and of the consequences of a bold assertion of opinion in all his speeches." He had a sharp, sarcastic tongue, and he used it often, sometimes in the presence of the recipient of his derision. In the Congress in 1777, he even publicly took on "the veneration which is paid to General Washington." Adams was not taken with politeness and hiding his feelings. "He was," as Rush put it, "a stranger to dissimulation"—the very characteristic Jefferson was often accused of having.[82]

These two men were so different from each other. How could they ever have become friends?

TWO

CAREERS, WIVES, AND OTHER WOMEN

REARED BY THE RANDOLPHS, Jefferson had no doubt that he would go to college. His maternal grandfather, Isham Randolph, and that grandfather's five brothers had attended the colony's college, which had been founded in 1693, the second college after Harvard in the North American colonies. Therefore it was natural that Jefferson would likewise attend the College of William and Mary, as he did in 1760, at age seventeen.

The situation at the college was not conducive to learning. The faculty was largely composed of Anglican clergymen who were embroiled in controversy. But fortunately for Jefferson the professor of natural philosophy, William Small, was not a clergyman. Small took Jefferson under his wing and opened his mind to the world of mathematics, science, and the liberal arts. Later Jefferson recalled that he had studied hard and read industriously under Small's influence. He believed that this Scottish professor had fixed the destiny of his life.

Yet based on the few surviving letters of Jefferson's college years, all of his time was scarcely spent studying. Jefferson immediately found friends and mingled easily with the sons of the great families of Virginia.

John Page of Rosewell, the largest and one of the grandest houses in the colony, became his closest companion. He and Page became members of the Flat Hat Society, America's oldest collegiate fraternity, founded at William and Mary in 1750. The society committed itself to friendship, mirth, learning, and perhaps, most important, holding parties in the taverns of Williamsburg. Although Jefferson had a reputation for burying his head in a book, he and his college friends obviously spent a good deal of time dancing and flirting with the young women of the colony. From the evidence in his early letters it seems that he and his close-knit social circle did little else but gossip about courtships and marriage.

One surviving letter, however, which was only recently discovered, reveals that the young student was thinking about some serious matters. He was interested in spiritual speculations and asked a friend when exactly he thought the soul departed from the body—an ancient issue that had fascinated even Homer. Jefferson was anxious that the "doubts" he had of the traditional religious opinion that the soul left the body at the instant of death might come to light and "do injustice to a man's moral principles in the eyes of persons of narrow and confined views." Consequently, to keep prying eyes from discovering their thoughts, he suggested that the two friends not address their letters or sign them.[1]

ALTHOUGH ADAMS AS A BOY may have expressed some doubts about attending college, he seems to have readily adapted to Harvard. The early entries to his diary, which he began at college in the early 1750s, were perfunctory, usually describing the weather. Although every once in a while he offered his thoughts on a chemistry experiment or a professor's lecture, he said nothing about his social life. In 1753, in one of his fullest entries, he briefly described a trip he and a cousin, a young preacher named Ebenezer Adams, took to New Hampshire, apparently the first time the undergraduate had traveled any distance. Only later, in 1821, did he fill out his memory of the trip. He recalled visiting the Reverend Joseph Whipple in Hampton Falls, New Hampshire. After dinner Parson Whipple invited Adams and his cousin to have a smoke in another room. Whipple's wife came in the room, "lifted up her hands and cried out" that she was "astonished to see that pretty little boy with a pipe in his mouth smoking that nasty poisonous tobacco." She said she couldn't "bear the sight." But young Adams was not about to give up his pipe. "I was as bashful and timorous as a girl," he remembered, "but resented so being called a little boy at 15 or 16 years of age and as stout as her husband, that I determined not to be frightened out of my pipe."[2]

Only after Adams had graduated from Harvard in 1755 did he begin to reveal to his diary his innermost thoughts and feelings, and then they came in torrents, and for good reason. Both he and Jefferson faced major issues upon leaving college: What career to follow and when and whom to marry?

In college Adams initially thought he might follow his father's wishes and become a minister, a career that was inconceivable for Jefferson. Adams, unlike Jefferson, had a strong religious sensibility, and "my Inclination I think was to preach."[3] He paid close attention to the debates taking place in Massachusetts over the strictness of traditional Calvinist determinism and its emphasis on original sin and the depravity of all humanity. While at college, he later told Jefferson, he thought he was "a Mighty Metaphis[ic]ian," and his friends "thought me so too; for We were forever disputing, though in great good humor." In order to impress them on his mind, he copied out in longhand various tracts and sermons, especially the popular writings of Dr. John Tillotson, the liberal late-seventeenth-century Anglican clergyman who had softened the harshness of orthodox Calvinism. Adams clearly responded to Tillotson's sermons, which were probably the most widely read religious writings in America during the first half of the eighteenth century. In place of what he called the "Frigid John Calvin," Adams came to favor a latitudinarian Congregationalism that played down the divinity of Christ and stressed the individual's moral agency in bringing about a better world.[4] But could he become a clergyman?

In his diary and letters to classmates, Adams expressed his mixed emotions over a possible career. Whatever he did, he said, had to be moral and uplifting. "Our proper business in Life," he wrote in 1756, "is

not to accumulate large Fortunes, not to gain high Honours and important offices in the State, not to waste our Health and Spirits in Pursuit
of the Sciences, but constantly to improve ourselves in Habits of Piety
and Virtue."[5] Becoming a clergyman would accomplish that and please
his father. But, as he recalled in his autobiography, he came to realize
that the study of theology and becoming a minister "would involve me in
endless Altercations and make my Life miserable, without any prospect
of doing any good to my fellow Men."[6]

The law was tempting and offered the possibility of fame, of making
a name for himself. But could that career be reconciled with habits of
virtue and piety? "The Study and Practice of Law, I am sure," he wrote,
"does not dissolve the obligations of morality or of Religion."[7] Besides,
as he told a classmate in 1756, a career in law had its own problems of
altercation. Not only did the law involve "fumbling and raking amidst
the rubbish of Writs, indightments, Pleas, ejectments, enfiefed, illate-
bration and 1000 other lignum Vitae words that have neither harmony
nor meaning," but it "often foments more quarrells" than it composes.
The law seemed to end up enriching the lawyers "at the expense of im-
poverishing others more honest and deserving."[8] Uncertain of what to
do, twenty-year-old Adams accepted a temporary post as a schoolmaster
in Worcester.

After nearly two years of teaching, Adams finally contracted with
James Putnam in Worcester to begin an apprenticeship in the law. "The
study of Law," he told his Harvard classmate Charles Cushing, did have
the advantage of being "an Avenue to the more important offices of the
state, and the happiness of human Society is an object worth the pursuit
of any man." But to Cushing at least, he played down the likelihood of
this avenue opening up to him. "The Acquisition of these important offices depends upon [so] many Circumstances of Birth and fortune, not
to mention Capacity, which I have not, that I can have no hopes of Being
Usefull that way." Later in his life he told Cushing's son that what he had
really wanted to do in 1756 was enlist in the army. Only the lack of influence and patronage, he said, had prevented him from becoming a
soldier.[9]

Adams was confident enough of his legal abilities that he turned down an offer to practice law in Worcester. Instead in 1758 he moved back to Braintree and the possibility of practicing law in the wider arena of Boston. He met with several senior Boston attorneys, including Jeremiah Gridley, the dean of the Boston bar. Gridley advised him not to marry too early and to avoid too much socializing, which would keep him from his law books. Most important, Gridley said, was "to pursue the Study of the Law rather than the Gain of it." But Adams was already reading philosophical works that were well beyond what other aspiring lawyers were reading. Adams knew what Gridley was getting at, for even before he met Gridley he had criticized a distant relative for his want of ambition in his legal career. "He is negligent of the Theory of his Profession, and will live and die unknown.—These driveling souls, oh! He aims not at fame, only at a Living and fortune." He criticized others too who were without "Courage enough to harbor a Thought of acquiring a great Character." [10]

Adams knew he was different from these other lawyers. He had the capacity for "hard study" and the passion for fame that the others lacked. His ambition was palpable. He desperately wanted to succeed in life, but could he do so in a manner worthy of that success? "Men of the most exalted Genius and active minds," he said, "are generally perfect slaves to the Love of Fame." He aspired to be one of those men of genius, but he mistrusted the pride that fed that desire. He knew that "the greatest men have been the most envious, malicious, and revengeful." [11]

Knowing something of Adams's ambitions, his friend Jonathan Sewall playfully held up the example of Cicero to him. As "Cicero's Name has been handed down thro' many Ages," he told Adams, "so may yours." It wasn't Cicero's offices or orations that created his fame. Fame, said Sewall, came when "a Man's Worth riseth in proportion to the Greatness of his Country." Perhaps it will happen to you, he told Adams in 1760. "Who knows but in future Ages, when New England shall have risen to its intended Grandeur, it shall be as carefully recorded among the Registrars of the Leterati, that *Adams* flourished in the second Century after the Exode of its first Settlers from Great Britain, as it is now, that *Cicero* was born in the Six-Hundred & Forty-Seventh Year after the Building of *Rome*."[12]

Adams replied that he was willing to join Sewall in "renouncing the reasoning of some of our last Letters"—all those fanciful expressions of youthful yearning. He admitted that he expected "to be totally forgotten within 70 Years of the present Hour." Nevertheless, he did not want to end up as one of "the common Herd of Mankind, who are to be born and eat and sleep and die, and be forgotten." As poor as his future possibilities seemed in 1760, he said that he was "not ashamed to own that a Prospect of an Immortality in the Memories of all the Worthy, to [the] end of Time would be a high Gratification of my Wishes."[13]

Adams hoped that once he had acquired not just expertise in the various kinds of law—natural, civil, common, and provincial—but also familiarity with the poetry, history, and oratory in Greek, Latin, French, and English, great results would follow. All this "critical Knowledge . . . will draw upon me the Esteem and perhaps Admiration, (tho possibly the Envy too) of the Judges of both Courts, of the Lawyers and of Juries, who will spread my Fame thro the Province." Still, were his motives in pursuing his legal career pure and proper? "Am I grasping at Money, or Scheming for Power? Am I planning the Illustration of my Family or the Welfare of my Country? These are great Questions," he said, and they were questions that he continually asked himself.[14]

At first, Adams thought his law practice would never take off. "I feel vexed, fretted, chafed, the Thoughts of no Business mortifies me, stings me." But then he urged himself to banish these fears. "Let me assume a Fortitude, and Greatness of Mind." He filled his diary with recriminations. Was he working hard enough? "What am I doing?" he asked. "I sleep away my whole 70 years." He reproached himself for his languor, his inattention, for being easily distracted.[15] He promised his diary that he would push himself into business. "I will watch my Opportunity, to speak in Court, and will strike with surprize—surprize Bench, Bar, Jury, Auditors and all."

What he needed most was to call attention to himself. "Reputation," he wrote, "ought to be the perpetual subject of my Thoughts, and Aim of my Behaviour. How shall I gain a Reputation? How should I spread an Opinion of myself as a Lawyer of distinguished Genius, Learning, and Virtue?" If his ascent to fame and fortune was gradual, the resulting pleasure would be "imperceptible." But with "a bold, sudden rise," he would "feel all the Joys" of fame and fortune "at once." Did he have the "Genius and Resolution and Health enough for such an achievement?" How to make his way in the law? "Shall I creep or fly?"[16]

Adams succeeded brilliantly. Although he had started from scratch, in time he became one of the leaders of the Massachusetts bar. He trained and befriended nearly a dozen law students and steadily developed his practice to the point where he became the busiest lawyer in the province. His clients came from all levels of the society, and his practice covered every kind of public and private law—cases involving real estate, torts, defamation, violations of the navigation acts, and crimes. Not only did he spend a great deal of time traveling between Braintree and Boston, but he rode two- and three-week circuits around eastern Massachusetts and tried cases in courts as far west as Worcester, as far south as Martha's Vineyard, and as far north as present-day Portland, Maine, which was then part of Massachusetts—"tossed about so much from Post to Pillar," he said, that he scarcely knew what "this Life of *Here and every where*" was about.[17]

LIKE ADAMS, Jefferson became a lawyer. There is no evidence, however, that he ever agonized over his decision to study law in the way Adams did. Indeed, law seemed a natural acquisition for an aristocratic planter. Even his friend James Madison, who never practiced law, nevertheless felt the need to educate himself in the law. After Jefferson graduated from William and Mary in 1762, he apprenticed to George Wythe in Williamsburg to study law, at which time he purchased numerous law books, along with other works of history and literature, including John Milton's *Works*, David Hume's *History of England*, William Robertson's *History of Scotland*, the *Thoughts of Cicero*, and George Sale's translation of the Koran.

Although Jefferson never purchased as many law books as Adams did, he bought many more books of other sorts, especially history books. Although in 1770 he lost all his books in a fire at his mother's home at Shadwell, within three years he had created a new library that numbered 1,256 volumes, which was three or four times larger than the one he had lost. This meant that since the fire he had purchased on average about one book per day. Eventually, Jefferson acquired the largest private library in the country.[18]

Adams expressed some misgivings over the money he was spending on law books. On the eve of the Revolution he realized that compared with other lawyers in Massachusetts he was poor, even though he had "done the greatest Business in the Province" and "had the very richest Clients in the Province." But, he confessed to his wife, Abigail, he also knew that he ought "to be candid enough to acknowledge that I have been imprudent. I have spent an Estate in Books."[19]

By contrast, Jefferson seems to have had no qualms whatsoever about the amount of money he was spending on books. Even though he was already in debt, he borrowed more money in order to buy more books. When Jefferson was compelled by his increasing debts to sell his extensive library to the U.S. government in 1815, he regretted the loss. When Adams learned of the sale, which went to form the nucleus of the second Library of Congress after the burning of the Capitol by the British in 1814, he congratulated Jefferson for the "immortal honour." But he admitted that he could not "enter into competition" with him, for his "books are not half the number of yours." Jefferson admitted that he hadn't sold all of his books; that would have been impossible. "I cannot live without books," he told Adams, "but fewer will suffice where amusement, and not use, is the only future object."[20]

Jefferson had the same expansive view of reading for the law as Adams did. After laying a foundation by reading the usual law books, Jefferson advised students to add to the study of the law "such of its kindred sciences as will contribute to its attainment," the most important of these being "Physics, Ethics, Religion, Natural Law, Belles Lettres, Criticism, Rhetoric, and Oratory."[21]

Both men were omnivorous readers and both agreed that reading was essential to wisdom. "How could any Man judge," wrote Adams in 1761, "unless his Mind had been opened and enlarged by reading." He never lost his love of reading. He said later in his life that he would even "sacrifice my eyes like John Milton rather than give up the Amusement without which I should despair."[22]

WYTHE SET JEFFERSON reading *Coke upon Littleton*, which was the first of four parts of Sir Edward Coke's *Institutes of the Lawes of England*, and students' usual introduction to English law. Like other students, Jefferson struggled with "the black letter text and uncouth but cunning learning" of Coke. He thought Coke's work was old and dull, and wished that the devil would take it. Adams too recognized the work's difficulty, but he was determined to keep reading it "over and over again," until he broke through it. As Adams told his diary, the difficulties involved in the study of law may have discouraged some students, "but they never discouraged me." Aware of the vanity expressed in this remark, he added: "Here is conscious superiority."[23]

Wythe was more than young Jefferson's law teacher; he introduced him to Francis Fauquier, the royal governor of Virginia, and together with William Small, the four men dined frequently at the Governor's Palace. At these dinners, Jefferson later recalled, he heard "more good sense, more rational & philosophical conversations" than at any other time in his life.[24] Connected to the governor's court in this manner, young Jefferson experienced as much grace and polish as provincial America had to offer. Governor Fauquier was a fine musician who helped Jefferson acquire his passion for music. Jefferson took his violin playing seriously, sometimes practicing three hours a day in preparation for performing in quartets at concerts at the palace. Adams, of course, never had this kind of experience.

After about three years of his apprenticeship with Wythe, Jefferson became a member of the bar in 1765; a year later he was appointed a justice of the Albemarle County Court. In 1769, at the age of twenty-six, he was elected to the House of Burgesses. The rapidity of his rise was a sign of his already established position in Virginia society. Although he knew the court system well, he never practiced in the county courts. Almost all of his cases were tried in the General Court of Virginia, which met semiannually in Williamsburg for four weeks in both April and October. Of the ten or so members of the General Court, Jefferson was the youngest and the only member from the west; all the others were from the Tidewater counties. A few lawyers practiced in both courts, but Jefferson did not; in fact, it was against Virginia law for a lawyer to practice in both courts unless he was a graduate of the Inns of Court in London. Although at the outset of his career he attended some county courts in order to drum up business, he was never a member of the county court bar, and thus he never rode circuit every month in the counties as the county court lawyers did. Thus, in addition to his attending the mid-June session of the governor's council, Jefferson spent roughly only two months of the year trying cases.

Jefferson's practice, such as it was, was not very remunerative. During his eight years of trying cases Jefferson's income in collected fees, before deducting expenses, was only about £1,200. Busy county court lawyers made considerably more than that. Jefferson's fees as a lawyer scarcely supported him; his plantations and his slaves were the principal source of his income. He was the patriarch of Monticello and his county and was never just a lawyer. While he was practicing law, he was deeply engaged in all sorts of efforts to improve the marketing of his tobacco and corn, including sponsoring legislation to clear obstructions on the James River.[25]

Unlike Adams, Jefferson did not seem to enjoy the law, or at least he seems to have become tired of it. Lawyers, he said in 1802, were just like priests, designed to "throw dust in the eyes of the people." Lawyers in legislatures were especially irritating, with their "endless quibbles, chicaneries, perversions, vexations, and delays." He came to hate the mystifications of the common law, especially as it was practiced by post-revolutionary pettifoggers—"Ephemeral insects," he called them. He wanted to exclude from the courts "the malign influence" of all English authorities cited since the reign of George III began in 1760 and free the unwritten common law from the "chaos of law-lore," perhaps by purifying it and codifying it in statutes. By 1810 he had concluded that the law was "quite overdone." It had "fallen to the ground; and a man must have great powers to raise himself in it to either honour or profit. The Mob of the profession get by it as little money, & less respect, than they would by digging the earth." Compared with a physician who tried to save lives and always had the respect of his neighbors, "the lawyer has only to recollect, how many, by his dexterity, have been cheated of their right, and reduced to beggary."[26]

By contrast, Adams believed that "a Lawyer, who confines himself to his practice and is careful to preserve his honor Intigrity, Humanity, Decency, and delicacy, may be as happy and useful a Citizen as any in society." Adams loved the mystery of the common law. "Law," he said, "is human Reason," and he never lost his "Veneration" for it.[27] He reveled in the law's complexity and was never happier in court than when he could pull out of the English law reports an authority or a precedent that no one had ever heard of. Mastering the difficulty and intricacy of the common law was the source of his success.

Perhaps a more important explanation for his admiration for the law was his belief that he had never known "a great Statesman in my sense of the Word who was not a lawyer." By his definition of great statesmen, he said in 1790, there were in America only three or four, and presumably he was one of them.[28]

As Adams was developing his law practice, he ignored the advice of his mentor Jeremiah Gridley that he not socialize too much and not be in a hurry to marry. Writing a former Harvard classmate in October 1758, Adams asked him about his marriage plans. "For my part, you know, that Women never fell within my Scheme of Happiness, altho' the world tells me I am over head and ears in love." Whether he was or not, he said, "I sincerely don't know."[29]

This reference may have been to Hannah Quincy, the twenty-two-year-old daughter of Colonel Josiah Quincy. She was attractive and flirtatious, and he enjoyed her company; but perhaps she was more taken with him than he with her. Her brother Samuel Quincy was absorbed in "Cards, Fiddles and Girls," which Adams was sometimes unable to resist. He was interested in women, but confessed that he didn't know how to talk with them, "so dull and confused at present is my mind." He filled his diary with the distractions of women, music, and parties, and his constant resolve to resist them. Keep to the law, he told himself. "Let no trifling Diversion or amuzement or Company decoy you from your Books, i.e. let no Girl, no Gun, no Cards, no flutes, no Violins, no Dress, no Tobacco, no Laziness, decoy you from your Books." Still, he could not help himself: for four days in a row, "All spent in absolute Idleness, or what is worse, gallanting the Girls."[30]

When Adams first met Abigail Smith in the summer of 1759, he was still seeing Hannah Quincy. Initially, neither John nor Abigail was impressed with the other. Since Abigail was not quite fifteen years old to Adams's twenty-three, she must have seemed immature compared with Hannah Quincy, who was only a year younger than Adams. Besides, he regarded Abigail's father, the Reverend William Smith of Weymouth, as a "crafty, designing Man," whose cynical and selfish manner he didn't at all like. Abigail and her older sister regarded themselves as "Wits," and he dismissed them as "not fond, not frank, not candid"; indeed, he thought both of them lacked the "Tenderness" of Hannah Quincy.[31]

But Adams was alarmed by the growing feelings he had for Hannah—feelings "that would have eat out every seed of ambition, . . . and every wise Design or Plan" he had for his future. Besides, his father told him he could not keep leading Hannah on if he wasn't serious about marriage. He came within a hairsbreadth of proposing to Hannah but was interrupted, fortunately, he said, for "Marriage might have depressed me to absolute Poverty and obscurity, to the end of my Life." So the relationship slackened, and Hannah married someone else the following year, which, Adams told his diary, "delivered me from very dangerous shackles, and left me at Liberty, if I will but mind my studies, of making a Character and a fortune."[32]

It may have been more complicated. Hannah's personality seems to have made Adams uneasy, and that uneasiness may have played into his hesitation. "Her face and Hart have no Correspondence," he noted. She knew how to check people with subtle sarcasm and ridicule. She could be sweet and charming on the outside, "when she is really laughing with Contempt" on the inside. And Adams, as he repeatedly confided to his diary, dreaded above all being the victim of sarcasm, ridicule, and contempt.[33]

Although the initial meeting between Adams and Abigail Smith had not gone well, they continued to see each other. Because Adams's friend Richard Cranch was courting Abigail's older sister, Mary, Adams often went along to the Smith household. By 1761 his earlier indifference had turned into affection. Abigail had matured both physically and emotionally. She had become more attractive, with a dark complexion and darker hair and eyes. And her sharp intelligence and her wide reading were bound to impress John. During his courtship he only once mentioned Abigail in his diary and that reference in 1763 was obscure, suggesting Adams's sudden seriousness and his unwillingness to say things even to his diary that he might regret. Calling her "Di," which was short for "Diana," the name he began using in correspondence with Abigail, he described her as a "friend," who was "Prudent, modest, delicate soft sensible, obliging, active."[34]

The courtship was not rushed. Not until 1764 did John and Abigail marry. John was nearly twenty-nine, Abigail soon to turn twenty. Marriage changed his life. He had matured as well. Fifteen months before the marriage, he broke off his diary and did not resume it until three months later. And when he did resume it, the diary entries were dramatically different. His writing became much less revealing of his inner feelings, less expressive of his insecurities and anxieties, and more objective and more straightforward in presenting facts.

Compared with the marriages of the other Founding Fathers, John and Abigail's was unusual, if not unique. It appeared to offer little financial advantage to either party. Although Abigail's father was the minister in Weymouth and her mother was a Quincy, a wealthy and important

Massachusetts family, John did not seem to worry much about his wife's estate or dowry. If anything, it was Reverend Smith who worried about his young daughter's marrying beneath her social station by taking as her husband the son of a modest Braintree farmer and shoemaker.

Much to her regret, Abigail had no formal education. "I never was sent to any school," she recalled. "I was always sick." Besides, she said, "female education in the best of families went no further than writing and arithmetic."[35] Instead, she set about educating herself. She read voraciously, taught herself French, borrowed books and took suggestions of what to read from her brother, William Smith, and exchanged ideas about her reading with other girls and young women. When she met John, she realized that he too was "a Lover of Literature." Indeed, she recalled, he "confirmed my taste, and gave Me every indulgence that Books could afford." In this way she was "taught at an early period of Life, that the true Female Character consisted not in the Tincture of Skin, or a fine set of Features, in lilly's white, or the Roses red, But in something still beyond the exterior form."[36]

She read many of the same works of history and poetry as John did and tried to match him in citing and quoting what she read. Abigail aimed to be her husband's intellectual partner, if not his equal. She once told an old friend that "a well-informed woman" was more capable "of engaging and retaining the affections of a man of understanding, than one whose intellectual endowments rise not above the common level."[37]

Most eighteenth-century marriages were not intellectual partnerships between equals. Most were still traditional and patriarchal. Women rarely had an independent existence, at least in law. In public records they were usually referred to as the "wife of," the "daughter of," or the "sister of" a male. Before marriage women legally belonged to their fathers, and after marriage they belonged to their husbands. A married woman was a *feme covert:* she could not sue or be sued, make contracts, draft wills, or buy and sell property. It went without saying that women could not hold political office or vote. They were considered to be dependent like children and were often treated like children by their husbands. Husbands might address their wives as "dear Child" or by their Christian names, but be addressed in return as "Mr."

For the eighteenth century the Adamses had an unconventional marriage, one that historians have called a companionate marriage, in which husbands, in the genteel wisdom expressed by Abigail, "willingly give up the harsh title of Master for the more tender and endearing one of Friend."[38] The Adamses were not just man and wife and lovers; each was also the other's intellectual partner and best friend. "Mrs. Adams," said Dr. Benjamin Rush, "in point of talent, knowledge, virtue, and female accomplishment was in every respect fitted to be the friend and companion of her husband in his different and successive stations."[39]

Ultimately what set off the Adams marriage from those of the other Founders was the quantity and quality of their correspondence with each other. Because John was so much away from home—at first riding the circuit courts as a young attorney, then attending the Continental Congress in Philadelphia, and later as minister in Europe—he and Abigail exchanged letters, about twelve hundred of them. For some of the Founders and their wives, we have virtually no letters at all. Even if we had letters between Jefferson, Washington, and their wives, it is hard to imagine that they would resemble those between John and Abigail. The Adamses' correspondence has an openness and candor and intellectual character that could come only from two people who regarded each other as intellectual comrades. Their correspondence, as John pointed out, was a conversation between "two friendly Souls."[40]

In their many letters John and Abigail exchanged views on everything from the politics of the Continental Congress to the price of clover seed. "I want to sit down and converse with you, every evening," wrote Abigail, and she did.[41] She told her husband about the local news of Braintree, her dinner guests, the local rumors, the weather, the state of their farm. She read widely and was eager to display to her husband the range of her knowledge. In her letters she quoted from an extraordinary array of writers, often from memory: John Dryden, Alexander Pope, William Collins, Edward Young, Shakespeare, the Bible, Polybius, and Charles Rollin's ancient history, among others. No issue was too small or too large for her comment, and she had strong views about everything, including slavery. In 1774 Abigail reminded John that slavery had "always appeared a most iniquitous Scheme to me—[to] fight ourselfs for what we are daily robbing and plundering from those who have as good a right to freedom as we have. You know my mind on this Subject."[42] She was especially outspoken on politics; indeed, she was, as Federalist Fisher Ames later observed, "as complete a politician as any lady in the old French Court."[43]

JEFFERSON'S EXPERIENCE in courting and marrying was different from Adams's. Although Jefferson was far more sophisticated and worldly than Adams, as a young man he seems to have been equally uncomfortable with women, especially with unmarried women. In Jefferson's youthful correspondence, which his chief biographer says he probably would have burned if he could, he expressed some of the same anxieties Adams voiced while courting.[44] While many of his friends courted and married, Jefferson remained single. Finally in October 1763, Jefferson at the age of twenty became smitten with an attractive seventeen-year-old named Rebecca Burwell and proposed marriage to her. But Jefferson mishandled the proposal—his carefully prepared speech, he told his friend John Page, dissolved into "a few broken sentences, uttered in great disorder, and interrupted with pauses of uncommon length."[45]

Miss Burwell gave Jefferson a second chance later that year, but he bungled that one as well. In the second meeting he revealed to her "the necessity of my going to England" and "the delays" that would follow from that. He told Page that he asked Rebecca Burwell "no question" that would require "a categorical answer," but he assured her "that such questions would one day be asked." Somehow Jefferson thought he had convinced Miss Burwell of his "sincerity" and he didn't have to do anything more. Months went on, and he avoided seeing her.[46]

Yet he was stunned when, in March 1764, he discovered that his prospective fiancée was going to marry the wealthy Jaquelin "Jack" Ambler.

"Can you believe it?" he asked his friend William Fleming. His dream of marriage was now "totally frustrated." He hadn't heard the decision from Rebecca Burwell herself, since he admitted that he had "been so abominably indolent as not to have seen her since last October," that is, six months earlier. Still, he was "as well satisfied that it is true as if she had told me." His immediate reaction was "Well the lord bless her I say."[47]

Jefferson went on to cite St. Paul's advice that "it is better to be married than to burn." To quench their sexual passions was the reason his friends Fleming and Page were determined to get married as soon as possible, and why they advised him to do the same. "No thank ye," said Jefferson, "I will consider it first. Many and great are the comforts of a single state." Besides, he said to Fleming, for young men burning with sexual passion there were "other means of extinguishing their fire than those of matrimony." Indeed, said Jefferson, if St. Paul had known about them, he would have earnestly recommended these "other means." Perhaps, it has been shrewdly suggested, Jefferson was simply acknowledging that young Virginia aristocrats had available female slaves to satisfy their sexual urges, something that St. Paul apparently had not anticipated.[48]

At any rate, the disappointment with Rebecca Burwell triggered the first of the many severe headaches brought on by tension and stress that would torment Jefferson through much of his life; only after he retired from the presidency in 1809 did they cease.[49]

Jefferson's frustration from the failed courtship of Miss Burwell also aggravated a deep mistrust of women that he may have developed early, even in his teenage years. He seems to have had problems with his mother—his few references to her in his papers were cold and unfeeling; and in the years between his courtship of Rebecca Burwell and his marriage in 1772 he found his relationship with women to be especially difficult and awkward.[50] From about 1760 or so until his marriage, he entered in his memorandum and commonplace books a number of passages drawn from his reading that expressed suspicion and hostility toward women.[51] In 1770, for example, he penned on the inside of the front cover of his memorandum book a Latin poem from the minor poet Pentadius that can be translated as:

Entrust a ship to the winds, do not trust your heart to girls.
For the surge (of the sea) is safer than a woman's loyalty:
No woman is good; but if a good one has befallen anyone
I know not by what fate an evil thing has become a good one.[52]

Notations like this run through his memorandum and commonplace books: "A fickle and changeful thing is woman ever" he quoted from Virgil. "Yes, men should have begotten children from some other source, no female race existing; thus would no evil ever have fallen on mankind" he selected from Euripides.[53] He copied two more passages from Milton's *Paradise Lost* that expressed mistrust of women. Misogynous lines in the plays of Restoration dramatist Thomas Otway especially caught his eye and his mood.

I'd leave the World for him that hates a Woman.
Woman the Fountain of all human Frailty!
What mighty ills have not been done by Woman?

Jefferson's irate response to news of Rebecca Burwell's engagement to Jack Ambler found expression in another passage copied from Otway's play *The Orphan; or, The Unhappy Marriage:*

—Wed her!
No! were she all Desire could wish, as fair
As would the vainest of her Sex be thought,
With Wealth beyond what Woman's Pride could waste,
She should not cheat me of my Freedom. Marry!
When I am old and weary of the World.
I may grow desperate,
And take a Wife to mortify withal.[54]

Too much should not be made of these youthful displays of misogyny, though historians, of course, have had a field day with them. Jefferson was probably merely expressing adolescent frustration over his inability to find a proper sexual partner. Once he married, his exquisitely polite manners seem to have made possible easy and normal relationships with women, better perhaps than Adams in his social awkwardness was able to manage.

ALTHOUGH ADAMS in his diary revealed his adolescent emotions and passions in the most open and fulsome manner, he never expressed anything resembling Jefferson's misogyny. Quite the contrary. In 1777 he reminded Abigail how often he had observed to her in conversation the fact that most "illustrious Men" owed "a great part of their Merit" to "some Female about them in the Relation of Mother or Wife or Sister."[55] Whatever personal problems Adams had with repression and resentment, they did not seem to involve his rapport with women, at least American women. He did later confess to being overawed by European women of "genius Taste Learning Observation and Reflection."[56] Once he had married Abigail, however, his subsequent relationship with other women was intellectual and not sexual. He took his marriage vows seriously.

Late in life he severely criticized the letters of Mademoiselle de Lespinasse, who had dominated the salons of Enlightenment philosophes, saying that he had "never read any thing with more ennui, disgust and loathing." That woman "was constantly in love with other women's husbands, constantly violating her fidelity to her own keepers with other women's husbands, constantly tormented with remorse and regrets . . . and constantly threatening to put herself to death." All in all, the letters revealed to Adams just how backward and decadent were the society and manners of the ancien régime of France during the "age of reason."[57]

Maybe it was the Puritan-soaked culture of Massachusetts or maybe it was his own moralistic restraint, but in matters of sex Adams seems to have been nowhere near as intense and lustful as Jefferson. In all the years of separation from Abigail there was never the slightest rumor of Adams making any advances on any woman. Indeed, in his autobiography he emphatically declared that he never had any improper relationship with any woman.[58] By contemporary French standards Jefferson was something of a puritan too, and there is no evidence that he was ever unfaithful to his wife while she was alive. But he certainly seems to have been more sexually passionate than Adams.

IN 1768, FOUR YEARS AFTER the ending of his courtship of Rebecca Burwell, Jefferson was unable to control his passions. Jefferson ended up trying to seduce the wife of a close college friend, John Walker. The Virginia government had commissioned Walker's father, Dr. Thomas Walker, and Colonel Andrew Lewis to attend a conference with several Indian tribes at Fort Stanwix in western New York. Walker's father wanted his son to accompany the mission as secretary. Knowing that the negotiations might take months, John Walker asked his good friend Jefferson to look after his wife, Elizabeth Moore Walker, and their infant daughter while he was away; he had in fact named Jefferson first among his executors. Elizabeth Walker was an attractive woman, and Jefferson tried to take advantage of the situation but was unsuccessful. When Walker returned four months later, Elizabeth Walker said nothing about Jefferson's advances during her husband's absence.

According to John Walker, Jefferson kept up his adulterous advances on Betsy Walker for a decade, even after Jefferson had married in 1772— a charge that was probably not true. Only after he had left for France in 1784 did Mrs. Walker reveal to her husband Jefferson's aggressive advances. Walker finally realized why his wife had constantly questioned the confidence he had placed in Jefferson in making him his executor. He said his wife apologized "for her past silence from her fear of its consequence which might have been fatal to me." The two former friends fell out, and Walker rewrote his will.[59]

Only during Jefferson's presidency was the affair publicly revealed, and it became a scandal. In the highly partisan atmosphere of 1802 the notorious journalist James Thomson Callender accused Jefferson of many things, including a relationship with a slave named Sally Hemings and the affair with Mrs. Walker. Both Walker and Jefferson tried to suppress news of the affair, and with Henry Lee, whose wife was a niece of Mrs. Walker, as mediator, Jefferson sought to assuage Walker's honor and prevent a duel. Finally, in 1805, Jefferson acknowledged to friends that he was willing to plead guilty to one of the charges against him—"that when young and single I offered love to a handsome lady. . . . It is," he said, "the only one, founded in truth among all their allegations against me."[60] He apparently never admitted that he might have made advances on Walker's wife after he himself was married.

Following the frustrations of his advances on Betsy Walker, Jefferson suddenly changed his mind about his earlier preference for the comforts of bachelorhood to marriage. Or perhaps, as has been suggested, the ease of his approach to Mrs. Walker convinced him that marriage might be possible with women who had already been married.[61] At any rate, in the fall of 1770 he made his first recorded visit to the Charles City County home of the twenty-two-year-old widow Martha Wayles Skelton.

Little is known of the courtship, but obviously Jefferson tried to make himself as appealing as possible. Early in 1771 he began investigating his genealogy with the hope of acquiring the coat of arms of his family—an acquisition common among the Virginia aristocrats. He asked his merchant-agent, who moved between Virginia and England, to search the Herald's Office in London. He said he had what he was told was the family's coat of arms, "but on what authority I know not." It was possible that the family had none. If so, he asked his agent to purchase one; and then he added jokingly, as if to cover his embarrassment at making such a request, he had Anglican Irish writer Laurence "Sterne's word for it that a coat of arms may be purchased as cheap as any other coat."[62]

Jefferson's ability to play the violin may have been more important to his courtship than a coat of arms. A story passed down through the family had two rival suitors arriving at Martha Wayles Skelton's house at the same time. Ushered into the hall, the two men heard from an adjoining room the young widow's harpsichord and soprano voice blending with Jefferson's violin and tenor voice in wonderful harmony. After listening for a stanza or two, the two suitors, realizing what they were up against, took their hats and retired, never to return.[63]

Jefferson had been playing the violin since he was a teenager. He may have been unusual, for in America, as he told his European correspondent, music was "in a state of barbarism."[64] Martha Wayles Skelton's musical talents made her all the more attractive to Jefferson. At the end of 1770 he initially planned on giving her a small clavichord. But by June 1771 he had seen a pianoforte and been "charmed" by it, and wanted it instead. He specified that the case should be "of fine mahogany, solid, not veneered," and "the workmanship of the whole very handsome, and worthy the acceptance of a lady for whom I intend it."[65] He married the young widow on New Year's Day 1772.

Martha Wayles Skelton had more than musical talent to make her attractive. As a widow she already possessed an ample estate with the promise of more from her father. She had married Bathurst Skelton in 1766, and her husband had died in 1768 after a sudden illness. Just before Martha's husband's death, Jefferson had taken on her father, John Wayles, as a legal client, and this is when he may have first met Martha Wayles Skelton.[66] John Wayles had been born in England and had acquired not only a large legal practice in Virginia but a large landed estate as well. A month after Martha was born in 1748, Wayles's first wife died. After losing two more wives, Wayles in 1761 began living openly with one of his slaves, a mulatto named Betty Hemings (her father was an English ship captain), and fathered six children with her, including one named Sally Hemings, who was born in 1773, the year Wayles died.[67]

Wayles left his son-in-law Jefferson a considerable amount of property, including Betty Hemings and all of her offspring. Jefferson brought the Hemings slaves to Monticello, where they were given special privileges. After all, not only were six of the Hemings slaves blood relatives of his wife, Martha, but because they possessed white blood they were in Jefferson's mind necessarily superior to pure blacks. Jefferson believed that blacks who were the offspring of racial mixing (as long as the mixing was between white men and black women) were improved in both "body and mind." Everyone knew this, he claimed; for him it proved that the black slaves' "inferiority is not the effect merely of their condition of life."[68]

Martha's share of her father's estate, Jefferson later wrote in his autobiography, "was about equal to my own patrimony, and consequently doubled the ease of our circumstances."[69] Indeed, he had acquired from the division of Wayles's estate more than eleven thousand acres of land and 135 slaves, which when added to the 52 slaves inherited from his father made him the second-largest slaveholder in Albemarle County. Jefferson now owned four major plantations in Virginia—Monticello, Poplar Forest ninety miles to the southwest, and Elk Hill and Willis Creek forty miles to the east; eventually only Monticello and Poplar Forest were retained. Although he had to sell about six thousand acres to settle some of Wayles's many debts, Jefferson had suddenly become one of the wealthiest planters in all of Virginia.[70]

Martha was beautiful and talented and a devoted wife. But she was not an intellectual companion to her husband in the way Abigail Adams was; indeed, none of the wives of the Founders resembled Abigail in that respect. Nor did Martha, like Abigail, arise at dawn to skim the milk; she had slaves to do that. Jefferson's marriage was a traditional patriarchal one, with his wife having the principal responsibility for promoting the well-being of her husband. That "trade" of being a dutiful housewife, as he once called it, was what he expected all marriages to be.[71] "Sweetness of temper, affection to a husband, and attention to his interests," Jefferson told his eldest daughter, Martha (sometimes called Patsy), on the eve of her own marriage, "constitute the duties of a wife and form the basis of matrimonial felicity." Wives, he said, must realize that their happiness depended "on the continuing to please a single person."[72]

In Jefferson's conception of the ideal marriage, even the husband's failings could be laid at the feet of his wife. If the marriage developed difficulties, Jefferson advised his daughter, the wife must not "allways look for their cause in the injustice of her lord," for "they may proceed from many trifling errors in her own conduct." Above all, a wife must never communicate to others any want of duty or tenderness she thinks she has perceived in her husband, for "this untwists, at once, those delicate cords, which preserve the unity of the marriage engagement." If third parties witness the failings of a marriage, "its sacredness is broken forever."[73]

He believed that husbands "expected to be pleased" by their wives who were "sedulous to please," and his wife, Martha, seems to have more than fulfilled that expectation. In his autobiography Jefferson called her "the cherished companion of my life" with whom he had lived "in unchequered happiness."[74] Happy as he was, he never regarded his wife, any more than he did his daughters, as his intellectual equal. When the Marquis de Chastellux visited Monticello in 1782, he described everything about his host and the house in minute detail, but he scarcely mentioned Martha. This was never true of Abigail: foreign visitors to the Adams household always felt her intellectual presence.

Jefferson was devoted to his wife, and the marriage was a happy one. The widowed Martha already had one child when she married Jefferson. She then gave birth to six children in ten years, with only two daughters reaching maturity. Her health was never strong, and four months after the birth of the last child she died, on September 6, 1782. Jefferson was devastated, and for six weeks he remained cut off from all society. Only in mid-October did he emerge from what he described to Chastellux as a "stupor of mind which had rendered me as dead to the world as was she whose loss occasioned it."[75]

On her deathbed Martha apparently extracted a promise from Jefferson that he would never marry again, a remarkable pledge given that most eighteenth-century widowers quickly remarried.

JEFFERSON WAS ONLY THIRTY-NINE when his wife died, and he lived another forty-four years. Since he considered sexual desire to be "the strongest of all the human passions," it is difficult to believe that he remained celibate the rest of his life.[76] In 1802 journalist James Callender wrote that President Jefferson, "the man, *whom it delighteth the people to honor*, keeps, and for many years past has kept, as his concubine, one of his own slaves. Her name is SALLY."[77]

This charge, which Jefferson never acknowledged and indirectly denied, has reverberated through the past two centuries. Many have doubted that he could have had any such relationship, some finding

Jefferson's liaison with a slave inconceivable, especially given his opposition to racial mixing. But DNA results showing that the Hemings children were fathered by someone in Jefferson's male line, together with the powerful arguments of historian Annette Gordon-Reed, give ample reason to conclude that Jefferson indeed took Sally Hemings as a concubine and fathered six of her children. Certainly, Jefferson as an eighteenth-century slaveholding Virginia planter would not have been unusual in having a black concubine.

In the 1850s a Richmond physician recalled that slave mistresses were "quite common in this city fifty years ago with gentlemen of the older time." Jefferson's neighbor General John Hartwell Cocke, who helped Jefferson establish the University of Virginia, said that "in Virginia this damnable practice prevails as much as any where." He could, he declared, "enumerate a score of such cases in our beloved Ancient Dominion." Indeed, Cocke, a prominent planter and politician, believed that "all Batchelors, or a large majority at least, keep as a substitute for a wife some individuals of their own slaves." Perhaps the examples could be numbered in the "hundreds," which was not "to be wondered at, when Mr. Jefferson's notorious example is considered."[78]

Jefferson could not be blind to the extent of racial mixing in Virginia; in fact, he saw it all around him. Visitors to Monticello were impressed by the number of mulatto slaves in the household. The Duc de La Rochefoucauld-Liancourt noted that many of Jefferson's slaves had "neither in their color nor features a single trace of their origin, but they are the sons of slave mothers and consequently slaves." The Comte de Volney was surprised to see so many slaves at Monticello who were "as white as I am."[79] Yet Jefferson never accepted this racial mixing. As he said in 1814, the black slaves' "amalgamation with the other colour produces a degradation to which no lover of his country, no lover of excellence in the human character can innocently consent."[80] Presumably the fact that Sally, according to the testimony of another Monticello slave, was "mighty near white" with "straight hair down her back" made Jefferson's "amalgamation" with an African American acceptable to him.[81]

Jefferson had inherited many of the mulattos from his father-in-law.

When John Wayles died in 1773, he had been living with Betty Hemings for over a decade. Betty already had four children, and with Wayles she had six more, the last being Sally. All the mulatto slaves who were the offspring of John Wayles and Betty Hemings were thus Martha Jefferson's half siblings. Over the next half century more than eighty members of the family of Betty Hemings—five generations of slaves—lived and worked at Monticello. By the time of Jefferson's death in 1826, one-third of the 130 slaves on his estate were members of the Hemings clan.[82]

When Jefferson went to Paris in 1784, he was accompanied by his eldest daughter, Martha, and his nineteen-year-old slave James Hemings, the brother of Sally. Jefferson intended to have James trained in cooking French style and bring him back to America to be his chef at Monticello. When Jefferson learned of the death of his two-year-old daughter, Lucy, in Virginia, he determined to have his other remaining daughter, Mary— or Polly, as she was called—join him in France. After many exchanges of letters back and forth across the Atlantic, in 1787 the nine-year-old Polly was finally able to sail to Europe, accompanied by her fourteen-year-old maid, Sally Hemings. According to Abigail Adams, who met the pair in London, Sally was "quite a child" and "wants more care" than Polly and was "wholy incapable of looking properly after her." Indeed, Mrs. Adams told Jefferson, the ship captain who brought the pair over thought that Polly's maid would be of "so little Service that he had better carry her back with him."[83]

Apparently over the next few years Sally matured quickly, becoming an unusually attractive young woman with a sweet temperament. She was thirty years younger than Jefferson, but such differences in age between females and males in relationships were not uncommon in eighteenth-century Virginia. Jefferson's father, Peter, had been in his early thirties when he married his wife of nineteen. The father of Jefferson's son-in-law, Col. Thomas Mann Randolph, Sr., married, at age fifty, seventeen-year-old Gabriella Harvie. And thirty-two-year-old James Madison's first engagement was with fifteen-year-old Kitty Floyd. Although the engagement eventually collapsed when Miss Floyd found someone else, no one thought it was a strange or unusual match. Jefferson's attraction to Sally may have been helped by the fact that she was the half sister of his deceased wife, and Jefferson knew that; she may even have resembled Jefferson's wife.[84]

Since slavery had no place in French law, James Hemings and his sister Sally knew that they could gain their freedom at any time while in France. Jefferson knew that too, and consequently he treated both James and Sally in a special manner. The lives of the two Hemings siblings were clearly transformed by their experience in France. They learned French and were often on their own in Paris. With Martha and Polly away at school, James Hemings doing the cooking, and French servants running the household, Sally naturally assumed a more prominent position at Jefferson's Parisian residence in the Hôtel de Langeac. Sally was particularly talented as a seamstress—a skill that Jefferson believed was one of the foundations of a woman's domestic life, even more valuable for women than the ability to read.

This Paris experience was bound to make the Hemings siblings think of themselves differently—not as typical Virginia slaves but as hired servants with special roles in the household. For some French friends of Patsy, Sally may not have even seemed to be a servant. One referred to Sally as "Mademoiselle Sally," a title that no normal servant would have been given. Before long, Sally was given a regular salary and began acting as a chambermaid to Jefferson, a role that she would continue to play at Monticello upon returning to America. During this time in France, as Sally's son Madison Hemings recalled, "my mother became Mr. Jefferson's concubine."[85]

When Jefferson planned his return to America in 1789, he was confronted with a problem. Sally Hemings was pregnant, and she did not want to go back to Virginia. According to her son Madison, in order to induce his mother to return, Jefferson "promised her extraordinary privileges, and made a solemn pledge that her children should be freed at the age twenty-one years."[86] At the same time James Hemings told Jefferson of his desire to remain in France and live off of his newly acquired skill as a chef. To induce him to return, Jefferson apparently promised James his freedom as soon as he trained another slave to cook in a French style.

After returning to America with Jefferson, James Hemings did teach another slave how to cook French style and was freed by Jefferson as promised. Sally Hemings remained at Monticello, with, according to one witness, "a room to her own" within the house.[87] She eventually gave birth to six or perhaps seven children, four of whom lived to adulthood. Two of them, Beverley and Harriet, left Monticello for freedom in 1822, apparently with Jefferson's acquiescence, and the other two, Madison and Eston, were freed by Jefferson's will along with three other Hemingses. Jefferson had kept his bargain with Sally. As octoroons, Jefferson and Sally's children were legally white by Virginia law in the 1820s. Of the four, only Madison chose to remain in the black community.

Jefferson mentioned Sally only a few times in his writings and then only in passing. Sally seems to have represented for him a medically necessary outlet for his sexual needs, and little more.[88] Sally's offspring were incidental to the relationship. Since Jefferson kept track of everything that went on at Monticello, he dutifully recorded in his farm book not only the new colts he acquired and the hogs he killed but the births of nearly all of his slaves as well, including Sally's children—that is, his children. Some other Virginia slaveholders with concubines often gave presents to their offspring or even recognized them in their wills, but not Jefferson. He never acknowledged his slave children publicly or privately and never made any effort to prepare for their financial futures. Apparently he did not even bother to teach them to read; the Hemings children had to coax the white children in the household to help them to learn to read. Madison Hemings admitted that although Jefferson "was affectionate toward his white grandchildren," he "was not in the habit of showing partiality or fatherly affection to us [Hemings] children."[89] Because Jefferson thought of all his slaves as children, all part of his extended "family," perhaps he had no emotional need to single out his own offspring from the rest.[90]

WHILE IN FRANCE, Jefferson befriended, corresponded with, and sometimes flirted with a number of different women—French, English, and American—including Alexander Hamilton's sister-in-law, Angelica Schuyler Church. But his most intense relationship was with Maria Hadfield Cosway, a woman who had everything—beauty, charm, intelligence, wealth, social prominence, and artistic and musical talent; indeed, Mrs. Cosway was probably the most fascinating woman Thomas Jefferson ever met in his entire life.[91]

Maria Cosway was born in Italy in 1760 of English expatriate parents. In 1781 she married Richard Cosway, a socially distinguished English miniaturist. She and her husband soon established one of the most fashionable salons in London. Cosway was an odd man who was almost twice her age and notoriously ugly, resembling a monkey, many said. He was foppish in manner with eccentric tastes in dress and companions. But Maria's parents were hard-pressed for money, and her marriage was one of convenience. She had many disappointed suitors, one of whom scoffed that Mr. Cosway "at that time adored her, though she always despised him." But another said that Maria's "capacity for the eccentric . . . made her a fitting wife for a husband who mingled not a little of charlatanism with very real gifts as an artist."[92] Maria Cosway was a celebrated painter in her own right, exhibiting over thirty works at the Royal Academy in London.

BUT SHE WAS NOT THE ADAMSES' kind of woman. In January 1786, months before Jefferson crossed paths with the Cosways, Abigail Adams and her daughter, Abigail—always known as Nabby—met Mrs. Cosway at a London party. Although Abigail never mentioned Mrs. Cosway in her correspondence, Nabby did, and she was not at all impressed by this brilliant young woman. In telling her brother John Quincy about the party, Nabby said that she and her group, which included her betrothed, William Stephens Smith, and her mother but not her father, had arrived late and had little choice of seats. She took one "next to a Mrs. Coswey, an Italian who is rather a singular Character." She noted that Mrs. Cosway "paintts and her subjects are the most singular that one can imagine." Nabby had seen some of Maria's paintings at an exhibition during the previous year. "One was a *Dream*, another the deluge, the mos[t] extraordinary things, that imagination could form." Mrs. Cosway, said Nabby, was reputed to speak English, Italian, and French "vastly well." She also played and sang well too, but, wrote Nabby, she had "the foibles, which attend these accomplishments." Sitting next to her for the whole evening was an ordeal, for Nabby had to witness "sollicidute from almost Every Person in the [room?]," all pleading with Mrs. Cosway "to Play and sing." All this begging met with Mrs. Cosway's "absolute refusal." She claimed that she was sick with a cold and had not sung for weeks. "At last," wrote Nabby, "after every one had given over their solicitude she, followed her own inclination and play[ed] and sang till she came away."

Nabby found this conduct inexcusable—unless the woman had "an ineshaustable fund of Wit and good Humour to display," which "this Lady had not." Maria Cosway struck her as "one of those soft gentle pretty Women, whose Compliance with the request of the company would please more than her Airs could possibly give her importance." Supposedly, Cosway gave musical parties at her house on Monday evenings, but Nabby had never been invited to any.[93]

Maria Cosway was twenty-five when she and her husband went to Paris in the summer of 1786. In September Jefferson was on an architectural excursion with John Trumbull, an aspiring young painter, when the two men ran into Richard and Maria Cosway. Trumbull knew the Cosways from London, and he introduced them to Jefferson. Unlike Nabby, Jefferson was immediately taken with Maria. She was coquettish, cultivated, and captivating, and straightaway she had Jefferson wrapped around her finger. For the next two weeks Jefferson and Maria wandered about Paris and its surroundings together.

Historians have been fascinated by Jefferson's relationship with Maria and have described it very differently.[94] Some have seen it as a passionate love affair that brought together a lonely widower and a woman unhappy in her arranged marriage. Others have seen it as a romantic friendship that was all playful talk with no consummation. Still others have described Maria as a coquettish young woman who loved to flirt with men and enjoyed nothing more than having a flock of besotted male admirers circling about her. She respected Jefferson and his learning and was obviously flattered by his infatuation with her, but she never saw their relationship as romantically serious. She relished her rich social life in London and never thought a moment about giving it up. If Nabby Adams had known about the relationship, she would have been appalled that Jefferson had been ensnared by this beautiful but narcissistic temptress.

Jefferson and Maria did not see each other in Paris for any great length of time; in fact, the relationship was much briefer than most historians have realized. Jefferson and Maria took their day trips and half-day trips around Paris on only ten or twelve days over several weeks. There were two more outings during the first week of October 1786, when Jefferson saw the Cosways for the last time just before their departure back to London. Jefferson and Maria's excursions were usually not private but often took place in the company of several people, including Richard Cosway, John Trumbull, and Jefferson's secretary, William Short. Historian Jon Kukla has persuasively concluded that the relationship was "a flirtatious friendship enhanced by shared cultural interests rather than a passionately erotic affair."[95]

After the Cosways went back to London, Jefferson and Maria kept in touch. Between 1786 and 1790 they exchanged three dozen letters with each other; then after a nearly five-year lapse they exchanged between 1794 and Jefferson's death in 1826 another fifteen letters. Jefferson was obviously more romantically smitten with her than she was with him. Her letters, as Kukla points out, were always characterized by "friendship, rather than romantic love."[96] The most famous of Jefferson's letters to Maria was one of twelve pages written shortly after the Cosways left Paris. He composed the letter as a dialogue between the Heart and the Head in which he expressed his feelings for her, reminded her of all the good times they had had together, and suggested a possible visit to America, "where strangers are better received, more hospitably treated, & with a more sacred respect." The dialogue was a curiously indirect way of expressing his feelings, but since such dialogues were a common literary device in the eighteenth century, Jefferson no doubt hoped to impress Maria with his imaginative use of it.[97] Abigail would not have been impressed.

THREE

THE IMPERIAL CRISIS

As John Adams launched his law practice in the 1760s, he began writing short pieces for Boston newspapers on a variety of topics. But 1765 changed everything for him and for the colonies. That was the year the British Parliament passed the Stamp Act, which levied a tax on legal documents, almanacs, newspapers, and nearly every form of paper used in the colonies. The tax sparked a firestorm of opposition in the colonies. The result, Adams told his diary, was to make 1765 "the most remarkable Year of my Life." The attempts by Parliament to batter down all the rights and liberties of America, he wrote, had "raised and spread thro the whole Continent, a Spirit that will be recorded to our Honor, with all future Generations." From Georgia to New Hampshire public resentment had forced the stamp agents to resign and had silenced everyone who had dared speak in favor of the Stamp Act. "The People, even to the lowest Ranks," he said, "have become more attentive to their Liberties, more inquisitive about them, and more determined to defend them, than they ever before known or had occasion to be. . . . Our Presses have groaned, our Pulpits have thundered, our Legislatures have resolved, and our Towns have voted. The Crown Officers had every where trembled, and all their little Tools and Creatures, have been afraid to Speak and ashamed to be seen."[1]

In response to the Stamp Act, Adams revised and expanded an essay that he had initially written for a private club of his fellow lawyers called Sodality. The revised piece, later entitled "A Dissertation on the Canon and Feudal Law," was published in four installments in the *Boston Gazette* in 1765.

His theme was the progress of liberty and the gradual enlightenment of the common people: since the Middle Ages the people had struggled to wrest their rights from the twin tyrannies of power—monarchs and the church. For centuries the great had exploited the ignorance and timidity of ordinary people in order to dominate and oppress them. When government was properly restrained by respect for the people's rights, it could be a useful force for good. "But when such restraints are taken off, it becomes an incroaching, grasping, restless, and ungovernable power." Up until the sixteenth century, the most effective weapons the great had used to oppress the common people were the canon and feudal law.

Canon law was framed by "the *Romanish* clergy" for the aggrandizement of their own order. Catholic priests had assumed an authority over all aspects of life—not only "a power of dispensation over all sorts of sins and crimes" but also "the mysterious, awful, incomprehensible power of creating out of bread and wine, the flesh and blood of God himself." Under feudal law, which was allied with that of the church, "the common people were held together in herds and clans, in a state of *servile* dependence on their lords; bound even by the tenure of their lands to follow them, whenever they commanded, to their wars."

As long as this confederacy between kings and clergy lasted and the people were kept in ignorance, "Liberty, and with her, Knowledge, and Virtue too, seem to have deserted the earth, and one age of darkness succeeded another." Then the Protestant Reformation broke the hold that canon and feudal law had on the common people, especially in England. As a result of the Reformation, the English people grew more and more conscious of the wrong that had been done them and became more and more impatient with their oppression until "under the execrable race of the Steuarts" the struggle between the people and the confederacy of temporal and spiritual tyranny "became formidable, violent and bloody."

It was this great struggle "that peopled America." In the seventeenth century Adams's Puritan forefathers had fled from the twin sources of Old World tyranny, the Stuart state and the hierarchical Anglican church, in search of both universal liberty and religious freedom. The Puritans came to New England and began their settlements and formed their plan of both ecclesiastical and civil governments "in *direct opposition* to the *cannon* and the *feudal* systems."

Adams conceded that the Puritans were enthusiasts in religion—not something valued by enlightened eighteenth-century liberals, but, he observed, everyone in Christendom was a religious enthusiast at that time. Besides, no great enterprise was ever accomplished without enthusiasm. Their settlement was "founded in revelation, and in reason too." They granted as much popular power in their new government as was consistent with human nature, but they focused their attention on religion. They sought to get rid of all the nonsense and delusions associated with canon law, and found their church on the Bible and common sense. This "at once imposed an obligation on the whole body of the clergy to industry, virtue, piety and learning and rendered that whole body infinitely more independent on the civil powers, in all respects, than they could be where they were formed into a scale of subordination, from a pope down to priests and fryers and confessors, necessarily and essentially a sordid, stupid wretched herd."

These Puritan adventurers denied that "most mischievous of all doctrines, that of passive obedience and non-resistance." Such a doctrine was inconsistent with "the constitution of human nature and that religious liberty, with which Jesus had made them free." They were convinced that nothing could preserve them from the twin tyrannies of feudal and canon law "but knowledge diffused generally thro' the whole body of the people." For this reason they founded a college and established schools, all publicly supported. The consequence was a highly literate people.

It was true, said Adams, that recently some High Churchmen, who were not descendants of the Puritans, had criticized these educational efforts as needlessly expensive and causing idleness among the people who ought to be working instead of going to school. But the people had "a right, an indisputable, unalienable, indefeasible divine right to that most dreaded, and envied kind of knowledge, I mean of the characters and conduct of their rulers." And contributing to the maintenance of that right was the press. Whenever the public interest and liberty were in danger from the ambition and avarice of great men, "whatever may be their politeness, address, learning, ingenuity, and in other respects integrity and honesty," the newspaper editors had done themselves honor "by publishing and pointing out that avarice and ambition."[2] This certainly was one of his many opinions that Adams would come to regret.

Since for Adams canon law was as threatening as feudal law, the conflict with Great Britain in the 1760s had to be about more than simply protecting the constitutional rights of the colonists. In his "Dissertation" he warned that the British government would ally with the Church of England to reverse the results of the Puritan revolution. As he told his diary, the Anglican clergy in Massachusetts were bigots and "devout religious Slaves." These "Church People," he said, "are many of them, Favourers of the stamp act."[3]

As he later recalled, the liberal Congregational minister Jonathan Mayhew had warned the people of Massachusetts that the Church of England was using the Society for Propagating the Gospel in Foreign Parts—an organization presumably designed to bring Anglican Christianity to the Indians—to undermine the Congregational churches. These warnings "excited a general and just apprehension, that bishops and dioceses, and churches and priests, and tithes, were to be imposed on us by Parliament. It was known that neither king, nor ministry, nor archbishops, could appoint bishops in America, without an act of Parliament; and if parliament could tax us, they could establish the Church of England, with all its creeds, articles, tests, ceremonies, and tithes, and prohibit all other churches, as conventicles, as schism shops."[4]

Not only was the "Dissertation" a powerful justification of American opposition to the recent policies of the British government, but it was Adams's first effort to set forth the importance of New England in the settlement of America.

As he said in a note added to later reprintings of the essay, he had always considered "the settlement of America with reverence and wonder, as the opening of a grand scheme and design of Providence for the illumination of the ignorant and the emancipation of the slavish part of mankind all over the earth."[5]

ALTHOUGH JEFFERSON had his own historical narrative about the struggle of liberty against tyrannical power, he would never have written anything like Adams's "Dissertation." For Adams, the Protestant Reformation always remained a powerful event. In 1815 he concluded "that all the Wars of the past fifty Years are only a continuation of the Wars of the Reformation." It was natural for him to draw analogies between the sixteenth century and the 1760s. "If [James] Otis was Martin Luther," he said, "Samuel Adams was John Calvin."[6] By contrast, the Reformation had almost no emotional significance for Jefferson. Since the origins of Virginia, unlike those of Massachusetts, had nothing to do with religious enthusiasts seeking freedom from Anglican tyranny, his story of the settlement of America had no place for the Protestant Reformation. Insofar as Jefferson found history useful in explaining the origins of America, he invoked in place of the Reformation the myth of a democratic Saxon period of independent landowning farmers that had been destroyed by the feudal laws of the Norman Conquest in 1066. For Jefferson this Saxon past was a lost utopian world that eighteenth-century Americans ought to emulate and recover. This was very different from Adams's understanding of history as a long, ongoing struggle against tyranny in which America had a central role to play.

ADAMS HAD BEEN THINKING about the theme of his "Dissertation"—America's place in world history—as early as 1755, the year he graduated from Harvard. That October, he outlined to his friend Nathan Webb his thoughts about the rise and fall of empires. Rome, he said, began as an "insignificant village" but gradually it rose "to a stupendous

Height," only to find itself in subsequent centuries sinking "into debauchery," which "made it att length an easy prey to Barbarians." Likewise, England had gradually risen "in Power and magnificence, and is now the greatest Nation upon the globe." Following the Reformation, "a few people came over into this new world for Conscience sake." Perhaps, he said, "this trivial incident may transfer the great seat of Empire unto America." The rapid growth of America's population and the increasing wealth of the country made its eventual dominance likely. Only the separation of the colonies one from another could "keep us from setting up for ourselves." With such thoughts it is obvious that Adams was already primed for the events that would take place over the next two decades.[7]

Although Adams later claimed that his "Dissertation" was the spark that ignited New England's opposition to the Stamp Act, in fact it was barely noticed at the time. However, Thomas Brand Hollis, an English radical, picked it up and published it in London in 1765; eventually the essay was printed in England without Adams's knowledge three times before 1776.

In 1765 Adams made another contribution to Massachusetts's resistance to the Stamp Act, with his draft of instructions for the town of Braintree to its representative in the General Court, as the Massachusetts legislature was known. His draft voiced defiance of recent British actions, which, he said, had been "pursued with a direct and formal Intention to enslave Us."[8] The draft was too radical for the town and it was moderated. Still, his influence over the final adopted instructions was unmistakable. He had obviously captured the attention of many of his fellow subjects in the colony.

But in Adams's mind there was a severe downside to the troubles provoked by the Stamp Act. All legal business had come to a halt, and Adams's legal career had been suddenly interrupted, just as it was about to take off. He had lived his life of thirty years in preparation for this moment of success. Now, however, his career was in danger. He had poverty to struggle with, and the malice of enemies to contend with, and only a few friends to assist him. It was as if the whole world were conspiring against him. He had, he told his diary, "groped in dark Obscurity, till of late, and had but just become known, and gained a small degree of Reputation, when this execrable Project was set on foot for my Ruin as well as that of America in General, and of Great Britain."[9]

For Adams resistance to British actions was not something abstract and distant. He knew his enemies personally and palpably—the Bernards, the Hutchinsons, the Olivers, the Grays—these were "my bitter Foes." They were all "Conspirators against the Public Liberty," all part of the "Conspiracy" that "was first regularly formed, and begun to be executed, in 1763 or 4." Thomas Hutchinson, above all, was his personal enemy. Hutchinson, the chief justice and lieutenant governor of the colony, and his family and friends had acquired all the highest honors and profits in Massachusetts, "to the Exclusion of much better Men." Adams believed that the province had more to fear from Hutchinson than from any other man in the world. By 1772 Adams had become convinced that Hutchinson was using all his "Art and Power" to destroy him personally just as he had sought to demolish the lives of other patriots.[10]

Nearly a half century later, Adams vividly recalled the way Chief Justice Hutchinson had abruptly interrupted his argument during an important trial, *Rex v. Corbet*, that took place during the tense atmosphere in Boston in 1769. Adams was defending several colonial seamen who were charged with murdering a British naval officer who was apparently trying to impress them. The trial was held before a special vice-admiralty court composed of fifteen dignitaries, including, in addition to Hutchinson, the governors of Massachusetts and New Hampshire, the judge of admiralty, a commodore of the Royal Navy, and some counselors from the other New England colonies. In the inflammatory atmosphere of Boston that year Hutchinson was more concerned with the politics than the legalities of the case, and he suddenly interrupted Adams and adjourned the trial. Four hours later, he and the court returned a hasty and unsubstantiated verdict of justifiable homicide. Even though Adams had won his case, he resented the court's lack of legal reasoning and the fact that he was prevented from presenting his legal discoveries to the public. To be cut off so brusquely by Hutchinson in front of so many worthies whom he was eager to impress angered and embarrassed him. "Never in my life," he recalled, "have I been so disappointed, so mortified, so humiliated as in that trial."[11]

JEFFERSON NEVER THOUGHT about his resistance to British policies in this personal manner. For him Parliament and the king were distant and abstract; they were institutions he knew about, but they never assumed the direct and personal character that they did for Adams. In fact, until near the very end of the colonial period Jefferson was intimate with royal officials, dining and playing music with Governor Fauquier in the mid-1760s. His opposition to Great Britain was intellectual and ideological, not tangible, not personal. And unlike Adams, he never let the law trump political reality.

Jefferson was only twenty-two in 1765 and, he recalled, was "but a student" of law in Williamsburg. He hadn't yet expressed anything resembling Adams's farsighted view of the future of America, and compared with Adams, he had a much more subdued reaction to the Stamp Act. At the end of May 1765, he wrote in his autobiography, he had gone to the Virginia capital to listen to the House of Burgesses debate the Stamp Act, and he had heard Patrick Henry let loose his "torrents of sublime eloquence" in opposition to British tyranny.[12]

Because of the fire at Shadwell in 1770 Jefferson lost most of his early papers, so we know little of his activities in the 1760s. He clearly spent a good deal of time engaged in his private affairs—establishing his law practice, wooing two women, and getting married. But he was obviously reading and thinking and developing enlightened ideas about what might be done in Virginia and in the empire. Once he began serving in the House of Burgesses, he introduced a measure for the emancipation of slaves in the colony, but it was rejected. Or as he recalled in his autobiography, "Indeed, during the regal government, nothing liberal could expect success," since Virginians were still paralyzed by a habitual subservience to the mother country. Although there is no record of any such measure being introduced, Jefferson, according to his first major biographer, Henry S. Randall, may have been referring to a bill he introduced to allow slave owners to emancipate their slaves. Or he may have wanted in his autobiography to embellish his liberal credentials at the outset of his career. At any rate he was certainly more radical on slavery and the imperial crisis than many of his colleagues in the House of Burgesses.

Jefferson was very much involved in the House's initial support of Massachusetts's resistance to British policies in the late 1760s. He joined other burgesses who met in Williamsburg's Raleigh Tavern in June 1770 to form an association pledged to the nonimportation of British goods as long as the Townshend Acts, which, in place of the repealed Stamp Act, had levied duties on a number of colonial imports, were in effect. But interest among the burgesses flagged, and so few members of the association showed up for a meeting scheduled for December 1770 that the effort finally collapsed.[13]

In the meantime, during the late 1760s Jefferson was busy planning and building his new mountaintop home, which he called Monticello. In an important sense this home became a symbol of his separation, not just from his mother and her home at Shadwell and the Randolphs in general, but also from the patrician society that he later derided. He originally called it Hermitage, a secluded place where he could escape from the people he did not like. In this respect he was very different from Adams, whose several homes in Braintree and Boston were nestled snugly into the community and possessed none of the size or architectural distinctiveness of Monticello.

Adams's final home in Quincy, which he purchased in 1787, was a simple New England farmhouse without a grand veranda or any of the pretensions of Monticello. Indeed, a French visitor in 1788 described the Adams homestead as "a small house, fifteen miles from Boston which no Paris advocate of the lowest rank would choose for his country-seat." Throughout his life Adams customarily covered any feelings of embarrassment with humor: he gave his modest home a variety of titles, many of them comical, beginning with "Peacefield," then "Stoney Field," later

"Mount Wollaston," and finally "*Montezillo* a little Hill" to rival Jefferson's "Monticello the lofty Mountain."[14]

Although Jefferson's house was supposedly designed in the manner of the sixteenth-century Italian architect Andrea Palladio, no one before Jefferson had ever conceived of building a country estate on the top of a deserted mountain. Not only did the peculiar location of Monticello violate all Palladian precedent, but the house's inaccessibility and the problems of supplying it with water made it expensive to erect and to maintain. But to Jefferson these difficulties did not matter. He had acquired a number of architectural books, surely more than any of his fellow planters ever owned, and read and studied them. He desired a building that would be a self-contained patriarchal enclave set apart from the hustle and bustle of the outside world, one that would be distinctive and reflect the superiority of his knowledge and taste.[15] As the Marquis de Chastellux pointed out, Monticello as a home resembled "none of the others seen in this country; so it may be said that Mr. Jefferson is the first American who has consulted the Fine Arts to know how he should shelter himself from the weather."

Chastellux's comment explains everything. The fact that Monticello did not resemble any of the great mansions of the other Virginia planters was precisely the point. Chastellux shrewdly deduced as much. Jefferson wanted a house that matched his intellect. Since "no object escaped Mr. Jefferson . . . ever since his youth he had placed his mind, like his house, on a lofty height, whence he might contemplate the universe."[16]

Jefferson never revealed his ambition in the fulsome way that Adams did. He never cared about becoming a great lawyer as Adams did. Instead, it seems clear that from the moment Jefferson began conceiving of Monticello he aimed at nothing less than becoming the supreme connoisseur of the best that was thought and known in the world.

By the time he moved to Monticello in the fall of 1770, the year his mother's house at Shadwell burned, he was already thinking about marriage. His only recorded reaction to the fire concerned the loss of his papers and books—nothing about what the loss of her home might have meant to his mother.[17]

. . .

DURING THESE SAME YEARS Adams's legal practice was booming. He recalled that by 1770 he "had more Business at the Bar, than any Man in the Province."[18] In 1766 he was elected a selectman of Braintree and continued to write newspaper pieces protesting British policies. In 1766–1767 he wrote nearly a dozen essays for the press attacking his old friend Jonathan Sewall, who, writing under the pseudonym "Philanthrop," had vigorously and publicly defended Governor Francis Bernard for his support of the Stamp Act.

In his pieces Sewall had promoted the importance of subordination in society and the need for the people to pay proper respect to their governing officials. In response Adams accused Sewall of trying "to deceive his countrymen," of seeking to fill "their minds with principles in government utterly subversive of all freedom." Behind all government, said Adams (and he knew of what he spoke) was the "infinite" power of "human Ambition." "We know it because We have felt the cruel oppressions, which Sprung out of it." In all ages and nations "the Prince and his favourites" have sought to cultivate "Reverence and Awe . . . Dread and Terror" among their inferiors. "The very first Maxim of Tyranny, is and always was, to puzzle the Understandings and excite the Admiration of the People."

In some of his attacks on Sewall, Adams took a strong populist line. Adopting in several essays the hick-farmer persona "Humphrey Ploughjogger," which he had also used earlier, Adams assailed Sewall for his display of "Pride and Vanity" and for the "Contempt" he had expressed "for the Generality of Mankind." He and his courtier ilk—"the better sort"—had too readily dismissed those whom they sneeringly referred to as "the Herd, Rabble, Mob, common People, Vulgar and such stuff."

No doubt in these essays Adams was releasing some of the pent-up resentments of the "Fleers and flounts, sneers and snubs" that he himself had felt from the better sort of Massachusetts. Above all, he wanted his newspaper readers to understand that "Parliament had no Authority" to pass the Stamp Act. But he went on to say that the Stamp Act at least had the unexpected benefit of resurrecting the dwindling spirit of the

people. "Calamities are the causticks and catharticks of the body poli-
tick," he said. "They arouse the soul. They restore original virtues. They
reduce a constitution back to its first principles."[19]

In 1768 he suddenly stopped keeping his diary, except for one entry
at the end of January, in which he once again worried about what he was
doing with his life. "What is the End and Purpose of my Studies, Journeys, Labours of all Kinds of Body and Mind, of Tongue and Pen?" he
asked on January 30. "Am I grasping at Money or Scheming for Power?
Am I planning the Illustration of my Family or the Welfare of my Country? These are great Questions."[20]

Sometime in that year he had an opportunity to answer these questions. His former friend Jonathan Sewall, who had been rewarded for
his support of the government with an appointment as special attorney
general of the province, asked whether Adams would accept an appointment as advocate-general in the court of admiralty. Adams knew the
office was lucrative and that it would be "a first Step in the Ladder of
Royal Favour and promotion." Despite the fact that this offer of a royal
office was "unexpected," he nevertheless, as he later recalled, was "in an
instant prepared for an Answer." And that was to promptly decline the
offer.[21]

Such a position would surely have fulfilled some of his earlier ambitions; and since he scarcely knew what was ahead of him, the offer must
have been tempting. Ten years later, after Thomas Hutchinson had fled
America and was exiled in England, he heard some Loyalist gossip related by two Massachusetts men, "Mr. [Richard] Clarke and [Samuel]
Quincy." The two reported that Adams had said to Sewall "that he was
at a loss which side to take, but it was time to determine." According to
this story, Sewall advised Adams to go with the government and proposed to Governor Bernard to make him a justice of the peace, "as the
first step to importance." But Bernard was piqued by something Adams
had done and delayed the offer, which in turn, said Hutchinson, irritated
Adams, who concluded that the governor had "some prejudice against
him, and resolved to take the other side."[22]

. . .

THERE IS NO OTHER EVIDENCE for this story, but since Hutchinson mentioned that the proposed office was merely a justice of the peace, and not the more important position of advocate-general in the court of admiralty mentioned by Sewall in 1768, the gossip was likely wrong or else referred to an earlier moment in the 1760s when the political situation was more fluid. But the fact that such a story was circulating in England two years after independence suggests that at some point some of Adams's fellow citizens had had doubts about where he stood—perhaps because his ambition had been so conspicuous.

In 1768 Adams actually seems to have hesitated for several weeks before replying to Sewall about the advocate-general position. But he must have realized that he had committed himself so completely to the patriot cause that to join the government as a royal office holder would be disastrous for his reputation. It may not have been simply lack of time that kept him from writing in his diary that year. Not knowing the future, he was becoming increasingly anxious over whether his closer involvement in patriot politics might hurt his practice as an attorney.

He certainly had been busy in 1768, and he had undoubtedly become much more deeply involved in patriot politics. In May he had written a piece in the *Boston Gazette* denouncing the creation of an Anglican bishopric in America. In June he had written instructions to the Boston representatives to the General Court protesting the seizure of John Hancock's sloop *Liberty;* and later he defended Hancock in admiralty court against charges of smuggling. In 1769, the year that he defended the three sailors accused of murdering the naval officer, he was engaged as co-counsel in bringing a civil case on behalf of one of Boston's leading patriots, James Otis, who had been assaulted by a customs commissioner. Also that year, he again drafted instructions for the Boston representatives opposing the power of the vice-admiralty court and the presence of British troops in Boston. In 1770 he was elected representative from Boston to the Massachusetts House of Representatives.

In effect, Adams had become the consigliere, the lawyer and counselor, of the Boston patriots and their organization, the Sons of Liberty.[23] And as such, ironically, he was assigned to defend the British officers and soldiers involved in the so-called Boston Massacre. In 1768 the British government, believing that all order had broken down in Massachusetts, had ordered two regiments to Boston. With nearly four thousand armed redcoats crammed into the seaport with fifteen thousand inhabitants, it was just a matter of time before a clash occurred. On March 5, 1770, a party of eight British soldiers fired upon a threatening crowd and killed five civilians. This was the "Boston Massacre."

Adams later described his role in defending the soldiers as one of the most courageous acts of his career. He recalled that taking on that un-popular task actually threatened him and his family with ruin and per-haps with his death; "for I could scarcely perceive a possibility that I should ever go through the Thorns and leap all the Precipices before me, and escape with my Life." And yet he assumed the dreadful responsibil-ity, and he did it, he said, "for nothing, except, what indeed was and ought to be all in all, a sense of duty."[24]

Despite all these later hand-wringing expressions of fear and anxiety, the actual circumstances of his appointment as defense attorney were more complicated. Josiah Quincy Jr., another successful Boston attorney, was appointed as co-counsel with Adams to defend the soldiers. When Quincy's father heard rumors of this appointment, he was appalled. He was filled "with anxiety and distress" over news that his son had "be-come an advocate for those criminals who are charged with the murder of their fellow citizens.—Good God!" he exclaimed to his son. "Is it possible?—I will never believe it." He thought that if the rumor was true, his son's reputation and interest were likely to be destroyed.

Young Quincy wrote back immediately to calm his father down. At first he took the high moral line that under English law everyone de-served a defense. But then he went on to say that he had initially declined the appointment as defense attorney—"until advised and urged to un-dertake it by an Adams, a Hancock, a Molineux, a Cushing, a Henshaw, a Pemberton, a Warren, and a Phillips"; in other words, until advised and urged by all the leading patriots of Boston to defend the soldiers.[25]

Apparently, Samuel Adams, John Hancock, Dr. Joseph Warren, and the other town leaders were concerned about Boston's reputation in the empire as a hotbed of mobs and fanatics; they thus sought through a fair trial for the soldiers to disabuse people of that reputation. As Adams later admitted, at the time "We knew not whether the Town would be supported by the Country: whether the Province would be supported by even our neighbouring States of New England; nor whether New England would be supported by the Continent." The stakes were high, and Adams and Quincy performed superbly. The captain and six of the eight soldiers were acquitted; two soldiers were found guilty of manslaughter but with pleas of benefit of clergy (the legal fiction that allowed for lesser sentences for first-time offenders) they were branded on their thumbs and released. The subsequent legal business of both Adams and Quincy, far from being damaged, actually flourished.[26]

Although the role of Adams and Quincy in the trial of the soldiers was sanctioned by his cousin Samuel Adams and the other patriot leaders, John Adams was sensitive to the feeling of the general public. In December 1772 Samuel Adams and Samuel Pemberton, a former Boston selectman, privately asked him to be the next orator in honor of the Massacre, March 5 already having been established as a day of remembrance. Adams declined, and told his cousin that although he thought the subject of the oration was quite compatible with his defense of the soldiers and the verdict of the jury, "I found the World in general were not capable or not willing to make the Distinction." Therefore, if he gave the Massacre oration, he told his colleagues, "I should only expose myself to the Lash of ignorant and malicious Tongues on both Sides of the Question." Samuel Adams and Pemberton reluctantly accepted his explanation and asked him to keep the invitation a secret.[27]

If Adams was at all accurate in his assessment of public opinion in 1772—that many Bostonians felt as Quincy's father had, that the defense of the soldiers was unpatriotic and outrageous—then his belief, which he expressed in his diary on the occasion of the March 5, 1773, oration, that his defense of the soldiers was "one of the most gallant, generous, manly, and disinterested Actions of my whole Life, and one of the best Pieces of Service I ever rendered my Country" may have considerable merit after all.[28]

IN 1772 THE BRITISH CROWN ATTEMPTED to add the superior court judges of Massachusetts to the royal civil list, which would mean that the judges' salaries would be paid by the Crown out of customs revenues rather than by the General Court, the province's legislature. This threatened to deprive the colonists of a traditional popular check on the judiciary. At a meeting in December 1772, the town of Cambridge condemned the idea of the Crown's paying the salaries of the judges as a violation of the colonists' ancient liberties.

At that meeting William Brattle, a wealthy landowner, military officer, and a member of the Council (the upper house of the General Court), defended the Crown's paying of the judges' salaries; and he challenged all patriots, including John Adams "by name," to debate him on the subject in the newspapers. Brattle contended that the judges in the province held their office with the same life tenure as judges in the mother country—that is, during good behavior, and not at the pleasure of the Crown. Thus the Crown's assumption of their salaries, said Brattle, did not threaten the judges' independence. Brattle argued that Parliament's Act of Settlement of 1701 had not created a new condition of judicial tenure but only reaffirmed the previously existing common law that granted life tenure in judicial offices.

Adams took up Brattle's challenge and with his usual profusion of citations and quotations from English history and law in seven weekly essays in the *Boston Gazette* overwhelmed the "absurdities" of Brattle's "vain and frothy Harrangues and Scribblings." Adams argued that prior to the Act of Settlement all English judges had not been independent but had served at the pleasure of the Crown. The Act of Settlement, he said, did not reaffirm old law, as Brattle claimed, but had created new law that unfortunately had not been extended to the colonies. This meant that the judges in Massachusetts, like the judges in the other colonies, remained totally dependent on the Crown.

Adams believed that his essays "contributed to spread correct Opinions concerning the Importance of the Independence of the Judges to Liberty and Safety." These opinions in turn, he claimed in his autobiography, influenced the strong affirmation of an independent judiciary in the Massachusetts constitution of 1780 and the federal Constitution of 1787. These principles prevailed almost everywhere in the nation, he wrote in his autobiography during the first decade of the nineteenth century, "till the Administration of Mr. Jefferson, during which they have been infringed and are now in danger of being lost."[29]

THE CONTROVERSY OVER the independence of the judiciary was only one of the many issues that were rapidly eroding the colonists' relationship with the mother country. Following the rioting by mobs and the development of nonimportation agreements by the colonists in the wake of the Stamp Act, the British Parliament in 1766 had repealed the act. Changing its mind so suddenly was so embarrassing that Parliament had to cover itself by accompanying the repeal with the passage of the Declaratory Act, which asserted Parliament's right to legislate for the colonies "in all cases whatsoever." This was a robust assertion of parliamentary sovereignty, which was the most important concept of political science in eighteenth-century British culture.

This doctrine of sovereignty, articulated most forcefully by the great English jurist William Blackstone in his *Commentaries on the Laws of England* (1765), held that there must be in every state "a supreme, irresistible, absolute, uncontrolled authority, in which the *jura summi imperii*, or the rights of sovereignty reside."[30] For the British, this sovereignty lay with the king-in-Parliament, since not only were all the estates of the realm—Crown, lords, and people—present in the Parliament, but the logic of the doctrine dictated that sovereignty or final authority had to be located in some institution in every state. Otherwise, there would be what was commonly called an *imperium in imperio,* a power within a power—a logical contradiction.

Although some British leaders, like William Pitt, did not accept the doctrine of parliamentary sovereignty, most did. Indeed, sovereignty became the central issue in the debate between the colonists and the British over the nature of the empire. In the end it was the colonists' inability to overcome the British insistence on the sovereignty of Parliament— that the colonists had to be totally under Parliament's authority or totally outside it—that ultimately drove them into their wholesale rethinking of the nature of the empire. Both Adams and Jefferson made major intellectual contributions to that rethinking.

The colonists had begun the imperial debate in 1765 by trying to explain their previous experience in the empire. They knew that since the late seventeenth century they had accepted parliamentary regulation of their trade. Controlling the flow of commerce was one thing; taking people's property through taxation was quite another. The Stamp Act of 1765 levied taxes on nearly all paper products in the colonies, and it aroused instant opposition. Americans knew instinctively that they could never accept Parliament's right to tax them and said so emphatically in the resolutions of the Stamp Act Congress, which met in New York in October 1765. At the same time, however, the Stamp Act Congress declared that the colonists owed Parliament all "due subordination"—presumably in matters of the Navigation Acts and the regulation of imperial trade.

Mistakenly believing that the Americans had rejected an "internal" tax such as the stamp tax, but would accept "external" taxes such as duties on imports, British officials led by Chancellor of the Exchequer Charles Townshend in 1767 tried imposing levies on glass, paper, paint, and tea imported into the colonies. But the colonists no more accepted these Townshend duties than they had the Stamp Act, and they exploded once more in opposition with riots and nonimportation agreements.

It was left to John Dickinson in his *Letters from a Farmer in Pennsylvania* (1768), the most popular patriot pamphlet of the 1760s, to explain that America opposed all forms of parliamentary taxation. Dickinson, however, was willing to recognize Parliament's right to levy duties in order to control the flow of commerce in the empire; after all, most colonists had not constitutionally challenged the duties levied by the Molasses Act of 1733 and by other trade regulatory measures. But how would the colonists distinguish between one kind of duty and the other? The answer, said Dickinson, would be based on the intention of the parliamentary act, whether it was to raise revenue or to regulate trade. So the colonists conceded that Parliament had some authority over them but not the authority to tax them.

To counter all the colonists' halting and fumbling efforts to divide parliamentary authority, the British offered a simple but powerful argument based on the sovereignty of Parliament.

Because the British polemicists could not conceive of the empire as anything but a single, unified community, they found absurd and meaningless all the American distinctions between trade regulations and taxation, between "external" and "internal" taxes, and between separate spheres of authority. If Parliament even "in one instance" was as supreme over the colonists as it was over the people of England, wrote a subministerial official and a spokesman for the British government, William Knox, in 1769, then the Americans were members "of the same community with the people of England." On the other hand, if Parliament's authority over the colonists was denied "in any particular," then it must be denied in "all instances," and the union between Great Britain and the colonies must be dissolved. "There is no alternative," Knox concluded. "Either the Colonies are part of the community of Great Britain, or they are in a state of nature with respect to her, and in no case can be subject to the jurisdiction of that legislative power which represents her community, which is the British Parliament."[31]

Since tyranny in British history had always come from the Crown, good Whigs like Knox found it inconceivable that anyone in his right mind would want to escape from Parliament's libertarian protection. In eighteenth-century English politics, Whigs were those who placed their confidence in Parliament—in opposition to the Tories, who tended to favor the Crown and the established Church of England. The Whigs knew that Parliament was the august author of the Bill of Rights of

1689, the historical guardian of the people's property, and the eternal bulwark of their liberties against the encroachments of the Crown.

Governor Thomas Hutchinson of Massachusetts, like Knox, could not imagine the colonists wanting to be outside of the authority of Parliament, and he unwisely invoked the doctrine of sovereignty in order to convince the colonists of the foolishness of their opposition to Parliament. In speeches to the Massachusetts General Court in January 1773, Hutchinson declared that he knew of "no line that can be drawn between the supreme Authority of Parliament and the total Independence of the Colonies. It is impossible there should be two independent Legislatures in one and the same State, for although there may be but one Head, the King, yet the two Legislative Bodies will make two Governments as distinct as the Kingdom of England and Scotland before the Union."[32]

In response, the Massachusetts Council wanted to avoid the stark alternatives the governor had laid down and sought instead to find some limits on Parliament's authority. But the members of the lower house, the House of Representatives, chose to take a more radical position. Dissatisfied with an initial draft of a reply to the governor, they asked John Adams, who was not at this point a member of the House, for help. They knew there was no one in the province who knew more law and more history than he. In fact, at this moment in January and February 1773 Adams was publishing his articles in opposition to the Crown's paying the salaries of judges of the superior court, which he believed compromised the independence of the colony's judiciary and was contrary to the English constitution.

Adams believed, as he told his diary, that the governor and the General Court were engaged in a debate "upon the greatest Question ever yet agitated"—the idea of sovereignty: that there must be in every state one final, indivisible, and supreme power.[33] Naturally, Adams wanted to be part of this great debate. According to his recollection, the initial draft of the House of Representatives was "full of very popular Talk and with those democratical Principles which have since done so much mischief in this Country." In the place of those democratic principles, he furnished the House "with Law Authorities and the legal and constitutional Reasonings" more in line with the governor's own argument.[34]

In writing the House's reply, Adams drew on his 1765 essay "A Dissertation on the Canon and Feudal Law" and invoked once again the twin tyrannies of kings and the Roman Catholic Church. These two sources of subjugation had long prevailed in the Old World "to the almost utter Extinction of Knowledge, Virtue, Religion, and Liberty," until they were undone by the Protestant Reformation. The knowledge produced by the Reformation "darted its Rays upon the benighted World, increas'd and spread among the People," and made them impatient under the "heavy Yoke" of oppression. "The most virtuous and sensible among them, to whose Steadfastness we in this distant Age and Climate are greatly indebted, were determined to get rid of it."[35]

Adams then entered into a long and detailed history, piling citations and examples one upon the other in the most lawyerlike fashion, all designed to reveal the manner in which the Stuart kings of the early seventeenth century issued charters to the various English colonies. The House contended that this history proved that "our Ancestors considered the Land which they took Possession of in America as out of the Bounds of the Kingdom of England, and out of the Reach and Extent of the Laws of England." Since the colonies were settled outside the realm, they were therefore beyond parliamentary jurisdiction. The seventeenth-century charters, said Adams, speaking for the House, were "repugnant to the Idea of Parliamentary Authority: And to suppose a Parliamentary Authority under such Charters, would necessarily induce that Solecism in Politics *Imperium in Imperio*."

In the end, the House of Representatives accepted the logic of sovereignty that Governor Hutchinson had set forth in his naïve belief that the Massachusetts colonists would never want to be independent of Parliament's protection. "If there be no such Line [between the supreme authority of Parliament and the total independence of the colonies]," it declared, "the Consequence is, either that the Colonies are the Vassals of Parliament, or, that they are totally Independent. As it cannot be supposed to have been the Intention of the Parties in the Compact, that we should be reduced to a State of Vassalage, the Conclusion is, that it was their Sense, that we were thus Independent." Since, as Governor Hutchinson had said, two independent legislatures in the same state were impossible, the colonies had to be "distinct States from the Mother Country," united and connected only through the king "in one Head and common Sovereign."[36] The logic of sovereignty was forcing a fundamental shift in the American position in the empire—a shift that Jefferson would soon quicken.

By 1770 the British government had repealed all the Townshend duties except that on tea. That levy was retained, said Prime Minister Lord North, to serve "as a mark of the supremacy of Parliament, and as an efficient declaration of their right to govern the colonies."[37] Many Boston patriots were looking for an opportunity to arouse opposition, and in 1773 the British government gave it to them. Parliament passed the Tea Act, which granted the East India Company the exclusive privilege of selling tea in America. Although the British government intended this Tea Act only to be a means of saving the East India Company from bankruptcy, it set off alarms throughout the colonies. In several ports colonists stopped the ships from landing the company's tea. After tea ships in Boston were prevented from unloading their cargoes, Governor Hutchinson refused to allow the ships to leave without landing the tea. In response, on December 16, 1773, a group of patriots disguised as Indians dumped about £10,000 worth of tea into Boston harbor.

Adams was ecstatic. "This is the most magnificent Movement of all," he exclaimed. "This Destruction of the Tea is so bold, so daring, so firm, intrepid, and inflexible, and it must have so important Consequences, and so lasting, that I cant but consider it an Epocha in History." "The Sublimity of it," he told his friend James Warren, "charms me!"[38]

DURING 1773 JEFFERSON and a few colleagues in the House of Burgesses, including Patrick Henry, the brothers Richard Henry Lee and Francis Lightfoot Lee, and Dabney Carr, had been meeting privately to discuss imperial issues. They believed, as Jefferson recalled, that older, senior members of the House lacked "the forwardness & zeal which the times required."[39] Many of the Virginia gentry were not pleased by the Bostonians' destruction of private property. And without Virginia, which was the biggest, richest, and most populous colony in North America, American resistance would go nowhere.

But the British government, increasingly frustrated by its repeated appeasement of the colonists, played into the radicals' hands. In response to the Boston Tea Party, Parliament in 1774 passed a succession of laws—the Coercive Acts or, as the colonists called them, the Intolerable Acts. These acts closed the port of Boston, altered the Massachusetts charter, reorganized the government, restricted town meetings, allowed for removing the venue for trials of certain crimes from the colonies to England, and strengthened the quartering of troops in the colonies. At the same time, Thomas Gage, commander in chief of the British army in America, was made governor of the colony of Massachusetts.

These Coercive Acts changed the Virginians' minds overnight. "Not the hundredth part of the inhabitants of that town [Boston]," wrote Jefferson, "had been concerned in the act complained of; . . . yet all were involved in one indiscriminate ruin, by a new executive power, unheard of till then, that of a British parliament." In other words, "property, of the value of many millions of money, was sacrificed to revenge, not repay, the loss of a few thousand." If Parliament could do what it did to Massachusetts, the Virginians became convinced that it could do the same to any other colony. [40]

In response to the Coercive Acts, Jefferson and some other members of the House of Burgesses, as he recalled, "cooked up a resolution" appointing June 1, 1774, which was the date the port of Boston was to be closed, as "a day of fasting, humiliation & prayer." When the royal governor of Virginia dissolved the House, the members convened informally at the Raleigh Tavern in Williamsburg and laid plans for the meeting of a provincial convention in August 1774, which would elect members to attend a Continental Congress in Philadelphia the following month.[41]

Because of illness, Jefferson was unable to attend the provincial convention in Williamsburg. Instead, he wrote out instructions for the Virginia delegates who were to attend the Congress with the hope that they would be embodied in an address to the king. Without his knowledge, his instructions were published in Williamsburg as *A Summary View of the Rights of British America*. He did not supply the title, nor was his name on the pamphlet. It was soon reprinted in Philadelphia and twice in England. It was the most radical statement of American rights yet to appear.

Convinced, like other Americans, that the British government was pursuing "a deliberate and systematical plan of reducing us to slavery," Jefferson came close to describing the colonies as independent states. He had nothing moderate or accommodating to offer. He defended the Tea Party as an "extraordinary interposition" by "an exasperated people" and commiserated with Adams's Boston, promoting a common sense of identity between Virginia and Massachusetts.[42]

To justify the colonies' near independence, he invoked the myth that represented the most alienated strain of Whig or anti-establishment thinking in the eighteenth century—the idea of a golden Anglo-Saxon age of pure liberty and equality that existed before the imposition of the Norman yoke in 1066.[43] Jefferson contended that Englishmen had settled the colonies in the seventeenth century in the same way the ancient Saxons had settled England a thousand years earlier. Just as the Saxons held their lands free of any feudal obligations before the Norman Conquest of 1066 and owed no allegiance to the German mother country from which they had migrated, so too, Jefferson suggested, did the American colonists own their lands outright and exist free of any allegiance to England. "America was not conquered by William the Norman, nor its lands surrendered to him, or any of his successors." The colonists settled the New World on their own and at their own expense, and not at the expense of the British public. Parliament, he said, was "a body of men, foreign to our constitutions, and unacknowledged in our laws," and it had "no right to exercise authority over us." Jefferson thus implied that whatever authority England claimed existed only at the sufferance of the colonies. The colonists, Jefferson said, had voluntarily decided to continue their union with England "by submitting themselves to the same common Sovereign, who was thereby made the central link connecting the several parts of the empire thus newly multiplied."[44]

Jefferson thus offered a conception of the empire similar to that presented by Adams and the Massachusetts House of Representatives a year earlier—an empire in which each of the colonies was independent of Parliament but remained voluntarily tied solely to the king. In 1774 other colonial writers—Benjamin Franklin, James Wilson, and Alexander Hamilton—reached conclusions similar to those of Adams and Jefferson about the nature of the empire. Historians have labeled this position the "dominion theory" of the empire because it anticipated the nature of the British empire worked out in the Statute of Westminster of 1931, which created the modern British Commonwealth, establishing the legislative independence of each of the separate dominions.

Jefferson in his radical pamphlet, however, went way beyond this dominion theory of the empire set forth by the other American polemicists. Jefferson was not content to deny all parliamentary authority over the colonies; he actually indicted the king himself for his failure to fulfill his duty in running the empire.

In fact, as historian Pauline Maier has pointed out, Jefferson's *Summary View* was "the first sustained piece of American political writing that subjected the King's conduct to direct and pointed criticism."[45] Relentlessly, one after the other, Jefferson described the colonists' grievances at the hands of the king. George III, he wrote, had the power to veto the harsh parliamentary legislation against the colonists, but he had refused to exercise it. Instead, he had applied his negative against the laws of the American legislatures. "For the most trifling reasons, and sometimes for no conceivable reason at all, his majesty has rejected laws of the most salutary tendency." And for his first example of the Crown's abusive behavior, Jefferson selected the problem of slavery. In an extraordinary admission for a slaveholding planter, Jefferson declared that "the abolition of domestic slavery was the great object of desire in those colonies where it was unhappily introduced in their infant state." But before that would be possible, the colonists needed to stop the slave trade. But unfortunately the king time and again had vetoed the colonists' efforts to prohibit the importation of slaves.[46]

Jefferson then went on to outline the other oppressive actions by the Crown, including neglecting to approve the colonies' laws in a timely manner, arbitrarily dissolving the representative legislatures and refusing to call others, interfering with the right of the colonists to purchase land, and sending armed forces to the colonies without their consent. Jefferson, in other words, was already primed for the listing of charges against the king that he would place in the Declaration of Independence two years later. He ended by "asserting the rights of human nature" and speaking directly to the king. "Open your breast, sire, to liberal and expanded thought. Let not the name of George the third be a blot in the page of history."[47]

Although Jefferson didn't go as far as Thomas Paine later did in calling George a "royal brute," nevertheless, by claiming that George III was "no more than the chief officer of the people" and that "kings are the servants, not the proprietors of the people," he came awfully close to delegitimizing the monarchy.[48]

BY EARLY 1774 Adams was even more deeply involved in the patriot cause than he had been earlier. He was delighted to see "so much of a Republican Spirit among the People" as they resisted the "Avarice and Ambition" of Hutchinson and his crowd, including the Oliver brothers, Andrew, the stamp agent and lieutenant governor, and Peter, the chief justice of the Massachusetts superior court. The independence of the judges was still a hot issue in Massachusetts, and mobs were threatening the judges if they accepted their salaries from the Crown. Most of the patriot leaders, including Adams, did not want the judges tarred and feathered, but, as he recalled in his autobiography, no one knew what to do. Out of the blue, Adams came up with a constitutional remedy for the problem. He suggested "an Impeachment of the Judges by the House of Representatives before the Council." His colleagues were stunned, or so he recalled. "Why such a thing is without Precedent," they said. But

Adams argued that just as "the House of Commons in England is the grand Inquest of the Nation, the House of Representatives is the grand Inquest of this Province." Many patriots "hardly knew what an Impeachment was," and they questioned whether this "strange Doctrine" could be extracted from the colony's charter. But Adams's impressive and unmatched display of legal scholarship convinced his colleagues that he was right, and the House went ahead and adopted articles of impeachment. Although the Council refused to participate in this unprecedented procedure, the impeachment of the judges of high crimes and misdemeanors was enough to bring the entire judicial process to a halt.[49]

If anyone in the colony still had doubts of Adams's incredible mastery of English law and history, this dredging up of the process of impeachment put them to rest. Adams was no longer just the consigliere of the patriot cause in Massachusetts; he had become one of the most important leaders and Whig spokesmen in the colony.

Thus there was little question that he would be selected in June 1774 as one of the colony's four delegates to attend the Continental Congress. In his diary Adams described the Congress as "an assembly of the wisest Men upon the Continent, who are Americans in Principle, i.e. against the Taxation of Americans, by Authority of Parliament." Yet at the same time he wondered whether these men were "fit for the Times."[50]

The Congress met in Carpenters' Hall in Philadelphia from September 5 to October 26, 1774. If Jefferson had been able to attend the Virginia convention that selected delegates to the Congress, he might have joined Adams. Even without the presence of Jefferson, Adams was impressed with the delegates from Virginia. "These Gentlemen from Virginia," he wrote in his diary, "appear to be the most spirited and consistent of any."[51]

Adams had never been outside of New England, and initially he was overawed by the task that lay ahead. He doubted his ability to adequately represent his colony of Massachusetts in what he called, in one of his typical flashes of learning, "the Court of Ariopagus, the Council of the Amphyctions, a Conclave, a Sanhedrim." He felt his "own insufficiency for this important Business" of being "an American Senator." He was, he confessed, "ignorant of the Characters which compose the Court of Great Britain, as well as of the People who compose the Nation." He didn't have "that Knowledge of the Commerce of the several Colonies, nor even of my own Province which may be necessary." He knew the risks in defying monarchy. "Hampden died in the Field. Sidney on the Scaffold, Harrington in Goal, &c." Engaging in high politics was dangerous, "yet someone must." Beneath all the doubts and fears, however, Adams was exhilarated at the prospect of his participating in what he called "a Nursery of American Statesmen." He was fulfilling his greatest ambitions.[52]

At first, he was overwhelmed by the "quick and constant Succession of new Scenes, Characters, Persons, and Events."[53] In Congress, he told his former law student William Tudor, were "Fortunes, Abilities, Learning, Eloquence, Acuteness equal to any I have met with [in] my Life."[54] But as he got to know his fellow delegates better and took their measure, his confidence rose. They turned out to be less impressive than he had imagined. In his diary he sketched unforgettable vignettes of some of his congressional colleagues that helped to bring them down to earth.

James Duane of New York had "a sly, surveying Eye, a little squint Eyed . . . very sensible, I think, and very artfull." Caesar Rodney of Delaware was "the oddest looking Man in the World. He is tall—thin and slender as a Reed—pale—his Face is not bigger than a large Apple. Yet there is Sense and Fire, Spirit, Wit and Humor in his Countenance." Edward Rutledge of South Carolina soon got on Adams's nerves. "He has the most indistinct, inarticulate Way of speaking. Speaks through his nose—a wretched Speaker in Conversation." He was "a perfect Bob-o-Lincoln—a Swallow—a Sparrow—a Peacock—excessively vain, excessively weak, and excessively variable and unsteady—jejune, inane, and puerile."[55]

JEFFERSON WAS A GRACEFUL WRITER, but he never described people the way Adams did. No other Founder, indeed, no other eighteenth-century American, could paint in prose such colorful and pungent pictures of individuals as Adams. Take, for example, his description in his diary of his Braintree minister:

> P[arson] W[ibird] is crooked, his Head bends forwards, his shoulders are round and his Body is writhed, and bended, his head and half his Body, have a list one Way, the other half declines the other Way, and his lower Parts from his Middle, incline another Way. . . . His Nose is a large Roman nose with a Prodigious Bunch Protuberance upon the Upper Part of it. His mouth is large and irregular, his teeth black and foul and craggy. . . . His Eyes are a little squinted, his Visage is long and lank, his Complexion wan, his Cheeks are fallen, his Chin is long, large, and lean. . . . When he prays at home, he raises one Knee upon the Chair, and throws one Hand over the back of it. With the other he scratches his Neck, pulls the Hair of his Wigg, strokes his Beard, rubs his Eyes, and Lips. . . . When he Walks, he heaves away, and swaggs on one side, and steps almost twice as far with one foot, as the other. When he sits, he sometimes lolls on the arms of his Chair, sometimes on the Table. . . . When he speakes, he cocks and rolls his Eyes, shakes his Head and jerks his Body about.[56]

Henry Fielding could not have done better. But when Adams tried to write seriously about history and politics, all his pungency and color disappeared, and his prose became ponderous and leaden. Unlike Jefferson, whose sensibility was predominantly intellectual, Adams's was largely visual.

ADAMS AND THE REST of the Massachusetts delegation at the Congress soon realized that many of the other delegates suspected them of having independence in mind. At this point, no one dared openly voice a desire for independence, but Adams was certainly thinking about it. He knew, however, that the other colonies were still hoping for reconciliation with the British, and therefore he and his Massachusetts colleagues would have to act "with great Delicacy and Caution."[57]

The task before the Congress, as he saw it, was to explain previous American experience in the empire and at the same time deal with the problem of parliamentary sovereignty. Parliament had been passing Navigation Acts regulating colonial trade for over a century. Could the colonies allow that to continue without conceding the authority of the Declaratory Act of 1766, which had asserted Parliament's right to legislate over the colonies "in all cases whatsoever"? Christopher Gadsden of South Carolina claimed that to acknowledge Parliament's power to regulate the trade of the colonies was to accept "a Right of Legislation, and a Right of Legislation in one Case, is a Right to all." Adams denied that this was true, but the issue was awkward. In the end the best the Congress could do (with Adams writing the draft) was "cheerfully consent" to Parliament's regulation of America's external commerce "from the necessity of the case and a regard to the mutual interest of both countries."[58]

Although Adams worked hard during this First Continental Congress, attending sessions from nine in the morning to three in the afternoon every day but Sunday, he and the other delegates spent a good deal of time dining and entertaining. Adams, alive and sensitive as he was to the world around him, soaked up as much of Philadelphia as he could. He was especially impressed by the number of different churches in the city, and each Sunday he went to two or three services in order to experience nearly all of them: Anglican, Methodist, Baptist, Presbyterian, Quaker, German Moravian, and Roman Catholic. He had never been in a Catholic cathedral before, and that experience, as he reported to Abigail, revealed not only his extraordinary sensuousness but also his religious sensibility.

> The poor Wretches, fingering their beads, chanting Latin, not
> a Word of which they understood; their Pater Nosters and
> Ave Maria's. Their holy Water; their crossing themselves
> perpetually; . . . their bowings and kneelings and genuflections

before the altar. The dress of the priest was rich with lace. His pulpit was velvet and gold. The altarpiece was very rich; little images and crucifixes about; wax candles lighted up. But how shall I describe the picture of our Saviour in a frame of marble over the altar, at full length, upon the cross in the agonies, and blood dripping and streaming from his wounds! The music, consisting of an organ and choir of singers, went all the afternoon except sermon time. And the assembly chanted most sweetly and exquisitely.

Despite his Puritan heritage and his strong anti-Catholic prejudice, which was common to all eighteenth-century Englishmen, he could not help being impressed by his experience. "Here," he told Abigail, "is every Thing which can lay hold of the Eye, Ear, and Imagination. Every Thing which can charm and bewitch the simple and ignorant. I wonder how Luther ever broke the spell."[59] One cannot imagine Jefferson having such a response to a Catholic Mass.

BY THE TIME THE CONGRESS ended its session in late October 1774, Adams had come to realize that he was the equal of any of the delegates. Most of them, he complained, were caught up in "nibbling and quibbling." He told his diary that "these great Witts, these subtle Criticks, these refined Genius's, these learned Lawyers, these wise Statesmen, are so fond of shewing their Parts and Powers, as to make their Consultations very tedious."[60]

After Adams returned to Massachusetts from Philadelphia, he confronted an imposing series of pseudonymous newspaper pieces by "Massachusettensis" defending the British actions. Although Adams thought the author was his old college friend Jonathan Sewall, Massachusettensis was actually another friend, Daniel Leonard, who had recently joined the colony's administration. Leonard offered a lucid defense of the existing relationship between the colonies and the mother country and warned of the dangers of too much popular power. Alarmed by the attention the Massachusettensis articles were getting, Adams in January 1775 began a response under the pseudonym of "Novanglus."

The patriots tended to adopt the English party name of Whigs to set themselves in opposition to those they labeled Tories, who were the traditional defenders of the Crown. Because there were very few Tories in Virginia compared with their numbers in Massachusetts, Jefferson, even if he had been so inclined, never had the same need that Adams and other Whigs in Massachusetts had to confront serious arguments by Loyalist native sons. For Jefferson his enemies were always three thousand miles away; for Adams they were his former friends and neighbors.

Adams began his Novanglus papers intending to "shew the wicked policy of the Tories—trace their plan from its rude sketches to its present compleat draught. Shew that it has been much longer in contemplation, than is generally known—who were the first in it—their views, motives and secret springs of action—and the means they have employed." He immediately quoted Massachusettensis's charges that the Whigs had been reminding "the people of the elevated rank they hold in the universe as men; that all men are by nature equal; that kings are but the ministers of the people; that their authority is delegated to them by the people for their good, and they have a right to resume it and place it in other hands, or keep it themselves, whenever it is made use of to oppress them." These charges only showed how out of touch Massachusettensis was with the colony's opinion. If this Tory polemicist thought that making such Whig views explicit would prove embarrassing to the Whigs, said Adams, he was sadly mistaken.[61]

For Adams, these Tory charges of excessive popular power were not at all awkward or disconcerting; he took all the popular power for granted as right and just. These descriptions of the people's authority, he said, were "what are called revolution principles," the principles of every major thinker in Western history, of Aristotle and Plato, of Livy and Cicero, of Algernon Sidney, James Harrington, and John Locke. They were "the principles of nature and eternal reason—the principles on which the whole government over us now stands."[62] If the Whigs of

Massachusetts were indeed to take these "revolution principles" to heart as completely as Adams suggested, then it was just a matter of time before an actual revolution broke out.

Adams eventually published twelve essays in response to Leonard's seventeen. Unlike Jefferson, Adams seemed to enjoy the give-and-take of these sorts of newspaper exchanges. But the bloated prose of his Novanglus essays was nothing like the clear and succinct writing of Jefferson's *Summary View*. Adams sought to overwhelm his readers with his many references to arcane legal authorities and historical sources, and thus his essays had little of the persuasive power of Jefferson's lean and lithe pamphlet.

At this point Adams was a very good Whig who overflowed with confidence in the people. When Leonard, like other Tories, raised the possibility that the democracy expressed in all the proliferating popular meetings and conventions might become despotic, Adams dismissed the notion out of hand. The idea that the people might tyrannize themselves was illogical. "A democratical despotism," he said, "is a contradiction in terms."[63] This was a popular position that Adams, but not Jefferson, eventually came to disavow.

By 1775 NEARLY ALL the debates over the nature of the empire sooner or later had to end up focusing on the problem of sovereignty. When Leonard writing as Massachusettensis followed the earlier arguments of Knox and Hutchinson and declared that "two supreme or independent authorities cannot exist in the same state," since that would result in "what is called *imperium in imperio,* the height of political absurdity," Adams could only agree. Obviously, he said, two supreme authorities could not exist in the same state, "any more than two supream beings in one universe." Therefore it was clear, he said, "that our provincial legislatures are the only supream authorities in our colonies."[64]

Like the other patriot polemicists, Adams eventually had given up trying to divide the indivisible and separate the inseparable and inevitably had surrendered to the logic of sovereignty—that there had to be only one supreme and indivisible power in each state. Adams and the other patriots finally accepted the idea of sovereignty, but placed it not in Parliament but in their provincial legislatures. The empire, Adams concluded in a common patriot reckoning, could be held together only by the connection that each of these thirteen legislatures had to the king.

And that connection, he later recalled, was solely through the seventeenth-century charter, which was "more like a treaty between Independent Sovereigns than like a Charter or grant of privileges, from a Sovereign to his subjects." In other words, Adams came to believe that the colony had been independent of the "English Church & State" from the very beginning in the seventeenth century. Thus the real authors of independence were "the first Emigrants." Adams and Jefferson and all the other patriotic polemicists of the 1760s and '70s "were only Awakeners & Revivers of the original fundamental principle of Colonization."[65]

By the spring of 1775 and the outbreak of fighting at Lexington and Concord, Adams surely saw that breaking that remaining connection to the British monarchy was just a matter of time, but he was reluctant to say so in print. For his part, Jefferson with his extraordinarily bold and radical pamphlet, *Summary View,* had already so severely shredded that tie to George III that it wouldn't take much to break it completely.

FOUR

INDEPENDENCE

I N T H E A F T E R M A T H O F Lexington and Concord, the Second Continental Congress convened on May 10, 1775. By this time royal government in several colonies had collapsed and the distant king in England was unresponsive to the Congress's petition asking for a redress of the colonists' grievances. Without any central authority to hold the colonies together, the Congress necessarily had to become a replacement for the far-off Crown. Which is why it assumed an authority far beyond what the colonists had conceded to Parliament. As a substitute for the Crown, it began doing all the things that the king had done in the colonies, from regulating Indian affairs to borrowing money and directing the army. The confusion and workload of government often overwhelmed the several dozen delegates from the colonies who made up the Congress. Because it was the entire central government for the colonies, blending legislative, executive, and judicial functions, the members of Congress ended up deciding not only major issues of policy but also the most mundane matters of administration, including whether to pay the bill submitted by a doorkeeper for his services. With only a handful of clerks to help the delegates, it is amazing that anything got done.

Adams was much busier in this Congress than he had been in the

First Continental Congress. With actual fighting having broken out, the stakes were higher and the delegates took their responsibilities much more seriously than they had earlier, entertaining and feasting much less than they had in the fall of 1774. The congressional sessions were longer and the delegates were working harder, with Adams working the hardest of all. He was soon serving on two dozen committees and chairing many of them. "Such a vast Multitude of Objects, civil, political, commercial and military, press and crowd upon Us so fast," he told his friend James Warren after several weeks of meetings, "that We know not what to do first."[1]

From Monday through Saturday Adams met in committees from seven to ten o'clock in the morning; then he participated in the debates in the full Congress from ten o'clock until the late afternoon, when the delegates broke for dinner. After dinner there were more committee meetings that went on from six until ten at night. For fear of British agents and spies, everything had to be done in secrecy, which added to the strain. Since each colony had only one vote, some delegates could take time off. Adams was not one of them.

At first Jefferson was not one of Virginia's seven delegates. But when Peyton Randolph had to return from Philadelphia, the thirty-two-year-old Jefferson was belatedly selected to be one of the colony's congressional representatives. Wealthier than many of the delegates, Jefferson spared no expense in traveling to Philadelphia, arriving with four horses. He took up luxurious quarters that were separated from the other delegates. By the time he arrived, the Congress had been in session for six weeks.

Unlike Adams, who seemed constantly on his feet, Jefferson remained silent in the public sessions. Adams later recalled that the whole time he sat with Jefferson in the Congress, "I never heard him utter three Sentences together." Jefferson was, however, very effective in committees and small groups, Adams recalled. He came to the Congress with "a reputation for literature, science, and a happy talent at composition"; indeed, the delegates passed Jefferson's writings about and praised their "peculiar felicity of expression."[2]

Adams learned of Jefferson's radical views in conversations and committees. Jefferson turned out to be "so prompt, frank, explicit and decisive," recalled Adams, even more so than his firebrand cousin Samuel Adams, "that he soon seized upon my heart."[3] Eight years older than Jefferson, Adams regarded the Virginian as his protégé, and Jefferson tended to assume that role. They complemented each other. Adams was often irascible and not comfortable in company, and was likely to erupt with tactless remarks. In the Congress he often resorted to sarcasm and satire to put down his opponents.[4] By contrast, Jefferson was always amiable and acutely sensitive to the feelings of whomever he was speaking with or writing to. He always went out of his way not to offend. His politeness was important to his success, but it was also a source of some mistrust.

Jefferson was certainly aware that many of the congressional delegates were lukewarm about independence. Even Adams realized that he had to curb his enthusiasm for independence if he was eventually to bring along the other delegates. He knew that the colonies were "not yet ripe" for such measures as forming a confederation and opening America's ports to all nations. "America," he said, "is a great unwieldy Body. Its Progress must be slow. It is like a large Fleet sailing under Convoy. The fleetest Sailors must wait for the dullest and slowest."[5]

Although Jefferson had been immediately asked to join John Dickinson in revising an earlier version of a Declaration on the Necessity of Taking Up Arms, he realized that he and Dickinson could not be as severe and radical in this document as he had been in his *Summary View*. Hence the declaration adopted by Congress on July 6, 1775, ended up assuring all the British subjects throughout the empire "that we mean not to dissolve that Union which has so long and so happily subsisted between us, and which we sincerely wish to see restored."[6]

Adams was one of the members who pushed the Congress to take the boldest stand. He repeatedly had to contend with the eloquence of the "Pennsylvania Farmer," John Dickinson, whom Adams in a letter captured and published by the British had called a "piddling Genius" who had "given a silly Cast to our whole Doings."[7] Dickinson had been one of the leading patriots in the late 1760s, but by 1775 he warned his colleagues that breaking from the British empire would cause the colonies to bleed from every vein.

Publicly both Jefferson and Adams had to suggest that they hoped for a restoration of the imperial relationship as long as American rights were fully acknowledged. This was especially true of Jefferson, who disliked personal controversy and tended to take account of what the recipient of his letters might prefer to hear. As late as August 1775, for example, he told his kinsman John Randolph, who was abandoning the colonies for England, that he was "looking with fondness towards a reconciliation with Great Britain." But it is clear that both Jefferson and Adams had privately determined on America's independence long before Thomas Paine published *Common Sense* in January 1776.[8]

Adams tended to be more frank and honest in displaying his feelings. No one in the Congress had any doubts where he stood, and no one did more to move the delegates toward independence. Adams, Jefferson later told Daniel Webster, "was our Colossus on the floor" of the Congress. He was "not graceful, not elegant, not always fluent." But, said Jefferson, Adams in debate could come out "with a power, both of thought and of expression which moved us from our seats."[9]

By early 1776, Adams began expressing his anger at the British and his desire for independence so openly that many thought he was the author of *Common Sense*, the boldest and most blatant call for an outright break from Britain that the colonists had ever read. By conventional eighteenth-century standards of rhetoric, *Common Sense* was so full of rage and indignation, so full of coarse and everyday imagery, that few would have thought the gracious and amiable Mr. Jefferson was the author. Although Adams confessed to Abigail that he "could not have written any Thing in so manly and striking a style," he believed he had a better understanding of how to construct governments than the author.[10]

Following the publication of Paine's pamphlet, the issue in the Congress was not as much when to declare independence as how to form new governments in each of the colonies. "To contrive some Method for the Colonies to glide insensibly, from under the old Government, into a peaceable and contented Submission to new ones," Adams in April 1776 told his learned friend Mercy Otis Warren, the sister of James Otis, was "the most difficult and dangerous part of the Business."

Adams and the other radicals in the Congress increased the pressure to move the Congress toward a general "Recommendation to the People of all the States to institute Governments"—a recommendation that would in effect move some of the reluctant colonies into independence. For, as Adams told Abigail, "no Colony, which shall assume a Government under the People, will give it up."[11]

With Congress's resolution of May 10, 1776, Adams saw his dreams fulfilled. This important resolution, which Adams drafted, urged the colonies to adopt new governments "where no government sufficient to the exigencies of their affairs have been established." Under Adams's leadership, Congress on May 15 added an extraordinary preamble to the resolution, which declared "that the exercise of every kind of authority under the . . . Crown should be totally suppressed" and called for the exertion of "all the powers of government . . . under the authority of the people of the colonies."[12]

When an unenthusiastic James Duane of New York told Adams that this preamble added to the May 10 resolution was really "a Machine for the fabrication of Independence," Adams, "smiling," retorted that "it was independence itself." He was not wrong. Not all the delegates who voted for the May resolution believed they were endorsing independence, noted Carter Braxton of Virginia, but "those out of doors on both sides [of] the question construe it in that manner."[13]

The May declaration, Adams told his friend James Warren, "was the most important Resolution that ever was taken in America." As he said to Abigail, it was "the last Step, a compleat Seperation" from Great Britain, "a total absolute Independence, not only of her Parliament but of her Crown." Since Adams was the delegate most responsible for "touching some Springs and turning some small Wheels which have had and will have such Effects" that few could have foreseen, it is not surprising that he should have felt "an Awe upon my Mind, which is not easily described."[14]

. . .

FOLLOWING THE MAY 1776 resolution and its preamble, which required a separate resolution, most delegates began thinking about creating new constitutions for their colonies. "It is a work of the most interesting nature," remarked Jefferson, "and such as every individual would wish to have his voice in." And it seemed to many as if that were indeed the case. Even the business of the Continental Congress was slowed by the lure of the constitution-making that was taking place in nearly every colony in the aftermath of the May resolutions. Many members of Congress, including the entire Maryland delegation, left for home in order to participate in the erection of new governments—and this before any declaration of independence. Except for waging the war, complained Robert Morris, the wealthy merchant from Pennsylvania, "this seems to be the present business of America." The Congress, grumbled Francis Lightfoot Lee of Virginia, was being left "too thin." For "Alass! *Constitutions* employ every pen." Nothing in 1776—not the creation of a confederation of the states, not an alliance with France, not even the war—engaged Americans more than did the framing of their new constitutions.[15]

Jefferson was one of the delegates who wanted to leave the Congress in order to participate in his colony's constitution-making. One day following Congress's May 15 preamble to the resolution of May 10, 1776, which had called on each colony to frame a government, Jefferson wrote to his colleagues in Virginia suggesting that the entire delegation be recalled to help in drawing up the new constitution. "In truth," he said, "it was the whole object of the present controversy." Sometime before the middle of June 1776, he drafted a constitution and had sent it to Virginia; but it arrived too late to substantially affect the state constitution that already had been written by George Mason and other colleagues. In frustration Jefferson sat in Philadelphia and pleaded with his colleagues in Virginia to call him back home.

The structure of the government that Jefferson proposed in his draft was basically similar to the constitution adopted by his fellow Virginians. He recommended a bicameral legislature together with an executive and judiciary whose "offices were to be kept for ever separate." Other suggestions, however, were controversial and, as George Wythe told Jefferson in July 1776, required much discussion and would have to be dealt with later—which Jefferson had every intention of doing. These included granting the right of citizenship and thus the suffrage to anyone who intended to live permanently in the state; recognizing full religious liberty for all persons and freeing the state from having to maintain any religious establishment; ending the importation of slaves; granting fifty acres of land freely to all adult white males who did not already have that many; and establishing a more equitable system of representation based on population.[16]

What the Virginia convention did take almost verbatim from Jefferson's draft was his preface that contained a series of charges against the king—most of which he would repeat in his Declaration of Independence. He ended his indictment by declaring that George III was "deposed from the kingly office in this government, and absolutely divested of all it's rights, powers, and prerogatives." If that weren't enough protection against tyranny, Jefferson's executive was to be elected by a House of Representatives for a one-year term and ineligible for reelection for three years.

Although Jefferson went on to say that the executive "shall possess the powers formerly held by the king," he made sure that very few of those powers actually remained in the executive's hands. Unlike Virginia's adopted constitution or the constitutions of the other states, Jefferson's draft spelled out in remarkable detail just what that executive could not do. He would have no negative or veto over legislation; he could not control the meetings of the legislature; he could not declare war or conclude peace; he could not raise armed forces; he could not coin money or regulate weights and measures; he could not erect courts, offices, corporations, markets, and ports; he could not lay embargoes; he could not even pardon crimes or emit punishments. All these traditional prerogative powers were to be given to the legislature or abolished. So much authority was stripped from the executive that Jefferson rightly labeled the office the "Administrator" rather than the term "governor" used by the other constitutions.[17]

Jefferson went into such detail in repudiating all semblances of the kingly office because, as he told his colleague Edmund Pendleton in August 1776, he was anxious about the possible "re-acknolegement of the British tyrant as our king. . . . Remember," he warned, "how universally the people run into the idea of recalling Charles the 2d. after living many years under a republican government." Such a caution suggests just how contingent everything seemed to those revolutionaries in 1776, who, of course, could not know their future.[18]

When it came to the upper house or the senate in his constitution, Jefferson expressed an early uncharacteristic mistrust of the people. All the senates of the state constitutions drawn up in 1776 were presumably to be made up of the wisest and most prominent men of the community. Unlike the lower houses, or houses of representatives, the senators were to have no constituents; they were not to represent anyone. But if elected by the people, as was the case in the Virginia constitution, the senators, Jefferson thought, might get to think they had constituents and were dependent on them; they would be just another house of representatives, thus undermining the idea of mixed government. To prevent this possibility, Jefferson's senate was to be elected by the lower house, not by the people directly. This was necessary, he claimed, in order "to get the wisest men chosen and to make them perfectly independent when chosen." Experience had taught him, he told Pendleton, "that a choice by the people themselves is not generally distinguished for it's wisdom. This first secretion from them is usually crude and heterogeneous." He had thus proposed that the senators be elected by the lower houses for a nine-year unrenewable term, so that they would not forever "be casting their eyes forward to the period of election (however distant) and be currying favor with the electors, and consequently dependent upon them." He could accept George Mason's plan for a system of electors to select the upper house. He could even submit to Pendleton's suggestion "to an appointment for life, or to any thing rather than a mere creation by and dependence on the people." But he took back much of this mistrust of the people when it came to suggestions that the senate should be confined to men who possessed a large amount of property. His experience told him that "integrity" was not "the characteristic of wealth." In the end, he believed that "the decisions of the people, as a body, will be more honest and disinterested than those of wealthy men."[19]

Making property the qualification for membership in the upper houses was a point on which Adams later would come to disagree dramatically with Jefferson. But in 1776 Adams was not that far away from Jefferson's ideas about the formation of the senates or from the Virginia constitution that the new state finally adopted. In fact, Adams had a greater influence on the Virginia constitution of 1776 than did Jefferson and probably anyone else.[20]

NO REVOLUTIONARY LEADER was more interested in constitutionalism than Adams. His understanding of constitutionalism was formed from his reading of history, and especially English history. Throughout the eighteenth century, Englishmen had described their centuries-long history as essentially a struggle between the king and the people, between the prerogative powers of an encroaching Crown and the rights of the people defended by their representatives in the House of Commons. This ancient conflict between monarchy and democracy had been mediated by the aristocracy in the House of Lords acting as the holder of the scales in the marvelously balanced English constitution. In his *Spirit of the Laws* (1748)—the political work most widely read by the revolutionaries—the French philosophe Montesquieu had accepted this conventional understanding of the English constitution and had emphasized the role of the nobility in the House of Lords in maintaining the balance between the major historic antagonists, the king and the people.[21] In 1776, at the moment of constitution-making in the states, this traditional view of the balance in the English constitution was one that Adams shared.

Adams had been committed to some sort of mixed or balanced

government well before the Declaration of Independence. "There are only Three simple Forms of Government," he declared in an oration delivered at Braintree in 1772, each of these simple forms undergirded by a social estate or social order. When the entire ruling power was entrusted to the discretion of a single person, the government, said Adams, was called a monarchy, or the rule of one. When it was placed in the hands of "a few great, rich, wise Men," the government was an aristocracy, or the rule of the few. And when the whole power of the society was lodged with all the people, the government was termed a democracy, or the rule of the many. Each of these simple forms of government possessed a certain quality of excellence. For monarchy, it was energy; for aristocracy, it was wisdom; and for democracy, it was virtue. But Adams knew that each one of these simple forms of government, left alone, tended to run wild and become perverted. Only by balancing and mixing all three in the government, only through the reciprocal sharing of political power by the social orders of the one, the few, and the many, could the desirable qualities of each be preserved and the government be free. As Adams put it in 1772, "Liberty depends upon an exact Balance, a nice Counterpoise of the Powers in the state. . . . The best Governments in the World have been mixed."[22]

And for Adams in 1772 the best government of all was the English constitution, properly mixed and balanced. Montesquieu and other eighteenth-century philosophes admired the English constitution precisely because it seemed to have achieved the balance and mixture that theorists since Aristotle and the ancient Greeks had only longed for. But it was not simply the expression of the three simple forms of government in the Crown, the House of Lords, and the House of Commons that made the English constitution seem extraordinary. More important was the fact that the whole society was embodied in these three governmental institutions. Each of the estates of the realm or, as Adams called them, "the powers of the society"—the king, peers, and people—was represented in the English government, that is, the king-in-Parliament. Not only were the three estates of the society embodied in the English government in this marvelous manner, but this tripartite English constitution corresponded beautifully with the three simple governments of antiquity—democracy, aristocracy, and monarchy. All this gave the English constitution its awesome reputation and the king-in-Parliament its sovereignty.

With talk of constitution-making already in the air following publication of Paine's *Common Sense*, the colony of North Carolina in early March 1776 asked its two congressional delegates, William Hooper and John Penn, to come home and bring some ideas about a form of government with them. Knowing that Adams was keenly interested in the science of politics, Hooper and Penn asked their Massachusetts colleague for advice. Sometime in late March, Adams wrote out a plan of government by hand and sent a copy to each of the Carolina delegates. George Wythe of Virginia and Jonathan Dickinson Sergeant of New Jersey learned of Adams's plan and asked for copies too. Finally, when Richard Henry Lee requested a copy, Adams decided to publish his plan as a pamphlet, *Thoughts on Government, Applicable to the Present State of the American Colonies*, printed anonymously in Philadelphia in April 1776. It was the most important and influential essay that Adams ever wrote.

Even though the pamphlet had originated, as the subtitle put it, as a hastily composed *Letter from a Gentleman to his Friend*, and was later considered by Adams to be "a poor Scrap," he actually had been thinking about creating new forms of government for the colonies ever since the possibility of independence had entered his head.[23] In working out his plan of government he realized that he needed to take the various colonial constitutions, which, with their assemblies, councils, and governors, were miniature versions of the mixed and balanced English constitution that he admired so much, and transform them into constitutions applicable to what he assumed the American colonies would soon become— independent republics.

Adams was sure the new American governments had to be republics. But for Adams this was not as much of an innovation as it was for others. In his Novanglus essays of 1775, borrowing from the seventeenth-century English theorist James Harrington, he had defined a republic as *"a government of laws, and not of men."* This definition, if just, he said, meant that "the British constitution is nothing more nor less than a republic, in which the king is first magistrate." This was one kind of republic the English had, but there could be other kinds. Because "the powers of society"—meaning the one, the few, and the many—could be combined in different ways, there was, he concluded, "an inexhaustible variety" of republics, including that of the British monarchy. Although he tried to explain that the British king "being hereditary, and being possessed of such ample and splendid prerogatives, is no objection to the government's being a republic as long as it is bound by fixed laws, which the people have a voice in making," he was never able to convince his fellow Americans that the British monarchy was really a republic; and the resultant confusion plagued him the rest of his life.[24]

HOWEVER MUCH HE DIFFERED with his fellow Americans over the definition of a republic, he at least agreed with them, and with Montesquieu, that as republics the new states would have to be founded on the principle of virtue. By classical standards virtue meant the willingness of people to sacrifice their private interests for the sake of the public, the *res publica*. For this reason Adams very much wanted his home state of Massachusetts to call its "Government a Commonwealth."[25]

Adams's republicanism was liberal and enlightened, not narrowly classical. Certainly neither Adams nor Jefferson was so enamored of antiquity that either believed that an individual belonged solely to the political community and that human flourishing could be achieved only within that political community. Their republicanism was not incompatible with the need to protect individual rights from an overweening government. Yet both Adams and Jefferson were classically educated enough to know that republics required sufficient virtue in the character of their citizens to prevent corruption and eventual decay. For this reason, they both knew that republics were very fragile polities, and always had been throughout history. A republic, said Adams, "is productive of every Thing, which is great and excellent among Men. But its Principles are as easily destroyed as human Nature is corrupted." Jefferson agreed.

Americans, he said, had to anticipate "a time, and that not a distant one, when corruption in this, as in the country from which we derive our origins, will have seized the heads of government, and be spread by them through the body of the people."[26]

Although Jefferson tended to see the corruption coming from the government while Adams believed it more likely inherent in human nature, both patriots knew that republics demanded far more morally from their citizens than monarchies did of their subjects. In monarchies, where authority flowed from the top down, each man's desire to do what was right in his own eyes could be restrained by patronage or honor, by fear or force. In republics, however, where authority came from below, from the people themselves, each citizen must somehow be persuaded to sacrifice his personal desires for the sake of the public good. In their purest form republics had no adhesives, no bonds holding their societies together, except their citizens' voluntary patriotism and willingness to obey public authority. Without virtue and self-sacrifice, republics would fall apart.

Did Americans have this "positive Passion for the public Good," this kind of virtue? That was the question that Adams anxiously asked himself as he outlined his plan of government. As he told Mercy Otis Warren in April 1776, he had seen "such Selfishness and Littleness even in New England, that I sometimes tremble to think that altho We are engaged in the best Cause that ever employed the Human Heart, yet the Prospect of success is doubtfull not for Want of Power or of Wisdom, but of Virtue." He knew that the new American governments would have to be popular, but he realized that "the degrees of Popularity in a Government are so various" that much might be done to prevent their corruption.[27]

To counter the possibility that the American people might not have sufficient virtue to sustain their new republics, Adams suggested a number of protective measures. In his pamphlet he urged a rotation of all offices, the creation of an independent judiciary that would be distinctly separated from the legislative and executive powers, laws for the liberal education of youth, and the passage of sumptuary laws. Advocating these sumptuary laws regulating personal expenditures on food and dress, he admitted, "will excite a smile." But, he contended, they would be good for the happiness of the people and the war effort. "Frugality is a great revenue, besides curing us of vanities, levities, and fopperies which are real antidotes to all the great, manly and warlike virtues."[28]

BUT MOST IMPORTANT IN COUNTERING the self-interestedness of human nature was his recommendation that the new constitutions possess some of the mixed and balanced features of the English constitution, which he claimed was "a fine, a nice, a delicate machine, and the perfection of it depends upon such complicated movements, that it is as easily disordered as the human body."[29] For Americans, however, he knew that this delicate machine would have to be republicanized. To prevent the people from having complete control of the government and running amok, all three "powers of society" had to be embodied in the constitution. This meant that the people would be represented in only one part of the legislature, in what most Americans called their houses of representatives. It was this "Popular Power, the democraticall Branch of our Constitution," he said, that had been invaded by the British government. This popular assembly, said Adams, "should be a miniature, an exact portrait of the people at large. It should think, feel, reason, and act like them."[30]

But once the people were represented in this one assembly, the "question arises whether all the powers of government, legislative, executive, and judicial, shall be left in this body?" Adams answered this question with as much passion as he felt about anything. "I think a people can not be long free, nor ever happy, whose government is in one Assembly." For this reason he never ceased expressing horror at what Pennsylvania did in 1776 in creating a constitution with a unicameral legislature and a plural executive. In fact, in subsequent years his well-known celebration of a two-house legislature became a major weapon wielded by those seeking to revamp the radical Pennsylvania constitution.[31] Adams confessed that "it would grieve me to the very Soul" if his own state of Massachusetts ever contemplated establishing "a single Assembly as a Legislature." For the rest of his life, this devotion to a bicameral legislature embodying two principal "powers of society" became the basis of all his political theory.[32]

To avoid all the evils that flowed from placing all the people's power in a single assembly, Adams urged that another distinct legislative body be created, which he labeled "a Council." This council or upper house would not be another representation of the people. Instead, it would be an embodiment of the social power of the few, the aristocracy, in accord with the traditional theory of mixed government. In this respect his upper house was no different from Jefferson's proposed senate.

With his proposal for a council, Adams was obviously thinking of his own Massachusetts colonial constitution, in which the Council (the upper house) had often tried to arbitrate the struggles between the royal governors and the people. "If the legislative power is wholly in one Assembly, and the executive in another, or in a single person," wrote Adams, "these two powers will oppose and enervate upon each other, until the contest shall end in war." To avoid this danger, another house in the legislature was necessary. The councils—or senates, as most states labeled the upper houses—would act, as the House of Lords in the English constitution did, "as a mediator between the two extreme branches of the legislature, that which represent the people and that which is vested with the executive."[33] This was how Montesquieu had described the role of the House of Lords in the English constitution. In other words, Adams conceived of his republicanized aristocracy mediating the classic struggle between monarchy and democracy that he and other Whigs assumed had gone on throughout the entire trajectory of English history.

If these aristocratic councils were to play their balancing role between the governors and people in the new mixed state constitutions, however, they would have to be a good deal stronger and more independent than the colonial councils had been. Even though the Massachusetts Council had been elected by both houses of the legislature, rather than appointed by the Crown, as was the case with the upper houses of the other colonies, it seldom had been able to resist the influence of the governor. "In disputes between the governor and the house," Adams wrote in 1775, "the council have generally adhered to the former, and in many cases have complied with his humour" rather than exercise its independent judgment.[34]

Adams proposed that both houses of the legislature, together, would annually elect the governor, who, like the king in England, would be "an integral part of the legislature," thus becoming an equal participant in lawmaking with the house of representatives and the senate. Although this governor would be "stripped of most of those badges of domination called prerogatives," he, like the English king, said Adams, ought to retain a veto power over all legislation. This was a far more powerful governor than Jefferson's proposed executive.

Although Adams's plan of a bicameral legislature and a separation of legislative, executive, and judicial powers very much influenced the state constitution-makers in 1776, his suggestion of a gubernatorial veto was too much for most of them. Except for the early constitution of South Carolina, and that only temporarily, all the revolutionary state constitutions prohibited their governors from having any role in legislation.

Even Adams's proposal that governors be granted a veto power over legislation was made timidly and without much assurance that it would be followed. As he told his colleagues in Massachusetts, he did not "expect, nor indeed desire that it should be attempted to give the Governor a Negative, in our Colony." Let the chief executive, he said, be only the head of the Council Board, a small executive advisory cabinet that, unlike the colonial Council, would have no legislative authority. "Our People will never Submit to more," and, as he conceded, it was "not clear that it is best they should."[35]

It was not just the elimination of the role of the governors in legislation that made the state constitutions of 1776 truly radical. Taking away all of the governors' traditional prerogative powers, as both Jefferson and Adams suggested, the framers of the state constitutions severely undermined, if they didn't entirely destroy, the chief magistrate's major responsibility for ruling the society—an abrupt departure from the English constitutional tradition. The eighteenth-century English monarch may have been severely confined by the Bill of Rights of 1689 and other parliamentary restrictions, but few Englishmen ever doubted that the principal responsibility for governing the realm still belonged to the Crown. With the 1776 state constitutions, this was no longer true. When the governors had even the pardoning power wrested from their hands and granted to the popular legislatures, then it became obvious that such an enfeebled executive could no longer be a magisterial ruler in any traditional sense, but could only be an "Administrator," as Jefferson had aptly named the office.

ADAMS WAS SURPRISED BY the rapid acceptance of the ideas expressed in his pamphlet. The adoption of republican governments, especially in the South, was "astonishing." Prior to 1774, who could have predicted it? "Idolatry to Monarchs and servility to Aristocratical Pride," he declared, "was never so totally eradicated, from so many Minds in so short a Time."[36]

Nevertheless, it was not long before Jefferson and Adams and many other constitution-makers of 1776 came to regret what they had done. When he became governor of Virginia in 1779, Jefferson came to appreciate only too clearly the weakness of the office his colleagues had created. As he looked back from 1816, he realized that he and his fellow Americans in 1776 had not truly understood republicanism. "In truth," he said, "the abuses of monarchy had so much filled all the space of political contemplation, that we imagined everything republican which was not monarchy." Out of our dislike of kings and former royal governors we had emasculated our new elected republican governors. "We had not yet penetrated to the mother principle, that 'governments are republican only in proportion as they embody the will of their people and execute it.'"[37]

Adams in 1816 would have agreed that the constitutional framers in 1776 had not fully understood what he had repeatedly called "the divine science of politicks." But it was not because they had failed to embody the will of the people in all parts of their governments. Rather, it was because they had granted too much power to the people in the houses of representatives. They should have offset that popular power with stronger and more distinctive senates and more powerful governors, who should never have had their prerogatives taken away from them in the first place. Above all, Adams believed, these senates and governors should never have been considered to embody the will of the people. They were the aristocracy and monarchy of a proper mixed constitution; the people, the democracy, existed only in the houses of representatives.[38]

MUCH OF THIS TALK OF NEW GOVERNMENTS and the planning for new constitutions had taken place as a result of the Congress's May 1776 resolutions and thus before the colonies actually declared their independence from Great Britain. So Adams had a point when he later argued that his May resolutions were more important than the Declaration of Independence, which in his mind became only a belated legal recognition of what already was taking place. Few Americans agreed with him, and certainly not Jefferson. But in May 1776 Jefferson was fortunate that Virginia ignored his wishes and refused to recall him. If he had gone home, he would have missed the most important moment of his life.

On June 11, 1776, the Congress appointed a committee of five delegates to draft a formal declaration of independence. The Congress aimed for geographical diversity: Jefferson from Virginia, Adams from Massachusetts, Roger Sherman from Connecticut, Robert R. Livingston from New York, and Benjamin Franklin from Pennsylvania. Adams in his autobiography claimed that this "Committee of Five" had appointed Jefferson and him as a subcommittee to draft the declaration. But Adams said that he had urged Jefferson to do the drafting by himself. He told Jefferson that it was important to have a Virginian take the lead. Adams said that he had been so obnoxiously zealous in promoting independence that a document he drafted would be more severely scrutinized and criticized by the Congress than one composed by Jefferson. Besides, he knew very well the "Elegance" of Jefferson's pen.[39]

Adams repeated this account in a letter to Timothy Pickering in 1822, some of which Pickering quoted in a Fourth of July oration in 1823 that was subsequently published. When this oration came to Jefferson's attention, he wrote his friend James Madison that Adams's memory was faulty—not surprising, he said, since Adams was nearly eighty-seven years of age and the events had taken place nearly a half century earlier.[40] Jefferson, who was himself eighty, claimed that he had some notes taken at the time that showed that the committee had appointed him alone to draft the Declaration. Although the notes have disappeared, if they ever existed, Jefferson was correct that he alone was appointed to draw up the document, something that Adams had previously noted in a diary entry of June 23, 1779.[41]

Of course, no one in 1776 realized how significant the drafting of the Declaration would become. Besides the May resolutions, which had called on the colonists to suppress Crown authority and set up independent governments, Adams thought the really important decision for independence had been taken on July 2, when the Congress voted to break away from the British empire. "The Second Day of July," he told Abigail, "will be the most memorable Epocha in the History of America." He believed that it "would be celebrated, by succeeding Generations, as the great Anniversary Festival. It ought to be commemorated, as the Day of Deliverance by Solemn Acts of Devotion to God Almighty. It ought to be solemnized with Pomp and Parade, with Shews, Games, Sports, Guns, Bells, Bonfires and Illuminations from one End of this Continent to the other from this Time forward forever more."[42]

Adams was so busy at this time that he was probably relieved that Jefferson was assigned the task of drafting the Declaration. At the same time as he was asked to serve on the Committee of Five to draft a declaration of independence, he was appointed to two powerful committees: one designed to form a Board of War that would oversee military operations, and a second assigned to prepare a plan of treaties that the country would make with foreign powers—assignments that surely Adams believed were more crucial than drawing up a declaration of independence.[43] By the early nineteenth century, however, both he and Jefferson knew better. The so-called authorship of the Declaration had taken on immense emotional significance for both men; indeed, it had become one of the most important issues dividing them.

Jefferson made no claim of originality in drafting the document. The object of the Declaration, he recalled later, in answer to the many requests for his sources, was "not to find out new principles, or new arguments, never before thought of, not merely to say things which had never been said before; but to place before mankind the common sense of the subject, in terms so plain and firm as to their assent, and to justify ourselves in the independent stand we are compelled to take." Jefferson said he had "turned to neither book nor pamphlet" nor to "any particular and previous writing." Instead, he said in 1825, the authority of the Declaration rested "on the harmonizing sentiments of the day." It was simply meant "to be an expression of the American mind."[44]

EVEN THE FAMOUS PHRASE from the Declaration that "all men are created equal" was not new, at least not to those who considered themselves modern and enlightened. This radical idea, of course, had roots in Christianity and Western culture that went back centuries, but by the eighteenth century it had taken on for many a literal and secular significance that is still the foundation of America's democratic faith. The slaveholding planter William Byrd, who was as much of an aristocrat as Virginia was ever to know, had read widely and was a learned member of the Royal Society, a London organization devoted to the advancement of knowledge. Nevertheless, despite his great distance from the common man, he wanted to be thought modern and enlightened and thus could not help affirming in 1728 that "the principal difference between one people and another proceeds only from the differing opportunities of improvement." Governor Francis Fauquier of Virginia, Jefferson's dining and music partner, made the point more bluntly: "White, Red, or Black, polished or unpolished," he declared in 1760, "Men are Men." James Boswell, Dr. Johnson's great biographer, during his tour to the Hebrides in 1773, was surprised to find a black African servant in the north of Scotland whose manners were no different from those of a white servant from Bohemia. But then he realized that he had forgotten the modern presumption that culture was socially constructed. "A man is like a bottle," he observed, "which you may fill with red wine or with white."[45]

Republicans especially had to believe that human nature could be shaped and molded and made more virtuous. If one held that human nature was "totally depraved, wicked, and corrupt," then, said Nathaniel

Chipman, a Yale graduate and eventually the chief justice of the Vermont Supreme Court, faith in the people's capacity for self-government was doomed. To be sure, Chipman admitted, there were numerous examples in history of tyranny and the abuses of power, even by the people. But these, he said, were not generally produced by "any malignity, any culpable disposition in the nature of man." They were instead "the effect of situation," of circumstances, of the environment. In other words, enlightened liberals had come to believe that what caused individuals to behave in an evil or corrupt manner and distinguished each of them from one another was the environment in which they were raised, the circumstances that molded and shaped them.[46]

John Adams agreed. He had to agree, at least at the beginning of his career, not simply because, like Byrd and Jefferson, he had read books and wanted to be thought enlightened, but, more important, because his personal experience told him that all men being created equal was true. As a young unconnected lawyer making his way in Massachusetts society, he had so often felt the arrogance and pretensions of the so-called great families that he could not help identifying emotionally with common ordinary people—"the multitude, the million, the populace, the vulgar, the mob, the herd and the rabble, as the great always delight to call them." These "meanest and lowest of the people," he wrote anonymously in newspaper publications in the 1760s, were far from being mere animals as some gentry called them; they were in fact "by the unalterable laws of God and nature, as well intitled to the benefit of the air to breathe, light to see, food to eat, and clothes to wear, as the nobles or the king." Adams believed devoutly—he had to believe—as he wrote in 1766, a decade before Jefferson's Declaration of Independence, that "all men are born equal." No patriot in the decade leading up to the Revolution defended with more passion common ordinary people against those who would have them "ridden like horses, fleeced like sheep, worked like cattle, and fed and cloathed like swine and hounds."[47]

Adams came to appreciate, as much as any American did, the capacity of individuals to transform themselves. Educated people came to believe—it was the basic premise of all enlightened thinking in the eighteenth century—that individuals were not born to be what they might become. As John Locke had written, the mind originally was "a white Paper, void of all Characters, without any *Ideas*," and it was filled up through time by "*Experience*."⁴⁸ As Adams pointed out in 1760, Locke, with the help of Francis Bacon, had "discovered a new World." He had demonstrated that human personalities at birth were unformed, impressionable things that could be cultivated and civilized. Experience gained through the senses was what molded and created people's characters; it inscribed itself on the blank slate, the tabula rasa, of people's minds. Hence, said Adams, by controlling and manipulating the sensations that people experienced, their character could be transformed. Adams took the image of cultivation seriously and literally. The "Rank and unwholesome Weeds" that had so dominated traditional society could now be "Exterminated and the fruits raised." Barbarism could be eliminated and civility increased. This kind of enlightenment had been denied to Cicero and the ancients. The idea that only cultivation separated one person from another was, he said, "the true sphere of Modern Genius."⁴⁹

In other words, nurture, not nature, was what mattered. This was the explosive eighteenth-century assumption that lay behind the idea that all men were created equal. Not everyone had the same capacity to reason, but since everyone had senses, this Lockean notion that all ideas were produced by the senses was inherently egalitarian.

MANY OF JEFFERSON'S COLLEAGUES in Virginia were not entirely happy with all this talk of being born equal. In the convention drawing up the new Virginia constitution in 1776, George Mason prefaced the document with a Declaration of Rights stating that "all men are by nature equally free and independent." Robert Carter Nicholas raised the question of the applicability of Mason's statement to black slaves. Could such a pronouncement be construed to free the slaves? Edmund Pendleton solved the problem by proposing to insert the clause "when they enter into a state of society," thus placing the African slaves outside of society and unentitled to enjoy the rights of citizenship.⁵⁰

In his *Notes on the State of Virginia*, Jefferson offered a more radical solution to the problem by doubting his own belief in the natural equality of all human beings. In a sense he had to. If one believed in the natural equality of blacks, then slavery became impossible, which is why most enlightened thinkers on both sides of the Atlantic came to oppose slavery. Like other slaveholding southerners, Jefferson sensed this and came to realize that black slavery could ultimately be justified and explained only if black Africans were considered a different order of being, a different race, one unequal to whites.

Although many white Americans explained the blackness of the Africans in environmental terms—the hot African sun had scorched their skin—and believed that in time living in a more moderate climate their skin would whiten, Jefferson suggested that there might be inherent differences between blacks and whites that climate and cultivation could not change. "It would be right," he conceded, "to make great allowances of the difference of condition, of education, of conversation, of the sphere in which they move." Nevertheless, he said, they had not taken advantage to learn from the conversation and manners of their masters. In other words, in his *Notes on the State of Virginia*, Jefferson suggested that black Africans might be so different from whites—that they did not begin life with blank slates similar to other human beings—that education and cultivation could never make them equal.[51]

He didn't feel that way about the Indians. In fact, he was quick to assert that the native Indians were "in body and mind the equal of the white man" and that any difference between them and whites was "not a difference of nature, but of circumstance." Indian women, for example, were "submitted to unjust drudgery," but that was true of "every barbarous people." If white Americans were "in equal barbarism, our females would be equal drudges." Once properly civilized, the Indian women would become domesticated and the equal of American white women. Although the Indians generally had few of the advantages the black slaves had in living in close proximity to the whites, they seemed to Jefferson to possess naturally the capacity for imagination and creativity. The oratory of the Indians was rich and sublime. They were able to carve out figures and crayoned pictures that were "not destitute of design and merit . . . , so as to prove the existence of a germ in their minds which only wants cultivation." In other words, they possessed at birth the same blank slates that whites possessed.[52]

Alas, however, he could not say the same for black Africans. Although he advanced his opinion "as suspicion only" and with "great diffidence," he claimed that black Africans were "inferior to the whites in the endowments of both body and mind." It was possible, he admitted, that their distinctiveness as a race was due to "time and circumstances," as many of his fellow white Americans believed, but in the end Jefferson seemed to favor the view that the Africans' presumed inferiority was the result of their nature at birth, not their condition as slaves. In bravery and in memory, Jefferson acknowledged, blacks were the equal of whites, and "in music they are more generally gifted than the whites with accurate ears for tune and time." But in reason they were "much inferior" to whites. And they lacked the capacity for poetry. Whereas the Indians' imagination was "glowing and elevated," the Africans' was "dull, tasteless, and anomalous." Although surrounded by black slaves, Jefferson said he had never yet found a black who "had uttered a thought above the level of plain narration," or who had displayed "even an elementary trait of painting or sculpture." So it wasn't their circumstances as slaves that explained their inferiority, he concluded. After all, the condition of the Roman slaves had not prevented them from becoming cultivated in ways that the African American slaves seemed unable to duplicate. Because Jefferson was unwilling to admit the great differences of circumstances between the slavery of antiquity, where the slaves were often literate and part of the households, and that of the plantations in eighteenth-century America, his entire analysis was fundamentally flawed.[53]

Although many Americans, especially southern Americans, may have agreed with Jefferson, many others did not. Most Americans who thought about the issue remained committed to the natural equality of all human beings, accounting for the obvious differences of people by their differing environments and differing degrees of cultivation. Adams became one of the conspicuous exceptions. By 1809 he was telling Benjamin Rush that he believed that "there is as much in the breed of men as there is in that of horses"—the kind of ancien régime comment that made people think Adams favored a hereditary aristocracy, which he emphatically denied. But within a decade of the writing of the Declaration of Independence, it was clear that Adams no longer believed that all men were born equal.[54]

The belief in the natural equality of all people had powerful implications. If all human beings were indeed equal at birth, if what separated one person from another was simply cultivation and education, then it followed that those who considered themselves enlightened suddenly felt morally responsible for the weak and downtrodden in their society. In the minds of the gentry, concern and compassion replaced smugness and indifference. If the culture—what people thought and believed—was man-made and could be changed, then the status of the lowly and deprived could be reformed and improved. Criminals were not born to behave in an evil manner and could be rehabilitated. Even "Savages," said Adams, could be civilized.[55] These Lockean assumptions lay behind all the reform movements of the revolutionary era, from antislavery to the changing ideas of criminal punishment, from the formation of dozens of benevolent societies to the obsession with education—not just the Americans' interest in formal schooling, but their concern with a variety of ways of remaking their culture and society. These comprised everything from the histories they wrote, and the advice manuals they read, to the many icons they created—including the Great Seal, Jefferson's Virginia capitol, John Trumbull's paintings, and the design of Washington, D.C.

IN 1776 BOTH ADAMS AND JEFFERSON, along with Benjamin Franklin, were interested in designing a device for the seal of the United States. It seemed as important as drawing up the articles of war. Adams proposed his favorite classical symbol—Hercules surveying the choice between Virtue and Sloth, which was probably the most popular emblem of the eighteenth century. Jefferson suggested of all things a scene from the Bible, "the Children of Israel in the Wilderness." Franklin proposed another biblical scene, that of Moses "lifting up his Wand, and dividing the Red Sea, and Pharaoh, in his Chariot overwhelmed with the Waters." But, as Adams admitted, these designs were "too complicated," and the job was turned over to the secretary of the Congress, Charles Thomson, who finally worked out the present Great Seal, which can be seen on the reverse side of the one-dollar bill.[56]

Both Jefferson and Adams were eager to leave the Congress and get back home. Jefferson was especially eager to return to Virginia. He told his colleagues in Virginia that he needed to return because of the health of his wife, Patty; but equally important was his intensifying desire to get back in order to begin to realize the many liberal reforms he had in mind. As he recalled in his autobiography, "I knew that our legislature under the regal government had many very vicious points which urgently required reformation, and I thought I could be of more use in forwarding that work."[57] Not in the Congress and not in Philadelphia, but only in what he called "my own country" of Virginia could he take advantage of the Revolution and fulfill his enlightened dreams.[58] Even something as small as the design of the state's seal commanded his attention, and he expressed some unhappiness with what his colleagues had done. What "for god's sakes," he asked, did the legislature mean by adopting *Deus nobis haec otia fecit* (God bestowed upon us this leisure) as the motto for the state's seal? The motto, he claimed, was puzzling to many members of Congress (but perhaps not to his Virginia colleagues who took for granted the slaves who gave them their leisure); besides, he said, the slogan was inappropriate for a country at war.[59] Finally, in early September Jefferson was able to get away and return to Virginia.

In the Virginia legislature that convened in October 1776, Jefferson immediately set about reforming his society in accord with enlightened reason. He introduced bills abolishing the legal devices of primogeniture (in which the estate passed to the eldest son) and entail (which kept the estate in the stem line of the family). "A distinct set of families," he wrote in his autobiography, had used these legal devices to pass on their wealth "from generation to generation" and had formed themselves into "a Patrician order, distinguished by the splendor and luxury of their establishments." By abolishing these legal devices, he hoped to destroy the privileges of this "aristocracy of wealth" in order "to make an opening for the aristocracy of virtue and talent" that was "essential to a well-ordered republic." He wanted Virginia's lands freely distributed as widely and as equitably as possible to its citizens.[60]

Although he had expressed some doubts about the people's ability to select the members of the upper house, he had no intention of limiting their participation in the government in general. He wanted to extend "the right of suffrage (or in other words the rights of a citizen) to all who had a permanent intention of living in the country." This could be measured by "either the having resided a certain time, or having a family, or having property, any or all of them." This meant granting every adult male the right to vote. Although women were thought dependent and thus without voting rights, still Jefferson's proposal for the suffrage was as broad as any made in 1776.[61]

At the same time he set forth elaborate plans for revising the state's laws. He aimed to overhaul the system of criminal punishment, introduce complete religious freedom, and create a system of public education. Having read *On Crimes and Punishments* (1764) by the Italian philosophe Cesare Beccaria, Jefferson was eager to liberalize the harsh penal codes of the colonial period, which had relied on the bodily punishment of whipping, mutilation, and especially execution. Like Beccaria, he wanted punishments that were proportionate to the crimes, and thus he proposed the *lex talionis,* the law of retaliation. So the death penalty was restricted to murder and perhaps treason, and those men guilty of rape, polygamy, or sodomy would be castrated. Over the next several years he gave more time to this reform of criminal punishment than to all the others put together, but much of it went beyond what most of his colleagues would accept.[62]

This was equally true of his other proposals for reform. He found, as he recalled in his autobiography, that in the 1770s "the public mind would not yet bear" his proposal to gradually abolish slavery, "nor," he wrote in 1821, "would it bear it even at this day." He knew John Locke had proposed religious toleration, but that was not enough. "Where he stopped short," he said, "we may go on" and establish true religious freedom. After all, toleration implied a religious establishment that merely allowed other religions to exist.[63] Unfortunately, his effort was delayed and was finally passed in 1786 only through the efforts of his friend James Madison. Jefferson's farsighted plan for creating a three-tiered—elementary school, grammar school, university—publicly funded educational system likewise was turned down by his colleagues. Still, he believed that his several reforms, as he stated in his autobiography, were based on his hope that "every fibre would be eradicated of antient or future aristocracy; and a foundation laid for a government truly republican."[64]

His Virginia colleagues must have been stunned by Jefferson's extraordinary enthusiasm for reform and the ambitious nature of his vision. His desire to transform the aristocracy of which he was a prime and wealthy member must have been challenging and bewildering to many of his fellow legislators. A few conservatives like Carter Braxton dismissed Jefferson as one of those "Men said to possess unbounded knowledge" who were full of "Chimerical . . . Schemes and Ideas" that tended to "injure more than they benefit mankind."[65]

Others, however, like the respected senior legislator Edmund Pendleton, took the proposals of the thirty-three-year-old Jefferson seriously, but tempered some of their impracticalities with doses of realism. Nevertheless, throughout all the debates and discussions, Jefferson kept the friendship and above all the respect of nearly all of his colleagues. He knew so much and had read so widely and was so intelligent and always amiable that they scarcely knew how to resist him. Besides, they realized that he was expressing the most liberal and enlightened thinking of the Western world, and they could not help wanting to be part of that Enlightenment.

It was an extraordinary moment in Virginia's history. These Virginia slaveholding planters knew—John Adams told them so in June 1776—that the Revolution was placing all traditional aristocracies under assault. All "the Dons, the Bashaws, the Grandees, the Patricians, the Sachems, the Nabobs, call them by what Name you please," said Adams in a letter that month to Patrick Henry, "sigh, and groan, and fret, and Sometimes Stamp, and foam, and curse—but all in vain." A more equal liberty was spreading throughout America, and, Adams told Henry, "that Exuberance of Pride, which has produced an insolent Dominion, in a few, a very few oppulent, monopolizing Families, will be brought down nearer to the Confines of Reason and Moderation, than they have been used."[66]

Even though they might have read Adams's letter to Henry or at least knew of its predictions, few of the dons, nabobs, and grandees of Virginia saw themselves threatened by the Revolution. Despite being heavily in debt, despite uneasiness over signs of corruption in their society, despite some apprehension over possible slave revolts, the slaveholding planters of Virginia remained remarkably sure of their position in society. Adams himself was surprised by the planters' eagerness to engage in the Revolution. But they had not just engaged in the Revolution; the Virginia aristocrats had in their own eyes taken the lead in breaking from Great Britain. Few aristocracies in history have ever undertaken a revolution with more confidence and enthusiasm than these southern aristocratic planters. And Jefferson was the most confident and enthusiastic of all.

ADAMS WAS AS MUCH AWARE as Jefferson of the spirit of enlightenment spreading throughout the Atlantic world, and like Jefferson, he expressed some longing to leave Philadelphia and get back home. But unlike Jefferson, he actually relished his participation in continental affairs, and was very eager to keep his seat in Congress. He was far more deeply involved in the business of the Congress than Jefferson. He was the chair of the Board of War, essentially in charge of the war, and was a member of the commission that met with British admiral Lord Richard Howe in August 1776 to discuss the possibility of peace. Adams missed his family, no doubt, but he returned to Massachusetts in

October mainly because he hoped to persuade the state legislature to increase his salary so he could bring Abigail and his family back to Philadelphia.

Unlike Jefferson, he had no interest in hurrying home in order to overhaul the society of his state. Of course, he realized only too keenly that the societies of New England already had many of the things that Jefferson desired for Virginia. In fact, Adams had written his *Thoughts on Government* with the hope that it might help to convert the aristocratic South to New England's ways. He knew he lived in a very different society from that of Virginia. By Virginia's standards, slavery scarcely existed in New England, and by 1776 it was already rapidly being eliminated. Massachusetts had possessed a public school system since the seventeenth century and was tackling its system of criminal punishment more effectively than the states of the South. Moreover, New England already had a broad suffrage and annual elections and possessed no social rank that resembled the great slave-owning planters of Virginia. In fact, Adams thought that the biggest problem that Massachusetts society faced in 1776 was not to be reformed by expanding the power of the people, but rather to control and restrain the already existing power of the people—popular power that was being dangerously aroused by the turmoil of the Revolution.

Hence, unlike Jefferson, who was so eager to get moving on reform, Adams advised patience. He told his Massachusetts colleagues to move "slowly and deliberately" in creating their government. He had no interest in reforming a society that needed no reform. Beware of "dangerous Innovations," he warned, especially since "the Spirit of Levelling" was abroad. He worried about "Duplicity" and "Hypocrisy" and the many reports that all kinds of wild proposals were flying about the province. "Are not these ridiculous Projects, prompted by disaffected Persons, in order to divide, dissipate, and distract, the Attention of the People, at a Time, when every thought Should be employed, and every Sinew exerted, for the Defence of the Country."[67] Reforming society was just not in his nature. Although he hated slavery and never owned any slaves, he hoped that a bill in the Massachusetts legislature in 1777 abolishing slavery would be allowed to "sleep for a Time. We have Causes enough of Jealousy Discord and Division, and this bill will certainly add to the Number."[68]

In Adams's eyes, the great danger of the Revolution was social disorder—something Jefferson never feared, at least not in 1776. "There must be a Decency, and Respect, and Veneration introduced for Persons in Authority, of every Rank, or We are undone," Adams told his friend James Warren in April of that year. "In a popular Government, this is the only Way of Supporting order."[69] Especially alarming were the numbers of new men taking advantage of the war to make money and to establish themselves as mushroom aristocrats. "When the pot boils the scum will rise," James Otis had warned at the outset. Primed as Adams was to think the worst of human nature, he was quick to appreciate how rapidly the scum was rising. By 1777 Adams feared "the Rage of Speculation and Flames of Passion" that were spreading throughout Massachusetts. "Our State," he lamented, "abounds with ambitious Men, in such Numbers, and with avaritious ones, who are still worse, and with others whom both Passions unite, in a great degree, who are the most dangerous of all," that he despaired of Massachusetts achieving any order and stability.[70]

Adams became especially troubled by suggestions that the qualifications for voting might be reformed. Don't touch the issue, he warned James Sullivan, a lawyer recently appointed to the Massachusetts superior court. "There will be no End of it," he predicted. "New Claims will arise. Women will demand a Vote. Lads from 12 to 21 will think their Rights are not enough attended to, and every Man, who has not a Farthing, will demand an equal Voice with any other in all Acts of State. It tends to confound and destroy all Distinctions, and prostrate all Ranks, to one common Levell."[71] He had none of the confidence that Jefferson expressed in his proposals for expanding the suffrage.

Of course, Jefferson, who was married to a conventional southern belle, could scarcely have imagined extending the franchise to women. He thought women were "too wise to wrinkle their foreheads with politics." Instead, "they are contented to soothe and calm the minds of their husbands returning from political debate." Women had "the good sense to value domestic happiness above all other, and the art to cultivate it beyond all others." As late as 1813, he believed that the participation of women in politics was "an innovation for which the public is not prepared, nor am I." Adams, married to Abigail, could never be so sanguine.[72]

Abigail was a woman of such wit, passion, and volubility—expressing her views about everything from education to forms of government—that she was bound to think about women participating in politics. In her now famous letter to John written on March 31, 1776, Abigail suggested to her husband, who she knew was busy in Philadelphia thinking about creating new governments, not to overlook the role of women.

> Remember the Ladies and be more generous and favorable to them than your ancestors. Do not put such unlimited power into the hands of the Husbands. Remember all Men would be tyrants if they could. If particular care and attention is not paid to the Ladies, we are determined to foment a Rebelion, and will not hold ourselves bound by any Laws in which we have no voice, or Representation.[73]

As biting as the passage is, it doesn't have quite the significance that many recently have attributed to it. John certainly did not take it seriously. "I cannot but laugh" at her ideas, he said in response. And he went on in the same amusing and saucy tone Abigail had used, telling her that men knew better than to repeal their "Masculine systems." Although those systems were "in full Force, you know," he said, "they are little more than Theory." Men were actually "the subjects. . . . We have only the Name of Masters," and giving that title up "would compleatly subject Us to the Despotism of the Peticoat."[74]

John's response clearly reveals the joking nature of their relationship. Abigail was not a modern feminist and she never became one. She was clever and witty and, proud of her sauciness, loved to tease and banter with her husband, which is what she was doing in this famous letter, to which John responded in a similar manner. Abigail kidded her husband about many things, including his being a big-shot delegate at the Continental Congress. At one point she suggested that their Braintree cows, suffering from drought, ought to petition the Congress, setting forth their grievances and their deprivations of ancient privileges that ought to be restored to them. She even joked with him about lawyers. Her "Remember the Ladies" letter was another example of her teasing. In her statement, Abigail was not expecting to fundamentally transform the role of women in her society.

Teasing, of course, can often make a serious point, and in her bantering remarks, Abigail was certainly expressing a self-conscious awareness of the legally dependent and inferior position of women—a provocative awareness that she never lost. In 1782 she noted once again the things women were denied. They were "excluded from honours and from offices" of government; "deprived of a voice in Legislation," they were "obliged to submit to those Laws which are imposed upon us." "Even in the freest countrys our property is subject to the control and disposal of our partners, to whom the Laws have given a sovereign Authority." Despite these sorts of complaints, however, Abigail did not seriously question the place of women in her society. She in fact listed the deprivations women suffered from simply to show how virtuous and patriotic women were.[75]

Although she did want women to be as well educated as men (itself a bold proposal), she was generally content merely with her domestic role as wife and mother. What she most disliked was having to act as the sole head of the household in John's absence, which she regarded as an unnatural sacrifice for the patriotic cause. Still, she always considered "it as an indispensable requisite that every American wife should herself know how to order and regulate her family; how to govern her domestics, and train up her children."[76]

Although Abigail became proud of her success as a manager of the family farm and the family finances, she wanted nothing more than to have her husband back so she could resume what she thought of as her rightful role as wife and mother. To conceive of Abigail as somehow yearning to be like her husband is not only anachronistic, it also trivial-izes and demeans her domestic character—as if the male model of politi-cal activity is the only standard of worth.[77] At the same time she certainly felt the equal of men, telling her sister in 1799 that she would "never consent to have our sex considered in an inferiour point of light." She admitted that God and nature designed men and women to move in dif-ferent orbits, but that didn't make them unequal: "If man is Lord, woman is *Lordess*." Although she accepted the fact that women did not hold the reins of government, she saw no reason that women could not judge how those governments were conducted.[78]

It is not surprising that John, knowing Abigail's feelings and having read her saucy letter about women voting, should have warned Sullivan not to contemplate changing the suffrage.

FIVE

MISSIONS ABROAD

ADAMS HAD LEFT the Continental Congress and arrived back home in Braintree in November 1776. He remained home only about nine weeks until, in January 1777, he left once again and returned to the Congress. In the meantime, the Congress in Philadelphia had been threatened by the British army and had temporarily relocated to Baltimore. Despite having suggested that he did not want to be separated any longer from his family, Adams returned to the Congress without them. Unlike Jefferson, whose heart and mind remained in Virginia, Adams realized that he needed to be in the Congress in order to fulfill his deepest ambitions. There was where he had accomplished the most; there was where he had acquired the respect of his countrymen; there was where he became something more than a provincial lawyer riding circuit in small-town courts.

Once back in Congress, Adams threw himself into its business. Once again he served on two dozen committees, chairing eight of them, with heading the Board of War taking most of his time. Perhaps out of guilt over having abandoned Abigail so quickly, his letters to her became more frequent. Perhaps too he had become more self-conscious of the Revolution as a historic event. Since, as he told his son John Quincy, he would be one of the "considerable Characters" in any history of the Revolution, his letters became all the more important.[1] But in his letters home he seemed to quickly forget that he was writing for posterity, for he continually filled them with complaints of the burdens of his service and the degree to which it was harming his health. Even the weather was often too much for him. "In the Midst of infinite Noise, Hurry, and Bustle," went one of his typical grumbles, "I lead a lonely melancholly Life, mourning the Loss of all the Charms of Life, which are my family, and all the Amusement that I ever had in Life, which is my farm."[2] As he was wont to do, he even raised the likelihood of his dying on behalf of the patriot cause. How often, he told Abigail, had he imagined her "a Widow and her Charming Prattlers Orphans, exposed to all the Insolence of unfeeling impious Tyrants!" Although he said the possibility of his death hadn't weakened his resolve, his melodramatic recounting of that possibility reduced Abigail to tears.[3]

In one of his complaints to Abigail in which he expressed once more his longings for home, and "for rural and domestic scenes, for the warbling of Birds and the Prattle of my Children," he abruptly stopped, and wrote, "Dont you think I am somewhat poetical this morning"—the kind of joking with "his dearest Friend" that helped make bearable all his moaning and groaning.[4]

In that same letter Adams went on to deny all political ambition. "I should prefer the Delights of a Garden to the Dominion of the World. I have nothing of Caesars Greatness in my soul. Power has not my Wishes in her Train. . . . Of that Ambition which has Power for its Object, I dont believe I have a Spark in my Heart." Later on, when rereading this letter, he inserted at this point, "But is not the Heart deceitfull above all Things?" It is this kind of occasional self-awareness that helps redeem Adams's egotism and self-pity.[5]

Finally, in November 1777 Adams obtained leave from Congress, and he returned to Braintree to resume his law practice. He told Abigail that he would not go back to Congress. But when Congress asked him to go to France as one of the commissioners to negotiate a treaty of alliance, he was surprised but excited. Abigail was full of anger and anguish. She said that if John must accept the appointment he should take his family with him. He convinced her that it was too dangerous in wartime for her to cross the Atlantic. But wanting some company, Adams took John Quincy, his ten-year-old son. They set sail on the *Boston* on February 15, 1778, and after a somewhat harrowing voyage they arrived in Europe six weeks later.

IN THE MEANTIME JEFFERSON remained in Virginia serving in the state legislature. Not only was he busy revising the state's laws and looking after the militia and local justice in his county, he was also preoccupied with the building and landscaping of Monticello. Although the war seemed far away, correspondents kept him informed of its progress. In May 1777 he wrote his first letter to Adams, who was still in the Congress. Jefferson was worried about the difficulties of maintaining the union of the states. Adams replied warmly, urging him to "come and help us. . . . Your Country is not yet, quite secure enough, to excuse your Retreat to the Delights of domestic Life."[6]

Adams did not intend this as a rebuke, and Jefferson did not take it as one. But Jefferson was not going to the Congress. Virginia was his "country" and that was where he wanted to be. Still, others, including Washington, found Jefferson's unwillingness to go to the Congress puzzling, because good men were needed there. Edward Rutledge of South Carolina even joked that he hoped Jefferson would soon condescend "to come from above and interest yourself in Human Affairs."[7]

All through the trying years of the war in 1777–1778, Jefferson remained optimistic that Britain could never conquer America. Thus he felt free "to indulge my fondness for philosophical studies," taking weather readings and viewing an eclipse of the sun.[8] In writing to David Rittenhouse, the ingenious Philadelphia inventor and scientist, he saw himself as one philosopher speaking to another. Since he had heard that Rittenhouse was deeply involved in "the civic government of your country"—that is, Pennsylvania—he suggested that he was wasting his talents. Some people were obliged to engage in public affairs, he said, but "there is an order of geniuses above that obligation, and therefore exempted from it.

No body can conceive that nature ever intended to throw away a Newton upon the occupation of a Crown." So he hoped he would be excused "the hazarding these free thoughts" in advising Rittenhouse to get back to science and let other men "do the commonplace drudgery of governing a single state." In fact, governing was "work which may be executed by men of an ordinary stature, such as are always and every where to be found."[9] So much for Adams's "divine Science of Politics."

Although Jefferson never explicitly compared himself with Rittenhouse, he did suggest to Edmund Pendleton in the late 1770s that he might retire completely from government in order to continue his philosophical studies. Pendleton was appalled at the suggestion and told Jefferson so. "You are too young to Ask that happy quietus from the Public," he said, "and should at least postpone it 'til you have taught the rising Generation, the forms as well as the Substantial principles of legislation."[10]

To keep Jefferson from retiring from public service in the midst of the war, Pendleton and many of his colleagues in the legislature decided in June 1779 that they had to elect him governor of the state. Granting Jefferson an honor that he could scarcely refuse was one way of getting him off his mountaintop retreat and back into politics. Jefferson quite correctly predicted that becoming governor would not add to his happiness.[11]

Before he became governor and experienced the war firsthand, Jefferson seemed not to have grasped the nature and severity of the conflict. He didn't think that the kind of hatred of the enemy that Adams expressed was good for the soul. While Adams in 1777 wanted to meet the "barbarian Britains" in the field, Jefferson sought to temper such "sweet and delicious" feelings of revenge.[12] Not only was Jefferson remarkably sanguine about the outcome of the war, but he assumed that the war was being waged in a more polite and civilized manner than it was in reality. While still in Congress he set forth his views of what war in the enlightened eighteenth century ought to be. "It is the happiness of modern times," he wrote, "that the evils of necessary war are softened by the refinement of manners and sentiment, and that an enemy is an object of vengeance, in arms and in the field only."[13] His idealism about the nature of war accounts for the way in which he treated the British and German soldiers who had surrendered at Saratoga in October 1777.

America's General Horatio Gates had signed a convention with Britain's General John Burgoyne allowing the return of his troops to Europe with the promise that they would not be used again in America. Because of a number of British actions, including the British treatment of American prisoners and Burgoyne's unwillingness to provide a list of his officers, Congress refused to agree with the convention and decided to keep the enemy soldiers in America until George III ratified it, which the Congress doubted would happen. In November 1778 this "Convention Army" was marched seven hundred miles from Boston, where it had been awaiting embarkation to Europe, to Charlottesville, Virginia, arriving in January 1779. These enemy soldiers were held in hastily constructed barracks until 1781, when the appearance of an invading British army forced their removal to Pennsylvania.

Jefferson was delighted with the presence of several thousand enemy officers and soldiers in his neighborhood not only because they brought some much-needed money to the area, but, more important, because they offered an opportunity for him to demonstrate the liberality and humanity of America in wartime. "It is for the benefit of mankind to mitigate the horrors of war as much as possible," he told Patrick Henry, his predecessor as governor, in March 1779. "The practice therefore of modern nations of treating captive enemies with politeness and generosity is not only delightful in contemplation but really interesting to all the world, friends, foes and neutrals." Jefferson urged Governor Henry to apply this enlightened practice to the Convention Army. If Virginians did not treat these enemy soldiers correctly, other nations, he warned Henry, would charge Americans with ignorance, whim, and cruelty. Jefferson wanted to demonstrate the possibility of civilizing war.[14]

Jefferson was especially pleased to have so many British and German officers in his neighborhood; they brought European charm and cultivation to what he often referred to as the cultural barbarism of his state. He was eager to show the European prisoners the polite and civilized nature of Americans, to convince them that his countrymen were not the mongrel savages that many Europeans presumed. He played music and talked art and philosophy with the European officers and invited them to dinner and accepted their invitations in return. He and his family developed an especially close relationship with the ranking Hessian officer, Major General Baron de Riedesel, and his wife, who had been with her husband at the Battle of Saratoga. In fact, it was common for as many as 15 percent of the soldiers in the British army to have their wives with them.[15] Jefferson obviously enjoyed the company of these European sophisticates and was eager to win their friendship and respect.

Releasing captured officers on parole and allowing them to move freely within a designated area was a common eighteenth-century practice in Europe; but the degree of intimacy Jefferson attained with the enemy prisoners in Charlottesville during the war was truly extraordinary. The hospitality he extended to the European officers went beyond all customary practice. After the war, he continued to correspond with some officers and met with them later when he went to Europe. One young Hessian officer, upon leaving America, wrote Jefferson how satisfied he had been in "conversing with a person in whom I find all the qualities which can arouse esteem and affection." Jefferson could scarcely have been more delighted at receiving such a compliment. He painstakingly worked over his response, eager to make it appear as gracious and polished as possible, lest the German gentleman think him uncultivated. Until Jefferson got to Europe itself, his consorting with these European prisoners was the next best thing.[16]

The burdens of being governor soon put a damper on his socializing with the enemy officers; it would be one of his many regrets at becoming his state's chief executive. His experience as the governor of Virginia for two years was rough. Jefferson, of course, knew that the executive was weak, and in 1776 he had wanted it weak; but the war graphically exposed to him and to the other state constitution-makers of 1776 their mistake in having so severely emasculated their chief executives. It was not long before Jefferson was longing to retire and return to the comforts of Monticello.

When the British forces under the command of Benedict Arnold invaded the state at the beginning of 1781, his difficulties became even more serious. He was slow to appreciate the danger and hesitated in calling out the militia, which allowed Arnold's relatively small raiding army to enter Richmond, which had replaced Williamsburg as the state capital, without opposition. At the same time the British general Lord Cornwallis invaded Virginia from the south and in May 1781, much to Jefferson's surprise, linked up with Arnold.

The invading British armies attracted thousands of slaves seeking freedom, including twenty-three of Jefferson's slaves from his several estates; he later recovered five of them. Ever since the November 1775 proclamation of Virginia's last royal governor, Lord Dunmore, offering freedom to all servants and slaves who were willing to join His Majesty's troops, the Virginia planters lived with the fear that their slaves would not just flee but would turn on them. In the weeks following that proclamation, hundreds of slaves had fled to Dunmore's Ethiopian Regiment; the governor's actions, said Jefferson, "raised our country into perfect phrenzy."[17]

Now the same thing was happening as slaves once again saw an opportunity for freedom. In 1781 he described his slaves as having "fled to the enemy," "joined enemy," or "ran away." Several years later he altered his verbs to the passive voice, so that the slaves became victims and no longer active agents.[18] By the mid- and late 1780s he claimed that Cornwallis had "carried off" his slaves, numbering them as thirty when it appears that he had lost at most nineteen. He used Cornwallis's destruction of his property and the taking of his slaves to justify his difficulty in paying his debts to his British creditors. "The useless and barbarous injury he did me at that instance," he explained to a British creditor, "was more than would have paid your debt, principal and interest." He went on to allege that the British had taken about thirty thousand slaves from Virginia plantations—a gross exaggeration, but one that he later used to explain the difficulty the Virginians in general had in paying their prewar debts to British creditors. Although he said in 1786 that he planned to pay his debts, the British had no right to expect prompt payment of prewar debts since they had withdrawn "American property contrary to express stipulation" in the 1783 Treaty of Paris.[19]

Perhaps five thousand or so slaves in the upper South ran away to the British lines between 1779 and 1781. By the end of the Revolutionary War, a total of about twenty thousand black slaves were estimated to have joined the British side, with roughly twelve thousand coming from the South. It was the greatest emancipation in America until the Civil War.[20]

BESET BY CRITICISM OF THE VIRGINIANS' capacity to wage war, especially from Baron von Steuben, a Prussian officer who had joined the American cause, Governor Jefferson tried to explain why his countrymen were having such trouble dealing with the enemy. "Mild Laws, a People not used to war and prompt obedience, a want of the Provisions of War and means of procuring them," he told the Marquis de Lafayette, "render our orders often ineffectual, oblige us to temporize and when we cannot accomplish an object in one way to attempt it in another."[21]

Just as his annual term as governor was ending in early June 1781, Jefferson came close to getting captured by the British. Surprised by approaching redcoats, he was forced to flee in embarrassment from Monticello. He compounded this embarrassment by suddenly deciding not to serve as governor the third and final year for which he was eligible, but he failed to issue a formal statement of his decision, leaving his fellow planters in the legislature befuddled. Consequently, the Virginia assembly had to scramble to elect his successor, which left the state with no chief executive for nearly a week.

It was hardly the time for a governor to retire. The situation in Virginia seemed so dire that, as Jefferson admitted in his *Notes on the State of Virginia*, there was talk in the legislature of setting up "a *dictator*" who would be "invested with every power legislative, executive, and judiciary, civil and military, of life and death" over persons and property.[22] Although at the time Jefferson condemned this talk of a dictator, in the autobiography written many years later he sought to exonerate himself by explaining that he had "resigned the administration at the end of my 2d. year" so that a military commander might be appointed governor. Such a combination of military and civil power, he said, "might be wielded with more energy and promptitude and effect for the defence of the state."[23]

Predictably, his retiring so abruptly as governor in the middle of this crisis angered some members of the assembly, including Patrick Henry. As a result the legislature resolved that at its next session "an inquiry be made into the conduct of the Executive of this State for the last twelve months."[24] For someone as confident as Jefferson of his social standing and his intellectual superiority, this was a harsh humiliation, and he never forgot it. It was by far the worst moment in his entire public career. No wonder he concluded that he found "the pain of a little censure, even when it is unfounded, is more acute than the pleasure of much praise."[25]

Despite this cloud hanging over him, he was once again pressured to get involved in the government. Congress even invited him to become one of the peace commissioners in Paris. If he hadn't already decided to avoid all public business, that office would have been agreeable to him. Indeed, he told Lafayette that by declining the European mission he was losing "an opportunity . . . of combining public service with private gratification, of seeing count[ries] whose improvements in science, in arts, and in civilization it has been my fortune to [ad]mire at a distance but never to see."[26] But, he told Edmund Randolph, a member of the Continental Congress, his decision was final. "I have . . . retired to my farm, my family and books from which I think nothing will evermore separate me."[27] Even when Randolph warned him that his "irrevocable purpose of sequestering yourself" was consigning "southern interests wholly to the management of our present ministers," Jefferson remained firm in his withdrawal from public life.[28]

The American and French victory at Yorktown in October 1781 reduced the fearful atmosphere in Virginia, with Jefferson congratulating the victorious General Washington "on your return to your native country" from years of military maneuverings in the North.[29] In December the House of Delegates, the name given to the lower house in the new Virginia state constitution, exonerated Jefferson's actions as governor. But his deep hurt was not soothed. Although in the spring of 1782 he was once again elected to the House of Delegates by his county, he refused to serve. James Monroe, Jefferson's young protégé, begged him to reconsider; in response Jefferson penned the most dispirited letter he ever wrote.

He was, he told Monroe, "thoroughly cured of every principle of political ambition." He was now reduced to a "mere private life," and in order to rest easy in it, he had to rid himself of every "lurking particle" of ambition. He was sure that "every fibre of that passion" had been "thoroughly eradicated." Besides, he had done enough. He had spent thirteen years engaged in public service at the expense of his private affairs. Despite his "constant sacrifice of time, labor, loss, parental and friendly duties," instead of gaining the affection of his countrymen, which was the only reward he ever wanted, he had lost even the small estimation he had once possessed. He might have accepted "disapprobation of the well-meaning but uninformed people," but the action of his legislative colleagues was an unexpected shock. To be sure, the legislature later issued "an exculpatory declaration," but in the meantime he had been suspected of "not mere weakness of the head," but of "treason of the heart." Only death, he said, would relieve him of "the wound on his spirit."

He then went on in this lengthy, bitter letter to complain that the state had no right to command the public services of its citizens. Fully cognizant of the classical republican tradition of the citizen's obligation to sacrifice his private interests for the sake of the public good, Jefferson was hard-pressed to justify his refusal to participate in government. All he could say was that everyone since independence was doing it. "Offices of every kind and given by every power, have been daily and hourly declined and resigned." His anxiety was acute, for he was confronting principles he had thoroughly imbibed in his extensive readings in the ancient classics. He knew he had political duties, but not at the expense of his whole existence. "If we are made in some degree for others, yet in a greater degree we are made for ourselves." In order to rationalize his uneasy position, he had to exaggerate what the republic was demanding. No state, he said, had "a *perpetual* right" to the services of its citizens. That would be slavery and not the liberty for which they fought the Revolution. It would "annihilate the blessing of existence," it would "contradict the giver of life who gave it for happiness and not for wretchedness." Anyway, he said, he was not so vain as to count himself "among those whom the state would think worth oppressing with perpetual service." He hoped that since he had spent "the whole of the active and useful part" of his life in service to the public, he would "be permitted to pass the rest in mental quiet." And then as a final gibe at his colleagues, he pointed out that at least he had been direct and honest in making "a simple act of renunciation." He had not tried to invoke the many legal disqualifications that others were using to justify their selfish withdrawal from governmental service.[30]

This angry outburst was not characteristic of Jefferson, and the intensity of his bitterness puzzled his colleagues. Even his close friend James Madison could not excuse his anger. "Great as my partiality is to Mr. Jefferson," Madison told Edmund Randolph, "the mode in which he seems determined to revenge the wrong received from his Country, does not appear to me to be dictated either by philosophy or patriotism."[31] Eventually, Jefferson's anger and self-pity subsided, his self-confidence returned, and he joined the world once more. It turned out that he was not as unambitious as he claimed in this moment of deep despair.

DURING THESE YEARS that Jefferson was philosophizing at Monticello and serving as governor of Virginia, Adams was abroad, except for six months in the latter half of 1779, when he briefly returned to Massachusetts to write the state's belated constitution. Adams was experiencing firsthand all the science, arts, and civilization of enlightened Europe that Jefferson could only admire at a distance.

Adams had been sent over to Paris to replace Silas Deane as one of the three commissioners to help negotiate treaties of alliance and commerce with France. By the time he got to Paris in April 1778 to join the two other commissioners, Arthur Lee and Benjamin Franklin, the treaties had already been signed. Adams and Lee were unknowns compared with Franklin. Indeed, Franklin was the most celebrated American in the world and the toast of France. Adams lamented that he was "a Man of no Consequence—a Cypher." When he first arrived in France, some mistook him for "Le fameux Adams," by which they meant Samuel Adams. Adams had great fun in his diary describing the difficulties he had in France convincing the French that he was not "the famous Adams." At least, he said, "No body went so far . . . as to say I was the infamous Adams."[32]

Adams had met Franklin in the Continental Congress and on one occasion in 1776 had shared a bed with him, a common practice in the eighteenth century. The two delegates had wrangled over shutting or not shutting the window while they slept. The incident was funny enough for Adams to recall it many years later in one of his incomparable anecdotes. Most of his memories of Franklin were not so humorous.[33]

From the outset Adams had problems being a diplomat at Versailles, the most elegant and protocol-laden court in all of Europe. As his former friend Jonathan Sewall pointed out in 1787, Adams was "not qualified, by nature or education, to shine in courts." Adams, of course, Sewall admitted, was quite capable of handling "the mechanical parts of his business" as a diplomat; but, said Sewall, this was "not enough. He cannot dance, drink, game, flatter, promise; in short, he has none of the essential arts or ornaments which constitute a courtier."[34]

And the lack of those arts and ornaments soon began to tell. Adams became more and more ill at ease amid the opulence and manners of the French aristocracy. He especially found it difficult to converse with learned French women. They terrified him and made him feel inferior. He realized that a person "must be of a Strange Disposition, indeed, who cannot be happy at Paris, where he may have his Choice, of all the Pleasures, Amusements and Studies, which human Life affords." Nevertheless, as a stern republican, he increasingly felt out of place. "The Richness, the Magnificence, and Splendor" of Paris and Versailles, he said, were "beyond all description." But he found little pleasure in beholding the grandeur of all the buildings, gardens, paintings, and sculptures. They were, he said, simply "Bagatelles, introduced, by Time and Luxury in Exchange for the great Qualities and hardy manly Virtues of the human Heart. . . . The more Elegance, the less Virtue in all Times and Countries."[35] This was certainly not a view that Jefferson shared.

Because Adams mistrusted Franklin, who did have the arts of a courtier, he never appreciated the extraordinary contribution that Franklin made to the American cause. No one but Franklin could have extracted from the French monarchy loan after loan in support of the Revolution. But all Adams could see was a celebrity who was lazy and not up to the responsibilities of his commission. Adams couldn't get the old man to attend meetings, make decisions, or even sign important documents that Adams had prepared. Adams admitted that Franklin was "a Wit and Humourist." "He may be a Philosopher, for what I know, but he is not a sufficient Statesman, he knows too little of American affairs or the Politicks of Europe, and takes too little Pains to inform himself of Either. He is too old, too infirm too indolent and dissipated, to be sufficient for the Discharge of all the important Duties" he had to fulfill. This was bad enough, but Franklin also revealed that he might be an atheist who didn't believe in a future state—something that horrified Adams. And to make matters worse, Franklin deferred to the French too often and allowed for too much French influence over American affairs.[36]

Adams particularly resented all the attention Franklin received from the French, especially from the women. Knowing only American women whose manners were "universally characterized at that time by Modesty, Delicacy and Dignity," he was puzzled by the behavior of the French ladies. They had, he lamented, "an unaccountable passion for old Age"— which explained the remarkable "Privilege" his "venerable Colleague" enjoyed with them. His Puritan sensibilities were scandalized by the flirting that took place between Franklin and the French women, especially with Anne-Louise de Harancourt Brillon de Jouy, Franklin's wealthy and beautiful neighbor. In the presence of her elderly husband, Madame Brillon would sit on Franklin's lap, stroke his hair, and call him "Cher Papa." Adams couldn't get over the fact that a "very plain and clumsy" woman who was often present in the company was not the friend of Madame Brillon, as he had assumed, but was actually the mistress of Monsieur Brillon. "I was astonished," he recalled, "that these People could live together in such apparent Friendship and indeed without cutting each others throats. But I did not know the World."[37]

The Massachusetts Yankee never got used to that world. The society of the French aristocracy, he found, "disgusts and shocks me more and more." It was slight and superficial, "a mere conformity to the fashion." Despite all its external politeness, that world of courtiers, he said, lacked real friendship and affection; instead, it was "full of Jealousy, Envy, revenge and rancor," a "deadly poison to all the calm felicity of Life."[38]

When Jefferson went to France, he would have a somewhat different take on both Franklin and this French world.

ADAMS KEPT URGING his colleagues in the Congress that the mission ought to be in the hands of a single minister, which he hoped would be himself.[39] Yet he continued to yearn to return to his farm and his law practice. Besides, he realized that his relationship with Abigail was suffering. Worrying that his letters might be intercepted by the British, he wrote far fewer of them to Abigail, only once every two or three weeks. Abigail was lonely and she too wrote far fewer letters than she had earlier.

Finally, in September 1778, Congress agreed to have only a single minister plenipotentiary in France, but unfortunately for Adams, it selected Franklin, mainly because France insisted upon it. Congress offered no clear directions for what Adams was to do. As he confided to Abigail, he was "left kicking and sprawling in the Mire," a victim of "total Neglect and Contempt."[40] Like Jefferson, he was criticized for his actions as a public official. The Congress seemed to include him in its censure to the commissioners for squabbling and factional fighting. But instead of being hurt, he was angry. He sent off a spate of letters to colleagues in the Congress, defending his actions as a commissioner and demanding access to the congressional journals. He told Abigail that he was coming home. "I will draw Writs and Deeds and harrangue Jurys and be happy."[41] He finally left France in June 1779 and arrived in Boston in August, just in time to participate in a convention called to write a constitution for Massachusetts.

Adams had not completed his drafting of the Massachusetts constitution when he learned that October that Congress had assigned him to Paris to negotiate a peace treaty with Great Britain, a process in which it was expected America's great ally France would be very much involved. He was eager to accept the appointment. Because his earlier mission had not gone well, he wanted to show the world that he was capable of diplomacy. He urged his disconsolate wife "to keep up your Spirits and throw off Cares as much as possible." The most he could promise her was that "We shall yet be happy."[42] After an absence in Europe of nearly eighteen months, he had been home only a little over three months. This time he took both John Quincy, now twelve, and his seven-year-old son, Thomas, with him to Europe.

He began his assignment in 1780 full of suspicion of the Comte de Vergennes, the French foreign minister. Vergennes, who thought Adams simple and naïve, with "so little Experience in the World," advised him to put off trying to negotiate peace with the British.[43] Adams, "having nothing else here wherewith to employ himself," as Franklin ruefully told the Congress, decided to try "supplying what he may suppose my Negociations defective in." Adams thought that Franklin was entirely wrong in the deferential way he approached the French. "He thinks as he tells me himself," reported Franklin in August 1780, "that America has been too free in Expressions of Gratitude to France; for that she is more obliged to us than we to her: and that we should shew Spirit in our Applications."[44] Unfortunately, in a series of undiplomatic letters, Adams said many of the same things directly to Vergennes, who became so angry with Adams's bumptious manner that the Frenchman ceased communicating with him; in fact, he tried to get Congress to recall Adams, or failing that, to appoint a "colleague capable of containing him."[45]

With little to do in Paris, Adams took off to Holland, negotiated loans and a treaty of amity and commerce with the Dutch republic, and became America's first minister to the Netherlands. Getting the Dutch to diplomatically recognize the United States was his greatest diplomatic achievement.

IN JUNE 1781 CONGRESS ASSIGNED the peace negotiations with Britain to a commission composed of Adams, Jefferson, John Jay, Henry Laurens, and Franklin.[46] Jefferson declined the initial invitation to be a member of the peace commission, but when the appointment was renewed in November 1782, he readily accepted. His wife had died that September and he welcomed the chance to relieve the burden of his grief. But because of winter ice and the threat of a British fleet, he was unable to get away. Then, with news of a provisional treaty in February 1783, his mission was suspended.

Since Jefferson could not join the peace commission, he was instead elected as delegate from Virginia to the Confederation Congress. He soon discovered that not only was the Congress having difficulty gathering a quorum (even to ratify the peace treaty with Britain), but its members who did attend were "afflicted with a morbid rage of debate." How could it be otherwise, he said, since the Congress was filled with lawyers "whose trade it is to question everything, yield nothing, & talk by the hour?" Unlike Adams, who was notoriously garrulous, Jefferson preferred "to listen." One way to lose friends, he said, was to engage in public debates.[47]

Adams ruefully agreed. "Few Persons," he said, "can bare to be outdone in Reasoning or declamation or Wit, or Sarcasm or Repartee, or Satyr, and all these things are very apt to grow out of public debate." These things anger people, so much so that in time "a Nation becomes full of a Mans enemies, or at least of such as have been galled in some Controversy, and take a secret pleasure in assisting to humble and mortify him." Adams never got over the feeling that all his eloquence and speech making in public assemblies had not brought him fame comparable with that of others. "Examples of Washington, Franklin, and Jefferson," he said, "are enough to shew that Silence and reserve in public are more Efficacious than Argumentation or Oratory."[48]

Despite the verbosity of his fellow congressmen, Jefferson accomplished a great deal during the few months he spent in Congress. He drafted two dozen or more papers and reformed the coinage system, substituting the dollar and decimal units in place of the English pounds, shillings, and pence. Jefferson enjoyed nothing more than the challenge of bringing order out of numbers. His later reports as secretary of state on uniform weights and measures led an Englishman to write him, saying, "I believe you are the first nation that ever produced statesmen who were natural philosophers."[49]

Jefferson also wrote the Ordinance of 1784, which shaped expansion across the American continent for the next century. Eager to ensure that the new nation would not have colonies, Jefferson established the principle that all new states would be admitted to the Union on an equal basis with the existing states. If he had had his way, the new states in the West would not have had slavery either. His provision to prevent the extension of slavery in the West after 1800, he said, lost by the vote of a single state. This provision, he later told the French philosophe Jean Nicholas Démeunier, who was writing encyclopedia entries on America, "would have prevented this abominable crime from spreading itself over the new country. Thus we see the fate of millions unborn hanging on the tongue of one man, and heaven was silent in that awful moment!"[50] An exaggeration, no doubt, but typical of Jefferson when he was writing about slavery to French liberals.

During his service in the Congress, Jefferson impressed everyone. His obvious intelligence, his range of knowledge, his cool and polite demeanor, his unusual serenity, and his willingness to work hard solidified his reputation as a prominent national statesman. Nothing seemed beyond his grasp, and in taking on all his numerous responsibilities he never seemed ruffled or stressed.

AT THE SAME TIME, ADAMS IN EUROPE was behaving in exactly the opposite manner. He was always nervous and passionate, never cool or serene. He worried about everything, about his salary and whether expenses should be charged to his personal account or that of the United

States, about whether he should accede to Vergennes's request and leave Holland and return to Paris, about how to respond to a Russian-Austrian plan for mediating the war between Britain and her enemies, about the way in which he was being treated by the Congress. The stress became unbearable, and in late August 1781 he collapsed with what he later described as "a nervous Fever, of a very malignant kind, and so violent as to deprive me of almost all Sensibility for four or five days." For six weeks Adams wrote no letters and carried on no business. Although his debilitating illness probably came from physical causes, the strain of work must have increased his vulnerability to disease.[51]

By the time Adams recovered, he had to deal with the peace commission of which he was one of five members, the increase in personnel explicitly designed to dilute his contentious influence. But because Jefferson declined the appointment and Laurens was captured at sea by the British and imprisoned in the Tower of London, the peace negotiations were left in the hands of just Franklin, Jay, and Adams—a combination that sparked Jefferson's interest. Although he had not seen Adams since their days together in the Continental Congress, he knew what he was like. As Jefferson confided to his friend James Madison, he wondered how his former colleague would act in the peace negotiations. "He hates Franklin, he hates Jay, he hates the French, he hates the English. To whom will he adhere?" Although Jefferson knew that Adams lacked "taste"— by which he meant judgment or a sense of appropriateness—he hadn't realized how vain he was. Nevertheless, he admitted that Adams did have "a sound head on substantial points," and he had "integrity," and conceded in a backhanded compliment that Adams would be a useful member of the peace commission. "His dislike of all parties, and all men, by balancing his prejudices, may give the same fair play to his reason as would a general benevolence of temper." Jefferson's conclusion said it all: "honesty may be extracted even from poisonous weeds."[52]

As one of the peace commissioners, Adams had been as obstreperous as Jefferson feared. He trusted no one, especially the French and their toady Franklin. He thought that Vergennes "means to keep us down if he can—to keep his Hand under our Chin, to prevent Us, from drowning, but not to lift our Heads out of Water."[53] Although Congress had instructed the commissioners to follow French advice and opinion in the peace negotiations, Adams and Jay decided to deal directly with the British without consulting Vergennes, and to Adams's surprise Franklin agreed. Adams said Congress could never have meant to bind the hands and feet of its ministers to the French government. "Those Chains I will never wear. They would be so galling to me that I could not bear them."[54]

Franklin's patience was worn down by Adams's undiplomatic behavior, and in a letter to Robert Livingston, the secretary of foreign affairs, he finally and famously characterized Adams as someone who "means well for his Country, is always an honest Man, often a Wise One, but sometimes and in some things, absolutely out of his Senses."[55] Actually Jefferson's description of Adams in his letter to Madison anticipated the nub of Franklin's characterization by several months. Fortunately for the friendship, Adams never saw Jefferson's letter to Madison, but he did see Franklin's portrayal of him soon after it was written. Elbridge Gerry had sent it to Abigail, who passed it on to her husband. This "private Stab to the Reputation of our Friend," as Gerry described the comment to Abigail, deepened Adams's hatred of Franklin.[56]

For all of his intelligence and learning, Adams was easily mocked, and he was often his own worst enemy. In February 1783 he wrote the president of the Congress suggesting that the United States immediately appoint a minister to Great Britain. He then described in great detail the qualifications of such a minister, qualifications that fit himself to a T: The minister "should have an Education in classical Learning, and in the Knowledge of general History, ancient and modern. . . . He should be well versed in the Principles of Ethicks; of the Law of Nature and Nations; of Legislation and Government; of the civil Roman law; . . . and in the Letters, Memoirs, and Histories of these great Men who have heretofore shone in the Diplomatick Order, and conducted the Affairs of Nations and the World." Finally, "he should be of an Age to possess a Maturity of Judgment arising from Experience in Business—He should be active, attentive, and industrious; above all he should possess an upright Heart and independent Spirit."[57]

After drawing this "picture of a fit character in which his own likeness is ridiculously and palpably studied," as Madison, a member of the Congress, derisively put it to Jefferson, Adams surprisingly recommended John Jay for the position. Yet Adams added, in an embarrassing display of wounded pride in what was after all an official report to the Congress, that if Jay was in fact appointed an "Injustice must finally be done to him, who was the first Object of his Country's Choice." By "the first Object" he obviously meant himself, and as Madison's comment on this "long and curious epistle from Mr. Adams" suggested, everyone in the Congress knew it. Since he had been charged with negotiating a commercial treaty with Britain, Adams believed he was already de facto minister to the Court of St. James's.[58] In fact, as he told his friend Charles Dumas, the indefatigable United States agent at The Hague, he thought he had "an incontestable Right to be Minister Plenipotentiary to the Court of Great Britain."[59]

WHEN JEFFERSON FINALLY had another opportunity to get to Europe and renew his friendship with Adams in person, he soon developed a less sardonic and more favorable attitude toward his former colleague. In May 1784 Congress elected him minister plenipotentiary to join Adams and Franklin in a commission to negotiate treaties of amity and commerce with sixteen European nations. All three commissioners shared an enlightened liberal view of international commerce. They hoped that "the increasing liberality of sentiments among philosophers and men of letters, in various nations," as Adams put it, might lead to "a reformation, a kind of protestantism, in the commercial system of the world."[60]

In 1776 the Congress, with Adams writing the draft, had drawn up a model treaty that would avoid the traditional kinds of political and military commitments and concentrate instead exclusively on commercial connections with other nations. Such a treaty promised the greatest amount of commercial freedom and equality among nations, which, if widely achieved, would eliminate the tensions and conflict of world politics. Absolute reciprocity in trade was the guiding principle of the model treaty. In duties and trade restrictions, foreign merchants would be treated as one's own nationals were treated. Even in wartime, trade was to be kept flowing. Neutral nations would have the right to trade with and carry the goods of the belligerent nations—the right expressed in the phrase "free ships make free goods."

The model treaty also provided that "the most Christian King," Louis XVI, would promise never to invade nor attempt to possess any portions of North America, which were to be exclusively possessed by the United States. At the same time as the treaty claimed America's right to all potential conquests in North America, it asserted that if this treaty with France resulted in Britain declaring war on France, the United States promised only to refrain from assisting Britain in such a war. This audacity of innocence did not last long.

Although the United States in 1778 was unable to avoid signing a conventional military treaty with France, the dream of tying nations together solely through commercial connections remained alive. The members of the commission, or at least Jefferson and Franklin, continued to hope that they might realize "an object so valuable to mankind as the total emancipation of commerce and the bringing together all nations for a free intercommunication of happiness."[61]

But, as Adams had anticipated, the world wasn't ready for such enlightened ideas. "No Facts are believed, but defensive military Conquests," he told Franklin in 1780; "no Arguments are seriously attended to in Europe but Force."[62] But Jefferson the enlightened dreamer hadn't given up. In 1785 he asked Adams what he thought of his draft of a model treaty to be presented to the courts of England and France. He admitted that the treaty went "beyond our powers; and beyond the powers of Congress too," but unfortunately it also went beyond the powers of possibility. It was truly radical. It not only proposed the free flow of commerce between the two signatory nations but also provided that "the intercourse between all the subjects and citizens of the two parties shall be free and unrestrained." While traveling in each other's territory, the peoples of each nation would be "considered to every intent and purpose as members of the nation where they are, entitled to all the protections, rights and advantages" of the natives of the other nation, but without any requirement for religious conformity. The signatory nations might confine their public offices to natives. Otherwise, this treaty that placed natives and aliens on an equal footing promised a mutuality of citizenship among nations. It was the fulfillment of an enlightened vision of a world that would exist virtually without borders.[63]

Adams politely told Jefferson that his model treaty was a fine idealistic effort, but unfortunately it was not appropriate to the realities of European politics. "We must not, my Friend, be the Bubbles of our own Liberal Sentiments. If we cannot obtain reciprocal Liberality, We must adopt reciprocal Prohibitions, Exclusions, Monopolies, and Imposts. Our offers have been fair, more than fair. If they are rejected, we must not be Dupes." By 1787 Adams had become convinced, as he told Jefferson, "that neither Philosophy, nor Religion, nor Morality, nor Wisdom, nor Interest, will ever govern nations or Parties, against their Vanity, their Pride, their Resentments or Revenges, or their Avarice or Ambitions. Nothing but Force and Power and Strength can restrain them." In ascribing personal passions to nations in this peculiar manner, Adams was merely expressing his deepening understanding of himself and his fellow human beings.[64]

In the end Adams's realism turned out to be more accurate than Jefferson's enlightened vision. Only three states—Sweden, Prussia, and Morocco, peripheral powers with little overseas trade—agreed to sign liberal commercial treaties with the United States, none of which involved more than most-favored-nation commercial relations. Most European states were indifferent to the Americans' enlightened ideas of commerce, ignorant, said Jefferson, to the power of American commerce.

THE COMMISSION'S FAILURES, however, were redeemed by the renewal of the friendship between Adams and Jefferson. Adams was delighted that his "old Friend" with whom he had labored at solving "many a knotty Problem" was joining him in Europe. Jefferson, he told James Warren, was someone "in whose Abilities and Steadiness I always found great Cause to confide."[65] But it was not just Jefferson who was joining him.

Abigail and his daughter Nabby would be arriving in Europe at about the same time as Jefferson arrived with his daughter Patsy. This news made Adams "twenty Years younger" and "the happiest Man upon Earth."[66]

The separation of John and Abigail over the previous decade had been extraordinary. During the ten years between August 1774 and August 1784, the couple had been together only about a quarter of the time. Between February 1778 and August 1784, they saw each other for just the fourteen weeks in 1779 that John returned to participate in the writing of the Massachusetts constitution. There were periods in Europe when John seemed to forget that he was married. No doubt his ambition to succeed as a great man was overriding his marital obligations. By contrast, Jefferson had turned down an appointment in Europe in 1777 because of his wife's uncertain health, even though he had long yearned to get to Europe. By 1781 Adams's letter writing to Abigail had declined considerably; during the first nine months of that year he sent only six letters to her. Abigail thought of herself as a widow and justifiably felt that she suffered from the separation more keenly than did her husband. She relieved her solitude by carrying on a flirtatious correspondence with James Lovell, a Massachusetts congressman. Finally she had had enough. If John wasn't coming home, then she would go to him.[67]

Abigail's presence in Europe helped to deepen the friendship of the two revolutionaries. She softened her husband's cantankerous personality, captivated the polite and reserved Jefferson, and enlivened the conversations that took place at the Adams home in the Parisian suburb of Auteuil. Accustomed to southern belles who knew their familial place and never discussed politics, Jefferson had his eyes opened by Abigail. Not only did Adams's wife fulfill her expected role as a household manager, being one of "the most attentive and honourable oeconomists" Jefferson had ever known, but she was also, and more remarkable, an intelligent, well-read, and politically knowledgeable person who had many opinions about the role and rights of women. Although Jefferson never accepted these opinions, he developed great affection and respect for Abigail; he described her to his friend Madison as "one of the most estimable characters on earth." In his eyes, Abigail, who could converse on history and philosophy, was no ordinary woman. "When writing to you," he said in one of his letters to her after the Adamses had gone to London, "I fancy myself at Auteuil, and chatter on till the last page of my paper awakens me from my reverie."[68]

JEFFERSON HAD MIXED FEELINGS about France. He was excited about being at long last at what he earlier had called "a polite court with literati of the first order." He certainly took to French fashion in dress more readily than Adams. He admired the refinement, art, music, and wine of France, but he found the bulk of the population to be oppressed. "The truth of Voltaire's observation, offers itself perpetually," he said, "that every man here must be either the hammer or anvil." But, as he told Mrs. Adams, he loved the French *"people* with all my heart." He thought that "with a better religion and a better form of government . . . their condition and country would be most enviable." Sensitive to Abigail's feelings about women's rights, Jefferson went on to point out that he had "used the term *people* and that this is a noun of the masculine as well as feminine gender."[69]

As someone who always valued politeness, certainly much more than did John Adams—who thought "the polite life in Europe is such an insipid round of head-dressing and play" as to be "beneath the character of a rational being"—Jefferson was especially taken with the good-humored manners of the French aristocracy. He even wished his countrymen would adopt some French politeness. Without abandoning "too much of the sincerity of language," perhaps his fellow Americans might try to "make all those little sacrifices of self which really render European manners amiable," and thus relieve their "society from the disagreeable scenes to which rudeness often exposes it." In France, he said, "it seems that a man might pass a life without encountering a single rudeness."[70]

Since good republicans always extolled sincerity and condemned courtierlike dissembling and deceit, too much politeness could appear monarchical and antirepublican. Coupled with his total admiration for all the French arts—he had no words, he said, to express his enjoyment of them—Jefferson's passion for French politeness could sometimes make him seem un-American. But ultimately "the empty bustle" of the French aristocracy, with its members "ever flying from the ennui" of their pointless lives, repulsed him; and he delighted in drawing contrasts between the worldly sophistication of Europe and the innocent simplicity of America. For the first time, he met individuals who were smarter and more knowledgeable than he, and that experience was bound to make him feel more American. He was no more at ease amid the libertine culture of the French nobility than the Adamses. The French aristocrats, Jefferson said, did not believe in conjugal love or domestic happiness; with all their lovers and mistresses they lived lives that offered only "moments of extasy amidst days and months of restlessness and torment."[71]

Living in Europe, advised Jefferson, was in fact dangerous for a young American. "He acquires a fondness for European luxury and dissipation, and a contempt for the simplicity of his own country." He becomes "fascinated with the privileges of the European aristocrats and sees with abhorrence the lovely equality which the poor enjoys with the rich in his own country." A young American abroad becomes "a foreigner, unacquainted with practices of domestic oeconomy necessary to preserve him from ruin." He is apt to be "led by the strongest of all the human passions into a spirit for female intrigue destructive of his own and others happiness, or a passion for whores destructive of his health." In either case, he "learns to consider fidelity to the marriage bed as an ungentlemanly practice and inconsistent with happiness."[72]

PRECISELY BECAUSE HE HIMSELF FELT these temptations and was so deeply drawn to the sophistication and the arts of Paris, Jefferson welcomed the company of the Adamses—in Jefferson's eyes, a down-to-earth domestic American family if there ever was one. Abigail, who was only a year younger than Jefferson, made the recent widower feel at home. She doted on him and helped him recover from a serious illness he suffered during his first winter in Paris. She consoled him when he learned that he had lost to whooping cough the two-year-old daughter he had left behind in Virginia. She urged him to bring his middle daughter, Maria, called Polly, to France and unite his family.

In 1787 Abigail met the nine-year-old Polly and her fourteen-year-old mulatto maid, Sally Hemings, in London. The little girl, who did not recognize her father from a portrait that was shown her, spent three weeks with the Adamses, and Abigail and Polly grew very attached to each other, with Abigail telling Jefferson that she was "really loath to part with her."[73]

Despite Abigail's sense that Jefferson should have come himself to London to pick up his daughter instead of sending his maître d'hôtel, she nevertheless continued to believe that he was "one of the choice ones of the Earth."[74] During the time Jefferson and Adams were in Paris together, the two families frequently intermingled. On one occasion Jefferson took Nabby and John Quincy to a concert, and at another time the two families visited Patsy's convent school together. Unlike the diplomatic guests whom the Adamses were obliged to invite to their home, Jefferson, said Abigail, was someone "who visits us in the Socially friendly way."[75] So close were the families that Adams later told Jefferson that he thought of John Quincy as "our John, because when you was at Cul de sac at Paris [the location of one of Jefferson's residences], he appeared to me to be almost as much your boy as mine."[76] Rarely had Adams had such an intimate and sociable friend. Indeed, Abigail told Jefferson that he was "the only person with whom my Companion could associate with perfect freedom, and unreserve."[77]

Adams enjoyed Jefferson so much because Jefferson was always amiable, always a good listener, and, most important, always deferential to him. Adams tended to think of Jefferson as a much younger man than he was in fact—only seven and a half years separated them. Jefferson, he once said, was "but a boy to me." Moreover, Adams had been abroad for most of the previous half-dozen years, and Jefferson naturally submitted to Adams's greater experience. Certainly Adams took great pleasure in the respect Jefferson paid him and regarded himself as Jefferson's "preceptor in politics." Indeed, Adams in 1809 claimed that he had "taught him everything that has been good and solid in his whole political conduct."[78]

Despite warnings from America that Jefferson was too idealistic and would "snuff up the incense of French adulation," Adams believed that Congress could not have sent a better man. He had studied Jefferson's character nine years earlier, and it was unaltered: "The Same industry, Integrity, and Talents remain without diminution." Jefferson was a "wise and prudent Man" with an "unquenchable Thirst of Knowledge." He was without "Party Passions or national prejudices, or any Partialities but for his own Country." With Franklin ill and indisposed, the two remaining members of the commission "lived together" in what Adams later recalled as "the most perfect friendship and harmony."[79]

Both Adams and Jefferson complained that the salaries paid them by the Congress were insufficient to maintain their households, especially if they wished to uphold the dignity of the United States. The Adamses tried desperately to avoid going into debt. Abigail told her sister Mary Cranch that "we spend no evenings abroad, make no suppers . . . and avoid every expence which is not held indispensable."[80] By contrast, Jefferson had no such qualms about borrowing money in order to sustain the patrician style of life to which he was accustomed. He was an aristocrat to his toes. He admitted as much when he told Madison that he disliked getting involved in any negotiations about money. "I do not understand bargaining nor possess the dexterity requisite to make them." Adams, he said, was better at it; he "stands already on ground for that business which I could not gain in years."[81] Perhaps he thought Yankees naturally had that skill.

As a good aristocrat, Jefferson inevitably had expensive tastes, and he denied himself few comforts. Unlike Adams, who lived on the outskirts of Paris, where the rents were cheaper, Jefferson chose to live closer to the center of the city, on the Champs-Élysées, where the price, as he complained to Abigail, was much more than that of his previous residence.[82] He kept changing houses, once paying rent to two houses at the same time, and remodeling them and furnishing them with new and more expensive furniture than he needed. He could scarcely refrain from sampling the vast array of goods that Paris offered—clothes, wine, candlesticks, silverware, and works of art. He especially couldn't stop buying books, sometimes purchasing books every day for weeks on end, and he borrowed money to do so. He admitted that the Adamses were living in a much plainer and more economical manner than he, which he attributed to the management skills of Abigail.[83]

IN 1785 JEFFERSON SUCCEEDED FRANKLIN as minister to France and Adams became minister to Great Britain, and the two friendly families had to separate. Jefferson immediately missed the camaraderie and told Adams that "the departure of your family has left me in the dumps."[84] But the families kept in touch through letters, Adams telling Jefferson that the "intimate Correspondence with you . . . is one of the most agreeable Events of my Life."[85] In her first letter from England, Abigail ruffled Jefferson's feathers a bit when she told him that London seemed "vastly superiour to Paris" in "wealth and grandeur," especially in its equipage of horses and carriages. In reply Jefferson said that he "always found it best to remove obstacles first," so he told her that her boast of London superiority was "a flout," and in a jesting manner went on to praise Paris and its people. A few months later and having experienced England more fully, Abigail now told Jefferson just what he wanted to hear: that the English were inferior to the French, "more constricted and narrow in their Sentiments notwithstanding their boasted liberality. . . . They affect to despise the French, and to hate the Americans. . . . So great is their pride that they cannot endure to view us as independent, and they fear our growing greatness."[86]

Abigail and Jefferson not only wrote to each other, but they shopped for each other, Jefferson, for example, buying shoes and table figurines for Abigail and she purchasing tablecloths and linen shirts for him. The relationship of Jefferson and Abigail was warm and for Jefferson remarkably playful, even flirtatious. In selecting the classical figurines, Jefferson told Abigail that he had been offered "a fine Venus, but I thought it out of taste to have two at table at the same time."[87] Although he believed, as he said to Angelica Schuyler Church, Alexander Hamilton's sister-in-law, that "the tender breasts of young ladies were not formed for political convulsion," he was more than willing to talk politics with Abigail. Suggesting that he was not getting enough political news from her husband, he asked Abigail if she would "be so good as to keep that office in your own hands." He was getting "little from any other quarter." Adams was so busy trying to open markets for whale oil—his "head," joked Jefferson, "was full of whale oil," but don't tell him this, he said—that he counted on Abigail to keep him informed about what was going on. Even if Mr. Adams could supply him with news, he said, "De tout mon coeur, I had rather receive it from you." In 1788 he asked Abigail if he could continue corresponding with her, to which she gratefully agreed.[88]

Jefferson was coming to realize that his friend Adams could be cantankerous, difficult, and "careless of appearances." He admitted to Madison, who had first suggested Adams's quirkiness, that Adams was indeed "vain, irritable and a bad calculator of the force and probable effect of the motives which govern men." During the time he had spent in Congress with Adams, Jefferson had not seen the vanity of the man, but the months together in Europe had opened his eyes. Still, he told Madison in 1787, that vanity is "all the ill" that could be said of Adams. He was a man "of rigorous honesty" and as "disinterested as the being which made him: he is profound in his views and accurate in his judgment except where knowledge of the world is necessary to form a judgment. He is so amiable, that I pronounce you will love him if ever you become acquainted with him."[89]

Although separated by the English Channel, the two families could scarcely have been closer. They not only exchanged gifts, portraits, and letters, and even joked about exchanging children, but the two ministers also collaborated in a number of matters. Jefferson and Adams, for example, shared in the expense of commissioning the French sculptor Jean-Antoine Houdon to do a bust of General Washington. In March 1786 Jefferson went to London to participate in the signing of a commercial treaty with Portugal and stayed six weeks, visiting often with the Adamses. He and Adams also hoped to negotiate a commercial treaty with Great Britain, but they were ignored by the British government and soon realized that such a treaty was impossible. Britain, said Jefferson, was now more hostile to America than it had been during the war.[90] The two ministers were presented at court, and, according to Adams family lore, George III turned his back on them.[91]

The two men spent a week touring England, visiting Birmingham, Oxford, Worcester, and Stratford-upon-Avon, among other places, as well as a number of the notable English country houses and gardens. Adams was taken with the sites of battles that had occurred in the English Civil War, where, he noted, "Freemen had fought for their Rights." He also described Shakespeare's birthplace and pondered the source of "this great Genius."[92]

For his part, Jefferson does not seem to have been much impressed by the battle sites or Stratford-upon-Avon; he was mainly interested in the gardens of the aristocratic country houses. Unlike Adams, he saw himself as one of these landed aristocrats, and he aimed to make Monticello the equal of any of their great houses. He walked through their gardens with a standard gardening book in hand, taking notes on "such practical things as might enable me to estimate the expense of making and maintaining a garden in that style."[93]

Adams admitted that the country houses and gardens and all of their embellishments of statuary and paintings were elegant and beautiful, but at what cost! The British national debt of "274 millions sterling" accumulated over "the Course of a Century might easily produce all this Magnificence." In his opinion all the obelisks and temples to Roman gods scattered about the grounds of the country houses were both "artificial" and "unnecessary" amusements. He hoped that it would be a long time before America would find such gardens and ornamental pleasure grounds fashionable. In America, he said, "nature has done greater Things and furnished nobler Materials there." Like many other Americans, Adams found that the sublime grandeur of America's rough landscape more than compensated for the nation's lack of great art. "The Oceans, Islands, Rivers, Mountains, Valleys," he said, "are all laid out upon a larger Scale."[94]

In Adams's opinion, the only artificial things in America worth noting were its state constitutions, and he had been responsible for the creation of most of them.

SIX

CONSTITUTIONS

LTHOUGH BOTH JEFFERSON and Adams were abroad in 1787 and thus missed attending the Philadelphia convention that drafted the new federal Constitution, they had been deeply involved in constitution-making from the very beginning of the revolutionary era. Jefferson had left the Continental Congress in 1776 and returned to Virginia in order to participate in creating Virginia's new republican constitution. For his part, Adams had written his *Thoughts on Government,* which became the most important pamphlet affecting the drafting of the state constitutions in 1776.

Although Virginia had drafted a constitution in 1776, Massachusetts had not. When royal authority in Massachusetts collapsed in 1775, the provincial congress had simply resumed the old charter of 1691, with the understanding that a more permanent constitution would be formed later. In 1778 the legislature finally got around to drafting a constitution for the state, which it submitted to the towns for approval. Because this constitution lacked a bill of rights and had problems with representation, the upper house, and the militia, the people in the towns turned it down. Some had criticized the constitution because it had not adequately protected property and the rights of creditors; others criticized it because it had been drafted by the legislature instead of by a body specially called for that purpose. How could a constitution be fundamental if it was created and alterable by the existing legislature?

Having a constitution that was different from ordinary statutes was a problem from the outset. To draft their constitutions, nearly all the states in 1776 had relied on congresses or conventions that were usually just their legislatures meeting without their royal governors. Because the constitutions were created by the legislatures, they presumably could also be changed or amended by the legislatures. Some of the constitution-makers in 1776 realized that their constitutions were supposed to be a kind of fundamental law, different from ordinary statutes, and they sought anxiously and confusedly to deal with the distinction. Delaware provided for a supermajority, five-sevenths of the legislature, for changing the constitution. Maryland said that its constitution could be amended only by a two-thirds vote of two successive legislatures. Most states, however, simply enacted their constitutions as if they were regular statutes. Everyone believed that the constitutions were special kinds of law, but no one knew quite how to make them so.

No one struggled with this problem of distinguishing fundamental from statutory law more persistently than Jefferson. His most detailed thinking on the subject appeared in his *Notes on the State of Virginia*. Jefferson wrote that book, the only one he ever authored, in response to the Marquis de Barbé-Mabois, the secretary to the French Legation, who in 1780 sought information about the American states for his government.

In the section Query XIII, entitled "Constitution," Jefferson began with a lengthy description of the seventeenth-century charter granted by the Crown to the planters and adventurers of the Virginia Company. Not only did the seventeenth-century charters granted to several colonies outline a structure of government for each colony, including a governor, council, and general assembly, but they also secured all the rights of Englishmen. Even when the king abrogated the charter in 1624 and made Virginia a crown colony, the structure of government and the rights of the people remained intact. When Parliament in the brief Commonwealth period during the English Civil War reinforced these articles and rights in 1651, the people of Virginia, said Jefferson, assumed that they had secured their autonomy and their "exemption from taxation but by their own assembly." This laid the constitutional basis for the colonists' opposition to British policies a century or so later.[1]

By his extensive description of all the written documents in seventeenth-century Virginian history, Jefferson demonstrated the importance of the early colonial charters as models for the constitution-making of 1776. Adams agreed. The charters, he said, were a kind of contract between the king and his subjects in which the king stipulated that his subjects "should enjoy all the rights and liberties of Englishmen forever."[2] Although the charters had been initially grants of the Crown to commercial companies to carry out certain public ends, by the eve of the Revolution they had been turned into defensive documents or, as Adams called them, contracts between the king and the people of each colony in which protection and allegiance were the considerations. These charters both prescribed forms of government and protected the rights of the people from encroaching power.

Consequently, by 1776 Americans were primed to think of a constitution as a written document set apart from the government and that somehow both ordered and delimited it. This was a very different understanding of a constitution from the way the English understood a constitution.

Englishmen tended to think of their constitution as including the operations of the government; it was the way in which the government was constituted or put together. It was, as the Tory Charles Inglis declared in 1776, *"that assemblage of laws, customs, and institutions which form the general system; according to which the several powers of the state are distributed, and their respective rights are secured to the different members of the community."*[3] The English constitution was not a single written document set apart from the government and ordinary lawmaking. For Englishmen, as William Blackstone declared, there could be no distinction between the "constitution" and the "system of laws." In other words, every act of Parliament was a part of the constitution, and all law, both customary and statutory, was thus constitutional. "Therefore," said William Paley, that acute summarizer of common eighteenth-century

British thought, "the terms *constitutional* and *unconstitutional* mean *legal* and *illegal*."[4]

That was not at all what Adams thought in 1773. He realized that "many people had different ideas from the words *legally* and constitutionally." The king and Parliament, he said, could do many things that were considered legal but were in fact unconstitutional. The problem was how to distinguish one from the other.[5]

MORE SO THAN ADAMS, Jefferson from the outset was eager to separate these two words—"legal" and "constitutional"—keen to ensure that the fundamental law of the constitution would be different from statutes that were legal. In 1776, in the first draft of his proposed constitution for Virginia, he proposed that the constitution could not be repealed except "by the unanimous consent of both legislative houses," a crude and impractical suggestion. By his second and third drafts, he had refined his thinking and now proposed that the constitution or "bill" be referred "to the people to be assembled in their respective counties and that the suffrages of two thirds of the counties shall be required to establish it," the constitution then being unalterable "but by the personal consent of the people on summons to meet in their respective counties." In 1776 he was the only one of his Virginia colleagues to object to the authority of the existing convention to frame a constitution without a new election.[6]

By 1779 Jefferson had become even more preoccupied with the problem of separating fundamental principles from statutory law. He knew from experience that no legislature "elected by the people for the ordinary purposes of legislation only" could restrain the acts of succeeding legislatures. Thus he realized that to declare his great Act for Establishing Religious Freedom in Virginia to be "irrevocable would be of no effect in law; yet we are free," he wrote into his 1779 bill in frustration, "to declare, and do declare, that . . . if any act shall be hereafter passed to repeal the present [act] or to narrow its operation, such act will be an infringement of natural right." All he could do, in other words, was place a curse on any future legislators who might violate his act.[7]

Jefferson realized that such a paper declaration was not enough and that something more was needed to protect natural rights and the fundamental laws of constitutions from legislative tampering. He was eager "to form a real constitution" for Virginia; the existing one, he said, was merely an "ordinance" with "no higher authority than the other ordinances of the same session." He wanted a constitution that would be "perpetual" and "unalterable by other legislatures." The only way that could be done was to have the constitution created, as he put it, "by a power superior to that of the legislature." By the early 1780s, the answer had become clear. "To render a form of government unalterable by ordinary acts of assembly," wrote Jefferson, "the people must delegate persons with special powers. They have accordingly chosen special conventions or congresses to form and fix their governments."[8] Moreover, the constitution had to be sent to the people for ratification.

MASSACHUSETTS HAD SHOWN THE WAY. It had demonstrated to the country the procedure by which a constitution could be created that was unalterable by ordinary statutory law. In 1779 the General Court authorized the election of a special convention to draft a new constitution. In order to further distinguish this constitution-making body from the regular legislature, for the election to this convention every male inhabitant over twenty-one years of age was allowed to vote—a broader suffrage than that for the legislature. Then the constitution had to be ratified by two-thirds of the state's free males twenty-one years and older.

The convention began meeting in September 1779, a month following Adams's return from Europe. A drafting committee of thirty named a subcommittee composed of James Bowdoin, president of the convention, Samuel Adams, and John Adams to draw up a constitution. This subcommittee turned over the writing of a draft to John Adams. Although it is clear that Adams was the principal framer of the constitution, he could not have done it alone. He returned to Europe in November 1779, and the convention continued to meet and revise the document until March 1780. Although Adams drew on the other state constitutions drafted in

1776 and 1777—"so many fine Examples have been so recently set [before] Us"—the most important influences on him were the discussions he had with his Massachusetts colleagues—"this society of Worthies," he called them—just after he had arrived back in the state.[9] The Massachusetts leaders had been increasingly alarmed by the dissident thinking and behavior in the western part of the state, and had been pondering the nature of a new constitution for Massachusetts for several years. So Adams was joining a conversation about constitutionalism that had been going on all the while he had been away in Europe.

Despite saying that he was drawing on the examples of the state constitutions framed in 1776, Adams and his colleagues created a constitution that was very different from those. The Massachusetts leaders had come to realize that the constitutions of 1776 had granted too little authority to the executives and too much authority to the popular assemblies.

By 1780 it had become increasingly clear to many gentry-elites that all the state legislatures were abusing their power and creating democratic excesses in the states that few Whigs in 1776 had anticipated. The "democratic despotism" that Adams in 1775 had declared to be "a contradiction in terms" had become all too real. State legislatures were assuming the powers of the executive and the judiciary to themselves. And they were passing multiple and mutable laws that were also unjust, including various kinds of debtor relief legislation and paper money issues that were hurting creditors. These vices, as Jefferson's friend James Madison put it, were bringing "into question the fundamental principle of republican Government, that the majority who rule in such governments are the safest Guardians both of public Good and private Rights."[10]

Although by 1780 gentry-elites in most of the states were contemplating reform of their original state constitutions, only Massachusetts was able to draft a constitution that was in accord with the revised thinking; this was made possible by the fact that the state had delayed the constitution-making process and learned from the mistakes of the other states. Consequently, the Massachusetts constitution not only influenced the revisions of the other state constitutions in the late 1780s and early 1790s, but decisively affected the nature of the national Constitution of 1787.

There exists no manuscript copy of Adams's draft of the Massachu-setts constitution, so the printed *Report of a Constitution* that went to the convention is all we have. It was probably largely but certainly not en-tirely the work of Adams. This *Report* presented a constitution that was by far the longest and most detailed of the revolutionary constitutions.

At the beginning the draft report adopted the term "Common-wealth" instead of "State," something that Virginia and Pennsylvania had done.[11] It also set forth a declaration of rights, largely borrowed from those of other state constitutions, and incorporated it in the constitution itself as chapter I. The opening phrase, taken from the declarations of rights in the Virginia and Pennsylvania constitutions of 1776, stated that "all men are born equally free and independent, and have certain natural, essential, and unalienable rights." Although Adams was willing to bor-row various passages from the 1776 Pennsylvania declaration of rights, he knew he would never borrow anything from the structure of that state's government, especially its unicameral legislature and plural exec-utive. In October 1779, while Adams was in the midst of writing the draft, Benjamin Rush, his friend from Pennsylvania, reminded him of his immediate response upon seeing a copy of the radical Pennsylvania constitution in 1776. "Good God! (said you) the people of Pensylvania in two years will be glad to petition the crown of Britain for reconciliation in order to be delivered from the tyranny of their constitution."[12]

Consequently, Adams's constitution created a structure of government that was very different from that of Pennsylvania. It provided for a bicam-eral legislature with a strong senate, and an independent judiciary whose members served during good behavior. The property qualifications for voting and holding office were considerably higher than those in the other states. Adams's constitution also created a much more powerful and inde-pendent governor than existed in the other states. The governor, who was required to have an estate worth at least a thousand pounds, was to be annually elected by the people at large rather than by the legislature, as was the case in most of the other state constitutions. The constitution cre-ated a council of nine members to advise the governor in his executive duties; although this council was to be drawn from the forty annually elected senators, it, unlike the old colonial Council, had no legislative authority whatsoever. Eager to enhance executive authority, Adams granted the governor some of the prerogative powers that had been stripped from the executives in the state constitutions drafted in 1776. His draft gave the governor not only the authority, along with the governor's council, to appoint judges, sheriffs, and militia officers, but, more important, the sole power to veto all laws passed by the legislature.[13]

Adams was especially proud of his section of the constitution that provided for the government's positive role in encouraging education, the principles of humanity and general benevolence, literature, science, and the arts in both public and private institutions—all premised on the belief that "wisdom and knowledge, as well as virtue, diffused generally among the body of the people [were] necessary for the preservation of their rights and liberties."[14]

ALTHOUGH MUCH OF THIS *Report of a Constitution* was the work of Adams, the full committee and the convention made some substantial changes in his draft. Not only did the convention formally divide the constitution into two parts, separating the declaration of rights from the frame of government, but it altered the opening phrase of the declaration of rights and transformed its meaning. Stating, as Adams had, that "all men are born equally free and independent" did not have quite the emphasis on equality that was in the Declaration of Independence or, for that matter, in Adams's earlier statement of 1766, that "all men are born equal."[15]

By 1779 Adams had lost much of his earlier enthusiasm for the enlightened view that all men were created equal; indeed, he was coming to believe the opposite—that all men were created unequal. That was too much for the convention, however, and so it changed his phrase to read that "all men are born free and equal"—a statement more in line with the Declaration of Independence.

Much more important to Adams was the change the convention made to the governor's role in lawmaking. The convention balked at Adams's desire to give the governor an absolute veto power over all legislation; instead, it granted the governor only a qualified veto power, which allowed two-thirds of each house of the legislature to override the governor's veto. This denial of the absolute veto that Adams wanted, as Theophilus Parsons, an eminent lawyer from Essex County, privately explained, was a concession made "to please the People."[16]

The convention also rejected Adams's proposal that the governor could be annually reelected no more than five times over a period of seven years, and his suggestion that all officeholders be Christians. Instead the convention limited this second restriction to the governor and lieutenant governor, but at the same time inconsistently required all councilors and legislators to swear or affirm a belief in the truth of Christianity upon assuming their offices. The convention eliminated Adams's reference to the right of free speech in the declaration of rights and did away with the right of the governor to appoint militia officers. The convention added some obvious things that Adams had overlooked, including the right of the house of representatives to judge the qualifications of its members, compensation for property taken for public uses, stipulating a quorum for the senate, and providing for amending the constitution.

These sorts of omissions came from the haste with which Adams worked. Also it is clear that he did not write certain sections of the *Report*. The most controversial part of the *Report* was article III, which stated that the government had the authority to provide at public expense for the public worship of God and for the support of teachers of religion. Although Adams claimed that he had nothing to do with this article, Isaac Backus, the celebrated leader of the Baptists in New England, later claimed that on the floor of the convention Adams had cited an incident from 1774 in which Backus and the Baptists had embarrassed the Massachusetts delegation at the Continental Congress, in order to inflame the convention and get it to vote for article III.[17]

OTHER ARTICLES IN THE DECLARATION of rights were lifted almost verbatim from other state constitutions, perhaps in some cases without much reflection. If Adams was the one who copied article V of the declaration of rights from the Pennsylvania and Virginia constitutions of 1776, for example, it appears that he hadn't given much thought to its implications. The article read that "all power residing originally in the people, and being derived from them, the several magistrates and officers of government, vested with authority, whether legislative, executive or judicial, are their substitutes and agents, and are at all times accountable to them." But as Adams set forth his thinking about mixed government, making all parts of the government substitutes and agents of the people was not what he believed at all—as his later exchanges with Samuel Adams, Roger Sherman of Connecticut, and John Taylor of Virginia demonstrated. It was Taylor who most fully drew out the implications of having all members of the government considered as agents of the people, implications that were far more in accord with the sentiments of the American people than Adams's fidelity to the English theory of mixed government.

The convention, anticipating Taylor, had none of Adams's devotion to the traditional theory of mixed government, and in its Address, which it sent to the people in March 1780, it made very explicit the significance of conceiving of all the officers of government, executive as well as legislative, as substitutes and agents of the people. This Address appeared five months after Adams had gone back to France and was not his work at all.

Although Adams certainly would have agreed with the Address's conventional emphasis on separating the executive, legislative, and judicial powers, he would probably not have labeled them, as the Address did, "the three capital powers of Government." For Adams, the three capital powers of government remained the house of representatives, the senate, and the governor—embodying the three orders or powers of the society. Nor would he have agreed with the Address's statement that "the Governor is emphatically the Representative of the whole People, being chosen not by one Town or County, but by the People at large." For Adams, continuing to think in traditional terms of mixed or balanced government, the people were represented solely in the house of representatives. Adams believed that the governor embodied the one, the monarchical order in the society, and had to be independent of the people, not their representative.

It was precisely because Adams thought the governor stood for an order or an estate in the society that he had wanted an absolute veto given to him. "I am clear for Three Branches, in the Legislature," he told Elbridge Gerry. "I am persuaded, We never shall have any Stability, Dignity, Decision, or Liberty without it." The executive "ought to be the Reservoir of Wisdom, as the Legislature is of Liberty." Without the weapon of a full voice in legislation, that is, an absolute veto, the executive "will be run down like a Hare before the Hunters."[18]

The reason Adams wanted the executive to be a full-fledged member of the legislature was that the king of Great Britain was a full-fledged member of Parliament, and the English constitution was his model for the Massachusetts constitution. The English constitution with the king-in-Parliament was, he believed, "both for the adjustment of the balance and the prevention of its vibrations, the most stupendous fabric of human invention." "Americans," he continued, "ought to be applauded instead of censured, for imitating it as far as they have done." Even back in 1775 he had written in his Novanglus essays that if a republic was *a government of laws not of men,* as great thinkers like Aristotle and Harrington had contended, then "the British constitution is nothing more or less than a republic, in which the king is first magistrate."[19]

Of course, conceiving of the English constitution as a republic made it easier for Adams to adopt it as a model. Of all the revolutionary state constitutions, the Massachusetts constitution came closest to the English constitution. Even the judiciary was modeled on it. Although Adams had granted judges tenure during good behavior, he had also provided that they, like the English judges, could be removed by the governor and council "upon the address of both Houses of the legislature." This was something less than the judicial independence touted by the constitution-makers in the other states.[20]

THE ENGLISH CONSTITUTION that Adams admired in 1779 was the one interpreted by the Swiss jurist Jean Louis De Lolme in his *La Constitution de l'Angleterre,* first published in French at Amsterdam in 1771. Although Adams never mentioned De Lolme in drafting the

Massachusetts constitution, he obviously had read his work and had been influenced by it.

De Lolme fundamentally revised Montesquieu's earlier understanding of the English constitution and helped to change the thinking of Adams and others on the nature of mixed or balanced government. Although Montesquieu in his *Spirit of the Laws* had spent a good deal of time extolling the English constitution, De Lolme's work was the first by a continental European devoted entirely to the subject. The first English translation of De Lolme's book, *The Constitution of England; or, An Account of the English Government*, appeared in 1775, and the work went on to have multiple printings over the succeeding decades.[21]

In his 1748 *Spirit of the Laws*, Montesquieu had accepted the conventional understanding of the English constitution as a struggle between the king and the people, between the prerogative powers of an encroaching Crown and the rights of the people defended by their representatives in the House of Commons. This ancient conflict between monarchy and democracy had been mediated by the aristocracy in the House of Lords, acting as the holder of the scales in the marvelously balanced English constitution.[22]

Adams in his *Thoughts on Government* had likewise accepted this traditional view of the balance in the English constitution and had urged his countrymen to draft their state constitutions with this historic contest between the executive and the popular assembly in mind. "If the legislative power is wholly in one Assembly and the executive in another, or in a single person, these two powers," he had written in this 1776 pamphlet, "will oppose and enervate upon each other, until the contest shall end in war, and the whole power, legislative and executive, be usurped by the strongest." An upper house embodying the aristocracy of the society, he concluded, would mediate this contest and bring about a proper balance.[23]

Contrary to Montesquieu, De Lolme in his work emphasized that the basic struggle in English history was not between the monarch and the people, but was actually between the House of Commons, or the democracy, on the one hand and the House of Lords, or the aristocracy, on the other, with the crucial role in maintaining the proper balance being played by the king. This was a major innovation in thinking about the English constitution. A strong executive, De Lolme wrote, was the best check against the ambitions of the aristocracy, which always posed the greater threat to the stability of the constitution. Too much democracy did not lead to anarchy but to oligarchy or aristocracy. Without a powerful executive, the freedom and stability of the English constitution and presumably any other balanced constitution, De Lolme concluded, could not be maintained.[24]

With good reason did Adams call De Lolme's book "the best defense of the political balance of three powers that was ever written."[25] He had closely followed De Lolme's argument and in the process had fundamentally altered his thinking about the nature of the proper balance in a constitution. Adams now claimed that the principal conflict in society was between the people and the aristocracy, a conflict, according to reports he had received from his colleagues in the late 1770s, that was much more in accord with the realities of Massachusetts society and politics. That is why he was so insistent on a strong executive for the Massachusetts constitution, one who was a full and equal participant in the legislative process with an absolute negative over all legislation and one who could balance the aristocracy and the democracy embodied in the other branches of the legislature. But to Adams's chagrin, the final constitution in chapter I, section I, article I, declared that "the department of legislation shall be formed by two branches," which meant that the governor possessed only a limited veto power.[26] Still, the executive in the Massachusetts constitution emerged as the strongest governor of any of the states.

WHEN IT CAME TO CREATING the senate or upper house, Adams was much more indebted to his colleagues who had been wrestling with the problem for months. During the debate over the proposed constitution of 1778 in Massachusetts, Theophilus Parsons in the *Essex Result*, the publication of the Essex County convention, had spent a great deal of time discussing the difficulty of constructing an upper house.

The proposed constitution of 1778 was defective, Parsons wrote, because it provided for the selection of the senate by all the freemen: "a trust is reposed in the people which they are unequal to." If Massachusetts wanted a proper senate containing "the greatest wisdom, firmness, consistency, and perseverance," it had to look beyond the common people. "These qualities," said Parsons, who later became chief justice of the Massachusetts Supreme Court, "will most probably be found amongst men of education and fortune," especially fortune. On behalf of the Essex convention, Parsons admitted that all men of property were not at present men of learning and wisdom, but surely, he said, it was among the wealthy that the largest number of men of education and character could be found. Hence the senate, declared the Essex convention, should represent the property of the state.[27]

Since the weakness of the senate was one of the reasons the proposed constitution of 1778 had been turned down, the convention of 1779–1780 was determined to remedy this defect. Adams had proposed that the senators had to own a freehold worth at least three hundred pounds. The convention doubled this amount to six hundred pounds and included personal property in the sum, thus opening up the office to wealthy individuals who may not have owned sufficient land. The Address of the convention went on to spell out the difference between the two houses in no uncertain terms: "The House of Representatives is intended as the Representatives of the Persons, and the Senate of the property of the Commonwealth."[28]

Making the senate the overt representative of property severely distorted the meaning of mixed government that the state constitution-makers of 1776 had applied. The framers of the revolutionary state constitutions had hoped that their upper houses would embody the wisdom and learning of the society, not just property and wealth. In 1776 William Hooper of North Carolina had suggested that senators should be "selected for their Wisdom, remarkable Integrity, or that Weight which arises from property and gives Independence and Impartiality to the human mind."[29] Although wisdom and integrity were difficult to measure, property was not. Out of frustration with the people's inability to perceive the wise and truly talented, the states fell back on property as the best practical source of distinction for their state senates. Some of the states required members of their upper houses to have more property than members of the lower houses, while other states required the senatorial electors to have more property than those electing the houses of representatives. Thus many American leaders found in property a criterion by which the "senatorial part" of their society could be distinguished from ordinary people. By stating that the upper house represented property, the Massachusetts constitution made glaringly explicit what was only implicit in the other states.

Making property the measure of wisdom was not what most framers of the revolutionary state constitutions had expected. In his experience, Jefferson had noted in 1776, "Integrity" was not "the characteristic of wealth."[30] Adams agreed. He never said that his idea of a senate was simply to represent property; the explicit statement to that effect made in the convention's Address to the people in 1780 was the view of his colleagues, not his view. Instead, for Adams the upper house embodied the aristocratic estate of the society, which, as he came to explain in his *Defence of the Constitutions of Government of the United States of America*, included much more than mere property.

EVEN THOUGH BOTH Adams and Jefferson in the early 1780s were working for the Confederation Congress, their focus was still on their individual states. Indeed, with the end of the war in 1783, Jefferson thought the Congress had lost most of its usefulness. "The constant session of Congress," he said, "can not be necessary in time of peace." After clearing up the most urgent business, the delegates should "separate and return to our respective states, leaving only a Committee of the states," and thus "destroy the strange idea of their being a permanent body, which has unaccountably taken possession of the heads of their constituents, and occasions jealousies injurious to the public good."[31]

Certainly Jefferson's mind was still on his own state of Virginia. At the very time Massachusetts was putting its new constitution into effect, he was thinking about reforming the Virginia constitution that had been adopted in 1776. Since "we were new and inexperienced in the science of government" in 1776, it was not surprising, he explained, "that time and trial have discovered very capital defects in it." The most important defect lay in the nature and behavior of the legislature. It had concentrated within itself all the legislative, executive, and judicial powers, which, said Jefferson, was "precisely the definition of despotism." The fact that the legislature was composed of many hands did not mitigate the problem: "173 despots would surely be as oppressive as one," he observed.[32]

Adams and many of the other leaders in Massachusetts and elsewhere would have agreed with this assessment. That was why they favored a stronger executive and a stronger senate. But their reforms came from a growing mistrust of the people at large. The assemblies were behaving tyrannically because they were only too representative of the people and their partial and narrow interests.

Jefferson believed the opposite. He had not lost faith in the people themselves. He assumed the assemblies, although elected, were not really the people; these elected legislatures had drifted away from the people and were not carrying out the people's true wishes. He was especially critical of some of his colleagues in the Virginia legislature who twice had panicked and called for a dictator to save them. Did they believe, he said, that the people of Virginia had substituted fear for virtue as their motivating principle? He knew that republicanism was risky and required an educated populace. Every government, including Virginia's, contained "some germ of corruption," and "when trusted to the rulers of the people alone" it was bound to degenerate. "The people themselves therefore are its only depositories."[33]

In Virginia the suffrage was too limited; "the majority of the men in the state who pay and fight for its support are unrepresented in the legislature." And "among those who share the representation, the shares are very unequal."[34] Counties in the western parts of the state did not have representation in proportion to their population. Unlike most reformers in the 1780s, Jefferson believed that a fuller and more equitable representation of the people could alleviate the problem of legislative abuses. He was one of those who paid little or no attention to what Madison later called that "essential distinction, too little heeded," between governments that became oppressive by opposing the will of the people and those governments that became oppressive by only too accurately embodying the will of the people.[35] For Jefferson the people themselves could never become oppressive; only their elected agents were capable of tyranny.

Jefferson was unable to persuade his Virginia colleagues to reform the state's 1776 constitution. Although equally unsuccessful, reformers in the other states, especially in Pennsylvania, did not cease trying to bring their constitutions more in line with the more conservative Massachusetts constitution of 1780. Only with the adoption of the new federal Constitution in 1787 were some states, but not Virginia, able to reform their constitutions.

THE FRENCH WERE FASCINATED by all these American state constitutions. Soon after Benjamin Franklin arrived in France in 1776, he arranged with the Duc de La Rochefoucauld-Liancourt to have the state constitutions translated into French. At least five different editions of the constitutions were published in France between 1776 and 1786. By 1784 Adams noted that "the Philosophers are speculating upon our Constitutions." He hoped that they "will throw out Hints, which will be of Use to our Countrymen."[36]

That same year, the British dissenting minister Richard Price published in London his *Observations on the Importance of the American Revolution and the Means of Making it a Benefit to the World*, and it was promptly republished in Boston. At the end of this pamphlet, Price included a letter he had earlier received from the French philosophe and former minister to Louis XVI Baron Anne-Robert-Jacques Turgot, who had died in 1781. In this 1778 letter, Turgot had criticized the revolutionary state constitutions drafted in 1776. Too many of them, he said, were based on the English constitution. "Instead of bringing all the authorities into one, that of the nation, they have established different bodies, a House of Representatives, a Council, a Governor, because England has a House of Commons, an House of lords, and a King." The constitution-makers, he said, had misunderstood what republics required. Monarchies, Turgot said, may have needed "different authorities" to balance and offset "the enormous preponderance of royalty," but republics, "formed on the equality of all citizens," had no such need. Indeed, by constituting "different bodies" in their governments, the Americans had created "a source of divisions." In other words, "by striving to prevent imaginary dangers, they have created real ones."[37]

Turgot had a point. In 1776 most Americans rather unthinkingly had followed the English example in creating bicameral legislatures and separate governors. Their experience with their colonial constitutions, which they had regarded as miniature copies of the English constitution, and the influence of Adams's *Thoughts on Government*, had dictated the structure of their new republics. But unlike Turgot or Adams, by creating such mixed constitutions most Americans had not assumed they were incorporating different bodies or estates in their governments; they simply had not thought through the implications of what they were doing.

When challenged on this issue that they were creating estates or separate bodies in their constitutions in the manner of the English constitution, most Americans began offering very different justifications of their bicameral legislatures and independent governors. By the 1780s it was becoming increasingly difficult, if not impossible, for political leaders in America to justify their mixed and balanced constitutions as embodying estates or powers of the society. It was Adams's unfortunate fate never to fully grasp this new development.

Reformers of the controversial Pennsylvania constitution of 1776, for example, very much wanted to replace the unicameral assembly with a legislature that contained a senate as well as a lower house. But as soon as they voiced this reform, defenders of the original constitution accused them of being "a junto of gentlemen in Philadelphia, who wished to trample upon the farmers and mechanics, to establish a wicked aristocracy, and to introduce a House of Lords, hoping to become members of it." In response, the critics of the unicameral legislature denied any intention of foisting an aristocracy on the state. Instead, they argued that the upper house was necessary only as a means of checking the power of a single

The young John and Abigail Adams by Benjamin Blyth (1766). These portraits, drawn in pastel by an obscure Massachusetts artist, reveal much more about Abigail than about John. While his picture portrays a plain, pudgy, and expressionless figure, Abigail's reveals a sharp, confident, and rather commanding personality.

Official presidential portrait of Thomas Jefferson by Rembrandt Peale (1800). This portrait expresses the confidence and optimism of Jefferson at the height of his powers.

Portrait of John Adams by Gilbert Stuart (1824). This likeness captures the sparkle and crustiness of Adams as an old man.

Portrait of Jefferson by Gilbert Stuart (1805). Stuart was not happy with a portrait he had done of Jefferson in 1800, and in 1805 he insisted on another sitting. Not until 1821 did Jefferson finally receive a portrait of himself painted by Stuart.

Portraits of Adams and Jefferson by Mather Brown (1788). In the 1780s Jefferson began collecting portraits of those he considered "worthies" in the history of America. He commissioned Brown, a young American artist who was abroad studying with Benjamin West, to do these portraits of himself and Adams. While Brown depicted Adams as rather old and tired looking, he portrayed Jefferson as aloof, aristocratic, and dressed to the nines in his elegant French clothes. This portrait is the earliest known likeness of Jefferson.

Adams's Montezillo (top) and Jefferson's Monticello (bottom). The difference
between their homes tells us much about the two men. That Adams in 1819
began calling his house "*Montezillo* a little Hill" reveals his characteristic
facetiousness, something Jefferson never displayed.

Portrait of Benjamin Rush by Thomas Sully (c. 1813). If it weren't for an intervention by Rush, a physician, Adams and Jefferson would never have been reconciled after the election of 1800.

Portrait of Abigail Adams by Gilbert Stuart (1800–1815). Stuart began
this portrait in 1800 but did not finish it until 1815. In her old age, Abigail
retained the same sharp and piercing look as in her youth.

Self-portrait of Maria Cosway (1787). In addition to being an accomplished painter who exhibited more than thirty of her paintings at the Royal Academy of Arts in London, Cosway was a talented composer and musician and a European celebrity.

Declaration of Independence by John Trumbull (1832). Trumbull initially thought he would paint only the famous battles of the Revolution, but Jefferson apparently suggested that he include the presentation of the draft of the Declaration of Independence in his depictions of great events.

Washington, D.C., in a watercolor by William Russell Birch (1800). In 1800 Abigail and her entourage got lost trying to make their way through the woods to the primitive city of Washington. One can travel miles, she said, "without seeing any human being."

Portrait of Benjamin Franklin by Joseph-Siffred Duplessis (1778). Duplessis's portrait was just one of many likenesses of Franklin that the French created. Franklin's image appeared everywhere—in numerous prints and on medallions, snuffboxes, candy boxes, rings, clocks, vases, dishes, handkerchiefs, and pocketknives, making him, as Adams complained, "one of the most curious Characters in History."

Portrait of the Marquis de Lafayette by Joseph-Désiré Court (1785).
An enlightened and enthusiastic liberal who initially promoted the
reforms that led to the French Revolution, Lafayette was beloved
by Jefferson but dismissed as ignorant and naïve by Adams.

Portrait of George Washington by Gilbert Stuart (1796).
Washington possessed what Adams and even Jefferson lacked:
the gift of natural charismatic leadership.

Portrait of Alexander Hamilton by John Trumbull (1806). Hamilton was the one founder who was hated by both Adams and Jefferson.

Portrait of James Madison by John Vanderlyn (1816). Madison was Jefferson's closest friend and confidant. He never quite understood what Jefferson saw in Adams.

Engraving of Thomas Paine by William Sharp (1793). Adams claimed in 1805 that the age he and Jefferson were living through was anything but Paine's "Age of Reason." But he had little doubt that this man Paine, "such a mongrel between pig and puppy, begotten by a wild boar on a bitch wolf," had had the greatest influence over all their lives. Never before in history, said Adams, had "the poltroonery of mankind" allowed anyone "to run through such a career of mischief. Call it then the Age of Paine."

legislature. It had no social significance whatsoever. It would simply be "a double representation of the people." The two houses "would both draw their power from the same source—from the people, the fountain of all authority." Therefore they would not have opposite interests, but only the single interest of the people. The very thing that Jefferson and others had worried about—the homogeneity of interests between the two houses in a bicameral legislature—was now celebrated as a good thing.[38]

Others began drawing out the implications of having a double representation of the people. If the people could be represented twice, why couldn't they be represented three or more times? It was this extraordinary expansion of the idea of representation that enabled the Massachusetts convention in 1780 to label the governor, simply because he was elected by the people at large, "emphatically the Representative of the whole People."[39] The process of popular election by itself made an official a representative of the people.

Everywhere in the states in the early 1780s, the traditional theory of mixed government was fast giving way to the idea that all parts of the state governments were in some way or another representatives of the people. Although Jefferson in his *Notes on the State of Virginia* had complained that the senate in Virginia, "being chosen by the same electors, at the same time, and out of the same subjects," was "too homogeneous with the house of delegates," he had no admiration whatsoever for the English constitution and did not see the senate as embodying any sort of aristocratic order or estate. Because in his *Summary View* pamphlet of 1774 he had declared that "kings are the servants, not the proprietors of the people," he was already primed to think of all officers of government as representatives of the people.[40]

JOHN ADAMS WAS A CONSPICUOUS EXCEPTION to all these popularizing developments. No American was more infatuated with the English constitution; even his old radical Whig English friend Thomas Brand Hollis chided him for being so excessively fond of the English constitution, especially since Hollis believed that it had become defective and unbalanced.[41] Certainly Adams more than any other American leader clung tightly to the traditional theory that underlay the English constitution—that the three powers or orders of society were embodied in all governments that contained bicameral legislatures and independent executives.

Because most Americans were rapidly abandoning the English theory of mixed government or had never firmly grasped it in the first place, they paid little or no attention to Turgot's criticism of their constitutions. Adams, however, was different. Being enamored of the English constitution and knowing exactly what Turgot was getting at, he was outraged by the Frenchman's criticism. Since he rightly believed that he had been most responsible for the form and structure of the revolutionary state constitutions, he took Turgot's criticism personally. In fact, he claimed "that Mr. Turgot's crude idea is really a personal attack upon me, whether he knew it or not." Therefore, it was only proper, he said, that the defense of the constitutions should come from Adams himself.[42]

The result was his *Defence of the Constitutions of Government of the United States of America*—that huge, three-volume, jumbled conglomeration of political glosses on a single theme. No government, Adams contended, could long remain stable and free unless it placed each of the principal social orders—the people and the aristocracy—in separate houses of the legislature and balanced them by an independent executive. The common people he knew about, from his background in Braintree and his law practice, if from nothing else, and he was well aware of their anarchical passions. All history was full of examples of the people robbing and plundering the rich. It was evident that the people, unrestrained, were "as unjust, tyrannical, brutal, barbarous, and cruel as any king or senate possessed of uncontrollable power."[43] Nevertheless, it was the aristocracy that he was most worried about.

ADAMS HAD BEEN THINKING ABOUT writing a book on aristocracy for several years, certainly by the early 1780s, when Jefferson first joined him in Paris.[44] In 1813 he reminded Jefferson how both of

them in 1784 had spent "a whole evening" in Jefferson's apartments being "harrangued" by the Marquis de Lafayette on "the plans then in
Operation to reform France." Adams recalled being "astonished at the
Grossness of his Ignorance of Government and History." It was what
others—"Turgot, Rochefaucault, Condorcet, and Franklin"—had been
saying for years. "This gross Ideology" of all those Frenchmen and those
Frenchified liberals like Franklin—their obsession with democracy and a
single-house legislature—was what "first suggested" to him the "thought
and inclination . . . of writing Something upon Aristocracy."[45]

But listening to Lafayette and reading the likes of Turgot could never
by themselves have provoked Adams's fascination with the subject of
aristocracy. He had read so much history—more, surely, than any other
American of his generation—and all that history, from ancient Rome to
Renaissance Italy and eighteenth-century England, had stressed over
and over the inevitability of patricians distinguishing themselves from
plebeians. For a moment in early 1786 he thought that this social distinction might not be inevitable after all; indeed, perhaps it could even
be eliminated.

In a letter written on January 21, 1786, to his eccentric French friend
Count Sarsfield, Adams said that he had "half a mind to devote the next
ten years to the making of a book on the subject of nobility." He wished
"to inquire into the practice of all nations, ancient and modern, civilized
and savage, under all religions,—Mahometan, Christian, and Pagan,—
to see how far the division of mankind into patricians and plebeians,
nobles and simple, is necessary and inevitable, and how far it is not." If
this distinction was man-made, created by art, then perhaps, he told
Sarsfield, it could be unmade, which would be a good thing.[46]

This notion that aristocracy might be done away with by artful means
was for Adams a momentary fancy tossed off playfully to a friend. Once
he got serious about his inquiry into the nature of aristocracy, he quickly
concluded that such patricians not only were inevitable in every society
but were based on the inequality of people that was rooted in nature.

Of course, there was nothing really new or unusual about Adams's
division of the society into the few and many, into gentlemen and com-

moners, aristocrats and democrats. Many Americans in the 1780s believed that every developed society always divided into the few and the many and that each needed to defend itself against the other. "Give all power to the many, they will oppress the few," said Alexander Hamilton in 1787. "Give all power to the few they will oppress the many."[47] By the 1780s the conflict between gentlemen and commoners had become conventional wisdom for many northern elites, but it had become increasingly politically incorrect to contend publicly that each house of a bicameral legislature should embody these two social contestants.

Adams distinguished himself from his contemporaries by his obvious willingness to boldly and publicly admit the need to represent the social orders in separate houses of the legislatures. But even more important in setting himself apart from his colleagues was his conviction that since the social division between aristocrats and commoners was inevitable and existed in every society, it needed to be understood scientifically. That is why his *Defence of the Constitutions* spent little or no time analyzing the American state constitutions themselves. In Adams's mind it was enough to demonstrate that their structure was based on a scientifically established principle of government that encompassed different peoples over centuries of time. "Nations," he said, "move by unalterable rules," by the same kinds of laws and regularities as the heavenly bodies.[48]

Others may have taken the social division between gentlemen and commoners for granted, but he wanted to know where this pervasive difference between the few and the many, the rich and the poor, came from. Why did some people always emerge as aristocrats while others remained as commoners? Adams, in effect, was trying to work out his own "iron law of oligarchy."[49]

HIS IRON LAW OF OLIGARCHY was reinforced by his personal experience with snobbery and inequality. He knew what aristocrats were like, not just those he experienced in Europe but also those he knew in America. As a young aspiring lawyer, he had resented "all the great Notions of high Family" displayed by the Winslows, Hutchinsons,

Leonards, Saltonstalls, and <u>Chandlers;</u> and he hated their presumption of superiority, for, he said, it was "vain and mean to esteem oneself for his Ancestors Merit."[50] Even as the Revolution made him one of the gentry-aristocratic leaders, his resentment of aristocracy continued to haunt him. Those who considered themselves his social superiors, he believed, had envied his outspokenness in the Continental Congress in the 1770s, and in subsequent years they had continued to throw out hints about the lowness of his birth and obscurity of his ancestry.

Although Adams always said that he was the last man in the world to claim any benefit in favor of blood, he was proud of his ancestry, and he was deeply angered by all the aspersions cast upon it. He believed his ancestry was comparable "with the Descent of any of the Grandees of any Part of America." He was bitter "at the low Cunning and mean Craft of those who talk and Scribble upon this Subject" of ancestry. But he was also angry "at the Meanness and Inconsistency of the American public for tolerating this Insolence and much more for encouraging it." In Adams's mind his behavior had been so virtuous that his enemies had nothing else "but lies about his Birth and Conduct, to get him out of the Way." The accumulation of resentments over the years lay behind much of his obsession with aristocracy.[51]

Even his own relatively egalitarian state of Massachusetts possessed aristocrats whose self-interestedness and power always impressed him. He was keenly aware of the social conflict between creditors and debtors in Massachusetts and saw how the state's elites exerted their powerful influence in handling it, especially during those several months in 1779 when he was drafting the state's new constitution.

From at least 1774 on, many farmers in the western counties of Massachusetts had been in a state of virtual rebellion. In Hampshire County the courts had been closed since 1774 and did not open again until 1778; in Berkshire County the courts did not open until the Massachusetts constitution of 1780 had gone into effect. Even after the formation of the new state constitution, extralegal committees and conventions continued to protest the existence of the senate and the overwhelming hard-money interests of eastern creditors in the government.

These eastern gentry-creditors, fearful of the social unrest and debtor protests, had influenced the design of the Massachusetts constitution of 1780, especially in creating the peculiar character of the senate as the representation of property. As the principal drafter of the constitution, Adams had felt their intense pressure to shape the senate to their liking. In 1779 he had seen the Massachusetts east-coast gentry up close, men such as John Lowell, George Cabot, Nathaniel Tracy, Jonathan Jackson, and Theophilus Parsons, many from Essex County, and he had been fascinated by the way in which they had exerted their influence in establishing the Massachusetts senate in the face of much popular opposition. Out of that experience Adams had come to appreciate more fully than ever before the power and influence of the aristocracy in public life. At the same time, he had come to realize that unless constrained and segregated, the rich and wellborn might pose an even greater danger to free government than the common people.

SUDDENLY JEAN DE LOLME'S new understanding of the English constitution as a struggle between aristocracy and democracy took on a heightened meaning for Adams. De Lolme's suggestion that the aristocracy was more dangerous than the democracy obviously impressed him. But he was not the only Massachusetts man to read De Lolme and experience the social conflict that lay behind the writing of the Massachusetts constitution.

Beginning in 1784, twenty-eight-year-old Benjamin Lincoln Jr., a Harvard graduate, son of the Revolutionary War general Benjamin Lincoln, and one of the eastern elites, published a series of articles under the pseudonym of "The Free Republican" that anticipated John Adams's *Defence* at nearly every major point.[52]

"Two distinct and different orders of men," Lincoln had written, "seems incident to every society," and these "two contending interests," fed by a "spirit of jealousy and distrust," would always be in dispute with each other. "Whether the parties to the contests style themselves the

Rich and the Poor, the Great and the Small, the High and the Low, the Elders and People, Patricians and Plebeians, Nobility and Commons, still," Lincoln had claimed, "the source and effects of the dispute are the same." This continual struggle between these two social interests—the many and the few—had "occasioned the greater part of those civil wars, with the sad relation of which the histories of the antient and modern nations of the world so generally abound."[53]

The common people or the many, wrote Lincoln, were those who possessed only the rights of persons; their "subsistence is derived from their bodily labours." The gentlemen or the few, on the other hand, were those who obtained "their riches and support, not from their own, but the labours of others." These men of property, wrote Lincoln, who certainly saw himself as one of this group, were "the merchant, the physician, the lawyer and the divine, and in a word, all of every kind whose subsistence is not derived from the labours of their body." Because the few gentry derived their support from the same source—that is, the labor of others— they collaborated and supported one another. "As a union of interests is the strongest cement of friendship, we find them, not only united in publick life, but associating together in private." Since these gentlemen possessed a sense of superiority and seldom stooped except with reluc- tance, they rarely associated with the laboring many and inevitably courted the society of their own genteel kind.[54]

Although these two social contestants had different names at different times, "with us," said Lincoln, "they are described by the gentlemen and the common people." Adams in his *Defence* agreed. All societies, Adams said, were "naturally divided into two sorts, the gentlemen and the sim- plemen, a word here chosen to signify the common people."[55] Both Ad- ams and Lincoln included the middling sort among the common people.

To us today, the designation of gentleman scarcely seems to represent anything similar to an aristocracy, let alone a separate social order. But for that very different eighteenth century the title of gentleman was very meaningful and even carried legal significance. For Adams and for young Lincoln, the distinction of being a gentleman was not just a convenient social label as it was for some. They saw it as something central to the organization of society; the aristocracy was a republican-style estate that required representation in a separate branch of the legislatures.[56]

This American aristocracy, however, was very different from that of Europe. European nobles, said Adams, had more pride, "that kind of pride which looks down on commerce and manufacturing as degrading." Perhaps this contempt for commerce, he said, played a useful role in Europe. Maybe it helped prevent the European nobility from becoming too rich and inhibited its acquiring too large a proportion of landed property. Or the aristocracy's valuing honor over money might have saved the European nations from being completely consumed by avarice. But in America such pretensions, such disdain for the making of money, said Adams, not only would be "mischievous" but would expose the aristocrats "to universal ridicule and contempt." The American aristocracy's preoccupation with money distinguished it from the European aristocracy and was one of its weaknesses.

Other European "hauteurs," such as "keeping the commons at a distance and distaining to converse with any but a few" of their own aristocratic kind, while impossible to pull off in America, survived in the Old World because they relieved the common people of a multitude of humiliating and troublesome compliances. This distance between the nobility and commoners in Europe may have helped prevent the aristocrats there from caballing with the people and influencing elections. But in America such a separation between gentry and commoners, such expressions of aristocratic snobbery, said Adams, "would justly excite universal indignation. . . . No such airs will ever be endured."

Despite America's aristocrats being less arrogant than their European counterparts, however, they turned out to be more sly and devious. By downplaying their distinctiveness and pretending that they were no different from the common people, the American gentry, said Adams, actually exerted more influence over their society than did the European aristocrats.[57]

Despite these differences between the European and American aristocracies, both Lincoln and Adams believed that American society, like that of Europe, was basically divided between two coherent social orders of gentlemen and commoners and that these two orders were in constant conflict with each other. Both writers offered the same solution to the conflict: each of the contending social interests had to be embodied in a separate house of the legislature, with the executive granted an unqualified negative over all legislation in order to preserve a balance between the two houses.

"A balance," wrote Lincoln, "supposes three things, the two scales, and the hand that holds it." Adams could not have put it better; indeed, he used the same image in the *Defence,* both he and Lincoln borrowing the figure directly from a 1701 piece by Jonathan Swift.[58] Only "three different orders of men," watching and balancing one another, said Adams, could preserve the constitution. Every legislature had to have separate chambers, one for the few on the top and another for the many on the bottom of the society, an organizing, segregating, and balancing of the two basic social estates, mediated by a third estate, an independent executive who shared in the lawmaking—that is, who possessed an absolute veto over all legislation. The perfect constitution, said Adams, was "the tripartite balance, the political trinity in unity, trinity of legislative, and unity of executive power, which in politics is no mystery."[59]

SINCE BENJAMIN LINCOLN JR.'s description of a constant struggle between the many and few in all societies was so close to Adams's later account in his *Defence,* and since there is no evidence that Adams ever read Lincoln—he certainly never mentioned "The Free Republican" in his papers—both political analyses had to have come from a common source, a common Massachusetts experience.[60] Both young Lincoln and Adams were clearly privy to the conversations and opinions of the eastern creditors who were involved in creating the Massachusetts constitution of 1780 and its aristocratic senate designed to protect eastern gentry-property against the radicalism of the western debtor farmers.

Adams certainly favored a strong senate, but his idea of what the senate was supposed to stand for was broader than simply protecting the property of the creditors against the rapaciousness of the people. Although Lincoln admitted that the few rich should never be in a position to deprive the commoners of their share in government and he voiced some concern over the power of the few over the many, he generally had a more generous attitude toward the aristocracy than Adams. Lincoln identified with the east-coast creditor-elites, and like them he was far more obsessed with property than Adams. He maintained that the security of property must "be ranked among the first objects of civil society" and that "men possessed of property are entitled to a greater share of political authority than those who are destitute of it."[61]

Adams never made claims for property in this blunt and barefaced manner, and he never said the rich deserved a greater share of political authority than the common people. Instead, more often than not, he repeatedly voiced apprehensions over the overweening power and influence of the aristocracy. "The great and perpetual distinction in civilized societies," he said over and over, "has been between the rich who are few, and the poor who are many." The struggle between the patricians and the plebeians was constant. But ultimately the few patricians generally outmaneuvered and outwitted the many plebeians. "The few have had most art and union, and therefore have generally prevailed in the end."[62]

He said in 1787 that he no longer shared Jefferson's conventional Whig fear of where the major threat to liberty lay. "You," he told Jefferson, "are afraid of the one—I, of the few. . . . You are apprehensive of Monarchy, I, of Aristocracy." Both of us, he said, "agreed perfectly that the many should have a full fair and perfect Representation" in the various houses of representation. Unlike the ancients, Adams had no desire whatsoever to exclude ordinary working people from citizenship. But Adams knew that he and Jefferson differed over the power to be granted the other two elements in the government. Whereas Jefferson wanted to reduce the power of executives, Adams said he would enhance the power of the executives and reduce that of the senates. For Adams it was the few, "the rich, the well-born, and the able," who, with their heightened sense of avarice and ambition, were the social order most dangerous to liberty and the stability of the society.[63]

Adams's fear that aristocrats were more threatening to society than kings came from his previous experience with the rich, the wellborn, and the able, reinforced by his extensive reading in history. As someone of middling origins who had made it to the top of the society, he necessarily had an ambivalent view of aristocracy. He certainly realized these gentlemen-aristocrats—2 to 12 percent of American society, with fewer in the South than in the North—generally represented the best the society could offer in honor and wisdom.

These few gentry may have been wealthy, but if they were to be ideal aristocrats Adams knew that they should not be preoccupied with work and the making of money. A thoroughly commercial people like the Dutch, he said, were not really aristocratic. They lacked the aristocratic passions—"the Love of Fame, the Desire for Glory, the Love of Country, the regard for Posterity, in short, all the brilliant and sublime Passions"—and they were therefore uninspiring and dull and interested in "nothing but the Love of Ease and Money." The problem with the Dutch, said Adams in a revealing remark, was that they were "not Ambitious, and therefore happy."[64] Happiness, Adams realized, was never to be his lot in life.

It was precisely because he himself was so possessed by those aristocratic passions, especially ambition and the love of fame, that he feared aristocrats. The aristocrats, he said, were so driven and were so powerful that they "acquire an influence among the people that will soon be too much for simple honesty and plain sense, in a house of representatives." How then, Adams asked, "shall the legislator avail himself of their influence for the equal benefit of the public? And how, on the other hand, shall he prevent them from disturbing the public happiness?" Only by taking "the most illustrious" of these rich and wellborn aristocrats and separating them "from the mass" and placing them by themselves in a senate, only then could the nation "have the benefit of their wisdom, without fear of their passions." This was to all intents and purposes, said Adams, "an ostracism."[65]

. . .

ADAMS WAS NOT THE ONLY ONE whose presumed fear of the aristocracy led to a desire to have the aristocrats isolated in a separate branch of the legislature. In 1787 Gouverneur Morris, the wealthy New Yorker representing Pennsylvania, made the same argument in the Constitutional Convention. Morris wanted an upper house that would exclusively represent property holders, but, he declared, placing the property-holding aristocrats in a separate house was not to protect them but only to limit their power. The rich, said Morris, would always "strive to establish their dominion & enslave the rest." If they mixed with "the poor" in a single house, they would overawe the commoners and "establish an Oligarchy." Yet if the "aristocratic interest" could be secluded in a separate branch of the legislature, "the popular interest will be combined against it." There would then be "a mutual check and mutual security."[66]

An ingenious argument, but for Morris, an aristocrat to his core, it was no doubt a disingenuous one. Later in the Convention Morris revealed his concerns more clearly. He invoked the fear of aristocracy once again but now as a means of justifying limitations on who could vote. He suggested that giving the suffrage to all freemen, including people who had no property, would only contribute to the aristocracy's domination of the government. Those voters without property, he said, will sell their votes "to the rich who will be able to buy them."[67]

Benjamin Lincoln Jr., in his "Free Republican" essays of 1785–1786, had made similar arguments. The few rich, he said, were dangerous because they could never be kept down. "Power, or the ability of controlling others, ever has been, and ever will be attached to property. . . . The glare of wealth, and the splendor of its favours" created an influence which was almost impossible to control. "Let us therefore," Lincoln concluded, "regulate an evil we cannot prevent." Segregate the few in a separate house of the legislature.[68]

Both Morris and young Lincoln were wellborn aristocrats whose arguments for ostracizing the wealthy in upper houses seem more self-serving than Adams's. They didn't really fear the aristocracy the way Adams did; they were much more interested than Adams in protecting their property from rapacious commoners.

Adams's difference from Morris, who was a scion of one of the wealthiest and most distinguished families in New York, probably goes without saying. But even in the case of young Lincoln, Adams's social status was different. Adams's view of the Massachusetts senate differed from Lincoln's because he had a different relationship to the eastern gentry-elites of the state than Lincoln did.

As the son of a prominent Revolutionary War general, Lincoln was born a full-fledged member of the eastern aristocracy; Adams was not. Shortly before his untimely death at thirty-one, Lincoln had married Mary Otis, youngest daughter of the revolutionary patriot James Otis, and was moving in genteel circles with many powerful political and judicial figures, including Francis Dana, Edmund Trowbridge, and other members of what the followers of Thomas Jefferson later called the "Essex Junto." Young Lincoln had become a Freemason in one of the most prestigious lodges in Massachusetts; Adams never became a Mason. Adams never liked such aristocratic fraternities; he believed that the Society of the Cincinnati, a hereditary organization of former revolutionary army officers whose Massachusetts chapter was headed by Lincoln's father, was "against the Spirit of our Government and the Genius of our People."[69]

Adams never felt fully at ease with the Cabots and Lowells, and he never shared Lincoln's confidence in these eastern gentry. The intermarrying aristocrats from Essex County were generally far richer and better born than he, and their often arrogant manner put him off. While he was away serving his country, they were amassing wealth from their mercantile and legal practices and from interest on their money out on loan.

Although Adams counted many of these aristocrats as friends and acquaintances, he was troubled by their blatant self-interestedness and their preoccupation with their prosperity and property. His relationship with these Massachusetts gentry became much worse after he became president and especially after he retired and began supporting some Jeffersonian policies that these aristocratic conservatives bitterly opposed. This Massachusetts experience—what Abigail called "the insolence of wealth" in the state—was a principal source of his mistrust of the few.[70]

A S   S U C C E S S F U L   A S   H E   W A S , Adams never entirely shed his middling origins and he never accepted the aristocratic sense that those who were rich and wellborn were naturally entitled to high political office. In the traditional society of prerevolutionary America, wealth and social distinction generally had been prerequisites to holding superior political offices. Consequently, access to government had often come quickly and easily to those who had the necessary social credentials. So wealthy Thomas Hutchinson became a Boston selectman and a member of the General Court at age twenty-six and began at once to amass political offices. That was just as true of Jefferson. Following his marriage to Martha Wayles Skelton, Jefferson emerged as one of the wealthiest planters in colonial Virginia. Whatever Jefferson's considerable talents may have been, his wealth and social rank alone entitled him to a prominent position in Virginia's government.

Adams was different. His family connections were meager, and he deeply resented the veneration for family that he saw all around him. "Go into every village in New England," he said, "and you will find that the office of justice of the peace, and even the place of representative, which has ever depended only on the freest election of the people, have generally descended from generation to generation, in three or four families at most."[71] Unlike Jefferson, Adams was a "new man"; he was completely a product of the Revolution in a way that Jefferson was not. Adams in his rise to public office dramatically reversed the relationship between social and political authority that existed in the traditional prerevolutionary society. In his case, his positions in government were the principal source of his social rank, not the other way around, as was the case with Jefferson, Washington, and many other leaders. For them their preexisting social preeminence and wealth gave them their claim, their entitlement, to high political office.

Precisely because Adams was not rich and did not possess outside sources of income from rents, interest, or slaves, he emphatically rejected the two-thousand-year-old classical tradition of aristocratic public service. In an ideal republican world, it was assumed that government officeholders would transcend economic interests and would serve without salary.

Washington was always concerned with his reputation for disinterestedness and had determined not to be paid a salary as commander in chief. Benjamin Franklin in the Constitutional Convention of 1787 proposed that all members of the executive branch, from the president on down, should serve without pay. Jefferson was also committed to a classical republican view of office holding, which should be, he said, in accord with what he called "the Roman principle." "In a virtuous government," he claimed, "public offices are, what they should be, burthens to those appointed to them, which it would be wrong to decline, though foreseen to bring with them intense labor, and great private loss." Public employment contributed "neither to advantage nor happiness. It is but honorable exile from one's family and affairs." In fact, the very drudgery of office and the bare "subsistence" provided for officeholders in a republic were, said Jefferson, "a wise & necessary precaution against the degeneracy of the public servants."[72]

Adams was in no position financially to accept this ancient tradition of public service, and in an extraordinary series of letters to his radical English friend John Jebb in 1785, he released all his pent-up anger at those rich aristocrats who claimed a virtuous superiority because they served the public without pay.

He was keenly aware, he said, that "the Word 'disinterested' turns the Heads of the People by exciting their Enthusiasm." By "disinterested," of course, he did not mean uninterested, as we usually do today; instead, he meant being impartial and possessing the capacity to rise above selfish interests—the meaning that Washington always gave to the term. Adams deeply resented Washington's serving as commander in chief without salary and his constant claim of being disinterested. Washington, he said, should have been paid a salary. "Would it Lessen his

Reputation? Why Should it?" If "the People were perfectly judicious," paying him a salary would have enhanced his reputation. "But if it did not surely the late revolution was not undertaken to raise one Great reputation to make a sublime Page in History, but for the Good of the People." Besides, Washington's example was dangerous. Knaves would take advantage of such promises to serve without salary. Such men would make the people believe that they were "perfectly disinterested" until they gained the people's confidence and excited their enthusiasm, and then they would "Carry that Confidence and Enthusiasm to market."

Rarely did Adams express more passion than he did in these letters to Jebb. To avoid the evils of a wealthy and overweening aristocracy, Adams, who certainly saw himself as one of the gentlemen-aristocrats, insisted that officeholders had to be paid a salary. If "no Man should hold an office who had not Private income sufficient for the subsistence and prospects of himself and family," he knew only too well what the consequence would be: "all offices would be monopolized by the rich— the Poor and the Middling Ranks would be excluded and an Aristocratical Despotism would immediately follow."[73]

From the outset of his career, he had seen these arrogant, wealthy aristocrats up close. Even after the expulsion of the Loyalists, rich families continued to dominate Massachusetts politics. The main reason he had wanted an absolute veto for the governor in 1779 was to counter the influence of the wealthy wellborn of the state. He told Elbridge Gerry in November 1780 that Massachusetts society had "so many Men of Wealth, of ambitious Spirits, of Intrigue, of Luxury and Corruption, that incessant Factions will disturb our Peace, without it."[74] Obviously, Adams viewed these Massachusetts elites ambivalently—with good reason: many of them eventually became his bitter enemies.

ADAMS PUT ALL THESE FEARS and anxieties over the social conflict he saw in America in the 1780s into what he told Jefferson was a "hazardous Enterprise"—his *Defence* of the United States constitutions. It became the work that he had intended to write on aristocracy, surely one of the most challenging subjects for any American then or now to write about.[75]

Adams began writing the *Defence* in October 1786 and completed the bulk of the first volume by the end of the year. He worked rapidly and drew extensively from a wide variety of sources—from historians, philosophers, and political theorists going back to the ancients. That haste and his habit of inserting many of his sources verbatim into the work lay behind the labored and ponderous style of his writing. His letters and diary were spontaneous expressions of his feelings and were always colorful and pungent. But, as the historian Zoltán Haraszti pointed out years ago, Adams lacked the patience to write longer sustained works of intellectual argument. Adams claimed that he didn't know how to revise, amend, correct, and polish his writing. He was so eager to get his thoughts on the page that in composing the *Defence* he was unable to digest his many sources and thus he failed to make his writing the product of his mind alone. "My great misfortune, through a pretty long life," he later admitted, "has been, that I have never had time to make my poor productions shorter."[76]

Nevertheless, Adams did display in his *Defence* a degree of erudition and knowledge of Western culture that few could match. In the preface to the first volume, Adams outlined his main theme of the need to balance the three orders of society in government if civil war was to be avoided. He framed the bulk of the volume as a series of fifty-five letters to his son-in-law, William Stephens Smith. In these letters he traced the history of two dozen or so different republics, including democratical, aristocratical, and monarchical republics. He indiscriminately added letters on the ideas of various philosophers, ranging from Plato and Polybius to Machiavelli and Harrington.

The material was hastily put together, badly organized, and ill digested. Three-quarters of the book consisted of lengthy quotations from other works, some of them carelessly translated and some unattributed. He believed that his argument "would be more useful and effectual" if he laid "facts, principles, examples, and reasoning" before his readers "from the writings of others than my own name." Unfortunately, he admitted, this borrowing from other writers had "given an air of Pedantry" to his work, but, he said, this was better than to have "contrived with more art, to promote my own reputation."[77]

This first volume was published at Adams's expense in London in January 1787. Adams sent copies to ten or so individuals, including Jefferson. He also sent a hundred copies to his wife's uncle, Cotton Tufts, instructing him to present two dozen copies to particular persons, with the rest to be turned over to a Boston bookseller. The volume arrived in the United States in mid-April 1787.

The timing was perfect. By more or less coinciding with the suppression of Shays' Rebellion, an uprising of several thousand debtor farmers in western Massachusetts, and with the creation of the new federal Constitution, the book was greeted favorably, at least at first.

Indeed, some New Englanders thought his volume had contributed to the antipopulist atmosphere that helped create the Constitution. In March 1788 James Freeman, a Boston clergyman with Unitarian leanings, sent a copy of the Massachusetts ratification debates to a fellow clergyman in London. He warned his correspondent that the Constitution was "less democratick, than might be expected from a people who are so fond of liberty." Freeman suggested that among the causes that had "conspired to render republican sentiments unfashionable" were "a late insurrection in the state of Massachusetts, . . . the corrupt proceedings of the legislature of Rhode Island," and "Mr. J. Adams's publications."[78]

With doubts about republicanism at a fever pitch in Massachusetts, praise from friends and relatives flooded in on him. Cotton Tufts thought that Adams's "Description of the Miseries of an unbalanced Democracy, is well calculated to serve as a Beacon to warn the People here of the Ruin that awaits them."[79] Abigail's brother-in-law, Richard Cranch, told him that the "Litterati" of Massachusetts were "amazed at the vastness of your Reading on the subject of Legislation and Government."[80] Because Adams's suggested ideal structure of government—with a bicameral legislature and an independent executive that shared in the law-making authority—closely matched that in the new federal Constitution, the *Defence* was warmly applauded; it seemed to be as much a defense of that new national Constitution as of the several state constitutions. With such praise it's not surprising that Adams immediately began working on a second and third volume.

From the outset, however, Adams sensed that his *Defence* would sooner or later get him in trouble with his countrymen. He told Benjamin Franklin that the work was his "confession of political faith, and if it is heresy, I shall, I suppose, be cast out of communion. But it is the only sense in which I am or ever was a Republican." "Popularity," he said to his friend James Warren, "was never my Mistress, nor was I ever, or shall I ever be a popular Man. This Book will make me unpopular."[81]

He had every reason to worry, for his *Defence* offered a devastating view of his fellow Americans.

SEVEN

THE FRENCH REVOLUTION

T HE FRENCH REVOLUTION severely strained the relationship of the two friends and brought to the surface differences that had remained latent and largely unacknowledged. But this awareness of difference did not occur suddenly. Thomas Jefferson and most Americans welcomed the outbreak of the French Revolution in 1789 as a promising expression of a people seeking merely to make their monarchical constitution less autocratic and more balanced. John Adams was unusual in not joining in this initial common enthusiasm; he was immediately skeptical of what the French were doing. Europe, he said at the outset, was trying to reconcile popular government with monarchy and the contradictory experiment would never work. When the ferocity of the French Revolution began to intensify, Adams's initial skepticism turned to outright horror. Under these circumstances, the two American statesmen sought desperately to hold their friendship together. In the end, they could do so only by ignoring what each other said and believed.

Adams wasn't just skeptical about the capacity of the French for self-government. He was skeptical about the character of his fellow Americans as well. Even before he knew of the outbreak of the French Revolution, he had worked out a chilling assessment of the moral fiber of his own countrymen, one that prepared him to see the worst of people everywhere.

Right from the beginning of his own American Revolution, Adams had deep misgivings about whether his fellow citizens had the proper moral character needed to sustain their republican governments. "The only foundation of a free Constitution," he said on the eve of America's declaring independence, "is pure Virtue, and if this cannot be inspired into our People, in a greater Measure, than they have it now, They may change their Rulers, and the forms of Government, but they will not obtain a lasting Liberty."[1]

During his long service abroad, Adams increasingly felt that his fellow Americans were showing less and less appreciation of virtue, particularly his virtue. By the mid-1780s Adams was filling his letters to confidants with complaints about the praise being lavished on Franklin and Washington while he was being ignored and mistreated. His hatred of Franklin knew no bounds. "His whole Life," he said, "has been one continued Insult to good Manners and to Decency." But worse, Franklin was dishonest and a liar. His reputation was grossly exaggerated. Indeed, "no Man that ever existed had such a reputation for Wisdom and such an Influence, with so many stupid opinions."[2] That someone like Franklin should be so celebrated was a reflection on America itself. Adams knew that the United States "was destined beyond doubt to be the greatest Power on Earth, and that within the Life of Man," but could that great power remain a republic?[3] He told his cousin Samuel Adams that for years he had "been in the belief that our Countrymen have in them a more ungovernable passion for Luxury than any People upon earth."[4]

For Adams the creation of the Society of the Cincinnati in 1783 especially seemed to be a sign of increasing American decadence. "It is sowing the Seeds of all that European Courts wish to grow up among Us, vizt. of Vanity, Ambition, Corruption, Discord, & Sedition." The country was clearly heading in the wrong direction. "While Reputations are so indiscreetly puffed; while Thanks and Statues are so childishly awarded, and the greatest real services are so coldly received, I had almost Said censured," he told his friend Elbridge Gerry, "we are in the high Road to have no Virtues left, and nothing but Ambition, Wealth and Power must keep them Company."[5]

By 1787 what he had feared all along had become too obvious to him to be denied. His fellow Americans had "never merited the Character of very exalted Virtue," and it was foolish to have "expected that they should have grown much better."[6] At the outset and even in 1779, when he drafted the Massachusetts constitution, he had hoped that education and the regenerative effects of republican government would be able to mold the character of the people—to extinguish their follies and vices and inspire their virtues and abilities. As late as 1786, he told a British acquaintance that education was still important. Before government could be studied and developed in the same way as geometry and astrometry had been studied and developed, he wrote, "a memorable change must be made in the system of Education and Knowledge must become so general as to raise the lower ranks of Society." Education of the nation must no longer be confined to a few; it "must become the National Care and expence, for the Information of the Many."[7]

But by the time he came to write his *Defence of the Constitutions of Government of the United States of America* a year later, he had lost much of his confidence that Americans could be educated to behave differently. Citizens in a small community might be taught to be wise and virtuous. "But the education of a great nation can never accomplish so great an end. Millions must be brought up, whom no principles, no sentiments derived from education can restrain from trampling on the laws."[8]

Something else would be required to save Americans from eventual tyranny and destruction, from the fate of Europe, indeed, from the fate of every people in history. He wrote the *Defence* to save his fellow Americans from ruin. "It appeared to me," he told the English radical Richard Price, "that my Countrymen were running wild, and into danger, from a too ardent and inconsiderate pursuit of erroneous opinions of Government."[9] They were too attracted to the ideas of Thomas Paine and the French philosophes, including the Marquis de Condorcet, La Rochefoucauld, and Pierre-Samuel du Pont de Nemours, the sorts of reform-minded dreamy intellectuals with whom Jefferson was most friendly.

ADAMS'S EXPERIENCE IN EUROPE was different from Jefferson's. For Jefferson the luxury and sophistication of Europe only made American simplicity and virtue appear dearer, while for Adams Europe represented what America was fast becoming—a society consumed by luxury and vice and fundamentally riven by a struggle between rich and poor, gentlemen and commoners.

All of Adams's long-simmering feelings and opinions—all his irritations, jealousies, and resentments—finally boiled over onto the pages of his *Defence*. In this huge, sprawling compilation of history and philosophy, Adams brought a lifetime of reading and personal experience to the working out of what he believed was the best scientific solution to the political problem of social inequality and the persistence of elites. The *Defence*, he said, was "an attempt to place Government upon the only Philosophy which can support it, the real constitution of human nature, not upon any wild Visions of its perfectibility."[10]

The years riding circuit in his law practice, the months spent in the Continental Congress since independence, his involvement with Massachusetts politics during the drafting of the state's constitution, the duplicitous behavior of diplomats abroad, his ill treatment by the Congress, the descriptions from home of the luxury and self-interestedness prevalent everywhere in the States, especially the news of the explosive conflict between western debtors and eastern creditors in his home state of Massachusetts—a conflict that led some to advocate abolishing the senate and creating a unicameral legislature—and above all, an understanding of human nature that sprang from his own tormented soul, all combined to shape his understanding of the ways societies were structured and worked.

In his rambling and long-winded volumes, Adams painted as dark and as pessimistic a portrait of the American people as anyone has ever rendered. Americans, said Adams, were as driven by the passions for wealth and superiority as any people in history. Ambition and avarice, not virtue and benevolence, were the stuff of American society. Those philosophers like Turgot who contended that the American republics were founded on equality could not have been more wrong. The promise of the Declaration of Independence could never be fulfilled. All men were not created equal; they were decidedly born unequal, which was why inequalities predominated in all societies everywhere. "Was there, or will there ever be," he asked, "a nation, whose individuals were all equal in natural and acquired qualities, in virtues, talents, and riches?" Every society, he said, had inequalities "which no human legislator ever can eradicate."[11]

To be sure, said Adams, in America there were "as yet" no legal or artificial inequalities—no hereditary dignities symbolized by garters, titles, and ribbons. And in America there were no political and moral inequalities of rights and duties. Everyone was equal before the law. But these were superficial equalities. What really mattered in America, and, in fact in every nation, said Adams, was the overwhelming presence of real and fundamental inequalities—inequalities of wealth, of birth, of talent. These inequalities were of momentous importance to any legislator faced with the need to create a constitution; for they had "a natural and inevitable influence in society."[12] Every society contained a hierarchy of inequalities, with the few aristocratic-gentry at the top. "Some individuals, whether by descent from their ancestors, or from greater skill, industry, and success in business, have estates both in lands and goods of great value," while others at the very bottom of society "have no property at all." Between these two extremes existed "all the variety of degrees" of middling sorts who constituted the bulk of common people.[13]

THESE MIDDLING SORTS RANGED from someone like William Findley, an ex-weaver from western Pennsylvania, to someone like William Manning, a farmer and small-time entrepreneur from Billerica, Massachusetts. These were men "in the various trades, manufactures, and occupations" who had to work for a living; and by work was meant not just laboring with one's hands but also running a business or trade. A master printer with a dozen or more journeymen and apprentices working for him was still considered to be a middling commoner. However wealthy he might be, as long as he was running his printing shop and engaging in trade, he was not generally regarded as a gentleman. By the 1780s and '90s these middling sorts were increasingly setting themselves in opposition to those aristocratic-gentry, as Manning put it, who "live without Labour."[14]

"Those that git a Living without bodily Labour," wrote Manning, whose own writings were inspired by his reading of Benjamin Lincoln's "Free Republican" essays, were "the merchant, phisition, lawyer & divine, the philosipher and school master, the Judicial & Executive Officers, & many others." These orders of men were generally "so rich that they can live without Labour." Once these gentry had attained their life of "ease & rest" that "at once creates a sense of superiority," wrote Manning, in phonetic prose that was real and not some gentleman's satiric ploy, they tended to "asotiate together and look down with two much contempt on those that labour." Although "the hole of them do not amount to one eighth part of the people," these gentry had the "spare time" and the "arts & skeems" to combine and consult with one another. They had the power to control the electorate and the government "in a veriaty of ways." Some voters they flattered "by promise of favors, such as being customers to them, or helping them out of debt, or other difficultyes; or help them to a good bargain, or treet them or trust them, or lend them money, or even give them a little money"—anything or everything if only "they will vote for such & such a man." Other voters the gentry threatened: "'if you don't vote for such & such a man,' or 'if you do' and, 'you shall pay me what you owe me,' or 'I will sew you'—'I will turne you out of my house' or 'off of my farm'—'I wont be your customer any longer.' . . . All these things have bin practised & may be again." This was how the "few" exerted influence over the many.[15]

Although Adams never read Manning's unpublished essays, he was equally concerned with this age-old distinction between those who worked for a living and those who did not. As he said in 1790, "the great question will forever remain, *who shall work?*" Not everyone could be idle, said Adams; not everyone could be a gentleman. "Leisure for study must ever be the portion of a few. The number employed in government, must forever be very small." Adams was so keen on this point of gentlemen and high public officials not being involved in any sort of demeaning manual labor that on a voyage to Europe, he—much to the surprise of foreign observers—"scorned working at the pump, to which all the other passengers submitted in order to obviate the imminent danger of sinking, arguing that it was not befitting a person who had public status in Europe." To risk drowning rather than to lose one's honor as a gentleman who was not supposed to engage in physical labor tells us just how important this distinction was to Adams.[16]

At the same time Adams had no desire to follow Aristotle and the other ancients in excluding working people from citizenship. Not only was Aristotle's antique view "the most unphilosophical, the most inhuman and cruel that can be conceived," but it misjudged the capacities of ordinary people. "The meanest understanding," said Adams, "is equal to the duty of saying who is the man in his neighborhood whom he most esteems, and loves best, for his knowledge, integrity, and benevolence." Moreover, the understandings of husbandmen, minor merchants, shopkeepers, mechanics, and other middling people were not always the meanest. From among them often arose "the most splendid geniuses, the most active and benevolent dispositions, and the most undaunted bravery." He ought to know; he had once been one of them.[17]

THIS DISTINCTION BETWEEN those who worked and those who did not was important to Jefferson too, but for different reasons. When he thought about the issue of work and leisure, he focused on the institution of slavery. In his indictment of slavery in his *Notes on the State of Virginia*, he mentioned the "miserable condition" of the slaves, but he was far more interested in the evils that slavery inflicted upon the manners of the slaveholders themselves. Not only did slavery tend to incite the crudest passions among the slaveholders, breed despotic attitudes, and undermine their morals, but "their industry also is destroyed. For in a warm climate no man will labour for himself who can make another labour for him." Only a few "proprietors of slaves" were "ever seen to labour."[18]

This was alarming to Jefferson not because aristocratic planters like him with hundreds of slaves were expected to engage in bodily labor, but because many ordinary farmers who might own only a few slaves (or owned none but wished to possess some) inevitably developed a contempt for work, which in turn encouraged their indolence. Jefferson, of course, hoped that "the mass of cultivators" would not become slaveholders but instead look "to their own soil and industry" for their subsistence. But the southern culture of slavery with its scorn for labor was powerful and pervasive. As many southerners pointed out, laziness had become the scourge of the South and a danger to its social health.[19]

In 1792 David Rice, a courageous Virginia-born Presbyterian minister in Kentucky, condemned slavery for just this reason—for sapping the moral foundations of the society. "Slavery," Rice declared, "produces idleness; and idleness is the nurse of vice. A vicious commonwealth is a building erected on quick-sand, the inhabitants of which can never abide in safety." When slavery becomes common, said Rice, who tried but failed to get an antislavery article inserted into Kentucky's constitution, it makes industriousness shameful. "To labour is *to slave;* to work is *to work like a Negro;* and this is disgraceful; it levels us with the meanest of the species; it sits hard upon the mind; it cannot be patiently borne." As a result, southern youth were "tempted to idleness, and drawn into other vices; they see no other way to keep their credit, and acquire some little importance."[20] Jefferson claimed over and over that "the cultivators of the earth" were the "most vigorous, most independent, the most virtuous" citizens.[21] But, in the 1780s at least, he shared a great deal of the Reverend Rice's sense that slavery and its promotion of idleness threatened the well-being of southern society.

As a slaveholder Jefferson naturally saw himself as a leisured aristocrat, but unlike most of his fellow southern planters, he had no contempt for those who worked. When he eventually realized that much of his political support in the North came from common people who lived by manual labor and not by their wits, he came to recognize that work was not something fit only for slaves. One of the reasons he disliked cities was because they were places where men sought "to live by their heads rather than their hands."[22]

Nevertheless, slavery and its effect on work were subjects too sensitive for Jefferson to dwell on. Consequently, he never had the same intense preoccupation that Adams had with the social division between a leisured aristocracy and the common people who labored for a living. For Adams, no issue was more important, because this division lay at the heart of his entire understanding of society and politics.

IN ADAMS'S ANALYSIS, THE SOURCES of the leisured gentry's separation from the laboring commoners were many and diverse, but slavery was not one of them. Wealth, he said, was crucially important in distinguishing one person from another. But merit and talent as well as service in the army or government could also earn "the confidence and affection of their fellow citizens to such a degree" that their advice and influence would be respected. Adams undoubtedly assumed he was among this group.

Birth was also important in distinguishing one person from another. Some individuals inherited position and privilege from their families. It was obvious, said Adams, that "the children of illustrious families have generally greater advantages of education, and earlier opportunities to be acquainted with public characters, and informed of public affairs, than those of meaner ones, or even those in middle life." Such families were very influential and were usually venerated and respected by the general public from generation to generation simply for their name—something that Adams, in 1787 at least, obviously scorned. Despite the importance of ancestry, however, in the end he believed that wealth always had "more influence than birth."

Then there were the liberally educated—"men of letters, men of the learned professions, and others"—who through "acquaintance, conversation, and civilities" were usually connected with the wealthy aristocracy. Alas, too many of these learned sort—"among the wisest people who live"—tended to get caught up in excessive admiration and respect for the wealthy aristocracy. Adams, who always valued his independence, clearly did not count himself among those who venerated the rich and wellborn.

Adams spent so much time describing the sources of this natural aristocracy because, like William Manning, he feared their "natural and inevitable influence in society." No doubt the aristocratic few contained "the greatest collection of virtues and abilities in a free government." They could become the "glory of the nation" and "the greatest blessing of society," but only if they were controlled and institutionalized—as he put it, only if they were "judiciously managed in the constitution." This is why he wanted to ostracize the aristocrats in a separate branch of the legislature that was balanced by a strong executive. Unless this was done, they were "always the most dangerous" order in the society; indeed, unless they were segregated in senates and checked by the executive, they never failed "to be the destruction of the commonwealth."[23]

Nothing was more certain to Adams than the existence of this sort of inequality in all societies at all times. These differences among people, he said, were "not peculiar to any age"; they were "common to every people, and can never be altered by any, because they are founded in the constitution of nature."[24] No American revolutionary leader talked quite this way, and none offered a more direct challenge to the assertion in the Declaration of Independence that all men were created equal.

Adams, in other words, was defying the Enlightenment dream that only cultivation and different opportunities for education separated one person from another. When in 1776 Jefferson declared that all men were created equal he was not simply saying that all had equal rights under the law. Since many Englishmen believed in equality under the law, such an idea would never have been radical. Instead, he was claiming that all men (in his case at least, all white men) were born with equal blank slates and that the natural and cultural environments inscribing these blank slates through time by themselves created the obvious differences that separated one person from another. When this enlightened assumption was coupled with the power of education, everyone had an equal opportunity to become somebody of distinction.

What made Adams's position in 1787 so unusual, so reactionary, was his denial of this optimistic assumption of 1776, which he himself had once taken so seriously. Although he had as early as 1766 declared that all men were born equal, he had changed his mind. Experience had convinced him of the opposite. All men, he now contended, were born decidedly unequal. Contrary to what many revolutionaries believed in 1776, people did not begin the race of life from the same starting point. At birth some were more intelligent, some were more handsome, and some were more wealthy. People were born possessing previously existing natural and cultural privileges. Therefore, the slates with which people began life were not blank but were already marked and engraved. Locke's white paper was already full of inscriptions. The obvious distinctions that arose in society were inherent in the inequalities of birth. Nature, not nurture, now was what counted. In other words, Adams was reviving the traditional assumptions of the ancien régime, the assumptions about differences of blood and birth that the Revolution presumably had laid to rest.

ADAMS OFFERED HIS COUNTRYMEN a terrifying picture of themselves. He described the two orders of society—the aristocracy and the commoners—engrossed in relentless struggles for supremacy. People were constantly scrambling for distinction—for wealth, for power, for privilege, for social eminence that they hoped could be passed on to their descendants. Everyone's desire to get ahead was limitless and all-consuming. Especially powerful were the "aristocratical passions"—avarice, vanity, and ambition. "The love of gold grows faster than the heap of acquisition." The love of praise was so great that "man is miserable every moment when he does not snuff the incense." As for ambition, it was voracious; it "strengthens at every advance, and at last takes possession of the whole soul so absolutely, that a man sees nothing in the world of importance to others or himself, but in his object."[25]

The numerous commoners and middling sorts, driven by the most ambitious, always attempted to ruin and displace the aristocratic leaders they envied and hated. Those in particular "whose fortunes, families, and merits in the acknowledged judgment of all" seemed closest to those at the top "will be much disposed to claim the first place as their own right."[26] Those few who struggled to the top of this anxiety-ridden society would seek only to stabilize and aggrandize their superior position by trying to influence or oppress the many below them who had been left behind. Hence America, like every society, had been and would continue to be ridden by this basic social conflict, its members impelled by a fundamental desire for distinction that was rooted in human nature. Anyone, said Adams, who didn't agree with his social analysis was simply denying reality.

Jefferson never saw society in the way Adams did. He took his leisured gentry status for granted; he never felt threatened by ambitious and scrambling middling sorts trying to displace him. Indeed, his Virginia had very few middling sorts anyhow—very few manufacturers, artisans, tradesmen, clerks, and petty merchants—and he celebrated their absence. People who were not farmers were detrimental to the society. He considered "the class of artificers as the panders of vice and the instruments by which the liberty of a country are generally overturned."[27]

SINCE ADAMS'S SOCIAL ANALYSIS was designed to create a science of politics that was applicable to all peoples at all times, his conclusion in the *Defence* was obvious. America was essentially no different from Europe. There was, said Adams, "no special providence for Americans, and their nature is the same with that of others." With all the high hopes of 1776 dissipating, Adams faced the formidable task of persuading his countrymen that they were, after all, "like all other people, and shall do like other nations." In all of American history, no political leader of Adams's stature, and certainly no president, has ever so emphatically denied the belief in American exceptionalism.[28]

Adams's description of his society as one inevitably divided in two and tortured by jealousy, envy, and resentment was so dark and so grim that no political solution could seem possible. But Adams had one: "Orders of men, watching and balancing each other, are the only security; power must be opposed to power and interest to interest."[29] A balanced constitution like that of England was the solution: the common and middling people had to be confined to the lower houses of the legislatures and the gentry-aristocrats had to be ostracized in the upper houses, with the balance maintained by a strong and independent executive.

The powerful executive was crucial to his system—the very part of government Jefferson most feared. "If there is one certain truth to be collected from the history of all ages," said Adams, "it is this: that the people's rights and liberties, and the democratical mixture in a constitution, can never be preserved without a strong executive." Only an alliance between the first magistrate and the common people was capable of putting down the cunning and craftiness of a rapacious aristocracy. "What is the whole history of the barons wars but one demonstration of this truth? What are all the standing armies in Europe, but another? These were all given to the kings by the people, to defend them against aristocracies." It was obvious to Adams that the executive power, by whatever name it might be called, was "the natural friend of the people, and the only defence which they or their representatives can have against the avarice and ambition of the rich and distinguished citizens."[30]

A bicameral legislature with a strong executive: this was Adams's constitutional remedy for the ferocious social struggle he had laid out in such terrifying detail in his *Defence*, a remedy that seems disproportionate to the severity of the social scramble he had depicted. Adams never explained how the aristocrats would remain segregated in the senates, or how such powerful elites could be kept from entering or influencing politics in the lower houses, or how the common people, even in alliance with the executive, would ever be able to control the influence of such wealthy and formidable men. Yet however inadequate his constitutional remedy, Adams at least had accurately diagnosed the problem of social inequality that was plaguing American politics in the 1780s; it was one that would continue to plague the nation that prided itself on its equality.

WITH HIS USUAL GOOD MANNERS, Jefferson told Adams that he had read the volume of the *Defence* Adams had sent him "with infinite satisfaction and improvement. It's learning and it's good sense," he said, "will I hope make it an institute for our politicians, old as well as young." He promised to try to get it translated into French, which he ultimately never did, probably because his French liberal friends objected strenuously to Adams's argument.[31]

From his favorable comments, it's clear that Jefferson did not read the book from cover to cover—who could blame him?—for if he had, he would have been deeply disturbed by so much that ran against the grain of his own thinking, indeed, that challenged almost everything he believed. Adams's dramatic descriptions of his countrymen's mania for distinctions and luxury, his denial of American equality, his celebration of executive authority, and his assertions that Americans were no different from Europeans—all these strongly voiced opinions expressed in his first volume would surely have shocked and alarmed Jefferson if he had read the book carefully.

Although Jefferson knew that people differed from one another, he could never accept Adams's harsh description of America's severe and permanent social inequalities. Confident of his position in society and believing that real hereditary aristocracies existed only in Europe, he saw his own country as peculiarly egalitarian. In America, said Jefferson, "no other distinction existed between man and man" except those separating government officials from private individuals. And among these private individuals, he said, "the poorest labourer stood on equal ground with the wealthiest."[32]

Like most people receiving a gift from a friend of such a dense and massive tome, Jefferson was eager to assure the author that he actually had dipped into the book, and the best way to do that was to object to a minor point in the conclusion in which Adams had said that the Congress was "only a diplomatic assembly." When Jefferson received the second volume of the *Defence* six months later, he admitted that he only had time to "look into it a little." But putting that brief look at the second volume together with his hasty reading of the first volume, he summarized what he thought Adams was getting at: "The first principle of a good government is certainly a distribution of it's powers into executive, judiciary, and legislative, and a subdivision of the latter into two or three branches." Since Jefferson's superficial summary seems to be the response of most modern scholars to Adams's *Defence,* it is perhaps understandable; but it scarcely did justice to Adams's powerful and pessimistic understanding of the way society operated.[33]

Adams was probably fortunate that most people found the writing in his *Defence* impenetrable. Like Jefferson, most of his contemporaries tended to ignore his references to social estates and orders and simply concluded that he was only defending the bicameral legislatures and the separation of powers that existed in most of the state constitutions and in the new federal government. Even Adams's notion that the senate should be socially different from the lower house was widely shared by anxious elites. But few followed his arguments about the corruption of American society and appreciated the degree to which his book challenged the basic enlightened premises of the American Revolution. To be sure, many of his fellow Americans sensed that he was enamored of the English constitution, but few grasped just how dark and forbidding and un-American a picture of their society he had painted.

BY 1787 JEFFERSON AND ADAMS had developed very different takes on what was happening in America, especially on the issue of aristocracy. Like Adams, Jefferson opposed the creation of the Society of the Cincinnati, and in 1784 he had politely outlined to George Washington his objections to this hereditary institution, which sought to preserve the fellowship of the military officers, including French officers, who served in the Revolutionary War. But once he arrived in Europe and discovered how passionately French reformers like the Comte de Mirabeau were attacking the Society of the Cincinnati, Jefferson found himself on the defensive, trying to explain to them why a nation dedicated to equality would create such an aristocratic institution.

In his observations on the entry on America in Jean Nicolas Démeunier's encyclopedia, Jefferson was eager to downplay the significance of the Cincinnati in America and to emphasize "the innocence of it's origins."

The criticism that arose in America, he said, was full of "exaggerations"; it had to be based on the critics' rich imaginations, "for to detail the real evils of aristocracy they must be seen in Europe." In the end, Jefferson claimed that Americans would have abolished the society except they did not want to insult and appear ungrateful to the French officers who had been elected to membership.[34]

Jefferson's claim that no real aristocratic distinctions existed in America and that "a due horror of evils which flow from these distinctions could be excited in Europe only" could not have been more at odds with Adams's belief that aristocracy and inequality were everywhere in America and that America, in this respect especially, was no different from Europe.[35]

Given their different attitudes toward America, Adams and Jefferson were bound to have different responses to Shays' Rebellion. In 1786 several thousand distressed debtor farmers in western Massachusetts, after years of rioting and complaining of high taxes and tight money, finally took up arms in protest against eastern creditors who were foreclosing their mortgages and seizing their farms. The rebels, led by a former militia captain named Daniel Shays, closed the much despised courts and threatened to seize a federal arsenal. Although the uprising was eventually put down by privately funded eastern militia, it frightened elites up and down America, especially since it occurred in the very state that was supposed to have the most balanced and strongest constitution of all the thirteen states.

Adams was disturbed by the rebellion, calling it "extremely pernicious." But in November 1786 he initially told Jefferson not to be alarmed, that "all will be well"; and he predicted that "this Commotion will terminate in additional Strength to Government." Since the uprising reflected badly on his home state and the constitution he had helped create, he naturally was eager to minimize its significance. Abigail had no such inhibitions, especially since by the time she wrote Jefferson in January 1787 news of the rebellion had become more frightening. She told Jefferson that "ignorant, wrestless desperadoes, without conscience or principals, have led a deluded multitude to follow their standard, under pretence of grievances which have no existence but in their imaginations."[36]

Jefferson took a much more sanguine view of Shays' Rebellion. He told Abigail in November 1786 that he was "not alarmed at the humor shown by your countrymen." He liked to see "the people awake and alert." The "spirit of resistance to government" was at times so valuable that he wished it would always be kept alive. "I like a little rebellion now and then," he declared in one of the most memorable of his statements. "It is like a Storm in the Atmosphere."[37]

A year later, when the rebellion had been put down and the new federal Constitution ratified, he was even more relaxed in his view of the uprising. Not only was it not worth worrying about, he wrote in a letter to Adams's son-in-law, but it was natural and healthy for a republic to have periodic uprisings of the people. It was the only way the people could correct misconceptions. "God forbid that we should ever be 20 years without such a rebellion." If the people remain quiet too long, "it is a lethargy, the forerunner of death to the public liberty." Rulers need to be warned every once in a while that the people have a spirit of resistance. What did a few lives lost every century or two matter? "The tree of liberty must be refreshed from time to time by the blood of patriots and tyrants. It is it's natural manure."[38]

With such expressions Jefferson revealed a political temperament very different from Adams's. He had none of Adams's doubts about the people and none of his worries that their ambitions and desires were a danger to the stability of the society. Jefferson believed that "the good sense of the people will always be found to be the best army" for putting down a rebellion. "They may be led astray for a moment, but will soon correct themselves."[39] With his revolutionary ideology of 1776 fixed and intact in his mind, he was essentially immune to the doubts about the people many American leaders had developed in the decade following the Declaration of Independence.

JEFFERSON SHARED FEW OF THE FEARS that his friend Madison had about the vices of the political system and the excesses of democracy in the states. Those fears led his fellow Virginian to lead a movement to scrap the Articles of Confederation in favor of an entirely new national government that operated directly on individuals rather than on the states. Like almost all Americans by 1786, Jefferson was open to revising the Articles by adding amendments that would give the Congress the powers to levy duties on imports and to regulate international trade. But he never fully grasped just how radical Madison's plans actually were. Madison and his colleagues took the consensus in favor of adding amendments to the Articles and ran with it, using the general acceptance of reform as an opportunity to convene a meeting in Philadelphia to do much more than simply amend the Articles. In fact, Madison was eager to drastically reduce the power of the states in the Union.

Because both Jefferson and Adams were abroad when the Constitutional Convention met in the summer of 1787, they had to learn about the new Constitution months after it was drafted. Although Jefferson thought the Convention was "an assembly of demi-gods," he objected to its vow of secrecy and was shocked by the Constitution it created. He told Adams he didn't think a new constitution was necessary. "Three or four new articles," he said, might have been "added to the good, old, and venerable fabric" of the Articles of Confederation. He especially objected to the office of the president. It seems, he said, "to be a bad edition of a Polish king," who, once elected, served for life—which is what Jefferson feared would happen with the American president. Instead, he wanted the president to serve for only four years and be ineligible for a second term.[40]

By contrast, Adams was pleased that the Articles had been scrapped. The new Constitution so much resembled the balanced government and the separation of powers he advocated in his *Defence* that he naturally was satisfied with much of it. Unlike Jefferson, he approved of the office of the president, and having the president chosen over and over was "so much the better." Since Adams feared aristocracy more than monarchy, he told Jefferson that he would "have given more Power to the President and less to the Senate," especially in the appointment of officers. "Elections to offices, which are great objects of Ambition," Adams told Jefferson, ought to be regarded "with terror"—an extraordinary remark for someone who was supposed to be a republican.[41]

Jefferson let this provocative remark pass. Perhaps that was because he and Adams in 1787–1788 were so caught up in issues involving negotiating loans, international trade, and a civil war in the Netherlands that offhand remarks about elections scarcely seemed to matter. But Jefferson also had a propensity to overlook important points in letters or, as in the case of the *Defence*, books that did not fit with his conceptual world. In the fall of 1787, Madison wrote Jefferson an incredibly lengthy letter, explaining in great detail the thinking that went into the making of the new federal Constitution. He especially emphasized his own ideas about the dangers of majority rule in a republic. In his response Jefferson scarcely acknowledged Madison's sophisticated account of the thinking behind the Constitution. Instead, he set forth his objection to a president who could be continually reelected, and reaffirmed his "principle that the will of the Majority should always prevail"—precisely the point that Madison had most systematically questioned.[42] Still, there is no doubt that Jefferson's growing appreciation of his friend Madison's great contribution to the creation of the Constitution helped him to come around and support the Constitution more enthusiastically than he had at the outset.[43]

One other "bitter pill" Jefferson found in the Constitution was its lack of a bill of rights.[44] Adams also raised that omission with Jefferson, mainly because he had included a declaration of rights in his draft of the Massachusetts constitution. But Jefferson seems to have desired a bill of rights at least partly out of embarrassment over what "the most enlightened and disinterested characters" among his liberal French friends might think, especially since they were busy drawing up drafts of possible declarations of rights for their own nation. No matter that Madison had tried to explain to Jefferson in great detail that the new government did not resemble traditional governments that had had to be bargained with and that writing out the people's rights might actually have the effect of limiting them. Jefferson knew, and that was enough, that "the enlightened part of Europe have given us the greatest credit for inventing this instrument of security for the rights of the people, and have been not a little surprised to see us soon give it up."[45]

. . .

WHILE HIS FELLOW AMERICANS back home were creating a new federal Constitution and debating its ratification, Jefferson, despite his official position as minister to France, was becoming more deeply involved in the efforts of Lafayette and his other French friends to reform the French monarchy. These efforts, which culminated in the French Revolution, ultimately changed Jefferson's attitude toward the world and in particular his attitude toward the American Revolution. He came to believe that the American Revolution was not simply an event whose significance was confined only to Americans. It became for him, much more clearly than he had realized in 1776, a historic event that had launched a republican revolutionary movement that would spread around the world. He came to see the French Revolution as a consequence of the American Revolution. He eventually concluded that France had become a sister republic to the United States, and because of that relationship he became much more emotionally invested in the success of the French Revolution than many of his countrymen and certainly more than John Adams. Indeed, Adams became skeptical of the French Revolution at the outset and thus began the estrangement of the two American friends.

It took a while for Jefferson to realize the seriousness of the emerging crisis in France. In August 1786 he had no inkling whatsoever of any trouble brewing among the French people. In contrast to England, which had experienced an assassination attempt on George III, the French people were engaged in "singing, dancing, laugh, and merriment." There were, he told Abigail Adams, "no assassinations, no treasons, rebellions or other dark deeds. When our king goes out, they fall down and kiss the earth where he has trodden: and then they go on kissing one another. . . . They have as much happiness in one year as an Englishman in ten."[46]

When the Assembly of Notables met early in 1787 and was widely mocked, Jefferson concluded that the French were not seriously interested in reform. But all the turmoil, he complained, was ruining social life in Paris. "Instead of that gaiety and insouciance which has distinguished it heretofore, all is filled with political debates into which both sexes enter with equal eagerness."[47] Although he said he was a mere spectator of events, he couldn't resist the requests from his liberal French friends—Lafayette, La Rochefoucauld, du Pont de Nemours, Condorcet, and others—for constitutional advice. Indeed, he periodically met in an informal seminar on political theory with these friends, members of what Jefferson called "the Patriotic party." He seemed to think that the Patriots were merely French versions of the American patriots of 1776. They were "sensible of the abusive government under which they lived, [and] longed for occasions of reforming it." They would "from the natural progress of things . . . press forward to the establishment of a constitution which shall assure them a good degree of liberty."[48] With his usual optimism Jefferson was sure that everything could be sorted out in a rational manner.

As early as December 1787, Adams, with his skeptical view of human nature, saw things quite differently. He realized that all of Europe was talking of reviving assemblies and calling for meetings of estates, with France taking the lead. Surely, he told Jefferson, some improvement, some lessening of superstition, bigotry, and tyranny, would result from all this ferment. But he had doubts that things could be kept under control. "The world will be entertained with noble sentiments and enchanting Eloquence, but will not essential Ideas be sometimes forgotten, in the anxious study of brilliant Phrases?" Europe, he said, had tried such experiments before, and they had never worked out. "Contradictions will not succeed, and to think of Reinstituting Republicks . . . would be to revive Confusion and Carnage, which must again End in despotism."[49]

In response Jefferson expressed none of these doubts. He was pretty sure that France's "internal affairs will be arranged without blood." The opposition was moderate, and if it could remain so, he said, "all will end well."[50] In November 1788 he asked John Jay, who was now the American secretary for foreign affairs in the Confederation government, for a leave of absence for five or six months to go home to attend to his plantation. Jefferson fully expected to return to France. When he learned that the Estates-General would convene in May 1789—the assembly of clergy, nobles, and the Third Estate of commoners hadn't met since 1614—he predicted that France in two or three years would probably enjoy "a tolerably free constitution, and that without it's having cost them a drop of blood."[51] He had come to realize, as he told Washington in December 1788, that "the nation has been awakened by our revolution, they are enlightened, their lights are spreading, and they will not retrograde."[52] Instead of a republic, however, he thought France would end up with a constitutional monarchy like that of England.

By May 1789, while his countrymen were getting their new national government on its feet, Jefferson was still in France and still enthusiastic about the course of its Revolution. "The revolution in this country has advanced thus far without encountering any thing which deserves to be called a difficulty," he reported to John Jay. But, he admitted, there had been riots in Paris and elsewhere, with several hundred Frenchmen killed by government troops. This was not a little rebellion feeding the tree of liberty; indeed, these mobs, he said, were composed of "the most abandoned banditti of Paris," and their rioting was totally unprovoked and unjustified. Believing that France was involved merely in a constitutional reformation, Jefferson had little sense of the deep rumbling anger of the French people that was beginning to erupt. None of these riots, he claimed in all innocence, had "a professed connection with the great national reformation going on."[53]

Sometimes Jefferson seemed to forget that he was the U.S. minister to a foreign country; instead of maintaining an official detachment from French affairs, he began acting as if he himself were one of the French reformers—in violation of all diplomatic protocol. He was in constant touch with his friends in the Patriot party, badgering them to create a constitution modeled on that of England. The king, he suggested, might be set over a bicameral legislature with the orders of the clergy and the nobility located in an upper house. He counseled his friends on the role of juries, and drafted a ten-point charter of rights that he sent to Lafayette. But the Third Estate ignored both his advice and his charter and, calling itself the National Assembly, persuaded many of the clergy and the nobility to join it and agree to vote by persons, not by "orders" or estates, thus creating a single uniform nation—the very sort of unicameral body Adams hated and feared. At this point Jefferson told Jay he wouldn't report to him as frequently as he had in the past, "the great crisis being now over."[54]

But events kept outrunning his high hopes for a compromise between the king and the people. On July 11, 1789, Jefferson assured Thomas Paine that the Revolution was once again effectively over, only to be confronted with the momentous events of the succeeding days, including the destruction of the Bastille. But even these bloody events did not shake Jefferson's confidence that all would soon be well, as long as his Patriot friends were in control. In August, he hosted at his house a six-hour meeting of eight of the leading French liberal reformers as they plotted what steps to take. The discussion, he recalled, was "truly worthy of being placed in parallel with the finest dialogues of antiquity, as handed down to us by Xenophon, by Plato, and Cicero."[55] (The next day he apologized to Louis XVI's minister of foreign affairs for this extraordinary diplomatic impropriety.)

His naïve faith in the future was breathtaking. He had witnessed the mobs destroying the Bastille and "saw so plainly the legitimacy of them" that he never lost a bit of sleep. Since "quiet is so well established here . . . there is nothing further to be apprehended." There was no want of bread, and the members of the National Assembly were in control. Being "wise, firm, and moderate. . . they will establish the English constitution, purged of it's numerous and capital defects." He had, he said, "so much confidence in the good sense of man, and his qualifications for self-government" and had such little fear of failure "where reason is left free to exert her force" that he was willing "to be stoned as a false prophet" if everything in France did not end well.[56]

Years later, in his autobiography, Jefferson set forth his account of what had happened and revealed how little understanding he had of the origins of the French Revolution. The queen, Marie Antoinette, he claimed in retrospect, was ultimately responsible for everything. If she, wallowing in her "inordinate gambling and dissipations," had not prevented her weak husband, Louis XVI, from acting sensibly, things would have been different. "I have ever believed," Jefferson concluded, "that had there been no queen, there would have been no revolution."

Despite this unsophisticated conception of the historical process, Jefferson by 1821 had nevertheless come to appreciate the world-shattering consequences of the French Revolution. It had unleashed forces that had spread everywhere, with the result being "the condition of man thro' the civilized world will be finally and greatly ameliorated." Like the American Revolution, which was sparked by "a two penny duty on tea," the French Revolution, he said, was "a wonderful instance of great events from small causes."[57]

IN 1789 ADAMS WROTE JEFFERSON that "your Friend" had come in second in electoral votes to Washington and was thus going to be vice president. With his usual protective sarcasm, he told Jefferson that "it may be found easier to give Authority than to yield Obedience."[58]

By December 1788, Jefferson had already heard that Adams—along with John Hancock, John Jay, and Henry Knox—was being suggested in the middle and northern states for vice president, it being taken for granted that Washington would become president. In October 1788, Madison had informed Jefferson that Adams and Hancock were "the only candidates in the Northern States brought forward with their known consent." Madison thought both men were "objectionable" and wished that they would be satisfied with lesser positions in the government. Adams, he said, had "made himself obnoxious to many particularly in the Southern states by the political principles avowed in his book." Others objected to Adams because he presumably had caballed against Washington during the war and was extravagantly self-important. Some wondered why, given his modest means, Adams preferred "an unprofitable dignity to some place of emolument better adapted to private fortune." It seemed that he might have his "eye on the presidency," and because of his "impatient ambition might even intrigue for a premature advancement," especially if some "factious characters . . .

should get into the public councils." At any rate, said Madison, many believed that "he would not be a very cordial second to the General."[59]

As it turned out, Adams received thirty-four votes to Washington's sixty-nine. With every elector allowed to vote for two persons from two different states, Washington received every possible electoral vote. Adams's thirty-four votes were just shy of a majority, with most of them coming from New England. The rest of the electoral votes were scattered among several individuals, with no one receiving more than John Jay's nine votes.[60] Adams knew that the southerners did not like him but was upset that the New Yorkers seemed to oppose him as well. With Washington, the Virginian, guaranteed to be president, it was natural for the electors to vote for a northerner, especially a New Englander, for their second choice; and Adams seemed to be the most famous New Englander. He made it clear to friends that he would not become a senator; in fact, he implied that he would accept nothing less than the vice presidency.

Although Adams had every right to feel that his election as vice president was a mark of respect for him, he nevertheless thought he had been elected "in a scurvy manner" and not out of "the Gratitude" that he thought was due him. Despite his election as vice president, he could not refrain from telling his friends privately how ignorant and inexperienced the American people were and how they had forgotten that "laws are the fountain of Freedom and Punctuality the source of Credit."[61] By 1789 Adams had become as fearful of the majority of commoners as he was of the aristocracy.

ALTHOUGH ADAMS, UNLIKE JEFFERSON, did not personally get involved in the French Revolution, his *Defence of the Constitutions* did. Early in 1789, Jefferson's liberal friends Condorcet, du Pont de Nemours, and the Italian physician and agent for Virginia during the Revolution Philip Mazzei brought out a French translation of John Stevens's *Observations on Government*, which had been originally published in New York in 1787.[62] Stevens's pamphlet was a severe attack on both Adams's *Defence* and on De Lolme's *Constitution of England*. Writing anonymously as a "Farmer of New Jersey," Stevens, a well-to-do future inventor, who seems to be one of the few Americans who actually read the *Defence* with care, condemned Adams for suggesting that American governments resembled the English constitution and for promoting aristocracy in America. Stevens denied that there were any orders or estates in America, and therefore Adams's rationale for a mixed or balanced government in the United States was misplaced. Since Stevens accepted a bicameral legislature with an independent executive, many, including some scholars, could not understand what his quarrel with Adams was about.[63] But Stevens rightly realized that Adams in his *Defence* was presuming a social order of aristocrats in America, and he wanted no part of that claim. For him and for most Americans by 1787, there were no estates or social orders in America that had to be embodied in separate parts of the government as in England; instead, all parts of America's governments—lower houses, senates, and executives—had become simply different kinds of representatives of the sovereign people. America had no aristocratic social power or an aristocracy of any sort, said Stevens. Adams was simply too caught up in his admiration for the English constitution to appreciate America's uniqueness.

"Had Mr. Adams been a native of the old, instead of the new world," wrote Stevens, "we should not have been so surprised at his system." In Europe, he said, "wealth and power [were] everywhere in the hands of a few—nobility almost universally established," especially in the English constitution.[64]

For Jefferson's liberal French friends this was precisely the point that attracted them to Stevens's pamphlet: they wanted to discredit the English constitution as a model for France and collapse that separate estate of the aristocracy into the Third Estate, so that everyone would become a commoner in a single body of the people. They issued their French edition of Stevens's pamphlet to boost their effort to do away with orders or estates in the French government. Condorcet and Du Pont added so many notes and commentary to Stevens's pamphlet that their version turned out to be several times longer than the original. They annotated and manipulated Stevens's work as they saw fit, turning his 56-page pamphlet into a 291-page book that included 174 pages of notes, a translation of the U.S. Constitution, and some notes from the Virginia ratifying convention. All this was done with the purpose of justifying a single assembly that would represent the whole nation. As their translation of Stevens's pamphlet was invoked repeatedly in the debates that took place in the National Assembly during 1789, Adams had become a whipping boy for the problems of French society.[65]

BEFORE JEFFERSON DEPARTED for his six-month leave in the United States, fully intending to return to Paris, he wrote a remarkable letter to Madison outlining his idea "that the earth belongs in usufruct to the living: that the dead have neither powers nor rights over it." Apparently discussions with his physician, Richard Gem, an elderly Englishman who was friendly with the philosophes and a supporter of the American Revolution, helped to gel his thinking about the issue of "whether one generation of men has a right to bind another." Jefferson had in fact discussed this problem of the rights of succeeding generations with Lafayette in January 1789. He was particularly interested in the burden of debt that one generation left for successive generations, understandable since he was just becoming aware of the extent of his own personal debts.[66] He suggested that these successive generations ought to be able to repudiate debts that had been incurred by previous generations. Constitutions ought to be treated in the same way. No single generation, which Jefferson with mathematical precision decided was nineteen years in length, should be able to "make a perpetual constitution, or even a perpetual law. . . . Every constitution then, and every law, naturally expires at the end of 19 years. If it be enforced longer, it is an act of force, and not of right."[67]

In his response, Madison very tactfully suggested that Jefferson's extraordinarily utopian idea was not "in *all* respects compatible with the course of human affairs," and he went on to point out its various impracticalities. Jefferson respected Madison's advice and never sought to implement his notion legally or constitutionally. Nevertheless, he remained stubbornly convinced for the rest of his life that the past should never be a burden to the present: it was central to his radical approach to the world, that people should never be held back by the dead hand of history.[68]

Adams, who probably had read more history than Jefferson and had certainly written more of it—three volumes of what he called "all genuine History"—never thought that society could ever be free of the past: it was a record of constant struggles between aristocrats and democrats from which mankind must learn the truths of politics. "Lessons," he told Jefferson, "are never wanting. Life and History are full" of them. Describing these lessons in his volumes had cost him "a good deal of Trouble and Expence." He had delved "into Italian Rubbish and Ruins," among many other sources, but he had found "enough of pure Gold and Marble . . . to reward the Pains." The past was the invaluable source of lessons for the present. Nearly all the commentators on the French Revolution, he lamented, had no sense of history whatsoever, which was why they so misjudged it. The only commentator, he said, who understood the importance of the past was Edmund Burke, in his *Reflections on the Revolution in France*.[69]

WHEN JEFFERSON ARRIVED back in the United States in the fall of 1789, both he and America had changed. Living in Europe had given him a new perspective on his country. In his *Notes on the State of Virginia*, written in the early 1780s, he had criticized his fellow Virginians for their backwardness and the likelihood of their losing all sense of virtue—often in terms similar to those of Adams. He had urged reform of everything—of the Virginia constitution, of the laws, of religion, of slavery. He had warned that "from the conclusion of this war we shall be going down hill." Our rulers would become corrupt and the people careless. The people would be forgotten and their rights disregarded. "They will forget themselves, but in the sole faculty of making money."[70]

But now he was no longer obsessed with reforming his state and society. Even eliminating slavery was no longer uppermost in his mind;

instead he emphasized ameliorating the conditions of his slaves at Monticello. His experience with European sophistication and luxury had given him a new appreciation of the plainness and provinciality of America. He was "savage enough," he told a German correspondent in 1785, "to prefer the woods, the wilds, and the independence of Monticello, to all the brilliant pleasures of this gay capital" of Paris. America didn't need reforming, but old decayed oppressive Europe did. Indeed, Jefferson returned from Europe convinced that America must avoid at all costs becoming more like Europe.[71]

But when he arrived in the temporary federal capital of New York in March 1790 to take up the position of secretary of state in the new federal government, a responsibility he accepted reluctantly, he discovered that many Americans wanted to do just that—become more like decadent, monarchical Europe. He was "astonished," he later recalled, "to find the general prevalence of monarchical sentiments," especially sentiments in favor of the English constitution. At dinner parties and other social occasions, he found very few Americans who seemed willing to support "republicanism."[72]

Jefferson's memory was not faulty. America had changed a great deal since he had left in 1784, and talk of royalism and monarchy had indeed become more prevalent, especially in New England and New York. Benjamin Tappan, the father of the future abolitionists, told Henry Knox in 1787 that "monarchy" had become "absolutely necessary to save the states from sinking into the lowest abyss of misery." Not only had the Constitution been created largely out of fear of too much democracy, but the strong independent president was very much welcomed as an elected monarch, resembling the Polish king that Jefferson had predicted.

In 1789 the president had been greeted with acclamations of "Long live George Washington!" with some calling his inauguration as president "a coronation." One of his future secretaries of war even saluted Washington, "You are now a King, under a different name"—may you "reign long and happy over us." With toasts being drunk to "his Highness," it was not surprising that, in the first draft of his inaugural address, Washington attempted to counter these monarchical expectations by pointing out that he had no offspring, "no family to build in greatness upon my country's ruins." Although Madison talked him out of this draft, Washington's desire to show the public that he entertained no kingly ambitions revealed just how widespread was the talk of monarchy in 1789.[73]

Jefferson recalled that the most anyone in 1790 would do in support of republican features in the new government was to say that the Constitution was inevitably going to become more monarchical in time.[74] Indeed, that was a common supposition of those who favored a stronger, more monarchical-like government in 1789—the Federalists, they called themselves, clinging to the name the supporters of the Constitution had adopted. Many of these Federalists thought that time was on their side. They were well versed in the theory of the Scottish social scientists that held that states progressed through four stages of development—from hunter-gathering, to herding, to an agricultural phase, and finally to the sophisticated commercial stage that characterized the modern states of Britain and France. As American society inevitably left the agricultural stage and became more mature, more unequal, and hierarchical, and came to resemble the societies of Europe, the Federalists concluded that the United States would necessarily have to become more monarchical. Rawlins Lowndes of South Carolina thought that America was halfway there. Its government, he said, so closely resembled the British form that everyone naturally expected "our changing from a republic to monarchy."[75]

As far as John Adams was concerned, the United States was already a monarchy, a republican monarchy, to be sure, but nevertheless a monarchy. "The Constitution of Massachusetts is a limited Monarchy," he said. "So is the new Constitution of the United States." No one could understand what he meant. By his lights, however, any state that had a strong independent executive was a monarchy of some sort, a concept that most Americans found confusing, if not absurd. Most, especially most southerners, were convinced that all Adams cared about was the monarchical English constitution.[76]

Since southern aristocrats were more confident of their position in the

society and less fearful of democracy than elites in the North, they became the most fervent supporters of liberty, equality, and popular republican government and at the same time the most severe critics of both
Adams and the northern talk of monarchy. Like Jefferson, these southern
aristocrats could claim to be full-fledged republicans without fearing the
populist repercussions their northern counterparts had come to dread.

It was not surprising, as Senator William Maclay from Pennsylvania
noticed, that most of those who supported titles and dwelled on other
monarchical formalities in government came from New England, where
the social structure was most equal and the gentlemen-aristocrats, such as
they were, were always more vulnerable to challenge. Southern slaveholding aristocrats, whose elite status could usually be taken for granted, could
therefore, as one Marylander did, easily mock Adams's talk of "the awful
distance which should be maintained between some and others" and more
readily ridicule his rants "upon the necessity of one of his three balancing
powers, consisting of the *well born*, or of those who are distinguished by
their descent from a race of illustrious ancestors." Where in America,
asked this sarcastic Marylander, "are those *well born* to be found?"[77]

Adams knew where they could be found. They existed all over
America, especially in his own state; indeed, he declared that Massachusetts possessed as many aristocratic families as any place on earth, and
these social inequalities were impossible to eradicate.[78] In his stubborn,
perverse way, Adams was defying the egalitarian assumptions of Jefferson shared by most Americans. By positing the inevitable presence of
aristocracy, he confronted American culture head-on.

By 1789 almost no political figure was willing to admit publicly that
he was a member of an American aristocracy. Even Alexander Hamilton, when accused by the sharp-witted anti-Federalist Melancton Smith
in the New York ratifying convention of being an aristocrat, felt compelled to deny the charge vehemently. Smith, Hamilton contended, would
certainly never admit that he was demagogically accusing men of being
aristocrats simply to arouse passions and create prejudices. "Why then are
we told so often of an aristocracy? For my part," said Hamilton, "I hardly

know the meaning of the word as it is applied." There was no aristocracy in America, said Hamilton, or else "every distinguished man is an aristocrat," which, if that was what Smith meant, he said, rendered the term meaningless.[79] But that was pretty close to what Adams eventually came to mean by an aristocrat.[80]

However confused his critics were by Adams's discussions of aristocracy, they were basically correct in claiming that he wanted to change the state constitutions and the federal Constitution. In 1789 only Massachusetts, New Hampshire, and the new federal government gave even a limited veto power to their executives; no government in America yet possessed the absolute executive veto power that Adams thought essential for a properly balanced constitution.

ALTHOUGH ADAMS PROTESTED that he was "as much a republican as I was in 1775," many of his ideas seemed out of place in the America of 1789–1790.[81] Since most of his fellow Americans had abandoned or never clearly held Adams's traditional conception of a mixed republic, with its balance of the social orders of monarchy, aristocracy, and democracy, his talk of "monarchical republics" and "republican monarchies" was bound to confuse people and raise suspicions. Couldn't his countrymen follow what he was saying? "How is it possible," he said, in frustration, "that whole nations should be made to comprehend the principles and rules of government, until they shall learn to understand one another's meaning by words?"[82]

Roger Sherman of Connecticut, for example, could not grasp Adams's unusual definition of a republic as "government where sovereignty is vested in more than one person." Adams actually celebrated the fact that this strange definition of republican government made England as much of a republic as America, "a monarchical republic, it is true," Adams admitted, "but a republic still." England was a republic, he said, to Sherman's bewilderment, because "the sovereignty, which is the legislative power . . . is equally divided between the one, the few, and the many, or in other words, between the natural division of mankind in society,—the monarchical, the aristocratical, and democratical."

For Sherman this made no sense at all. For him a republic was the opposite of a monarchy, "a commonwealth without a king," a government in which all parts, executives as well as the two branches of the legislature, were elected agents of the people. What especially made a state "a republic," said Sherman, was "its dependence on the public or people at large, without any hereditary powers."[83]

To Adams, Sherman's definition was just another example of the "peculiar sense to which the words republic, commonwealth, popular state" were being used by people "who mean by them a democracy, or rather a representative democracy." But for most Americans by 1789 that was precisely what the United States had become—a representative democracy, even though it contained single executives and bicameral legislatures at both the state and federal levels. For Sherman and most other Americans, all these various parts of their governments had become different kinds of representatives of the people—at least that was what they were calling them in public.

Captivated as he was by the historical meaning of mixed government as a balancing of social estates and lacking any sense of political correctness, Adams could not understand what Sherman and others were talking about. For him a democracy or a representative democracy was simply "a government in a single assembly, chosen at stated periods by the people, and invested with the whole sovereignty." If the government contained a single executive and a senate, Adams believed that it necessarily had to be something other than a democracy, or even a representative democracy; indeed, it had to be a "limited monarchy" or "a monarchical republic." That gap in understanding between him and his countrymen was never closed.

Because America to Adams was a monarchical republic, its president being a kind of elective king and an embodiment of the order of the "one" in the society, "it is essential to a monarchial republic," he declared, "that the supreme executive should be a branch of the legislature, and have a negative on all the laws." Without a full and proper share in the legislature by the monarchical order, he told Sherman, the desired balance of the state "between the one, the few, and the many" could not be preserved.[84]

By 1789 this justification for the executive veto was peculiar to Adams and was not at all shared by Sherman and most other Americans. An absolute veto, said Sherman, may have made sense in England where the rights of the people and the rights of the nobility had to be offset by the Crown's possessing a complete negative power over all laws. But the American republics, "wherein is no higher rank than that of common citizens," had no such social orders to balance. The qualified veto power given to executives in America, said Sherman, had nothing to do with embodying a monarchical social order in the government; it was designed "only to produce a revision" of the laws and to prevent hastily drawn legislation.

As a final blow to Adams's conception of government and society, Sherman claimed that there were "no principles in our constitution that have any tendency to aristocracy." Since "both branches of Congress are eligible from the citizens at large, and wealth is not a requisite qualification, both will commonly be composed of members of similar circumstances in life." Thus there could be no social struggle between the several branches of government; all were equal agents of the people, "directed to one end, the advancement of the public good."[85]

In his conventional republican rhetoric, Sherman may have understood correctly how Americans had come to conceive of their government, but by so casually and mindlessly denying the existence of any aristocracy in America, he, like other Americans, did not do justice to the power and complexity of Adams's analysis of their society. Adams may have misunderstood the rationale Americans now gave for the structure of their balanced governments, but he realized better than most of his countrymen the inherent inequality of their society and the inevitability of elites.

In the face of this kind of mounting criticism, Adams clung to his unorthodox views of government only more firmly. He published two more volumes of his *Defence* in which he laid out even more fully his pessimistic but realistic analysis of American society. He realized that his critics conceived of aristocracy in formal legal terms, but they were letting their predilections get in the way of the truth; their ideology was obscuring social realities. "Perhaps it may be said," Adams declared, "that in America we have no distinctions of ranks, and therefore shall not be liable to those divisions and discords which spring from them." But this was just wishful thinking. "All we can say in America is, that legal distinctions, titles, powers, and privileges, are not hereditary." The craving for distinction—basic to human nature—was as strong in America as anywhere. Weren't the slightest differences of rank and position, between laborers, yeomen, and gentlemen, "as earnestly desired and sought, as titles, garters, and ribbons are in any nation of Europe"?[86]

In fact, said Adams, almost a half century before Tocqueville made the same penetrating observation, the desire for distinction was even stronger in egalitarian America than elsewhere. Aristocrats, of course, had to keep up their distinctiveness, "or fall into contempt and ridicule." But in America "the lowest and the middling people," despite their continual declamations against the rich and the great, were really no different. They were as much addicted to buying superfluities as the aristocracy. Indeed, "a free people," said Adams, "are the most addicted to luxury of any." Their republican emphasis on equality hurried them into buying more than they needed. A man would see his neighbor "whom he holds his equal" with a better coat, hat, house, or horse. "He cannot bear it; he must and will be on a level with him." In the 1780s, said Adams, the American people "rushed headlong into a greater degree of luxury than ought to have crept in for a hundred years." Indeed, he told Benjamin Rush, because America was "more Avaricious than any other Nation that ever existed," it would be foolish to expect the country to free itself from the passion for distinctions.[87]

In April 1790 Rush told Adams that he and Jefferson in the previous month had had a conversation about Adams. "We both deplored your attachment to monarchy and both agreed that you had changed your principles since the year 1776." Adams replied to Rush immediately and vehemently denied both charges. So by the time Jefferson joined the administration in the spring of 1790, he had at least an inkling of his friend's strange monarchical thinking. But as yet the two had not directly confronted each other over their differences. That was soon to change.[88]

EIGHT

FEDERALISTS
AND REPUBLICANS

WHEN THOMAS JEFFERSON arrived in New York in the spring of 1790 to take up his post as secretary of state in the Washington administration, he realized, as his conversation with Benjamin Rush indicated, that his friend John Adams was contributing to the surprising prevalence of monarchical sentiments in the city. Many people were claiming that "the glare of royalty and nobility, during his mission to England, had made him believe their fascination a necessary ingredient in government." Adams, it appeared, had become a crypto-monarchist, very much in love with the English constitution.[1]

Adams's initial behavior as vice president certainly helped convince many people that he had indeed been too long at the Court of St. James's. Worried about too much democracy, Adams, like many other conservatives, assumed that the new national government needed a certain amount of monarchical ceremony and ritual to offset the populism of the country. He advised President Washington that his office required a "large and ample" household and an entourage of chamberlains, aides-de-camp, and masters of ceremonies to conduct the formalities of the office and give it a necessary show of "Splendor and Majesty."[2]

. . .

ADAMS TOOK HIS OWN position in the government quite seriously, not as vice president (in which "I am nothing, but I may be everything"), but as president of the Senate.³ He rode to the Senate each day in an elaborate carriage with six horses, attended by four servants, "two Gentlemen before him," and a driver in livery—"no more state," said Abigail, "than is perfectly consistent with his station."⁴ And then, dressed in European-court style with a powdered wig and small sword, he presided over all the Senate's meetings and engaged fully in its debates—contrary to what subsequent vice presidents have done.

When some senators resisted his initial efforts to inject into the Senate some ceremonial practices borrowed from the British government— charging that such rituals represented "the first Step of the Ladder in the Assent to royalty"—Adams declared that as colonists Americans had been happy using those practices and that all he wanted was a respectable government. He went on to suggest that perhaps he had indeed been abroad too long and the temper of the American people had changed. At any rate, he said, if he had known in 1775 that it would come to this, that the American people would not accept a dignified government, "he never would have drawn his Sword."⁵ Such an astonishing statement revealed the extent of his growing frustration with his countrymen's unwillingness to recognize the social chaos they faced.

Such an exaggerated remark came from a real anxiety that the authority of the new government might not be properly "supported with dignity and Splendor." It was "not to gratify individuals that public Titles are annexed to offices," he said. "It is to make offices and laws respected," especially among "the Profligate," who had "little reverence for Reason, Right or Law divine or human."⁶ As vice president, Adams became obsessed with titles for governmental officials, especially for the president, and this at a time, as some opponents noted, when revolutionary France was busy abolishing titles and all traces of feudalism.

The Senate took up the issue of titles and debated it for a month, with Adams constantly haranguing the senators from the chair. The president's title, he told his friend William Tudor, could not be simply "His Excellency," which was what governors of states were called. Only something like "His Highness, or, if you will, His Most Benign Highness" would do. If the governors of the states got to thinking that they were superior to the president, "they will infallibly undermine and overturn the whole system"—a not unfounded fear.[7]

It was obvious to Adams that the chief executive had to be addressed as something other than mere "President." After all, he informed the Senate, there were "Presidents of Fire Companies & of a Cricket Club." Finally, under Adams's prodding the Senate agreed on the title "His Highness the President of the United States of America, and Protector of Their Liberties." But because Adams's "grasping after Titles has been observed by every body," he hurt himself with Washington and some of his colleagues. During the debate, some senators, especially from the South, began mocking him and calling him "His Rotundity."[8]

Meanwhile, under James Madison's leadership, the House of Representatives rejected the Senate's suggestion and prevailed with the simple title of "Mr. President"—which worked because Washington's inherent authority gave it weight. When Jefferson learned of Adams's preoccupation with titles, he could only shake his head in wonderment and remind Madison of Benjamin Franklin's characterization of Adams as someone who was "always an honest man, often a great one, but sometimes absolutely mad."[9]

Jefferson soon had firsthand evidence of his friend's admiration for the English constitution. Before leaving for a tour of the southern states in the spring of 1791, President Washington asked the cabinet to meet and discuss what should be done in his absence; he suggested that Vice President Adams also be present, "the only occasion," said Jefferson, "on which that officer was ever requested to take part in a Cabinet question." Jefferson offered to host a dinner party for the discussion. After business was done, the conversation turned to other matters, including the English constitution. Jefferson was stunned to hear the English constitution extolled by his guests and he wrote up what was said as soon as his guests had left.[10] "Purge that constitution of it's corruption," he reported Adams saying, "and give to it's popular branch equality of representation, and it would be the most perfect constitution ever devised by the wit of man." What Adams meant by corruption was the members of Parliament being simultaneously ministers of the Crown, by American standards a clear violation of separation of powers. As if to twist the knife that Adams had planted in Jefferson, Secretary of the Treasury Alexander Hamilton went on to say, following a suggestion of the Scottish philosopher David Hume, that he preferred the English constitution with its corruption. Corruption, said Hamilton, was precisely what made the English constitution workable, for it allowed for ministerial responsibility to Parliament. And, of course, that is precisely how the British parliamentary system of cabinet government has worked right up to today.[11]

HAMILTON'S REMARK ONLY REINFORCED Jefferson's suspicion of what the secretary of the treasury was up to. With the support of President Washington, Hamilton had set forth in 1790–1791 an ambitious program designed to turn the United States into a fiscal-military state that in time—perhaps three or four decades—would be able to take on any of the great European powers on their own terms. Hamilton and other Federalists wanted the United States to move as rapidly as possible into the final stage of commercial and industrial development. "Notions of equality," he told Washington, were as "yet . . . too general and too strong" for the distinctions and hierarchy appropriate to a mature, advanced nation.[12] But with his program America in time would develop all the elements of the modern society of Great Britain—banks, stock markets, stock companies, and manufacturing firms. If the United States remained the predominantly agricultural society that Jefferson preferred, then Hamilton and the other Federalists believed that America would remain a rude and stagnant society.

Although Adams, like Hamilton, certainly thought that the nation would mature and would need hereditary institutions in order to maintain social stability, and "that in no very distant Period of time," he was a moderate on the issue of commercial development.[13] He was less confident than Hamilton on the wisdom of the Federalist program, believing that "the Science of political Economy is but a late Study and is not generally understood among Us." Nevertheless, he agreed that "a discreet and judicious Encouragement of Manufactures" was essential for the good of the nation. Other Federalists were bolder. "An agricultural nation which exports its raw materials and imports its manufactures," declared a New Englander in 1789, could never become either "opulent" or "powerful."[14]

Nothing could be a more blatant challenge to Jefferson's vision of what America ought to be: an agricultural society supported by yeoman farmers growing staple crops for overseas export—whether tobacco, rice, or cotton. Because, like southerners in general, Jefferson thought of markets for these agricultural staples as mainly existing abroad, he attached a special importance to overseas commerce. Indeed, he defined the word "commerce" in traditional terms, as Montesquieu had: "the exportation and importation of merchandise with a view to the advantage of the state."[15] And for him and other southerners, exports were especially valuable. "The commodities we offer are either necessities of life, or materials for manufacture, or convenient Subjects of Revenue," he wrote in his "Report on Commerce" in 1793; "and we take in exchange, either manufactures, when they have received the last finish of Art and Industry; or mere luxuries."[16]

Because Americans exported necessities and imported mere luxuries, Jefferson and other southern leaders came to believe that the United States was in a strong position to use its trade as a weapon in international conflicts. As Jefferson told Madison in 1793, this ability to withhold America's international trade was an alternative to war; it gave America "a happy opportunity of setting another example to the world, by shewing that nations may be brought to do justice by appeals to their interests as well as by appeals to arms."[17] These were the assumptions behind Jefferson's and Madison's experiments with nonimportation legislation and embargoes.

Since America had land enough to last for generations to come, Jefferson thought he could freeze time and simply expand the agricultural stage of society in space. Because yeoman farmers, his "chosen people of

God," were the only ones who could prevent the nation from becoming corrupt, they must continue to dominate American society. "While we have land to labour then," he wrote, "let us never wish to see our citizens occupied at a work-bench, or twilling a distaff." As manufacturing cities were sores on the body politic, "let our work shops remain in Europe." If Americans should ever "get piled upon one another in large cities, as in Europe," he said, "they will become as corrupt as in Europe." To be sure, cities, he admitted, did "nourish some of the elegant arts, but the useful ones can thrive elsewhere" than in cities. Better, he said, to have fewer of the fine arts if it meant "more health virtue & freedom"—an extraordinary concession to his vision of an agricultural America.[18]

As much as Jefferson had loved Paris and its art, he could not help viewing "great cities as pestilential to the morals, the health, and the liberties of man."[19] By seeking to stymie social development and preserve farming in America and prevent the emergence of cities, Jefferson knew that he was defying the trajectory of progress as understood by the best social science of the day. Whether consciously or not, he was protecting the agricultural slave society of the South as he knew it.

Both Jefferson and Adams, each in his own way, had a foreboding of America's future. Jefferson wanted to hold back social maturation and halt America at the agricultural stage of development, or the society would become irreversibly corrupted and lose its capacity for republicanism. Adams thought that America was already well along in corruption and was wallowing in such luxury and inequality that it needed to adopt some monarchical elements in its governments if it were to maintain some modicum of freedom. Neither one predicted the future accurately.

Hamilton was more accurate, at least in the long run: the United States in time did become a great fiscal-military state. The secretary of the treasury's program involved the federal government assuming the Revolutionary War debts of the states, combining them with the federal debts, and funding them—that is, issuing new bonds paying interest on a regular basis—in order to put the nation's finances on a firm footing and turn the United States into an attractive place for investment by moneyed people both abroad and at home. His program also included an experiment for developing manufacturing in the country. To cap his plans Hamilton created a national bank, the Bank of the United States, to handle the federal government's finances and to issue paper money. It was an extraordinary program, and it established Hamilton's reputation as one of the great statesmen of modern Western history.

Since Hamilton's program was modeled on the early-eighteenth-century experience of Great Britain, which had enabled it to become the greatest power in the world, it was bound to raise fears among those who were already anxious about all the talk of monarchy and titles and admiration for the English constitution. Since the only alternative to the new national government seemed to be disunity and anarchy, opposition to the administration developed slowly, especially because of the confidence everyone had in President Washington. Besides, no one as yet could conceive of a legitimate opposition in a republican government. Most people condemned parties as symptoms of disease in the body politic and signs that partiality and selfishness were replacing devotion to the public good, the *res publica*.

AT FIRST JEFFERSON DID NOT FULLY GRASP the implications of Hamilton's program. He had been away, he later explained, and had "lost all familiarity" with what had been going on. To his subsequent embarrassment, he actually arranged the dinner party at which the compromise of 1790 was worked out between Hamilton and Madison. This compromise, which located the national capital on the Potomac in return for allowing the federal assumption of state debts, showed that most congressmen were still willing to bargain for the sake of union. But the chartering of the Bank of the United States in February 1791 in emulation of the Bank of England seemed a step too far and alarmed many Americans, especially southern aristocrats like Madison and Jefferson.

In 1791 most Americans were not all that familiar with banks. A decade earlier, the Continental Congress had set up the Bank of North America in Philadelphia, and by 1790 there were three more banks established in New York, Boston, and Baltimore. Yet compared with England, with its dozens upon dozens of private and county banks all regulated by the Bank of England, banking in America was new and undeveloped. When the Bank of North America was first opened in 1781, it was "a novelty," said its president, Thomas Willing. Banking in America, he said, was "a pathless wilderness ground but little known to this side of the Atlantic." English rules, arrangements, and bank bills were then unknown. "All was to us a mystery."[20]

Banking was certainly a mystery to both Jefferson and Adams, and it remained a mystery for the rest of their lives. Neither understood how banks worked. Jefferson hated the Bank of the United States not only because it was a bank, but also because he considered that Congress's chartering of it was unconstitutional. Anyone acknowledging the legitimacy of the Bank of the United States was committing "an act of *treason*" against the states, he told Madison in 1792; those who tried to "act under colour of the authority of a foreign legislature" (that is, the federal Congress) and issue and pass notes ought to be "adjudged guilty of high treason and suffer death accordingly, by the judgment of the state courts." Calling the new federal Congress "a foreign legislature" revealed just how much of an anti-Federalist Jefferson really was, and his outrageous remark about treason suggested just how passionate he could get, at least in private letters.[21]

It wasn't just the Bank of the United States that Jefferson hated; he hated all banks—"banking establishments," he said, "are more dangerous than standing armies." He especially hated the paper money they issued, which, he said, was designed "to enrich swindlers at the expense of the honest and industrious part of the nation." He never understood how "legerdemain tricks upon paper can produce as solid wealth as hard labor in the earth. It is vain for common sense to urge that *nothing* can produce but *nothing*." Jefferson thus saw little of value in Hamilton's program. The buying and selling of stock and the raising of capital were simply licentious speculations and wild gambling, all symptoms of commercial avarice and corruption. Like most Virginians, he thought the only real wealth lay in land, not money.[22]

. . .

ALTHOUGH ADAMS AS VICE PRESIDENT was presumably a member of the administration, he had nothing to do with Hamilton's program. He did cast twenty-eight tie-breaking votes in the Senate during his eight years as vice president, most of which strengthened the national government, but he was rarely ever consulted on the administration's policies.[23] By the summer of 1790, the French chargé d'affaires reported to his government that "the popularity of Mr. Adams . . . is falling lower and lower." As far as his relationship with the president was concerned, "the influence of Mr. Adams was almost nil." The French chargé concluded that "he will never be President."[24]

Of course, it didn't help matters that Adams soon began spending nearly three-quarters of each year at his farm in Quincy, especially after Abigail decided she no longer wanted to stay in Philadelphia, which in 1790 had replaced New York as the capital of the country. Apparently, the couple decided in 1792 that they could cut expenses if Abigail remained in Quincy, though publicly they claimed it was for reasons of health.

In Philadelphia, Adams sorely missed Abigail, complaining often of his "tedious days! and lonesome nights!"[25] Unlike his tours in Europe, when he went weeks without writing, he now sent to her a steady stream of letters, at least one each week and sometimes more frequently. Abigail reciprocated. She lamented that "we are grown too old to live separate," but she added that "our present seperation is much mitigated by the frequent intercourse we are enabled to hold by Letter."[26] Indeed, during the eighteen months spanning January 1794 through June 1795, the couple exchanged 145 letters.

It was not just his frequent absences in Quincy, however, that contributed to the administration's neglect of him. Hamilton and Washington surely realized that he had little to offer them, for Adams was as innocent of banking and finance as Jefferson. To the end of his life he was convinced that "every dollar of a bank bill that is issued beyond the quantity of gold and silver in the vaults, represents nothing and is therefore a cheat upon somebody."[27] Of course, the only way a bank could earn any money for its investors was to issue more paper than it had gold or silver in its vaults.

These banks issuing notes were the means by which the states got around article I, section 10, of the Constitution, which prohibited the states from issuing paper money, one of the most notorious vices Madison had been concerned about in 1787. The states simply chartered banks, which then issued the paper money that everyone needed to carry on business with one another. Without that paper money, the economy would have been stifled. But some banks did sometimes get overextended. In 1808 the Farmers' Exchange Bank of Gloucester (now Glocester), Rhode Island, emitted over $600,000 of paper notes, but had only $86.45 in gold and silver to support these notes; it went bankrupt and became the first bank to fail in United States history.[28]

That was the kind of incident that convinced Adams that banking was some sort of fraud. Because most gentry, especially those in the North, tended to live on rents, interest from money out on loan, official salaries, and other forms of fixed income, they feared inflation—that is, depreciated currency—above all. Adams was no different. He hated the paper money favored by debtors, most of whom were entrepreneurial-minded farmers and artisans borrowing money in order to carry on and enhance their commercial activities. "The Cry for Paper Money," Adams said, "is downright Wickedness and Dishonesty. Every Man must see that it is the worst Engine of Knavery that ever was invented."[29]

This dislike of paper money issued by the state-chartered banks alone made him a good Federalist. But his credentials as a Federalist were reinforced by his suspicion of France, his admiration of the English constitution, his dread of popular disorder, and his desire that due respect be paid to public officials. But because, like Jefferson, he had little understanding of banking and high finance, he was not quite Hamilton's kind of Federalist. In fact, at times he could talk about the Federalists as if he were not one of them. "They are Seeking Popularity and Loaves and Fishes as well as the Anti's," he told Abigail in 1794, "and find it inconvenient to act a decided open Part in any Thing." What he wanted above all was to "keep himself forever independent of the Smiles or Frowns of political Parties."[30]

THE INITIAL ESTABLISHMENT of the new federal government did not allay Adams's fears for the country, and the continued American enthusiasm for the rampaging French Revolution was deeply alarming. His three-volume *Defence of the Constitutions of Government of the United States of America* had not been enough to persuade his countrymen to reform their governments and prepare for a violent and disorderly future. In 1790 he concluded that he had to take up his pen once again in order to further educate his fellow Americans on the dangers they faced, this time more from the populace than from the aristocracy. Reading the work of the seventeenth-century Italian historian Enrico Caterino Davila, Adams was provoked into writing thirty-two essays called *Discourses on Davila* that were serially published anonymously over the period 1790–1791 in John Fenno's Federalist New York *Gazette of the United States*. (Adams later claimed that his Davila essays were the fourth volume of his *Defence*).

Davila's *Historia della guerre civili de Francia*, originally published in 1630, described the intrigues, battles, and assassinations that occurred in France in the last half of the sixteenth century, in Adams's mind a portent of the disasters that were currently afflicting revolutionary France. Most of Adams's essays were straight translations of the first five books of Davila's history. But fourteen of them had nothing to do with Davila, and instead contained Adams's "useful reflections" on ambition, emulation, envy, and fame, what he called "the constitution of the human mind."[31]

Apparently, Adams had been reading Adam Smith's *Theory of Moral Sentiments*, and a particular chapter in that work entitled "The Origins of Ambition and the Distinction of Ranks" struck a chord with him. When Smith in this chapter emphasized people's powerful desire for reputation—men striving to have the eyes of the whole world gazing at them in admiration—Adams realized at once whom the author might have been talking about. When Adams, in effect responding to Smith's interpretation of human psychology, wrote that nature had wrought the passion for distinction "into the texture and essence of the soul," he knew only too keenly what soul he meant.[32]

More fearful now of the social war raging in revolutionary France, which Adams thought America might eventually duplicate, he became even more eager to emphasize the power of the passion for superiority and reputation that he believed lay behind what was happening in France and, indeed, behind all social upheavals. That passion for distinction, which, he said, was "the great spring of social activity," existed in everyone in all societies. Every individual, no matter how lowly, wanted to be approved, talked about, and respected by those about him. If society was to avoid all the evils that overweening ambition and the desire for dominance created—the family rivalries, the mobs and seditions, and the "hissing snakes, burning torches, and haggard horrors" that came from civil war—it had to control and manage these passions.

Ultimately, said Adams in his extraordinary final discourse—one that appeared in Fenno's paper but was never reprinted in the subsequent 1805 volume of the collected essays—the best means of regulation was to make the offices of government hereditary. History demonstrated this, said Adams. Nearly all the nations of the earth had eventually given all power over to hereditary monarchs, and they had done so after they had tried "all possible experiments of elections of Governors and Senates." They had found "so much emulation in every heart, so many rivalries among the principal men, such divisions, confusions and miseries" that they concluded that "hereditary succession was attended with fewer evils than frequent elections." Adams agreed with that perspective, saying emphatically that this was "the true answer and the only one."[33]

WITH SUCH VIEWS, it was not surprising that Adams's *Discourses on Davila* aroused a storm of controversy and eventually turned Jefferson and others against Fenno's paper. Jefferson had been following the Davila essays from their beginning in April 1790 and had actually tried to counter them by inserting into Fenno's *Gazette* translated pro-republican pieces from a Dutch paper in Leyden; he saw these insertions as "an Antidote" to Adams's quasi-monarchical views.[34] The insertions came to an end in July 1790, when Fenno's paper turned decisively against the French Revolution and its "barbarous spirit of democracy."[35] Instead of simply defending the federal Constitution, the *Gazette,* in Jefferson's opinion, had become a mouthpiece for the Federalist program, spouting antirepublican sentiments. With the change in Fenno's paper, Jefferson became convinced that he should create a newspaper that supported pure republicanism.

Adams remained extraordinarily naïve. He seemed to have little awareness of the effect his statements and writings had on people. When his longtime friend Mercy Otis Warren asked him to find positions for her husband and son in the new government, instead of simply telling her that he had no control over patronage and leaving it at that, he went on to proclaim his virtue in never allowing his personal attachment to family or friends to interfere with his public duties. And if that weren't enough, he then proceeded to criticize her husband, General James Warren, for his support of the Shaysite rebels. Their long friendship began to unravel. He was irritated by the Warrens' more radical politics, and they in turn were angered by his manner. When Adams as minster to the Court of St. James's was unable to get Mrs. Warren's history play *The Sack of Rome* published in England, telling her "nothing American sells here," she was offended. Although she had originally dedicated the play to Adams, when it was finally published in America in 1790, she changed the dedication to George Washington.[36]

Jefferson would never have responded to his enemies, never mind his friends, in the blunt manner Adams did with the Warrens. He was always far more in control of his personal and political views than Adams. Jefferson knew instinctively what his fellow Americans wanted and needed to hear. If the United States was to be a nation, he realized it had to be fundamentally different from the European nations and especially England; and he spent a good deal of time stressing America's exceptionalism. By contrast, Adams risked his reputation for patriotism by emphatically denying America's uniqueness at the same time as he celebrated the greatness of the English constitution.

Even Hamilton was infuriated by Adams's naïveté, and he condemned his writings, particularly his Davila essays, saying that because they so publicly favored the English constitution, they tended to undermine, not strengthen, the new national government in the public's eyes. Hamilton told Jefferson that he was sure that Adams's intentions were pure—what dark motive could he have?—but that didn't absolve the vice president of blame for blundering and disturbing "the present order of things."[37]

Unlike Jefferson, whose political antennae were generally quite alert, Adams seemed to have had no political sense whatsoever. When President Washington asked him if he wished to accompany him on a tour of the northern states in the fall of 1789, he balked at the invitation and reminded Washington that there was much business to be done in the capital. No wonder Jefferson later declared that Adams was someone whom Washington "certainly did not love." Abigail, whose political instincts were often better than her husband's, was surprised that her husband had turned down the president's invitation, and she encouraged him to join him. Instead, Adams made his own separate journey north.[38]

Adams often appeared to be living in his own mind. When in February 1790 John Trumbull informed him of what his enemies were saying about him, Adams denied that anyone disliked him. "I am the Enemy of no Man living," he said; "and I know of none who is an Enemy to me." That didn't mean, however, that he wasn't envied. "But Envy is not Enmity." When Trumbull told Adams that his behavior in the Senate, particularly his mingling in debates, had been criticized, Adams replied that "you are the first who has ever hinted to me, that any exception has ever been taken in the senate."

He sloughed off other criticisms as well. The accusation of his favoring "'the splendor of monarchical Court' has no Effect on me." All he had done was publish under his name "my honest sentiments of Government, with the Reasons on which they were founded, at great length in three solid perhaps ponderous Volumes." If his countrymen disapproved of these sentiments, so be it; they were free to reject them. He did admit, however, that sometimes when he had felt "very easy and happy" with friends at his own table, he had been known to express himself too warmly in response to some "Strange sentiments" and thus he had unintentionally hurt some people's feelings—something that "Mrs. Adams sometimes objects to me on this head."[39]

APPARENTLY JEFFERSON, or so Jefferson claimed, had been calling Adams "a heretic" freely to his face for some time, but doing so in a joking enough manner as to not endanger the friendship.[40] When Jefferson arrived in New York in late March 1790, he immediately began socializing with the Adamses—Abigail telling her sister that the new secretary of state "adds much to the social circle."[41] Although Jefferson told Benjamin Rush early that year, at least a month before the publication of any of the Davila essays, that he deplored the change he saw in Adams's opinion on republican forms of government, he, according to Rush, still spoke of Adams "with respect and affection as a great and upright man."[42]

Adams, having expressed to Jefferson in 1789 "an affection that can never die," was as yet scarcely capable of sensing any hostility coming from his friend; but he was clearly more restrained in expressing his monarchical ideas with Jefferson than he was with Benjamin Rush, with whom he had become very intimate.[43]

With Rush, Adams issued his opinions, feelings, and resentments in an effusive and candid manner that he felt he could not duplicate with Jefferson.[44] Corresponding with Rush, he seemed to hold nothing back. For every conventional bromide about American exceptionalism and American republicanism timidly offered by Rush—the bromides that Jefferson spouted all the time—Adams let loose a torrent of his eccentric opinions that left Rush stunned.

Weren't Americans, asked Rush hesitantly, different from other people, freer of faction, and peculiarly qualified for republican governments? That was absurd, responded Adams. The only republic appropriate for Americans was "the Aristo-Democratical-Monarchy," and that was "because they are more Avaricious than any other Nation." Boston, New York, and Philadelphia were as vicious and licentious as London. "How can you say," he demanded of Rush, "that Factions have been few in America? . . . Have not our Parties behaved like all Republican Parties? Is not the History of Hancock and Bowdoin, the History of the Medici and Albizi."

When Rush said that he abhorred all titles, Adams fired back that Rush was simply deceiving himself. Titles were "indispensably necessary to give Dignity and Energy to Government." In fact, he said, "Government is nothing else but Titles, Ceremonies and Ranks." This was a far cry from what he had said as a young man when he had railed against the pomp and vanities of the great families of Massachusetts. "Formalities and Ceremonies," he had told his diary in 1770, "are an abomination in my sight." But in two decades he had changed his mind. To Rush's horror, Adams even praised hereditary institutions not only as possessing "admirable wisdom and exemplary Virtue in a certain Stage of Society in a great Nation," but also "as the hope of our Posterity." Indeed, Adams added, Americans must eventually resort to a hereditary monarchy and a hereditary aristocracy "as an Asylum against Discord, Seditions, and Civil War, and that in no very distant Period of time." Therefore Americans should cease mocking those hereditary institutions.[45]

Maybe Adams enjoyed getting a rise out of Rush by saying outrageous things that he would never have said to Jefferson. "Limited monarchy is founded in Nature," he told Rush. "No Nation can adore more than one Man at a time." Adams conceded that America was fortunate in having Washington as that one man. Yet he realized how "the Trumpetts, the Puffs" can distort the past. "The History of our Revolution," he informed Rush, no doubt with his tongue somewhat in cheek, "will be one continued Lye from one End to the other. The Essence of the whole will be *that Dr. Franklins electrical Rod, smote the Earth and out Sprung General Washington. That Franklin electrified him with his Rod. And thence forward these two conducted all the Policy Negotiations, Legislation and War.*" He realized that someone a hundred years later reading these lines might conclude that "the envy of this J.A. could not bear to think of the Truth!"

Adams was mocking himself with this caricature, but he knew it contained a kernel of truth—that often the real movers of events were forgotten and others got all the credit.[46]

ADAMS NEVER HAD AS FREE and easy a relationship with Jefferson as he had with Rush—perhaps because Rush paid him such deference. By 1790 the relationship with Jefferson had become decidedly uneven. Jefferson knew what Adams thought about politics and the French Revolution from Adam's writings and from observation and stories of his odd behavior and what Jefferson called "his apostasy to hereditary monarchy and nobility."[47] But Adams did not really know just how deeply contrary his political views were to those of his friend. Jefferson may have teased Adams privately with being "a heretic," but because of his natural reserve and his aversion to personal confrontations, Jefferson never spelled out to Adams just how profound his differences were over government and the French Revolution.

In fact, Jefferson's enthusiasm for the French Revolution knew no bounds; it even matched the revolutionary zeal of Thomas Paine. Jefferson had come to believe that the future of liberty in Europe depended on the favorable outcome of what was taking place in France. "For the good of suffering humanity all over the earth," he hoped that "that revolution will be established and spread thro' the whole world." But more important, he also believed that the success of that "so beautiful a revolution" could even determine the fate of the American Revolution. If the French Revolution should fail, he told George Mason, America was in danger of "falling back to that kind of Half-way-house, the English constitution."[48]

Although Adams may not have fully comprehended Jefferson's view of the French Revolution, Jefferson knew only too well from the Davila essays where Adams stood on what was happening in France. Jefferson believed that there was a sect in the government that was opposed to the French Revolution and standing in the way of reason and progress. "The members of this sect have, many of them, names and offices which stand high in the estimation of our countrymen." Fortunately, he said, "the great mass of our countrymen is untainted by these heresies, as is it's head"—that is, President Washington.[49] Indeed, Jefferson at the outset exempted Washington from all of his criticism of the administration. Although he still esteemed Adams as a friend and, as he told the president, he considered him "one of the most honest and disinterested men alive," Jefferson nevertheless did not exclude Adams from this heretical sect. After reading Adams's final Davila essay on the value of hereditary succession over elections, Jefferson could only conclude that Fenno's *Gazette* had become "a paper of pure Toryism, disseminating the doctrines of monarchy, aristocracy, and the exclusion of the influence of the people."[50]

That was a private comment made to his son-in-law. The last thing that Jefferson wanted was to be caught up in a public controversy over the Davila essays. But inadvertently he did get thrust into the public arena. In April 1791, he received a copy from England of the first part of Thomas Paine's *Rights of Man*. The book was a direct reply to Edmund Burke's *Reflections on the Revolution in France* and an impassioned assault on monarchy and hereditary aristocracy. It also ardently defended the rights of the living generation over those of the dead and mocked titles as a sort of foppery in the human character. It ridiculed mixed governments of monarchy, aristocracy, and democracy and declared that there was but one element of human power, that of the people. It thus opposed much of what Adams favored and said everything Jefferson believed in. Indeed, if Jefferson had ever systematically written out his thoughts on government, the book would have resembled *The Rights of Man*.

Because his ardent republican friend John Beckley had asked him to, Jefferson forwarded Paine's work to a printer in Philadelphia. He made the mistake, however, of including a covering note, expressing his pleasure that "something is at length to be publicly said against the political heresies which have sprung up among us," not doubting that "our citizens will rally a second time around the standard of Common sense." By "political heresies" Jefferson admitted that he meant Adams's *Discourses on Davila*.[51]

When Jefferson received a printed copy of Paine's pamphlet, he was stunned to discover that a preface to the work included his note to the publisher. By identifying the secretary of state as the author of the note

and the person who had passed on a copy of Paine's pamphlet for repub-
lication, the printer implied that Jefferson was the sponsor of the American edition of *The Rights of Man*—a work and its tendency that Adams
declared he detested from the bottom of his heart.

Paine's pamphlet and especially Jefferson's note created a sensation in
America. As Tobias Lear, one of Washington's secretaries, remarked,
"This publication of Mr. Jefferson's sentiments respecting Mr. Paine's
pamphlet will set him in direct opposition to Mr. Adams's political tenets." Jefferson was mortified over having been "thus brought forward
on the public stage," which he told Washington was "against my love of
silence and quiet, and my abhorrence of dispute."[52]

Jefferson knew Adams would be displeased. He said to Madison that
Adams was one of "those gentlemen, fast by the chair of government,
who were in sentiment with Burke and as much opposed to the sentiments of Paine." But Madison told him not to worry about it. Adams
had been acting recklessly and had no right to complain of criticism.
"Under a mock defence of the Republican Constitutions," said Madison,
Adams had "attacked them with all the force he possessed, and this in a
book with his name to it whilst he was the Representative of his Country
at a foreign Court." And as vice president, "his pen has constantly been
at work in the same cause." If one public servant can attack the government as he has done, said Madison, then surely "it can not be very criminal or indecent in another to patronize a written defence of the principles
on which that Government is founded." Madison had none of Jefferson's
affection for Adams.[53]

In response to Paine's pamphlet and Jefferson's note, someone writ-
ing as "Publicola" published a series of letters in the Boston *Columbian
Centinel* attacking *The Rights of Man* and its sponsor Jefferson for assuming that the work was a kind of "Papal Bull of infallible virtue."[54] Since
"the stile and sentiments" of Publicola seemed to be those of Adams,
Jefferson like many others presumed that he was the author. Actually,
Publicola was John Quincy Adams, the twenty-four-year-old son of
Adams. The public assumed, however, at least at first, that the secretary
of state and the vice president were at odds over fundamental principles

of government—a personal confrontation that had serious political implications.[55]

Jefferson's inclination was not to get involved at all in this brouhaha. But since both his name and that of Adams had been "thrown on the public stage as public antagonists," he felt he had to write to Adams and explain what had happened. It would not be easy, and he put off writing to Adams for two months. When he finally wrote, he told Adams that he had taken up his pen a dozen times only to lay it down again. He then decided that he would write "from a conviction that truth, between candid minds, can never do harm."

Unfortunately, the harm had already been done. "That you and I differ in our ideas of the best form of government is well known to us," he said to Adams; "but we differed as friends should do, respecting the purity of each other's motives, and confining our differences of opinion to private conversations." He told Adams that he had had no intention whatsoever of having their names brought before the public in this manner. "The friendship and confidence which has so long existed between us required this explanation from me."[56]

Two weeks later Adams replied to what he called Jefferson's "friendly Letter" in a letter that was not quite so friendly; indeed, Adams revealed that he had been deeply hurt by Jefferson's note that had been attached to Paine's work. He described how that note had been reprinted in many newspapers and considered "as a direct and open personal attack on me." It appeared to countenance "a false interpretation of my Writings as favouring the Introduction of hereditary Monarchy and Aristocracy into this Country." The newspapers had asked, What heresies was the secretary of state talking about? And the answer they had given, said Adams, was "the Vice Presidents notions of a limited Monarchy, an hereditary Government of Kings and Lords, with only elective commons." Adams said he had not written the Publicola essays, and he categorically denied that he had ever in his public writings or private letters attempted to introduce hereditary executives and hereditary senates into America's governments. He then told Jefferson that he did not realize, as Jefferson stated, that their ideas differed over the best form of government. How would he have known? "You and I have never had a Serious conversation together that I can recollect concerning the nature of Government. The very transient hints that have ever passed between Us," he said, "have been jocular and Superficial, without ever coming to any explanation."

Adams concluded by telling Jefferson that "it was high time that you and I should come to an explanation with each other." The friendship of fifteen years had always been and was still "dear to my heart." Just as he knew Jefferson's motives in writing to him were pure and friendly, he trusted that Jefferson would think of his motives "in the same candid Light."[57]

It is obvious that Adams was not as honest as he thought he was in his letter. By the time he wrote his letter, if not well before, he knew that he and Jefferson had very different ideas of government. He had told Henry Knox a month earlier that he would not allow "Paine's Nonsense" or its preface by "his Godfather" to much affect him, the "Godfather" being, of course, Jefferson. "It only grieves me," he added, "that a Character who stood high is so much lowered in the public Esteem."[58] Although Adams believed that technically he had never advocated that hereditary executives and senates be introduced immediately into America's governments, his final Davila essay—in which he suggested that hereditary succession was preferable to elections—certainly opened him to that charge.

But Jefferson was not honest either. In his reply to Adams he placed all the blame for the controversy on the writings of Publicola, "the real aggressor in this business." If Publicola hadn't attacked Paine's principles, "which were the principles of the citizens of the U.S.," and hadn't "thought proper to bring me onto the scene," Paine's pamphlet and his note, Jefferson claimed, would have gone "unnoticed." Jefferson was so anxious to exculpate himself that he told Adams that "so far from naming you, I had not even in view any writing which I might suppose to be yours" when he wrote his covering note. Then as if to compensate for this blatant lie, Jefferson went on to praise Adams for "the disinterestedness of character which you are known to possess by every body who knows your name." He hoped Adams would see that he was "as innocent *in effect*" as he "was in intention." He trusted that "the business is now over," and its effects too, "and that our friendship will never be suffered to be committed [meaning to be put away and forgotten], whatever use others may think proper to make of our names." He ended by asking Adams to present him "to Mrs. Adams with all the affection I feel for her."[59]

At the same time, however, Jefferson was telling Thomas Paine that there were in America "high and important characters," Adams, of course, being one of them, who were "preaching up and panting after an English constitution of king, lords, and commons, and whose heads are itching for crowns, coronets and mitres." He congratulated Paine for his book, which had awakened people to the English monarchical thinking expressed by the "*Defence* of the American constitutions" and the "*Discourses of Davila*." He had rescued republicanism from the sect, "high in names but small in numbers," that was trying to destroy it.[60]

This sort of duplicity by Jefferson came from his compulsive politeness and from an intense desire to avoid all personal confrontations. Despite knowing that his political views were nearly diametrically opposite of those of his old friend, he desperately wanted to maintain his connection with Adams. Over the next two years, Jefferson wrote a pair of businesslike letters to Adams, one in November 1791, the second in March 1793, with no response from Adams. Although the two men were in the federal capital together much of the time and had less need of letters, it was clear that the relationship had greatly cooled.[61]

THE ENTIRE CONTROVERSY over Paine's *Rights of Man* had elevated Jefferson into the champion of the republican cause. As an English dinner partner observed in 1792, Jefferson in conversation had become "a vigorous stickler for revolutions and for the downfall of an aristocracy. . . . In fact, like his friend T. Payne, he cannot live but in revolution, and all events in Europe are only considered by him in the relation they bear to the probability of a revolution to be produced by them."[62]

Jefferson was a thorough Francophile who was eager to demonstrate

his new cosmopolitanism to America's political world. In his Philadelphia home in the early 1790s, he sought to re-create his Paris residence
of the 1780s. He had a French housekeeper, a French coachman, French
wine, French food, French paintings, and French furniture. In fact, he
returned from France with eighty-six packing crates of furnishings,
mostly in the Louis XVI style, which included fifty-seven chairs, two
sofas, six large mirrors, wallpaper, silver, china, linen, clocks, scientific
equipment, a cabriolet, and a phaeton, not to mention all the books,
artworks, wine, and French dogs he brought back. At the same time, he
began remodeling and enlarging Monticello in line with what he took to
be the highest standards of an elegant Parisian town house.[63] Just as opponents of the Federalists thought that John Adams had spent too long
at the British court, so too did the Federalists come to believe that Jefferson had spent too much time in Paris imbibing all those radical doctrines of the French philosophes.

Just as the scandal over Jefferson's note was breaking in the spring of
1791, Jefferson and Madison were on a trip up the Hudson Valley on
holiday. In the minds of the Federalists, however, the two Virginians
were using the trip to meet with some New Yorkers to plan their opposition to Hamilton's program. Certainly Jefferson and Madison were
alarmed enough by the support of the administration in Fenno's paper to
want a paper of their own. They entered into negotiations with the poet
Philip Freneau, who had been Madison's classmate at the College of
New Jersey in Princeton, to edit a newspaper that could oppose the Federalists' program.

After being offered a position in the State Department as a translator
and other promises of support, Freneau finally agreed. The first issue of
his *National Gazette* appeared at the end of October 1791, and the paper
immediately took an anti-British and pro-French tone. By early 1792
Freneau's newspaper was claiming that Hamilton was plotting to subvert
liberty and establish monarchy and aristocracy in America. At the same
time, the paper hailed Jefferson as the distinguished patriot who was
defending republicanism against Hamilton's monarchical system of
corruption.

Although the opponents of the administration were not as yet organized as a party, something labeled the "republican interest" emerged in the Congress in 1791, with the Virginia delegation at its center.

Freneau and his newspaper effectively altered the terms of the national debate. His *National Gazette* now openly declared that "the question in America is no longer between federalism and anti-federalism, but between republicanism and anti-republicanism."[64] As Hamilton quickly realized, casting the dispute as one between supporters of monarchy and republicans was not at all favorable to the Federalists.

Finally, in the summer of 1792, Hamilton had had enough, and he began writing in Fenno's *Gazette* and attacking Jefferson directly. He stated that the secretary of state, though "the head of a principal department of the Government," was "the declared opponent of almost all the important measures which had been devised by the Government." In a stream of newspaper pieces under different anonymous names, Hamilton accused Jefferson of having hired Freneau to set up a newspaper that was "an exact copy of the politics of his employer" and had him "regularly pensioned with the public money." He accused Jefferson of wanting to become president.[65]

Jefferson was obviously upset by Hamilton's attacks, but, as he explained to Attorney General Edmund Randolph, he was not going to counter with newspaper pieces of his own. He had, he said, "preserved through life a resolution, set in a very early part of it, never to write in a public paper without subscribing my name, and to engage openly an adversary who does not let himself be seen, is staking all against nothing."[66] Besides, he realized that two ministers of the government squabbling in the public press would be utterly indecent. But even squabbling in cabinet meetings was indecent, and President Washington was alarmed.

In February 1792 Jefferson privately mentioned to Washington his concern over the overweening influence of the Treasury Department, which threatened "to swallow up the whole Executive powers." The discontent in the country, he told the president, flowed from the actions of that department. It had created a system that enticed the citizens into "a species of gambling, destructive of morality, & which had introduced it's poison into the government itself." He suggested to Washington that people were wondering whether Americans lived "under a limited or unlimited government," but he hoped the elections of 1792 would settle the dissatisfaction of people and keep "the general constitution on it's true ground."[67]

On May 23, 1792, in an extraordinary and lengthy letter to Washington, Jefferson spelled out all of his mounting apprehensions about what Hamilton and the Federalists, including Adams, were up to. Hamilton had organized a "corrupt squadron of paper dealers" that had bought off the Congress. This squadron had the "ultimate object" of preparing "the way for a change from the present republican form of government, to that of a monarchy, of which the English constitution is to be the model." Indeed, "the Monarchical federalists" with their program had threatened to separate the Union into northern and southern parts. They had broadly construed the Constitution for their own ends and had interpreted "the new government merely as a stepping stone to monarchy." Only Washington himself, said Jefferson, held the country together, and thus he must stay on for a second term.[68]

By 1792 THE REPUBLICAN INTEREST IN the Congress had spilled out into the country and had become the Republican Party, organized to win elections, with Jefferson and Madison as its leaders. But the emergence of this Republican Party, which eventually became the Jeffersonian Democratic-Republican Party, did not yet signify modern party politics. Politics in the 1790s retained much of its eighteenth-century character. It was still very much a personal and elitist business—resting on friendship, private alliances, personal conversations, letter writing, and intrigue. Such politics was regarded as the prerogative of gentry-aristocrats who presumably had sufficient reputations to gather supporters and followers. Although no one as yet thought parties were a healthy thing in a republic, some were coming to realize that they might be impossible to avoid.

The two parties that emerged were something other than modern political parties. Neither accepted the legitimacy of the other and neither saw itself as permanent. The Federalists did not even think of themselves as a party. They were the government, the administration, not a party. The Republicans did call themselves a party, but they claimed they were only a temporary organization, like the Whigs in the 1760s designed to combat the Tories. They assumed that once they had displaced the "monocrats," the "Eastern men," and the "British party"—the terms they applied to the Federalists—they could safely disband. For their part, the Federalists saw their Republican opponents as illegitimate threats to order, labeling them "Jacobins," the "Virginia party," or the "French party."

Jefferson, who described his followers as "the Friends of the People," was pleased by the 1792 elections for Congress, which, he told Thomas Pinckney, the American minister to Britain, had "produced a decided majority in favor of the republican interest." He thought the Federalist interest in the country had peaked and that beginning with the next session of Congress in 1793, the government would "subside into the true principles of the Constitution."[69]

For his part, Adams could only express his astonishment "at the blind Spirit of Party which has Seized on the whole Soul of this Jefferson. There is not a Jacobin in France more devoted to Faction." Jefferson realized that some members of the new Republican Party wanted to deprive Adams of the vice presidency in the election of 1792. They had seized upon the election of the vice president as a proper way of "expressing the public sense on the doctrines of the Monocrats." Jefferson therefore knew that there would be "a strong vote against Mr. Adams, but the strength of his personal worth and his services will I think prevail over the demerit of his political creed."[70]

Although Adams complained constantly of the impotence of the vice presidency—"my Country," he said, "has in its Wisdom contrived for me, the most insignificant Office that ever the Invention of Man contrived or his Imagination conceived"—he was proud of his having achieved the second office in the land, and he knew too that it was the stepping-stone to the presidency.[71]

In the election of 1792 Washington again received every possible electoral vote, 132, with Adams gaining 77 votes for the second-place position, elected this time by what Jefferson called "a great majority."[72] On behalf of the newly formed Republican Party, 50 electors, including all 21 of Virginia's votes, supported Governor George Clinton of New York. Jefferson received 4 votes from Kentucky, and would have received 21 more if the electors of Virginia could have voted for both him and Washington; but the Constitution required that one of the two votes each elector cast be for a person outside his own state.[73]

This competition between Adams and Jefferson for the vice presidency in 1792 strained their relationship but didn't break it. In February 1793, Adams informed Abigail that "Mr. Jefferson was polite enough to accompany me" to a meeting of the American Philosophical Society, to which Adams had been newly elected; "so you see," he told Abigail, "we are still upon Terms." He didn't perceive that Jefferson's Philosophical Society had "any great superiority" over his own American Academy of Arts and Science in Boston, "except in the President." Of course, Adams was playing at being modest, since he had helped found the American Academy in 1780 and in 1793 was its president.[74]

Adams even contributed twenty dollars to support Jefferson's dream of a proposed scientific expedition into the West. As vice president of the American Philosophical Society, Jefferson had enthusiastically helped organize this western expedition to be conducted by the French botanist André Michaux, but unfortunately it never came off.

Instead, Edmond Genet, the French minister to the United States, persuaded Michaux to join up with some Kentucky forces and liberate Louisiana from Spain. As secretary of state, Jefferson could scarcely endorse such a venture against a foreign state. But, he noted, with his usual finesse in making fine distinctions, Genet communicated these filibustering plans to him, "not as Secy. of state, but as Mr. Jeff." He told Genet that Michaux would have to travel as a private citizen and not as a French consul, as Genet wanted. Jefferson warned that if Michaux and the Kentucky soldiers were caught taking up arms against a friendly country, they might be hanged. "Leaving out that article," he coolly told Genet, he "did not care what insurrection should be excited in Louisiana."[75]

Adams continued to suggest that all Jefferson's enthusiasm for the French Revolution stemmed from his burden of personal debts. Because of all "his French Dinners and Splendid Living," he had run further into debt and was being forced to sell his furniture and horses. Adams wished "somebody would pay his Debt of seven Thousand Pounds to Britain and the Debts of his Country men," meaning his fellow Virginians, and then, said Adams, "his Passions would subside, his Reason return, and the whole Man and his whole State become good Friends of the Union and its Govt."[76]

BUT ADAMS KNEW THE PROBLEMS facing the country were really more serious than Jefferson's debts. The conflict that was emerging was not simply between elite members of the cabinet or the administration; it reached deep into the society and involved tens if not hundreds of thousands of people. Through parades, festivals, songs, political societies, and the unprecedented proliferation of newspapers, the populace was making itself felt as never before, and the public "out of doors" took on a heightened significance. Jefferson was delighted by these new expressions of popular politics. "Our constituents," he told Madison, "seeing that the government does not express their mind, perhaps rather leans the other way, are coming forward to express it themselves."[77]

Adams, like other Federalists, was alarmed by the spread of popular politics, especially by the emergence of self-created Democratic-Republican societies existing outside of the formal institutions of government.[78] He realized that the new American government was "still but an Experiment." Elective politics being as licentious as it was, he could not help but feel that the United States might eventually have to resort to some hereditary offices. When he saw the pressure that Hamilton as secretary of the treasury was under from the Congress, he wondered "whether the Ministers of state under an elective Executive will not be overborne, by an elective Legislature."[79] But most despairing to Adams were the "Personal hatreds and Party Animosities" that consumed the capital. The

"Altercations" between the followers of the two leading ministers had spilled out into the streets, he told Abigail, harming the reputations of both Hamilton and Jefferson. "Ambition is imputed to both, and the Moral Character of both Suffered in the Scrutiny."[80]

When Adams learned of the killings and upheavals in France, he could only express astonishment that Louis XVI and Jefferson's liberal friends—Lafayette, La Rochefaucauld, and others—"should have had So Little Penetration as to believe that the late Constitution [of 1791] could long endure." He thought his fellow citizens were much too enthusiastic in their support of the French Revolution. Even before hearing of Louis XVI's execution, which took place in January 1793, he expressed little hope for the outcome of the Revolution. Indeed, in a conversation with Jefferson and Edmund Randolph, Adams, according to Jefferson's notes, launched into one of his usual diatribes that "men could never be governed but *by force*," and that "neither virtue, prudence, wisdom nor anything else sufficed to restrain their passions." Adams predicted that the French revolutionaries would create and demolish one constitution after another, hanging each successive group of constitution-makers, "until force could be brought into place to restrain them." Sooner or later, he said, the French people would find themselves so exhausted and so irritated that they would "unite in a military Government for the defense of their Persons and Property."[81]

When Adams did finally learn of Louis XVI's death, which suddenly dampened many Americans' enthusiasm for the Revolution, he emphasized once again his pessimistic view of human nature and the constant dangers of uncontrolled power. "Majorities, banishing, confiscating, massacring, guillotining Minorities, has been the whole History of the French Revolution," which he had "told them would be the Case in three long Volumes before they began—But they would not believe me."[82]

Although Adams had come to realize that Jefferson had become the ideological leader of a party passionately committed to the French Revolution and opposed to the Federalist administration, he scarcely knew the half of it. If he could have read Jefferson's letter of January 3, 1793, to his protégé William Short, he would have been appalled at just how much of a fanatical ideologue Jefferson had become.

Short had written Jefferson from Europe, telling him that many of his former French friends were being guillotined. Jefferson's response was extraordinary. He told Short that he deplored the fact that some innocent lives were being lost in the struggle, but, he said, the fate of the French Revolution—indeed, "the liberty of the whole earth"—was at stake. "Was ever such a prize won with so little innocent blood?" No doubt the Revolution was devouring the lives of many of his friends, and he was hurt by that; "but rather than it should have failed, I would have seen half the earth desolated. Were there but an Adam and Eve left in every country, and left free, it would be better than as it now is." Jefferson did not see his sentiments as unusual or extreme; they were, he said, "really those of 99 in an hundred of our citizens."[83]

(Presumably this was another example of what Madison referred to as Jefferson's habit, shared by "others of great genius, . . . of expressing in strong and round terms impressions of the moment."[84])

BY 1793 THE TWO GREAT POWERS of Europe, Britain and France, were at war, locked in a titanic struggle for supremacy in the Western world. Although the Washington administration adopted a formal policy of neutrality, the two American parties, the Federalists and the Republicans, felt that they had to choose sides. While the Federalists were horrified by what was happening in France and most of them looked to England as a source of stability in a world gone mad, Jefferson and the Republicans celebrated their new sister republic, France, and passionately wished for its success.

Neither Hamilton nor Jefferson wanted the United States to get involved in a European war, and both secretaries accepted Washington's Proclamation of Neutrality of April 1793. But Jefferson knew that such a policy of neutrality would in fact mean "a mere English neutrality."[85] As he told Madison, it "will prove a disagreeable pill to our friends, tho' necessary to keep us out of the calamities of a war."[86] Believing as he did in "the love of the people for the French cause and nation," Jefferson was embarrassed by the policy of neutrality that he had supported, especially since France and the United States had an alliance dating from 1778.

Although Vice President Adams insisted that "a Neutrality, absolute Neutrality is our only hope," Jefferson immediately began to distance himself from the proclamation. Jefferson, who, as one British observer noted, had "a degree of finesse about him, which at first is not discernable," took great pains to tell his friends that he had not written the proclamation, explaining that at least he had been able to have the word "neutrality" omitted from it. Thus the actual proclamation stated only that the United States would "pursue a conduct friendly and impartial towards the belligerent powers."[87] Yet this Jeffersonian nicety scarcely satisfied the most avid Republicans, who believed that the cause of France was the cause of republicanism everywhere.

Naturally the leaders of each of the warring powers looked to the respective American parties for support. Just as the French saw the Republicans as fervent advocates for their Revolution, so were the British encouraged by the Federalists' many expressions of their ties with England. As one of Jefferson's American informants in England reported, the British were "confident that we wish to return to the Arms of the mother Country," and were using the writings of Vice President Adams to bolster their claims. These "Advocates of Tyrants here . . . extol our Aristocrats to the Skies, seem highly interested about who shall succeed the President—and . . . wish to have a Finger in the Business."[88]

Jefferson's position as a member of the government whose policies he strongly opposed became increasingly untenable. Having lost the battle with Hamilton over the financial program and neutrality, and eager, so he informed Hamilton's sister-in-law, "to be liberated from the hated occupation of politics" and return to "the bosom of my family, my farm and my books," he finally informed Washington that he would resign as secretary of state on December 31, 1793, and return to Monticello.[89] He told the president that every day he had become "more and more convinced that neither my talents, tone of mind, nor time of life fit me."[90]

He had been thinking about retiring for over a year, but delayed only because Washington had urged him to remain in office.

Adams had mixed feelings when he learned of Jefferson's plans. He told Abigail that he had "so long been in habit of thinking well of [Jefferson's] Abilities and general good dispositions" that he could not but have some regret at the secretary of state's resignation. But he added that Jefferson's "Want of Candour, his obstinate Prejudices both of Aversion and Attachment: his real Partiality in Spite of his Pretensions and his low notions about many Things," including having a "soul poisoned with Ambition," made it difficult for Adams to weep over Jefferson's leaving Philadelphia. In a letter to his son John Quincy, Adams went into great detail speculating about all the reasons why Jefferson might have decided to retire. In his mind, every one of Jefferson's motives was dark and dirty. Jefferson couldn't support his luxurious style of living on his salary. His heavy debts meant that he did not want to spend his private income on public service. As secretary of state, he found it awkward having the French minister, Citizen Genet, celebrate Thomas Paine's principles, since those principles were his principles. Moreover, "he could not rule the Roast in the Ministry." And the "Subtlest Beast" of all, said Adams, was Jefferson's ambition, which he concealed from himself. By retiring, said Adams, Jefferson hoped to gain a reputation as a "humble, modest, meek Man, wholly without ambition or Vanity," which would then set him up to be called back to Philadelphia as president.[91]

By the time Jefferson actually left for Monticello, Adams was ready to wish "a good riddance of bad ware." He only hoped that retirement would cool Jefferson's temper and make his principles more reasonable. He knew the man had talent and perhaps integrity, "but his mind is now poisoned with Passion Prejudice and Faction."[92]

Despite his harsh view of Jefferson's character and motives, Adams wrote to him, congratulating him on his retirement. He envied him, he said, being on his plantation, "out of the hearing of the Din of Politicks and the Rumours of War." He enclosed a book on Swiss politics, perhaps as something of a peace offering.[93]

Eager to maintain the relationship, Jefferson quickly answered, and, commenting on the issues in the book Adams had sent him having to do with competing claims between the French-speaking Pays de Vaud and the German-speaking city of Berne, declared that these claims were "on grounds which I fancy we have taught the world to set little store by. The rights of one generation will scarcely be considered hereafter as depending on the paper transactions of another," a reference to his idea, which he had expressed to Madison in 1789, that the earth belongs in usufruct to the living.[94]

With his habit of turning a conversation into an argument, Adams took issue with this remark, pointing out, as Madison had in 1789, some of its impracticalities. "The Social Compact and the Laws," said Adams, "must be reduced to Writing. Obedience to them becomes a national Habit and they cannot be changed but by Revolutions which are costly Things." Then he dryly added, to the man who had a reputation for loving revolutions, "Men will be too Œconomical of their blood and Property to have recourse to them very frequently." He ended by saying to Jefferson that if he had "Your Plantation and your Labourers," he too might think of retiring and escaping from the corruption of Philadelphia.[95]

Adams had not gotten over his anger at Jefferson and said so in conversations with people, including the British minister in Philadelphia. He and Jefferson kept up a businesslike relationship in the mid-1790s, exchanging several letters with each other annually, usually prompted by some common request from a foreigner. Business or not, Adams didn't hide his feelings about the foolishness of the French Revolution—"Reasoning has been all lost. Passion, Prejudice, Interest, Necessity has governed, and will govern, and a Century must roll away before any permanent and quiet System will be established."[96]

For his part Jefferson kept repeating how much he enjoyed being tranquilly retired and how he felt about politics—"a subject I never loved, and now hate." And in extolling the greatness of America's experiment in government, he managed to suggest to Adams that he was "sure, from the honesty of your heart, you join me in detestation of the corruption of the English government," adding that no one in his right mind, and certainly not Adams, would want that English system introduced into America.[97]

Inserting these little digs in their letters, knowing they would irritate, indicates that the warm friendship that the two revolutionaries had enjoyed in the 1780s was gone.

PERHAPS MORE THAN ANYTHING ELSE, Adams's attitude toward the French Revolution divided him from Jefferson and other Republicans. In a conversation with Senator John Taylor of Virginia and Senator John Langdon of New Hampshire in 1794, Adams declared that the people of France were too ignorant and corrupt to sustain republican government. According to Taylor, who kept notes of the discussion, Adams went on to predict that America would eventually go the way of Europe and that Taylor and the other Republicans would sooner or later have to acknowledge that "no government could long exist, or that no people could be happy, without an hereditary first magistrate, and an hereditary senate."[98]

Jefferson's excessive enthusiasm for the French Revolution was matched by his intense hatred of Britain. In fact, he seems to have generated his identity as an American from his loathing of England—understandably so, since the Americans and the English had once been one people but were now presumably two. It was not easy to get Americans to think of themselves as a distinct people. John Jay, who was three-eighths French and five-eighths Dutch, without any English ancestry whatsoever, nevertheless had declared in *Federalist* No. 2 that the Americans were "a people descended from the same ancestors, speaking the same language, professing the same religion, attached to the same principles of government, [and] very similar in their manners and customs."

How could such a people differentiate themselves from the people of the former mother country? How could they become a nation? In Jefferson's case, hating the British helped to sustain his sense of American nationalism. By contrast, Adams shared little of Jefferson's loathing of the British, and like many Federalists, he was proud of his English heritage. He told Joseph Priestley, the English scientist and Unitarian minister, that he couldn't imagine any Englishman wanting to destroy "the sublime and beautiful fabric of the English Constitution." It would mean the end of "their liberties and Property."[99]

With Jefferson's hatred of Britain and passion for the French Revolution growing ever more extreme, his relationship with Adams was bound to deteriorate. He had no sympathy for those Federalists opposed to the French Revolution; they were, he said, "conspirators against human liberty."[100] Whenever he thought about all those European tyrants, those "scoundrels," who were attacking France and resisting the spread of the French Revolution, his blood boiled. He could only hope that France's eventual triumph would "bring at length kings, nobles and priests to the scaffolds which they have been so long deluging with human blood."[101]

With Jefferson's followers rejoicing over the Revolution—parading and singing the "Marseillaise," passing liberty caps around, and calling one another "citizen" to emphasize the egalitarianism of republicanism— Adams and other Federalists could only shake their heads in despair. They feared, as Adams said, that the "Anarchy, Licentiousness and Despotism" of the French Revolution were being brought to America.[102]

Late in his life, Adams vividly recalled the frenzied atmosphere of "Terrorism" that ran through the nation's capital in the 1790s: "Ten thousand People in the Streets of Philadelphia, day after day, threatened to drag Washington out of his House and effect a Revolution in the Government, or compel it to declare War in favour of the French Revolution, and against England."[103]

THE REPUBLICANS IN THE CONGRESS were certainly eager to use the power of American trade to change British policy. Since three-quarters of all American exports and imports were exchanged with the former mother country, Jefferson and the other Republicans thought the British were susceptible to American pressure and that they might be able to use trade restrictions to break up Britain's navigation system. Relying on the arguments set forth by Jefferson in his December 1793 report to

Congress on the state of America's foreign commerce—arguments in favor of free trade that went back to the model treaty of 1776—the Republicans in Congress in early 1794 demanded that Britain agree to neutral rights and to commercial reciprocity with the United States. If Britain refused, the United States would retaliate with tariffs and trade restrictions.

Although trade with America constituted only one-sixth of Britain's total commerce, the Republican leaders nevertheless assumed that American commerce was absolutely vital to Great Britain. If the United States ceased buying luxuries from Britain, British manufacturers would be thrown out of work, riots would follow, and the British government would be compelled to capitulate. Consequently, the Republican leaders did not expect their commercial retaliation to result in war. "If it does," said Jefferson, "we will meet it like men: but it may not bring on war, and then the experiment will have been a happy one." And America will have given "the world still another useful lesson, by shewing to them other modes of punishing injuries than by war, which is as much a punishment to the punisher as the sufferer."[104]

The experiment Jefferson referred to was part of the Republican dream that embargoes and commercial restrictions could become alternatives to war. Enlightened liberals in the eighteenth century assumed that war was the consequence of aggrandizing monarchs. The needs of kings—the requirements of their bloated bureaucracies, their standing armies, their marriage alliances, their restless dynastic ambitions—lay behind the prevalence of war. Eliminate monarchy and all its accouterments, Jefferson and other Republicans believed, and war itself would be eliminated.

A world of republican states would encourage a different kind of diplomacy, a peace-loving diplomacy—one based not on the brutal struggle for power of conventional diplomacy but on the natural concert of the commercial interests of the people of the various nations. If the people of the various nations were left alone to exchange goods freely among themselves—without the corrupting interference of selfish monarchical courts, irrational dynastic rivalries, and the secret double-dealing diplomacy of the past—then, it was hoped, international politics would become republicanized, pacified, and ruled by commerce alone. This kind of thinking was what made the stakes behind the success of the French Revolution so high.

Adams and the other Federalists had different assumptions about the world. Ever since the failure to sign commercial treaties with many European states in the mid-1780s, Adams had lost faith in the utopian dreams of 1776. Force was all that worked in the world. And far from yearning to republicanize Europe, Adams was opposed to the "Fanaticism of the times" that was encouraging "the present Spirit of Crusade against European kings." Republican elections simply didn't work well in Europe, and people were discovering "that unbridled Majorities, are as tyrannical and cruel as unlimited Despots." He was convinced that "the great Nations of Europe must and will return to hereditary elections or become barbarians."[105]

With such views Adams, like other Federalists, was opposed to the Republicans' commercial measures. The Federalists realized cutting off trade with Britain would unsettle the economy and undermine Hamilton's entire financial program. Financing the funded national debt was dependent on the customs duties levied on foreign imports, most of which were British. The Republicans were able to get their restrictive measures through the House, but they failed in the Senate when Adams broke a tie with a negative vote.

The Republicans' attempt to use trade restrictions in order, as Madison put it, to attack Britain "thro' her commerce" was stymied. Instead, President Washington decided "to supplicate for peace" by sending John Jay in 1794 to negotiate a commercial treaty with Britain, a decision that Adams wholeheartedly supported. "May the gentle Zephers waft him to his Destination," he told Abigail, "and the Blessings of Heaven succeed his virtuous Endeavors to preserve Peace." He concluded that Jay's negotiations with Britain were "temperate, grave, and wise, . . . and the Results judicious."[106]

Jefferson and his fellow Republicans could not have disagreed more. In fact, nothing the Federalists did in the 1790s aroused more Republican anger than this treaty with Great Britain. Protests and riots broke out everywhere, and Jay was burned in effigy in nearly every city up and down the continent. Jefferson said that the treaty "excited a more general disgust than any public transaction since the days of our independence."[107]

Despite America's tilt toward Britain represented by Jay's Treaty (as the agreement came to be known), Jefferson nevertheless looked forward to an ultimate French victory over Britain. In fact, in 1795 he believed that the French were just about to invade England. So sure was he of French success that he was tempted, he said, to leave Monticello and travel to London the following year in order to dine there with the victorious French general and "hail the dawn of liberty and republicanism in that island."[108]

ADAMS THOUGHT THAT THE French Revolution was breeding "false Notions of equality" and that these were being picked up by "the Democrats of this Day" and undermining the stability of American society. These developments inspired Adams to write a series of letters to his son Charles on just what "the modern Doctrine of Equality" really meant.

Declarations of equality in the state constitutions and the Declaration of Independence meant "not a Phisical but a moral Equality." Of course, common sense, said Adams, told us that we were not equal in fact, "not all equally tall, Strong, wise handsome, active," but we were equal in the sight of God, equal in "Rights and Obligations, nothing more." But this emphasis on moral equality in so many documents should not blind us to the actual inequalities among individuals, inequalities that were present from birth. These physical inequalities among men in a state of nature were infinite. They were "so obvious so determinate and so unalterable, that no Man is absurd enough to deny them." They "lay the Foundation for Inequalities of Wealth Power Influence and Importance, throughout human Life. Laws and Government have neither the Power nor the Right to change them." Even "the Simplest democracy" would have inequalities. "A few will Start forth more Eloquent more Wise, and more brave than the rest and acquire a superiour Influence Reputation & Power." Inequality was inevitable in any developed society. Once the arts and sciences, manufactures, and commerce were admitted into the society, inequalities of property would naturally arise and were impossible to eradicate. Plato had tried to equalize property in his commonwealth and failed.[109]

Why were Jefferson's followers so eager to deny the reality of inequality? If they were "so anxious lest Aristocracy should take root," Adams suggested to his son, why didn't they "eradicate all the seeds of it," including the use of titles? He had been burned so badly over his preoccupation with titles in 1789 that he couldn't pass up an opportunity to mock his opponents' desire to do away with them. If the Republicans hated titles so much, why not address the Speaker of the House as "Freddy Mulenbourg" (Frederick Muhlenberg)? Why not call the Republican congressman from Virginia "Billy Giles" (William Branch Giles)? Insurgents, said Adams, always sought to simplify society and level people. During Shays' Rebellion in 1786 and the Whiskey Rebellion in 1794, for example, "Gaffer and Gammar, Mr and Mrs were laid aside." Once the insurgents have destroyed everything, "We may hope that We shall be out of Danger of Titles and Aristocracy." He told his son that "this must be quite a Secret between you and me: but I will laugh a little with my Children at least, at the Follies of the Times."[110]

To the end of his life Adams always felt a deep need to emphasize the natural inequality of people. Somehow or other it became an explanation and a vindication of his own extraordinary rise from mediocrity. Jefferson, of course, never felt such a need.

NINE

THE PRESIDENT vs.
THE VICE PRESIDENT

WHEN WASHINGTON ASSUMED the presidency in
1789 many people, including Thomas Jefferson, thought that
he might serve for life. That was why Jefferson claimed that
the office of the president resembled a Polish king—an elective monarch,
something that was not out of the question in the eighteenth century. As
James Wilson, one of the initial justices of the Supreme Court, noted, in
the distant past "crowns, in general, were originally elective."[1] But Washington had no intention of serving for life. He had tried to retire in 1792,
but was talked out of it. But by 1796 he was determined to leave the office
at the end of his second term. That posed an ominous threat to the Union.
As the Spanish minister pointed out, Washington's special status in the
eyes of the people had saved the nation from "internal dissention." But
that could not last, "because it seems impossible that there could be found
another man so beloved of all. . . . Disunion will follow."[2]

Rumors of Washington's stepping down left Adams, who was clearly
not beloved by all, excited and nervous, and he sent off a series of anxious
letters to Abigail that she was to show no one. He told her that they
faced a momentous decision—"Either We must enter upon Ardours

more trying than any ever yet experienced; or retire to Quincy Farmers for Life." He assumed he was the "Heir Apparent" to the presidency, but he was not sure what to do politically. By attempting to represent Adams "as a Man of Moderation," the "Southern Gentry," he said, were playing "a very artful Game." Although they conceded that Adams was "inclined to limited Monarchy and somewhat Attached to the English," they claimed he was much less so than John Jay or Alexander Hamilton. Adams thought that this insidious southern scheme was designed to have him remain as vice president, "provided the Northern Gentlemen would consent that Jefferson should be president."[3]

This, however, was the one thing he was sure of: he was "determined," he said, "not to serve under Jefferson." He could never be vice president under someone other than Washington, "especially if that other should entertain sentiments so opposite to mine as to endanger the Peace of the Nation." Given the nature of the electoral process, where the person who received the most votes became president and the runner-up became vice president, having the two chief executive officials possess contrasting political views was quite possible and perilous. "It will be a dangerous Crisis in public affairs," he warned, "if the President and Vice President should be in opposite Boxes."[4]

Neither Adams nor Jefferson had anticipated the United States becoming riven by parties. Jefferson thought that allegiance to a party would be "the last degradation of a free and moral agent," a denial of being an independent and disinterested citizen. "If I could not go to heaven but with a party," he said, "I would not go there at all." Adams agreed. Parties were "the greatest political Evil" imaginable. He dreaded nothing as much as "a Division of the Republick into two great Parties, each arranged under its Leader, and concerting Measures in opposition to each other."[5]

Yet that was precisely what was happening. By February 1796, Adams saw that "the Electioneering Campaign is opened already," and his worst fears of "the silly and the wicked Game" were being realized. Jefferson as "'the good Patriot, Statesman, and Philosopher'" was being "held up as the Successor." "The Accursed Spirit which actuates a vast Body of People," including the anti-Federalists, desperate debtors, and "frenchified Tools," would, if victorious, "murder all good Men among Us and destroy all the Wisdom & Virtue of the Country."[6] Despite all this—despite his dread of parties and his belief that politics had become just a "Game" that he was weary of and actually not very good at—Adams nevertheless didn't "know how I could live out of it."[7]

Jefferson, who by contrast was very good at the game of politics, never admitted even privately that he enjoyed it; in fact, he always denied having any great yearning for political office. In his "younger years" he may have had a "spice of ambition," he told James Madison in 1795, but that "has long since evaporated." To Madison's entreaties that he come out of retirement and lead the Republicans, he said that his two dozen years of service meant that the public no longer had any claim on him.[8] Yet this repeated insistence that he wanted nothing more than to be home with his family and his books may not have been entirely honest. He later confessed to his daughter Mary that those years of retirement from the public, between 1793 and 1797, were the most depressing of his life. Withdrawing from the world had led to "an anti-social & misanthropic state of mind." Ultimately, he was every bit as ambitious as Adams.[9]

Although Jefferson never acknowledged that he wanted to become president, neither did he ever pretend, publicly or privately, to be a disinterested spectator standing above all parties. If the two parties were simply divided over their greed for office, as in England, then not taking sides might make sense. "But," he told William Branch Giles of Virginia, "where the principle of difference is as substantial and as strongly pronounced as between the republicans and the Monocrats of our country, I hold it as honorable to take a firm and decided part, and as immoral to pursue a middle line, as between the parties of Honest men, and Rogues, into which every country is divided."[10] This, of course, was precisely the opposite of Adams's position, which always sought to maintain a middle line above parties.

SINCE WASHINGTON HAD BEEN UNANIMOUSLY acclaimed as president in 1788 and 1792, the election of 1796 became the first contest for the presidency in American history. It was conducted by two rival political parties in a culture that disparaged and condemned political parties and partisanship. And these two parties, which had substantial numbers of followers, were led by two famous revolutionaries and two former friends, Adams and Jefferson.

"Led" is a misnomer, for neither man campaigned for the presidency in any modern sense. Neither left his home to meet people and shake hands, and neither made speeches or wrote essays on his own behalf. Both thought in traditional terms that a gentleman should never directly seek an office, only be called to it. Because the Federalists were making "continual insinuations in the public papers" that the former secretary of state had secret desires to become president, Jefferson believed that it would have been indecent even to acknowledge these insinuations. But now that the Republicans themselves had begun urging him to seek the presidency, Jefferson told Madison that he at last felt free to declare that the question of the presidency was "for ever closed with me." It was important that this be clearly understood so that the Republicans not divide their votes, "which," he said, "might be fatal to the Southern interest"—a revealing slip, later altered to read "the Republican interest," that showed that Jefferson and many other Republicans in 1795 were thinking very much in sectional terms. Indeed, Jefferson was increasingly coming to identify the Federalists with northern values—finance, paper money, and religious fanaticism.[11]

Madison became fearful that pressuring Jefferson too much might make him even more adamant in his refusal to consider the presidency, and thus he cut off all communication with his friend for six months. Adams likewise resisted telling Federalist visitors of any plans he might have for the presidency. When they suggested that Hamilton might make a good vice president and hinted that support for Adams might depend on his attitude toward the funding system, he recorded in his diary that he remained "wholly silent."[12]

Washington had planned on announcing his retirement in June 1796, but Hamilton urged him to "hold the thing until the last moment" in September, which would hinder the Republicans' electioneering and give the Federalists time to undermine Jefferson's candidacy. Ironically, the Federalists' continual attacks on Jefferson in the press as the silent leader of the opposition elevated his status as a presidential candidate. When Washington's Farewell Address was published in September 1796, the leading Republican newspaper, the Philadelphia *Aurora,* declared that the two obvious candidates to succeed Washington were Thomas Jefferson and John Adams. The choice was now clear: "Whether we shall have at the head of our executive a steadfast friend of the Rights of the People, or an advocate for hereditary power and distinctions."[13]

Although the Republicans by 1796 obviously wanted Jefferson for president, many of the Federalists weren't sure they preferred Adams for president. Hamilton and several other Federalist leaders thought he was too irascible and indiscreet and doubted whether he was a firm supporter of the Bank of the United States and the government's financial program. Hoping to cut into support for Jefferson, Hamilton favored a southerner as an alternative to Adams, first suggesting Patrick Henry, and after some second thoughts, Thomas Pinckney of South Carolina, the diplomat who had recently negotiated an important treaty with Spain.

Hamilton and other Federalists were fearful of Jefferson's being elected to either the presidency or the vice presidency. If Jefferson became president, said Oliver Wolcott Jr., the Connecticut Federalist who had replaced Hamilton as secretary of the treasury in 1795, he would "innovate upon and fritter away the Constitution." But, continued Wolcott, Jefferson as vice president might be even worse. "He would become the rallying point of faction and French influence," and "without any responsibility, he would . . . divide, and undermine, and finally subvert the rival administration."[14] Better to support Pinckney as president, some Federalists declared, than to see Jefferson in any high office, even if it cost Adams the presidency.

Adams heard these rumors and was appalled at the idea that Hamilton was intriguing "to give Pinckney a Sly slide over my head." The idea that Jefferson might come in ahead of him was disturbing enough, he said, but that "such an unknown being as Pinckney" might become president, "trampling on the bellies of hundreds of other men infinitely his superiors in talents, services, and reputation," made him afraid for the safety of the nation. The possibility of a nobody like Pinckney becoming president made him change his earlier opinion about Jefferson as chief executive. "I had rather hazard my little Venture in the ship to the pilot-age of Jefferson," he told Abigail in mid-December 1796, "than that of Pinckney." Adams was coming to realize that he disliked some Federal-ists more than he did his former friend, despite the fact that Jefferson was being hailed as the leader of the opposition Republican Party.[15]

The campaign was rancorous, with the followers of Jefferson and Ad-ams using the writings of each against him. In an attempt to weaken Jef-ferson's support among southern slaveholders, Federalists drew on his antislavery remarks in his *Notes on the State of Virginia* and on his 1791 correspondence with the black mathematician Benjamin Banneker, in which he referred to "our black brethren" and his desire to be shown that they had "talents equal to those of other colours of men." The Federalists also used Jefferson's comments on religion in the *Notes*—"It does me no injury for my neighbor to say there are twenty gods or no god; it neither picks my pocket nor breaks my leg"—to accuse him of being hostile to Christianity. Other Federalists criticized his soft, sentimental, and "wom-anish" affection for France, his cowardice as governor during the Revolu-tion, and—in contrast to Adams, whose public service was untiring—his neglect of his public duties by his retirement to Monticello. Jefferson, de-clared the Federalists, was merely a soft and weak intellectual—someone perhaps suited to be a college professor or the head of a philosophical so-ciety, "but certainly not the first magistrate of a great nation."[16]

In the case of Adams, the Republicans had more writings to work with, since Adams had published so much. His *Defence of the Constitu-tions of Government of the United States of America* had been reissued in London in 1794, an edition that reached the United States just in time to be used against Adams in the campaign. The Republicans claimed that his volumes were a "Eulogium of Monarchy and the British," writ-ten, they noted, "whilst Minister at the Court of London." In the *De-fence*, the Republicans asserted, Adams had questioned the whole idea of popular government. He had admitted that elections were fine, if "soberly made." But since electing high officers was such a "hazardous experiment," so liable to be disturbed by parties, factions, drunkenness, and bribes, the people sooner or later would discover that the electoral process was not working well. They would find that the only recourse they had was to reduce the frequency of elections by lengthening the terms of the chief magistrate and senators gradually "till they become for life; and if this is not found to be an adequate remedy, there will remain no other but to make them hereditary."[17] Adams had expressed such antipopular sentiments so frequently that denial was impossible. Not that he ever tried. But people had heard his eccentric views so often that perhaps they had begun discounting them.

Adams was in fact pleased that so many people were paying attention to his *Defence,* even if it was for the purpose of criticizing him. In a hundred years, he said, "it would not have been so much read" as it was during the election campaign. A new third edition was on the way, and he told Abigail, with his usual self-protective sarcasm, that he expected "it will be got by Heart by All Americans who can read."[18]

The electors met in their respective state capitals in December 1796 and, although the ballots would not be certified until they were opened in February 1797, the results began leaking out. In mid-December Madison was preparing his friend Jefferson for the probability that he would become vice president. "It seems *essential,*" he told his fellow Virginian, "that you should not refuse the station which is likely to be your lot." Besides, Madison said, serving with your former friend Adams as his vice president "may have a valuable effect on his councils," especially in foreign policy and America's relations with France, which were verging on war. Adams would not necessarily follow the domestic policies of the Washington administration either. His censures of the paper systems and his anger at the efforts of New York to put Pinckney above him had separated him from "the British faction." In addition, Madison told Jefferson, Adams was now speaking of you "in friendly terms" and would "no doubt be soothed by your acceptance of a place subordinate to him." But, he said, all these calculations might be worth nothing in the face of Adams's "political principles and prejudices."[19]

In the final tally Adams received seventy-one electoral votes, mostly from New England and New York and New Jersey. Jefferson was next with sixty-eight, all from Pennsylvania and the states in the South. Pinckney received fifty-nine votes and Aaron Burr, the presumed Republican vice presidential candidate, received thirty, but only one vote from Virginia. Because personal ambitions, local interests, friendships, and sectional ties tended to override national party loyalties, the election was confused and chaotic. The Constitution provided for the electors to select any two candidates that suited them, even if they were from opposing parties, as long as they were from two different states. So in Pennsylvania one elector voted for both Jefferson and Pinckney. In Maryland an elector voted for Adams and Jefferson. And all the electors of South Carolina voted for both Jefferson and Pinckney. Despite these examples of crossing party lines, however, eight of sixteen states did vote a straight Adams-Pinckney or Jefferson-Burr ticket. Yet, as the vote of the South Carolina electors suggests, the election in fact reflected more of a sectional than a party split.

Adams believed that the "narrow Squeak" of three votes by which he had beaten Jefferson was humiliating, and he never got over it.[20] He was especially upset by the prospect of men he considered his friends voting against him. When he learned that Thomas McKean, the chief justice of Pennsylvania, had voted for Jefferson, he was hurt. "All Confidence between Men and Men," he told Abigail, "is suspended for a time." In fact, he hated the whole process of elections, believing it a disgrace to republicanism. Hearing in the Senate chamber that some electors had actually voted for George Clinton, Adams gritted his teeth and exclaimed, "Damn 'em' Damn 'em' Damn 'em' you see that an elective government will not do."[21]

THE COUNTRY WAS INITIALLY excited by the election of the Federalist John Adams as president and the Republican Thomas Jefferson as vice president. It seemed to promise an end to factionalism and a new era of good feelings. Since both men were thought to have a mutual respect for each other, it seemed possible that they might renew their friendship and restore the revolutionaries' dream of nonpartisan government.[22] During the campaign Adams had scarcely thought of Jefferson as his opponent. He had directed his anger more at Hamilton, who, he said, was "a proud Spirited, conceited, aspiring Mortal always pretending to Morality, with as debauched Morals as old Franklin who is more his Model than any one I know." Comparing him with Franklin was about as damning a comment about Hamilton as Adams could have made.[23] Having a common enemy in Hamilton made a reconciliation of Adams and Jefferson appear all the more promising.

Abigail was certainly pleased by Jefferson's election as vice president. Despite his support for Tom Paine and his being "frequently mistaken in Men & Measures," he was, she said, not "an insincere or a corruptable Man." She had "not a Doubt but all the Discords may be tuned to harmony by the Hand of a skillful Artist."[24] Although John Adams was certainly no skillful artist in politics, probably no president could have created political harmony in 1797. Jefferson realized that Washington was getting out at the right moment. "The President," he told Madison, "is fortunate to get off just as the bubble is bursting, leaving others to hold the bag."[25] Certainly this premonition made Jefferson's willingness to serve under Adams more comprehensible. But neither he nor Adams foresaw just how bad things would get.

Some Republicans doubted whether Jefferson would accept the vice presidency. He had been willing to become president, but only, he told Madison, in order "to put our vessel on her republican tack before she should be thrown too much in leeward of her true principles." He had been less sure about the vice presidency, but with Adams elected as president, he no longer had any misgivings about playing a secondary role. "I am his junior in life, was his junior in Congress, his junior in the diplomatic line, his junior lately in our civil government." In addition, Jefferson believed that if Adams could be "induced to administer the government on it's true principles, and to relinquish his bias to an English constitution," he could become "the only sure barrier against Hamilton's getting in." He had written a letter to Adams to encourage these friendly feelings but had not yet sent it. He wanted Madison to look it over first.[26]

In this draft of a letter to Adams, dated December 28, 1796, Jefferson told Adams that although he had not followed the campaign closely, he knew that the press had placed him and Adams in opposition to each other. He was sure, however, that very little of this opposition "has been felt by ourselves personally." He had no doubts at all that Adams would be elected president and that he had never wished otherwise. The only way Adams could be "cheated of your succession" was through the trickery of "your arch-friend of New York." Fortunately, he himself was beyond Hamilton's reach. Secure at home in his warm berth among his friends and neighbors, he left "to others the sublime delights of riding in the storm." He declared, in one of his many self-denying comments, that "I have no ambition to govern men." All he knew was that no one would congratulate Adams for becoming president "with purer disinterestedness than myself." Jefferson left it up to Madison to decide whether or not to post this letter to Adams.[27]

Madison decided it should not be sent and outlined his reasons. Adams, he told Jefferson, already knew of Jefferson's conciliatory feelings toward his old friend and any attempt to better those feelings might make them worse. He next suggested that there was in Jefferson's draft "a general air on the letter which betrays the difficulty of your situation in writing it," and Adams might be put off by that tone. Moreover, he said, might not Jefferson's disavowing "the sublime delights of riding in the storm, etc." be misconstrued as an insult to Adams, who seemed to enjoy riding the whirlwind of politics? Madison admitted that Jefferson knew Adams's temper better than he did, but he always thought it to be "rather a ticklish one." Any attempt to play down or depreciate the partisan differences between Jefferson's backers and Adams was bound to create resentment among the Republicans. And finally, given the uncertainty of the future and the possibility that the actions of the Adams administration might generate "opposition to it from the Republican quarter," the possession of this letter by Adams, filled as it was with

Jefferson's polite expressions of confidence in Adams due to "your personal delicacy and friendship," was apt to cause "real embarrassments" in the months to come.[28]

Jefferson thanked Madison for his discretion and agreed not to send the letter. Isolated as he was at Monticello from the hurly-burly of Philadelphia politics, he had not appreciated how "an honest expression" of his feelings toward Adams might be misused. He reiterated his affection for Adams, which went back to the beginning of the Revolution. Since their return from Europe, there had been some little incidents, he said, "which were capable of affecting a jealous mind like his." Despite their political differences, however, Jefferson had not become "less sensible of the rectitude of [Adams's] heart: and I wished him to know this." He also wanted Adams to understand how pleased he was that he had become president. He informed Madison that he had written John Langdon of New Hampshire and told him the same thing: how he was willing to serve as vice president under Adams and how being secondary to Adams was natural, since he had been "secondary to him in every situation in which we ever acted together in public life for twenty years past." The reverse would have been "the novelty," and Adams would rightly have been offended by it. He was sure that his letter to Langdon would be conveyed to Adams.[29]

Actually, Madison, without telling Jefferson, had leaked another letter to Benjamin Rush, an amiable one Jefferson had written on December 17, 1796, in which he had expressed his willingness to serve under Adams, even if they should end in a tie with the same number of electoral votes, since Adams had always been his senior in every respect. Rush in turn had conveyed the contents of this letter to Adams, who was delighted. Adams excitedly told Abigail that Jefferson had written that "Mr. Adams's services have been longer more constant and more important" than his. Jefferson's letter to Madison, he told Abigail, had circulated everywhere and was "considered as Evidence of his Determination to accept [the vice presidency]—of his Friendship for me—and of his Modesty and Moderation." Adams concluded that he and Jefferson "should go on affectionately together and all would be well."[30]

. . .

AT THIS POINT BOTH MEN SEEMED emotionally ready to bury their political differences and resume the friendship that had meant so much to them in earlier years. Jefferson, however, was politically more sensitive than Adams, more willing to accept the necessity of party. Although he once had said that he disliked parties, he had become the reluctant leader of a transatlantic republican cause, a cause that was threatened by the English monarchy abroad and the Federalist monocrats at home. He and his fellow Republicans sincerely feared for the fate of their sister republic France, and thought that the destiny of the American republic was tied up with that of revolutionary France. For Jefferson the Republicans' organization as a party was essential but temporary. As soon as republicanism was firmly established in Europe and the United States, the Republican Party could wither away.

Hence, with Madison's advice very much in mind, Jefferson concluded that as the leader of an opposition party he ought not to get involved in the administration's affairs in any way. His excuse was that his participation would be constitutionally impossible. As president of the Senate, he was a "member of a legislative house" and forbidden by the Constitution to meddle in executive business.[31]

Adams was less politically astute, and for a moment he actually seemed to think that he and Jefferson might be able to collaborate in running the government. As president, he did not see himself as the leader of something called the Federalist Party. He admitted that he was a Federalist, by which he meant that he was a friend of government, of hierarchy, and of law and order. Although he was as suspicious of banks and Hamilton's financial program as Jefferson, he hated the French Revolution with a passion and thus he tilted toward England in its titanic struggle with France. That alone identified him as a Federalist and set him at odds with Jefferson and the Republicans.

All Adams had to guide him as president was his image of an independent executive set forth in his writings. Despite all his theoretical emphasis on the executive, he had actually never served in any executive capacity. He had never been a governor or a cabinet officer. Even as vice president he had not been involved in the discussions and decisions of the Washington administration.

He immediately revealed his political naïveté by retaining the members of Washington's cabinet, whose loyalties were not with him but with Hamilton. He was determined, he later claimed, "to make as few removals as possible," and certainly none "from personal malice" or "from mere Party Considerations." Besides, he recalled, Washington had asked him to keep his cabinet, and he feared that if he removed any one of them "it would turn the world upside down." According to Madison, Adams at the beginning was uncertain over whether or not he could remove his predecessor's ministers without the Senate's advice and consent. Madison suggested that either "the maxims of the British Govt. are still uppermost in his mind" or Adams believed his election was "a continuation of the same reign."[32]

Although Adams later realized that keeping Washington's cabinet members was the greatest political error of his presidency, at the time he had "no particular objections to any of them." But Jefferson understood his mistake at once. By May 1797 he knew that Adams's cabinet had been working from the outset to alienate the president from his vice president. These "Hamiltonians by whom he is surrounded," he told Elbridge Gerry, "are only a little less hostile to him than to me." He realized that these "machinations" by the followers of Hamilton were bound to affect the cordiality of his relationship with Adams, but he didn't know how to convince Adams that he wasn't trying to undermine his government. Although he realized that not knowing each other's motives "may be a source of private uneasiness with us," he was confident that neither he nor Adams would allow it to harm "our public duties."[33]

Jefferson arrived in Philadelphia on March 2, 1797, and he promptly called on Adams, who the following morning returned the call. According to Adams's recollections published in the *Boston Patriot* in 1809, he had sought out Jefferson on March 3 because he trusted him. He had been his friend for twenty-five years, sometimes in very perilous situations, and he had "always found him assiduous, laborious, and as far as I could judge, upright and faithful." They had differed over the French Revolution, but Adams said that he had no reason to think that they differed over the U.S. Constitution. He thought that the slurs and slanders of partisan politics should not prevent him from consulting someone like Jefferson, with all his experience and talent.[34]

In Jefferson's account based on notes he had taken at the time, Adams said he was glad to find Jefferson alone, for he wanted to have "a free conversation" with him. He explained that because of French seizures of American merchant ships, the situation with France had become dire and threatened to end in war. Adams wanted to send a mission at once to France and wished that Jefferson could be a member of it, but he realized that it might be improper to send the vice president abroad.[35] If so, he hoped to send Madison instead, along with two others, in a high-level commission that would represent all sections of the country.

Jefferson told Adams that his participation was out of the question. He also doubted Madison would join a mission either, given that he had turned down an earlier invitation to go abroad. Adams was disappointed, but said that he would appoint Madison anyway "and leave the responsibility on him."[36] According to Adams, he and Jefferson "parted as good friends as we had always lived."[37]

The next day, March 4, was Adams's inauguration as president, the most trying day in his life, he told Abigail. Washington attended and seemed serene and peaceful, as if he were enjoying "a Tryumph" over Adams. "Methought I heard him think Ay! I am fairly out and you fairly in! see which of Us will be happiest." But Adams knew very well the historic importance of the occasion. "The Sight of the Sun Setting full orbit and other rising tho less Splendid was a novelty." He and many others were deeply moved, with much weeping. "Exchanging Presidents without Tumult," said Adams, was no small thing.[38]

In his inaugural address Adams tried to counter some of the impressions his publications had made. It was as if he suddenly realized that as president he couldn't talk to the country in the blunt way he had in his writings. He praised the Constitution and said that there had never been "any objection to it in my mind that the Executive and Senate were not more permanent." Nor had he ever thought of "promoting any alteration" of it except as the people themselves might desire in the future and in accord with the amendment process set forth in the document. He urged that Americans encourage education and religion as "the only means of preserving our Constitution from its natural enemies, the spirit of sophistry, the spirit of party, the spirit of intrigue, the profligacy of corruption, and the pestilence of foreign influence, which is the angel of destruction to elective governments." At the end, he felt it necessary to express his "veneration for the religion of a people who profess and call themselves Christians," remarks that Jefferson would never have made. Adams apparently thought that affirming "a decent respect for Christianity" was much needed as an important qualification for public service in light of Thomas Paine's recent publication of *The Age of Reason*, which had dismissed Christianity as an absurdity.[39]

The next day Adams excitedly told Abigail that all agreed that his inauguration "taken all together . . . was the sublimest Thing ever exhibited in America." But when some high-toned Federalists criticized his address as too soft on France and the Republicans, he became indignant. "If the Federalists go to playing Pranks," he told Abigail, "I will resign the office and let Jefferson lead them to Peace, Wealth and Power if he will." He then launched into one of his characteristic outbursts against ambition and emulation, which he feared "will turn our Government topsy turvy." Although he had written endlessly about "Jealousies & Rivalries," with "Checks and Ballances as their Antidotes," never had they "stared me in the face in such horrid forms as at present."[40]

Jefferson said nothing about Adams's inaugural address. In fact, he seems to have had no misgivings whatsoever over Paine's harsh criticism of Christianity or over anything else Paine wrote. Several weeks later he received a long letter from Paine predicting the bankruptcy and likely downfall of England. Paine warned Jefferson that as vice president he had to keep an eye on Adams, for Adams had "a Natural disposition to blunder and to offend." With his bad temper, said Paine, he could "do nothing but harm."[41]

On the day following his inauguration, March 5, Adams met with his secretary of the treasury, Oliver Wolcott, and told him about his plans for sending a mission to France with Madison as a member. He was surprised to find Wolcott cool to the whole idea of a mission and especially concerned about Madison being a member. That, Wolcott said, would stir "the passions of our parties" in Congress and throughout the country, and he offered to resign.

Adams was taken aback. He consulted two other department heads, Secretary of State Timothy Pickering and Secretary of War James McHenry, and he came to realize that "the violent party spirit of Hamilton's friends" made Madison's appointment impossible. "I could not do it," he recalled, "without quarreling outright with my ministers, whom Washington's appointment had made my masters."[42]

According to Jefferson, the next day, March 6, he and Adams came away together from a dinner at Washington's house. As Jefferson tried to explain his attempts to persuade Madison to join the commission, Adams immediately became embarrassed and said that "some objections to that nomination had been raised." He was going on with excuses when the two men had to part to go to their respective residences. Adams, noted Jefferson, "never after that said one word to me on the subject, or ever consulted me as to any measures of the government." Jefferson correctly concluded that Adams in his innocence and in the enthusiasm of his inauguration had forgotten about his Federalist connections and, as he was wont to do, had allowed himself to be governed by "the feeling of the moment." But as soon as Adams had met his cabinet the next day, he had realized his mistake "and returned to his former party ways."[43]

ADAMS FELT ISOLATED IN PHILADELPHIA, with "no Society but Statesmen" and with no one he could fully trust. His vice president was no confidant, and besides, he told Abigail, who was back in Quincy, Jefferson had left for Virginia. "He is as he was," he said. What he needed was her presence. "I must go to you or you must come to me. I cannot live without you."[44]

The most pressing challenge facing the president was dealing with the deteriorating relations with France. Angered by Jay's Treaty with Great Britain, the French had begun seizing American ships and confiscating their cargoes. John Quincy Adams, the president's son, who was now minister to the Netherlands, alerted his father to France's goals in a remarkable series of letters. In 1795 France had turned the Netherlands into a satellite and renamed it the Batavian Republic and, relying on French republican sympathizers in various countries, was now seeking to expand its republican revolution elsewhere in Europe. More alarming, France had its eye on the United States as well. It was, said John Quincy, bent on undermining the Federalists and bringing about the "triumph of French party, French principles, French influence in the United States." The French government had been led to believe that "the *People* of the United States have but a feeble attachment to their Government, and will not support them in a contest with that of France." Young Adams even suggested that France planned to invade the South and, with the support of Jefferson and the Republican Party there and in the West, break up the Union and turn the United States into another puppet republic.[45]

By the time Adams took office, the French had decided to confront the United States directly. The French government refused to receive as minister Charles Cotesworth Pinckney, Thomas Pinckney's elder brother, and intensified its seizure of American ships carrying British goods.

In response, the president called for a special session of Congress for May 16, 1797, the first president to do so. Adams requested a buildup of American military forces, especially the navy, and condemned the French for trying to separate the American people from their government. Americans, he declared, must convince the French that "we are not a degraded people, humiliated under a colonial spirit of fear and sense of inferiority, fitted to be the miserable instruments of foreign influence."[46]

Jefferson was incensed by Adams's actions. He thought that Adams's calling Congress "out of season" was totally unnecessary. Convening Congress in a special session was simply an attempt by the administration "to see how far and in what line they could count on it's support." The president's speech, he told a Maryland follower, was "too bold" and actually endangered "the peace of our country."[47]

A relative of this Maryland recipient read this letter and, despite being told that he should make no improper use of it, communicated the substance of it to Adams. The president found Jefferson's comments "serious," and reason enough among "*many* others . . . to be upon my guard." Gone was his earlier confidence in his vice president. He now had "evidence of a mind, soured, yet seeking for popularity, and eaten to a honeycomb with ambition, yet weak, confused, uninformed and ignorant."[48]

Adding to Adams's awareness of the vice president's hostility was the publication in the press of a letter Jefferson had written the previous year to his Italian friend Philip Mazzei. In its translation from English to Italian to French back to English, Jefferson was quoted as describing a separation between the "Anglo-Monarchical-Aristocratic party" that dominated the government and the mass of the American citizens who were still "faithful to republican principles." The government, he said, was under the control of "apostates" who once were "Solomons in council and Sampsons in combat, but whose hair has been cut off by the whore England." Although Jefferson was embarrassed and never publicly acknowledged the letter, the Federalists were delighted with it and never ceased using it against the leader of the Republicans. The comment seemed to indict Washington most directly, but it could also be construed as a criticism of Adams. Indeed, the French émigré the Comte de Volney observed that although most Federalists were not devoted to England, many did have "a taste for its constitution and M. Adams is at the head."[49]

Hoping against hope that Jefferson in 1797 had moderated his views from what they had been a year earlier, Abigail described the Mazzei letter as something written when Jefferson "was anxious to convert all political Hereticks to French Faith." Still, she told her son John Quincy, she was sure it would "never be forgotten by the Characters traduced."[50] In his reply, John Quincy told his mother that the Mazzei letter was "more than imprudent: it shows a mind full of error, or an heart full of falsehood." But he could not believe the latter. "My old sentiments of respect veneration and attachment still hang about me with regard to that man"—evidence of how strong and warm the friendship between the Adams family and Jefferson had been in Europe. Nevertheless, said young Adams, the letter did reveal "a very weak man" and a hypocritical one. Indeed, "there could not be a stronger proof of the misrepresentations and calumnies" that lay behind recent French policy toward the United States. It showed just "how much the French depended upon an internal party in America to support and justify their treatment of us."[51]

Adams himself was anxious about the strength of Jefferson's attachment to France. He was convinced that from the beginning France had "invariably preserved a Course of Intrigue to gain an undue Influence in these states, to make Us dependent upon her, and to keep up a quarrel with England."[52] By the middle of 1797, he felt that the United States and France were on the verge of war.

Jefferson and the other Republican leaders dismissed the Federalists as warmongers, threatening a war that France did not want, and they urged delay. To Jefferson and the other Republicans, war with America's sister republic was inconceivable. It would play into the hands of the English party in the United States and destroy the republican experiment everywhere. Besides, Jefferson believed that a French invasion of Britain was imminent and that its success would solve all of America's problems with France.

Adams's earlier plans to send a commission to France now became even more urgent, and he decided on John Marshall of Virginia, Elbridge Gerry of Massachusetts, and Charles Cotesworth Pinckney, who was already in France, to make up the diplomatic commission.

By November 1797, Abigail had lost all hope for Jefferson. "He is a child," she said, "the dupe of party, . . . a Man whose Mind is so warped by prejudice, and so Blinded by Ignorance as to be unfit for the office he holds."[53] Adams himself was deeply discouraged. Congress was giving him little or no support in his dealings with France. And for over a year since his inauguration he had had no contact whatsoever with his predecessor, Washington.[54]

. . .

FOR SOMEONE LIKE JEFFERSON, who placed such a high value on politeness and social harmony, the political passions dividing the society were truly alarming. "Men who have been intimate all their lives," he lamented, "cross the street to avoid meeting and turn their heads another way, lest they should be obliged to touch their hats." He could have been speaking about his personal relations with Adams when he said that "party animosities" had "raised a wall of separation between those who differ in political sentiments."[55]

That November, the Republican majority in the House of Representatives rejected Adams's appeal to build up a naval force. Jefferson dismissed Adams's efforts to call attention to French depredations as "inflammatory," designed only to promote his desire to arm America's merchant ships. Jefferson was delighted that the merchants themselves were becoming less and less interested in arming their ships. As far as the French government itself was concerned, the Americans seemed hopelessly divided and thus no threat whatsoever.[56]

Bad as things were, Adams and Jefferson were still speaking to each other, though not intimately. Jefferson recorded a conversation he had with the president when they sat next to each other at the end of a large dinner party in mid-February 1798. After discussing the high price of labor and rents and concurring in holding the banks and their issues of paper money responsible, the two turned to the Constitution. In the course of the conversation, which Jefferson recorded in notes shortly thereafter, Adams contended that no republic could long exist without a strong senate, "strong enough to bear up against all popular storms & passions." He thought the U.S. Senate was probably "as well constituted as it could have been," but still it was "not durable enough"; and eventually that would be its undoing. Certainly, trusting "a popular assembly for the preservation of our liberties . . . was the merest chimaera imaginable." Although Adams was aware that Jefferson supported the French Revolution, he nevertheless told him to his face that "in France anarchy had done more mischief in one night than all the despotism of their kings had ever done in 20 or 30 years."[57]

Polite as usual, Jefferson never fully revealed to Adams just how much of a true believer he was—someone thoroughly convinced that the success of the French Revolution would determine the fate of America's experiment in republicanism. Just as Adams and the Federalists were frightened by the fifth-column-like activities of the Republicans, so too did Jefferson see the Federalists using their mercantile and financial connections to draw America "into war on the side of England" in order ultimately "to break up our union."[58] Jefferson believed that war with France would be a calamity and would play into the hands of monarchies everywhere.

Adams was the very opposite of a true believer. He was pessimistic, cynical about human nature, and sure about only one thing—that the French Revolution was an unmitigated disaster. He lacked Jefferson's confidence in the future and was uncertain about what to do. In contrast to some High Federalists who favored war with France, he preferred a peaceful resolution of the crisis, "provided that no Violation of Faith, no Stain upon Honour is exacted. But," he told his son John Quincy, "if Infidelity, Dishonour, or too much humiliation is demanded, France shall do as she pleases and take her own course. America is not *Scared*."[59]

Adams realized that England was as much a violator of America's neutral rights as France. "If we believe Britain's less hungry for plunder than Frenchmen," he told his secretary of state, "we shall be deceived." Still, unlike Jefferson, he was proud of his English heritage. Impressed by England's skill and perseverance in the war at sea, he told Abigail "we are a Chip of that Block."[60] Since he believed in order, hierarchy, and the inevitability of social inequality, and was an admirer of the English constitution and suspicious of democracy, he was necessarily a Federalist, but he was not really a party man. And many of his fellow Federalists sensed that, which made him suspect in their eyes.

IN THE END FRANCE ITSELF RESCUED Adams from his despairing uncertain situation. The French government refused to recognize the credentials of the commissioners Adams had sent to France. French agents, later referred to as "X, Y, and Z" in dispatches published in America, demanded of the American envoys that the U.S. government apologize for President Adams's allegedly unfriendly May 1797 speech to Congress and assume responsibility for any outstanding French debts owed to Americans. To top this off, the French agents insisted that the United States in effect give a bribe to the French government of fifty thousand pounds. Only then might the French government receive the commissioners.

In April 1798, after months of haggling, a disgusted Marshall and Pinckney returned to the United States. Gerry, fearful that a war with France would "disgrace republicanism & make it the scoff of despots," decided to remain behind.[61] Before returning, Marshall had sent to the president records of the XYZ Affair and the collapse of the negotiations with France. Without revealing the contents of the commission's dispatches, Adams on March 19, 1798, informed the Congress of the failure of the diplomatic mission and called for arming America's merchant vessels and other defensive measures. On March 23, he also called for "a day of solemn humiliation, fasting and prayer" to be held on May 9, 1798.

Jefferson was horrified by what he took to be Adams's warlike message. He called it "insane." Madison agreed, and said the message was evidence that "the violent passions, and heretical politics" that had long governed Adams privately had at last been publicly exposed. Desperate to avoid conflict with America's sister republic, the Republican leaders sought to find some way of delaying action by Congress. "To do nothing, and to gain time is everything with us," Jefferson told Madison. If war could be put off for six months or so, he said, events in Europe would save us. England was on its last legs, and a French invasion of the British Isles was bound to happen soon.[62]

The Republicans thought that Adams's initial refusal to make the envoys' dispatches public was a cover-up, and, unaware of how damaging they were to their cause, they called for their release. On April 4, 1798, Abigail told her son John Quincy that the Republicans wanted the dispatches, and she said, with smiling anger, "today *they will receive them*."

The dispatches exhibited "a picture of National Degradation and unparalleled corruption" and were so insulting, she said, that America ought to cut off all connection with that regicide republic.

When Americans finally learned how the French government had humiliated their commissioners in the XYZ Affair, most of them exploded in anger against France and the Republican Party. "The Jacobins in senate and House were struck dumb," said Abigail, and not having received instructions from their French emissaries spread all over America, they didn't know what to do.[63]

Jefferson himself was stunned. The publication of the dispatches, he told Madison, "produced such a shock on the republican mind as has never been seen since our independence." Especially embarrassing were the French agents' references to the "friends of France" in the United States, suggesting that there existed quislings in the country willing to aid the French. Many of the "vibrators" and "wavering characters" in the Republican Party, Jefferson groaned, were so anxious "to wipe out the imputation of being French partisans" that they were going over in droves to "the war party." He himself felt especially persecuted. "At this moment," he told James Monroe, "my name is running through all the city as detected in a criminal correspondence with the French directory."[64]

Over the remainder of 1798 and into 1799, the Federalists won election after election, even in the South, and gained control of the Congress.

Following his initial shock, Jefferson soon recovered his natural optimistic faith in the French Revolution, and he began assuring his correspondents that only "the merchants & satellites of the administration" favored war. The farmers of America did not. He began making excuses for the French, arguing that the Directory in charge of the government knew nothing of the corrupt behavior of its foreign minister and his agents. The only real obstacle to negotiations, he claimed, was President Adams's speech of May 16, 1797. It will be "the real cause of war, if war takes place." If that "insult from our Executive should be first wiped away," the French seemed willing to settle all other differences. It was certain, he said, that the revelations of these dispatches "do not offer one

motive the more for our going to war." The Republicans, or what he often called "the whig-party" in contrast to the monarch-minded Tories,
were "willing to indulge the war-gentry with every reasonable measure
of internal defense & preparations, but will oppose everything external."
He expected time would heal passions, "unless the Executive should be
able to plunge us into war irrecoverably."[65]

THE REVELATION OF THE XYZ AFFAIR suddenly made
President Adams and the Federalists popular in a way they had not been
before. "Millions for defense but not one cent for tribute!"—the reply the
American envoys supposedly had given to the French demand for a
bribe—became the Federalists' rallying cry. Songs and plays celebrated
the president, and theater audiences that earlier had rioted on behalf of
the French now sang praises of President Adams.

Acclamations and addresses cascaded upon the president—hundreds
of them, from state legislatures, town meetings, college students, grand
juries, Masonic lodges, and military companies. They congratulated
him for his leadership, for his patience, for his impartiality, and for his
wisdom in upholding the honor and independence of the United States.
The addresses condemned those "characters in the United States who
call themselves Americans and who . . . are endeavoring to poison the
minds of the well-meaning citizens and to withdraw from the government the support of the people."[66]

Beside himself with excitement, Adams answered all the addresses,
sometimes with bellicose statements against the "inordinate Ambition
and Avarice" of France and at other times with indictments of "designing men" who have appealed to "the Passions and Prejudices of the People" in an attempt "to separate the People from the Government." In his
answer "To the Young Men of the City of Philadelphia," an answer that
greatly upset Jefferson, Adams declared that, "without wishing to damp
the ardor of curiosity, or influence the freedom of inquiry," he guessed
that after much impartial research the longest liver among the young
men would "find no principles, institutions, or systems of education more

fit, in general, to be transmitted to your posterity, than that you have received from your ancestors." In other words, the wisdom of the past trumped the promises of the future. Nothing could be more contrary to Jefferson's outlook on the world.[67]

Jefferson was fascinated by Adams's answers, and he systematically compiled a list of all that were published, categorizing them under various headings: "favor to England," "abuse of the French," "libels against his fellow-citizens," "anti-republican heresies," and "egoisms." He complained that these presidential responses were "full of extraordinary things" and were more boastful and more damaging to the possibility for peace than the addresses themselves. Foreign nations might be able to pardon indiscreet and passionate statements made by local governments and private organizations, but, he said, they could scarcely ignore statements made by the president of the United States.[68]

All of Adams's responses troubled Jefferson, but the one that most outraged him and the one he never forgot was Adams's astonishing advice given to the young men of Philadelphia. It was, Jefferson exclaimed, "precisely the doctrine which the present despots of the earth are inculcating, & their friends here re-echoing; & applying especially to religion and politics." He could hardly believe what Adams had said: "we are to look backwards then, & not forwards for the improvement of science, & to find it amidst feudal barbarisms and the fires of Spital-fields"—that is, amid the cremations from the Roman era discovered in London in the sixteenth century. "But thank heaven," he said, "the American mind is already too much opened, to listen to these impostures."[69]

Because Adams was finally receiving the popular praise and respect that he had long yearned for, all his doubts about his actions suddenly disappeared. He could only conclude that "the French and many Americans have miscalculated. They have betrayed to the World their Ignorance of the American Character."[70] Adams took the responsibility for answering all these addresses so seriously that Abigail feared for his life.[71] But he himself was never happier than he was during the summer of 1798, lecturing his countrymen on the ignorance and dishonesty of both France and the Republican Party.

. . .

DESPITE ADAMS'S NEWFOUND CONFIDENCE, the situation in 1798 was exceedingly perilous. Groups of Republicans and Federalists adopted different cockades—the Federalists assumed a black ornament to contrast sharply with what they took to be the French tricolor cockade worn by the Republicans. Mobs wearing these contrasting cockades became involved in skirmishes, fistfights, and other violence, even at church doors. Abigail was beside herself with anger and anguish. She hoped that people were at last uniting against "foreign influence" in the capital and would crush "the Hydra Monster of Jacobinism" and prevent it from ever rising again. To some frightened observers, society seemed to be coming apart. "Friendships were dissolved, tradesmen dismissed, and custom withdrawn from the Republican party," bemoaned the wife of a prominent Republican in Philadelphia. "Many gentlemen went armed."[72]

Rumors spread everywhere that a conspiracy was afoot to burn Philadelphia on May 9, 1798, the day Adams had designated for fasting and prayer. On the eve of that day, riots and brawling erupted in the capital between supporters of Britain and backers of France, and mobs attacked Republican newspaper editors. Many years later the events of that night were still vivid in Adams's memory. "What think you of Terrorism, Mr. Jefferson?" asked Adams, in one of his many letters to Jefferson written in retirement. "I have no doubt You was fast asleep in philosophical Tranquility," he sarcastically reminded Jefferson, "when ten thousand People, and perhaps many more, were parading the Streets of Philadelphia."[73]

Adams had been scared. The governor of Pennsylvania had to order patrols of horse and foot to preserve the peace. Crowds—numbering ten thousand persons, said Abigail—were everywhere. "Market Street was as full as Men could stand by one another." A mob of over a thousand even came to the president's door, so close that some of his servants, who were in a "Phrenzy," said Adams, offered "to sacrifice their Lives in my defence." His "Domesticks" were about to make "a desperate Sally among the multitude," when others, "with difficulty and danger," dragged them back. Adams himself had ordered "Chests and Arms" to be brought surreptitiously to his house, which he was determined to defend "at the expense of my Life, and the lives of the few, very few Domesticks and Friends within it."[74]

John and Abigail both blamed the terrorism on the Republican newspaper editors, such as Benjamin Franklin Bache, the grandson of Benjamin Franklin; William Duane, who succeeded Bache as editor of the Philadelphia *Aurora;* and the notorious James Thomson Callender, who had vilified the president and other Federalist officials in the years leading up to 1798. "The vile incendiaries" in the Republican newspapers, exclaimed Abigail in April 1798, were filled with "the most wicked and base, violent & caluminiating abuse" of Federalist officeholders. "But," she said, "nothing will have an effect until congress pass a Sedition bill." Indeed, there was no stronger advocate for limiting the scurrility of the press than Mrs. Adams. She and many other Federalists thought that all authority was under attack, with French sympathizers everywhere and a French army on the verge of invading the country.[75]

John Randolph, Jefferson's brilliant but eccentric second cousin, later claimed in the Congress that "the grand Army of Richmond was intended to put down the Yankee Administration." Adams later said that he had no doubt that this was true, and "Mr. Jefferson and Mr. Madison were privy to the design."[76]

THESE WERE INDEED FRIGHTENING TIMES, perhaps the most frightening moment in all of American history—something most historians have not appreciated. The only comparable period of terror might be the months following the attack on Pearl Harbor on December 7, 1941, when the country, worried over possible Japanese espionage and an invasion of the West Coast, interned well over a hundred thousand people of Japanese ancestry, 60 percent of whom were American citizens. Bad as the situation was in 1941–1942, 1798–1799 seems scarier because the nation then was so new and so militarily weak and the enemy that threatened to invade was the strongest land power in the world.

A French invasion of America was not far-fetched. French armies were dominating Europe. Not only had France annexed Belgium and parts of Germany outright, but, more alarming, it had also used native collaborators to create puppet republics in the Netherlands, Switzerland, and much of Italy. It might do the same in America. France after all had sent a huge army across the Atlantic two decades earlier. And there were large numbers of Americans and recent immigrants, both French and Irish, who were sympathetic to the French Revolution and who might welcome a French invasion. So strong was the French influence in the capital that one historian has called Philadelphia in the 1790s "an American Paris."[77]

Jefferson, of course, was right when he said that the Federalists were mistaken in presuming that the Republicans' attachment to France and their hatred of the Federalist monarchists trumped their love of their own country.[78] At the time, however, that was not at all clear to the Federalists. All they could see were the Republican expressions of sympathy for France and the threat of a French invasion; and, of course, they, like everyone else, did not know the future. Even Jefferson realized that he had expressed enough affection for France and support of the French Revolution that his loyalty might be suspect. In fact, the Federalist press was calling him "that traitor to his country."[79] When the French philosophe the Comte de Volney left America to return to France, Jefferson asked him not to write to him, fearing that letters from any Frenchmen at this critical time were bound to arouse suspicion.[80]

Because none of the Federalists' fears actually materialized and no invasion occurred, historians have never been able to fully appreciate the Federalists' apprehensions. Yet if the Federalists' actions during the crisis of 1798–1799 are to be understood, their fears, which were genuine and deeply felt, must be taken seriously, however wrongheaded they turned out to be.

The most devout Federalists in Congress began enacting measures to prepare the county for war with France. In the absence of a formal declaration of war, they sanctioned a Quasi-War, or what Adams called "the half-war with France."[81] Congress formally abrogated all treaties with France and laid an embargo on all French trade. It authorized American naval vessels to attack armed French ships that were seizing American merchant vessels. In addition to levying new taxes, providing for loans, and making plans for beefing up the army, Congress approved the building of fifteen warships. To supervise the new fleet Congress created an independent Navy Department—one of Adams's proudest accomplishments. The "one thing wanting," said Abigail, was a formal declaration of war. It "ought undoubtedly to have been made," except for Elbridge Gerry's "unaccountable Stay" in France. The people wanted war, but their representatives in Congress, she said, were too timid, too full of "party spirit, and Jacobinism." Apparently, Adams himself, at least at this moment, was equally bent on a declaration of war.[82]

At the same time the Federalists in Congress thought they had to do something about what they believed were the sources of Jacobin influence in America—the increasing number of foreign immigrants and the scurrilous behavior of the Republican press. In response, in the summer of 1798 they passed and President Adams signed the Alien and Sedition Acts, measures that turned out to be a horrendous mistake. In fact, more than anything else, these acts have so tarnished the historical reputation of Adams and the Federalists that it can probably never be recovered. Yet it is important to put these acts in context and explain why they made sense to the Adamses and to the Federalists.

AT THE OUTSET OF THE NEW GOVERNMENT in 1789, the Federalists, especially the big land speculators, had been very eager to receive foreign immigrants, and in 1790 they had passed a fairly liberal naturalization measure that required only two years of residency for free white persons to become citizens. By contrast, Jefferson and the Republicans were not initially as welcoming to immigrants. Believing in a more active hands-on role for the people in politics, they had worried that European immigrants might lack a proper appreciation of liberty and self-government to become good citizens. In his *Notes on the State of Virginia*, Jefferson had thought that too many European immigrants might come to America with monarchical principles "imbibed in their early youth" and would pass these principles on to their children and infuse into

American culture "their spirit, warp and bias its direction," ultimately turning America into "a heterogeneous, incoherent, distracted mass."[83]

In the subsequent years, however, the Federalists and the Republicans changed their minds. In the 1790s alone, nearly one hundred thousand immigrants came to the United States. Many of these were political or religious refugees, driven from Britain and Ireland because of their dissenting beliefs, and they tended to support the Republican Party. A disproportionate number of them became newspaper editors, usually writing on behalf of the Republican cause.

At the same time, thousands of Frenchmen in the 1790s, escaping the convulsions in their homeland and in the French Caribbean colony of Saint-Domingue (modern-day Haiti), entered the United States, and these French immigrants naturally made many Federalists uneasy. It has been estimated that as much as 10 percent of the population of Philadelphia in the mid-1790s was French, with French shops, French craftsmen, and French newspapers everywhere in the city. Jefferson's French friend the Comte de Volney, who arrived in Philadelphia in 1795, thought the city had "a penchant for our arts, our manners, our language."[84] By 1798 the Federalists were frightened enough by the presence of all these foreigners that they were prepared to limit their ability to influence American politics.

The Naturalization Act of June 18, 1798, extended the period of residence required before an alien could become a citizen to fourteen years, and prevented aliens who were citizens or subjects of a nation with which the United States was at war from becoming citizens. This legislation was followed a week later by the Alien Friends Act, which allowed the government to restrain aliens even in peacetime.

Although the United States had not actually declared war on France, nevertheless, "in times like the present," Abigail told her sister, "a more careful and attentive watch ought to be kept over foreigners."[85] John Adams much later justified his signing the Alien Friends bill as president on the grounds that "we were then at War with France: French Spies then swarmed in our Cities and in the Country. . . . To check them was the design of this law. Was there ever a Government," he asked Jefferson, "which had not Authority to defend itself against Spies in its own Bosom?" Jefferson vehemently opposed the act and scorned it as "a most detestable thing," something "worthy of the 8th or 9th century."[86]

Following the passage of the Alien Friends Act, more than a dozen shiploads of frightened Frenchmen sailed for France or Santo Domingo, the former Spanish colony adjoining Saint-Domingue that France had acquired in 1795. Adams wanted no more Frenchmen, no matter how enlightened, to enter the United States. "We have had too many French Philosophers already," he told Secretary of State Pickering in September 1798; "and I really begin to think or to suspect, that learned academics not under the immediate Inspection and Control of Government have disorganised the World and are incompatible with social order." When Médéric Louis Elie Moreau de St. Méry, a refugee from the Reign of Terror who in 1794 had established a bookstore in Philadelphia, asked why he was on the president's list for deportation, he was told of President Adams's blunt reply: "Nothing in particular, but he's too French."[87]

In the end, however, because so many foreigners left before the act was enforced and because of Adams's strict interpretation of the statute, the Federalist government never actually deported a single alien under the Alien Friends Act.

But it was the Sedition Act of July 14, 1798, that aroused the most Republican anger. It made it a crime to "write, print, utter or publish . . . false, scandalous, and malicious" writings that brought the president or members of either house of Congress "into contempt or disrepute." (Significantly, the vice president was not protected by the act.) It was designed, said Jefferson, for "the suppression of the whig presses," especially the Philadelphia *Aurora*. If the Republican papers were silenced, he said, "republicanism will be entirely brow-beaten."[88]

The partisan newspapers were truly scandalous. Indeed, never in American history has the press been more vitriolic and more scurrilous than it was in the 1790s. Although the Federalist press had its own share of malicious charges against the Republicans, it was the growing number of Republican newspapers that filled the air with vicious attacks on the president and Federalist officeholders. Federalist officials were denounced for being "Tory monarchists" and "British-loving aristocrats." Adams was singled out for being "a mock Monarch" who was "blind, bald, toothless, and querulous" and "a ruffian deserving of the curses of mankind."[89]

By the early nineteenth century, all Adams could recall of the press during his presidency was that it was full of "the most envious malignity, the most base, vulgar, sordid, fishwoman scurrility, and the most palpable lies." Indeed, based on what the pamphlets and newspapers of both parties had said about him, he had to be judged nothing less than "the meanest villain in the world."[90]

The traditional common law of seditious libel that ran in most state courts was designed to protect authority and promote order in this still premodern world. In a society that lacked police forces and modern mechanisms for maintaining order, magistrates and rulers, it was thought, had to rely on their inherent social authority—their wealth, their learning, and their social respectability—to command the obedience of those below them. If that social respectability was brought into question by scurrilous charges in the press, then the capacity of these magistrates and rulers to maintain order would be endangered. As Adams's Harvard classmate Jonathan Sewall had put it in 1766, "the *person* and the *office* are so connected in the minds of the greatest part of mankind, that a contempt of the *former* and a veneration for the *latter* are totally incompatible."[91] This was the rationale behind the common law of seditious libel.

Americans believed in freedom of the press and had written that freedom into their Bill of Rights. But they believed in it as Englishmen did.[92] Indeed, the English had celebrated freedom of the press since the seventeenth century, but they meant by it, in contrast with the French, no prior restraint or censorship of what was published. Under English law, people were nevertheless held responsible for what they published. If a person's publications were calumnious enough to bring public officials into disrespect, then under the common law the publisher could be prosecuted for seditious libel. The truth of what was published was no defense; indeed, it even aggravated the offense. Furthermore, under the common law, judges, not juries, had the responsibility to decide whether or not a publication was seditious. Although this common-law view of seditious libel had been challenged and seriously weakened by John Peter Zenger's trial in New York in 1735, it had never been fully eradicated from American thinking or practice in the state courts.

In this regard the Sedition Act passed by Congress in 1798 was a liberalization of the common law. It said the statements had to be true in order to be libelous, and it allowed for juries to decide whether a piece was seditious. Unlike Madison and many other of his fellow Republicans, who were more libertarian than he, Jefferson objected to the Sedition Act solely on federalist grounds—that is, that the national Congress had no constitutional right to enact such a law. But he fully accepted the right of the state courts to use the traditional common law of seditious libel in order to punish scurrilous writers who attacked government officials.

Not only did he dislike the press nearly as much as Adams—"nothing in a newspaper," he said, "is to be believed"—but when he became president he wrote to Republican governors and attorneys general in the states and urged them to prosecute some scandalmongering Federalist editors for seditious libel under the common law. In 1803 he told Thomas McKean, by then governor of Pennsylvania ("what I say must be entirely confidential"), that "a few prosecutions of the most eminent offenders would have a wholesome effect in restoring the integrity of the presses— not a general prosecution, for that would look like persecution: but a selected one." Although Jefferson did allow for truth to be a defense in these trials of seditious libel, his efforts to go after Federalist editors surreptitiously have not endeared him to some later historians.[93]

EXPELLING ALIENS and stifling the scurrility of the Republican press were only parts of the Federalist program designed to save the nation from the evils of Jacobinism. Many Federalists remained convinced that a French army would sooner or later invade the United States and the country had to be prepared. Consequently, in the summer of 1798,

Congress immediately enlarged the army to twelve thousand men and authorized ten thousand more in case of an actual invasion. Adams, who doubted the possibility of a French invasion, had never called for these increases in the army. They were pushed by Hamilton and other Federalists, and the president felt himself carried along. In fact, sometimes Adams acted as if he were not the chief executive at all and someone else was making the decisions.

In the summer of 1798, Adams confessed to his predecessor his sense of helplessness in the face of the crisis. If the country was to be saved, he told Washington, it had to "depend upon Heaven, and very little on any thing in my Power." Since he had no martial experience, he wished the Constitution would allow him to change places with Washington or permit him to become vice president once again under his leadership. Without getting Washington's final permission, Adams went ahead and commissioned the former president as the commander in chief of all the armies. Washington, however, declared that he would serve only if Hamilton was second in command and the de facto commander. Adams wanted Henry Knox as second in command, because he had outranked Hamilton in the Revolutionary War. Under pressure from Washington and his cabinet, Adams finally gave way. He was furious that he had to promote Hamilton, who became for Adams "the most restless, impatient, indefatigable and unprincipled Intriguer in the United States, if not in the world."[94]

Hamilton did have grandiose plans. He was a Napoleonic figure who wanted glory both for himself and for the nation. He wanted to strengthen the Union, extend the judiciary, and amend the Constitution to break up the large states, especially Virginia. He thought a war with France would allow the United States, in cooperation with Britain, to seize both Florida and Louisiana. He even raised the possibility of aiding the Venezuelan patriot Francisco de Miranda in liberating South America from Spanish control.

At first Jefferson remained sanguine in the face of all the Federalist talk of crisis and a French invasion. In June 1798, he sought to soothe the fears of John Taylor of Virginia, who had criticized the Federalists' plans and raised the possibility of the southern states seceding from the Union. "A little patience," he told Taylor, "and we shall see the reign of the witches pass over." The Federalists in Massachusetts and Connecticut, "marked like the Jews with a peculiarity of character," were now in control, but that was unnatural and only temporary. "The body of our countrymen is substantially republican through every part of the union."[95]

With the passage of the Alien and Sedition Acts in the summer of 1798, however, Jefferson became more apprehensive, fearing that the Federalists might build on the success of their oppressive legislation. He saw that legislation as "an experiment on the American mind to see how far it will bear an avowed violation of the constitution." If the people accept these acts, Congress might next attempt to grant the president life tenure, which would lead to making the office hereditary, followed by establishing the Senate for life. Since these attempts "to worm out the elective principle" were what Adams had long predicted, Jefferson had little doubt the Federalists were contemplating making them, and given the degree to which the American people had been duped so far, he was no longer confident of being able to resist them.[96] Even more alarming was the possibility of Hamilton, "our Buonaparte, surrounded by his comrades in arms," invading Virginia in order to put down the Republican opposition.[97]

In the end Jefferson, actually now more fearful of what was happening than Adams, became convinced that he had to do something to combat the Federalist plans. With the Federalists in control of Congress and the presidency, he had come to think of the federal government as "a foreign jurisdiction." Over the previous decade, he said, the general government had "become more arbitrary, and has swallowed up more of the public liberty than even that of England." By contrast, "our state governments are the *very best in the world*." Consequently, he and Madison plotted to use the state legislatures as the most effective instrument for contesting the constitutionality of the Alien and Sedition Acts.[98]

Jefferson's draft of the state resolutions was intended for the Virginia legislature, but when Madison's draft went to Virginia, his ended up in the Kentucky legislature. In it Jefferson described the Constitution as "a compact" among the several states, with each state retaining final authority to declare acts of the federal government that exceeded its delegated powers, in this case, the Alien and Sedition Acts, "void & of no force" within that state's jurisdiction. Jefferson labeled this remedy for abusive federal actions "nullification," but, fortunately for his subsequent reputation, the Kentucky legislature edited out this inflammatory term when it adopted Jefferson's draft in a set of resolves issued in November 1798.[99]

ADAMS'S EARLIER APPREHENSIONS about what the French and their Republican sympathizers might be up to were now overwhelmed by his hatred of Hamilton and the High Federalists. He had come to detest the entire Hamiltonian financial program, declaring that "there is not a democrat in the world who affects more horror than I really feel, at the prospect of that frightful system of debts and taxes, into which imperious necessity seems to be precipitating us." Having been humiliated by Washington and the Hamiltonians over the appointment of the army's generals, Adams was very bitter. His loathing of Hamilton was so intense that he came to regard him as something other than an American, calling him nothing but "a foreigner," and "not a native of the United States."[100]

Sharing none of his fellow Federalists' fears of a French invasion—he told Secretary of War James McHenry in October 1798 that "at present there is no more prospect of seeing a French army here, than there is in Heaven"—Adams was finally prepared to defy Hamilton and the High Federalists and defuse the warlike atmosphere they had created.[101] In a December 8, 1798, speech to Congress, the president opened the door to further negotiations with France.

Jefferson was impressed with its "moderation," but doubted that it revealed Adams's genuine feelings.[102] But Adams had changed. Learning from various sources that France was finally ready to reach an agreement with the United States, Adams, without consulting anyone, including his own cabinet, decided in February 1799 to send another mission to France.

This extraordinary action stunned the Federalists and divided the party. It was as if Adams's long pent-up hostility to being attached to a party with which he had little in common could at last be released. "If anyone entertains the Idea that, because I am President of three votes only, I am in the Power of a party," he told Charles Lee, his attorney general, they had another think coming. The president was ready to take on the "Combinations of Senators Generals and Heads of Departments" that had formed against him. So little had he come to think of himself as a Federalist that he even suggested that he would form a new party made up of independent-minded men from both existing parties.[103]

He even saw himself as a kind of republican king ruling above all parties. He asked his ministers' advice as to whether or not the president could establish "a Gazette in the Service of the Government." After all, the king of England had a gazette, and "without running a Parallel between the President of the United States and the King of England, it is certain that the honor Dignity and Consistency of Government is of as much importance to the People, in one case as the other." This remarkable proposal suggests just how much Adams modeled the American executive on that of England and just how out of touch he was with the realities of American politics.[104]

Adams was no politician and certainly no party leader; and he had very little political sense. In 1799 he seemed oblivious to the political implications of counseling a federal judge to surrender to British authorities a sailor named Jonathan Robbins, alias Thomas Nash, who was accused of a bloody mutiny on H.M.S. *Hermione* in 1797. Only after Robbins was given up to the British did the sailor claim to be a U.S. citizen impressed into the British navy—a false claim, as it turned out. British subject or not, mutineer or not, Robbins and his extradition and subsequent quick execution by the British became a political disaster for Adams. The Republicans relentlessly criticized him in the press for being complicit in the murder of a "martyr to liberty," and under the leadership of Edward Livingston in the House of Representatives, they threatened to censure and even impeach him.

Jefferson followed these proceedings very closely and was well aware of the implications of the Robbins affair for the upcoming presidential election. As early as October 1799, he thought that "no one circumstance since the establishment of our government has affected the popular mind more" than the Robbins case. As an American presumably seized by the British navy, Robbins embodied the evil of British impressment. Indeed, many, including Jefferson, thought that Robbins's martyrdom was a major reason for Adams's defeat in 1800.[105]

As his behavior over the Robbins affair indicated, Jefferson was a superb politician and party leader. While Adams did little or nothing to plan for his reelection, Jefferson was exchanging letters with his Republican colleagues, tallying votes state by state and plotting strategy. It was as if Adams didn't care about the election. He told members of his cabinet that at their upcoming meeting there should be no discussion of the election. He knew where he stood in the eyes of the people and he was going to be "a President of three votes or no president at all"—the difference in his opinion being "not worth three farthings."[106]

Since for Adams party had lost all meaning, he now felt free enough to criticize Hamilton openly and to do what he should have done long before—dismiss the Hamiltonians in his cabinet, Pickering and McHenry. In an explosive expression of rage, which had become increasingly common, Adams accused McHenry of being "subservient to Hamilton," who was "a man devoid of every moral principle, a Bastard," and the cause of all the Federalists' problems. Jefferson, said Adams, was an "infinitely better" and "wiser" man than Hamilton, and if he should become president he "will act wisely." Adams went on to say that he would rather be vice president under Jefferson, or even minister at The Hague, than be "indebted to such a being as Hamilton for the Presidency."[107] So strange and eccentric did Adams's actions seem that some Federalists thought that he and Jefferson must have come to some secret agreement.[108]

Learning of Adams's tirade, and especially the reference to his illegitimacy, an irate Hamilton could only conclude that the president was "more mad than I ever thought him" and perhaps because of his praise of Jefferson "as wicked as he is mad."[109] Others too thought that Adams had become emotionally unhinged. Even the British minister described him as "the most passionate, intemperate man he ever had anything to do with."[110] Some Federalists questioned Adams's mental stability and sought to find some alternative as president. In 1799 a few had even tried to talk Washington into standing once again for the presidency—an effort the ex-president in anger and despair dismissed out of hand, saying that in this new era of political parties even "a broomstick" properly supported by its party could win an election.[111]

Hamilton was especially desperate. In the summer and fall of 1800, he composed a fifty-four-page privately published *Letter from Alexander Hamilton, Concerning the Public Conduct and Character of John Adams, Esq., President of the United States*. In this pamphlet Hamilton criticized Adams for his "eccentric tendencies," his "distempered jealousy," his "extreme egoism," his "ungovernable temper," and his "vanity without bounds." He declared that Adams and his many "paroxysms of anger" had undone everything that the Washington administration had established. If Adams were to continue as president, he might bring the government to ruin. Despite stating that Adams was unfit to be president, Hamilton ended his invective polemic by supporting the president's reelection. Apparently, he was hoping for some combination of electoral votes that would result in the election of Charles Cotesworth Pinckney as president.

Although Hamilton's *Letter* may not by itself have prevented Adams's reelection, its publication revealed the deep division among the Federalists that made Jefferson's election as president more or less inevitable. That division was caused by Adams's courageous decision to send a new mission to France, the issue that Hamilton most emphasized in his pamphlet and the one that stunned and destroyed Adams's reputation among many Federalists.

Writing from Federalist-dominated Massachusetts, Abigail told her husband that his decision "universally electrified the public. . . . It came so sudden, was a measure so unexpected, that the whole community were like a flock of frightened pigeons: nobody had their story ready; Some call'd it a hasty measure; other condemned it as an inconsistent one; some swore, some cursed."[112]

Adams actually enjoyed angering the Hamiltonian Federalists, showing them that he was his own man. He considered this decision to try once more to negotiate with France, as he never tired of telling everyone, "the most disinterested, prudent, and successful conduct in my whole life." He desired no other inscription on his gravestone than: "Here lies John Adams, who took upon himself the responsibility of the peace with France in the year 1800."[113]

Although presidents probably should not make controversial decisions without consulting someone, Adams was right to be proud of his determination to send a new mission to France. Not only did his decision vindicate his theory of an independent executive—someone who stood above all parties—but it put an end to the war crisis, a crisis that in the minds of some Federalists and Republicans had threatened a civil war. News of Admiral Horatio Nelson's destruction of the French fleet at the Battle of the Nile in October 1799 undercut the threat of a French invasion and made Adams's mission possible. The plans of the extreme Federalists to strengthen the central government and the military establishment of the United States crumbled, and consequently they have never been taken seriously by historians.

After months of negotiations, France, now headed by First Consul Napoleon Bonaparte, who would soon make himself emperor, agreed to terms and in 1800 signed the Treaty of Mortefontaine with the United States; it brought the Quasi-War to a close and suspended the Franco-American treaty of 1778 (and its related convention of 1789), thus freeing America from its first of what Jefferson would refer to as "entangling alliances."[114]

Adams realized that the "imprudent and disorganizing opposition and Clamor" of the High Federalists to his decision to send another peace mission had severely delayed the departure of the envoys, and that delay might very well endanger his reelection as president. So be it, he said. He was prepared to lose, he told John Trumbull in September 1800. "Age, Infirmities, family Misfortunes have conspired, with the Unreasonable Conduct of Jacobins and insolent Federalists, to make me too indifferent to whatever can happen."[115] He actually didn't mean that.

He was right to worry about the delay. News that the conflict was ended did not reach America until the Republicans had won the presidency. Jefferson received seventy-three electoral votes to Adams's sixty-five. The twelve electoral votes of New York for Jefferson and for Aaron Burr, who had guaranteed those votes, made all the difference.

TEN

THE JEFFERSONIAN
REVOLUTION OF 1800

L IKE THE OTHER FEDERALISTS, John Adams had misjudged the future. He assumed that American society would
eventually mature and become less egalitarian, more hierarchical, and more like the societies of Europe. He was so sure of the process
of maturation that he wanted to prepare for it by having political officeholders serve for longer terms and perhaps for life. By contrast, Thomas
Jefferson did end up on the right side of history, but inadvertently. He
saw the future no more clearly than Adams. In 1800, however, he and
his fellow Republicans did rightly see their electoral victory as more than
one party replacing another.

Jefferson sincerely believed that the Hamilton-led Federalists, fearful of the popular forces unleashed by the Revolution, had sought to
turn the United States into a European-type state with an enlarged bureaucracy, a standing army, a national bank, high taxes, and a credit
system that tried to tie the financial interests of the country to the government. Jefferson and the Republicans set out to repudiate as much as
they could all of those Federalist dreams. Jefferson wanted no part of the
hereditary aristocracies, gross social inequalities, bloated executives, oppressive debts, and the huge and expensive military establishments that

characterized the traditional European monarchies. Despite the excesses and perversions of the French Revolution, he remained faithful to its goal of destroying the old monarchical world. He believed that his election had saved the United States from monarchy and had brought the entire revolutionary venture of two and a half decades to successful completion. Indeed, he was convinced that his election, "the Revolution of 1800," as he later called it, "was as real a revolution in the principles of our government as that of 1776 was in its form."[1]

Instead of the fiscal-military state the Federalists had wanted, Jefferson, as he said in his inaugural address, sought only "a wise and frugal government," one that kept its citizens from injuring one another but otherwise left them "free to regulate their own pursuits of industry and improvement" while at the same time avoiding taking "from the mouth of labor the bread it has earned." He contemplated "a rising nation, spread over a wide and fruitful land, traversing all the seas with the rich productions of their industry, engaged in commerce with nations who feel power and forget right, advancing rapidly to destinies beyond the reach of mortal eye." For Jefferson, America had become "the world's best hope" for the future of agrarian republicanism. It was "a chosen country, with room enough for our descendants to the thousandth and thousandth generation." For those who thought republican governments were too weak to sustain themselves, Jefferson replied that the United States, based as it was on the sovereignty of the people, was "the strongest Government on earth."[2]

Adams never witnessed Jefferson's inauguration since he left before sunrise, becoming the first and only president not to greet his successor. It was an insult that Adams's onetime friend Elbridge Gerry thought had "wounded his real [friends] & been severely censured by his pretended friends." Gerry thought that Adams's recent conduct toward himself had "by no means been satisfactory."[3]

DESPITE SELF-PROTECTIVELY suggesting that he was indifferent to the results of the election, Adams had taken his defeat hard. It was humiliating. He believed that, like Washington, he should have been able to serve until he voluntarily stepped down. In the eyes of some observers, his "unexpected displacement" was unnatural and had to be an act of God. Sometimes Adams could not hide his bitterness, telling his son Thomas, for example, that "if I were to go over my Life again I would be a Shoemaker rather than an American Statesman." Although that was never serious, the statement was a measure of his disappointment.[4]

It had been a brutal campaign, perhaps the most vicious and scurrility-ridden in American history. Some Federalists feared that if the Republicans won, "the air will be rent with the cries of distress, the soil will be soaked with blood, and the nation black with crimes." For their part, the Republicans claimed that if the Federalists won, they would sell out the country to Great Britain and establish a monarchy. Adams was accused of being a "poor old man . . . in his dotage," who "merely pretended to be a true friend of revolutionary republicanism." He even had the gall, the Republicans charged, to negotiate with Toussaint-Louverture, the black leader of the slave rebellion in the French colony of Saint-Domingue, and to dine personally in the White House with one of the island's black representatives.[5]

Jefferson had been especially alarmed by Adams's decision to open up trade with the black rebel state. Allowing "Toussaint's subjects to a free commerce" with the southern states and "free ingress & intercourse with their black brethren" made him very uneasy. "If this combustion can be introduced among us under any veil whatsoever," he told Madison, "we have to fear it." Since the Federalists were willing to accept this migration of blacks into America, he said sarcastically, then they ought not to worry so much about a possible French invasion of the country. "If they are guarded against the Cannibals of the terrible republic," he declared, "they ought not to object to being eaten by a more civilized enemy."[6]

Although neither Adams nor Jefferson had campaigned personally, Jefferson had kept tabs on what was happening in each state, promoted with advice and funds the writings of Republican scandalmongers, and in numerous letters to key Republicans set forth his principles and ideas.

He became as much of a party leader as any presidential candidate in American history.

JEFFERSON LATER RECALLED THAT HE had met Adams on the day they had learned of the vote of New York that gave the Republicans the victory. Adams was "very sensibly affected" and told Jefferson that although he had been beaten "in this contest," he would be "as faithful a subject as any you will have." Jefferson replied that he did not see the election as a "personal contest" between him and Adams, but as a division between two parties, with different principles of government, which had put each of them at their head. According to Jefferson, Adams said, "You are right . . . that we are but passive instruments, and should not suffer this matter to affect our personal dispositions." Unfortunately, recalled Jefferson, Adams "did not long retain this just view of the subject."[7]

Since the inauguration of the new president was not until March 4, 1801, Adams had several months remaining in his term. The lame-duck Federalist Congress passed a Judiciary Act and other legislation that created six new circuit courts with sixteen new judges along with many new marshals and district attorneys and justices of the peace. Before surrendering the presidency to Jefferson, Adams appointed Federalists to these new offices, at the same time selecting his new secretary of state, John Marshall, as chief justice of the United States. Because Adams signed the commissions of many of these appointments shortly before Jefferson's inauguration, the infuriated Republicans exaggeratedly labeled them "midnight appointments" and vowed to repudiate the Judiciary Act as soon as possible.

Since Jefferson and his presumed vice president, Aaron Burr, had inadvertently ended up with the same number of electoral votes, the election was thrown into the House of Representatives. Adams played no role in the resolution of the crisis, but both he and Abigail much preferred Jefferson to Burr. Adams saw Burr as an upstart, "rising like a balloon," whose political manipulations could only encourage "party intrigue and corruption!" Abigail said "his private Character will not bear the scrutiny which Mr. Jefferson's will." He had Napoleonic ambitions and was "a much more dangerous Man than Mr. Jefferson."[8]

Abigail recorded a conversation she had with Jefferson (recorded perhaps because such conversations had become so rare) at a large presidential dinner held in January 1801, two months before Jefferson took office. Knowing that congressmen would soon decide his fate, Jefferson asked her to identify several members attending the dinner, since he never went into the House of Representatives and thus knew only about one in twenty of them. Pointing at one member, she said, "You surely know him, Smiling. He is a democrat." "No, I do not," he answered. His ignorance had proved embarrassing, he told Abigail, because some congressmen had complained that he did not take off his hat to them when passing. Besides, said Jefferson, he wouldn't go into the House because he knew "there are persons there who would take a pleasure in saying something purposefully to affront me." Abigail declared she knew nearly all of the congressmen, "a few violent demos excepted," but she had recently avoided attending the House for the same reason as Jefferson: "party spirit is much alike upon both sides [of] the Question." When Jefferson replied that there was "more candor and liberality upon one side than there is upon the other," she said, "I differ with you, Sir." Jefferson then asked her what she thought the House would do about the tie vote for president. She said she didn't know, but she quoted a clergyman who declared that when people "do not know what to do, they should take great care that they do not do—they know not what." At this, said Abigail, Jefferson "laught out, and here ended the conversation."[9]

Abigail's recording of her exchange with Jefferson revealed her ambivalent feelings—her saucy sarcasm directed at the leader of what many Federalists caustically labeled the "dems" mingled with her respect for his civility and politeness.

Despite his preference for Jefferson over Burr, Adams was not happy with Jefferson's election, for it meant that the country would be tossed "in the tempestuous sea of liberty for years to come and where the bark can land but in a political convulsion I cannot see." Americans, he said, "have sett up pretensions to superior information, intelligence and public virtue in comparison with the rest of mankind." Those pretensions "will very soon be found wanting, if they have not already failed in the trial." He doubted whether America's experiment in republicanism could last.[10]

BY CONTRAST, Jefferson was filled with optimism. He told John Dickinson in 1801 that America's ship of state had passed through a storm promoted by individuals seeking to sink it, but his administration would right the ship and put it on its proper republican tack. The spirit of 1776, he said, had finally been fulfilled, and the United States could at last become a beacon of liberty for the world. "A just and solid republican government" of the kind he sought to build "will be a standing monument & example for the aim & imitation of the people of other countries." Expanding on the theme of his inaugural address, he told Dickinson that the American Revolution had excited the minds of "the mass of mankind." Its "consequences," he said, "will ameliorate the condition of man over a great portion of the globe."[11] With Napoleon's assuming the office of consul for life and the apparent stifling of the French Revolution, America's role as the sole emblematic republic became all the more important. It was Jefferson, more than any other single figure, who created the idea of America's exceptionalism and its special role in the world.

With the end of a decade of Federalist delusion, the new Democratic-Republican president had recovered his confidence in the future. America had thrown off its momentary fantasies, he told Joseph Priestley, a fellow supporter of the French Revolution noted for his radical religious views. The forces of "bigotry in Politics & Religion," said Jefferson, had been routed. "We can no longer say that there is nothing new under the sun, for this whole chapter in the history of man is new." He told Priestley that his predecessor, President Adams, had never understood the progressive wave of popular opinion sweeping the country and had never appreciated innovation. Adams was one of those who pretended to encourage education, but it was "the education of our ancestors" that he meant.

Jefferson invoked once again Adams's 1798 response to the young men of Philadelphia whose reactionary character had so shocked him. Adams, he told Priestley, had claimed in his answer that there could be no real progress in science and religion and that "we were to look backwards not forwards for improvement." Jefferson believed that Adams and the Federalists—"the barbarians"—had sought "to bring back the times of Vandalism, when ignorance put every thing into the hands of power & priestcraft." This was the sort of ignorance that had forced Priestley to flee Britain in 1791 and more recently had embroiled him in controversy in America. All those "who live by mystery and charlatanerie," said Jefferson, "fear being rendered useless" by those like Priestley who sought to simplify "the Christian philosophy." No doubt, he said, Christianity was "the most sublime & benevolent" religion, but it was also the "most perverted system that ever shone on man."[12]

Despite his disparaging remark about Adams in his letter to Priestley, he had wanted, as he told Madison in December 1800, to reach "a candid understanding with mr A." He didn't think Adams's feelings or his interest would object to some sort of rapprochement. Confident of his ability to soothe Adams's quirky sensibilities, Jefferson hoped "to induce in him dispositions liberal and accommodating."[13] Anticipating his major means of politicking as president, Jefferson on January 17, 1801, invited Adams to dinner.[14]

Jefferson's friends were bewildered and mortified by his persistent praise of Adams, praise that they felt was undeserved. "Your minds are not congenial," one friend told him, "his being too contracted to contain a generous or disinterested sentiment and his conduct towards you has evinced it—he has done all he cou'd to injure you and he hates you on that account." But Jefferson tended to ignore such advice, and he remained confident of his ability to conciliate not just Adams but most of the Federalists as well. Consequently, he inserted in his inaugural address an appeal for unity. Although Americans were called by different names, he declared that "we are all republicans: we are all federalists."[15]

Adams likewise had hesitated to criticize Jefferson publicly during the campaign, which puzzled some of his fellow Federalists. Instead of condemning Jefferson, complained Fisher Ames, the arch-Federalist from Adams's own state of Massachusetts, Adams tended to praise

Jefferson as "a good patriot, citizen and father." He "acts as if he did not hate or dread Jefferson."[16]

Still, Adams was pained by his defeat. During the crisis over the electoral tie between Jefferson and Burr, Jefferson met Adams and told him that a Federalist plan to override the election by congressional action "would probably produce resistance by force and [have] incalculable consequences." Adams showed no sympathy for Jefferson's plight and, "with a vehemence" he had not shown before, said that the problem could be quickly solved if Jefferson would simply give assurances that he would honor the public debt, maintain the navy, and not remove the federal officers. Jefferson replied that he would not enter the office "but in perfect freedom to follow the dictates of my own judgment." Then, said Adams, "things must take their course." With that abrupt remark, the conversation ended. It was "the first time in our lives," Jefferson recalled, that he and Adams "had ever parted with any thing like dissatisfaction."[17]

The two former friends exchanged several businesslike letters that showed little or no warmth. Several weeks before the inauguration, Adams informed Jefferson that he was leaving seven horses and two carriages in the stables for the new president's use. Unfortunately, Congress discovered that Adams had purchased the horses and carriages out of the wrong federal fund, and the issue became embarrassing to Adams. (The British chargé in the new capital city of Washington, D.C., thought this was one of the reasons Adams skipped the inauguration.) Jefferson didn't want the horses and carriages anyhow and purchased his own.[18]

On March 8, 1801, Jefferson forwarded to Adams a private letter that had mistakenly been delivered to him. The letter had contained information about the funeral of Adams's son Charles, who had died recently of alcoholism at age thirty. Adams told Jefferson that if he had read the letter, it "might have given you a moment of Melancholly or at least of Sympathy with a mourning Father." Adams went on to say that he hoped that Jefferson would never experience anything similar. The tone suggested that Adams had been hurt that Jefferson never acknowledged

Charles's death. Adams concluded by rather belatedly wishing Jefferson "a quiet and prosperous Administration."[19] They would not correspond again with each other for eleven years.

BELIEVING THAT MOST OF THE EVILS afflicting human beings in the past had flowed from the abuses of inflated political establishments, Jefferson set out to regain what he believed was the original aim of the Revolution: to reduce the overweening and dangerous power of government. He sought to create a general government that could rule without the traditional attributes of power—with as few offices, as little debt, as low taxes, and as small a military establishment as possible.

Jefferson advocated his kind of minimal government because, like such other eighteenth-century radicals as Thomas Paine and William Godwin, he believed that society was naturally harmonious and benevolent and did not need much government. This eighteenth-century radicalism was determined by how much faith theorists had in the inherent sociability of people. Carry this belief in the natural sociability of people far enough and a thinker ended up, as William Godwin did, with a kind of anarchism. Jefferson and Paine never wanted to go that far, but they both sought to disparage government and shrink its power as much as possible. Get rid of the intrusive elements of monarchy—its titles, privileges, excessive taxes, perquisites of offices, monopolies, and corporate grants—and society could sustain itself.

In the opening of *Common Sense,* Thomas Paine had drawn a sharp distinction between society and government. "Society," he wrote, "is produced by our wants and government by our wickedness." Society "promotes our happiness *positively* by uniting our affections"; government "*negatively* by restraining our vices. The one encourages intercourse, the other creates distinctions." Later in his *Rights of Man,* which Jefferson completely agreed with, Paine went even further in denigrating the importance of government. Since "society performs for itself almost every thing which is ascribed to government," Paine thought that government contributed little or nothing to civilized life. Instead of

THE JEFFERSONIAN REVOLUTION OF 1800 · 329

ordering society, as Adams and other Federalists believed, government, said Paine, "divided it; it deprived it of its natural cohesion, and engendered discontents and disorder, which otherwise would not have existed."[20] If only the natural tendencies of people to love and care for one another were allowed to flow freely, unclogged by the artificial interference of government, particularly monarchical government, Paine and Jefferson both believed, society would prosper and hold itself together.

This would occur because people were innately sociable; they possessed a social sense that naturally bound people together. Such an inherent social predisposition was needed to counter the problems raised by Lockean sensationalism. Although Jefferson generally accepted the premises of Lockean sensationalism—that the character and personality of individuals were formed by the environment operating through the senses—he and other liberals were not such out-and-out sensationalists that they counted on men and women being able by reason alone to control the environment's chaotic bombardment of their senses. Something else was required in individuals to help structure their sensuous experiences. Otherwise human personalities, as James Wilson pointed out in 1790, citing David Hume's *Treatise of Human Nature*, would become "a bundle or collection of different perceptions, which succeed each other with an inconceivable rapidity, . . . in a perpetual flux and movement."[21]

A society composed of such variable and unstable personalities would be impossible. Something had to bind people together intuitively and naturally and bring order out of all the various sensations flying about. As Jefferson said, "The Creator would indeed have been a bungling artist, had he intended man for a social animal, without planting in him social dispositions." Jefferson and others modified their stark Lockean environmentalism—their belief that circumstances by themselves shaped people's character—by positing a natural sense of sociability and sympathy in every human being. "Nature," said Jefferson, "hath implanted in our breasts a love of others, a sense of duty to them, a moral instinct in short, which prompts us irresistibly to feel and to succor their distresses." Jefferson admitted that this moral sense did not exist in everyone and was imperfect in others. But that there were exceptions did not contradict the rule that such a social disposition was "a general characteristic of the species." When this moral sense was lacking, he said, "we endeavor to supply the defect by education, by appeals to reason and calculation."[22]

Although the idea of such a moral gyroscope in the English-speaking world went back at least to Anthony Ashley Cooper, 3rd Earl of Shaftesbury, and Bishop Joseph Butler, by the late eighteenth century it was generally identified with the Scottish moral or commonsense philosophy associated with Francis Hutcheson, Lord Kames, Thomas Reid, and other Scots; but it was much too prevalent among enlightened liberals like Jefferson to be linked to any single writer or group of writers. It resembled the categories of Immanuel Kant, which were likewise designed to counteract the worst and most frightening implications of pure Lockean sensationalism. If man's character were simply the consequence of the "impressions" made upon him "from an infinite variety of objects external and internal," Nathaniel Chipman, the federal district judge in Vermont, wrote in 1793, "he would be the sport of blind impulses." In order "to prevent the utmost capriciousness of conduct" by individuals beset by multitudes of fluctuating impressions, "some constant regulator is necessary." In wild and changing environments, people needed "a balancer, as well as some arbiter of moral action."[23]

And this regulator, balancer, or arbiter was not reason, which was too unequally distributed in people, but a common moral disposition hardwired in nearly every person's heart or conscience, however humble and however lacking in education that person may have been. "State a moral case to a ploughman and a professor," said Jefferson; "the former will decide it as well, and often better than the latter, because he has not been led astray by artificial rules." Despite his jaundiced view of the inferiority of blacks in reason and imagination, Jefferson did concede that the African slaves possessed the same moral sense and sympathy for others as whites. They had the same endowments of "the heart" and the same feelings of "benevolence, gratitude, and unshaken fidelity" as whites.[24]

This belief in the natural benevolence and sociability of people made modern republican government possible. People's social disposition and fellow feeling became the sources of eighteenth-century virtue—modern substitutes for the ascetic and Spartan virtue of the ancient republics. This new modern virtue, as Hume pointed out, was much more in accord with the growing commercialization and polite refinement of the enlightened and civilized eighteenth century than the austere and militaristic virtue of the ancients. Virtue in antiquity had flowed from the citizen's participation in politics; government had been the source of the citizen's civic consciousness and public spiritedness. But the modern virtue of Jefferson, Paine, and other eighteenth-century liberals flowed from the citizen's participation in society, not in government.

It was Jefferson's assumption that society was naturally benevolent and self-ordering that lay behind his belief in minimal government. He was not a nineteenth-century laissez-faire liberal trying to promote capitalism by reducing the power of government, but an eighteenth-century radical who hated monarchical power and all that it entailed. In fact, calling him a believer in minimal government doesn't do justice to his deep disdain for hereditary monarchical government. Monarchy for Jefferson was silly and contemptible, and his scorn for the European monarchs was boundless. All the kings, he said, were fools or idiots. "They passed their lives in hunting, and dispatched two courtiers a week, one thousand miles, to let each other know what game they had killed the preceding days."[25]

Adams, like anyone who believed at all in republicanism, had to acknowledge that humans had some sort of moral sense, but he never shared the confidence of Jefferson and Paine in the natural harmony and benevolence of society.[26] Because in his mind aggrandizing governments were not the real source of evils in the society, as Jefferson and Paine and other utopians believed, minimizing government and allowing individuals freely to engage in their separate pursuits of happiness were recipes for disaster. For without government constraining, controlling, and balancing the human passions of ambition, envy, and jealousy, society would fall apart.

Consequently, Adams thought Paine's distinction between an evil government and a benign society "a Species of airy Anticks," empty and vaporous. It was not possible to separate the two: "Society," he said, "cannot exist without Government, in any reasonable sense of the Word." There could be "Single Acts of Sociability," but, he asked his son Thomas in 1803, "can you conceive of any thing which can be properly called Society, which signifies a Series of Acts of Sociability, without Government? Nay can you conceive of a Single Act of Sociability without Government?" No matter how minutely these things were traced out, he said, "you will find Government, by Hope, or fear, Force, Influence or Consent in every conceivable Social Act." He saw "no Symptom of any Society or any Social Act, or exertion of Sociability without Government."[27]

Adams may not have been as cynical about human nature as Hamilton, but he was certainly closer to the Federalists' end of the political spectrum than he was to Jefferson's. All society, he said, including marriage and the family, was impossible without authority, and "Government is nothing more than Authority reduced to practice." As he had repeated over and over, that authority had to be bolstered by ceremonies, rituals, and titles—in other words, by all the paraphernalia of monarchy.[28]

FROM THE VERY OUTSET JEFFERSON was determined to get rid of all that monarchical paraphernalia. He wanted to establish a new tone of republican simplicity in place of the stiff formality and regal ceremony with which Washington and Adams had surrounded the presidency. No elaborately ornamented coach drawn by four or six horses for Jefferson: the president-elect walked from his boardinghouse on New Jersey Avenue to his inauguration, dressed, as a reporter noted, as "a plain citizen, without any distinctive badge of office." The day he became president, wrote Jefferson anonymously in the Philadelphia *Aurora*, "buried levees, birthdays, royal parades, and the arrogation of precedence in society by certain self-stiled friends of order, but truly stiled friends of privileged orders."[29] Since the Federalist presidents Washington and Adams, like the English monarchs, had delivered their addresses to the

Congress "from the throne," Jefferson chose to deliver his message in writing to which no formal answer from the Congress would be expected; this set a precedent that was not broken until the presidency of Woodrow Wilson. Much to the chagrin of foreign dignitaries, he brought a new republican informality to the president's residence. Unlike Washington and Adams, Jefferson ("his Democratic majesty," as one person called him) made himself easily accessible to visitors, all of whom, no matter how distinguished, he received, as the British chargé reported, "with a most perfect disregard to ceremony both in his dress and manner." He was unwilling "to admit the smallest distinction that may separate him from the mass of his fellow citizens."[30]

Jefferson, unlike Adams, was a superb administrator who intended to centralize information and affairs in his own hands. He told his cabinet at the outset that Adams as president had made a mess of things. Because of "his long & habitual absences from the seat of government," he was removed "from any share in the transactions of affairs." Instead, the government under Adams had been parceled out "among four independent heads, drawing sometimes in opposite directions." As president, Jefferson would have none of that.[31]

The new president aimed to create a much smaller central government, one that resembled the old Articles of Confederation rather than the European-type state that the Federalists had sought to build. The federal government, Jefferson declared in his first message to Congress in 1801, was "charged with the external and mutual relations only of these states." All the rest—the "principal care of our persons, our property, and our reputation, constituting the great field of human concerns"—was to be left to the states, which Jefferson thought were the best governments in the world.[32] The Sedition Act lapsed, and a new liberal naturalization law was adopted. Because of what Jefferson called the Federalist "scenes of favoritism" and "dissipation of treasure," strict economy was ordered to root out corruption.[33]

Jefferson inherited from Adams a governmental establishment that was minuscule by modern standards and small even by eighteenth-century European standards. In March 1801, the headquarters of the War

Department, for example, consisted of only the secretary, an accountant, fourteen clerks, and two messengers. The secretary of state had a staff consisting of a chief clerk, six other clerks (one of whom ran the patent office), and a messenger. The attorney general did not yet even have a clerk. Nonetheless, Jefferson believed that this tiny federal bureaucracy had become "too complicated, too expensive," and offices under the Federalists had "multiplied unnecessarily."[34] He especially resented all the appointments that Adams had made after the election results were known. He considered these so-called midnight appointments as "mere nullities," with the candidates having no claim whatsoever to the offices. Adams, he said, especially in contrast to Washington, had "degraded himself infinitely by his conduct on this subject."[35]

Jefferson was appalled by the abuses and "disregard of legal appropriations" practiced by the previous two administrations. There were "expenses . . . for jobs not seen; agencies upon agencies in every part of the earth, and for the most useless or mischievous purposes, & all of these opening doors for fraud & embezzlement far beyond the ostensible profits of the agency." Hence his administration, he told colleagues, had become busy "hunting out & abolishing multitudes of useless offices, striking off jobs &c."[36]

His government eliminated all tax inspectors and collectors, which shrunk the number of treasury employees by 40 percent. The diplomatic establishment was reduced to three missions—in Britain, France, and Spain. If Jefferson could have had his way completely, he said he would have gotten rid of all the missions and maintained only consuls. Like other enlightened believers in the possibility of universal peace, Jefferson longed to have only commercial connections with other nations.

The one nation he wanted nothing to do with was the new Republic of Haiti. In 1802–1803 he supported France's attempt to recover the island and restore slavery on it, but when that failed he refused to extend diplomatic recognition to the independent black republic—the only sister republic in the New World. The United States did not recognize the Haitian government until the administration of Abraham Lincoln.

Jefferson wanted no part of the Federalist dream of creating a modern army and navy like those of European nations. When he learned early in 1800 of Napoleon's coup d'état of November 1799, which had overthrown the French Republic, he did not draw the lesson that Adams did: that too much democracy led to dictatorship. Instead, he said, "I read it as a lesson against standing armies."[37] Upon taking office, he immediately cut the military budget in half. Since the armed forces had been the largest cause of non-debt-related spending in the 1790s, amounting to nearly 40 percent of the total federal budget, this reduction severely decreased the overall expenditures of the national government. Jefferson left the army with three thousand regulars and only 172 officers. The state militias were enough for America's defense, he said.

Although the navy had only a half-dozen frigates, Jefferson sought to replace this figment of a standing navy with several hundred small, shallow-draft gunboats, which were intended simply for inland waters and harbor defense. They would be the navy's version of the militia, unquestionably designed for defense of the coastline and not for risky military ventures on the high seas. Such small, defensive ships, said Jefferson, could never "become an excitement to engage in offensive maritime war" and were unlikely to provoke naval attacks from hostile foreign powers. Not only were the standing armies and navies that the Federalists had desired expensive and a threat to liberty, but they were the cause of all the monarchical-bred wars that had gone on for the past three centuries.[38]

Since Hamilton's financial program had formed the basis of the political power of the federal government, it above all had to be dismantled—at least to the extent possible. It mortified Jefferson that his government inherited "the contracted, English, half-lettered ideas of Hamilton. . . . We can pay off his debt in 15 years, but we can never get rid of his financial system." He had to keep the Bank of the United States with its twenty-year charter, but other aspects of Hamilton's program could be abolished. All the internal excise taxes the Federalists had designed to make the people feel the energy of the national government were eliminated. For most citizens the federal presence was now reduced to the delivery of the mail. Such an inconsequential and distant government, noted one observer in 1811, was "too little felt in the ordinary concerns of life to vie in any considerable degree with the nearer and more powerful influence produced by the operations of the local governments."[39]

Jefferson believed that his election had occurred in just the nick of time. If the Federalists had continued in office much longer, he said, "it would have been long & difficult to unhorse them." But they had brought about their own downfall. "Their madness" over the preceding three years had accomplished "what reason acting alone" might not have been able to do in decades. With the Republicans having taken over the presidency and the House of Representatives, with a fairly even balance in the Senate, he now intended "to establish good principles" and "to fortify republicanism behind as many barriers as possible."

The Federalists, however, had not been completely routed. "They have retired into the Judiciary as a strong hold." There, Jefferson lamented, they hoped to preserve the "remains" of their party. "From that battery all the works of republicanism are to be beaten down & erased by a fraudulent use of the constitution." Since judges were not constitutionally removable, the Federalists with their lame-duck legislation had "multiplied useless judges merely to strengthen their phalanx."[40] Jefferson and the new Republican Congress moved swiftly to repeal the Judiciary Act of 1801, thus eliminating the offices of sixteen federal judges, and then set about using impeachment to remove otherwise immovable Federalist judges and justices of the Supreme Court. Jefferson realized that impeachment, which was designed for "high crimes and misdemeanors," was "a bungling way" of removing judges with life tenure, but unfortunately there seemed no alternative.[41]

IN RETIREMENT ADAMS had trouble getting over his hurt and anger. He began a lengthy answer to Hamilton's malicious *Letter,* which helped to calm some of his emotional turmoil, but he never published it. He wondered what he would do in retirement. Having been so active for so many years, could he suddenly come to a stop? He dismissed out of hand the notion that he could resume his law practice or become a minister at a foreign court. No, he concluded, he "must be Farmer John of Stoneyfield and nothing more, (I hope nothing less) for the rest of my Life" (Stoneyfield being one of the several names he gave to his home in Quincy).[42]

Fuming over the way he had been treated, in October 1802 he began writing an autobiography, designed, as he said, to show his posterity by his own hand "proof of the falsehood of that Mass of odious Abuse of my Character, with which News Papers, private Letters and public Pamphlets and Histories have been disgraced for thirty Years."[43] But after only a few pages and getting up to only 1751, the year he entered college, he abandoned the memoir.

Two years later, in November 1804, John Quincy, unaware of his father's earlier effort, urged his father to write "an account of the principal incidents of your own life."[44] Adams's reply was swimming in self-pity: "Alass! Alass! What can I say? I can recollect no part of my Political Life, without pain." All he saw was "so much jealousy, Envy, Treachery, Perfidy, Malice without cause or provocation and revenge: without Injury or Offence" that he couldn't imagine recovering a credible account of his life. "You may depend on this, I am a Man more Sinned against than sinning." He feared that if he wrote "the whole Truth and nothing but the Truth," not only would very few believe him, but he would also have to "reveal to posterity the Weaknesses of many great Men," which would result in his work being dismissed as "an Hymn to Vanity." Far from soothing his passions, as his son hoped, the effort to write his memoir would only inflame them, reminding him of all "my Mortifications, Disappointments or Resentments" in a life forsaken even by God. Like the memoirs of the Duc de Sully, the early-seventeenth-century minister to Henri IV of France, his would be "a melancholly Book."[45]

Melancholy or not, Adams nevertheless resumed his autobiography, and wrote doggedly for the next seven months, carrying the jumbled story of his life up to 1776.

· · ·

LEARNING OF THE ATTEMPT by Jefferson and the Republicans to use the process of impeachment to remove hostile Federalist judges, Adams was reminded of his 1773 defense in the Massachusetts press of an independent judiciary, and he included the events in his memoir. He said he had embodied these principles of an independent judiciary in the Massachusetts constitution of 1780, and they had prevailed in America until the administration of Jefferson, "during which they have been infringed and are now in danger of being lost." This was alarming, he wrote in his autobiography, because "we shall have no balance at all of Interests or Passions, and our Lives, Liberties, Reputations and Estates will lie at the mercy of a Majority, and of a tryumphant Party."[46]

In June 1805, Adams paused in the writing of his memoir, perhaps because he began writing many more letters to friends, family members, and acquaintances. At this time he resumed his friendship with Benjamin Rush, with whom he had not corresponded since he had become president in 1797. In December 1806, however, he once again returned to his memoir and worked on it for another seven months or so, bringing his life up to 1780, when he was in France. He abruptly stopped there, and never completed it.

Perhaps he ceased writing his memoir in 1807 because he couldn't stomach reliving the duplicity of Franklin in the 1780s and the arrogance of Hamilton in the 1790s; or because he had critics like Mercy Otis Warren whom he had to answer; or because he began contributing to the *Boston Patriot* numerous pieces defending his role in the Revolution; or because his interest in the actions of the Jefferson administration was absorbing more and more of his time.

AT FIRST ADAMS had no confidence whatsoever in Jefferson's administration. He thought the new president was unreliable. His "sayings are never well digested, often extravagant, and never consistently pursued," he told his son Thomas in July 1801. Jefferson did not have "a clear head"; he "never pursues any question through. His Ambition and his cunning are the only steady qualities in him. His Imagination and Ambition are too strong for his Reason."[47]

Adams objected to Jefferson's assertion that his election had saved republicanism from monarchism. That was false, Adams said. The reason he had failed to get reelected as president, he claimed, was that the Federalists had become divided, not because of "any change in favor of Republicanism in the People, . . . nor by any opinion that the new president was more of a Republican than the old former one." He was also offended by the Republicans' charge of his "aggrandizing Executive Power." In fact, he said in June 1801, there had been "more acts of the Executive of more Power in 4 months past, than were in 12 years preceeding." He especially resented Jefferson's being hailed as a great enlightened philosopher. "The harmonious voice of Europe and America," he said, "pronounce Jefferson the greatest Man who ever was in America." This was the man who "had the affectation to go to Italy for an outlandish name for his Hill."[48]

It was all too much to bear. "That part of the World of Science called Academicians, if not the Universal," he told his brother-in-law, "are at this day, prone to Epicureanism to such a degree, that they instantly become the puffers and Trumpeters of every man of genius and Learning who despises the Church."[49]

Yet gradually Adams's resentments softened. Not wanting his administration to be dismissed as some sort of monarchical ancien régime that had to be overthrown, he continued to play down Jefferson's claim that his election represented a radical revolution. He admitted to his son John Quincy in 1804 that he had some regrets about what was happening under the Republicans, especially the assaults on the judiciary and the cashiering of so many public offices. But generally, he said, things at present were not "so very terrible."[50]

Adams appreciated that Jefferson was trying to avoid taking sides in the great struggle for supremacy taking place between Britain and France. The ferocity of that war, which had gone on more or less continually since 1793, had convinced Adams of "the absolute necessity of keeping aloof from all European Powers and Influences; and that a Navy was the only Arm by which it can be accomplished." He was especially pleased to learn that Jefferson seemed to endorse this need for a strong navy in order to keep foreign powers off America's shores. He was mistaken in this hope, as Jefferson had no such plans.[51]

Adams concluded that Jefferson had borrowed, indeed, stolen, the basic principle that Adams himself had advocated and upheld ever since the model treaty of 1776—"to do Justice of all Nations, to have alliances with none without necessity." Emotionally, Adams needed to see continuity, not change, in Jefferson's administration. Forgetting how bellicose he had been at times during 1798–1799, Adams claimed that as president he had "established Peace with both France and England in such a manner that it was almost impossible for my Successor to break it."[52]

He still worried about Jefferson's enthusiasm for the French Revolution—an enthusiasm that Bonaparte's 1799 coup had not diminished. Initially, Jefferson had not seen Napoleon, as Adams had, as the inevitable outcome of a revolution that had gone terribly awry. Instead, Jefferson simply dismissed Bonaparte as a bigoted Italian usurper who offered "nothing which bespeaks a luminous view of the organisation of rational government." Napoleon's assumption of power was "not serious enough to disturb the course of [French] military operations." Besides, Bonaparte had "but a few days to live," for he was likely to be assassinated soon by fervent French revolutionaries. Jefferson had so much vested in the French Revolution that he just knew that if Bonaparte tried to stop it and declare for royalty either for himself or for Louis XVIII, "the enthusiasm of that nation would furnish a million of Brutus's who would devote themselves to death to destroy him."[53]

But if Bonaparte was not killed, there was some consolation, said Jefferson. He might settle the question that had been undecided between the two transatlantic sister republics for nearly a decade—whether the single executive in the United States was better than the plural executive of the Directory in France.[54] Jefferson hoped that Napoleon would use his head and realize "how much superior is the glory of establishing a republic to that of wearing a crown." If he chose the crown, he feared "the influence of the example on our countrymen"—suggesting just how fragile America's experiment in republicanism still seemed to Jefferson. All Americans could do, he said, was "wait with patience" until the French got it right. If it went wrong and the French republic blew up, the United States was at least far enough away to be safe.[55]

By contrast, Adams had no illusions about Napoleon. To him the man was an extraordinary force of nature. Neither Julius Caesar, Oliver Cromwell, nor even Alexander the Great, he said, could "bear a Parallel with Bonaparte." He was "Sui generis." Of course, he admitted, no one could predict what would happen in France. The Revolution there resembled nothing before in history, "and Bonaparte differs from all the Conquerors we know of." But at least Napoleon was bringing order and tranquillity to a society that was "weary of blood, disgusted with murder, and indignant at rapine." He told Lafayette that he wished Napoleon "a greater Glory than ever yet fell to the Lott of any Conqueror before him, that of giving Peace to Europe and Liberty and Good Government to France."[56]

Perhaps because of his appreciation of what military force could achieve, Adams had come around to Jefferson's handling of the continuing problems with North African pirates. Ever since independence, the Barbary states had been capturing and imprisoning American merchant sailors in the Mediterranean Sea and then asking for ransom to free them. Back in the 1780s, Adams had differed with Jefferson over how these Muslim states ought to be treated. Believing that Congress would never pay for the warships necessary to use force, he advocated following the example of Britain and France and simply paying tribute to the pirates. It would, he said, be cheaper than going to war with them.

Jefferson, on the other hand, had taken a hard line. He believed that the North African states were so caught up in Islamic fatalism and Ottoman tyranny that their backward and indolent societies could only be dealt with by force. Although he was opposed to a standing army and preferred using commercial pressure to war in dealing with international problems with the great powers, the Barbary pirates were different. Paying tributes and ransoms, he said, was just "money thrown away." The

North African states kept upping their requests and breaking their promises. "I am an enemy to these douceurs, tributes and humiliations," he explained to Madison, who was now his secretary of state, and "I know that nothing will stop the eternal increase of demand from these pirates but the presence of an armed force."[57]

Now thanks to the half-dozen frigates that his predecessor Adams had built to engage in the Quasi-War with France—a war and a naval buildup Jefferson had opposed—President Jefferson was at last able to use naval power against the Barbary pirates and teach them a lesson.

As far as Jefferson's domestic policies were concerned, Adams saw little that was really new or radical. Substituting messages for speeches and holding dinners every day for a dozen instead of levees twice a week for a large number were "mere Trifles." Even Jefferson's "twenty other little Sacrifices to a very vulgar popularity" didn't bother him. He claimed disingenuously that he had never really favored the Alien and Sedition Acts, and therefore he did not regret their repeal. He did think the Republicans had made the naturalization process "too easy." All "the irreligion, the Immorality and Venality which are creeping in and gaining ground" he blamed on "French intrigue," and Jefferson couldn't stop it anyhow. Adams predicted, correctly, that the Republicans' catering to the press would in the future turn newspaper editors into "the principal Instruments" of party ambition and activity.

In the end, the worst the Republicans had done was to shift the basis of American politics. "Public Virtue is no longer to rule: but Ambition is to govern the Country. . . . Call it Vanity or what you will," but Adams believed that his and Washington's administrations were the last expressions of selfless disinterested government. In the future, all the American people could hope for was that they might "be governed by honorable, not criminal ambition." Since America's Constitution seemed to lack "any Mediating Power capable of uniting or controlling Rival Factions, and maintaining a ballance between them, our Government must forever be a kind of War of about one half the People against the other." This to Adams was what political parties portended.[58]

The only solution he could imagine was to make the president more independent and more respectable, presumably by making him president for life. "Till this is done, the Government will be a ride and a tye, a game at leap frog, one Party once in eight or twelve years leaping over the head and shoulders of the other, kicking and spurring when it rides"—a rather perceptive prediction of what eventually did become normal American politics. He wanted the president to resemble a monarch and be the head of the nation, not the head of a party. He saw himself standing above all the factional fighting.[59]

Adams kept up a relentless patter of cynicism in his correspondence, describing, for example, "the Philosophers of the eighteenth Century and almost all the Men of Science and Letters" as cracked and fit only for Bedlam. Indeed, judging "by the Conduct and Writings of the Men of Science," it seemed to him that the earth had become the place where "the Sun, Moon, and Stars send all their Lunaticks . . . for confinement." He often made sly references in one way or another to the dreaminess of Jefferson. He mocked philosophers who believed in "a universal and perpetual Peace among all Nations and all Men." He made fun of those who feared having "any thing more powerful at sea than Gun Boats." He loved emphasizing the Virginians' belief that in their state "Geese are all Swans." He enjoyed pointing out that all men have the "universal Passion" of self-love in an equal degree, but, unlike knaves, "honest Men do not disguise it." Someone like Jefferson who prided himself on his modesty, he said, was bound to be "as vain a fellow as lives."[60]

When told that he knew Jefferson better than anyone, he denied it outright. "In truth," he said, "I know but little concerning him." Even when they had been abroad together, "there was no very close intimacy between us."[61] Adams was still angry and hurt. His sarcasm was unmistakable when he called Jefferson's government "our Monarchical, Antirepublican Administration" and compared it with his own, led by a real and "zealous Republican." He was more serious and direct in his criticism of Jefferson's handling of the 1807 trial of Aaron Burr for treason. (In 1806 the former vice president had organized a mysterious expedition to the West that seemed to threaten a breakup of the Union.) "Mr. Jefferson," Adams told Benjamin Rush, "has been too hasty in his

Message in which he has denounced him by Name and pronounced him guilty." Even if Burr's guilt was "as clear as the Noon day Sun," he said, "the first Magistrate ought not have pronounced it so before a Jury had tryed him." It is a point many historians and jurists have subsequently made as well.[62]

GRADUALLY, HOWEVER, Adams found himself agreeing more and more with Jefferson's administration than with the views of his fellow Federalists. In fact, he became increasingly hostile to the so-called Essex Junto in Massachusetts, who he believed had turned against him in the election of 1800. While some northern Federalists plotted secession from the Union over the Louisiana Purchase in 1803, Adams and his son John Quincy, newly elected by the Massachusetts legislature to the U.S. Senate, celebrated it. With Jefferson, he strongly opposed the British practice of impressing sailors on American ships. He and John Quincy even approved of Jefferson's Embargo Act of 1807—a policy that devastated trading communities in New England and became anathema to the Federalists. Indeed, John Quincy's support for the embargo cost him his seat in the Senate.

When in 1807 a British warship fired on the U.S.S. *Chesapeake*, killing several seamen, and went on to impress four others, the United States was brought to the brink of war. But Jefferson hated war so much—it bred monarchism—that he hoped he might coerce Britain by withholding American trade as the colonists had done in the 1760s and '70s. "War is not the best engine for us to resort to," he said; "nature has given us one in our commerce, which, if properly managed, will be a far better instrument for obliging the interested nations of Europe to treat us with justice."[63] He and his Republican Congress thus instituted the embargo, which barred American ships and goods from all overseas trade.

Although Adams termed the embargo "a cowardly measure," he supported it as "a wise and prudent" but temporary action designed only to protect America's seamen and property.[64] Not liking armies, Adams understood the attractiveness of Jefferson's grand experiment in peaceful coercion—what we today call economic sanctions. In the end, however, he realized that not only was the embargo "extremely difficult if not absolutely impossible to carry into Execution," but he had "never believed that we could coerce or intimidate or bring to serious consideration the Government of Great Britain by embargo's or non-importations or non-intercourses."[65] Such economic sanctions never worked for long; he realized that ultimately Americans might have to fight, but only if "we are compelled to it, and then only by Sea unless we are invaded."[66] When the war with Britain finally came, in 1812, Adams favored the military conflict, believing that war was needed to bring Americans together and preserve the Union.

BY THIS TIME ADAMS had become more of an outsider among the Federalist elite of Massachusetts than he had ever been. He had been in "Enemies Country" before—France, England—but now, he said, that country was "Boston, Massachusetts." Some of these Massachusetts Federalists flirted with the British and even threatened secession. At a convention in Hartford in the winter of 1814–1815, several dozen of these angry and frightened Federalists from all the New England states brought to a head all their accumulated grievances against Virginia's Republican dominance over the Union. Adams scoffed at the disloyal behavior of these Federalists, expressing astonishment that "so many of his Country-Men, still cherish a fond attachment to the people of England." It seemed that some aspects of the Revolution had not been completed. In 1776 it had been "necessary to destroy the ignorant bigoted Attachment of the People to Great Britain. And this never has yet been half done."[67]

Although Adams's position as an ex-president earned him the presidency of several boards in the state, including the American Academy of Arts and Sciences, the Massachusetts Society for Promoting Agriculture, and the Visitors of the Professorship of Natural History at Harvard, he found himself at the meetings of these boards the odd man out. He told his friend Rush that there were twelve men on these boards, and they met once a month. "Every one, but myself, is a Staunch Anti-Jeffersonian and Anti-Madisonian. . . . They were all real Gentlemen; all but me, very rich, have their City Palaces and Country Seats, their fine Gardens and greenhouses and hot Houses &c &c &c."[68]

This was the aristocracy Adams had long worried about. In the opinion of these well-to-do Federalists, Adams's separation from them was puzzling and his support for "Mr. Madison's War" against Great Britain incomprehensible. He advised his controversial Republican friend Dr. Benjamin Waterhouse of the dangers of writing in the press against the Essex Junto. "They will not," he warned Waterhouse, "hesitate to destroy, if they can, both you & your family."[69] The fact that John Quincy had joined the Republican Party only further convinced them that Adams had become a Jeffersonian. (JQA began as a Federalist but after the Embargo of 1807–8 he joined the Republican Party.) Before long, the High Federalists in Massachusetts were relishing the fact that Adams had "few friends" left, which Adams had to admit was all "too true."[70]

By the time the nation was at war with Great Britain, the New England states, much to Adams's horror, were threatening secession. This moment in 1813, he told Jefferson, was the most serious that he had ever experienced. But the northern states were only copying what they had learned from the examples of Virginia and Kentucky in 1799. He didn't know which party, the Federalists or the Republicans, had "the most unblushing Front, the most lying Tongue, or the most impudent and insolent not to say the most seditious and rebellious Pen."[71] All he knew was that the Union was in danger.

THE ISSUE THAT THREATENED the Union most was slavery. Adams had never commented on Jefferson's involvement with slavery, but when the press brought it up, he could hardly avoid the subject. In the late summer and fall of 1802, James Callender, the former Republican scandalmonger who had recently turned against Jefferson, published in the Richmond *Recorder* several accounts of the relationship between Jefferson and his slave Sally Hemings. Callender claimed that he had earlier heard hints of Jefferson's relationship with a slave but had dismissed them as Federalist calumny. But he now believed that "by this wench Sally our president has had several children." There was no one in the neighborhood of Charlottesville, he wrote, who did not believe the story.

Callender claimed he was no prudish Scottish Presbyterian pastor. He understood boys and bachelors having relations with slaves, but Jefferson was the president, "the favorite! the first born of republicanism! the pinnacle of all that is good and great!" It was amazing that Jefferson should have a black concubine, given what he had previously written "so smartly concerning negroes." When he had "endeavoured so much to *belittle* the African race" in his *Notes on the State of Virginia*, Callender had not expected that he would become "the ringleader" in showing this opinion to be erroneous or that he would choose "an African stock" on which he would "engraft his own descendants." Because of this interracial relationship, the Republicans no longer had any right to criticize President Adams's treaty with Haiti. Indeed, Jefferson was fortunate that the revelation came after he became president. If Americans had known about Sally in 1800, that "SINGLE FACT would have rendered his election impossible."[72]

These charges were picked up and spread everywhere in the press, becoming in the course of a year increasingly crude and more malicious in tone. The Republicans tried to deny them, while the delighted Federalists wrote endless poems and satires about "Dusky Sally." Even John Quincy Adams, who generally tried to moderate some of the harshest Federalist criticism of Jefferson, joined in the fun with a loose imitation of Horace's "Ode to Xanthia Phoceus." He attributed the piece to Thomas Paine, "THE SOPHIST OF THETFORD," and in a note he cited Jefferson's *Notes on the State of Virginia* on "the amatory propensities of the blacks." The poem opened:

> Dear Thomas, deem it no disgrace
> With slaves to mend thy breed.
> Nor let the wench's smutty face
> Deter thee from the deed.[73]

348 · FRIENDS DIVIDED

Jefferson made no response whatsoever to all these charges and satires, but he knew about them. His friends usually dismissed them as
slander. Adams did not. "Callender and Sally will be remembered as
long as Jefferson has Blotts in his Character." The story, he told a Massachusetts correspondent in 1810, was "a natural and almost Unavoid-
able Consequence of the foul contagion in the human Character [of]
Negro Slavery." He had heard said by a great lady that there was not "a
Planter in Virginia who could not reckon among his Slaves a Number of
his Children." Still, he added, none of Jefferson's scandals, including
that involving his youthful attempts to seduce Mrs. Walker, were as bad
as the "much more atrocious" tales involving Hamilton.[74]

Although Adams liked to brag that "never in my Life did I own a
slave," he was no abolitionist and was much more a man of his own time
than ours. In 1790 he had been disgusted when the Abolition Society of
Pennsylvania had introduced into Congress a petition, signed by Benjamin Franklin, calling for the abolition of slavery in the United States.
"What motives the eastern members can have to support the silly petition
of Franklin and his Quakers, I never could conceive."[75] For most leaders
in 1790, that was certainly the realistic position. Although Franklin's petition sparked outrage from southern congressmen, one of them saying
the Pennsylvanian proposal if accepted would result in a civil war, most
elites, including President Washington, agreed with Adams that the petition was ill timed, for it threatened to break up the Union just as it was
getting on its feet.

In 1795 Jeremy Belknap, a Boston clergyman and a major founder of
the Massachusetts Historical Society, asked Adams how slavery had been
abolished in Massachusetts. Adams replied that although he had been involved in several cases before the Revolution in which slaves had sued for
their freedom, the rise and progress of slavery was "a subject to which I
have never given any very particular attention." The fact that in at least
four recorded cases Adams was the counsel for the master and lost three
of them may have helped account for his lack of interest in the subject.[76]

In his answer to Belknap, Adams assumed that slavery would decline elsewhere just as it had in Massachusetts. One thing was clear: it had not been abolished by intellectual arguments or court decisions. "The real Cause was the multiplication of labouring White people, who would no longer Suffer the Rich to employ these Sable Rivals, So much to their Injury." These common white people turned black slaves into unprofitable servants. "Their Scoffs & Insults . . . filled the Negroes with Discontents, made them lazy idle, proud, vicious and at length wholly useless to their Masters: to such a Degree that the Abolition of slavery became a measure of Oeconomy." This same principle had "kept Negro slavery out of France England and other Parts of Europe."[77]

At any rate, Adams did not think it wise to suddenly turn the slaves "loose upon a World in which they have no Capacity to procure even a Subsistence." He asked Belknap, "What would become of the old? The young? The infirm?" The only just way to abolish slavery, said Adams, was "to prohibit the Importation of new Negroes," and "soften the Severity of the Condition of old ones, as much as possible." This would buy time "until the increasing Population of the Country shall have multiplied the Whites to such a superiority of Numbers, that the Blacks may be liberated by Degrees, with the Consent of Master and Servant."[78]

In 1801 he repeated his admonition to two antislavery Quakers that "the Abolition of slavery must be gradual and accomplished with much caution and Circumspection." To do it forcefully and abruptly, he said, "would produce greater violations of Justice and Humanity than the continuance of the practice." He presumed that neither of his Quaker correspondents "would be willing to venture on Exertions which would probably excite Insurrections among the Blacks to rise against their Masters and imbue their hands in innocent blood." Besides, he said, there were "many other Evils in our Country" that were a more immediate threat to the United States "than the oppression of the blacks . . . hatefull as that is." These evils, he said, at the very moment the Jeffersonian Republicans were about to take office, were "a general Debauchery as well as dissipation, produced by pestilential phylosophical Principles of Epicurus" that were undermining both government and education.

These were more pressing social evils than slavery. Like many other leaders in the early nineteenth century, Adams thought that "the practice of slavery was fast diminishing."[79]

Actually, at this point Adams's position on biding time and softening the condition of the slaves was not all that different from Jefferson's. By the time Jefferson had returned from France in 1789, he had essentially abandoned his earlier goal of abolishing slavery outright. Instead, he had come to terms with the institution and had begun concentrating on what he called "ameliorating" the condition of the slaves. It was part of his new appreciation of the superiority of America over Europe. Despite its fine arts and culture, the Old World was no longer the measure of civilization. America may have had slaves, but he thought most of them were better off than the great mass of oppressed peasants in Europe.[80]

When he had left the Washington administration at the end of 1793, he had told people he was returning to Monticello "to watch out for the happiness of those who labor for mine." Masters and slaves were no longer in the state of war he had described in his *Notes on the State of Virginia*. Jefferson had come to believe that a paternalistic slaveholder could have the best interests of the slaves at heart. He had witnessed the way prisoners were treated at the Walnut Street Prison in Philadelphia, where the aim was to eliminate corporal punishment and create rational and useful members of society; and he now sought to apply those principles to the running of Monticello.

He introduced incentives of rewards and distinctions and began doling out random acts of leniency and paying money for some jobs. He established a nail factory, in which young enslaved boys aged ten to sixteen would learn self-discipline and efficiency. He wanted to use "the stimulus of character" rather than "the degrading motive of fear" to get the boys to work productively. Using the whip on the boys (except "in extremities") would "degrade them in their own eyes" and thus destroy the value of Jefferson's experiment.[81]

This was only a respite, however; the burden of slavery on Jefferson would only get heavier as time went on.

. . .

BOTH ADAMSES RETAINED an interest in Jefferson's life. Abigail learned that in April 1804 Jefferson's younger daughter, Mary Eppes, known as Polly, died at age twenty-five of a lingering illness following the birth of her second child. Learning of Jefferson's loss, Abigail wrote Jefferson in May to offer her condolences. Since Abigail had not been in touch with Jefferson for three and a half years, she said she had at first hesitated to write for "reasons of various kinds." But her feelings for Polly, whom as a nine-year-old arriving in Europe she had cared for, "burst through the restraint." Having lost her son Charles in 1800, Abigail knew what Jefferson was going through. With what Jefferson called his "evening prospects" now hinging on "the slender thread of a single life"—his elder daughter, Martha Randolph—he had been utterly devastated by Polly's death. Abigail knew that he needed all the sympathy he could get. She signed her letter as someone "who once took pleasure in subscribing Herself as your Friend."[82]

On June 13, 1804, Jefferson responded warmly, recalling the friendship "with which you honoured me," and expressing "regret that circumstances should have arisen which have seemed to draw a line of separation between us." He reminded Abigail of his long friendship with Mr. Adams that went back to the very beginning of the Revolution. He said that the political difference that had produced "a rivalship" in the minds of their respective followers was not duplicated in their minds, and thus the "mutual esteem" that each man had for the other was never lessened. This was "sufficient to keep down all jealousy between us, and to guard our friendship" from any sense of rivalry.

Jefferson seems to have assumed that the old friendship was unbroken and that Abigail valued it as much as he did. Perhaps too eager to reconcile, he misinterpreted the tone of Abigail's letter. He apparently thought their friendship was strong enough that he could invoke it as a reason for excusing Adams for something offensive he had done. He told Abigail "with truth" that there was "only one act of Mr. Adams's life, and one only," that ever displeased him. And that was Adams's many lame-duck appointments to the judiciary. These Jefferson considered "personally unkind." He believed "it seemed but common justice to leave a successor free to act by instruments of his own choice." But after brooding for some time, Jefferson said he had "cordially" forgiven Adams's action because of their friendship and had restored all the esteem and respect for Adams that he had earlier felt. Mentioning this one act that had displeased him was a disastrous mistake.[83]

Abigail answered Jefferson immediately. She said that if Jefferson had written only the first page of his letter there would have been no further need to write. But his comments about the lame-duck appointments called for a response, and she gave him a long and passionate one. Adams, she said, had assumed that all officeholders with the exception of the cabinet officials would be kept on. Then she launched into a bitter diatribe against the way in which Jefferson's supporters carried on the campaign for the presidency. She was very angry, and she decided to "freely disclose" to Jefferson just what he had done to sever "the bonds of former Friendship."

Abigail told Jefferson that one of the first acts of his administration had been to liberate that "wretch" James Callender, who had vilely slandered Adams in the campaign and deserved to remain in jail. Actually, Callender had completed his prison sentence, but Jefferson had pardoned him, thus remitting his fine, which Abigail regarded as "a public approbation of his conduct." She was furious and cut Jefferson no slack whatsoever. She said "the Chief Magistrate of a Nation, whose elevated station places him in a conspicuous light," should never forget that his behavior, giving "countenance to a base Calumniater," for example, could have a very bad effect on the manners and morals of the community. She blamed Jefferson for encouraging Callender and financially supporting him and she couldn't help reminding the president that this "serpent" whom he had "cherished and warmed" had turned and "bit the hand that nourished him." She regarded the whole business of Callender "as a personal injury." She ended by saying that there was one other act of his administration that she considered "personally unkind," but since "it neither affected character, or reputation," she decided not to describe it. She told Jefferson that she wrote in confidence and no one had seen her letter. "Faithful are the wounds of a Friend." Often, she said, she had wished that Jefferson had behaved differently. She bore no malice, she said, but of course she did.[84]

Jefferson quickly protested. He knew nothing of Callender's character and his "charities to him were no more meant as encouragements to his scurrilities than those I give to a beggar at my door are meant as rewards for the vices of his life." Besides, he paid no more attention to what Callender was writing than Mr. Adams paid to the Federalist scandalmongers. He said he pardoned all the victims of "the pretended Sedition law." His motives ought to be judged, he said, "by the general tenor of my life."[85]

Abigail wrote back with "the freedom and unreserve of former Friendship," to which she would gladly return if all the causes could be removed. These causes went beyond mere differences of opinion, differences, for example, over the Sedition Act. She wouldn't judge its constitutionality. She presumed that was the job of the Supreme Court. All she knew was that "in no Country has calumny falsehood, and reviling stalked more licentiously than in this." Not appreciating that the Sedition Act had expired when Jefferson assumed office, she accused Jefferson of taking it upon himself, like a despot, to annul the law. "You exculpate yourself from any intentional act of unkindness towards any one." She then told him that the other act she faulted him for was his removal of her son John Quincy from a district judgeship.[86]

By this time, Jefferson must have been wondering what he had gotten himself into. He patiently explained that he knew nothing about John Quincy's removal as a bankruptcy judge, and if he had known he would have been pleased to have appointed him over anyone else. He then went on to deny Abigail's suggestion that the Supreme Court alone could decide the validity of the Sedition Act. The executive had an equal right to decide for itself the constitutionality of acts. Indeed, each branch of government had a coordinate power to determine the constitutionality of a law. For Jefferson the Constitution was primarily a political, not a legal, document, and judges had no monopoly on interpreting it. If slander by the press needed to be curbed, then leave it to the states, "and their exclusive right, to do so." The First Amendment prohibited the Congress, but not the states, from controlling the press.

Jefferson hoped that Abigail would understand his position. He accepted wide differences of opinion. Both political parties wanted to promote the public good but differed over means. "One fears most the ignorance of the people: the other the selfishness of rulers independent of them." Time will tell which is right; the body of the nation would decide. All he knew was that these differences of opinion and his anxieties over the future had never allowed him to use anything but "fair and honorable means, of truth and reason" in his politics. Nor had these differences and anxieties "ever lessened my esteem for moral worth; nor alienated my affections from a single friend who did not first withdraw himself." When friends had become estranged from him, he had kept himself "open to a return of their justice." The ball of friendship was in the Adamses' court.[87]

Abigail wrote one final letter explaining to Jefferson at length why she had been hurt by his actions and why she had withdrawn her esteem for him. She grudgingly accepted his explanation for his behavior, but added that she did not believe that the First Amendment prohibited the Congress from protecting the national government from a scurrilous press. She hoped that posterity would judge "with more candour, and impartiality" than the opposing parties just what measures had best promoted the happiness of the people. She also hoped that he as president would contribute to that happiness. But with her underlying anger unabated, she asked "whether in your ardent zeal, and desire to rectify the mistakes and abuses as you may consider them, of the former administration, you are not led into measures still more fatal to the constitution, and more derogatory to your honour, and independence of Character? Pardon me Sir if I say, that you are." This was candor with a vengeance.

In a postscript added three weeks later to Abigail's letter-book copy of this extraordinary letter, John Adams noted that at Abigail's request he had just read "the whole of this Correspondence," and wanted posterity to know that it "was begun and conducted without my Knowledge or Suspicion." He had "no remarks to make upon it at this time and in this place."[88] The friendship between the Adamses and Jefferson was as dead as ever.

Having won the election in 1800 and riding high in popularity with the Louisiana Purchase of 1803, Jefferson was certainly more open to a renewal of the friendship in 1804 than Abigail. If he had avoided any criticism whatsoever of Adams in his letter of June 13, and had instead fulsomely praised him, he might have gradually warmed Abigail up. But her anger was so pervasive and powerful that the slightest criticism of her husband was bound to touch it off.

ELEVEN

RECONCILIATION

Benjamin Rush had been a good friend of both Adams and Jefferson ever since the meeting of the Continental Congress in 1775. When Adams returned from Europe in 1789, he and Rush had become especially close, with Adams feeling free to express the most outrageous opinions—opinions that sometimes left Rush flabbergasted. Although Rush's support for Jefferson and the Republicans in the 1790s had cooled the relationship, it didn't prevent President Adams from helping Rush out financially by appointing him treasurer of the Mint in 1797. Rush was grateful but told Adams that he was not changing his political principles. According to Rush, Adams took him "by the hand and with great kindness said, 'You have not more pleasure in receiving the office I have given you, than I had in conferring it upon an old Whig.'"[1]

In 1805 Adams and Rush were thus emotionally prepared to renew their friendship. Adams initiated the correspondence by telling Rush "that you and I ought not to die without saying Goodbye or bidding each other Adieu."[2] Rush responded warmly and for the next eight years the letters flowed back and forth, with Adams once again engaging in his usual "facetiousness" on some subjects, which unfortunately was "seldom understood," except by those, like Rush, who knew him well.[3]

. . .

As Adams and Rush exchanged letters, they were bound to mention Jefferson. When Jefferson's second term was nearing its end in 1808, Adams wondered how the president would deal with his guilt after he retired. "He must know," he said to Rush, "that he leaves the Government infinitely worse than he found it and that from his own error or Ignorance." But since Jefferson had "a good Taste for Letters and an ardent curiosity for Science," Adams assumed that the president would be able to amuse and console himself after leaving office. He told Rush that he had no resentment toward Jefferson, "though he has honoured and salaried almost every villain he could find who had been an enemy to me."[4]

On the day in March 1809 that Jefferson turned over the presidency to his friend James Madison, Adams asked Rush, who had often spoken of his many dreams, "to take a Nap, and dream for my Instruction and edification a Character of Jefferson and his Administration."[5] Rush didn't respond to this request, but seven months later, in October, he told Adams of a dream he did have, involving "one of the most extraordinary events" of the year 1809—"the renewal of the friendship" of Adams and Jefferson. In the dream Rush briefly related the careers of the two ex-presidents, who were now retired to their homes just waiting to be reconciled. According to the dream, Adams had written a short note to Jefferson congratulating him "upon his escape to the shades of retirement and domestic happiness" and expressing "good wishes for his welfare." Only a man like Adams, someone possessing "a Magnanimity known only to great minds," could initiate the renewal of the friendship.

Rush went on to describe the letters between these two great patriots that followed from the renewal of their friendship, letters full of "many precious aphorisms, the result of observation, experience, and profound reflection." After these two "rival friends" had outlived their parties and were "sunk into the grave nearly at the same time," the nation would benefit greatly from such a correspondence.[6]

"A Dream again!" exclaimed Adams in his quick response. "I wish you would dream all day and all Night, for one of your Dreams puts me in spirits for a Month. I have no other objection to your Dream, but that it is not History. It may be Prophecy."[7]

As indeed it was, but not immediately. In the meantime, Rush knew he had to work on Jefferson and prepare him for a renewal of the friendship. Although he corresponded regularly with Jefferson, two or three letters a year, Rush did not have an intimate relationship with him, certainly nothing like the one he had with Adams.

On January 2, 1811, Rush wrote to Jefferson and in the middle of his letter casually mentioned that "now and then" he exchanged letters with Adams, who, he said, glowed with his recollections of the patriot years of 1774–1776. Knowing how Jefferson felt about banks, Rush cited some hostile remarks that Adams had made about banks and the aristocracy they bred. After softening Jefferson up in this way, he mentioned Jefferson's "early attachment" to Adams and stressed the degree to which their concerted labors had contributed to independence. Finally Rush told Jefferson how much he "ardently wished a friendly and epistolary intercourse might be revived" between him and Adams before they died. Such an exchange of letters, he said, not only would honor their talents and their patriotism, but would also be useful to republicanism in the United States and all over the world. "Posterity will revere the friendship of two ex-Presidents that were once opposed to each other."[8]

Jefferson soon answered Rush in a long letter, explaining that he was not responsible for the discontinuance of the correspondence. He recalled that during the early years of the Revolution he and Adams had possessed "a high degree of mutual respect & esteem" for each other. "Certainly no man," he said of Adams, "was ever truer than he was, in that day, to those principles of rational republicanism" that underlay America's new governments. "Altho' he swerved afterwards towards the principles of the English constitution, our friendship did not abate on that account." Unlike Hamilton, Jefferson said, "Adams was honest as a politician as well as a man." But during the crisis of 1798, Adams, overwhelmed by lurid accounts of the ferocities of the French Revolution, had gleefully expressed his "new principles of government" to Jefferson, mingling his kindness with "a little superciliousness." Even Mrs. Adams, "with all her good sense & prudence," had been "sensibly flushed."

He described his immediate anger over Adams's "midnight appointments," but he told Rush how "a little time and reflection" had restored to him "that just estimate" of Adams's "virtues & passions" made familiar by their long friendship. Knowing that Adams "was not rich," he had first considered appointing him to a lucrative office in Massachusetts. But when his fellow Republicans objected, he "dropped the idea." Still, he yearned for an opportunity to renew the friendship, but he believed that his awkward exchange with Mrs. Adams in 1804 made any reconciliation very difficult. To convince Rush of his good intentions, he sent the 1804 correspondence with Abigail to Rush for his perusal.

Jefferson said that he believed Adams to be "an honest man" and "a powerful advocate" for independence. Unfortunately, however, Adams had become alienated from him by listening to lies "contrived for electioneering purposes"—lies that accused Jefferson of having been involved in the intrigues against and slander of his former friend. He believed that Adams's conduct had been likewise honorable toward him, but that it was "part of his character to suspect foul play in those of whom he is jealous," and it was not easy for him "to relinquish his suspicions." Jefferson told Rush that he supplied all these details so that he might have a full picture of the relationship in order to be able to judge the possibility of a revival of the friendship.[9]

Rush quickly replied, assuring Jefferson that he had been more than fair with Mrs. Adams. Indeed, he was struck by "the kindness, benevolence, and even friendship" expressed in his letters to Mrs. Adams— "genuine effusions of your heart." Many, he said, were "the evils of a political life," but none was so great "as the dissolution of friendships." He repeated his hope that he and Adams might be brought back together and mentioned again how much Adams hated banks and that he had "expressed favorable sentiments towards you."[10]

Something was needed to break the impasse—something that would convince Jefferson that the bad ending of his correspondence with Abigail in 1804 was not irreparable. In the summer of 1811, two young

Virginian brothers, John and Edward Coles, who were neighbors and friends of Jefferson, traveled north and paid a two-day visit to Adams in Quincy. They reported their discussion to Jefferson, who in turn related to Rush the nature of their conversation with Adams. During the Coleses' visit, Adams apparently spoke very freely, "without any reserve," about his presidential administration. He said that "his *masters,* as he called his heads of departments," had acted "above his control, & often against his opinions."[11]

According to a much fuller account given by Edward Coles in 1857 to Jefferson's biographer Henry S. Randall, Adams had voiced his grievances over the way he had been treated by Jefferson in the election of 1800. The Coleses told Adams that they could not reconcile his remarks with the complimentary things they had often heard Jefferson say about Adams, even to his fellow Republicans. After the election results were known, Jefferson had hesitated about paying a call on Adams, unsure of the proper time, "fearing that if he called too soon, it might have the appearance of exulting over him," but at the same time afraid that if he delayed too long, Adams's "sensitive feelings might construe it into a slight, or the turning a cold shoulder to him." When Jefferson finally made his call, he realized that it was gone too soon, for Adams was "deeply agitated." Only with difficulty did Jefferson compose him by stressing that their competition was political, not personal. Adams apparently agreed with the brothers' account of the meeting, but was "astonished" to learn that Jefferson had given so much thought to the timing of his visit. At this he burst out, "I always loved Jefferson, and still love him."[12]

This last spontaneous outburst, so characteristic of Adams, Edward Coles had relayed to Jefferson. Deeply touched, Jefferson in turn related this cherished remark to Rush, concluding, "this is enough for me." All he needed, he said, was this knowledge of Adams's feelings "to revive towards him all the affections of the most cordial moments of our lives." He told Rush he would change only a single part of Franklin's famous characterization of Adams, by replacing "absolutely out of his senses" with "sometimes incorrect & precipitate in his judgments." Since Adams possessed "so many other estimable qualities, why should we be dissocialized by mere differences of opinion in politics, in religion in philosophy, or any thing else"—an extraordinary statement that revealed Jefferson's deep affection for Adams the man. He went on to say that Adams's "opinions are as honestly formed as my own," and concluded in good Lockean sensationalist manner that their different views on the same subject were "the result of a difference in our organization & experience." Since he had never withdrawn from the society of anyone because of these sorts of differences of opinion, "altho' many have done it from me," why would he do so with someone "with whom I had gone thro' with hand & heart, so many trying scenes"?

He told Rush that all he needed was an appropriate occasion in order to express to Adams his "unchanged affections for him." He realized that because of his previous correspondence with Mrs. Adams that she must be separated from any resumption of "this fusion of mutual affections." So much had he been taken aback by her coldness that he thought that it would "only be necessary that I never name her." He hoped that Rush's suggestion to Adams of his "continued cordiality towards him" might prompt "the natural warmth of his heart" into writing.[13]

Rush wrote immediately to Adams, incorporating passages from Jefferson's letter that expressed Jefferson's *unchanged affection* for his former colleague. "And now, my dear friend," said Rush, "permit me again to suggest to you to receive the olive which has been offered to you by the hand of a man who still loves you."

Rush then launched into a peroration that he hoped would clinch his appeal: "Fellow laborers in erecting the great fabric of American independence!—fellow sufferers in calumnies and falsehoods of party rage!—fellow heirs of the gratitude and affection of posterity!—and fellow passengers in a stage that must shortly convey you both into the presence of a Judge with whom the forgiveness and love of enemies is the condition of acceptance!—embrace—embrace each other!"

Rush told Adams to forget all that had caused the separation. Explanations may be required between lovers, he said, "but are *never so* between divided friends." If he were with Adams, he would put a pen in his hand and guide it to write: "Friend and fellow laborer in the cause of the liberty and independence of our common country, I salute you with the most cordial good wishes for your health and happiness."[14]

The next day, December 17, 1811, Rush wrote to Jefferson, telling him what he had said to Adams, including his peroration. He hoped this second effort to revive the friendship would be successful. "Patriotism, liberty, science, and religion would all gain a triumph by it."[15]

Adams replied to Rush on Christmas with self-protective joshing. How should he answer Rush's letter? he asked. "Shall I assume a sober Face and write a grave Essay on Religion philosophy, Laws or Government? Shall I laugh like Bacchus among his Grapes, wine vats and Bottles? or Shall I assume the Man of the World, the Fine Gentleman, the Courtier and Bow and scrape, with a smooth smiling Face, Soft Words, many Compliments and Apologies? think myself highly honoured, bound in gratitude? &c. &c. &c."

Realizing that Rush had been teasing him and Jefferson to write to each other, Adams said the image of an olive branch was misplaced, since he and Jefferson had never been at war. He claimed that he and Jefferson had no difference of opinion over "the Constitution, or Forms of Government in General." Then Adams outlined the differences he did have over several measures of Jefferson's administration. But he had raised no public clamor over these measures. "The Nation approved them, and what is my Judgment against that of the Nation." They had differed over the French Revolution. Jefferson "thought it wise and good and that it would end in the Establishment of a free Republick." He, on the other hand, had seen through the falseness of the Revolution, even before it broke out, and had predicted that it would "end only in a Restoration of the Bourbons or a military Despotism, after deluging France and Europe in blood." Since Rush had likewise supported the French Revolution and he and Adams were still friends, Adams saw no reason that issue should make enemies of him and Jefferson.

He then went on to describe the differences he had with Jefferson over republicanism as trivial and meaningless: they were differences of speeches over messages, and levees over dinners. Eager to belittle what after all had been very serious disagreements, Adams joked that Jefferson was "for Liberty and Strait Hair," while he "thought curled Hair was as Republican as Strait." Rush had been so solemn and sincere in his exhortations that Adams couldn't restrain his "inclination to be ludicrous" with him. "Why do you make so much ado about nothing." What use could an exchange of letters between him and Jefferson have? Neither could have anything to say to each other except to wish each other "an easy Journey to Heaven when he goes." But Adams ended his letter by hinting that time and chance, "or possibly design," might soon produce a letter between him and Jefferson.[16]

He meant it. A week later, on New Year's Day 1812, he sent Jefferson a humorous and affable letter. Knowing that Jefferson was a friend of American manufactures, he had taken the liberty of sending him "a Packett containing two Pieces of Homespun lately produced in this quarter by One who was honoured in his youth with some of your Attention and much of your kindness."[17] The "two Pieces of Homespun" were the two volumes of John Quincy's *Lectures on Rhetoric and Oratory*, prepared while he was a professor at Harvard in 1806–1809.

Because the volumes hadn't yet arrived by the time Jefferson received Adams's letter and had replied, he had forgotten how facetious Adams could be and simply assumed that some real manufactured items were on their way to him. Consequently, in response he wrote a short dissertation on the state of manufacturing in Virginia that must have amused Adams.[18]

At the same time Jefferson wrote a brief note to Rush, enclosing copies of his and Adams's letters. He told Rush that because of his "kind interposition" in bringing two old friends together, he had a right to know how the first approaches had been made. He explained that he had written "a rambling, gossiping epistle" to Adams in order to avoid mentioning "the subject of his family," meaning Abigail, "on which I could say nothing." But he hoped his letter expressed his "sincere feelings" and would at least furnish Adams with "ground of reciprocation."[19]

When the two books Adams had sent arrived a day after his letter, an embarrassed Jefferson sent off a quick letter to Adams, apologizing that "a little more sagacity of conjecture" on his part would have saved Adams from having to read his "long dissertation" on manufacturing in Virginia. Jefferson recovered nicely by showering praise on John Quincy's books, saying they were "a mine of learning and taste" that revealed that young Adams, who had written some acute reviews of the works of leading Federalists, excelled "in more than one character of writing." By making a point of equally criticizing both France and England, describing "one as a den of robbers, and the other of pirates," Jefferson, courteous as always, revealed his acute sensitivity to Adams's feelings. Perhaps realizing what had happened with his correspondence with Abigail in 1804, Jefferson was determined from the outset to make this reconciliation work. Without his patience and courtesy and willingness to put up with numerous affronts and provocations, the correspondence could easily have been terminated.[20]

WITH THE ICE FINALLY BROKEN, the letters began flowing freely. Adams immediately answered Jefferson with two letters, a week apart, explaining the actual nature of the gift and telling Jefferson that his dissertation on Virginia's manufacturing was "a feast to me." He then responded to Jefferson's claim that he had given up politics and newspapers "in exchange for Tacitus and Thucydides, for Newton and Euclid." Adams said that he wished he had spent more time with Newton, contemplating the heavens instead of wasting time "on Plato, and Aristotle, Bacon, (Nat) Acherly, Bolingbroke, De Lolme, Harrington, Sidney, Hobbes, Plato Redivivus, Marchmont Nedham, with twenty others upon Subjects which Mankind is determined never to Understand, and those who do Understand them are resolved never to practice, or countenance." He then went on to complain about how he had sacrificed his popularity in New England for the sake of the Union. But instead of receiving thanks from the great families of Virginia he had suffered their mistreatment.[21]

This initial exchange clearly revealed the nature of the 158 letters the two men would write to each other over the next fourteen years. Adams seemed to enjoy the correspondence more than Jefferson, telling Jefferson that he couldn't write "a hundredth part of what" he wished to say to him. Although he apologized at one point for writing four letters to one of Jefferson's ("Never mind it, my dear Sir . . . ; your one is worth more than my four"), overall he actually wrote only three times as many as Jefferson.[22] In the summer of 1813, he wrote a dozen letters in a row before Jefferson replied. But, of course, Jefferson was an international celebrity, "the man," said the French philosophe Antoine Destutt de Tracy, "whom I respect most in the universe and from whom I crave approval the most."[23] Since Jefferson's many correspondents ranged from the tsar of Russia to the Polish patriot Tadeusz Kosciuszko, from the wife of Napoleon's youngest brother to the great German naturalist Alexander von Humboldt, Jefferson had many more letters to write than Adams. In 1822 Jefferson claimed that he had received 1,267 letters in 1820, most of which he answered. By contrast, in that same year of 1820, Adams received 123 letters and wrote 121, a mere fraction of Jefferson's enormous correspondence. It's not surprising that Adams put more into his exchanges than Jefferson did.[24]

Adams knew very well that he was in a different celebrity league from Jefferson. He was embarrassed that "all the literary Gentlemen" of New England had "an Ambitious Curiosity to see the Philosopher and Statesman of Monticello," and they all applied to him for introductions. If only he had received one introduction from Jefferson, he said he wouldn't feel so bad in foisting so many young men on Jefferson.[25]

Jefferson's relationship with Abigail remained stilted. In July 1813, at the end of one of Adams's letters to Jefferson, Abigail broke the silence by penning a short note, in which she offered "the regards of an old Friend, which are still cherished and preserved through all the changes and v[ic]issitudes which have taken place since we first became acquainted."[26] Jefferson responded awkwardly, explaining that his neglect of his "duty of saluting you with friendship and respect" was due to "the unremitting labors of public engagement." He went on to ask after her health, to describe a bit of his health, and to compare numbers of grandchildren.[27]

Abigail responded with a letter full of her feelings over the loss of Nabby, who had died at age forty-eight after a terrible struggle with breast cancer. Aware that Jefferson had suffered a similar loss of an adult daughter, she knew he could "sympathize with your bereaved Friend." Although political calumny had interrupted their "friendly intercourse and harmony," she was pleased that "it is again renewed."[28]

Since Jefferson had been initially told of Nabby's death by Adams, he did not reply directly to Abigail, but expressed his condolences to both Adamses in a letter to John.[29] Fifteen months later Abigail sent some letters written by John Quincy that contained accounts of the Destutt de Tracy family that she thought Jefferson might be interested in. She expressed her continued friendship with "the philosopher of Monti-cello."[30] Jefferson replied politely enough, but the correspondence between him and Abigail never achieved the intimacy it had possessed in the 1780s. Before her death in October 1818, Abigail wrote one more businesslike letter to Jefferson, requesting a letter of introduction for a young Massachusetts man traveling to France.[31]

Thus the exchanges were almost totally confined to the two revolu-tionary heroes. "You and I," said Adams at one point, "ought not to die, before We have explained ourselves to each other."[32] But they were writing to posterity as well as to themselves. Their styles expressed their personali-ties. Adams's writing spewed forth from him with extraordinary exuber-ance and unrestrained passion (he called it "incoherent rattle"); and it was often loaded with provocative and sometimes facetious remarks.[33] Some-times the provocations could be cruel. Knowing that Jefferson had greatly admired the engineer-scientist David Rittenhouse, Adams nevertheless described him as "a good simple ignorant well meaning Franklinian Democrat, totally ignorant of the World, as an Anachorite, an honest Dupe of the French Revolution."[34]

Whenever Adams sat down to write to Jefferson, he said he could not see the forest for the trees; "so many Subjects crowd upon me," he said, "that I know not, with which to begin."[35] Besides, what could he say to the man who knew everything? Writing Jefferson about any subject was like "sending Coal to Newcastle." Nevertheless, Adams continually reported what he was reading and made all sorts of joshing comments about it. John Marshall's five-volume *Life of George Washington* he described as "a

Mausolaeum, 100 feet square at the base, and 200 feet high."[36] But other times he could be quite serious, as when he quoted extensively from the account by the French revolutionary Armand-Gaston Camus concerning the fifty-two volumes entitled *Acta Sanctorum* (Acts of the Saints). Adams concluded that the work was "the most complete History of the corruptions of Christianity, that has ever appeared."[37]

Adams told anecdotes from his reading in ancient literature and related gossip from the present. A scandal involving the wife of James Bowdoin III, son of the former governor of Massachusetts, set him off on a chaotic account of the race of Boudouins in France that went back to the twelfth century. He ended the story by telling Jefferson that in 1804 he, President Jefferson, had immortalized the name Bowdoin by appointing this cuckold as minister to Spain. In commenting on John Taylor's prolix writing style, which was based on Taylor's precept "Gather up the Fragments that nothing be lost," he said that such a rule was "of inestimable Value in Agriculture and Horticulture," but perhaps not for books. "Every Weed Cob, Husk Stalk ought to be saved for manure." He agreed completely with Jefferson's view that Plato's *Republic* was full of "sophisms, futilities, and incomprehensibilities." All he ever got out of "the tedious toil" of reading Plato were two things: one, that Franklin's idea of exempting farmers and mariners from military service was borrowed from Plato, and two, "that Sneezing is a cure for the Hickups." Adams's persistent theme, he said, was drawn from Horace: "What forbids a man to speak the truth by joking."[38]

Jefferson was always graceful and polite in response to Adams's effusive and often teasing banter, and he tended to ignore Adams's flippant provocations. Indeed, anyone else might have broken off the correspondence; but Jefferson knew that beneath Adams's outward irascibility lay a warm and amiable heart.

Occasionally Jefferson did try to match some of Adams's playfulness; and his letters became less somber and serious than was usual in his correspondence. Both men enjoyed showing off their wide knowledge of Greek, Latin, and modern literature. Indeed, their letters often exploded with kaleidoscopic displays of learning in classical and Christian texts that are bound to leave a modern reader thoroughly abashed. At age seventy-five, Jefferson offered a long disquisition on the difference between the pronunciation of ancient and modern Greek, followed by a learned discussion of the changes in the pronunciation of American English. For his part Adams once mentioned Archytas, the fourth-century BC Greek philosopher, and followed that up by pointing out that "John Gram a learned and honourable Dane has given a handsome Edition of his Works with a latin translation and an ample Account of his Life and Writings."[39]

Jefferson fed Adams's vanity by expressing wonder over Adams's extensive reading. "Forty three volumes read in one year, and 12 of them quartos! Dear Sir, how I envy you!" Adams's reading of the twelve volumes of Charles François Dupuis's *Origine de tours les cultes* was, he said, "a degree of heroism to which I could not have aspired even in my younger days." But Jefferson had an explanation for why he could not match Adams's reading: He didn't have the time, he was so busy answering his many correspondents, some of whom he had "never before heard." All his letter writing, he said, was "the burden of my life." He wished he could get rid of the strangers and concentrate on friends he loved like Adams. He was mortified that he had not been able to keep up with his letters.

Adams had his own answers to this burden. One was to simply ignore many of the letter writers and neglect to answer their letters, which, he said, he had done, and it had cost him many correspondents from whom he might have learned something. The other expedient was to give "gruff, short, unintelligible, mysterious, enigmatical, or pedantical Answers." He told Jefferson that this solution was "out of your power," since it was "not in your nature."[40]

OF COURSE, PUBLISHERS eventually discovered that the two former presidents were exchanging letters and, much to Jefferson's disgust, wanted to publish them. "These people," he said, "think they have a right to everything however secret or sacred." Adams confessed that no printer had approached him, but that was not surprising, since Jefferson's writing was famous and his was not. He said that "our Correspondence is thought such an oddity by both Parties, that the Printers imagine an Edition would soon go off and yield them a Profit."[41]

Although Adams realized that both he and Jefferson were "weary of Politicks," he nevertheless couldn't stay away from the subject. He used the fact that he had received some books on Virginian prophets as an excuse to mock all those prophets of the 1780s and '90s, including Joseph Priestley, who had predicted that the French Revolution was the beginning of the millennium. Priestley, Adams reported, had told him, "soberly, cooly and deliberately," that "he fully believed upon the Authority of Prophecy that the French Nation would establish a free Government and that the King of France who had been executed, was the first of the Ten Horns of the great Beast, and that all the other Nine Monarchs were soon to fall off after him."[42] Knowing what Jefferson had thought about the French Revolution, Adams obviously was trying to get a rise out of him.

Because Adams in passing had mentioned the Prophet of the Wabash, Tenskwatawa, who with his brother Tecumseh had been defeated in November 1811 at the Battle of Tippecanoe, Jefferson was able to ignore Adams's provocative statements about the French Revolution and instead concentrate on giving Adams a detailed description of the beliefs and visions of this Shawnee religious leader.[43] It was a technique that Jefferson used over and over to deflect Adams's baiting comments. It didn't stop Adams, however, from coming right back at Jefferson with another attempt at needling. After thanking Jefferson for his account of the Shawnee Prophet, Adams suggested that all modern prophets ought to be put in the stocks as they had been in biblical times: they might thus be prevented "from spreading so many delusions and shedding so much blood."[44]

Adams brought up the case of Timothy Pickering and the other extreme Federalists who had earlier tried to separate the northeastern states from the Union. He told Jefferson he had long opposed these High Federalists, at a cost of his popularity in New England, but if the national government under the Republican administrations continued to employ embargoes and oppose a buildup of naval power, it would play into the hands of these arch-Federalists, resulting not only in making Adams and his son John Quincy more unpopular in New England than they already were, but, more alarming, in provoking "a Convulsion as certainly as there is a Sky over our heads."[45]

When Adams asked about books on Indian antiquities, Jefferson jumped at the opportunity to get away from sensitive subjects, and he responded with a scholarly and informative discussion of the issue. He respected the Indians and knew a great deal about their culture and languages. Adams, by contrast, confessed that he knew very little about Indians and had never collected any books on the subject. He remembered seeing Indians in his youth, but he thought, mistakenly, that they had disappeared from New England. He was not very sympathetic to their plight. He conceded that they had "a Right to Life Liberty and Property in common with all Men." But could "a few handful of Scattering Tribes of Savages have a right of Dominion or Property over a quarter of the Globe capable of nourishing hundreds of Millions of happy human Beings?" He admitted that his ancestors had not puzzled themselves with the "Refinements" over who actually possessed the land prior to "civil Society," but had simply entered into negotiations with the Indians, "purchased and paid for their Rights and Claims whatever they were, and procured Deeds, Grants and Quit-Claims of all their Lands, leaving them their Habitations Arms Utensils huntings and Plantations." For Adams, the land unquestionably belonged to the whites. During the Revolutionary War, he had told Abigail that any tribes that fought on the side of the British "deserve Extermination."[46]

Jefferson was never so harsh, but by 1812 he did believe that those Indians who were not becoming civilized and were falling under the sway of the English in Canada would soon be conquered. This was a measure of his confidence in the outcome of the war that was soon to be declared against Great Britain.[47]

AS LONG AS THE LETTERS were confined to the history of Mount Wollaston in New England and the origins and nature of the Indians, they went on swimmingly. But when Adams discovered a volume that contained several of Jefferson's letters to Joseph Priestley in 1801 and 1803, there was a moment of tense embarrassment. One was the letter in which Jefferson criticized the Federalists for being "barbarians," and Adams in particular, for looking backward and not forward in his 1798 "To the Young Men of the City of Philadelphia." Adams denied Jefferson's charge and explained that he had written so many answers to addresses in that hectic year that he couldn't recall what he had said. But he couldn't drop the issue and had to defend his statement about our ancestors being the best source of knowledge by suggesting that by ancestors he meant none other than Jefferson and himself. In fact, he said, Americans were so different in religion and ethnicity that only the general principles coming out of the Revolution could unite them. Those were, he said, "the general Principles of Christianity, in which all those Sects were United: and the *general Principles* of English and American Liberty."[48]

Adams was very upset by Jefferson's letters to Priestley and had a hard time letting them go. He anguished over what Jefferson had said about his election in 1800 being something new under the sun. He told Jefferson he had been elected by merely the narrowest margin, and that had been made possible by one Federalist changing his vote; consequently, he mocked Jefferson's phrase about his election resulting from a mighty wave of public opinion rolling over the nation. "Oh! Mr. Jefferson!" he exclaimed. "What a Wave of public Opinion has rolled over the Universe." And he went on to describe all the many waves of changing opinion in Western history.[49]

Jefferson was clearly embarrassed by the revelation of his letters to Priestley. He said his letters were private communications only, not intended to be made public. He went on to explain that each political party would interpret the events of 1798–1799 differently and posterity would have to judge between them. He said that he did not consider Adams's statement about respecting only his ancestors' views as "your deliberate opinion." Jefferson tried to suggest that his comments were directed at the Federalists, whom both he and Adams hated, and not at Adams himself. He followed with another letter emphasizing that he had no intention of reviving these "useless and irksome" quarrels of the past. It was clear that Jefferson was acutely worried that the Priestley letters might wreck the restored friendship.[50]

Adams quickly reassured him. "Be not surprised or alarmed." The statements in the Priestley letters "will do no harm to you or me." Neither man wanted to endanger the reconciliation that had been so long in coming. Adams assured Jefferson that he had no intention of publishing their letters in the way someone had published Jefferson's letters to Priestley. If they were eventually published, he told Jefferson, "your Letters will do you no dishonor." As for his own letters, Adams cared "not a farthing." His reputation had been "the Sport of the public for fifty years, and will be with Posterity, . . . a bubble, a Gossameur, that idles the wonton Summer Air."[51]

Adams made this kind of self-deprecating remark over and over, but always wished that it were not so. He was not wrong, however, about how posterity would view his reputation. He told Jefferson he had suffered from more terror, often verbal terror, than any other American. "Name another if you can." He had "been disgraced and degraded," and he had "a right to complain." But he had "always expected it," and had "always submitted to it, perhaps often with too much tameness." He had been treated "with the Utmost Contempt" by Republicans in the Congress, including being threatened "with Impeachment for the murder of Jonathan Robbins," the British sailor who falsely claimed to be an American when the British had impressed and executed him.[52]

Adams knew what future histories of their respective presidencies would say. "Your Administration," he told Jefferson, "will be quoted by Philosophers, as a model, of profound Wisdom; by Politicians, as weak, superficial and short sighted." "Mine . . . will have no Character at all." Adams's complaints were endless. "How many Gauntletts am I destined to run? How many Martyrdoms must I suffer." Jefferson, he said, knew him better than most, "yet you know little of the Life I have led, the hazards I have run."[53]

When reading all of Adams's moaning and groaning, Jefferson must have shaken his head and smiled—but with affection. He realized that this was the warmhearted friend he had always known.

AFTER WRITING SIX LETTERS in a row in two weeks during the summer of 1813, Adams was thoroughly wound up and was able to release the tension only by reminding Jefferson once again of his wrongheaded support for the French Revolution. It was, he said, the first issue on which they had differed. What he most hated about the French Revolution, he told Jefferson, was the way it set back, perhaps for a century or more, the progress that was "advancing by slow but sure Steps towards an Amelioration of the conditions of Man, in Religion and Government, in Liberty, Equality, Fraternity Knowledge Civilization and Humanity." The French patriots were like young students or sailors flushed with recent pay, mounted on wild horses, lashing and spurring, until they killed the horses and broke their own necks.

He had written his *Defence of the Constitutions of Government of the United States of America* and Davila essays to try to head things off. Although his "poor, unprotected, unpatronised Books" had said new things about government that other theorists—from Locke to Montesquieu to Rousseau—had never said, his books never had a chance. They were "overborne by Misrepresentations and will perish in Obscurity." Unfortunately, his works laid the foundation of the immense unpopularity that had befallen him, while "your steady defence of democratical Principles," he told Jefferson, "laid the foundation of your Unbounded Popularity."[54]

Adams enjoyed needling Jefferson over the apparent failure of the French Revolution. All those naïve French philosophes—Voltaire, d'Alembert, Diderot, Rousseau, and others—could have been of some service to humanity "if they had possessed Common Sense. But they were all totally destitute of it." They assumed that all of Christendom was as convinced as they were that every religion was visionary and that "their effulgent Lights had illuminated the World." These dreamers seemed to believe that "whole Nations and Continents had been changed in their

Principles Opinions Habits and Feelings by the Sovereign Grace of their Almighty Philosophy." Their effort "to perfect human Nature and convert the Earth into Paradise of Pleasure" had come to nothing.[55]

Where now were the "Perfection and perfectibility of human Nature?" he asked Jefferson, who in Adams's mind had been as dreamy as the philosophes. "Where is now the progress of the human Mind? Where is the Amelioration of Society?" The ravings of men like Dr. Thomas Young and Thomas Paine who attacked all organized religion were no answer; "for," said Adams, "I hold there can be no Philosophy without Religion."[56] He then picked up on Jefferson's statement in one of his letters to Priestley, in which he had said that Christianity, though benevolent, was also "the most perverted System that ever shone on Man." Priestley had said that Jefferson was "generally considered an unbeliever."[57]

Adams said he considered Jefferson to be as good a Christian as Priestley. But that was not much of a compliment, since Adams later went out of his way to disparage Priestley "as absurd inconsistent, credulous and incomprehensible as Athanasius" and no different from all those other so-called "rational Creatures," the utopian French philosophes. Adams claimed that he had been a student of religion for sixty years and had read books whose titles Jefferson had never seen. Although Priestley had been dead for ten years, Adams said that he had many questions about the Apocryphal epistles of the Bible that he would ask Priestley about—"when I see him."[58]

Jefferson took all this amiably enough and suggested that people did not differ in religious opinions as much as was supposed. He agreed with Priestley, who had declared that if people candidly examined themselves, "they would find that Unitarianism was the religion of all." It was "too late in the day," Jefferson said, "for men of sincerity to pretend they believe in the Platonic mysticisms that three are one, and one is three; and yet the one is not three, and the three are not one."[59]

Along with the French Revolution, religion was a major issue that divided the two men. Both Jefferson and Adams agreed in the belief in a supreme being who organized the universe, and both, like many other enlightened rationalists of the age, denied the divinity of Christ and thus the central Christian doctrine of the Trinity. For Jefferson, Jesus was just "an extraordinary man," and for Adams, claims for the divinity of Jesus had become an "awful blasphemy."[60]

Nevertheless, Adams had a much more acceptable view of religion than Jefferson. Although he did not put much stock in creeds or ecclesiastical authorities, he never became as hostile to organized religion or to orthodox Christianity as Jefferson. Adams certainly agreed that ancient Christianity had been corrupted and debased by "Greeks, Romans, Hebrews, and Christian Factions, above all the Catholicks"—"Miracles after Miracles have rolled down in Torrents"—but he never mocked the Trinity as Jefferson did, never ridiculed it as "mere Abracadabra" foisted on the people by "the mountebanks calling themselves the priests of Jesus."[61] Although Adams was certainly a Unitarian in his beliefs, he treated "the doctrine of the Trinity" not as a joke but as "a Part of an immense system of doctrines of too inormous faith for me to digest." "Let the Wits joke; the Phylosophers sneer!" he said, but that was not his approach to religion. He always was, as he said in 1811, "a Church going Animal."[62]

Adams believed that there was "in human nature, a solid, unchangeable and eternal foundation of Religion." All he felt was awe and adoration in the face of "the Author of the Universe," a universe that was infinite and eternal and in which Adams himself was "but an Atom, a Molecule." Indeed, to Adams God was so beyond all human understanding, so "altogether incomprehensible, and incredible" that he could just "as soon believe the Athanasian Creed, which asserted the traditional Roman Catholic belief in the Trinity."[63]

Adams's sense of religious liberty and ecumenical toleration—"all Religions have Something good in them"—came from this sense of humility in an "inscrutable and incomprehensible" universe, from his deeply held belief that Christianity was "Resignation to God." When Adams was minister to Great Britain, he had worked hard to get the Anglican hierarchy to consecrate American bishops in the Episcopal Church without having to swear allegiance to the king. In fact, he said in 1814 that "there is no part of my Life, on which I look back and reflect with more Satisfaction, than the part I took, bold, daring and hazardous as it was to myself and mine, in the introduction of Episcopacy into America." He even admired the Episcopal Church service. It was "very humane and benevolent, and sometimes pathetic & affecting: but rarely gloomy, if ever." It was certainly "more cheerful and comfortable" than the Presbyterian Calvinists, but he really couldn't criticize the Calvinists either. Since all his family and his ancestors were Calvinists, he would have to be "a very unnatural Son to entertain any prejudices against Calvinists or Calvinism." Indeed, he had "never known any better people than the Calvinists." And as infidelity became associated with Jefferson and Paine's beloved French Revolution, Adams's esteem for Christianity went up. Christianity, Adams told his diary in 1796, was the "Religion of Wisdom, Virtue, Equity and Humanity, let the Blackguard Paine say what he will."[64]

Jefferson never conceived of himself as an insignificant speck in an infinite universe, nor did he ever have anything good to say about the Episcopal hierarchy or Calvinism. As far as he was concerned, Calvinism had "introduced into the Christian religion more new absurdities than its leader had purged it of old ones."[65]

But what most separated Jefferson from Adams was Jefferson's view, at least as he expressed it in his younger years, that religion was exclusively private and personal and did not have much to do with society. Not only had Jefferson revealed in his *Notes on the State of Virginia* his indifference to the social significance of religion, but in the first section of his Bill for Establishing Religious Freedom, which had taken effect in Virginia in 1786, he had claimed that "our civil rights have no dependence on our religious opinions, any more than our opinions in physics and geometry."[66]

This was a position that most Americans, including Adams, found totally unacceptable. However liberal and however tolerant American leaders might have become, nearly all of them continued to believe that religion was essential for the maintenance of order and morality in society, which was especially important for a republic. Indeed, in contrast to Jefferson, most Americans were convinced that America's civic rights were absolutely dependent on religion. And religion for them was a matter of faith, not, as it was for Jefferson, a mere matter of opinion. As president, Jefferson would have nothing to do with proclaiming national days of fasting and prayer as Adams had done; they were anathema to him.

Although Adams, like Jefferson, had come to deny the divinity of Jesus and the miracles of the Bible, he never doubted the need the society had for Christianity. At the outset of the Revolution, he told Abigail that New England was superior to other parts of America because it obliged "every Parish to have a Minister, and every Person to go to Meeting."[67] Adams later said he was not responsible for article III in the Massachusetts Declaration of Rights, which authorized the state legislature to maintain an established church in the towns, and in the Massachusetts constitutional convention of 1820 he favored complete religious freedom. Nevertheless, he was not opposed to the public support of religion. As much as he worried that the clergy, especially the New England divines, could foster "spiritual tyranny and ecclesiastical Dominion" and endanger liberty, he nevertheless believed that America could not "do without them in this wicked world." He even regretted that the federal Constitution did not at least pay "Homage to the Supreme Ruler of the Universe."[68]

Although both men proclaimed themselves Unitarians, they could not have differed more on religious matters. It was inconceivable that Jefferson would ever have said, as Adams did in 1817, that "without Religion this world would be Something not fit to be mentioned in polite Company, I mean Hell."[69]

During the election for the presidency in 1800, Jefferson's radical comments on religion had come back to haunt him. The Federalists had accused him of being an atheist, an infidel, and a Paine-like opponent of Christianity. If he were to become president, they warned, all religion and morality would be destroyed and the bonds of society would come apart. So vicious had been the criticism of his religious views that Jefferson felt the need to explain his understanding of the role of Christianity in society. He had been anticlerical since his college years, but reading the works of Joseph Priestley helped to clarify his religious ideas and to reconcile them with Christianity.

When Jefferson read Priestley's *History of the Corruption of Christianity* sometime in the mid-1790s, he had been deeply impressed. Priestley had argued that Christianity was originally a simple religion subsequently corrupted by the church and that Jesus was not divine but a great moral teacher. By 1801 Jefferson was telling correspondents that "the Christian religion when divested of the rags in which [the clergy] have inveloped it, and brought to the original purity & simplicity of it's benevolent institutor, is a religion of all others most friendly to liberty, science, and the freest expansions of the human mind."[70] Priestley's work helped Jefferson to conceive of himself as a genuine Christian.

In reading Priestley's new pamphlet, *Socrates and Jesus Compared*, in 1803, Jefferson realized that he could give the ancients "their just due, & yet maintain that the morality of Jesus, as taught by himself & freed from the corruptions of later times, is far superior" to that of the ancient philosophers.[71] In 1803 Jefferson wrote out his thoughts in what he called his "Syllabus of an Estimate on the Merit of the Doctrines of Jesus, compared with Those of Others." Anxious to dispel the impression held by many that he was antireligious and especially anti-Christian, Jefferson sent copies of this thousand-word essay to several friends and members of his cabinet and family. (He belatedly sent a copy to Adams in 1813.)

In 1804 Jefferson followed up this essay with a scissors-and-paste version of the New Testament in which he cut out all references to supernatural miracles and Christ's divinity and kept all the passages in which Jesus preached love and the Golden Rule. He called this collection "The Philosophy of Jesus." He told a friend that this "wee little book" was "proof that I am a *real Christian*, that is to say, a disciple of the doctrines of Jesus, very different from the Platonists, who call *me* infidel, and *themselves* Christians and preachers of the gospel, while they draw all their characteristic dogmas from what it's Author never said nor saw."[72] In 1820 Jefferson expanded his work into the "Life and Morals of Jesus of Nazareth." By 1819 he had become, he said, "a sect by myself."[73]

Although both Jefferson and Adams denied miracles and the divinity of Jesus, they both accepted the existence of a hereafter. Jefferson was somewhat more circumspect than Adams. When he was young, he had hoped to gain "some insight into that hidden country," but eventually had come to rest easy with his ignorance and simply trust in God's goodness. Adams assumed that God would not have created all these human beings if there were no life after death. "Take away hope and What remains?" he asked Jefferson. People wouldn't put up with earthly existence if there were no hope of a hereafter. He said if he did not believe in "a future state I should believe in no God." Adams put it more colorfully to his friend Francis Adrian Van der Kemp: "Let it once be revealed or demonstrated that there is no future State, and my Advice to every Man Woman and Child would be, as our Existence would be in our own power, to take opium."[74] In other words, if there were no afterlife, life on earth would not be worth living—a truly extraordinary notion.

ADAMS KEPT INTERRUPTING the discussion of religion with what interested him even more—his old bugaboo, aristocracy. Perhaps because he was surrounded by all those Essex Junto Federalists who were plotting secession in opposition to "Mr. Madison's War," he couldn't stay away from the subject. He reminded Jefferson in 1813 that thirty years before, Jefferson had encouraged him to write something on aristocracy, and he had "been writing Upon that Subject ever since." No society, including republican America, could rid itself of its aristocracy. "It is entailed upon us forever." All we could do, he said, was manage our aristocrats, but they were "the most difficult Animals to manage" in every kind of government. "They not only exert all their own Subtilty Industry and courage, but they employ the Commonalty to knock to pieces every Plan and Model that the most honest Architects in Legislation can invent to keep them within bounds." And unfortunately, said Adams, the aristocrats were usually not the best men in the society. "Birth and Wealth together have prevailed over Virtue and Talents in all ages."[75]

Jefferson told Adams that parties, such as Whigs versus Tories, had always existed and would continue to exist, one taking the side of the many, the other the few. Adams agreed. The aristocracy and the democracy would always quarrel, and all those like Rousseau and Helvétius (and, he might have added, Jefferson in the Declaration of Independence) who proclaimed "the natural Equality of Mankind" were wrong. "Inequalities of Mind and Body are so established by God Almighty in his constitution of Human Nature that no Art or policy can ever plain them down to a Level." The only equality Adams would admit was equality before the law, but he knew that was not at all what Jefferson and most others in 1776 had meant by equality.[76]

Jefferson understood there was a natural aristocracy in every society, but he wanted that natural aristocracy distinguished from those he called an artificial or pseudo-aristocracy, which, he said, was "founded on wealth or birth, without either virtue or talents." He considered the natural aristocracy based on wisdom and virtue to be "the most precious gift of nature for the instruction, the trusts, and government of society." In fact, he said, governments should be judged by their capacity to ensure that these natural aristocrats were selected into the offices of government.[77]

He realized that Adams had a different take on this issue. "*You* think it best to put the Pseudo-aristoi into a separate chamber of legislation where they may be hindered from doing mischief by their coordinate branches, and where they may be a protection to wealth against the Agrarian and plundering enterprises of the Majority of the people." This was a mistake, he told Adams. Giving the wealthy aristocrats power in order to prevent them from doing mischief was "arming them for it, and increasing instead of remedying the evil." He didn't feel that wealthy aristocrats had to be protected anyhow. "Enough of them will find their way into every branch of the legislation to protect themselves." The best remedy was to let the citizens in free elections separate the natural aristocrats from the pseudo-aristocrats, the wheat from the chaff. "In general," he said, "they will elect the real good and wise." Only in a few instances would the citizens be corrupted by wealth and birth, but never enough to endanger the society. This, of course, was the view of an aristocrat who had never lost an election in his life.[78]

Jefferson accounted for their differing opinions on the aristocracy from the different societies in which he and Adams lived. Because of the established Calvinist churches in Massachusetts and Connecticut, Jefferson claimed that the New England clergy tended to encourage "a traditional reverence for certain families."[79] This was not true in Virginia, he claimed. The clergy had no influence over the people, and the great families that had been allied with the Crown had been discredited by the Revolution and undone by the abolition of primogeniture and entail and the separation of the church from the state.

Jefferson only regretted that his plans for a system of public education in which the geniuses and future leaders would be "raked from the rubbish annually" had not been implemented by the Virginia legislature.[80] He went on to describe his plans for small wards of four or five miles square that would be responsible for the schools and for local self-government in Virginia. When finally put into effect, these plans for public education and small ward-republics would raise "the mass of the people to the high ground of moral responsibility necessary to their own safety," and would qualify them "to select the veritable aristoi, for the trusts of government, to the exclusion of the Pseudalists."[81]

Jefferson's plan for publicly supported education had no place for women. In fact, he admitted he had never systematically contemplated the subject, and had thought about it only insofar as his daughters were concerned. Their education was designed so that when they became mothers they could educate their own daughters; they would not be responsible for educating their sons unless the "fathers be lost, be incapable, or be inattentive." Although women might read some great poets— Pope, Dryden, Shakespeare—"with pleasure and improvement," Jefferson advised that "too much poetry should not be indulged," and novel reading should be avoided altogether. Because the French language was the universal language among nations and "now the depository of all science," it was "an indispensable part of education for both sexes." Education allowed for some attention to be paid to the amusements of life, and for women these were "dancing, drawing & musick."[82]

Adams had a different approach to women's education. Marriage to Abigail helped to make him remarkably respectful of women of intelligence and learning. He even joked with his friend Van der Kemp that he was terrified of "learned Ladies"; he felt "such a consciousness of Inferiority to them" that he could "scarcely speak in their presence." That may have been true with some aristocratic women he had known in France, but once a learned lady, such as Mercy Otis Warren or John Quincy's wife, Louisa Catherine, became his friend, he treated her as his intellectual equal. When in 1820 the educator and women's rights activist Emma Willard sent Adams her pamphlet proposing publicly supported women's seminaries, Adams endorsed the plan enthusiastically. "The Feminine Moiety of Mankind," he told Willard, "deserve as much honour Esteem, and Respect, as the Male." He advised his granddaughter that since she would be responsible for educating all her children, sons and daughters alike, she should become acquainted with all the great writers, bar none, who had dealt with both the "little Aerial World within us"—of intelligence and sensibility—as well as "the great World without us—of Heaven, Earth and Seas."[83]

This respect for female education did not mean that Adams was a supporter of modern feminism. He never advocated the suffrage for women, and he had nothing good to say about Mary Wollstonecraft's *Vindication of the Rights of Women*, regarding it as another one of those crazy tracts thrown up by the French Revolution. But he was troubled enough by her book to spend hours reading it and filling its margins with his jeering objections.[84]

Jefferson never felt the need to confront Wollstonecraft and her ideas. As an aristocrat presiding over his scores of slaves, he took his patriarchy for granted, calling himself at one point "the most blessed of the patriarchs."[85] He regarded his slaves as childlike dependents in his patriarchal household and thus members of what he called his "family." He believed these patriarchal relationships were important to the health of the nation. Indeed, one of his principal objections to French society, which he otherwise so admired, was the fact that "the domestic bonds" were "absolutely done away," and there was nothing put in their place. French women were flirtatious and voluptuous, and consequently they continually strained the bonds of marriage. To his great surprise, women in France, he once told Washington, actually engaged in politics. "The manners of the nation allow them to visit, alone, all persons in office, to solicit the affairs of the husband, family, or friends." By contrast, he said, American women were superior because they looked after their husbands and their households and were devoted to simple republican domesticity.[86]

Although Adams was far more permissive about women in politics than Jefferson—encouraging his daughter-in-law Louisa Catherine in her promotion of her husband's career—he also emphasized the importance of patriarchy to the society. In fact, he claimed that "the Source of Revolution, Democracy, and Jacobinism" was the "Systematical dissolution of true Family Authority." There could be no regular government in a nation, he told his son Thomas, "without a marked Subordination of Mothers and children to the Father." But, probably thinking of Abigail, he warned his son not to tell anyone what he had said. "If you divulge it to any one, it will soon be known to all, and will infallibly raise a Rebellion against me." Unlike Jefferson, Adams could never take patriarchy in his household for granted.[87]

Like Adams, many New England leaders tended to be obsessed with stability. Faced with popular instability and disorder that the slaveholding planters of Virginia rarely experienced, the New England Federalists understandably favored order and hierarchy, even to the point of yearning for elements of monarchy and hereditary offices. Unlike Jefferson and the other Virginia aristocrats, who overwhelmingly supported the libertarian and egalitarian ideology of the Republican Party, the New England aristocrats did not have the confidence that the people would always elect the natural aristocracy of the wise and good. It was so much easier to believe in democracy when the aristocratic elites didn't have to worry about the quirks and whims of the electorate.

Adams thought Jefferson was engaging in "a little merriment upon this solemn subject of aristocracy." He agreed with Jefferson that men of talents were the aristocrats. But what did Jefferson mean by talents? For Adams, the talents were innumerable. "Education, Wealth, Strength, Beauty, Stature, Birth, Marriage, graceful Attitudes and Motions, Gait, Air, Complexion, Physiognomy, are Talents, as well as Genius and Science and learning." Anyone possessing any of these talents that allowed him to command influence in the society was an aristocrat to Adams. All literature, all history, proved "the existence of inequalities, not of rights, but of moral and intellectual and physical inequalities in Families, descents and Generations."[88]

Consequently, concluded Adams, Jefferson's distinction between natural and artificial aristocracy was not well founded. Some men were born smarter, stronger, and more beautiful than others. These were the natural aristocrats. The only artificial aristocrats Adams recognized were those whose titles and honors were conferred on them by municipal laws and political institutions. These kinds of artificial aristocrats could be easily done away with, but the natural aristocrats that Adams conceived of could never be eliminated, for they were the result of nature, of some individuals being born more intelligent, shrewder, and more wily than others.

Before Adams was done talking about aristocracy he came to see it everywhere. Indeed, he ended up democratizing the aristocracy—declaring that anyone who could influence the vote of one other person was an aristocrat, "in my Sense of the Word; whether he obtains his one Vote in Addition to his own, by his Birth Fortune, Figure, Eloquence, Science, learning, Craft Cunning, or even his Character for good fellowship and a bon vivant." This was a peculiar kind of aristocracy, an enlarged and uniquely middle-class American aristocracy. Such aristocrats—men who could simply influence the vote of one other person—were so numerous as to render the term virtually meaningless.[89]

These sorts of aristocracies—middling men with some influence claiming gentlemanly status—were springing up everywhere in America. They were arising, said Adams, "not from Virtues and Talents so much as from Banks and Land Jobbing." Adams denied over and over to

Jefferson that he had ever favored hereditary honors and offices. All he meant to say was "that Mankind have not yet discovered any remedy against irresistible Corruption in Elections in Offices of great Power and Profit, but making them hereditary."[90]

ADAMS BOMBARDED JEFFERSON with five letters on aristocracy and religion before his Virginian friend responded. "Give yourself no concern," he told Jefferson. "Answer my Letters at Your Leisure." He wrote, he said, only as "a refuge and protection against Ennui."[91]

When Jefferson did finally respond, he avoided Adams's curious notion of a democratized aristocrat who needed to influence only one other person to become an aristocrat; instead, he chose to return to the more comprehensible subject of religion. He admitted that he had never read many of the histories of religion that Adams had, but he agreed that much about religion had been invented and perverted over the centuries.

The perversions of religious writers led Jefferson to the fraudulent manipulation of the laws of Alfred, the ninth-century Saxon ruler who had issued an extensive legal code. These in turn reminded him of the ways in which modern English judges had been "willing to lay the yoke of their own opinions on the necks of others," especially in their efforts to make revealed religion part of the common law. These judges, especially William Murray, 1st Earl of Mansfield, who served as lord chief justice of the King's Bench for over thirty years, had set forth a "string of authorities all hanging by one another on a single hook, a mistranslation by Finch of the works of Prisot, or on nothing."

"Our cunning" Chief Justice Marshall was no better, said Jefferson; he was able to find "many sophisms" with which to twist the law out of all kinds of documents, just "as he did to twist Burr's neck out of the halter of treason." Knowing that Adams loved the common law and perhaps eager to pay Adams back a bit for all the needling he was getting, he quoted Jesus: "Woe unto you, ye lawyers, for ye laden men with burdens grievous to bear."[92]

In contrast to Adams's effusiveness and gushing emotion, Jefferson remained his usual cool and collected self. He liked to be optimistic and disliked those with "gloomy and hypochondriac minds" who were "disgusted with the present and despairing of the future; always counting that the worst will happen, because it may happen." Too much introspection was unhealthy. Better to be hopeful than to dwell on failure. The emotions and passions ought to be controlled and kept in their place. Indeed, he wondered, for example, about the purpose of the emotion of grief. He wished that "the pathologists" would tell us what use it did have and what good it did do.[93]

Jefferson should have realized that such queries were just what Adams craved. Adams exploded with lengthy discourses on grief and its uses and abuses, to which Jefferson could only reply, "You have exhausted the subject."[94] Adams realized, as he told his son John Quincy, that there was "a Rage; a Mania, a delirium or at least an Enthusiasm" in him that needed to be corrected. He would stop and say to himself, "Be not carried away by sudden blasts of Wind, by unexpected flashes of Lightening, nor terrified by the sharpest Crashes of Thunder."[95]

The dialogue between the two patriots tended to be dominated by Adams. He made comments, often challenging or facetious ones, that Jefferson either ignored entirely or answered earnestly and courteously. When Jefferson mentioned the three volumes on ideology by Antoine Destutt de Tracy—"the ablest writer living on intellectual subjects," said Jefferson—Adams mocked the work. "3 vols. of Idiology!" he exclaimed. "Pray explain this Neological Title! What does it mean?" When Napoleon first used the word "ideology," Adams said he had been delighted with it, "upon the Common Principle of delight in every Thing We cannot understand." Did it mean "Idiotism? . . . The Science of Lunacy? The Theory of Delerium?"[96]

Jefferson ignored Adams's flippancy and replied to his lighthearted taunts with a serious explanation of Destutt de Tracy's work. He told Adams that William Duane had published Destutt de Tracy's *Commentary and Review of Montesquieu's Spirit of the Laws* in 1811. Without mentioning that he had once called it "the most valuable political work of the present age" and had actually translated the section of the book on public liberty and constitutions, Jefferson promised to have a copy sent to Adams if it was still in print. Despite the scorn Adams had expressed for Destutt de Tracy's books, Jefferson sought to make a strong case for their importance. The Frenchman's logic, he said, "occupies exactly the ground of Locke's work on the understanding."[97]

When the copy of Destutt de Tracy's book on Montesquieu arrived as promised, Adams, obviously embarrassed by his ridiculing of the Frenchman, replied that "in our good old English language of Gratitude" he was deeply in Jefferson's debt. He had read a hundred pages of the book and would read the rest. Destutt de Tracy was "a sensible Man and is easily understood," not like another one of Jefferson's former French friends, that "abstruse, mysterious, incomprehensible Condorcet." Even while praising Destutt de Tracy, Adams couldn't help pointing out that he was really just another idealistic French philosophe who "supposes that Men are rational and conscientious Creatures." He said he agreed with that, but lest Jefferson think he was getting soft, he couldn't let it rest there; he had to add that men's "passions and Interests generally prevail over their Reason and their conscience; and if Society does not contrive some means of controlling and restrain[in]g the former the World will go on as it has done."

Adams then went on to criticize other writers whose works contained "a compleat drought of the Superstitions, Credulity and Despotism of our terrestrial Universe." They had shown how all the sciences and all the fine arts of architecture, painting, statuary, poetry, music, eloquence—"which you love so well and taste so exquisitely"—had been used everywhere to support priests and kings at the expense of the poor.

Adams ended his letter by saying that it would be delivered by a young man eager to meet Jefferson. In fact, he added, all the young gentlemen of New England who had any sort of mind and the money to travel had "an ardent Curiosity to visit, what shell I say? the Man of the Mountain? The Sage of Monticello? Or the celebrated Philosopher and Statesman of Virginia."[98]

To make all these sorts of taunting and teasing remarks, Adams must have become completely confident of his relationship with Jefferson. Jefferson was so self-contained, so polite, and so smart that Adams knew deep in his soul that the Sage of Monticello had something that he, Adams, would never have, and that no matter how many books he read and how many wisecracks he made, Jefferson would always be his superior.

TWELVE

THE GREAT REVERSAL

Americans commonly regarded the War of 1812 as their second American Revolution. With Andrew Jackson's overwhelming victory over the British army at New Orleans in January 1815—two weeks after the peace treaty had been signed in Ghent, Belgium—they celebrated what they took to be a reaffirmation of their independence from the former mother country. The war had vindicated their republican institutions and had established their national character, the existence of which so many seemed to have doubted. John Adams appreciated this renewed sense of nationhood and mischievously suggested to Thomas Jefferson that his revolution of 1800 might not have been so important after all, not compared with what his successor had accomplished. "Notwithstand[ing] a thousand Faults and blunders," he told Jefferson, James Madison's administration had "acquired more glory, and established more Union than all his three Predecessors, Washington, Adams, Jefferson, put together."

Jefferson agreed that the war had secured the nation. The Federalists were discredited and the threat they once posed was gone. "Our government is now so firmly put on its republican tack," Jefferson assured Lafayette, "that it will not be easily monarchised by forms."[1]

Suddenly everyone seemed interested in the original Revolution.

Many realized that documents from the Revolution were being neglected and in danger of disappearing. The men who had led the Revolution were dying off and the survivors needed to be interviewed before they passed on. Antiquarians and would-be historians wrote Adams and Jefferson, along with the other revolutionary leaders, requesting information about the great events they had experienced. Some suggested that the two great revolutionaries ought to write their own histories of the Revolution.

Both Adams and Jefferson doubted that anyone would be able to write a really accurate history of the Revolution. "Who can write it?" asked Adams. "Who would ever be able to write it?" The most essential documents—the debates and deliberations in Congress from 1774 to 1783—were "all in secret, and are now lost forever." Most of the speeches in the Congress, including his, had been "universally extemporaneous," and had never been written down. Adams was reminded of the problem by reading a review in the May 1815 issue of the *Analetic Magazine* of a history of the American Revolution by the Italian Carlo Botta. The reviewer, said Adams, claimed that Botta's book "is the best history of the revolution that ever has been written." Botta, like the historians of ancient Greece and Rome, solved the problem of the lack of documents by simply "composing speeches for his Generals and Orators." "How faithful" to reality were these speeches Adams left Jefferson to judge.[2]

Jefferson agreed that no one could write an accurate history of the Revolution. For that reason, he worried about how he would be treated. "We have been too careless of our future reputation while our tories will omit nothing to place us in the wrong," he complained to Supreme Court justice William Johnson of South Carolina in 1823. He thought that Adams's biography would be left to his son John Quincy, "whose pen, you know, is pointed and his prejudices not in our favor."[3] Somehow he sensed that his legacy might depend on a comparison between him and Adams—that any praise of Adams would mean a diminution of him.

At any rate, said Jefferson, historians would get only the "external facts" of history. All the designs and discussions were behind closed doors, and since no one, as far as he knew, had taken notes, all the "life and soul of history must forever be unknown." Despite Botta's practice of inventing speeches and putting them in the mouths of characters who never made them, Jefferson thought that his book, published in Italian in Paris in 1809 and soon translated into French and English, was "a good one, more judicious, more chaste, more classical, and more true than the party diatribe" of *The Life of George Washington* (1804–1807) written by Chief Justice John Marshall during Jefferson's presidency. Botta's "greatest fault" was that he borrowed too much from Marshall.

Jefferson had an abiding dislike of his Federalist cousin, who had been Adams's secretary of state and had been appointed to the Supreme Court by Adams. Not only did Jefferson despise the way Marshall was using the Court to strengthen the national government at the expense of the states, but he resented the fact that in his *Life of Washington* Marshall had relegated Jefferson's writing of the Declaration of Independence to a footnote. Marshall had written in that footnote that "the draft reported by the committee has been generally attributed to Mr. Jefferson"—a remarkable playing down of Jefferson's actual contribution.[4]

Since Adams several years earlier had dismissed Marshall's biography as a mere moneymaking "Mausolaeum," he sidestepped Jefferson's effort to bait him. What he wanted to do instead was set forth what he regarded as his "peculiar, perhaps singular" ideas about a history of the Revolution. "The War?" he said. That was no part of the Revolution. "It was only an Effect and a Consequence of it." The real Revolution took place not on the battlefield but in the minds of the people, and "this was effected, from 1760 to 1775, in the course of fifteen Years before a drop of blood was drawn at Lexington."[5]

No doubt Adams's view of the Revolution, which he repeated to many of his correspondents, was self-serving. Instead of Washington and his military exploits, what counted in the Revolution were all the publications of men like Adams that preceded the clash of arms. By all these writings, he said, "the public Opinion was enlightened and informed concerning the Authority of Parliament over the Colonies." He knew the world would think he was envious, but he could not help objecting to orators calling Washington the "Father of his Country." He thought that lawgivers ought to be exalted above military heroes, but he realized that "military glory dazzles the Eyes and Eclipses all civil and political Lustre."[6]

As someone who read a lot of history, Adams had long thought about the nature of history writing. He had told Benjamin Rush in 1806 that he took the duties of a historian seriously. He repeatedly had declared that no history should be written except under the oath of the late-sixteenth- and early-seventeenth-century French historian Jacques-Auguste de Thou: "To the truth of my history I invoke God himself as a witness." If someone could write a history of the period from 1760 to 1806 and at the end truly repeat Thou's maxim, that work, Adams told Rush, would be "a great blessing to Mankind."[7]

He could never write such a history, for his papers were a mess. Besides, what could he say of his "own Vanity and Levity"? Thank God, he had no crimes, but "Follies, indiscretions and trifles enough and too many." What about all "the Jealousy and Envy of those who have been my most intimate friends, Colleagues and Coadjutors? What of the malice and vengeance of unprovoked enemies?" It was said that Washington had "an insatiable thirst" for fame, but that Adams was "excessively careless of it." He believed the saying was correct, that he had neglected his role in history. He could never bring himself "seriously to consider that I was a great Man, or of much importance or consideration in the world." The few traces of his life must therefore go down to posterity "in as much confusion and distraction, as my life has been passed."[8]

Three years later, in 1809, he was still pondering the problems of history writing. He reminded Rush that he had "very solemn notions of the sanctity of History," and once again invoked de Thou's oath. Although he would not write his own history but leave it to others, he doubted "whether faithful History ever was or ever can be written."[9]

By the time Adams received clergyman Jedidiah Morse's request for assistance in writing a history of the Revolution, in 1815, he could only sigh and shake his head, saying that he did not know "whether I ought to laugh or cry." He had, he said, "little faith in history." He read history as he read romances, he said, "believing what is probable and rejecting what I must." The history of the past half century in America was already corrupted. If he were to write a true and honest history of that period, in accord with de Thou's oath, a hundred critics from America, France, England, and Holland "would immediately appear and call me, to myself, and before the world, a gross liar and a perjured villain." He despaired that all the concealed and unknown facts, those that "mark characters," would ever see the light of day.[10] He told Jefferson in 1817 that he had been "so little satisfied with Histories of the American Revolution, that I have long since, ceased to read them. The Truth is lost, in adulatory Panegyricks, and in vituperary Insolence."[11]

ALL THIS INTEREST IN THE HISTORY of the Revolution created disputes over which state had actually initiated the Revolution. Was it Adams's Massachusetts or Jefferson's Virginia? In 1817 an excited Dr. Benjamin Waterhouse, a man who was friendly with both Jefferson and Adams, wrote Jefferson about William Wirt's *Life of Patrick Henry*, which had just been published. He told Jefferson that Wirt had quoted Jefferson saying that Henry "certainly gave the first impulse to the ball of the Revolution." Waterhouse then went on in his impassioned letter with a lengthy critique of Wirt's claim for Henry's priority in beginning the Revolution. If Jefferson was correct about Henry, he said, "we in New England have been brought up in error." Waterhouse said that he had been taught to believe that the Revolution began not with the Stamp Act in 1764, the time when, as Wirt claimed, Henry had made his mark, but three years earlier, in 1761, with James Otis of Massachusetts and his opposition to the writs of assistance (search warrants used by royal customs officials).

Waterhouse said that he had derived his information about Otis from "the venerable" John Adams, "who in his old age shines in the full brightness of his faculties." Quoting from letters he had received from Adams, Waterhouse wrote that "it was the wonderful powers of James Otis's oratory that electrified *Samuel Adams;* who electrified & enlightened *John Hancock,* when they in combination with the worthies already mentioned, enlightened France, & the rest of the world." By the worthies already mentioned, Adams meant young Washington, who at that time still "dwelt on the banks of the Patomack"; Jefferson, who "was a youth of fifteen"; and Henry, "the Demosthenes of Virginia," who "had not yet raised his powerful voice against the insidious encroachments of Britain."

Perhaps not aware of how well the two ex-presidents knew each other, Waterhouse reminded Jefferson what a wonderful character the old New Englander was. "There is a good humour & facetiousness about him, which makes his company very agreeable to young people of both sexes. He is venerated visited, consulted & followed, as were some of the ancient Philosophers in Greece."

Waterhouse said that he had written Adams about Jefferson's statement in Wirt's book, and he quoted Adams's reply. "As Mr. Jefferson has made the revolution a game of billiards, I will make it a game of shuttlecock." Henry might have given the first impulse to the ball in Virginia, "but Otis' battledore had struck the Shuttlecock up in the air in Massachusetts; and continued to keep it up for several years before Henry's ball was touched." According to Waterhouse, Adams had gone on to explain why he had said that Jefferson in 1761 was but a youth in college, "too intent on his classicks & sciences to know, think, or care about anything in Boston." Since Adams was only twenty-five in 1761, and "Mr. Jefferson is at least nine, or ten years younger than me," he could not have been more than fifteen or sixteen; "and he probably knew more of the eclipses of Jupiter's satellites than he did of what was passing in Boston."[12]

Jefferson replied at once to Waterhouse, well aware that whatever he said would be passed on to Adams. He admitted that he did say to Wirt something about Henry's setting the ball going, but explained that Wirt in citing his remark had probably meant Virginia alone. But even if he didn't, the question of "who commenced the revolution" was impossible to answer.[13] Anxious to head off any trouble with Adams, Jefferson also wrote to inform him of Waterhouse's letter. Appealing to Adams's legal professionalism, he said that lawyers know that words always needed to be put in context and that in Wirt's case that context was Virginia. "It would moreover be difficult to say at what moment the revolution began, and what incident set it in motion, as to fix the moment that the embryo becomes an animal, or the act which gives him a beginning."[14]

In response Adams agreed that it was difficult to say when the Revolution began. In his opinion it had actually started in the seventeenth century "as early as the first Plantation of the Country. Independence of Church and Parliament was a fixed Principle of our Predecessors in 1620 as it was of Sam. Adams and Chris. Gadsden in 1776." Of course, 1620 was when the Pilgrims arrived on the *Mayflower*, and it was not the first plantation in America. Like many New Englanders, Adams tended to ignore the founding of the colony of Virginia in 1607, for it had had nothing to do with independence from the Church of England and Parliament.[15]

Adams's views about the priority of the revolutionary movement soon became public and aroused controversy. In March 1818, a very agitated Thomas Ritchie, the publisher of the *Richmond Enquirer*, wrote to Jefferson that he had read in a Baltimore paper John Adams's letter to Hezekiah Niles "in which he attempts to strip Virginia of the merit of originating the War of Independence, and transferring it to Massachusetts." In his letter to Niles, the founding editor of *Niles' Weekly Register*, Adams claimed that the awakening and revival of American principles had taken place in Massachusetts as early as 1750 with a sermon by Jonathan Mayhew, well before Patrick Henry supposedly got the ball of revolution rolling. Ritchie told Jefferson that he was grateful for what the Massachusetts patriots had done, but as a proud Virginian he couldn't sit by patiently and have his state stripped of the laurels to which he always had assumed it was entitled. He asked Jefferson to clarify this matter and settle the issue.[16]

Jefferson replied at once and sent Ritchie an extract of his letter to Waterhouse. As usual, he was calm and reasonable, saying that he did not think the issue was "susceptible of dispute." Everyone will decide for himself who first set the ball of revolution in motion. Some will think an opinion voiced in private conversation would count. Others will believe a lawyer's argument denying the validity of a law would be the initial impulse. Still others would think that nothing short of a formal declaration would satisfy. He then went on to disparage all this jealousy between the states. He thought a state, like an individual, ought not to be praising itself. Leave that judgment to the world. Americans weren't noted for their modesty. "It has been said, and I am afraid not entirely without foundation, that ours is the most boasting and braggadocio nation on earth." We Virginians, he said, "have been held up as arrogating all praise and power to our own state, and it has not been without some ill effect." It might have been wiser for Virginia to have been more delicate and unassuming, which would help "conciliate the suffrage of our sister states." As always, Jefferson's sensibility was highly refined—it was what made him so attractive.[17]

LATE IN HIS LIFE AND AFTER A DECADE of his renewed correspondence with Adams, Jefferson had to bear with embarrassing revelations of Adams's earlier opinion of his presidency. In 1823 the publication of Adams's correspondence with William Cunningham, a distant relative, could well have destroyed the reconciliation. In 1804 Cunningham had asked Adams for information that could be used against Jefferson's reelection. With his usual frankness, Adams had declaimed against "the awful spirit of democracy" that, like an artful villain, was seducing the people and would bring about their ruin. And he had told Cunningham of his experience with Jefferson's "intrigues." He admitted that Jefferson had talent, but he said that "candour and sincerity belong to other people," not to him. With Jefferson, "cool, dispassionate, and deliberate insidiousness never arrived at greater perfection."[18]

Although Cunningham had promised never to publish Adams's letters during the ex-president's lifetime, he committed suicide in May 1823, and his son immediately published the correspondence for political purposes. Young Cunningham claimed that Adams had written the letters in 1803–1804 in order to destroy Jefferson's reputation and raise "himself and his family upon the ruins of republicanism."[19] Cunningham hoped their publication would discredit the character of the Adams family and thus undermine John Quincy Adams's upcoming campaign for the presidency, in 1824.

Of course, Adams was mortified that Jefferson would read what Adams had said about him in the bitter aftermath of Adams's defeat for the presidency and feared that the reconciliation would be damaged, if not destroyed.

With his usual good manners and his deep desire to maintain the friendship, Jefferson immediately dismissed this "wicked" attempt "to draw a curtain between you and myself." He assured Adams that he was "incapable of receiving the slightest impression from the effort now made to plant thorns on the pillow of age, worth and wisdom, and to sow tares between friends who have been such for near half a century." Indeed, he said, "it would be strange . . . if, at our years, we were to go back an age to hunt up imaginary, or forgotten facts, to disturb the repose of affections so sweetening to the evening of our lives." He beseeched Adams to ignore the whole business and put it "among the things which have never happened."[20]

According to Adams, his entire family read Jefferson's letter and universally exclaimed that it was "the best letter that ever was written. . . . How generous! How noble! How magnanimous!" everyone said. But Adams believed it was just such a letter as he expected from Jefferson, "only it was infinitely better expressed." This was exactly the heartwarming response that Jefferson wanted.[21]

Jefferson seems to have valued the correspondence and the renewed relationship so much that he scrupulously avoided mentioning any of his views of Adams's earlier monarchical beliefs. While carrying on his correspondence with Adams in their retirement years, he certainly remained convinced that Adams had once been a monarchist, even if he wasn't one now.

Shortly before his death, Jefferson vividly recalled returning from France and confronting all the monarchical sentiments in New York in 1790. The Federalists of the 1820s, he told his protégé William Short in 1825, were trying to whitewash the monarchical history of their party and "prove that the sun does not shine at mid-day." The Federalists in

1790 were monarchists. Hamilton was one and so was Adams. "Can anyone read Mr. Adams' defence of the American constitutions," he asked, "without seeing that he was a monarchist?" Yet he would never have brought up Adams's monarchism with Adams himself, sensing what an explosion of passion it would set off.[22]

As the signers of the Declaration of Independence died off, more and more attention was paid to the survivors. In fact, Jefferson and Adams kept a tally of who among the signers were still alive. When Robert R. Livingston died in 1813, Adams and Jefferson became the last two survivors of the committee that had drafted the Declaration (Benjamin Franklin had died in 1790 and Roger Sherman in 1793). In January 1812, Jefferson informed Adams that "of the signers of the Declaration of Independence I see now living not more than half a dozen on your side of the Potomak, and on this side, myself alone." (Actually there were ten signers of the Declaration, including Jefferson and Adams, still alive in 1812.) Benjamin Rush and George Clymer died the same year as Livingston, 1813. Rush's death—"a better man than Rush could not have left us"— prompted Jefferson once again to write Adams to ask how many were left. He knew of four, including Adams and himself. He said he was the only one south of the Potomac. And "we too must go; and that ere long."[23]

Conscious of himself as the principal author of the Declaration, Jefferson was obviously more interested in the document and its signers than Adams. Initially, he and others had not made much of the preamble or his authorship. Attention at first focused on the document's conclusion: "That these United Colonies are, and of Right ought to be, Free and Independent States." Jefferson's authorship of the Declaration was not widely known; indeed, one of the first references to his writing the Declaration was made by Yale College president Ezra Stiles in 1783, in which he said that Jefferson had "poured the soul of the continent into the monumental act of independence." During the 1780s, Jefferson was mentioned as one of the members of the committee that drafted the Declaration, but he was not singled out and celebrated as the author.[24]

Jefferson himself actually helped draw attention to the significance of the Declaration. While hosting the young painter John Trumbull in Paris in the 1780s, Jefferson listened to the artist's ambitious plans to paint a series of military battles of the Revolution. Apparently, Jefferson suggested to Trumbull that he ought to consider painting the committee's presentation of the Declaration of Independence. He even sketched out the scene in Independence Hall; unfortunately, it contained some architectural inaccuracies that Trumbull included in his painting.[25]

When Adams learned of Trumbull's intention to paint the Declaration of Independence, he urged him to be accurate. "Truth, Nature, Fact, should be your guide. Let not our Posterity be deluded by fictions under pretence of poetical or graphical Licenses." But Adams was not very encouraging. Not only did he question whether debates or arguments could ever be depicted on canvas, but he told Trumbull that all the arts, including painting, had always been "enlisted on the Side of Despotism and Superstition" to the detriment of "the Rights of Mankind." He further deflated Trumbull's ambitions by claiming that no Americans were interested in the history of the Revolution anyway. "I see no disposition to celebrate or remember, or even Curiosity to enquire into the Characters, Actions, or Events of the Revolution."[26]

Despite the cantankerous letters he had received from Adams, Trumbull thanked him for his support, telling him that in painting a great moral and political event he had enabled the United States to break from previous artistic conventions. He hoped "the Example thus set will be hereafter followed, in employing the Arts in the Service of Religion, Morality and Freedom."[27]

Jefferson dealt with Trumbull very differently. He praised Trumbull's plans and hoped that their fellow citizens in the Congress would "honor themselves, their country and yourself by preserving these monuments of our revolutionary achievements."[28]

SINCE TRUMBULL'S PAINTING of the Declaration was officially exposed to public view only in 1819, it was not the source of the heightened interest in the document or in Jefferson's authorship. Actually, Jefferson's authorship of the Declaration first became well known during the partisan struggles of the 1790s. To counter the vicious Federalist attacks on Jefferson, his Republican followers had begun touting his writing of the Declaration. They made much of the preamble that emphasized equality, inalienable rights, and the right of revolution—dangerous ideas to the Federalists frightened by the French Revolution. Republican newspapers began referring to the Declaration as "our great American charter" drawn up by "the immortal Jefferson." When someone mentioned the similarity of the Declaration to some of the writings of John Locke, the Federalists were quick to pick this up and use it to disparage the originality in Jefferson's authorship. Whenever the Federalists had asked what services Mr. Jefferson had ever rendered the country, the Republicans had always replied that "he was the author of our Declaration of Independence." But now, the Federalists gloated, it turned out that he had "borrowed" or "compiled" the Declaration from Locke's writings. All this Federalist belittling of Jefferson's authorship was to no avail. When Jefferson served as president, his sole authorship of the Declaration became even more firmly established.[29]

Adams did not take this claim of Jefferson's authorship well. Back in 1776, he had not believed that drafting the Declaration was all that important, especially compared with the heavy burden of congressional committee work that he was bearing. By 1805 he had come to realize that Jefferson was being lavishly celebrated for writing the Declaration. This in turn led him to lament to Rush that the scenery surrounding the activity of public life was often more important than the character of the actors. "Was there ever a Coup de Theater, that had so great an effect as Jefferson's Penmanship of the Declaration of Independence?" Adams felt that the real business of bringing about the Revolution had been behind the scenes, where he had done much of the work. He had never put much stock in the addresses and documents of the Congress. They were "Dress and ornament rather than Body, Soul or Substance." Although he later confessed that he was wrong about denigrating the addresses of the Congress, "for these things were necessary to give Popularity to Our cause both at home and abroad," he nonetheless felt that Jefferson's writing of the Declaration had been a mere "Theatrical Show," a performance, something decorative that had captured the attention of people but was not substantially significant. But alas, he moaned, "Jefferson ran away with all the stage effect of that: all the Glory of it."[30]

Adams was obviously jealous of the fame Jefferson was getting as the author, not the draftsman, of the Declaration. In 1809 he even suggested to William Cunningham that he, Adams, had made his own declaration of independence from Great Britain as early as 1755. In a letter written in the year he graduated from college, he had predicted that as America became more populous than the mother country, the American people would inevitably transfer the seat of empire and set up for themselves in the New World. This 1755 letter was first published in 1807 and was widely circulated. In 1809 Adams referred to it as "my boyish letter" and playfully claimed that this 1755 letter was "*demonstrative evidence* that John Adams' Declaration of Independence was one and twenty years older than Thomas Jefferson's."[31]

In 1816 in a letter to Benjamin Rush's son Richard, then James Madison's attorney general, Adams offered a parody of some lines of Jonathan Swift's "Verses on the Death of Dr. Swift." In his poem, Swift, whose view of human nature was even darker than Adams's, developed a cynical maxim of La Rochefoucauld's that stated "in the misfortunes of our best friends we always find something that does not displease us." Adams imitated Swift's lines, which had referred to his close friend John Arbuthnot, by saying

> Jefferson is no more my Friend,
> Who dares to Independence to pretend
> Which I was born to introduce
> Refin'd it first and Shewed its Use.

Adams went on in this letter to Richard Rush to offer his own maxims concerning the arbitrariness of who was allowed into "the Temple of Fame." "Mankind," he said, "never give Credit to their true Benefactors," and "deliberately rob the real Sages and Heroes of their Laurells and confer them on others who have done nothing to deserve them." As an example, he pointed out that "Dr. Rush was a greater and better Man than Dr. Franklin; yet Rush was always persecuted and Franklin always adored." For an additional example in a postscript, he told young Rush to look in the Journals of Congress for the 1774 Declaration of the Rights of the Colonies and for the resolutions of May 1776, and "then consider whether the Declaration of Independence of 4 July 1776 is any thing more than a juvenile declamation founded on these two Documents"— documents that were drawn up by Adams himself. His jealousy was so palpable and was expressed so bluntly that more often than not his correspondents found it endearing.[32]

When Jefferson was asked about the contributions of Franklin and Adams to the writing of the Declaration, he said that "the rough draught was communicated to those two gentlemen, who each of them made 2 or 3 short and verbal alterations only, but even this is laying more stress on mere composition than it merits; for that alone was mine." But averse as he was to seeming vain, he wanted it understood that "the sentiments were of all America."[33]

Still, Jefferson had become increasingly proud of being the author of the Declaration and sensitive to suggestions that he was a mere draftsman who derived his ideas from elsewhere. Thus he was not at all happy when he learned from Adams in 1819 that an earlier declaration of independence had anticipated his famous document. Adams informed Jefferson that a resolution of independence supposedly issued by militia companies in Mecklenburg County, North Carolina, on May 20, 1775, had been recently discovered. This declaration, he told Jefferson, was "fifteen months before your Declaration of Independence." A physician named Joseph McKnitt Alexander had written an article for the *Raleigh Register and North Carolina Gazette* on April 30, 1819, within which he had included the resolves issued by the Mecklenburg militia companies. The resolves were republished in the June 5, 1819, issue of a Salem newspaper, the *Essex Gazette*, where Adams discovered them.

In his article, Dr. Alexander contended that when the Mecklenburg militia companies had learned of the Battles of Lexington and Concord, they had passed a set of resolutions that dissolved "the political bands, which have connected us to the Mother Country, and hereby absolve ourselves from all allegiance to the British Crown." After mentioning "the inherent and inalienable rights of man" and declaring themselves "a free and independent People," the militia companies went on in language eerily similar to Jefferson's Declaration to "solemnly pledge to each other our mutual cooperation, our lives, our fortunes, and our most sacred honor."[34]

Adams was obviously excited by this discovery and initially thought the Mecklenburg resolutions were authentic. He told Jefferson that "the Genuine sense of America at that Moment was never so well expressed before or since." By comparison, he said, Thomas Paine's *Common Sense* (and by implication perhaps Jefferson's Declaration) was "a poor ignorant, Malicious, short-sighted, Crapulous Mass." Adams wrote the Reverend William Bentley of Salem that Jefferson "must have seen" the Mecklenburg declaration in 1775, since he "copied the spirit, the sense, and the expressions of it *verbatim* into his Declaration of the 4th of July, 1776." He asked Bentley to have the printer of the *Essex Gazette* send him a half-dozen copies of the issue in which the Mecklenburg declaration had appeared, "whatever they may cost."[35]

Jefferson responded to Adams at once and claimed that the document was "spurious." He thought it strange that no one in North Carolina or Virginia had ever mentioned it until now. Would not every advocate for independence have rung the glories of Mecklenburg County in the ears of all the doubters in 1775? he asked. Yet no one ever did. Now anyone who could authenticate the resolves was dead and the original document had burned. He couldn't affirm that the document was "a fabrication," but he would continue to believe it was, "until positive and solemn proof of it's authenticity shall be produced."[36]

Jefferson made such a convincing case for the fraudulent character of the document that Adams agreed at once that it was a "fiction." Contrary to what some historians have claimed, Adams was not guilty of any "duplicity."[37] He wrote immediately to Reverend Bentley to tell him that

Jefferson's explanation was "correct and exact" and "intirely satisfactory in all its parts." Jefferson had persuaded him that "the pretended Mecklenburg Resolutions" were a fake or a hoax, and "ought to be called forgery's" with the authors exposed to public resentment. "It will be difficult for Posterity to detect the Multitudinous falsehoods which were published from day to day during the Revolution, and ever since—but fictions of this kind, five and forty years after the pretended fact, ought to be discountenanced by every man of honor."[38]

As his initial excitement over the Mecklenburg resolutions suggests, Adams undoubtedly had a secret desire that Jefferson would turn out to be a plagiarizer, for the Declaration of Independence had taken on a sacred character that no one in 1776 had anticipated. It had become, as the Board of Visitors of Jefferson's University of Virginia declared, "the fundamental act of union" of the United States. As such, Jefferson told Madison in 1823, our goal ought to be "to cherish the principles of the instrument in the bosoms of our own citizens."

Federalist critics of his role in writing the Declaration, such as Timothy Pickering (who claimed that he had gotten his information from John Adams), did not know what they were talking about. They claimed that the document "contained no new ideas, that it is a commonplace compilation, it's sentiments hackneyed in Congress for two year before, and its essence contained in [James] Otis's pamphlet." This "may all be true," Jefferson told Madison; he was not to be the judge. All he knew was that he had "turned to neither book nor pamphlet while writing it." He had not been seeking originality. He then went on in his letter to Madison to defend Adams's role in the Congress. "He supported the Declaration with zeal and ability fighting fearlessly for every word of it."[39]

In 1824 Secretary of State John Quincy Adams, acting under a resolution of Congress, sent Jefferson two facsimile copies of the Declaration. Jefferson was delighted, and took the Congress's act as "evidence afforded of reverence for that instrument, and view in it a pledge of adhesion to its principles and of a sacred determination to maintain and perpetuate them." This, he told John Quincy, was a "holy purpose."[40]

All the queries Jefferson was receiving about his authorship of the

Declaration convinced him that the document had taken on a hallowed character; and he began to realize that the writing box or desk on which he had composed the Declaration might become sacredly significant. In 1825 he told his granddaughter Ellen Wayles Coolidge that he had been recently impressed with the reverence accorded William Penn's chair in Philadelphia and it got him thinking. "If then things acquire a superstitious value because of their connection with particular persons, surely a connection with the great Charter of our Independence may give a value to what has been associated with that." Although the writing box was plain and ordinary, he wanted Joseph Coolidge, his granddaughter's husband, to have it. "Its imaginary value will increase with years, and if he lives to my age, or another half century, he may see it carried in the procession of our nation's birthday, as the relics of the saints are in those of the Church."[41]

No wonder that in working out a brief list of his life's achievements for his tombstone, Jefferson chose to have engraved "Author of the Declaration of Independence" first, followed by his authorship of the Virginia statute for religious freedom and his founding of the University of Virginia.

BY THE EARLY 1820s Jefferson's authorship of the Declaration had become a consolation, a justification, for a life that otherwise seemed to be spinning out of control. The final decade of Jefferson's life was not a happy time. To be sure, he had become the Sage of Monticello, relaxing among his family and friends and holding court on the top of his mountain for the hordes of visiting admirers. Against much opposition, he had fulfilled his dream of establishing the University of Virginia in his neighborhood. And he had his thousands of exchanges with his many correspondents and his reconciliation with Adams, which became increasingly meaningful to him. But there was not much else to comfort him.

The world around him, the world that he had done so much to create, was rapidly changing, and changing in ways that he found bewildering and sometimes even terrifying. The Revolution was unfolding in a radical and unforeseen manner. American society was becoming more democratic and more money-minded than he had anticipated. The economy had become wild and risky and unbelievably speculative. The people in whom he had put so much trust were behaving in ways he had not expected. During the final years of his life, he had moments of apprehension that the American Revolution to which he had devoted his life was in danger of failing. In response, he spoke and acted in ways that tended to violate the principles that he had lived by. He turned inward and began conjuring up thoughts, stirring up demons, and spouting dogmas that many subsequent historians and biographers have found embarrassing and puzzling.[42]

He feared the dynamic commercial society that was emerging in the aftermath of the Revolution and hated all the capitalistic accouterments that went with it—banks, stock markets, liquid capital, and especially paper money. As a southerner used to thinking of commerce as the selling of staples to international markets, he had little or no understanding that all this credit and capital—the proliferation of paper money—was feeding the enormous expansion of America's economy, an economy increasingly dominated by domestic trade in which the people of the nation carried on innumerable exchanges with one another and not with markets abroad. He told Adams; Albert Gallatin, who had been his secretary of the treasury; and all his other correspondents that the "Mania" for banknotes was ruining both individuals and the country. "All the members of our governments, general, special, and individual" have been "siesed by it's delusions and corruptions."[43]

The only hope for the country, he told Adams in 1818, lay in the West. "Our greediness for wealth, and fantastical expense has degraded and will degrade the minds of our maritime citizens. These are the peculiar vices of commerce," commerce for him still being identified with overseas trade. As far as he was concerned, the issue of hundreds of millions of dollars of paper currency was benefiting only speculators and gamblers. The paper money was merely "frothy bubbles" that no one was confident in holding. "We are now without any common measure of the value of property, and private fortunes are up or down at the will of the worst to our citizens."[44]

Although Jefferson thought that paper money was destroying the country, people seemed to want even more of it. How to convince them otherwise? He expected no relief from the state legislatures, "as little seems to be known of the principles of political economy as if nothing had ever been written or practiced on the subject." Perhaps if he could bring into print an English translation of Destutt de Tracy's *Treatise on Political Economy,* which he declared was "the best work on Political economy that has ever appeared," he could expose the problems of the banks and the excessive printing of paper money.[45]

Jefferson became almost desperate to bring this *Treatise* to the American public, and he worked hard—four to five hours a day for three months—to translate it into English. If the people and their representatives in the legislatures could read Destutt de Tracy's *Treatise,* they would be impressed by its rationality and its science and so find evidence for curbing the excesses of paper money.

No matter that Destutt de Tracy's book had nothing to say about the kind of staple-producing economy of the South that was dependent on international markets and instead celebrated the kind of domestic economy that was emerging in the North. No matter that Destutt de Tracy directly denied some of Jefferson's dearest and most fundamental convictions, including his belief that farmers had a special role to play in the nation. No matter too that this French liberal's book condemned slavery and the "drones" and the "truly *sterile* class" of "the idle, who do nothing but live, *nobly* as it is termed, on the products of labours" of others. In contrast to the South, which remained "in languor and stagnation," Destutt de Tracy praised the North for being "full of vigour and prosperity."[46]

Ultimately, what Jefferson was taken with was Destutt de Tracy's strong condemnation of the wildcat banks and the issuing of paper money. "Paper money," the French philosophe had written, "is the most culpable and most fatal of all fraudulent bankruptcies." Indeed, "all paper money" was *"a frenzy of despotism run mad."*[47]

Jefferson agreed. In fact, he told Albert Gallatin that "we are undone, my dear Sir, if this banking mania be not suppressed." Either the banks must be destroyed or the country would be. If translating and publishing

Destutt de Tracy's *Treatise* didn't solve the problem of paper money, then things looked hopeless. Everyone, Jefferson said, would just have to sit back and endure the evils of paper money the way they endured hurricanes, earthquakes, and other natural phenomena.[48]

ADAMS ALSO THOUGHT the dynamic world of the early republic was going to hell in a handbasket. He hated all the banks and their proliferating issues of paper money as much as Jefferson. He even called the rage for them "a Mania," as Jefferson had. They were "the Madness of the Many for the Profit of a Few."[49] He told Jefferson that he agreed with him that all the state banks had created "a system of national Injustice," by which public and private interest was sacrificed "to a few Aristocratical Friends and Favourites."[50]

Despite sharing Jefferson's view on the evils of banks, Adams responded very differently to the wild and hellish world of the early republic. He was not surprised by it and came to believe that it was what he had expected all along. He praised Jefferson's translation of Destutt de Tracy's book as accurate and elegant and told him he had read as much of it as he could. "If it can destroy the Parasite Institutions of our country it will merit immortal honor." But he wondered "how it has happened that religious liberty, fiscal science, coin and commerce, and every branch of political economy should have been better understood and more honestly practiced in that Frog land, than in any other country in the world."[51]

In fact, Adams told Jefferson that he felt detached from the whole speculative and gambling mess, just as if he were viewing it from the hereafter. "We cannot choose," he told Jefferson, "but smile at the gambols of Ambition Avarice Pleasure, Sport and Caprice here below." He reminded Jefferson of a French fable in which the angels, thinking of man and his fine qualities, especially his being "a rational Creature," set the whole of heaven into laughter. Man a rational creature! "How could any rational Being even dream that Man was a rational Creature?"[52]

Adams enjoyed teasing Jefferson about all the failures of reason. Reason was unable, for example, to sort out the differences between the

Spiritualists and the Materialists. "We may read Cudworth Clark Leibnitz, Berkly Hume Bolingbroke and Priestley and a million other Volumes in all Ages and be obliged at last to confess that We have learned nothing. Spirit and matter," he told Jefferson in 1817, "still remain Riddles." It was foolish to count on reason. "Vain Man! Mind Your own Business! Do no Wrong! Do all the good you can! Eat your Canvas back ducks, drink your burgundy, sleep your Siesta, when necessary, and Trust in God!"[53]

ADAMS WAS MUCH BETTER prepared intellectually and emotionally to deal with the emerging democratic and commercial circumstances of the early republic. Not that he favored them. He simply had many more doubts about the rationality and virtue of the American people than Jefferson had. Adams was never as bewildered and frightened as Jefferson by the new dynamic and popular world developing in the early nineteenth century. Profiteering, speculation, and corruption were only to be expected in a government as popular and democratic as America's. Adams's cynicism and low expectations of human nature protected him from the kind of disappointments Jefferson was experiencing.

Adams was never much committed to democracy in the first place. From the beginning in 1776, he had doubted the capacity of Americans to sustain their republic. He never had Jefferson's faith in the virtue of the people, and he never assumed that democracy was the be-all and end-all of government.

Where Jefferson was sincere and earnest, Adams was ironic and facetious. As he put it in 1817, he was never able to "contemplate human Affairs, without laughing or crying."[54] He had few illusions about the world and thus was much less likely to become disillusioned. By contrast, Jefferson was full of illusions and was unprepared intellectually and emotionally for the rapidly changing world of the early republic.

Jefferson had always been the ultimate optimist, a virtual Pollyanna about everything. His expectations always outran reality. He thought he would have more rain to supply water for his mountaintop home than he had. His elaborate plans for flowers and vegetables at Monticello were never fulfilled. He was surprised by the immature and riotous behavior of the students at his new university in violation of the honor code. And of course there was his deep faith in a French Revolution that had gone awry. He was the pure American innocent. He had little understanding of man's capacity for evil and had no tragic sense whatsoever. That is, he possessed no sense of the circumstances impinging on and limiting human action, little or no appreciation of the blindness of people struggling with a world they scarcely understood.[55]

More than any of the revolutionary leaders, Jefferson had placed unquestioning trust in the people and in the future. All the problems of the present would be taken care of by the people, if not now, then eventually. As he told Adams in 1816, he always liked "the dreams of the future better than the history of the past."[56] While Adams was complaining about the society's corruption and the direction it was taking, Jefferson had nearly always remained calm and hopeful. Even when he had moments of apprehension over the future, as he did in 1808, he did not allow them to get him down. He told his daughter Martha that "not being apt to deject myself with evils before they happen, I nourish the hope of getting along." He expected problems to be solved by themselves, that sooner or later something would turn up. He saw his financial troubles coming at him and his household "as an approaching wave in a storm. Still I think we shall live as long, eat as much, & drink as much, as if the wave had already glided under our ship. Somehow or other these things find their way out as they come in, & so I suppose they will now."[57] Jefferson had always believed that the future was on his side and on the side of the people. A liberal democratic society would be capable of solving every problem, if not in his lifetime, then surely in the coming years.

It was the same with every difficulty. In one way or another, he expected things eventually to work out. He knew slavery was a great evil, but he believed his generation could do little about it. Instead he counseled patience and a reliance on the younger generation who would follow. When one of those younger men, Edward Coles, actually called on Jefferson in 1814 to lend his voice in the struggle against slavery, he could only offer his confidence in the future. "The hour of emancipation is advancing, in the march of time. It will come."[58]

ALAS, DURING THE LAST DECADE of his life Jefferson came to have increasing doubts that the future would work out as he had expected. His correspondence in these years was punctuated with laments over "the rising generation, of which I once had sanguine hopes."[59] American society, including that of Virginia, was not progressing after all, but seemed to be going backward. Although Jefferson always celebrated common ordinary people, he hadn't anticipated their entering and actually wielding the powers of governments. He had not foreseen the popular middle-class revolution that he and his Democratic-Republican Party had inspired. He was frightened by the popularity of Andrew Jackson, regarding him as a military man of violent passions and unfit for the presidency. He was dismayed that the American people were not learning to love one another but were increasingly engaged in partisan, sectarian, and sectional strife.

Although Jefferson had always prided himself on his cosmopolitanism, in the final years of his retirement he became more narrow-minded and localist than he had ever been. He tended to cut himself off from many of the current sources of knowledge of the outside world, and became, as one of his visitors, George Ticknor, noted, "singularly ignorant & insensible on the subjects of passing politics." Jefferson read avidly, but, he admitted, "not of newspapers, these I have discarded."[60] He actually took only one newspaper, the *Richmond Enquirer*, and seemed to have no strong interest in receiving his mail, perhaps because he dreaded having to answer all of his many letters.

It was almost as if Jefferson couldn't face what was happening around him in his beloved "country" of Virginia. Decay was everywhere in early-nineteenth-century Virginia, and Jefferson felt it at Monticello. According to one observer, Jefferson's home county, Albemarle, had become a "scene of desolation that baffles description." Farms were "worn out, washed and gullied, so that scarcely an acre could be found in a place fit for cultivation."

By 1820 Virginia, which once had been the most populous state by far, had already been surpassed by Pennsylvania and New York. The growth of its population had slowed dramatically, and it no longer possessed its earlier confidence that it would be in charge of the nation. Although cotton had come to dominate the exports of the lower South, Virginia had no secure staple. Its climate prevented the growing of cotton, and the old standby tobacco had depleted the state's land. Some planters, including Jefferson, were trying to grow wheat for export, but it was not enough. Unable to farm the exhausted soil, many of Virginia's vigorous and ambitious younger people were fleeing the state, moving with their slaves to the new territories of Alabama and Mississippi.[61]

Despite his contempt for the politicians and priests of New England, Jefferson had a half-conscious admiration for the society the Federalists had created. His dream of a three-tiered educational system and his desire to establish participatory democracy in little ward-republics resembled nothing so much as the townships of Adams's New England.[62] Jefferson knew there were great differences between the North and the South, and if he had forgotten, he had his granddaughter Ellen Randolph Coolidge, who had moved to New England in 1825, to remind him. When she told him of the beauty and prosperity of New England that the southern states could never hope to emulate, not as long as "the canker of slavery eats into their hearts, and diseases the whole body by this ulcer at the core," he could only agree. If only "one single circumstance" could be changed, he told his granddaughter, Virginia would be the equal of Massachusetts in beauty. "One fatal stain," he said, "deforms what nature has bestowed on us of her fairest gifts." He knew, however—it had become the dread of his life—that that awful stain could not be easily eradicated.[63]

Jefferson's personal situation aggravated his sense that things were spinning out of control. Despite his lifelong aversion to public debts, his private debts kept mounting as he took out new loans to meet old ones. The enormous debt of £4,000 he had inherited from his father-in-law, John Wayles, loomed over him, and he realized that he might never be able to pay it off. He feared that he might even lose Monticello. Although he complained constantly of his debts, he refused to cut back on his lavish hospitality and his expensive wine purchases. In 1819 he cosigned a note for $20,000 for former Virginia governor William Cary Nicholas, whose daughter had married a Jefferson grandson. When Nicholas defaulted on the note, Jefferson became responsible for the debt. But he never let that responsibility affect his relationship with his granddaughter-in-law or with Nicholas. He was a gentleman to the end.[64]

Ordinary people in whom he had placed so much confidence were not becoming more enlightened after all. In fact, superstition and bigotry, which Jefferson identified with organized religion, were actually reviving, released by the democratic revolution he had led. Unlike Adams, he was temperamentally incapable of appreciating the deep popular strength of the evangelical forces that were seizing control of American culture in these early decades of the nineteenth century. He became a confused and embattled secular humanist in the midst of real moral majorities. Although he was still hopefully predicting that there was not a young man now alive who would not die a Unitarian, in 1822, Methodists, Baptists, and other evangelicals were gaining adherents by the tens of thousands in the Second Great Awakening and transforming American society.

Since he thought the priests of New England, with all their "pious whining, hypocritical canting, lying & slandering," were behind this attempt "to evangelize the nation," he dismissed the effort as simply an insidious scheme by New England, "having lost it's political influence by disloyalty to it's country, . . . to recover it under the mask of religion."[65]

Jefferson's solution to this perceived threat from New England and its "pious young monks from Harvard and Yale" was to hunker down in Virginia and build a university that would perpetuate true republican principles.[66] "It is in our Seminary," he told Madison, "that that Vestal flame is to be kept alive," where it would then "spread anew over our own and the sister states."[67]

Yet even building the University of Virginia brought sorrow and shock. Jefferson thought he had retired as president with a degree of popularity at least among Republicans, but that hadn't been borne out in his own state of Virginia. His attempt to found a university in order "to procure an improvement in the moral condition of my native state . . . ran foul of so many local interests, of so many personal views, and of so much ignorance" that he could only count on posterity to vindicate his public service.[68]

He admitted to Adams that the Virginia legislature was not as eager to spend money for higher education as he had expected. The members were "a good piece of a century behind the age they live in," and they had "so many biasses, personal, local, fanatical, financial, etc. that we cannot foresee in what their combinations will result."[69] Although Adams congratulated Jefferson on his new university, he was hardly comforting. He told Jefferson that with such esteemed supporters as Madison, Monroe, and himself, much was expected of the university. "But if it contains any thing quite original, and very excellent," Adams feared that "prejudices are too deeply rooted to suffer it to last long." It would not always have "such a noble Tryumvirate" to maintain it. He especially objected to Jefferson's "sending to Europe for Tutors and Professors." He thought that American professors had "more active ingenuity, and independent minds" than the Europeans, who were "all deeply tainted by prejudice both Ecclesiastical and Temporal."[70]

Actually, Jefferson's position in Virginia was such that his support for the university became more of a political liability in the legislature than an asset. "There are fanatics both in religion and politics," he told Joseph Cabell, his collaborator in promoting the university, in 1818, "who, without knowing me personally, have long been taught to consider me as a raw head and bloody bones." Even some in his own county were opposed to his promotion of higher education in Virginia.

Consequently, he even came to doubt the viability of popular republican government. "There is some flaw, not yet detected in our principle of representation," he told Thomas Cooper, the British émigré scientist, "which fails to bring forth the wisdom of our country into it's councils." Just as Adams had predicted, the people weren't electing into office the natural aristocrats after all. Where this would end he did not know, but it was bound to lead to "a state of degradation, which I thank heaven I am not to live to witness."[71]

. . .

ALTHOUGH JEFFERSON was always opposed to the past binding the present and as late as 1816 had urged the need to accommodate governments and institutions to changing circumstances in order "to keep pace with the times," he became increasingly fearful of the federal government's usurpation of authority at the expense of the states.[72] In the presidential election of 1824, he favored William H. Crawford of Georgia, the southern candidate, and was deeply disappointed in Crawford's third-place finish behind Andrew Jackson and John Quincy Adams. The electoral result, he said, weakened his confidence in the discretion of his fellow citizens. "The ignorance of character, the personal partialities and the inattention to those questions which ought to have guided their choice, augur ill of the wisdom of our future course."[73]

Although he politely congratulated Adams on the election of his son to the presidency, he feared that John Quincy's election would only lead to a further consolidation of federal authority, especially since the new president proposed using the powers of the federal government to promote internal improvements and the general welfare. Most alarming was the fact that the government seemed to be expressing the will of the people. Although the members of Congress were behaving badly in looking for "objects whereon to throw away the supposed fathomless funds of treasury," Jefferson realized "that in one of their most ruinous vagaries, the people were themselves betrayed into the same phrenzy with their Representatives."[74]

Yet the Congress and its members were not the branch of government to be most feared. "Taxes and short elections will keep them right." It was the judiciary that was most dangerous. The federal judges were "a subtle corps of sappers and miners constantly working under ground to undermine the foundations of our confederated fabric," with the aim of turning America's state-based government into a single supreme national government. It was a good thing for judges to be independent of a king, but it was a gross error to make them independent of "the will of the nation."[75]

Consequently, Jefferson became a bitter critic of the usurpations of the Supreme Court, which were "driving us into consolidation." He denied the Court "the right they usurp of exclusively explaining the constitution." He claimed that the other branches had an equal and coordinate right of interpreting the Constitution, including deciding issues between the federal government and the states. If Chief Justice Marshall's theory of judicial review was allowed to stand, Jefferson believed that the Constitution would become "a mere thing of wax in the hands of the judiciary, which they may twist and shape into any form they please."[76]

Jefferson thought that the state governments were granted power over "all legislation and administration in affairs which concern their own citizens only," and to the federal government was "given whatever concerns foreigners, or the citizens of other states." Hence the United States was a single confederation, with the states being "the domestic, the other the foreign branch of the same government, neither having control over the other, but within it's own department." If serious conflicts should arise between the two levels of government, "a Convention of the states must be called" as an umpire to settle the differences.[77]

As much as he hated slavery, he loved Virginia and its culture more. Suddenly he realized that the North was eager to interfere with the southern way of life. With the Revolution, the northern states had begun eliminating slavery, and by 1804 all of the states north of the Mason-Dixon Line had legally abolished the institution. By the second decade of the nineteenth century, antislavery sentiment in the North was spreading, making the future for Jefferson seem increasingly ominous. The Missouri crisis of 1819–1820, provoked by northern efforts to limit the spread of slavery in the West, became for Jefferson and other southerners "a fire bell in the night" that marked "the knell of the Union" and a threat to the revolutionary dream of republican self-government.[78]

Like many other southerners, Jefferson believed that the Missouri crisis was "merely a question of power," not of morality. He thought the Federalists, "despairing of ever rising again under the old division of whig and tory," had devised a new division, "of slave-holding & non-slave-holding states." This sectional division had "a semblance of being

Moral," but it was really about northern efforts to gain ascendancy over the South in the nation. Indeed, he told Gallatin, if there was any morality in the Missouri crisis, it lay with the South. By spreading and diffusing slavery over the territories of the West, the southern slaveholders were actually increasing the "happiness" of the slaves and helping to make possible their "future liberation."

Using the federal government, as the northerners were trying to do, to restrict the right of the people of Missouri to own slaves was a serious violation of the Constitution and an ominous threat to self-government. Congress, Jefferson said, had no right "to regulate the conditions of the different descriptions of men composing a state." Only each state had the "exclusive right" to regulate slavery. If the federal government arrogated to itself that right, then it would next declare all slaves in the country free. "In which case all the whites within the United States South of the Potomak and Ohio must evacuate their states; and most fortunate those who can do it first." A breakup of the Union was possible, and bad as that would be, it would have the additional deplorable consequence of discouraging the European nations from overthrowing "their oppressive and Cannibal governments."[79]

Indicative of how superficial at times his relationship with Adams could be, Jefferson tried to avoid even mentioning the Missouri crisis to his Massachusetts friend. Adams, of course, was less inhibited, but even he realized there were limits to what he could say on the sensitive issue of slavery. Invoking the nautical image that Jefferson had often used, Adams hoped that the crisis over the expansion of slavery into the West would "follow the other Waves under the Ship and do no harm." Although he realized, he told Jefferson, that it was "high treason to express a doubt of the perpetual duration of our vast American Empire," he feared that there were demagogues who "might rend this mighty Fabric in twain" or even "produce as many Nations in North America as there are in Europe."[80]

With no response from Jefferson, Adams two months later expressed a further wish that the Missouri question would "not sett too narrow limits to the Power and Respectability of the United States," and hoped that "some good natural way or other will be found out to untie this very intricate knot."[81] Privately, he was opposed to allowing slavery in Missouri, and, as he told his daughter-in-law, he had "no doubt of the right of Congress to stop the progress of slavery."[82]

After a year of silence, Jefferson finally revealed his anxieties on the Missouri question to Adams. He wondered what "the Holy alliance, in and out of Congress" meant to do "with us," meaning slaveholding southerners. Those who called it "the Missouri question," he said, scarcely scratched the surface of the problem. The real issue, he told Adams, in terms that vividly exposed his fears for the future of the South, involved those "in the states afflicted with this unfortunate population." Were "our slaves to be presented with freedom and a dagger?" If Congress had "the power to regulate the conditions of the inhabitants of the states, within the states, it will be but another exercise of that power that all shall be free." Would there then be two confederacies like Athens and Sparta and another Peloponnesian war "to settle the ascendancy between them?" Or was the tocsin announcing merely a servile war, a war between blacks and whites that he had long predicted? He could only hope that events would be delayed long enough for both he and Adams to get out of the way.[83]

Jefferson's belated disclosure of his feelings on the Missouri crisis allowed Adams an opening to respond. He said that he had seen slavery hanging over the United States "like a black cloud for half a Century." He had actually envisioned "Armies of Negroes marching and countermarching in air, shining in Armour." He had been "so terrified with this Phenomenon" that he always said to southern gentlemen that he could not "comprehend this object; I must leave it to you." He would never force a measure against Jefferson's judgment.[84]

FEARFUL AND APPREHENSIVE over the future of slavery to a degree he had never felt before, Jefferson became a more strident defender of states' rights than he had been even in 1798, when he penned the Kentucky resolution justifying the right of a state to nullify federal laws. In 1825 he proposed sending to the Virginia assembly a "Solemn

Declaration and Protest" against the possibility of the federal government promoting internal improvements of roads and canals in violation of the strict principles of the Constitution. Although his proposal did not advocate breaking up the Union, it declared that there were worse calamities than that: "submission to a government of unlimited powers." It was "only when the hope of avoiding this shall become absolutely desperate that further forbearance could not be indulged." In the meantime, the state would urge its citizens to comply with the acts of the federal Congress, until the state legislature should decide otherwise, even though those acts were "usurpations, and against which, in point of right, we do protest as null and void, and never to be quoted as precedents of right."[85]

His friend Madison talked him out of submitting this extraordinary document, arguing that Virginia ought not any longer be taking leadership "in opposing the obnoxious career of Congress, or, rather of their Constituents." Given the "prejudices" against Virginia in the country, the state would be better off letting others take the lead. Besides, said Madison, "the Phalanx" in favor of internal improvements and consolidation might break apart of its own accord.[86]

While Madison remained a nationalist, even upholding the right of the Supreme Court to interpret the Constitution, Jefferson lent his wholehearted support to the views of the most dogmatic, impassioned, and sectional-minded elements in Virginia, including the arch-states'-rightists John Randolph of Roanoke and Spencer Roane. His anguish over "the degeneracy of public opinion from our original and free principles" intensified.[87] As he became more and more parochial and increasingly alarmed by northern aggrandizement, his zeal for states' rights became fanatical.

IN THE END JEFFERSON'S supreme faith in the people became riddled with doubts. The people did not seem to know who he was, what he had done. Was this the new generation on which he had rested all his hopes? Because of the Missouri crisis over the expansion of slavery, he sensed that he was to die in the apprehension that all the sacrifices of the generation of 1776 to acquire self-government and happiness for their country were "to be thrown away by the unwise and unworthy passions of their sons." During the last year of his life, at a moment when he was experiencing "a kind of uneasiness I never had before," Jefferson was pathetically reduced to listing his contributions during sixty-one years of public service in order to justify a legislative favor. He realized he had overvalued himself, and the reluctance of the Virginia legislature to respond to his request was "a deadly blast to all my peace of mind during my remaining days." When his grandson Thomas Jefferson Randolph suggested that he might have to sell Monticello to cover his debts, he "turned quite white & set for some time silent." No wonder he felt "over whelmed at the prospect of the situation in which I may leave my family," and no wonder he felt cast off. "All, all dead!" he wrote in 1825 to his and Adams's mutual friend Adrian Van der Kemp, "and ourselves left alone midst a new generation whom we know not, and who know not us."[88]

On the eve of the golden jubilee of the nation, Jefferson had become deeply depressed over both its fate and the fate of his family. Ultimately, he had been victimized by his own rosy temperament, by his absolute confidence in the people, and by his naïve hopefulness in the future.

As Jefferson became more troubled and pessimistic, Adams became more serene if not optimistic. The two friends seemed to reverse their outlooks on the world. Not only was Adams being elected to many committees, but his fellow citizens in Massachusetts were honoring him more than they ever had before. "You cannot imagine of how much importance I am become," he told his son John Quincy in 1816. Although this was said jokingly, Adams felt the difference. "After being buffeted calumniated courted, neglected by turns all my Lifetime, I am lately invited into all Societies and much caressed." His home became a gathering place "where," according to young Josiah Quincy, who had occasionally read and been an amanuensis for the ex-president, "the fair ones of Milton and Quincy met in harmony." Adams was in his element: he told amusing anecdotes and entertained young girls on the "ancient belles and beaux of this place." On Adams's eighty-ninth birthday, Quincy said that he had never seen him "look better or converse with more spirit."[89]

When Adams reached his eighties, he became more accepting of things and actually conceded that progress had occurred. The world was "better than we found it," he told his old friend and Harvard classmate David Sewall. "Superstition, persecution and Bigotry are some what abated, Governments are a little ameliorated, science and Literature are greatly improved and more widely spread."[90] Adams became more mellow and more forgiving of his enemies. Not only had he reconciled with Jefferson, but he patched up his quarrel with Mercy Otis Warren before her death.[91] He was less and less bothered by the critics who buzzed about him. "Their bite in former times tingled," he told his son John Quincy, "but I am grown almost as insensible, as a Boston Dray horse, in September."[92]

In 1824 even John Taylor, the conscience of the Republican Party and the severest critic of Adams's *Defence of the Constitutions of the Government of the United States of America*, came around. Taylor knew he was dying and wanted to write Adams to express his admiration for his integrity and patriotism despite their great differences over political theory. In the exchange of dozens of letters, Adams's honesty and willingness to engage with Taylor's arguments—Adams may in fact have been the only person who actually read Taylor's lengthy and convoluted book—had won over the Virginian's heart, and Adams was touched by the compliments.[93]

Others too were writing him to tell him how much they admired his *Defence*, "a Book," Adams believed, "that has been misunderstood, misrepresented and abused more than any other, except the Bible." In fact, some even apologized for having formerly maligned the book before having actually read it. One such person, "convinced of his errour," had become an admirer after belatedly reading the work. "Great is Truth," said Adams, "and it will prevail." "My plain Writings had been misunderstood by many, misrepresented by more, and Vilified and Annathematised by multitudes, who never read them." They had nothing to recommend them "but stubborn facts." He had the consolation to know that his writings had been translated into French, German, and Spanish, and that "they are now contributing to introduce Representative Governments into various Nations of Europe" just as they had influenced the establishment of America's constitutions, "both of the Individual States and the Nation at large." Now the Latin American states were using his writings.[94]

At last he felt his great work might be properly appreciated. Thomas Cooper, a friend of Dr. Priestley, had recently published in the *Port Folio* "a very handsome eulogium on the Work." And most important, as Adams bragged in 1820 to one of the recent converts to his point of view, "the learned and scientific President Jefferson has in letters to me acknowledged that I was right, and that he was wrong"—an exaggeration no doubt, but emotionally accurate. Adams apologized to his correspondents for the vanity he was expressing, but he believed that all the injustice he had suffered over the years ought to excuse his egotism. At long last he felt that he might achieve the fame that all the Founders sought.[95]

With all of his grandchildren and great-grandchildren multiplying around him ("You have no idea of the prolific quality of the New England Adamses," he told Van der Kemp), he was as happy as he ever had been. Having all these children surrounding him was "as delightful as any thing we find in this pleasant world, as I call it." Certainly, he said, he could not call it "a vale of tears."[96]

Given some of his personal circumstances, Adams had every reason to feel the world to be "a vale of tears." His son Charles had died in 1800 at age thirty of alcoholism, and he had lost his daughter Nabby to cancer in 1813. Although John Quincy's career was progressing brilliantly, his son Thomas had moved back to Quincy and was drinking heavily. No doubt Abigail's death in 1818 devastated him, but he recovered. Six months later, he told Jefferson that although "the World is dead" and he could no longer hold a pen, "I still live and enjoy life."[97]

Knowing of Jefferson's ballooning debts, Adams could take comfort that his personal affairs were in order. He felt increasingly sure of his judgment and of his assessments of reality. He had never been happy with Jefferson's idea of withholding commerce as a weapon in international conflicts. It was true that he had accepted a temporary embargo against Britain in 1794 to protect American seamen and ships, "but not with the faintest hope that it would influence the British Councils." In fact, he had come to believe that a war was preferable to trying to enforce nonimportation laws and embargoes.[98] His predictions about the futility of Jefferson's embargo and the War of 1812 had been borne out. He told Benjamin Waterhouse in 1813 that he may not have the "Foresight of the Tumble-Bug: Yet in my Conscience, I believe, I have more and clearer, than this Nation or its Government for fourteen years past."[99]

He had been right about so many things, especially about the French Revolution. "What a mighty bubble!" he said to Jefferson. The French Revolution had failed, and by 1815 the Bourbons—Louis XVIII—were back on the throne of France, and the whirlwind that had raised Napoleon had "blowed him a Way to St. Helena." Adams hoped that "Liberty, Equality, Fraternity, and Humanity will never again . . . blindly surrender themselves to an unbounded Ambition for national Conquests." Adams never taunted Jefferson directly by saying "I told you so" over his mistaken faith in the French Revolution, but indirectly he did. He delighted in re-minding Jefferson how the Poet Laureate Robert Southey had become the laughingstock of Britain, America, and all of Europe over the 1817 repub-lication of his poetic pro-republican drama of 1794, *Wat Tyler*. Since "poor Laureate Southey" was "writhing in Torments" and suffering as much as Bonaparte, perhaps Jefferson—who had held out equally high hopes for republicanism in Europe—was writhing and suffering as well.[100]

Jefferson had ignored Adams's gibes and had put the best face on af-fairs in France as he could. He observed that "friends of a limited mon-archy there consider the popular representation as much improved by the late alteration, and confident it will in the end produce a fixed govern-ment in which an elective body, fairly representative of the people will be an efficient element." Adams, of course, had no such assurance and doubted whether the French had the character to sustain even a mixed monarchy.[101]

Adams had always had qualms about Jefferson's dreams and illusions, and at last events had vindicated him. He became more confident with

Jefferson than he had been earlier. His letters became more ebullient and more self-assured. He told Jefferson that "every line" from him "exhilarates my spirits and gives me a glow of pleasure." He lifted Jefferson's own spirits by telling him that "I look back with rapture to those golden days when Virginia and Massachusetts lived and acted together like a band of brothers." He was more optimistic about the future than Jefferson. He hoped that it would not be long before people would be saying "the golden age is returning," and then the world would hear no more of Hartford conventions or Virginian threats of 1798 to the Union.[102]

He knew that slavery was the greatest threat to this vision and that he could not easily discuss it with Jefferson. Adams told Richard Rush that he had "the sweet consolation to reflect, that I never owned a slave" and had always been opposed to the institution of slavery.[103] "The bible itself has not authority in these days to reconcile negro slavery to reason, justice, & humanity." He shuddered when he thought of the "calamities which slavery is likely to produce in this country." While Jefferson was struggling mightily with the problem, Adams was confident that on this most complicated issue facing the country he had always been on the right side of history.[104]

To top off his new sense of contentment, his son John Quincy in March 1825 became president of the United States. Many saw what this meant to Adams. Young Josiah Quincy and his mother visited Montezillo, the Adams home, to congratulate the ex-president on the election of his son. They found him "considerably affected by the fulfillment of his highest wishes." Mrs. Quincy compared Adams to "that old man who was pronounced by Solon to be the happiest of mortals when he expired on hearing of his son's success at the Olympic Games." The comparison visibly moved Adams and "tears of joy rolled down his cheek." But he retained enough of his cynicism to predict that his son would pay for this honor. "He will make one man ungrateful and a hundred men his enemies for every office he can bestow."[105]

According to Quincy, Adams actually looked forward to his death, when like Cicero he would meet up with all those he had known. "Nothing," he said, "would tempt me to go back" and relive his life, which was what Jefferson was willing to do. "I agree with my old friend, Dr. Franklin, who used to say on this subject, 'We are all invited to a great entertainment. Your carriage comes first to the door; but we shall all meet there.'" If Franklin had become his "old friend," then Adams had indeed mellowed.[106]

THE NATIONAL JUBILEE

T HE TWO OLD PATRIOTS were well aware of the approaching golden jubilee of the nation on July 4, 1826, the fiftieth anniversary of the Declaration of Independence. Several weeks before the jubilee, various organizations had invited the aged expresidents to participate in celebrations of the anniversary. Adams expressed his regrets to a committee of the citizens of Quincy, explaining that the "feeble State" of his health prevented his attendance at the town's festivities. He told the committee that the day that *these United States* became independent was "a Memorable epoch in the annals of the human race, destined, in future history, to form the brightest or the blackest page, according to the use or the abuse of those political institutions by which they shall, in time to come, be shaped, by the *human mind*."[1]

This response, so typical of Adams's ambivalence about America and the future, was very different from the one Jefferson made to the committee representing the citizens of Washington, D.C. Jefferson also expressed his regrets, but with far more effusive politeness than Adams, saying that he could not attend the celebration on account of "ill health." But he hoped that the American people would continue to approve the choice the men of 1776 had made in declaring independence. He then went on with one of his greatest perorations, which outdid anything that

Adams could have said. May the American experiment in democracy, he declared,

> be to the world, what I believe it will be, (to some parts sooner, to others later, but finally to all,) the signal of arousing men to burst the chains under which monkish ignorance and superstition had persuaded them to bind themselves, and to assume the blessings and security of self-government. . . . All eyes are opened, or opening, to the rights of man. The general spread of science has already laid open to every view the palpable truth, that the mass of mankind has not been born with saddles on their backs, nor a favored few booted and spurred, ready to ride them legitimately, by the grace of God.[2]

This was vintage Jefferson, the old Jefferson whose confidence in America and the future was once again clear and absolute.

BY EARLY 1826 BOTH MEN sensed they were near the end of their lives. Adams had lost most of his teeth, his eyesight was poor, and he could walk only with great difficulty. Jefferson was losing his hearing and was suffering from a painful inflammation of his prostate, for which he was regularly taking laudanum. By mid-June Jefferson knew he was dying, and he summoned his doctor. "I am like an old watch," he said, "with a pinion worn out here, and a wheel there, until it can go no longer."[3] By early July he was in and out of consciousness and desperate to reach the Fourth, the anniversary of his Declaration. On at least one occasion during the night of July 3, he asked if it was yet the Fourth, and his doctor replied that it soon would be. Early the next morning he awoke briefly and called for his servants. Finally, at fifty minutes past noon on the Fourth of July he died, his last hope fulfilled. For someone who liked to be in control, it was fitting that he had managed his own death.

At the same time five hundred miles away in Massachusetts, Adams too lay dying and, like Jefferson, was struggling to reach the Fourth. A story later circulated that on July 3 Daniel Webster visited Adams and asked how he was. "Not very well," Adams was supposed to have replied. "I am living in a very old house, Mr. Webster, and, from all that I can learn, the landlord does not intend to repair." If the story is not true, it ought to be, for it captured Adams's characteristic humor. According to a memoir published in 1827 by William Cranch, who was Abigail's nephew and the chief judge of the U.S. Circuit Court of the District of Columbia, Adams awoke on the Fourth of July to bells ringing and cannons firing. Asked whether he knew what day it was, he was said to have replied, "O yes, it is the glorious 4th of July—God bless it—God bless you all." He then slipped into unconsciousness, but before he died at about six p.m., according to legend, he briefly awoke to say "Thomas Jefferson survives."[4]

If Adams indeed did say this, he was of course technically wrong, for Jefferson had died five hours before him. But in a larger, more meaningful sense Adams turned out to be prophetically correct. In the mind of Americans Jefferson did survive Adams, and he survived him with a powerful significance for the nation that Adams, despite all his revolutionary efforts, all his contributions to American constitutionalism, and all of his realism, could never match.

No doubt, Adams said many things applicable to the nation he helped to create. He was a constitutionalist concerned with the abuses of governmental power and a realist concerned with the inequality of society. Because Americans could not count on the natural benevolence of people, he thought they must have institutional restraints to control the anarchic impulses of people and the selfish interests of the oligarchs. He was always the realist, quick to mock the foolishness of the world. As he said in his defense of the British soldiers in the Boston Massacre trials in 1770, "Facts are stubborn things; and whatever may be our wishes, our inclinations, or the dictates of our passion, they cannot alter the state of facts and evidence."[5] He was pessimistic, even cynical, about human nature. He didn't deny the existence of "human Reason and human Conscience," but he thought they were "not a Match, for human Passions, human Imaginations and human Enthusiasm." All the passions of ambition, avarice, love, resentment, and so on, he told Jefferson, possessed so much subtlety and eloquence "that they insinuate themselves into the Understanding and the Conscience and convert both to their Party."[6] He sought always to ensure that the facts of life were not hidden and distorted by people's passions and their tendency to dissemble.

Adams knew it was easy for facts to get buried and twisted, for people were naturally selfish and power-hungry. "Ambition is one of the more ungovernable Passions of the human Heart," he said in 1772. "The Love of Power is insatiable and uncontrollable." In retirement he was repeating the same thing to Jefferson. "Power always thinks it has a great Soul, and vast Views, beyond the Comprehension of the Weak; and that it is doing God service when it is violating all his Laws." However much "you and your Party may have ridiculed . . . Checks and Ballances," he told Jefferson in 1813, they were "our only Security." Even every one of the various Christian denominations would persecute the others "if it had unchecked and unbalanced Power. . . . Know thyself, human Nature." In perhaps the most profound statement he ever made, and surely his greatest contribution to American constitutionalism, he declared "that Power must never be trusted without a Check."[7]

NEARLY EVERYTHING ADAMS said about human nature and the character of his countrymen may have been utterly accurate and grounded in fact, but there was nothing inspiring about it, nothing that could sustain a nation. Adams even doubted whether America could be a real nation. Could Americans become the "one people" that Jefferson promised in the opening paragraph of the Declaration of Independence? In America, he said, there was nothing like "the Patria of the Romans, the Fatherland of the Dutch, or the Patrie of the French." All he saw in America was an appalling diversity of religious denominations and ethnicities. In 1813 he counted nineteen different religious sects in the country. "We are such an Hotch potch of people," he concluded, "such an omnium gatherum of English, Irish, German, Dutch Sweedes,

French &c. that it is difficult to give a name to the Country, characteristic of the people."[8]

In denying Jefferson's enlightened assertion that all men were created equal, Adams thought he was just being honest and realistic and that those who believed in equality were living with an illusion. "None will pretend," he said, "that all are born of dispositions exactly alike,—of equal weight; equal strength; equal length; equal delicacy of nerves; equal elasticity of muscles; equal complexions; equal figure, grace, or beauty." In 1814 he recalled visiting a foundlings' hospital in France in the 1780s. Examining the babies, who were all less than four days old, he had never seen "a greater variety, or more striking inequalities" anywhere in Europe. Some were ugly, others beautiful; some were stupid, others sensible. "They were all born to equal rights, but to very different fortunes; to very different success and influence in life."[9]

People might be equal in the sight of God or in having equal rights in law, but to Adams the fact that "every being has a right to his own, as clear, as moral, as sacred, as any other being has" did not negate the obvious natural inequalities among individuals; these were inevitable and impossible to eradicate. People were born unequal, and these inequalities were the products of nature, not nurture. "To teach that all men are born with equal powers and faculties, to equal influence in society, to equal property and advantages through life," he said, "is as great a fraud, as glaring an imposition on the credulity of the people, as ever was practiced by monks, by Druids, by Brahmins, by priests of the immortal Lama, or by the self-styled philosophers of the French revolution."[10]

Inequality was a fact of life: some people were born smarter, more handsome, more personable, more wealthy than others. Education—the great American panacea—could not really change things. To be sure, education and the dissemination of knowledge were important for the common people: "May every human being,—man, woman, and child,—be as well informed as possible." But, Adams warned, Americans must not assume that increased knowledge among ordinary people would make them equal to the aristocracy, to the elites. On the contrary: it would just accentuate the inequality natural to every society. "Knowledge, therefore, as well as genius, strength, activity, industry, beauty, and twenty other things, will forever be a natural cause of aristocracy."[11]

Unlike most of his countrymen, Adams was preoccupied with the existence of inequality, not equality. He believed that aristocracies would inevitably emerge to dominate all societies, including that of the United States, and these aristocracies would not necessarily be based on talent and merit; ancestry and money, especially money, would be more important.

Such views were too dark, too pessimistic, too contrary to the hopes of the Enlightenment, to be acceptable. Adams's ideas were not at all what his fellow Americans wanted or needed to hear. In fact, there was scarcely an American myth, an American belief, and an American dream that Adams did not challenge. While his countrymen were celebrating the uniqueness of their nation and its special role in history, he claimed the opposite: he said the United States was no different from other nations; it was just as corrupt, just as sinful, just as vicious, as other countries. America's future was as likely to be tragic as well as comic, "for," said Adams, "we have no Patent of Exemption from the common Lot of Humanity."[12]

However true, however correct, however in accord with stubborn facts Adams's ideas might have been, they were incapable of inspiring and sustaining the United States, or any nation for that matter. Jefferson, by contrast, could and did inspire and nourish the people of the United States. Despite or perhaps because of his innocence and naïve optimism, he offered his fellow Americans a set of stirring ideals that has carried them and their country through all of their many ordeals.

Hezekiah Niles, the most important journalist of the early nineteenth century, knew the importance of Jefferson. Niles wanted to help establish "a NATIONAL CHARACTER" for Americans, and despite the victory over Britain in the War of 1812, he knew that eliminating the old English habits of mind was essential to establishing that national character. If we were to have a new nation, Niles declared in a public appeal to Jefferson in 1817, we needed new principles, new ideas, new ways of thinking. "We seek a new revolution, not less important, perhaps, in its consequences than that of 1776—a revolution in letters, a shaking off of the fetters of the mind." To do this, he said, "we must begin with the establishment of first principles," which were best found in the Declaration of Independence. Thus the Declaration "shall be the base of all the rest—the *common reference* in cases of doubt and difficulty."[13]

Abraham Lincoln probably never saw Niles's appeal to Jefferson, but he had the same insight. When he said in 1858 "all honor to Jefferson," he paid homage to the one Founder who he knew could explain why the breakup of the Union could not be allowed and why so many lives had to be sacrificed to maintain that Union. Lincoln knew what the Revolution had been about and what it implied not just for Americans but for all humanity—because Jefferson had told him so. The United States was a new republican nation in a world of monarchies, a grand experiment in self-government, conceived in liberty and dedicated to the proposition that all men are created equal.

Half the American people, said Lincoln in 1858, had no direct blood connection to the Founders of the nation. Either these German, Irish, French, and Scandinavian citizens had come from Europe themselves or their ancestors had, and they had settled in America, "finding themselves our equals in all things." Although these immigrants may have had no actual connection in blood with the revolutionary generation that could make them feel part of the rest of the nation, they had, said Lincoln, "that old Declaration of Independence" with its expression of the moral principle of equality to draw upon. This moral principle, which was "applicable to all men and all times," made all these different peoples one with the Founders, "as though they were blood of the blood and flesh of the flesh of the men who wrote that Declaration." This emphasis on liberty and equality, he said, was "the electric cord . . . that links the hearts of patriotic and liberty-loving men together, that will link those patriotic hearts as long as the love of freedom exists in the minds of men throughout the world."[14]

With words like these, drawing on the meaning of the American Revolution best voiced by Jefferson, Lincoln expressed what many Americans felt about themselves and the future of all mankind. Liberty and equality, said Lincoln, were promised "not alone to the people of this country, but hope to the world for all future time." The Revolution, he said, "gave promise that in due time the weights should be lifted from the shoulders of all men, and that *all* should have an equal chance" in the race of life. But if the American experiment in self-government failed, then this hope for the future would be lost. That was why the Civil War was worth all the sacrifices.[15]

These were Jefferson's words, Jefferson's ideas, Jefferson's principles, that Lincoln drew upon. Adams was too questioning, too contrarian, too cynical, to offer any such support for America's nationhood. Adams had no answer for the great problem of American diversity: how the great variety of individuals in America with all their different ethnicities, races, and religions could be brought together into one nation. Jefferson did have an answer. As Lincoln grasped better than anyone, Jefferson offered Americans a set of beliefs that through the generations have supplied a bond that holds together the most diverse nation that history has ever known. Since now the whole world is in the United States, nothing but Jefferson's ideals can turn such an assortment of different individuals into the "one people" that the Declaration says we are. To be an American is not to be someone, but to believe in something. And that something is what Jefferson declared.

That's why we honor Jefferson and not Adams.

ACKNOWLEDGMENTS

Someone who has been teaching and writing history as long as I have accumulates a host of debts that can never be repaid, let alone adequately acknowledged. So I thank all those who have helped me in a variety of ways over the past several decades. I especially want to thank my wife, Louise, my editor in chief and my chief supporter over the years. I am also grateful for all the help I received from the editors and their associates at Penguin Random House, including Kiara Barrow, Christopher Richards, Jane Cavolina, Trent Duffy, Sophie Fels, and Bruce Giffords. My thanks too to the staff of the Rockefeller Library at Brown University, where this book was written; they couldn't have been more helpful.

For this book I am once again grateful for the support given me by Scott Moyers, the publisher of Penguin Press. Not only has he edited and published several of my books (and recommended titles for a couple of them), but he also suggested the topic of this book. I had originally intended to write about only John Adams, but he proposed comparing Adams with Thomas Jefferson. Fortunately, I took his suggestion, and I learned more about both men by pitting them against each other.

I have dedicated this book to the editors of the *Papers of John Adams* and *The Papers of Thomas Jefferson*. I could not have written the book, at least not in a decent amount of time, without the documents they have edited and made available to the public. We historians write monographs and books that are inevitably ephemeral;

but the editors of the papers of these two great patriots, indeed all the many documentary editors of America's past, are producing work for the ages.

All these documentary editors seldom receive the recognition and acclaim they deserve. We historians, indeed, the entire country, are deeply indebted to them for making available to us in print, whether online or in letterpress editions, the many documents of America's past. Because the coming generations of students no longer read cursive handwriting, the documentary collections like those of Adams and Jefferson will become all the more important. For most scholars and students in the future the original handwritten documents of American history will remain more or less inaccessible, expressed in a foreign language not easily deciphered.

NOTES

Because spelling and other forms of grammar were still unsettled in the late eighteenth century, reproducing the writing of that time in modern form presents some difficulty. John Adams tended to capitalize all his nouns, and Jefferson always spelled the possessive "its" as "it's." To acknowledge all the peculiarities of these writers would inevitably clutter up the text with numerous usages of "[*sic*]." Therefore, I have chosen to reproduce as accurately as possible the writing of the period as the people at the time wrote it and to leave it to the reader to adjust to the eccentricities of the various writers.

ABBREVIATIONS OF SOURCES

AA	Abigail Adams
AFC	L. H. Butterfield et al., eds., *Adams Family Correspondence,* 12 vols. to date (Cambridge, Mass.: Belknap/Harvard University Press, 1963–)
AFC–MHS	Adams Family Correspondence in uncorrected typescript at the Massachusetts Historical Society
AHR	*American Historical Review*

BR   Benjamin Rush

Cappon   Lester J. Cappon, ed., *The Adams-Jefferson Letters:*
                                The Complete Correspondence Between Thomas Jefferson
                                and Abigail and John Adams, 2 vols. (Chapel Hill:
                                University of North Carolina Press, 1959)

JA   John Adams

JA, *Diary;* JA,   L. H. Butterfield et al., eds., *Diary and Autobiography*
Autobiography   *of John Adams,* 4 vols. (Cambridge, Mass.: Harvard
                                University Press, 1961)

JA: Revolutionary   Gordon S. Wood, ed., *John Adams: Revolutionary*
Writings,   *Writings, 1755–1783,* 2 vols. (New York: Library of
1755–1775; JA: America, 2011)
Revolutionary
Writings,
1775–1783

JA: Writings from   Gordon S. Wood, ed., *John Adams: Writings from the*
the New Nation   *New Nation* (New York: Library of America, 2016)

JER   *Journal of the Early Republic*

JM   James Madison

JQA   John Quincy Adams

Letters of Rush   Benjamin Rush, *Letters,* ed. L. H. Butterfield, 2 vols.
                                (Princeton, N.J.: Princeton University Press, 1951)

Old Family Letters   Alexander Biddle, ed., *Old Family Letters*
                                (Philadelphia: J. B. Lippincott, 1892)

PJA   Robert J. Taylor et al., eds., *Papers of John Adams,*
                                18 vols. to date (Cambridge, Mass.: Belknap/Harvard
                                University Press, 1977–)

PJA–MHS   Papers of John Adams in uncorrected typescript
                                at the Massachusetts Historical Society

PTJ   Julian P. Boyd et al., eds., *The Papers of Thomas Jefferson,*
                                41 vols. to date (Princeton, N.J.: Princeton University
                                Press, 1950–)

PTJ: RS   J. Jefferson Looney et al., eds., *The Papers of Thomas*
                                Jefferson: Retirement Series, 12 vols. to date (Princeton,
                                N.J.: Princeton University Press, 2004–)

Republic of Letters	James Morton Smith, ed., *The Republic of Letters: The Correspondence Between Thomas Jefferson and James Madison, 1776–1826*, 3 vols. (New York: Norton, 1995)
Spur of Fame	John A. Schutz and Douglass Adair, eds., *The Spur of Fame: Dialogues of John Adams and Benjamin Rush, 1805–1813* (San Marino, Calif.: Huntington Library, 1980)
TJ	Thomas Jefferson
TJ: Writings	Merrill D. Peterson, ed., *Thomas Jefferson: Writings* (New York: Library of America, 1984)
WMQ	*William and Mary Quarterly*, 3d. Ser.
Works of JA	Charles Francis Adams, ed., *The Works of John Adams, Second President of the United States*, 10 vols. (Boston: Little, Brown, 1856)

PROLOGUE: THE EULOGIES

1. "Eulogy Pronounced at Boston, Massachusetts, August 2, 1826, by Daniel Webster," in *A Selection of Eulogies Pronounced in the Several States, in Honor of Those Illustrious Patriots and Statesmen, John Adams and Thomas Jefferson* (Hartford: D. F. Robinson and Co., 1826), 193. On the Jubilee, see L. H. Butterfield, "The Jubilee of Independence July 4, 1826," *Virginia Magazine of History and Biography* 61 (1953): 119–40; and Andrew Burstein, *America's Jubilee* (New York: Knopf, 2001).
2. Samuel L. Knapp, "Eulogy, Pronounced at Boston, Massachusetts, August 2, 1826," and Caleb Cushing, "Eulogy, Pronounced at Newburyport, Massachusetts, July 16, 1826," in *Selection of Eulogies*, 175, 23, 175.
3. Samuel Smith, "Eulogy, Pronounced in Baltimore, Maryland, July 20th 1826," and William Wirt, "Eulogy, Pronounced at the City of Washington, October 19, 1826," in *Selection of Eulogies*, 72, 379.
4. Cushing, "Eulogy," and Peleg Sprague, "Eulogy, Pronounced at Hallowell, Maine, July, 1826," in *Selection of Eulogies*, 7, 300, 48, 149.
5. Knapp, "Eulogy," in *Selection of Eulogies*, 184.
6. Cushing, "Eulogy," in *Selection of Eulogies*, 28.
7. Knapp, "Eulogy," in *Selection of Eulogies*, 185.
8. Wirt, "Eulogy," Cushing, "Eulogy," and Smith, "Eulogy," in *Selection of Eulogies*, 380, 51, 88.
9. Cushing, "Eulogy," and Wirt, "Eulogy," in *Selection of Eulogies*, 25, 380.
10. Cushing, "Eulogy," and Webster, "Eulogy," in *Selection of Eulogies*, 20, 233.
11. John Tyler, "Eulogy, Pronounced at Richmond, Virginia, July 11, 1826," and William Johnson, "Eulogy, Pronounced at Charleston, South Carolina, August 3, 1826," in *Selection of Eulogies*, 7, 300.

12. Sprague, "Eulogy," and William F. Thornton, "Eulogy Pronounced at Alexandria, District of Columbia, August 10, 1826," in *Selection of Eulogies*, 149, 341.
13. Merrill Peterson, *The Jeffersonian Image in the American Mind* (New York: Oxford University Press, 1960), 234.
14. BR to JA, 17 Feb. 1812, *Letters of Rush*, 2:1127.

ONE: CONTRASTS

1. JA to Adrian Van der Kemp, 20 Feb. 1806, PJA–MHS. Russell Kirk, in his influential work *The Conservative Mind: From Burke to Eliot*, 7th ed. (Washington, D.C.: Regnery, 1985), considered Adams "the founder of true conservatism in America" (p. 71).
2. *Documentary History of the First Federal Congress, 4 March 1789–5 March 1791*, ed. Kenneth R. Bowling and Helen Veit, vol. 9, *The Diary of William Maclay and Other Notes on Senate Debates* (Baltimore: Johns Hopkins University Press, 1988), 275, 306.
3. JA, *Diary*, 2:362; *Diary of William Maclay*, 278, 19, 11, 33.
4. "The Memoirs of Madison Hemings," in Annette Gordon-Reed, *Thomas Jefferson and Sally Hemings: An American Controversy* (Charlottesville: University of Virginia Press, 1997), 247.
5. Jonathan Sewall to Judge Joseph Lee, 21 Sept. 1787, *AFC*, 1:136–37n. The editors point out that by 1787 Sewall had taken to spelling his name "Sewell." (Sewall spelled the possessive "its" the way Jefferson always did, "it's.") Adams's personality seems to have resembled that of Dr. Samuel Johnson as described by James Boswell: "hard to please and easily offended, impetuous and irritable in his temper, but of a most humane and benevolent heart." Frederick A. Pottle and Charles H. Bennett, eds., *Boswell's Journal of a Tour to the Hebrides with Samuel Johnson, LL.D* (New York: The Literary Guild, 1936), 7.
6. JA to JQA, 22 Jan. 1817, AFC–MHS.
7. JA to Charles Carroll, 2 Aug. 1820, PJA–MHS; JA to TJ, 12 Dec. 1816, Cappon, 2:499.
8. TJ to Nathaniel Burwell, 14 Mar. 1818, *PTJ: RS*, 12:532. In 1771 Jefferson told a young man who had asked for advice about building a library that "the entertainments of fiction are useful as well as pleasant." But since the young man admitted that he possessed only the "capacity of a common reader who understands but little of the classics and who has not leisure for any intricate or tedious study," Jefferson wasn't necessarily speaking for his own tastes, which as an adult did not involve much reading of fiction and novels. TJ to Robert Skipwith, 3 Aug. 1771, *PTJ*, 1:76–77; Skipwith to TJ, 17 July 1771, ibid., 1:74–75; Douglas L. Wilson, *Jefferson's Books* (Lynchburg, Va.: Monticello, 1993), 21–22.
9. TJ, *Notes on the State of Virginia*, ed. William Peden (Chapel Hill: University of North Carolina Press, 1955), 64. See Garry Wills, *Inventing America: Jefferson's Declaration of Independence* (Garden City, N.Y.: Doubleday, 1978), 91–164.
10. TJ to JM, 20 Sept. 1785, *Republic of Letters*, 1:385; TJ to Giovanni Fabbroni, 8 June 1778, *PTJ*, 2:195–96.
11. Hugh Howard, *Dr. Kimball and Mr. Jefferson: Rediscovering the Founding Fathers of American Architecture* (New York: Bloomsbury, 2006), 11.

12. Seymour Howard, "Jefferson's Art Gallery," *The Art Bulletin* 59 (1977): 583–600.

13. *PTJ*, 7:383; James Traub, *John Quincy Adams: Militant Spirit* (New York: Basic Books, 2016), 124.

14. Marquis de Chastellux, *Travels in North America in the Years 1780, 1781 and 1782*, ed. Howard C. Rice (Chapel Hill: University of North Carolina Press, 1963), 2:391.

15. JA to J. B. Binon, 7 Feb. 1819, PJA–MHS.

16. JA to George Washington Adams, 27 May 1816, AFC–MHS.

17. JA to AA, 10 May 1777, *AFC*, 2:235; JA to Henry Laurens, 24 Oct. 1779, *PJA*, 8:224. Adams's vivid description of the painting was as follows: "The Picture represents a Coach, with four Horses, running down a steep Mountain, and rushing on to the middle of a very high Bridge, over a large River. The Foundations of the whole Bridge, give Way, in a Moment, and the Carriage, the Horses, the Timbers, Stones, and all, in a Chaos are falling through the Air down to the Water. The Horror of the Horses, the Coachman, the Footman, the Gentlemen and Ladies in the Carriage, is Strongly painted in their Countenances and Gestures, as well as the Simpathy and Terror of others in Boats upon the River and many others on shore, on each side of the River." The editors of the Adams Papers did not identify the painting, but it is almost certainly *The Collapse of a Wooden Bridge*, by Casanova, who painted several such disaster paintings. It is now in the Musée des Beaux Arts in Rennes and can be viewed online. I owe the identification of this painting to Christopher S. Wood.

18. JA, *Autobiography*, 3:305. According to Christopher S. Wood, the painting that Adams recalled was probably *The Last Supper* by Jacob Jordaens, now located in the Royal Museum of Fine Arts, Antwerp.

19. JA to AA, 27 Apr. 1777, *AFC*, 2:225; JA to AA, 28 Apr. 1777, ibid., 2:227; JA to John Trumbull, 1 Jan. 1817, PJA–MHS; JA to Benjamin Waterhouse, 26 Feb. 1817, ibid.

20. JA to AA, Apr.–May 1780, *AFC*, 3:332–33.

21. TJ to JM, 20 Sept. 1785, *Republic of Letters*, 1:385.

22. TJ to Benjamin Harrison, 12 Jan. 1785, *PTJ*, 7:600; George Washington to TJ, 1 Aug. 1786, ibid., 10:186; TJ to Nathaniel Macon, 22 Jan. 1816, *PTJ: RS*, 9:384–87. By 1800 the much copied Houdon statue of Washington was erected in the Virginia state capitol. The statue by Antonio Canova was installed in the capitol of North Carolina in 1822, but was destroyed by fire in 1831.

23. TJ to Charles McPherson, 25 Feb. 1773, *PTJ*, 1:96.

24. TJ to Harrison, 12 Jan. 1785, *PTJ*, 7:600; Washington to TJ, 1 Aug. 1786, ibid., 10:186; TJ to Macon, 22 Jan. 1816, *PTJ: RS*, 16:385–86.

25. JA to AA, post 12 May 1780, *AFC*, 3:342.

26. JA to Cotton Tufts, 9 Apr. 1764, *AFC*, 1:20.

27. JA, "Thoughts on Government," *PJA*, 4:86; JA to James Warren, 17 June 1782, ibid., 13:128; JA to Benjamin Franklin, 27 July 1784, ibid., 16:285.

28. TJ to Charles Clay, 29 Jan. 1815, *PTJ: RS*, 8:212.

29. TJ to JA, 28 Oct. 1813, Cappon, 2:389.

30. TJ to Marquis de Chastellux, 2 Sept. 1785, *TJ: Writings*, 826–28.

31. Ellen Randolph Coolidge to TJ, 1 Aug. 1825, in *The Family Letters of Thomas Jefferson*, eds. Edwin Morris Betts and James Adam Bear Jr. (Columbia: University of Missouri Press, 1966), 454–57.

32. JA to Jeremy Belknap, 21 Mar. 1795, *JA: Writings from the New Nation*, 313–14. Prior to the Revolution, JA was involved in four cases in which slaves in Massachusetts sued for their freedom. In each case he was the attorney for the master. "Slavery," in *The Legal Papers of John Adams*, ed. L. Kinvin Wroth and Hiller B. Zobel (Cambridge, Mass.: Belknap/Harvard University Press, 1965), 2:48.

33. Gordon S. Wood, *The Radicalism of the American Revolution* (New York: Knopf, 1992), 51.

34. JA to Robert J. Evans, 8 June 1819, *JA: Writings from the New Nation*, 647.

35. JA to Evans, 8 June 1819, *JA: Writings from the New Nation*, 647–48.

36. JA, *Diary*, 1:39.

37. Lewis Preston Summers, *History of Southwest Virginia, 1746–1786* (Richmond: J. L. Hill Co., 1903), 79, 26, 27.

38. Rufus Rockwell Wilson, ed., *Burnaby's Travels Through North America* (New York: A. Wessels Co., 1904), 55. Andrew Burnaby, an English clergyman, traveled in Virginia in 1759–1760.

39. TJ to William Wirt, 5 Aug. 1815, *PTJ: RS*, 8:641–46; William Wirt, *Sketches of the Life and Character of Patrick Henry* (Philadelphia, 1817), 33–34; TJ, *Notes on the State of Virginia*, 164.

40. TJ to Stevens Thompson Mason, 27 Oct. 1799, *PTJ*, 31:222; TJ to Thomas Leiper, 21 Feb. 1801, ibid., 33:50; Annette Gordon-Reed and Peter S. Onuf, *"Most Blessed of the Patriarchs": Thomas Jefferson and the Empire of the Imagination* (New York: Norton, 2016), 78.

41. Christa Dierksheide, *Amelioration and Empire: Progress and Slavery in the Plantation Americas* (Charlottesville: University of Virginia Press, 2014), 49–50; Lucia Stanton, "Thomas Jefferson: Planter and Farmer," in *A Companion to Thomas Jefferson*, ed. Francis D. Cogliano (Chichester, U.K.: John Wiley and Sons, 2012), 260–61; TJ to Joel Yancey, 17 Jan. 1819, in Edwin Morris Betts, ed., *Jefferson's Farm Book* (Charlottesville, Va.: Thomas Jefferson Memorial Foundation, 1999), 43.

42. Jack McLaughlin, *Jefferson and Monticello: The Biography of a Builder* (New York: Henry Holt, 1988), 46–47.

43. McLaughlin, *Jefferson and Monticello*, 47.

44. TJ, Autobiography, in *TJ: Writings*, 32, 3.

45. TJ, Autobiography, in *TJ: Writings*, 3.

46. JA, *Autobiography*, 3:256.

47. JA, *Autobiography*, 3:257; Peter Shaw, *The Character of John Adams* (Chapel Hill: University of North Carolina Press, 1976), 4–6, 50–51.

48. JA, *Diary*, 1:12.

49. JA, *Diary*, 1:33.

50. JA, *Diary*, 1:25.

51. JA, *Diary*, 1:67–68.

52. JA, *Diary*, 1:7–8, 37, 10.

53. TJ to Nichols Lewis, 11 July 1788, *PTJ*, 13:339–44.

54. Herbert E. Sloan, *Principle and Interest: Thomas Jefferson and the Problem of Debt* (New York: Oxford University Press, 1995).

55. Douglas L. Wilson, "Thomas Jefferson's Early Notebooks," *WMQ* 42 (1985): 433–41.

56. TJ to Vancey, 17 Jan. 1819, in Betts, *Jefferson's Farm Book*, 43.

57. James Reid, "The Religion of the Bible and Religion of K[ing] W[illiam] County Compared," in *The Colonial Virginia Satirist: Mid-Eighteenth Century Commentaries on Politics, Religion, and Society*, ed. Richard Beale Davis, Transactions of the American Philosophical Society, new ser. 57, pt. 1 (1967), 567.

58. Rhys Isaac, *The Transformation of Virginia, 1740–1790* (Chapel Hill: University of North Carolina Press, 1982), 61.

59. JA to Joseph Hawley, 25 Nov. 1775, *PJA*, 3:316.

60. JA to Hawley, 25 Nov. 1775, *PJA*, 3:316; JA to James Warren, 15 June 1776, ibid., 4:316.

61. William Manning, a Billerica farmer and entrepreneur, claimed that in Massachusetts in the 1790s gentlemen constituted one out of eight male citizens. Samuel Eliot Morison, ed., "William Manning's The Key of Libberty," *WMQ* 13 (1956): 220. For a modernized version, see Michael Merrill and Sean Wilentz, eds., *The Key of Liberty: The Life and Democratic Writings of William Manning, "A Laborer," 1747–1814* (Cambridge, Mass.: Harvard University Press, 1993), 138.

62. Carl Bridenbaugh, *Cities in Revolt: Urban Life in America, 1743–1776* (New York: Knopf, 1955), 137.

63. George Washington to Lund Washington, 20 Aug. 1775, in Philander D. Chase, ed., *The Papers of George Washington: Revolutionary War Series* (Charlottesville: University of Virginia Press, 1985–), 1:336; G. Washington to Major General Philip Schuyler, 28 July 1775, ibid., 1:188.

64. G. Washington to Richard Henry Lee, 29 Aug. 1775, in Chase, *Papers of George Washington*, 1:372; G. Washington to L. Washington, 20 Aug. 1775, ibid., 1:335. Other officers from outside New England had similar experiences with the New England soldiers. "The New England troops," complained General Richard Montgomery, a former officer in the British army, "are the worst stuff imaginable. There is such an equality among them, that the officers have no authority. . . . The privates are all generals." Hal T. Shelton, *General Richard Montgomery and the American Revolution: From Redcoat to Rebel* (New York: New York University Press, 1994), 106.

65. JA, *Diary*, 1:198.

66. JA, *Diary*, 1:198.

67. JA, *Diary*, 2:107.

68. JA, *Defence of the Constitutions of Government of the United States of America*, in *Works of JA*, 6:185.

69. Lisa B. Lubow, "From Carpenter to Capitalist: The Business of Building in Postrevolutionary Boston," in *Entrepreneurs: The Boston Business Community, 1700–1850*, ed. Conrad Edrick Wright and Katheryn P. Viens (Boston: Northeastern University Press, 1997), 181; Jayne E. Triber, *A True Republican: The Life of Paul Revere* (Amherst: University of Massachusetts Press, 1998).

70. George Rudé, *Hanoverian London, 1714–1808* (Berkeley: University of California Press, 1971), 37, 56–57.

71. Lubow, "From Carpenter to Capitalist," 185; Howard B. Rock, *Artisans of the New Republic: Tradesmen of New York City in the Age of Jefferson* (New York: New York University Press, 1979), 295–322.

72. JA, *Diary*, 2:38.

73. JA, *Diary*, 1:294.

74. JA, *Diary*, 1:54; JA, *Diary*, 2:99, 107, 105.

75. JA, *Diary*, 2:61–62, 38.

76. JA, "IV. 'U' to the *Boston Gazette*," 18 July 1763, *PJA*, 1:71; Humphrey Ploughjogger to Philanthrop, ante 5 Jan. 1767, ibid., 1:179.

77. Fiske Kimball, "Jefferson and the Arts," American Philosophical Society, *Proceedings* 87 (1943): 239.

78. Dumas Malone, *Jefferson the Virginian* (Boston: Little, Brown, 1948), 49–87; TJ to John Page, 25 May 1766, *PTJ*, 1:19–20.

79. TJ to Marquis de Lafayette, 11 Apr. 1787, *PTJ*, 11:285.

80. J. A. Leo Lemay and P. M. Zall, eds., *Benjamin Franklin's Autobiography: An Authoritative Text, Backgrounds, Criticism* (New York: Norton, 1986), 108.

81. TJ to Thomas Jefferson Randolph, 24 Nov. 1808, *TJ: Writings*, 1195–96.

82. George W. Corner, ed., *The Autobiography of Benjamin Rush: His "Travels Through Life" Together with His Commonplace Book for 1789–1813* (Princeton, N.J.: Princeton University Press, 1948), 140–42.

Two: Careers, Wives, and Other Women

1. TJ to——, 26 July 1764, *PTJ*, 27:665.

2. L. H. Butterfield et al., eds., *The Earliest Diary of John Adams* (Cambridge, Mass.: Harvard University Press, 1966), 49–50.

3. JA, *Diary*, 1:43.

4. JA to TJ, 14 Sept. 1813, Cappon, 2:374; JA to Nathan Webb, 1 Sept. 1755, *PJA*, 1:1; Norman S. Fiering, "The First American Enlightenment: Tillotson, Leverett, and Philosophical Anglicanism," *New England Quarterly* 34 (1981): 307–44.

5. JA, *Diary*, 1:23

6. JA, *Autobiography*, 3:262.

7. JA, *Diary*, 1:43.

8. JA to Charles Cushing, 1 Apr. 1756, *PJA*, 1:12–13.

9. JA to Cushing, 1 Apr. 1756, *PJA*, 1:12–13; JA to Charles Cushing Jr., 13 Mar. 1817, *Works of JA*, 1:38. In the immediate aftermath of the Battles of Lexington and Concord, Adams was overwhelmed by the military spirit that was running through the continent. "Oh that I was a Soldier!—I will be.—I am reading military Books—Every Body must and will be a soldier." In 1776 he recalled he had once "longed more ardently to be a Soldier than I ever did to be a Lawyer." But at last he had come to realize that the moment had passed; besides, he had also realized that what he was doing in the Continental Congress was as dangerous as being in the army. In his autobiography, he said that in 1776 he believed that "Courage and reading were all that were necessary to the formation of an Officer." JA to AA, 29 May 1775, *AFC*, 1:207; JA to AA, 13 Feb. 1776, ibid., 1:347; JA, *Autobiography*, 3:446.

10. JA, *Diary*, 1:55, 53, 51.

11. JA, *Diary*, 1:8.

12. Jonathan Sewall to JA, 13 Feb. 1760, *PJA*, 1:39–40.

13. JA to Sewall, Feb. 1760, *PJA*, 1:41–42.

14. Butterfield, *Earliest Diary of John Adams*, 77; JA, *Diary*, 1:337.

15. JA, *Diary*, 1:80, 73, 72.

16. JA, *Diary*, 1:80, 73, 78.

17. JA, *Diary*, 1:337–38.

18. Douglas L. Wilson, *Jefferson's Books* (Lynchburg, Va.: Monticello, 1993), 22.

19. JA to AA, 29 June 1774, *AFC*, 1:113–14.

20. JA to TJ, 28 Oct. 1814, Cappon, 2:440; TJ to JA, 10 June 1815, ibid., 2:443.

21. Henry S. Randall, *The Life of Thomas Jefferson* (Philadelphia: Lippincott, 1888), 1:53.

22. JA, *Diary*, 1:220; JA to AA, 31 Jan. 1796, *AFC*, 11:154.

23. TJ to John Page, 25 Dec. 1762, *PTJ*, 1:5; Dumas Malone, *Jefferson the Virginian* (Boston: Little, Brown, 1948), 70; JA, *Diary*, 1:174, 55.

24. TJ to L. H. Girardin, 15 Jan. 1815, *PTJ: RS*, 8:200.

25. On Jefferson's law practice, see Frank L. Dewey, *Thomas Jefferson, Lawyer* (Charlottesville: University of Virginia Press, 1986).

26. TJ to Elbridge Gerry, 28 Aug. 1802, *PTJ*, 38:308; TJ, Autobiography, *TJ: Writings*, 53, 40; TJ to Judge John Tyler, 17 June 1812, *PTJ: RS*, 5:135–36; TJ to Judge David Campbell, 28 Jan. 1810, ibid., 2:187.

27. JA to Charles Adams, 10 Jan. 1787, *AFC*, 7:428; JA, *Diary*, 1:117.

28. JA to William Tudor, 9 May 1789, PJA–MHS.

29. JA to John Wentworth, ? Oct. 1758, *PJA*, 1:26.

30. JA, *Diary*, 1:109, 72, 57.

31. JA, *Diary*, 1:108–9.

32. JA, *Diary*, 1:87, 118–19.

33. JA, *Diary*, 1:68–69, 83.

34. JA, *Diary*, 1:234.

35. Woody Holton, *Abigail Adams* (New York: Free Press, 2009), 7.

36. AA to Elizabeth Smith Shaw Peabody, 12 Feb. 1796, *AFC*, 11:173.

37. AA to Peabody, 12 Feb. 1796, *AFC*, 11:173; Jon Kukla, *Mr. Jefferson's Women* (New York: Knopf, 2007), 143–44.

38. AA to JA, 31 Mar. 1776, *AFC*, 1:370.

39. George W. Corner, ed., *The Autobiography of Benjamin Rush: His "Travels Through Life" Together with His Commonplace Book for 1789–1813* (Princeton, N.J.: Princeton University Press, 1948), 144.

40. JA to AA, 28 Apr. 1776, *AFC*, 1:400.

41. David McCullough, *John Adams* (New York: Simon and Schuster, 2004), 441.

42. AA to JA, 22 Sept. 1774, *AFC*, 1:162.

43. McCullough, *John Adams*, 506.

44. Malone, *Jefferson the Virginian*, 80.

45. TJ to John Page, 7 Oct. 1763, *PTJ*, 1:11.

46. TJ to Page, 10 Oct. 1763, *PTJ*, 1:13–15.

47. TJ to William Fleming, 20 Mar. 1765, *PTJ*, 1:15–17.

48. TJ to Fleming, 20 Mar. 1765, *PTJ*, 1:15–17; Kukla, *Mr. Jefferson's Women*, 36; Philip D. Morgan, "Interracial Sex in the Chesapeake and British Atlantic World, c. 1700–1820," in *Sally Hemings and Thomas Jefferson: History, Memory, and Civic Culture*, ed. Jan Ellen Lewis and Peter Onuf (Charlottesville: University of Virginia Press, 1999), 52–84.

49. Kukla, *Mr. Jefferson's Women*, 35, 226–27. Historians have often described Jefferson's headaches as migraines. But Kukla points out that TJ himself never used that term even though migraine headaches had been known for centuries. "Recent scholarship," writes Kukla, "suggests that Jefferson suffered not from migraines but from severe muscular-contraction headaches triggered by tension or stress." Ibid., 35, 226–28. See also John D. Battle Jr., "The 'Periodical Head-achs' of Thomas Jefferson," *Cleveland Clinic Quarterly* 51 (1984): 531–39; and A. K.

Thould, "The Health of Thomas Jefferson (1784–1826)," *Journal of the Royal College of Physicians of London* 23 (1989): 50–52.

50. Jack McLaughlin, *Jefferson and Monticello: The Biography of a Builder* (New York: Henry Holt, 1988), 47–51.

51. Douglas L. Wilson, ed., *Jefferson's Literary Commonplace Book* (Princeton, N.J.: Princeton University Press, 1989), 3–20; Kenneth A. Lockridge, *On the Sources of Patriarchal Rage: The Commonplace Books of William Byrd and Thomas Jefferson and the Gendering of Power in the Eighteenth Century* (New York: New York University Press, 1992), 47–73.

52. James A. Bear Jr. and Lucia C. Stanton, eds., *Jefferson's Memorandum Books* (Princeton, N.J.: Princeton University Press, 1967), 154. The minor poet Pentadius, who wrote in the third or fourth century AD, entitled his verse "De Femina." Jefferson did not identify the name of the poet or the poem.

53. Wilson, *Jefferson's Literary Commonplace Book,* 82, 73.

54. Wilson, *Jefferson's Literary Commonplace Book,* 118, 117; Kukla, *Mr. Jefferson's Women,* 37–39, 231–32; Brian Steele, *Thomas Jefferson and American Nationhood* (Cambridge: Cambridge University Press, 2012), 53–90.

55. JA to AA, 11 Aug. 1777, *AFC,* 2:306.

56. JA to Francis Adrian Van der Kemp, 8 Apr. 1815, PJA–MHS.

57. JA to TJ, 13 Feb. 1819, Cappon, 2:533.

58. JA, *Autobiography,* 3:260–61.

59. Kukla, *Mr. Jefferson's Women,* 56; Thomas A. Foster, *Sex and the Founding Fathers: The American Quest for a Relatable Past* (Philadelphia: Temple University Press, 2014), 60–61.

60. TJ to Robert Smith, 1 July 1805, *Founders Online,* National Archives.

61. Kukla, *Mr. Jefferson's Women,* 69; Winthrop D. Jordan, *White over Black: American Attitudes Toward the Negro* (Chapel Hill: University of North Carolina Press, 1968), 462.

62. TJ to Thomas Adams, 20 Feb. 1771, *PTJ,* 1:62.

63. Sarah N. Randolph, *The Domestic Life of Thomas Jefferson* (1871; repr., Charlottesville: University of Virginia Press, 1978), 44; Randall, *Life of Jefferson,* 1:64; Kukla, *Mr. Jefferson's Women,* 68.

64. TJ to Giovanni Fabbroni, 8 June 1778, *PTJ,* 2:195–96.

65. TJ to T. Adams, 1 June 1771, *PTJ,* 1:71.

66. Kukla, *Mr. Jefferson's Women,* 68.

67. Lucia Stanton, *"Those Who Labor for My Happiness": Slavery at Thomas Jefferson's Monticello* (Charlottesville: University of Virginia Press, 2012), 167.

68. Annette Gordon-Reed and Peter S. Onuf, *"Most Blessed of the Patriarchs": Thomas Jefferson and the Empire of the Imagination* (New York: Norton, 2016), 144; TJ, *Notes on the State of Virginia,* ed. William Peden (Chapel Hill: University of North Carolina Press, 1955), 141.

69. TJ, Autobiography, *TJ: Writings,* 5.

70. Stanton, *"Those Who Labor for My Happiness,"* 56.

71. TJ to Elizabeth Wayles Eppes, 12 July 1788, *PTJ,* 13:347.

72. Kukla, *Mr. Jefferson's Women,* 70; TJ to Martha Jefferson Randolph, 4 Apr. 1790, in Edwin Morris Betts and James Adam Bear Jr., eds., *The Family Letters of Thomas Jefferson* (Columbia: University of Missouri Press, 1966), 51.

73. Kukla, *Mr. Jefferson's Women,* 70–71.

74. Kukla, *Mr. Jefferson's Women*, 69; TJ, Autobiography, *TJ: Writings*, 46.
75. TJ to Marquis de Chastellux, 26 Nov. 1782, *PTJ*, 6:203.
76. TJ to John Banister Jr., 15 Oct. 1785, *PTJ*, 8:636.
77. Richmond *Recorder*, 1 Sept. 1802, *PTJ*, 38:323n–325n.
78. Kukla, *Mr. Jefferson's Women*, 118–19; Henry Wiencek, *Master of the Mountain: Thomas Jefferson and His Slaves* (New York: Farrar, Straus and Giroux, 2012), 196–97.
79. Joshua D. Rothman, "James Callender and Social Knowledge of Interracial Sex in Antebellum Virginia," in Lewis and Onuf, *Sally Hemings and Thomas Jefferson*, 87.
80. TJ to Edward Coles, 25 Aug. 1814, *PTJ: RS*, 7:604.
81. "Memoirs of a Monticello Slave," in James A. Bear Jr., ed., *Jefferson at Monticello* (Charlottesville: University Press of Virginia, 1967), 4.
82. Stanton, *"Those Who Labor for My Happiness,"* 167.
83. AA to TJ, 26 June 1787, Cappon 1:178; AA to TJ, 27 June 1787, ibid., 1:179; AA to TJ, 6 July 1787, ibid., 1:183.
84. Annette Gordon-Reed, *The Hemings of Monticello: An American Family* (New York: Norton, 2008), 283–84, 345.
85. Gordon-Reed, *Hemings of Monticello*, 250, 264; "The Memoirs of Madison Hemings," in Annette Gordon-Reed, *Thomas Jefferson and Sally Hemings: An American Controversy* (Charlottesville: University of Virginia Press, 1997), 246.
86. "Memoirs of Madison Hemings," 246.
87. Gordon-Reed, *Hemings of Monticello*, 507.
88. For a particularly sensitive study of TJ's relationship with Sally Hemings and his medically based sexual needs, see Andrew Burstein, *Jefferson's Secrets: Death and Desire at Monticello* (New York: Perseus, 2005), 146–49, 153–60. Burstein persuasively emphasizes the number of medical treatises TJ owned and relied upon to maintain his health, including his sexual health.
89. "Memoirs of Madison Hemings," 247.
90. Stanton, *"Those Who Labor for My Happiness,"* 4.
91. Kukla, *Mr. Jefferson's Women*, 86.
92. Kukla, *Mr. Jefferson's Women*, 88–89.
93. Abigail Adams 2d to JQA, Jan.–Feb 1786, *AFC*, 7:15–16.
94. Kukla, *Mr. Jefferson's Women*, 102.
95. Kukla, *Mr. Jefferson's Women*, 103.
96. Kukla, *Mr. Jefferson's Women*, 104.
97. TJ to Maria Cosway, 12 Oct. 1786, *TJ: Writings*, 866–99. Much to TJ's surprise, Maria Cosway eventually retired to the Catholic convent and girls' school that she had founded in Lodi in northern Italy.

THREE: THE IMPERIAL CRISIS

1. JA, *Diary*, 1:263.
2. JA, "A Dissertation on the Canon and Feudal Law," no.1, *JA: Revolutionary Writings, 1755–1775*, 114–25.
3. JA, *Diary*, 1:280.

4. JA to Hezekiah Niles, 18 Feb. 1818, *Works of JA*, 10:288. On the "Dread of the Hierarchy" of the Anglican Church as a much neglected cause of the Revolution, see JA to Jonathan Mason, 31 Aug. 1820, PJA–MHS.

5. JA, "A Dissertation on the Canon," *JA: Revolutionary Writings, 1755–1775*, 691.

6. JA to Adrian Van der Kemp, 20 May–11 June 1815, PJA–MHS; JA to Jedidiah Morse, 5 Dec. 1815, *Works of JA*, 10:190.

7. JA to Nathan Webb, 12 Oct. 1755, *PJA*, 1:5.

8. JA, "Instructions to Braintree's Representatives," Sept.–Oct. 1765, *PJA*, 1:133.

9. JA, *Diary*, 1:264–65.

10. JA, *Diary*, 2:11, 90, 55; 1:306.

11. "Admiralty–Criminal Jurisdiction," in *The Legal Papers of John Adams*, ed. L. Kinvin Wroth and Hiller B. Zobel (Cambridge, Mass.: Belknap/Harvard University Press, 1965), 2:275–335; JA to William Tudor, 30 Dec. 1816, PJA–MHS; JA to JQA, 8 Jan. 1808, ibid. In a diary entry of December 1769, six months after the trial, JA was still brooding over the trial and expressing resentment that he had not been allowed to present his learned argument, which "would be well worth the Perusal of the Public." He thought that "a great Variety of useful Learning might be brought into a History of that Case. . . . I have half a Mind to undertake it." JA, *Diary*, 1:347.

12. William Wirt, *Sketches of the Life and Character of Patrick Henry* (Philadelphia, 1817), 60–61.

13. TJ, Autobiography, *TJ: Writings*, 5; Henry S. Randall, *The Life of Thomas Jefferson* (Philadelphia: Lippincott, 1888), 1:58.

14. François La Rochefoucauld-Liancourt, *Travels Through the United States of North America* (London: R. Phillips, 1799), 1:408; JA to Richard Rush, 24 Nov. 1814, PJA–MHS.

15. Jack McLaughlin, *Jefferson and Monticello: The Biography of a Builder* (New York: Henry Holt, 1988), 51.

16. Marquis de Chastellux, *Travels in North America in the Years 1780, 1781 and 1782*, ed. Howard C. Rice (Chapel Hill: University of North Carolina Press, 1963), 2:389–91.

17. TJ to John Page, 21 Feb. 1770, *PTJ*, 1:34–35.

18. JA, *Autobiography*, 3:294.

19. Replies to Philantrop, Defender of Governor Bernard, ante 9 Dec. 1766–16 Feb. 1767, *PJA*, 1:199, 195, 179, 189, 192.

20. JA, *Diary*, 1:337.

21. JA, *Diary*, 3:287–88; JA to Tudor, 25 Nov. 1816, PJA–MHS.

22. Peter Orlando Hutchinson, ed., *The Diary and Letters of His Excellency Thomas Hutchinson, Esq.* (1884–1886; repr., New York: Lenox Hill, 1971), 2:220.

23. I owe the idea of Adams as the consigliere of the Boston patriots to Hiller Zobel.

24. JA, *Autobiography*, 3:294.

25. Josiah Quincy Sr. to Josiah Quincy, 22 Mar. 1770, and Josiah Quincy to Josiah Quincy Sr., 26 Mar. 1770, in Daniel R. Coquillette and Neil Longley York, eds., *Portrait of a Patriot: The Major Political and Legal Papers of Josiah Quincy Junior: Correspondence and Published Political Writings* (Boston: Colonial Society of Massachusetts, 2005–2014), 6:50–52.

26. JA, *Autobiography*, 3:292.

27. JA, *Diary*, 2:74. The defense of the soldiers and his patriotic activities had taken a toll on him. He collapsed with illness in 1771 and took a while to recover. He attributed his illness to the "labour and Anxiety" caused by his public service. JA, *Autobiography*, 3:294.

28. JA, *Diary*, 2:79. The March 5, 1773, oration that JA declined was delivered by Dr. Benjamin Church, who later became a spy for the British and a Loyalist.

29. JA, *Diary*, 2:77–78; JA, "On the Independence of the Judges," 11 Jan.–22 Feb. 1773, *PJA*, 1:252–309; JA, *Autobiography*, 3:297–98.

30. William Blackstone, *Commentaries on the Laws of England* (1765; repr., Chicago: University of Chicago Press, 1979), 1:49.

31. William Knox, *Controversy Between Great Britain and Her Colonies Reviewed* (London, 1769), in *The American Revolution: Writings from the Pamphlet Debate*, ed. Gordon S. Wood (New York: Library of America, 2015), 1:638.

32. *The Speeches of His Excellency Governor Hutchinson to the General Assembly . . . with the Answers of His Majesty's Council and the House of Representatives Respectively* (Boston, 1773), in Wood, *The American Revolution: Writings from the Pamphlet Debate*, 2:10.

33. JA, *Diary*, 2:77.

34. JA, *Autobiography*, 3:305.

35. *Speeches of His Excellency Governor Hutchinson*, in Wood, *The American Revolution: Writings from the Pamphlet Debate*, 2:62–63.

36. *Speeches of His Excellency Governor Hutchinson*, in Wood, *The American Revolution: Writings from the Pamphlet Debate*, 2:68, 28, 39.

37. Lawrence Henry Gipson, *The Coming of the Revolution, 1763–1775* (New York: Harper and Bros., 1954), 198.

38. JA, *Diary*, 2:85–86; JA to James Warren, 17 Dec. 1773, *PJA*, 2:1.

39. TJ, Autobiography, *TJ: Writings*, 6.

40. TJ, *A Summary View of the Rights of British America* (Williamsburg, Va., 1774), in Wood, *The American Revolution: Writings from the Pamphlet Debate*, 2:99.

41. TJ, Autobiography, *TJ: Writings*, 8–9.

42. TJ, *A Summary View*, in Wood, *The American Revolution: Writings from the Pamphlet Debate*, 2:96, 98.

43. H. Trevor Colbourn, "Thomas Jefferson's Use of the Past," *WMQ* 15 (1958): 56–70. Jefferson had been reading *An Historical Essay on the English Constitution* (London, 1771) and had entered passages from it in his commonplace book.

44. TJ, *A Summary View*, in Wood, *The American Revolution: Writings from the Pamphlet Debate*, 2:105, 101, 96, 93.

45. Pauline Maier, *American Scripture: Making the Declaration of Independence* (New York: Knopf, 1997), 112.

46. TJ, *A Summary View*, in Wood, *The American Revolution: Writings from the Pamphlet Debate*, 2:101, 102.

47. TJ, *A Summary View*, in Wood, *The American Revolution: Writings from the Pamphlet Debate*, 2:106–7.

48. TJ, *A Summary View*, in Wood, *The American Revolution: Writings from the Pamphlet Debate*, 2:91, 106.

49. JA, *Autobiography*, 3:298–302.

50. JA, *Diary*, 2:96, 93, 97.

51. JA, *Diary*, 2:120.

52. JA, *Diary*, 2:96; JA to James Warren, 25 June 1774, *PJA*, 2:99–100; JA to Warren, 17 July 1774, ibid., 2:109.

53. JA, *Diary*, 2:131.

54. JA to Tudor, 29 Sept. 1774, *PJA*, 2:176.

55. JA, *Diary*, 2:106, 121, 156.

56. JA, *Diary*, 1:92–93.

57. JA to Tudor, 29 Sept. 1774, *PJA*, 2:177.

58. "Declaration and Resolves of the First Continental Congress, Oct. 14, 1774," in Jack P. Greene, ed., *Colonies to Nation, 1763–1789: A Documentary History of the American Revolution* (New York: Norton, 1975), 245.

59. JA to AA, 9 Oct. 1774, *AFC*, 1:166–67.

60. JA, *Diary*, 2:156.

61. [JA] Novanglus, no. 1, 23 Jan. 1775, *JA: Revolutionary Writings, 1755–1775*, 1:387.

62. [JA] Novanglus, no. 1, 23 Jan. 1775, *JA: Revolutionary Writings, 1755–1775*, 1:387–88.

63. [JA] Novanglus, no. 5, 20 Feb. 1775, *JA: Revolutionary Writings, 1755–1775*, 1:473.
   Massachusettensis [Daniel Leonard], no. 1, 12 Dec. 1774, *JA: Revolutionary Writings, 1755–1775*, 1:329; Massachusettensis, no. 5, 9 Jan. 1775, ibid., 1:366; Massachusettensis, no. 11, 20 Feb. 1775. ibid., 1:451; [JA] Novanglus, no. 7, 6 Mar. 1775, ibid., 1:516; Gordon S. Wood, *The Creation of the American Republic, 1776–1787* (Chapel Hill: University of North Carolina Press, 1969), 351.

64. JA to William Tudor Sr., 18 Sept. 1818, PJA–MHS.

Four: Independence

1. JA to James Warren, 21 May 1775, *PJA*, 3:11.

2. JA to Timothy Pickering, 6 Aug. 1822, PJA–MHS.

3. JA to Pickering, 6 Aug. 1822, PJA–MHS.

4. Character of Mr. Adams by Benjamin Rush, post April 1790, PJA–MHS.

5. JA to AA, 17 June 1775, *AFC*, 1:216.

6. TJ and John Dickinson, "Declaration of the Causes and Necessity for Taking Up Arms," 6 July 1775, *PTJ*, 1:217.

7. JA to J. Warren, 24 July 1775, *PJA*, 3:89.

8. JA to William Tudor, 12 Apr. 1776, *PJA*, 4:118.

9. "Eulogy Pronounced at Boston, Massachusetts, August 2, 1826, by Daniel Webster," in *A Selection of Eulogies Pronounced in the Several States, in Honor of Those Illustrious Patriots and Statesmen, John Adams and Thomas Jefferson* (Hartford: D. F. Robinson and Co., 1826), 212.

10. JA to Tudor, 12 Apr. 1776, *PJA*, 4:118; JA to AA, 19 Mar. 1776, *AFC*, 1:363.

11. JA to Mercy Otis Warren, 16 Apr. 1776, *PJA*, 4:124; JA to AA, 17 May 1776, *AFC*, 1:411.

12. Worthington C. Ford, ed., *Journals of the Continental Congress, 1774–1789* (Washington, D.C.: Government Printing Office, 1904–1937), 1:342, 357.

13. JA, *Autobiography*, 3:335, 386; Carter Braxton to Landon Carter, 17 May 1775, in Paul H. Smith et al., eds., *Letters of Delegates to Congress, 1774–1789* (Washington, D.C.: Library of Congress, 1976–2000), 4:19.

14. JA to J. Warren, 15 May 1776, *PJA*, 4:186; JA to AA, 17 May 1776, *AFC*, 1:410.

15. TJ to Thomas Nelson, 16 May 1776, *PTJ*, 1:292; Robert Morris to Horatio Gates, 27 Oct. 1776, and F. L. Lee to Carter, 9 Nov. 1776, in Smith, *Letters of Delegates to Congress*, 5:412, 462–63; Gordon S. Wood, *The Creation of the American Republic, 1776–1787* (Chapel Hill: University of North Carolina Press, 1969), 128.

16. TJ, "Third Draft of Constitution," *PTJ*, 1:356–64; George Wythe to TJ, 27 July 1776, *PTJ*, 1:476–77.

17. TJ, "Third Draft of Constitution," *PTJ*, 1:357, 359–61.

18. TJ to Edmund Pendleton, 13 Aug. 1776, *PTJ*, 1:492.

19. TJ to Pendleton, 26 Aug. 1776, *PTJ*, 1:503–4.

20. Richard Alan Ryerson, *John Adams's Republic: The One, the Few, and the Many* (Baltimore: Johns Hopkins University Press, 2016), 180.

21. Montesquieu, *Spirit of the Laws*, trans. Thomas Nugent, ed. Franz Neumann (New York: Hafner, 1949), 1:bk. xi, sect. 6, p. 156; Donald S. Lutz, "The Relative Influence of European Writers on Late Eighteenth-Century American Political Thought," *American Political Science Review* 78 (1984): 190.

22. Adams, "Notes for an Oration at Braintree," 1772, JA, *Diary*, 2:57–60.

23. JA to Francis Dana, 16 Aug. 1776, *PJA*, 4:466.

24. [JA] Novanglus, no. 7, 6 Mar. 1775, *JA: Revolutionary Writings, 1755–1775*, 1:517; JA, "Thoughts on Government," *PJA*, 4:87. In his draft for the Massachusetts constitution of 1780, JA included in the second paragraph of his chapter 2, The Frame of Government, the phrase "a government of laws and not of men." The convention moved the phrase to article XXX of the declaration of rights. See "Report of a Constitution or Form of Government for the Commonwealth of Massachusetts," 1 Sept. 1779, *PJA*, 8:242; "Massachusetts Constitution of 1780," in Oscar Handlin and Mary Handlin, eds., *The Popular Sources of Political Authority: Documents on the Massachusetts Constitution of 1780* (Cambridge, Mass.: Belknap/Harvard University Press, 1966), 447–48.

25. JA to Dana, 16 Aug. 1776, *PJA*, 4:466.

26. JA to M. O. Warren, 16 Apr. 1776, *PJA*, 4:124; TJ, *Notes on the State of Virginia*, ed. William Peden (Chapel Hill: University of North Carolina Press, 1955), 121.

27. JA to M. O. Warren, 16 Apr. 1776, *PJA*, 4:124–25; JA to John Penn, 28 Apr. 1776, ibid., 4:149–50.

28. JA, "Thoughts on Government," *PJA*, 4:91. Benjamin Rush recalled asking JA in 1777 whether Americans were qualified for republican government. "He said 'No, and never should be 'till we were *ambitious to be poor.*'" BR to JA, 24 Feb. 1790, *Letters of Rush*, 1:535.

29. [JA], *Boston Gazette*, 8 Feb. 1773, *PJA*, 1:292.

30. JA, *Diary*, 2:60; JA, "Thoughts on Government," *PJA*, 4:87.

31. JA to AA, 4 June 1777, *AFC*, 2:255.

32. JA to Dana, 16 Aug. 1776, *PJA*, 4:466–67; JA, "Thoughts on Government," ibid., 4:88.

33. JA, "Thoughts on Government," *PJA*, 4:89. Ryerson, in his *John Adams's Republic* (p. 197), quotes this passage about the upper house acting "as a mediator" between the House of Representatives and the executive without assessing its implications for Adams's theory of mixed government. By 1780 and more explicitly by 1787, the mediator in JA's idea of balanced government was no longer the upper house; it had become the governor, standing between the people and the aristocracy.

34. Novanglus [JA], no. 5, *JA: Revolutionary Writings, 1755–1775*, 1:457.
35. JA, "Thoughts on Government," *PJA*, 4:89; JA to J. Warren, 12 May 1776, ibid., 4:182; JA to Dana, 16 Aug. 1776, ibid., 4:466.
36. JA to Richard Cranch, 2 Aug. 1776, *AFC*, 2:74.
37. TJ to Samuel Kercheval, 12 July 1816, *TJ: Writings*, 1396.
38. JA, "Thoughts on Government," *PJA*, 4:86.
39. JA, *Autobiography*, 3:336–37.
40. JA to Pickering, 6 Aug. 1822, *Works of JA*, 2:512–14.
41. JA, *Diary*, 2:391–92.
42. JA to AA, 3 July 1776, *AFC*, 2:30.
43. Pauline Maier, *American Scripture: Making the Declaration of Independence* (New York: Knopf, 1997), 102.
44. TJ to JM, 30 Aug. 1823, Cappon, 3:1175-76; TJ to Henry Lee, 8 May 1825, *TJ: Writings*, 1501.
45. William Byrd, "History of the Dividing Line . . . 1728," in Louis B. Wright, ed., *The Prose Works of William Byrd of Westover* (Cambridge, Mass.: Harvard University Press, 1966), 221; Gov. Fauquier to Jeffrey Amherst, 5 Oct. 1760, in Julie Richter, "The Impact of the Death of Governor Francis Fauquier on His Slaves and Their Families," *The Colonial Williamsburg Interpreter* 18, no. 3 (Fall 1997): 2; Frederick A. Pottle and Charles H. Bennett, eds., *Boswell's Journal of a Tour of the Hebrides with Samuel Johnson, LL.D.* (New York: The Literary Guild, 1936), 57. In 1815 the Scottish philosopher Dugald Stewart summed up what the Western world had learned since the mid-eighteenth century: "That the capacities of the human mind have been in all ages the same, and the diversity of phenomena exhibited by our species is the result merely of the different circumstances in which men are placed, had been long received as an incontrovertible logical maxim." Dugald Stewart, *Dissertation, Exhibiting the Progress of Metaphysical, Ethical, and Political Philosophy, Since the Revival of Letters in Europe* (1815), quoted in Silvia Sebastiani, *The Scottish Enlightenment: Race, Gender, and the Limits of Progress* (New York: Palgrave, 2013), 1.
46. Nathaniel Chipman, *Sketches of the Principles of Government* (Rutland, Vt., 1793), 78, 81.
47. Humphrey Ploughjogger to Philanthrop, ante 5 Jan. 1767, *PJA*, 1:179; Earl of Clarendon to William Pym, 27 Jan. 1766, ibid., 1:167–68; JA, "IV. 'U' to the *Boston Gazette*," 18 July 1763, ibid., 1:71.
48. John Locke, *An Essay Concerning Human Understanding*, ed. Peter H. Nidditch (Oxford: Oxford University Press, 1975), bk. II, ch. I, p. 104.
49. JA to Jonathan Sewall, Feb. 1760, *PJA*, 1:42–43.
50. John E. Selby, *The Revolution in Virginia, 1775–1783* (Williamsburg, Va.: Colonial Williamsburg Foundation, 1988), 107–8.
51. TJ, *Notes on the State of Virginia*, 138–42.
52. TJ, *Notes on the State of Virginia*, 58–62, 141–43.
53. TJ to Marquis de Chastellux, 7 June 1785, *PTJ*, 8:184–86; TJ, *Notes on the State of Virginia*, 58–62, 141–42.
54. JA to BR, 25 Oct. 1809, *Spur of Fame*, 158.
55. JA to Sewall, Feb. 1760, *PJA*, 1:43.
56. Frank H. Sommer, "Emblem and Device: The Origins of the Great Seal of the United States," *Art Quarterly* 24 (1964): 57–77.
57. TJ, Autobiography, *TJ: Writings*, 32.

58. TJ to Charles François, Chevalier d'Anmours, 30 Nov. 1780, *PTJ*, 4:168.

59. TJ to John Page, 30 July 1776, *PTJ*, 1:482.

60. TJ, Autobiography, *TJ: Writings*, 32.

61. TJ to Pendleton, 26 Aug. 1776, *PTJ*, 1:504.

62. TJ, "A Bill for Proportioning Crimes and Punishments in Cases Heretofore Capital" (1776–1786), *PTJ*, 2:492–507; Dumas Malone, *Jefferson the Virginian* (Boston: Little, Brown, 1948), 269.

63. TJ, "Notes on Locke and Shaftesbury," Oct.–Dec. 1776, *PTJ*, 1:548.

64. TJ, Autobiography, *TJ: Writings*, 43–44, 44.

65. Selby, *The Revolution in Virginia*, 140.

66. JA to Patrick Henry, 3 June 1776, *PJA*, 4:235.

67. JA to John Lowell, 12 June 1776, *PJA*, 4:250; JA to J. Warren, 16 Apr. 1776, ibid., 4:122; JA to John Winthrop, 23 June 1776, ibid., 4:332–33.

68. JA to J. Warren, 7 July 1777, *PJA*, 5:242.

69. JA to J. Warren, 22 Apr. 1776, *PJA*, 4:137.

70. James Otis, quoted in Wood, *Creation of the American Republic*, 476; JA to Samuel Freeman, 27 Apr. 1777, *PJA*, 5:161.

71. JA to James Sullivan, 26 May 1776, *PJA*, 4:208.

72. TJ to Anne Willing Bingham, 11 May 1788, *PTJ*, 13:151–52; Gordon S. Wood, *Empire of Liberty: A History of the Early Republic, 1789–1815* (New York: Oxford University Press, 2009), 507.

73. AA to JA, 31 Mar. 1776, *AFC*, 1:370.

74. JA to AA, 14 Aug. 1776, *AFC*, 1:382.

75. AA to JA, 17 June 1782, *AFC*, 4:328.

76. AA to Mary Cranch, 1809, AFC–MHS.

77. On the various interpretations of Abigail, see Edith B. Gelles, "The Abigail Industry," *WMQ* 45 (1988), 656–83. See also Edith B. Gelles, *First Thoughts: Life and Letters of Abigail Adams* (New York: Twayne Publishers, 1998); and Edith B. Gelles, *Abigail and John: Portrait of a Marriage* (New York: William Morrow, 2009).

78. AA to Elizabeth Smith Shaw Peabody, 19 July 1799, AFC–MHS.

FIVE: MISSIONS ABROAD

1. JA to JQA, 27 July 1777, *AFC*, 2:289–90.

2. JA to AA, 26 Apr. 1777, *AFC*, 2:224; JA to AA, 15 May 1777, ibid., 2:239.

3. JA to AA, 8 July 1777, *AFC*, 2:277; AA to JA, 5 Aug. 1777, ibid., 2:301.

4. JA to AA, 10 July 1777, *AFC*, 2:278; JA to AA, 16 Mar. 1777, ibid., 2:176–77.

5. JA to AA, 16 Mar. 1777, *AFC*, 2:176–77.

6. TJ to JA, 16 May 1777, Cappon, 1:4; JA to TJ, 26 May 1777, ibid., 1:6.

7. Edward Rutledge to TJ, 12 Feb. 1779, *PTJ*, 2:234.

8. TJ to Giovanni Fabbroni, 8 June 1778, *PTJ*, 2:195.

9. TJ to David Rittenhouse, 19 July 1778, *PTJ*, 2:203. Actually, Benjamin Franklin had argued the opposite, saying that participation in public affairs always trumped science. In 1750 he cautioned his fellow scientist Cadwallader Colden, the lieutenant governor of New York, not to "let your Love of Philosophical Amusements have more than its due weight with you. Had Newton been Pilot of but a single common Ship the finest of his discoveries would scarce have

excus'd, or attone'd for his abandoning the Helm one Hour in Time of Danger, how much less if she had carried the Fate of the Commonwealth." Gordon S. Wood, *The Americanization of Benjamin Franklin* (New York: Penguin Press, 2004), 67.

10. Edmund Pendleton to TJ, 11 May 1779, *PTJ*, 2:266.

11. TJ to William Phillips, 25 June 1779, *PTJ*, 3:15.

12. JA to AA, 19 Aug. 1777, *AFC*, 2:319.

13. TJ, "Draft of a Declaration on the British Treatment of Ethan Allen," 2 Jan. 1776, *PTJ*, 1:276.

14. TJ to Governor Patrick Henry, 27 Mar. 1779, *PTJ*, 2:237–44.

15. See Don N. Hagist, "The Women of the British Army in America," http://www.revwar75.com/library/hagist/britwomen.htm. I owe this reference to Philip C. Mead.

16. Johann Ludwig von Unger to TJ, 13 Nov. 1780, *PTJ*, 4:117; TJ to Johann Ludwig von Unger, 30 Nov. 1780, ibid., 4:171; Dumas Malone, *Jefferson the Virginian* (Boston: Little, Brown, 1948), 295.

17. TJ to Edmund Randolph, 29 Nov. 1775, *PTJ*, 1:268–70.

18. Lucia Stanton, *"Those Who Labour for My Happiness": Slavery at Thomas Jefferson's Monticello* (Charlottesville: University of Virginia Press, 2012), 132.

19. TJ to William Jones, 5 Jan. 1786, *PTJ*, 11:16; TJ to Alexander McCaul, 19 Apr. 1788, ibid., 9:388; TJ to John Jay, 23 Apr. 1786, ibid., 9:404; Cassandra Pybus, *Epic Journeys of Freedom: Runaway Slaves of the American Revolution* (Boston: Beacon Press, 2006), 48–49, 104–5.

20. Gary B. Nash, "The African Americans' Revolution," in *The Oxford Handbook of the American Revolution*, ed. Edward G. Gray and Jane Kamensky (New York: Oxford University Press, 2013), 261. Historians, following the often exaggerated claims of the slaveholding planters, have tended to overestimate the numbers of runaway slaves. See Cassandra Pybus, "Jefferson's Faulty Math: The Question of Slave Defections in the American Revolution," *WMQ* 62 (2005): 243–64.

21. TJ to Marquis de Lafayette, 10 May 1781, *PTJ*, 5:113.

22. TJ, *Notes on the State of Virginia*, ed. William Peden (Chapel Hill: University of North Carolina Press, 1955), 126.

23. TJ, Autobiography, *TJ: Writings*, 45.

24. Malone, *Jefferson the Virginian*, 361.

25. TJ to Francis Hopkinson, 13 Mar. 1789, *PTJ*, 14:650–51.

26. TJ to Lafayette, 4 Aug. 1781, *PTJ*, 6:112.

27. TJ to E. Randolph, 16 Sept. 1781, *PTJ*, 6:118.

28. E. Randolph to TJ, 9 Oct. 1781, *PTJ*, 6:128.

29. TJ to George Washington, 28 Oct. 1781, *PTJ*, 6:129.

30. TJ to James Monroe, 20 May 1782, *PTJ*, 6:184–86.

31. JM to E. Randolph, 11 June 1782, in JM, *Papers*, ed. William T. Hutchinson and William M. E. Rachal (Chicago: University of Chicago Press, 1962–), 4:333.

32. JA, *Diary*, 2:351.

33. JA, *Autobiography*, 3:418–19.

34. *Works of JA*, 1:58n.

35. JA to AA, 12 Apr. 1778, *AFC*, 3:17, 10; JA to Richard Henry Lee, 12 Feb. 1779, *PJA*, 7:407; JA to Francis Adrian Van der Kemp, 8 Apr. 1815, PJA–MHS.

36. JA, *Diary*, 2:367; JA to Thomas McKean, 20 Sept. 1779, *PJA*, 8:162.
37. JA, *Autobiography*, 4:36; JA to Mercy Otis Warren, 18 Dec. 1778, *PJA*, 7:282; JA to AA, 25 Apr. 1778, *AFC*, 3:17; JA, *Autobiography*, 4:47.
38. JA to James Warren, 2 Dec. 1778, *PJA*, 7:245; JA, *Autobiography*, 4:47.
39. JA to Samuel Adams, 21 May 1778, JA, *Diary*, 4:107.
40. JA to AA, 28 Feb. 1779, *AFC*, 3:181.
41. JA to AA, 20 Feb. 1779, *AFC*, 3:175.
42. JA to AA, 13 Nov. 1779, *AFC*, 3:324.
43. JA, *Autobiography*, 4:247.
44. Benjamin Franklin to Samuel Huntington, 9 Aug. 1780, in Leonard Labaree et al., eds., *The Papers of Benjamin Franklin* (New Haven: Yale University Press, 1959–), 33:162.
45. John Ferling, *John Adams: A Life* (1992; repr., New York: Henry Holt, 1996), 228.
46. Because Jefferson originally declined the invitation to join the peace commission and later was prevented from sailing and Henry Laurens was captured on the high seas by the British and imprisoned in the Tower of London, only Adams, Jay, and Franklin negotiated the final treaty with Britain.
47. TJ, Autobiography, *TJ: Writings*, 53.
48. JA, *Autobiography*, 3:336.
49. Benjamin Vaughn to TJ, 6 July–3 Nov. 1790, *PTJ*, 17:619–20.
50. "TJ's Observations on Démeunier's Manuscript," 1786, *PTJ*, 10:58.
51. JA to the President of Congress, 15 Oct. 1781, *PJA*, 12:15. See also JA to Franklin, 25 Aug. 1781, in Paul H. Smith et al., eds., *Letters of Delegates to Congress, 1774–1789* (Washington, D.C.: Library of Congress, 1976–2000), 14:469–70. John Ferling and Lewis E. Braverman have suggested that Adams may have suffered from hyperthyroidism, which would account for some of his ailments and his occasional bouts of illness. See their article "John Adams's Health Reconsidered," *WMQ* 55 (1998): 83–104.
52. TJ to JM, 14 Feb. 1783, *PTJ*, 6:241.
53. JA to Jonathan Jackson, 8 Nov. 1782, *PJA*, 14:44.
54. JA to Arthur Lee, 10 Oct. 1782, *PJA*, 14:525.
55. Franklin to Robert Livingston, 22 July 1783, in Gordon S. Wood, *The Americanization of Benjamin Franklin* (New York: Penguin Press, 2004), 195. TJ, like many others, learned of Franklin's characterization of JA and invoked it later himself. See TJ to JM, 29 July 1789, *PTJ*, 15:316.
56. Elbridge Gerry to AA, 18 Sept. 1783, *AFC*, 5:250.
57. JA to the President of Congress, 5 Feb. 1783, *PJA*, 14:242.
58. JM to TJ, 6 May 1783, *PTJ*, 6:205; JA to the President of Congress, 5 Feb. 1783, *PJA*, 14:242–45. JA's reasoning was based on the Dutch precedent. Before the Netherlands formally recognized the United States, JA had been commissioned to negotiate a Dutch-American commercial treaty. Once diplomatic relations were established, he had become the first minister to the Dutch republic. He thus assumed that the authority to negotiate a commercial treaty with a foreign country was inseparable from the authority normally granted to the minister of a foreign country.
59. JA to C. W. F. Dumas, 28 Mar. 1783, *PJA*, 14:373.
60. JA to John Jay, 10 Aug. 1785, *Works of JA*, 8:298.

61. American Commissioners to Friederich Wilhelm, Baron von Thulemeier, 14 Mar. 1785, *PTJ*, 8:28.
62. JA to Franklin, 17 Aug. 1780, *PJA*, 10:78.
63. TJ to JA, 28 July 1785, *PTJ*, 8:317–19. See also TJ to JA, 31 July 1785, Cappon, 1:46–47, where TJ noted JA's objection to placing natives and aliens on an equal footing.
64. JA to TJ, 4 Sept. 1785, Cappon, 1:61; JA to TJ, 9 Oct. 1787, ibid., 1:202.
65. JA to James Warren, 27 Aug. 1784, *PJA*, 16:309.
66. JA to AA, 26 July 1784, *AFC*, 5:399.
67. Adams believed that what he and the other diplomats were doing abroad was indispensable. Indeed, he told James Warren in 1784 that "the Character and the System of our Country had been entirely decided by our foreign affairs." JA to Warren, 30 June 1784, *PJA*, 16:262.
68. TJ to JM, 25 May 1788, *Republic of Letters*, 540; TJ to AA, 25 Sept. 1785, Cappon, 1:71.
69. TJ to Franklin, 13 Aug. 1777, *PTJ*, 2:27; TJ to Charles Bellini, 30 Sept. 1785, ibid., 8:568; TJ to AA, 21 June 1785, Cappon, 1:34. See also Gaye Wilson, "'Behold me at length on the vaunted scene of Europe': Thomas Jefferson and the Creation of an American Image Abroad," in *Old World, New World: America and Europe in the Age of Jefferson*, ed. Leonard Sadosky et al. (Charlottesville: University of Virginia Press, 2010), 155–78.
70. JA to Abigail Adams 2d, 14 Apr. 1783, *AFC*, 5:123; TJ to Charles Bellini, 30 Sept. 1785, *PTJ*, 8:569.
71. TJ to Anne Willing Bingham, 7 Feb. 1787, *PTJ*, 11:122–23; TJ to Bellini, 30 Sept. 1785, ibid., 8:569.
72. TJ to John Banister Jr., 15 Oct. 1785, *PTJ*, 8:636–37.
73. AA to TJ, 6 July 1787, Cappon, 1:183.
74. AA to Elizabeth Cranch, 8 May 1785, *AFC*, 6:119.
75. AA to E. Cranch, 8 May 1785, *AFC*, 6:119.
76. JA to TJ, 22 Jan. 1825, Cappon, 2:606–7.
77. AA to TJ, 6 June 1785, Cappon, 1:28.
78. JA to BR, 25 Oct. 1809, *Spur of Fame*, 159.
79. Arthur Lee to JA, 12 Aug. 1784, *PJA*, 16:296; JA to Arthur Lee, 31 Jan. 1785, ibid., 16:510; JA to William Knox, 15 Dec. 1784, ibid., 16:469; JA to Gerry, 12 Dec. 1784, ibid., 16:451; JA to BR, 25 Oct. 1809, *Spur of Fame*, 159.
80. AA to Mary Cranch, 5 Sept. 1784, *AFC*, 5:442.
81. TJ to JM, 20 June 1787, *PTJ*, 11:482.
82. TJ to AA, 4 Sept. 1785, Cappon, 1:57–58.
83. TJ to JM, 25 May 1788, *Republic of Letters*, 540. For a superb account of AA's management skills and her financial talents, see Woody Holton, *Abigail Adams* (New York: Free Press, 2009).
84. TJ to JA, 25 May 1785, Cappon, 1:23.
85. JA to TJ, 1 Mar. 1787, Cappon, 1:177.
86. AA to TJ, 6 June 1785, Cappon, 1:29; TJ to AA, 21 June 1785, ibid., 1:33; AA to TJ, 12 Aug. 1785, *PTJ*, 27:749.
87. TJ to AA, 25 Sept. 1785, Cappon, 1:69. In 1788 TJ asked AA if he could continue corresponding with her, to which she gratefully agreed. But it was sixteen years before Abigail and Jefferson resumed their correspondence, which soon went sour.

88. TJ to Angelica Schuyler Church, 21 Sept. 1788, *PTJ*, 16:623–24; TJ to AA, 27 Dec. 1785, Cappon, 1:110; TJ to AA, 9 Aug. 1786, ibid., 1:149. For a similar account see Cassandra Good, *Founding Friendships: Friendships Between Men and Women in the Early American Republic* (New York: Oxford University Press, 2015), 16.

89. TJ to JM, 25 May 1788, *Republic of Letters*, 540; TJ to JM, 30 Jan.–5 Feb. 1787, in JM, *Papers*, ed. William T. Hutchinson and William M. E. Rachal (Chicago: University of Chicago Press, 1962–1991), 9:247–52. TJ's critical comments were written in code.

90. TJ to David Ross, 8 May 1786, *PTJ*, 9:474.

91. *Works of JA*, 1:420.

92. JA, "Notes on a Tour of England with Thomas Jefferson," April 1786, *JA: Writings from the New Nation*, 49–51.

93. TJ, "Notes of a Tour of English Gardens," Apr. 1786, *PTJ*, 9:369.

94. JA, "Notes on a Tour of England with Thomas Jefferson," 49–51.

Six: Constitutions

1. TJ, *Notes on the State of Virginia*, ed. William Peden (Chapel Hill: University of North Carolina Press, 1955), 117.

2. [JA] Novanglus, no. 8, 20 Mar. 1775, *JA: Revolutionary Writings, 1755–1775*, 540.

3. [Charles Inglis], *The True Interest of America Impartially Stated, in Certain Strictures on a Pamphlet Intitled Common Sense (1776)*, in *The American Revolution: Writings from the Pamphlet Debate, 1773–1776*, ed. Gordon S. Wood (New York: Library of America, 2015), 2:721.

4. Gordon S. Wood, *The Creation of the American Republic, 1776–1787* (Chapel Hill: University of North Carolina Press, 1969), 261.

5. JA, *Boston Gazette*, 8 Feb. 1773, *PJA*, 1:292.

6. TJ, "Drafts of the Virginia Constitution" (1776), *PTJ*, 1:345, 354, 364.

7. TJ, "Bill for Establishing Freedom of Religion" (1779), *PTJ*, 2:546–47.

8. TJ, Proposed Revision of the Virginia Constitution, *PTJ*, 6:280; TJ, *Notes on the State of Virginia*, 121–25.

9. JA to BR, 10 Sept. 1779, *PJA*, 8:140.

10. JM, "Vices of the Political System of the United States, April 1787," in *James Madison: Writings*, ed. Jack N. Rakove (New York: Library of America, 1999), 69–80.

11. Adams had liked the term "Commonwealth," which Virginia had employed in its constitution of 1776, and had wanted other states, including Massachusetts, to adopt it. JA to Jonathan Dickinson Sergeant, 21 July 1776, *PJA*, 4:397; JA to Francis Dana, 16 Aug. 1776, ibid., 4:466. Near the end of the convention of 1779–1780, an unnamed delegate, not JA, proposed that the state rename itself the "Commonwealth of Oceana," after James Harrington's seventeenth-century republican utopia. *PJA*, 8:261–62n.

12. BR to JA, 12 Oct. 1779, *PJA*, 8:200.

13. *Report of a Constitution or Form of Government for the Commonwealth of Massachusetts*, 28–31 Oct, 1779, *PJA*, 8:236–71. For the final adopted Massachusetts constitution, see Oscar Handlin and Mary Handlin, eds. *The Popular Sources of Political Authority: Documents on the Massachusetts Constitution of 1780* (Cambridge, Mass.: Belknap/Harvard University Press, 1966), 441–72. See also

Robert J. Taylor, "Construction of the Massachusetts Constitution," American Antiquarian Society, *Proceedings* 90 (1980): 317–40.

14. *Report of a Constitution or Form of Government*, 8:260.

15. JA, "The Earl of Clarendon to William Pym," 27 Jan. 1766, *PJA*, 1:168. Some Virginian planters in 1776 had found Mason's softer statement that men were "by nature equally free and independent" too radical for a slaveholding society and had forced the addition of the phrase "when they enter into a state of society," thus excluding the black slaves from the declaration of rights. Pauline Maier, *American Scripture: Making the Declaration of Independence* (New York: Knopf, 1997), 195.

16. David H. Fischer, "The Myth of the Essex Junto," *WMQ* 21 (1964): 214.

17. Taylor, "Construction of the Massachusetts Constitution," 333.

18. JA to Elbridge Gerry, 4 Nov. 1779, *PJA*, 8:276.

19. JA, *Defence of the Constitutions of Government of the United States of America*, in *Works of JA*, 4:358; [JA] Novanglus, 6 Mar. 1775, *PJA*, 2:314.

20. *Report of a Constitution or Form of Government*, *PJA*, 8:257.

21. John Louis De Lolme, *The Constitution of England; or, An Account of the English Government*, ed. David Lieberman (1784; repr., Indianapolis: Liberty Fund, 2007).

22. Montesquieu, *Spirit of the Laws*, trans. Thomas Nugent, ed. Franz Neumann (New York: Hafner, 1949), 1:bk. xi, sect. 6, p. 156.

23. Adams, *Thoughts on Government, Applicable to the Present State of the American Colonies* (1776), in *JA: Revolutionary Writings, 1775–1783*, 2:52.

24. De Lolme, *Constitution of England*, book II, chs. i–ii, pp. 139–52.

25. Adams, *Defence*, in *Works of JA*, 4:358. De Lolme's *Constitution of England* was one of the few books the newly elected vice president in 1789 asked Abigail to have sent to him in New York. JA to AA, 24 May 1789, *AFC*, 8:358.

26. "Massachusetts Constitution," in Handlin and Handlin, *Popular Sources of Political Authority*, 448.

27. Theophilus Parsons, *Essex Result* (1778), in Handlin and Handlin, *Popular Sources of Political Authority*, 349, 333–34.

28. "Address of the Convention," March 1780, in Handlin and Handlin, *Popular Sources of Political Authority*, 437. The Massachusetts constitution of 1780 granted the senate the power to amend but not the power to initiate money bills. It soon became evident that this limitation, applied in emulation of the practice of the House of Lords, made no sense if the senate was supposed to represent the property of the state. Many pointed out the anomaly, and by the mid-1780s the senate had begun ignoring this constitutional limitation.

29. Wood, *Creation of the American Republic*, 217.

30. TJ to Edmund Pendleton, 26 Aug. 1776, *PTJ*, 1:508.

31. TJ to François Barbé de Marbois, 5 Dec. 1783, *PTJ*, 6:374.

32. TJ, *Notes on the State of Virginia*, 120.

33. TJ, *Notes on the State of Virginia*, 126–28, 148.

34. TJ, *Notes on the State of Virginia*, 118.

35. Drew R. McCoy, *The Last of the Fathers: James Madison and the Republican Legacy* (Cambridge: Cambridge University Press, 1989), 115.

36. JA to Benjamin Franklin, 27 July 1784, *PJA*, 16:285.

37. Richard Price, *Observations on the Importance of the American Revolution and the Means of Making It a Benefit to the World* (London, 1784; repr., Boston: Powars and Willis, 1784), 76. The letter is reprinted in *Works of JA*, 4:278–81.

38. Wood, *Creation of the American Republic*, 247–55.

39. "Address of the Convention," 437.

40. TJ, *Notes on the State of Virginia*, 119; TJ, *A Summary View of the Rights of British America* (Williamsburg, Va., 1774), in Wood, *The American Revolution: Writings from the Pamphlet Debate*, 2:106.

41. Thomas Brand Hollis to JA, 15 May 1789, PJA–MHS.

42. JA to Richard Price, 4 Feb. 1787, PJA–MHS.

43. JA, *Defence*, in *Works of JA*, 6:10, 95.

44. TJ to JA, 6 Feb. 1787, Cappon, 1:170.

45. JA to TJ, 13 July 1813, Cappon, 2:355.

46. JA to Count Sarsfield, 21 Jan. 1786, *Works of JA*, 8:370.

47. Max Farrand, ed., *The Records of the Federal Convention of 1787* (New Haven: Yale University Press, 1911, 1937), 1:288.

48. JA, *Defence*, in *JA: Writings of the New Nation*, 158.

49. For a rich account of JA's obsession with oligarchy, see Luke Mayville, *John Adams and the Fear of Oligarchy* (Princeton, N.J.: Princeton University Press, 2016). The theory of the "iron law of oligarchy" was developed by the German sociologist Robert Michels in his *Political Parties: A Sociological Study of the Oligarchical Tendencies of Modern Democracy* (1911).

50. JA, *Diary*, 2:38; 1:207.

51. JA to John Trumbull, 12 Mar. 1790, PJA–MHS.

52. Apparently, neither C. Bradley Thompson nor Richard Alan Ryerson in their monumental works on JA's political theory (Thompson, *John Adams and the Spirit of Liberty* [Lawrence: University Press of Kansas, 1998]; Ryerson, *John Adams's Republic: The One, the Few, and the Many* [Baltimore: Johns Hopkins University Press, 2016]), consulted the essays by "The Free Republican," even though they both knew that Lincoln's essays anticipated some of the same issues of balanced government as Adams.

53. Free Republican, no. 5, *Independent Chronicle*, 22 Dec. 1785, in *Essays by "The Free Republican" 1784–1786*, ed. Philip C. Mead and Gordon S. Wood (Indianapolis: Liberty Fund, 2016), 37–38.

54. Free Republican, no. 5, *Independent Chronicle*, 22 Dec. 1785, in Mead and Wood, *Essays by "The Free Republican,"* 38–39.

55. Free Republican, no. 5, *Independent Chronicle*, 22 Dec. 1785, in Mead and Wood, *Essays by "The Free Republican,"* 39; JA, *Defence*, in *Works of JA*, 6:185.

56. Unlike Benjamin Lincoln, JA at one point felt compelled to explicitly deny that America contained different orders of men, by which he simply meant, however, that there was no hereditary nobility in America. "Out of office," he said, "all men are of the same species, and of one blood." He made this comment out of defensive reaction to French charges that by creating senates Americans had recognized a European-type nobility. Yet his analysis clearly presumed that his aristocracy was an order or power of society different and distinct from that of the common people. All "three branches of power," he said, "have an unalterable foundation in nature," and they existed "in every society, natural and artificial." JA, *Defence*, in *Works of JA*, 4:380, 100.

57. JA, *Defence*, in *Works of JA*, 4:395.

58. Free Republican, no. 3, *Independent Chronicle*, 8 Dec., 1785, in Mead and Wood, *Essays by "The Free Republican,"* 23. In his *Defence*, JA accurately quoted from Jonathan Swift's *A Discourse of the Contests and Dissensions Between the Nobles and*

the Commons in Athens and Rome, with the Consequences They Had upon Both Those States (London, 1701), 5: "The true meaning of a balance of power is best conceived by considering what the nature of a balance is. It supposes three things,— first, the part which is held, together with the hand that holds it; and then the two scales, with whatever is weighed therein." JA, *Defence*, in *Works of JA*, 4:385.

59. JA, *Defence*, in *Works of JA*, 4:557; 6:128.

60. In December 1785, JA said that young Lincoln was "personally unknown to me," but he believed that he had "an undoubted Character as a Man of Honour and abilities in his Profession" of law. JA to Elizabeth Brown, 10 Dec. 1785, PJA–MHS.

61. Free Republican, no. 10, *Independent Chronicle*, 9 Feb. 1786 in Mead and Wood, *Essays by "The Free Republican,"* 74–75.

62. JA to Hollis, 11 June 1790, PJA–MHS.

63. JA to TJ, 6 Dec. 1787, Cappon, 1:213; JA, *Defence*, in *Works of JA*, 4:290, 414.

64. JA to President of Congress, 27 May 1781, *PJA*, 11:340; JA to AA, 4 Sept. 1780, *AFC*, 3:410.

65. JA, *Defence*, in *Works of JA*, 4:290, 414. De Lolme had written that a seat in the House of Lords was supposedly a reward, but in fact for the recipient it was "a kind of Ostracism." The "favourite of the People" appointed to the House of Lords, said De Lolme, "does not even find in his newly acquired dignity, all the increase of greatness and eclat that might at first be imagined." Instead, he discovers that he has taken "a great step towards the loss of that power which might render him formidable." William Pitt's elevation to the House of Lords as Lord Chatham was often cited as an example of this point. De Lolme, *Constitution of England*, bk. II, ch. i, pp. 147, 145–46.

66. Farrand, *Records of the Federal Convention*, 1:512–13.

67. Farrand, *Records of the Federal Convention*, 2:202–3, 209–10.

68. Free Republican, no. 10, *Independent Chronicle*, 9 Feb. 1786, in Mead and Wood, *Essays by "The Free Republican,"* 67.

69. JA to Marquis de Lafayette, 28 Mar. 1784, *PJA*, 16:104.

70. AA to JA, 21 July 1783, *AFC*, 5:210.

71. JA, *Defence*, in *Works of JA*, 4:393.

72. TJ to William Duane, 1 Oct. 1812, *PTJ: RS*, 5:366; TJ to Richard Henry Lee, 17 June 1779, *PTJ*, 1: 298; TJ to Francis Willis, 18 Apr. 1790, ibid., 16:352–53; TJ to Jean Nicholas Démeunier, 29 Apr. 1795, ibid., 28:340–41.

73. JA to John Jebb, 21 Aug. 1785, 10 Sept. 1785, *JA: Writings from the New Nation*, 29–38.

74. JA to Elbridge Gerry, 4 Nov. 1779, *PJA*, 8:276.

75. JA to TJ, 1 Mar. 1787, Cappon, 1:176.

76. Zoltán Haraszti, *John Adams and the Prophets of Progress* (Cambridge, Mass.: Harvard University Press, 1952), 43; JA to BR, 28 Aug. 1811, *Old Family Letters*, 357; JA to John Taylor, 21 Jan. 1815, *Works of JA*, 6:515. Adams told Francis Adrian Van der Kemp that the *Defence* "was not the fruit of twenty years labor, like Montesquieu's and Gibbon's," but "was written in haste." If he had more time, "the Book would have been shorter by one half." JA to Van der Kemp, 25 Dec. 1799, 30 Jan. 1800, PJA–MHS.

77. JA to Price, 20 May 1789, PJA–MHS.

78. George William Van Cleve, "The Anti-Federalists' Toughest Challenge: Paper Money, Debtor Relief, and the Ratification of the Constitution," *JER* 34 (2014): 549.

79. Cotton Tufts to JA, 15 May 1787, PJA–MHS.

80. Richard Cranch to JA, 24 May 1787, *AFC*, 8:59–60.

81. JA to Franklin, 27 Jan. 1787, PJA–MHS; JA to James Warren, 9 Jan. 1787, in Massachusetts Historical Society, ed., *Warren-Adams Letters, Being Chiefly a Correspondence Among John Adams, Samuel Adams, and James Warren* (Boston: Massachusetts Historical Society, 1917–1925), 2:281.

SEVEN: THE FRENCH REVOLUTION

1. JA to Zabdiel Adams, 21 June 1776, *AFC*, 2:21.

2. JA to James Warren, 13 Apr. 1783, *PJA*, 14:402–3; JA to Stephen Higginson, 4 Oct. 1785, ibid., 17:492.

3. JA to John Jay, 8 May 1785, *PJA*, 17:102.

4. JA to Samuel Adams, 15 Aug. 1785, *PJA*, 17:336.

5. JA to Elbridge Gerry, 25 Apr. 1785, *PJA*, 17:42.

6. JA to J. Warren, 9 Jan. 1787, in Massachusetts Historical Society, ed., *Warren-Adams Letters, Being Chiefly a Correspondence Among John Adams, Samuel Adams, and James Warren* (Boston: Massachusetts Historical Society, 1917–1925), 2:280.

7. JA to Matthew Robinson-Morris, 23 Mar. 1786, PJA–MHS.

8. JA, *Defence of the Constitutions of Government of the United States of America*, in *Works of JA*, 4:557.

9. JA to Richard Price, 20 May 1789, PJA–MHS.

10. JA to William Walter, 24 Oct. 1797, PJA–MHS.

11. JA, *Defence*, in *Works of JA*, 4:392.

12. JA, *Defence*, in *Works of JA*, 4:392.

13. JA, *Defence*, in *Works of JA*, 4:392.

14. JA, *Defence*, in *Works of JA*, 4:392; Samuel Eliot Morison, ed., "William Manning's The Key of Libberty," *WMQ* 13 (1956): 218–23.

15. Morison, "William Manning's The Key of Libberty," 218–23. Michel Merrill and Sean Wilentz have edited a modern edition, *The Key of Liberty: The Life and Democratic Writings of William Manning, "A Laborer," 1747–1814* (Cambridge, Mass.: Harvard University Press, 1993), but unfortunately they have corrected all his phonetic spelling. In his opening remarks Manning described the 1785–1786 "Free Republican" essays of Benjamin Lincoln Jr. as the best thing he had ever read on the division "between the few & Many." Manning never mentioned JA's *Defence*.

16. JA, *Discourses on Davila* (1805; repr., New York: Da Capo Press, 1973), 91; Antonio Pace, ed., *Luigi Castiglioni's Viaggio: Travels in the United States of North America, 1785–87* (Syracuse: Syracuse University Press, 1985), 335.

17. JA, *Defence*, in *Works of JA*, 5:457.

18. TJ, *Notes on the State of Virginia*, ed. William Peden (Chapel Hill: University of North Carolina Press, 1955), 162–63.

19. TJ, *Notes on the State of Virginia*, 162–63; David Bertelson, *The Lazy South* (New York, Oxford University Press, 1967).

20. Philanthropos [David Rice], *Slavery Inconsistent with Justice and Good Policy* (Lexington, Ky., 1792), 17–18.

21. TJ to Jay, 23 Aug. 1785, *PTJ*, 8:426.

22. TJ to David Williams, 14 Nov. 1803, *PTJ*, 41:728.

23. JA, *Defence*, in *Works of JA*, 4:392–93, 397.

24. JA, *Defence*, in *Works of JA*, 4:392–93, 397.

25. JA, *Defence*, in *Works of JA*, 4:406–7.

26. JA, *Defence*, in *Works of JA*, 4:399–400.

27. TJ to Jay, 23 Aug. 1785, *PTJ*, 8:426.

28. Adams, *Defence*, in *Works of JA*, 4:401; Mercy Otis Warren to JA, 28 July 1807, recalling a comment JA made in 1788, Massachusetts Historical Society, *Collections*, 5th ser., 4 (1878): 361.

29. JA, *Defence*, in *Works of JA*, 4:557.

30. JA, *Defence*, in *Works of JA*, 4:290, 355, 585.

31. TJ to JA, 23 Feb. 1787, Cappon, 1:174–75. Joyce Appleby, "The Adams-Jefferson Rupture and the First French Translation of John Adams' *Defence*," *AHR* 73 (1968): 1084–91, has made a persuasive case that TJ permitted the "suppression" of a translation. Certainly his liberal French friends eager to reform their own government found the *Defence* and its preoccupation with a separate legislative house for an aristocracy deeply objectionable and probably prevented any translation. Whether TJ connived at the suppression of a translation or simply quietly accepted what his French friends wanted seems to be the point of disagreement between Appleby and Julian Boyd. See Julian P. Boyd, "*Rights of Man:* The 'Contest of Burke and Paine in America,'" *PTJ*, 20:279.

32. TJ, "Observations on Démeunier's Manuscript," 1786, *PTJ*, 10:52.

33. TJ to JA, 23 Feb. 1787, Cappon, 1:174.

34. TJ to George Washington, 16 Apr. 1784, *PTJ*, 7:105–8; TJ to Washington, 14 Nov. 1786, ibid., 10:532; TJ, "Observations on Démeunier's Manuscript," 10:49–52.

35. TJ, "Observations on Démeunier's Manuscript," 10:52.

36. JA to M. O. Warren, 7 May 1789, PJA–MHS; JA to TJ, 30 Nov. 1786, Cappon, 1:156; AA to TJ, 29 Jan. 1787, Cappon, 1:168.

37. TJ to AA, 21 Dec. 1786, Cappon, 1:159; TJ to AA, 22 Feb. 1787, ibid., 1:173.

38. TJ to William Stephens Smith, 13 Nov. 1787, *PTJ*, 12:356.

39. TJ to Edward Carrington, 16 Jan. 1787, *PTJ*, 11:49.

40. TJ to JA, 30 Aug. 1787, Cappon, 1:196; TJ to JA, 13 Nov. 1787, ibid., 1:212.

41. JA to TJ, 6 Dec. 1787, Cappon, 1:213–14.

42. While Madison was describing to the Italian physician and agent for Virginia during the Revolution Philip Mazzei that "the real danger to America & to liberty lies in the defects of *energy* & *stability* in the present establishments of the United States," TJ was telling JM that he was "not a friend to a very energetic government—It is always oppressive." JM to Philip Mazzei, 8 Oct. 1788, in JM, *Papers*, ed. William T. Hutchinson and William M. E. Rachal (Chicago: University of Chicago Press, 1962–1991), 11:278; TJ to JM, 20 Dec. 1787, *Republic of Letters*, 514.

43. TJ to JM, 20 Dec. 1787, *Republic of Letters*, 513–14. Concern for what TJ might think about his fears of excessive democracy in the states led JM to revise some of his notes of the proceedings of the Constitutional Convention. Mary Sarah Bilder, *Madison's Hand: Revising the Constitutional Convention* (Cambridge, Mass.: Harvard University Press, 2016).

44. TJ to Carrington, 21 Dec. 1787, *PTJ*, 12:446.
45. JA to TJ, 10 Nov. 1787, Cappon, 1:210; TJ to John Jay, 23 May 1788, *PTJ*, 13:190; JM to TJ, 17 Oct. 1788, ibid., 14:16–21; TJ to Francis Hopkinson, 13 Mar. 1789, ibid., 14:650–51.
46. TJ to AA, 9 Aug. 1786, Cappon, 1:149.
47. TJ to Madame de Bréhan, 9 May 1788, *PTJ*, 13:150.
48. TJ to Richard Price, 8 Jan. 1789, *PTJ*, 14:421.
49. JA to TJ, 10 Dec. 1787, Cappon, 1:214–15.
50. TJ to JA, 2 Aug. 1788, Cappon, 1:230.
51. TJ to James Monroe, 9 Aug. 1788, *PTJ*, 13:489.
52. TJ to Washington, 4 Dec. 1788, *PTJ*, 14:330.
53. TJ to Jay, 8 May 1789, *PTJ*, 15:110–11.
54. TJ to Jay, 29 June 1789, *PTJ*, 15:223.
55. TJ, Autobiography, *TJ: Writings*, 96.
56. TJ to Count de Jean Diodati-Tronchin, 3 Aug. 1789, *PTJ*, 15:325–26; TJ to Edward Bancroft, 5 Aug. 1789, ibid., 15:333.
57. TJ, Autobiography, *TJ: Writings*, 92, 97.
58. JA to TJ, 1 Mar. 1789, Cappon, 1:236.
59. JM to TJ, 17 Oct. 1788, *Republic of Letters*, 1:563.
60. Prior to the ratification of the Twelfth Amendment in 1804, the electors simply voted for two individuals for president, only one of whom could be from the same state as the elector; the one with the most votes became president, the runner-up, vice president.
61. JA to BR, 17 May 1789, *Old Family Letters*, 36; JA to William Tudor, 9 May 1789, PJA–MHS; JA to M. O. Warren, 2 Mar. 1789, ibid.
62. A Farmer of New Jersey [John Stevens], *Observations on Government, Including Some Animadversions on Mr. Adams's Defence of the Constitutions of Government of the United States of America: and on Mr. De Lolme's Constitution of England* (New York, 1787). The French liberals wrongly attributed the work to William Livingston, the longtime governor of New Jersey.
63. C. Bradley Thompson, for example, says that Stevens and JA did not differ over the form of government—a bicameral legislature with an independent executive. "Stevens's principal disagreement with Adams was over how that government was to be explained and justified." That's correct, but Thompson seems to believe that such an explanation and a justification were just minor matters. "For Stevens, government was an artificial construction and delegation of the people's power. Adams saw government in the very same way but he also thought it necessary to go a step further and take into account the social manifestations of human nature." Those "social manifestations of human nature" involved the inevitable emergence of aristocracies that, according to Adams, had to be ostracized in upper houses of the legislatures: in other words, JA believed in social orders like those in the English constitution—precisely Stevens's point. C. Bradley Thompson, *John Adams and the Spirit of Liberty* (Lawrence: University Press of Kansas, 1998), 255.
64. [Stevens], *Observations on Government*, 25.
65. *Examen du Gouvernement D'Angleterre, Comparé aux Constitutions des États-Unis* (Paris, 1789). Joyce Appleby says that TJ brought home with him a copy of the *Examen* though he never mentioned the book to JA. Appleby, "The Adams-Jefferson Rupture," 1091.

66. Herbert E. Sloan, *Principle and Interest: Thomas Jefferson and the Problem of Debt* (New York: Oxford University Press, 1995), 81–85.

67. TJ to JM, 6 Sept. 1789, *Republic of Letters*, 1:631–36.

68. JM to TJ, 4 Feb. 1790, *Republic of Letters*, 1:650–53.

69. JA to TJ, 25 Aug. 1787, Cappon, 1:192; JA to TJ, 9 Oct. 1787, ibid., 1:202; *Documentary History of the First Federal Congress, 4 March 1789–5, March 1791*, ed. Kenneth R. Bowling and Helen Veit, vol. 9, *The Diary of William Maclay and Other Notes on Senate Debates* (Baltimore: Johns Hopkins University Press, 1988), 254.

70. TJ, *Notes on the State of Virginia*, 161.

71. TJ to Baron von Geismar, 6 Sept. 1785, *PTJ*, 8:500; Annette Gordon-Reed and Peter S. Onuf, *"Most Blessed of the Patriarchs": Thomas Jefferson and the Empire of the Imagination* (New York: Norton, 2016), 156–72.

72. TJ to William Short, 8 Jan. 1825, in *The Writings of Thomas Jefferson*, ed. Paul Leicester Ford (New York: G. P. Putnam's Sons, 1892), 10:332–34. See also Mary Sarah Bilder, *Madison's Hand: Revising the Constitutional Convention* (Cambridge, Mass.: Harvard University Press, 2015), 204, for the difficulty TJ had in 1789–1790 adjusting to "the new political world."

73. Gordon S. Wood, *Empire of Liberty: A History of the Early Republic, 1789–1815* (New York: Oxford University Press, 2009), 54, 74–75; JA to Tudor, 9 May 1789, PJA–MHS.

74. TJ to Short, 8 Jan. 1825, in *The Writings of Thomas Jefferson*, ed. Andrew A. Lipscomb and Albert Ellery Bergh (Washington, D.C.: Jefferson Memorial Association, 1903), 16:93–95.

75. Louise Burnham Dunbar, *A Study of Monarchical Tendencies in the United States from 1776 to 1801* (1922; repr., Urbana: University of Illinois Press, 1970), 99.

76. JA to Benjamin Lincoln, 19 June 1789, PJA–MHS; TJ to Short, 8 Jan. 1825, in *Writings of TJ*, 10:332.

77. *Diary of Maclay*, 9; Baltimore *Maryland Journal*, 6 July 1787.

78. JA, *Defence*, in *Works of JA*, 4:392.

79. Bernard Bailyn, ed., *The Debate on the Constitution* (New York: Library of America, 1993), 2:760, 770.

80. Adams later declared that an aristocrat was anyone who could influence a single person, which certainly expanded the category of the aristocracy. JA to TJ, 15 Nov. 1813, Cappon, 2:398.

81. JA to BR, 9 June 1789, *Old Family Letters*, 37.

82. JA, *Defence*, in *Works of JA*, 5:453.

83. JA to Roger Sherman, 17 July 1789, *Works of JA*, 6:427–28; Sherman to JA, 20 July 1789, ibid., 6:437.

84. JA to Sherman, 18 July 1789, *Works of JA*, 6:430; JA to Sherman, 17 July 1789, ibid., 6:428–29.

85. Sherman to JA, 20 July 1789, *Works of JA*, 6:438; Sherman to JA, post–20 July 1789, ibid., 6:441.

86. JA, *Defence*, in *Works of JA*, 5:488.

87. JA, *Defence*, in *Works of JA*, 6:95. 97; JA to BR, 4 Apr., 1790, *Old Family Letters*, 57.

88. BR to JA, 13 Apr. 1790, *Letters of Rush*, 1:546; JA to BR, 18 Apr. 1790, *Old Family Letters*, 59.

Eight: Federalists and Republicans

1. TJ, "The Anas, 1791–1806," in *The Writings of Thomas Jefferson,* ed. Paul Leicester Ford (New York: G. P. Putnam's Sons, 1892), 1:165–66.
2. JA to George Washington, 17 May 1789, PJA–MHS.
3. *Documentary History of the First Federal Congress, 4 March 1789–5 March 1791,* ed. Kenneth R. Bowling and Helen Veit, vol. 9, *The Diary of William Maclay and Other Notes on Senate Debates* (Baltimore: Johns Hopkins University Press, 1988), 6.
4. AA to Mary Smith Cranch, 9 Aug. 1789, *AFC,* 8:399–400.
5. *Diary of William Maclay,* 16–17.
6. *Diary of William Maclay,* 27; JA to BR, 5 July 1789, *Old Family Letters,* 42–43.
7. JA to William Tudor, 3 May 1789, quoted in Page Smith, *John Adams* (New York: Doubleday, 1962), 2:755; JA to Benjamin Lincoln, 8 May 1789, PJA–MHS.
8. *Diary of William Maclay,* 16–17, 19, 28–29, 33; John Ferling, *John Adams: A Life* (1992; repr., New York: Henry Holt, 1996), 304; Jack D. Warren Jr., "In the Shadow of Washington: John Adams as Vice-President," in *John Adams and the Founding of the Republic,* ed. Richard Alan Ryerson (Boston: Northeastern University Press, 2001), 130–31.
9. TJ to JM, 29 July 1789, *PTJ,* 15:316.
10. TJ, "The Anas," Ford, *Writings of TJ,* 1:162–66.
11. TJ, "The Anas," Ford, *Writings of TJ,* 1:164–65.
12. Alexander Hamilton to Washington, 5 May 1789, *The Papers of Alexander Hamilton,* ed. Harold C. Syrett and Jacob Cooke (New York: Columbia University Press, 1961–1987), 5:335–37.
13. JA to BR, 9 June 1789, *Old Family Letters,* 38.
14. JA to Tench Coxe, May 1792, PJA–MHS; Gordon S. Wood, *Empire of Liberty: A History of the Early Republic, 1789–1815* (New York: Oxford University Press, 2009), 100.
15. Montesquieu, *Spirit of the Laws,* trans. Thomas Nugent, ed. Franz Neumann (New York: Hafner, 1949), 1:bk. xx, ch. 13, p. 323.
16. TJ, "Final State of the Report on Commerce," 16 Dec. 1793, *PTJ,* 27:574.
17. TJ to JM, 25 Mar. 1793, *Republic of Letters,* 765–66.
18. TJ, *Notes on the State of Virginia,* ed. William Peden (Chapel Hill: University of North Carolina Press, 1955), 105; TJ to JM, 20 Dec. 1787, *Republic of Letters,* 514.
19. TJ to BR, 23 Sept. 1800, *PTJ,* 32:167.
20. Bray Hammond, *Banks and Politics in America from the Revolution to the Civil War* (Princeton, N.J.: Princeton University Press, 1957), 66.
21. TJ to JM, 1 Oct. 1792, *Republic of Letters,* 740.
22. TJ to John Taylor, 28 May 1816, *PTJ: RS,* 10:89; TJ to Col. Charles Yancey, 6 Jan. 1816, ibid., 9:329; Dumas Malone, *The Sage of Monticello* (Boston: Little, Brown, 1981), 139–46 (quote at 141), 148–50.
23. The most important of these tie-breaking votes determined that the president did not have to have the consent of the Senate in order to remove an individual from an office that had required the Senate's approval for appointment. Wood, *Empire of Liberty,* 87–88.
24. Warren Jr., "In the Shadow of Washington," 132.

25. JA to AA, 23 Nov. 1794, *AFC*, 10:270.
26. AA to JA, 12 Jan. 1794, *AFC*, 10:36.
27. JA to AA, 9 Jan. 1793, *AFC*, 9:376; Hammond, *Banks and Politics*, 188–89, 196.
28. Jane Kamensky, *The Exchange Artist: A Tale of High-Flying Speculation and America's First Banking Collapse* (New York: Viking, 2008), 9, 160.
29. JA to Richard Cranch, 4 July 1786, *AFC*, 7:240–41.
30. JA to AA, 11 Mar. 1794, *AFC*, 10:109.
31. JA, *Discourses on Davila: A Series of Papers on Political History*, in *Works of JA*, 6:227–399 (quote at 232).
32. JA, *Discourses on Davila*, in *Works of JA*, 6:246. Zoltán Haraszti, in *John Adams and the Prophets of Progress* (Cambridge, Mass.: Harvard University Press, 1952), 169–70, claims that JA borrowed largely from Adam Smith's chapter on "The Origins of Ambition and the Distinction of Ranks" in his *Theory of Moral Sentiments* (1759). Although JA did tend to borrow heavily from writings that seemed to answer his emotional needs at the moment, his account of the passion for distinction seems actually richer than Smith's treatment, at least in that particular chapter.
33. JA, *Discourses on Davila*, in *Works of JA*, 6:233–34, 245, 256; "Discourse on Davila," *Gazette of the United States*, 27 Apr. 1791. In 1805 all the essays of *Discourses on Davila*, except the last one (dated 21 April 1791), were gathered together and published in Boston as a book. Presumably because it so emphatically endorsed hereditary succession over elections, this final essay was omitted from the 1805 reprint and from Charles Francis Adams's edition of the work.
34. TJ to C. W. F. Dumas, 23 June 1790, *PTJ*, 16:552.
35. Julian P. Boyd, "Jefferson's Alliance in 1790 with Fenno's *Gazette of the United States*," *PTJ*, 16:244.
36. JA to Mercy Otis Warren, 25 Dec. 1787, PJA–MHS.
37. Notes of a Conversation Between A. Hamilton and TJ, 13 Aug. 1791, Ford, ed., *Writings of TJ*, 1:168–69.
38. JA to Washington, 17 May 1789, in *The Papers of George Washington: Presidential Series*, ed. Dorothy Twohig (Charlottesville: University of Virginia Press, 1987–), 2:313–14; TJ to BR, 4 Oct. 1807, *PTJ*, 41:471; AA to Cranch, 11 Oct. 1789, *AFC*, 8:421; AA to JA, 20 Oct. 1789, ibid., 8:426; T. H. Breen, *George Washington's Journey* (New York: Simon and Schuster, 2016), 66, 17–18.
39. JA to John Trumbull, 9 Mar. 1790, PJA–MHS.
40. TJ to JM, 9 May 1791, *PTJ*, 20:293.
41. AA to Cranch, 3 Apr. 1790, *AFC*, 9:40.
42. George W. Corner, ed., *The Autobiography of Benjamin Rush: His "Travels Through Life" Together with His Commonplace Book for 1789–1813* (Princeton, N.J.: Princeton University Press, 1948), 181.
43. JA to TJ, 2 Jan. 1789, Cappon, 1:234.
44. Rush assured JA that in his correspondence "you may rely upon secrecy whenever your letters are confidential." BR to JA, 21 Feb. 1789, *Letters of Rush*, 1:502.
45. JA to BR, 4 Apr. 1790, *Old Family Letters*, 57; JA to BR, 19 June 1789, ibid., 40; JA to BR, 5 July 1789, ibid., 41; JA to BR, 28 July 1789, ibid., 48; JA to BR, 24 July 1789, ibid. 46–47; JA to BR, 9 June 1789, ibid., 37–38; JA, *Diary*, 1:355.
46. JA to BR, 4 Apr. 1790, *Old Family Letters*, 55–57.
47. TJ to Washington, 8 Mar. 1791, *PTJ*, 20:291.

48. TJ to Sir John Sinclair, 24 Aug. 1791, *PTJ*, 22:72; TJ to George Mason, 4 Feb. 1791, ibid., 19:241.

49. TJ to Mason, 4 Feb. 1791, *PTJ*, 19:241.

50. TJ to Mason, 4 Feb. 1791, *PTJ*, 19:241; TJ to Washington, 8 May 1791, ibid., 20:291; TJ to Thomas Mann Randolph Jr., 15 May 1791, ibid., 20:416.

51. TJ to Jonathan B. Smith, 20 Apr. 1791, *PTJ*, 20:290. In this volume, the last he edited, Julian P. Boyd composed several lengthy notes, one of which was "*Rights of Man:* The 'Contest of Burke and Paine in America,'" *PTJ*, 20:268–90.

52. Tobias Lear to Washington, 8 May 1791, quoted in Boyd, "*Rights of Man,*" *PTJ*, 20:277; TJ to Washington, 8 May 1791, ibid., 20:292.

53. TJ to T. M. Randolph Jr., 3 July 1791, *PTJ*, 20:296; JM to TJ, 12 May 1791, ibid., 20:294.

54. [JQA] Publicola, "Observations on Paine's Rights of Man," Boston *Columbian Centinel,* 8 June 1791.

55. Madison told TJ that Publicola was not Adams himself, but probably his son John Quincy Adams. JM to TJ, 13 July 1791, *PTJ*, 20:295–99.

56. TJ to JA, 17 July 1791, *PTJ*, 20:302.

57. JA to TJ, 29 July 1791, *PTJ*, 20: 305–7.

58. JA to Henry Knox, 19 June 1791, PJA–MHS. Abigail too was much offended by TJ's note, blaming "envy and jealousy" for the incident. AA to Martha Washington, 25 June 1791, *AFC*, 9:218–19.

59. TJ to JA, 30 Aug. 1791, *PTJ*, 20:310–11.

60. TJ to Thomas Paine, 29 July 1791, *PTJ*, 20:308–9; TJ to Paine, 19 June 1792, ibid., 20:312.

61. TJ to JA, 25 Nov. 1791, Cappon, 1:252; TJ to JA, 1 Mar. 1793, ibid., 1:252–53.

62. S. W. Jackman, "A Young Englishman Reports on the New Nation: Edward Thornton to James Bland Burges, 1791–1793," *WMQ* 18 (1961): 110.

63. Jack McLaughlin, *Jefferson and Monticello: The Biography of a Builder* (New York: Henry Holt, 1988), 248–55, 364; Annette Gordon-Reed and Peter S. Onuf, "*Most Blessed of the Patriarchs": Thomas Jefferson and the Empire of the Imagination* (New York: Norton, 2016), 249.

64. *National Gazette,* 20 Feb. 1792.

65. Stanley Elkins and Eric McKitrick, *The Age of Federalism: The Early American Republic, 1788–1800* (New York: Oxford University Press, 1993), 285.

66. TJ to Edmund Randolph, 17 Sept. 1792, *PTJ*, 24:387.

67. TJ, "Notes of Conversations with the President," 28–29 Feb. 1792, in Ford, *Writings of TJ*, 1:174–78.

68. TJ to Washington, 23 May 1792, *PTJ*, 23:535–40.

69. TJ to Thomas Pinckney, 3 Dec. 1792, *PTJ*, 24:696.

70. JA to AA, 28 Dec. 1792, *AFC*, 9:360; TJ to Pinckney, 3 Dec. 1792, *PTJ*, 24:697.

71. JA to AA, 19 Dec. 1793, *AFC*, 9:477.

72. TJ to David Humphreys, 2 Jan. 1793, *PTJ*, 25:9.

73. On JA's unpopularity in Virginia, see Archibald Stuart to TJ, 6 Dec. 1792, *PTJ*, 24:704–5. Governor George Clinton of New York was spreading rumors that Hamilton in 1787 had sought to establish a monarchical government in the United States and that JA at the same time had endorsed British overtures to help bring this about. There is no credible evidence for either plan, and TJ remained skeptical upon hearing the rumors. *PTJ*, 26:220–22n.

74. JA to AA, 3 Feb. 1793, *AFC*, 9:390.
75. TJ, "Notes of a Cabinet Meeting and Conversations with Edmond Charles Genet," 5 July 1793, *PTJ*, 26:438.
76. JA to AA, 28 Dec. 1792, *AFC*, 9:360; JA to AA, 3 Feb. 1793, ibid., 9:390. TJ's heavy lingering debts came not simply from his lavish style of living but also from the debts incurred when he inherited his father-in-law's estate in 1774.
77. TJ to JM, 19 May 1793, *Republic of Letters*, 2:775.
78. JA to Henry Marchant, 4 May 1794, PJA–MHS.
79. JA to AA, 27 Jan, 1793, *AFC*, 9:381.
80. JA to AA, 17 Feb. 1793, *AFC*, 9:406.
81. JA to Charles Adams, 18 Mar. 1793, *AFC*, 9:419; TJ, "Notes on John Adams and the French Revolution," 15 Jan. 1793, *PTJ*, 25:63–64; JA to Francis Van der Kemp, 11 Dec. 1793, PJA–MHS.
82. JA to John Stockdale, 12 May 1793, PJA–MHS; JA to C. Adams, 19 May 1794, *AFC*, 10:183.
83. TJ to William Short, 3 Jan. 1793, *PTJ*, 25:14. With its extreme statements, this letter led the Irish historian and journalist Conor Cruise O'Brien to say that "the twentieth-century statesman whom Thomas Jefferson of 1793 would have admired most is Pol Pot," the brutal leader of the Khmer Rouge, which killed an estimated two million people in Cambodia in the 1970s. O'Brien, *The Long Affair: Thomas Jefferson and the French Revolution, 1789–1800* (Chicago: University of Chicago Press, 1996), 150.
84. Drew R. McCoy, *The Last of the Fathers: James Madison and the Republican Legacy* (Cambridge: Cambridge University Press, 1989), 144.
85. James Roger Sharp, *American Politics in the Early Republic: The New Nation in Crisis* (New Haven: Yale University Press, 1993), 79.
86. TJ to JM, 28 Apr. 1793, *PTJ*, 25:619.
87. JA to Coxe, 25 Apr. 1793, PJA–MHS; TJ to JM, 11 Aug. 1793, *PTJ*, 26:652; Joanne B. Freeman, *Affairs of Honor: National Politics in the New Republic* (New Haven: Yale University Press, 2001), 45.
88. Enoch Edwards to TJ, 28 Oct. 1793, *PTJ*, 27:276.
89. TJ to Angelica Schuyler Church, 27 Nov. 1793, *PTJ*, 27:449.
90. TJ to Washington, 31 July 1793, *PTJ*, 26:593.
91. JA to AA, 26 Dec. 1793, *AFC*, 9:484-85; JA to JQA, 3 Jan. 1794, *AFC*, 10:3–4.
92. JA to AA, 6 Jan. 1794, *AFC*, 10:29–30.
93. JA to TJ, 4 Apr. 1794, Cappon, 1:252, 253.
94. TJ to JA, 25 Apr. 1794, Cappon, 1:254.
95. JA to TJ, 11 May 1794, Cappon, 1:255.
96. JA to TJ, 31 Jan. 1796, Cappon, 1:259.
97. TJ to JA, 28 Feb. 1796, Cappon, 1:259–60.
98. "Documents Relating to the 1796 Campaign for Electors in Virginia," *PTJ*, 29:194.
99. JA to Joseph Priestley, 12 May 1793, PJA–MHS.
100. Dumas Malone, *Jefferson and the Ordeal of Liberty* (Boston: Little, Brown, 1962), 71.
101. TJ to Coxe, 1 May 1794, *PTJ*, 28:67.
102. JA to AA, 9 Feb. 1794, *AFC*, 10:74.
103. JA to TJ, 30 June 1813, Cappon, 2:346–47.

104. TJ to Coxe, 1 May 1794, *PTJ*, 28:67.
105. JA to Jeremy Belknap, 18 Feb. 1793, PJA–MHS; JA to Stockdale, 12 May 1793, PJA–MHS.
106. JM to TJ, 25 May 1794, *Republic of Letters*, 2:845; JA to AA, 19 Apr. 1794, *AFC*, 10:148, JA to AA, 14 June 1795, ibid., 10:450.
107. TJ to Philip Mazzei, 8 Sept. 1795, *PTJ*, 28:457.
108. TJ to William Branch Giles, 27 Apr. 1795, *PTJ*, 28:337.
109. JA to C. Adams, 9 Jan 1794, *AFC*, 10:19–20; JA to C. Adams, 24 Feb 1794, ibid., 10:27–29; JA to C. Adams, 11 May 1794, ibid., 10:173–74.
110. JA to C. Adams, 24 Dec. 1794, *AFC*, 10:319–20. In December 1794 the Virginia congressman William Branch Giles proposed an amendment to the naturalization bill requiring aliens to renounce all hereditary titles before being granted American citizenship. *AFC*, 10:349n.

NINE: THE PRESIDENT VS. THE VICE PRESIDENT

1. TJ to David Humphreys, 18 Mar. 1789, *PTJ*, 14:679; James Wilson, "Lectures on Law" (1790–91), in *The Works of James Wilson*, ed. Robert Green McCloskey (Cambridge, Mass.: Harvard University Press, 1967), 1:288.
2. Diego de Gardoqui, quoted in Kathleen DuVal, *Independence Lost: Lives on the Edge of the American Revolution* (New York: Random House, 2015), 339.
3. JA to AA, 5 Jan. 1796, *AFC*, 11:122; JA to AA, 20 Jan. 1796, ibid., 11:141; JA to AA, 7 Jan. 1796, ibid., 11:130; JA to AA, 2 Feb. 1796, ibid., 11:149.
4. JA to AA, 5 Jan. 1796, *AFC*, 11:122; JA to AA, 7 Jan. 1796, ibid., 11:131.
5. TJ to Francis Hopkinson, 13 Mar. 1789, *PTJ*, 14:650; JA to Jonathan Jackson, 2 Oct. 1780, *PJA*, 10:192.
6. JA to AA, 10 Feb. 1796, *AFC*, 11:171.
7. JA to AA, 10 Feb. 1796, *AFC*, 11:172.
8. TJ to JM, 27 Apr. 1795, *Republic of Letters*, 2:877; TJ to JM, 9 June 1793, ibid., 2:781.
9. TJ to Mary Jefferson Eppes, 3 Mar. 1802, *PTJ*, 36:676; Annette Gordon-Reed and Peter S. Onuf, *"Most Blessed of the Patriarchs": Thomas Jefferson and the Empire of the Imagination* (New York: Norton, 2016), 74.
10. TJ to William Branch Giles, 31 Dec. 1795, *PTJ*, 28:566.
11. TJ to JM, 27 Apr. 1795, *Republic of Letters*, 2:877. Sometime later, someone crossed out "Southern" and substituted "Republican" on TJ's copy of the letter. Madison's recipient copy reads "Southern." Since Jefferson later claimed that "the republicans are the *nation*," it is likely that it was he who made the change. TJ to William Duane, 28 Mar. 1811, *PTJ: RS*, 3:8. See also TJ to JM, 27 Apr. 1795, in JM, *Papers*, ed. William T. Hutchinson and William M. E. Rachal (Chicago: University of Chicago Press, 1962–1991), 16:2n; and James Roger Sharp, "Unraveling the Mystery of Jefferson's Letter of April 27, 1795," *JER* 6 (1986): 411–18.
12. Joanne B. Freeman, "The Presidential Election of 1796," in *John Adams and the Founding of the Republic*, ed. Richard Alan Ryerson (Boston: Northeastern University Press, 2001), 145.
13. Jeffrey L. Pasley, *The First Presidential Contest: 1796 and the Founding of American Democracy* (Lawrence: University Press of Kansas, 2013), 224.

14. James Roger Sharp, *American Politics in the Early Republic: The New Nation in Crisis* (New Haven: Yale University Press, 1993), 149.

15. JA to AA, 18 Dec. 1796, *AFC*, 11:447; JA to Charles Adams, 30 Dec. 1796, ibid., 11:469; JA to Henry Knox, 30 Mar. 1797, *JA: Writings from the New Nation*, 336–37; Freeman, "The Presidential Election of 1796," 148; JA to AA, 12 Dec. 1796, *AFC*, 11:444.

16. TJ to Benjamin Banneker, 30 Aug. 1791, *PTJ*, 22:97–98; TJ, *Notes on the State of Virginia*, ed. William Peden (Chapel Hill: University of North Carolina Press, 1955), 159; Pasley, *First Presidential Contest*, 29, 263, 254.

17. JA, *A Defence of the Constitutions of Government of the United States of America: A New Edition* (London: John Stockton, 1794), 3:296; Pasley, *First Presidential Contest*, 283.

18. JA to AA, 9 Jan. 1797, *AFC*, 11:487.

19. JM to TJ, 19 Dec. 1796, *Republic of Letters*, 2:951.

20. JA to AA, 20 Dec. 1796, *AFC*, 11:451.

21. TJ, "Notes on Comments by John Adams," 26 Dec. 1796, *PTJ*, 29:593.

22. AA to Elbridge Gerry, 31 Dec. 1796, *AFC*, 11:476; Gerry to AA, 7 Jan. 1797, ibid., 11:486; Sharp, *American Politics in the Early Republic*, 158.

23. JA to AA, 9 Jan. 1797, *AFC*, 11:487; JA to AA, 27 Dec. 1796, ibid., 11:451.

24. AA to JA, 15 Jan. 1797, *AFC*, 11:499.

25. TJ to JM, 8 Jan. 1797, *Republic of Letters*, 2:955.

26. TJ to JM, 17 Dec. 1796, *Republic of Letters*, 2:950; TJ to JM, 1 Jan. 1797, ibid., 2:953.

27. Enclosure, TJ to JA, 28 Dec. 1796, *Republic of Letters*, 2:954.

28. JM to TJ, 15 Jan. 1797, *Republic of Letters*, 2:957.

29. TJ to John Langdon, 22 Jan. 1797, *PTJ*, 29:270.

30. TJ to JM, 15 Jan. 1797, *Republic of Letters*, 2:957; JA to AA, 1 Jan. 1796, *AFC*, 11:480–81; JA to AA, 3 Jan. 1796, ibid., 11:482.

31. TJ to Thomas Mann Randolph, 22 Jan. 1797, *PTJ*, 29:273–74.

32. JA to Benjamin Lincoln, 10 Mar. 1800, PJA–MHS; JA to BR, 19 Mar. 1812, *Spur of Fame*, 214; JM to TJ, 11 Feb. 1797, *PTJ*, 29:304–5. Actually, as vice president and president of the Senate, Adams had cast a crucial tie-breaking vote denying that the Senate's consent was needed for presidential removals from office.

33. JA to BR, 23 Aug. 1805, *Spur of Fame*, 36; JA to BR, 19 Mar. 1812, ibid., 214; TJ to Gerry, 13 May 1797, *PTJ*, 29:362.

34. JA, "Correspondence Published in the *Boston Patriot*," 1809, *Works of JA*, 9:284–86.

35. JA to Gerry, 6 Apr. 1797, PJA–MHS.

36. TJ, "The Anas, 1791–1806," in *The Writings of Thomas Jefferson*, ed. Paul Leicester Ford (New York: G. P. Putnam's Sons, 1892), 1:272–73; TJ, "Notes on Conversations," post 13 Oct. 1797, *PTJ*, 29:551–52.

37. JA, "Correspondence Published in the *Boston Patriot*," 9:285.

38. JA to AA, 5 Mar. 1797, *AFC*, 12:9; JA to AA, 9 Mar. 1797, ibid., 12:17.

39. JA, Inaugural Address, 4 Mar. 1797, *JA: Writings from the New Nation*, 330, 333.

40. JA to AA, 5 Mar. 1797, *AFC*, 12:10; JA to AA, 17 Mar. 1797, ibid., 12:33.

41. Paine to TJ, 1 Apr. 1797, *PTJ*, 29:340–44.

42. JA to BR, 23 Aug. 1805, *Spur of Fame*, 36; JA, "Correspondence Published in the *Boston Patriot*," 9:284–86. Ironically, on this issue JA's ministers were more High Federalist than Hamilton himself; he had actually suggested that Madison be part of a commission to negotiate with the French. Only someone with JM's

Republican credentials, Hamilton had said, could convince the French of America's good faith.

43. TJ, "The Anas," Ford, *Writings of TJ*, 1:273.

44. JA to AA, 13 Mar. 1797, *AFC*, 12:23.

45. JQA to JA, 4 Apr. 1796 and 3 Feb. 1797, *Founders Online*, National Archives; Richard H. Kohn, *Eagle and Sword: The Federalists and the Creation of the Military Establishment in America, 1783–1802* (New York: Free Press, 1975), 205–6.

46. JA, "Speech to Congress," 16 May 1797, *Works of JA*, 9:114.

47. TJ to Peregrine Fitzhugh, 4 June 1797, *PTJ*, 29:416–17.

48. JA to Uriah Forrest, 28 June 1797, *Works of JA*, 8:546–47.

49. "Extract Printed in the New York *Minerva*," 2 May 1797, *PTJ*, 29:86; for the original letter, see TJ to Mazzei, 24 Apr. 1796, *PTJ*, 29:82. See also François Furstenberg, *When the United States Spoke French: Five Refugees Who Shaped a Nation* (New York: Penguin Press, 2014), 358.

50. AA to JQA, 15 June 1797, *AFC*, 12:164–65.

51. JQA to AA, 29 July 1797, *AFC*, 12:224–25.

52. JA to Gerry, 3 May 1797, PJA–MHS.

53. AA to JQA, 3 Nov. 1797, *AFC*, 12:278.

54. AA to Thomas Boylston Adams, 16 July 1797, *AFC*, 12:207; TJ, "Notes on a Conversation with Benjamin Rush," 5 Apr. 1798, *PTJ*, 30:248.

55. TJ to Edward Rutledge, 24 June 1797, *PTJ*, 29:455–56; TJ to Angelica Schuyler Church, 11 Jan. 1798, ibid., 30:23.

56. TJ to JM, 8 Feb. 1798, *Republic of Letters*, 2:1017.

57. TJ, "Notes on a Conversation with John Adams," 15 Feb. 1798, *PTJ*, 30:113.

58. TJ to Gerry, 13 May 1797, *PTJ*, 29:363.

59. JA to JQA, 31 Mar. 1797, *AFC*, 12:56.

60. JA to Timothy Pickering, 23 Sept. 1799, PJA–MHS; JA to AA, 1 Jan. 1799, AFC–MHS.

61. George A. Billias, *Elbridge Gerry: Founding Father and Republican Statesman* (New York: McGraw-Hill, 1976), 274.

62. TJ to JM, 21–22 Mar. 1798, *Republic of Letters*, 2:1029; JM to TJ, 2 Apr. 1798, ibid., 2:1032.

63. AA to JQA, 4 Apr. 1798, *AFC*, 12:481, AA to Mary Cranch, 9 Apr. 1798, ibid., 12:491; AA to Cranch, 4 Apr. 1798, ibid., 12:485.

64. TJ to JM, 6 Apr. 1798, *Republic of Letters*, 2:1035; TJ to JM, 19 Apr. 1798, ibid., 2:1039; TJ to James Monroe, 5 Apr. 1798, *PTJ*, 30:247.

65. TJ to JM, 6 Apr. 1798, *Republic of Letters*, 2:1035; TJ to Peter Carr, 12 Apr. 1798, *PTJ*, 30:267; TJ to T. M. Randolph, 12 Apr. 1798, ibid., 30:269–70; TJ to T. M. Randolph, 19 Apr. 1798, ibid., 30:283.

66. "Address from the Grand Inquest of the United States of America, for the District of Pennsylvania," 13 Apr. 1798, in James Morton Smith, *Freedom's Fetters: The Alien and Sedition Laws and American Civil Liberties* (Ithaca, N.Y.: Cornell University Press, 1956), 97; "Address from the Inhabitants of Richmond," 1 June 1798, PJA–MHS.

67. JA, "To the Second Battalion of Militia of Prince George County, Virginia," 6 June 1798, in *JA: Writings from the New Nation*, 367; JA, "To the Grand Jury for Plymouth County, Massachusetts," 28 May 1798, ibid., 366; JA, "To the Young Men of the City of Philadelphia, the District of Southwark, and the Northern Liberties, Pennsylvania," 2 May 1798, in *Works of JA*, 9:188.

68. TJ, "Notes on JA's Replies to XYZ Addresses," ante 6 Oct. 1800, *PTJ*, 32:196–202; TJ to JM, 3 May 1798, ibid., 30:322; TJ to T. M. Randolph, 3 May 1798, ibid., 30:326. Jefferson sent his notes on Adams's answers to the Philadelphia *Aurora*, believing that excerpts from them could benefit the Republican cause.

69. TJ to William G. Munford, 18 June 1799, *PTJ*, 31:128.

70. JA, "To the Society of the Cincinnati, South Carolina," 15 Sept. 1798, PJA–MHS.

71. AA to Cranch, 13 May 1798, AFC–MHS.

72. TJ to JM, 17 May 1798, *PTJ*, 30:353; AA to JQA, 21 Apr. 1798, in Edith Gelles, ed., *Abigail Adams: Letters* (New York: Library of America, 2016), 617; Alexander DeConde, *The Quasi-War: Politics and Diplomacy of the Undeclared War with France, 1797–1801* (New York: Scribner, 1966), 82; TJ to A. Church, 11 Jan. 1798, *PTJ*, 30:23.

73. JA to TJ, 30 June 1813, Cappon, 2:347.

74. JA to TJ, 30 June 1813, Cappon, 2:347; AA to Cranch, 10 May 1798, in Gelles, *Abigail Adams: Letters*, 622–24.

75. AA to Cranch, 26 Apr. 1798, 21 Apr. 1798, *AFC*, 12:531, 520.

76. JA to William Tudor, 19 Jan. 1817, PJA–MHS.

77. Furstenberg, *When the United States Spoke French*, 115.

78. TJ to JM, 6 Apr. 1798, *Republic of Letters*, 2:1034–35.

79. Smith, *Freedom's Fetters*, 26.

80. Furstenberg, *When the United States Spoke French*, 375.

81. DeConde, *The Quasi-War*, 328.

82. AA to JQA, 14 July 1798, AFC–MHS; AA to JQA, 29 Mar. 1798, in Gelles, *Abigail Adams: Letters*, 608; AA to JQA, 26 May 1798, ibid., 626; Page Smith, *John Adams* (New York: Doubleday, 1962), 2:979.

83. TJ, *Notes on the State of Virginia*, 84–85.

84. Furstenberg, *When the United States Spoke French*, 97, 91, 109.

85. AA to Cranch, 20 May 1798, in Smith, *Freedom's Fetters*, 53.

86. JA to TJ, 14 June 1813, Cappon, 2:329; TJ to JM, 31 May 1798, *PTJ*, 30:379; TJ to T. M. Randolph, 9 May 1798, ibid., 30:341.

87. JA to Pickering, 17 Sept. 1798, PJA–MHS; Kenneth Roberts and Anna M. Roberts, eds., *Moreau de St. Méry's American Journey, 1793–1798* (Garden City, N.Y.: Doubleday, 1947), 253.

88. TJ to JM, 19 Apr. 1798, *Republic of Letters*, 2:1042.

89. Smith, *Freedom's Fetters*, 116; John C. Miller, *The Federalist Era, 1789–1801* (New York: Harper, 1960), 233.

90. JA to James Lloyd, 11 Feb. 1815, *Works of JA*, 10:117; JA to BR, 28 Aug. 1811, ibid., 9:636.

91. Boston *Evening Post*, 1 Dec. 1766.

92. For JA's evolving ideas of free speech, see Richard D. Brown, "The Disenchantment of a Radical Whig: John Adams Reckons with Free Speech," in *John Adams and the Founding of the Republic*, ed. Richard Alan Ryerson (Boston: Northeastern University Press, 2001), 171–85.

93. TJ to Monroe, 5 May 1811, *PTJ: RS*, 3:607; TJ to Thomas McKean, 19 Feb. 1803, *PTJ*, 39:553; Leonard W. Levy, *Jefferson and Civil Liberties: The Darker Side* (Cambridge, Mass.: Harvard University Press, 1963), 42–69.

94. JA, *Boston Patriot*, 10 June 1805, *Works of JA*, 9:305–6.

95. TJ to John Taylor, 4 June 1798, *PTJ*, 30:388–89.

96. TJ to Stevens Thomas Mason, 11 Oct. 1798, *PTJ*, 30:560; TJ to Gerry, 26 Jan. 1799, ibid., 30:646.

97. TJ to T. M. Randolph, 2 Feb. 1800, *PTJ*, 31:358; TJ to BR, 23 Sept. 1800, ibid., 32:167.

98. TJ to Monroe, 7 Sept. 1797, *PTJ*, 29:527; TJ to Taylor, 26 Nov. 1798, ibid., 30:589.

99. TJ, "Draft of Kentucky Resolutions of 1798," ante 4 Oct. 1798, *PTJ*, 30:531–32, 536–41.

100. JA to Oliver Wolcott Jr., 24 Sept. 1798, *Works of JA*, 8:603–4. Although this letter was never sent, it fully expressed JA's passionate feelings at the time. Hamilton was born in Nevis in 1755, which, of course, was then just as much a British colony as Massachusetts.

101. JA to James McHenry, 22 Oct. 1798, *Works of JA*, 8:613.

102. TJ to JM, 3 Jan. 1798, *PTJ*, 30:610.

103. JA to Charles Lee, 29 Mar. 1799, PJA–MHS.

104. JA to Pickering, 23 Apr. 1800, PJA–MHS.

105. A. Roger Ekirch, *American Sanctuary: Mutiny, Martyrdom, and National Identity in the Age of Revolution* (New York: Pantheon, 2017), 133, 143–67; TJ to Charles Pinckney, 29 Oct. 1799, TJ to T. M. Randolph, 2 Feb. 1800, TJ to JM, 4 Mar. 1800, TJ, "Notes on John Marshall's Speech," post 7 Mar. 1800, *PTJ*, 31: 227, 358, 408, 421, 181–82n.

106. Noble E. Cunningham Jr., *The Jeffersonian Republicans: The Formation of Party Organization, 1789–1801* (Chapel Hill: University of North Carolina Press, 1957), 116–74; JA to Benjamin Stoddert, 21 Sept. 1799, PJA–MHS.

107. McHenry to JA, 31 May 1800, PJA–MHS, recounting the conversation of the previous day.

108. Stephen G. Kurtz, *The Presidency of John Adams: The Collapse of Federalism, 1795–1800* (Philadelphia: University of Pennsylvania Press, 1957), 397.

109. Alexander Hamilton to McHenry, 6 June 1800, in *The Papers of Alexander Hamilton*, eds. Harold C. Syrett and Jacob E. Cooke (New York: Columbia University Press, 1961–1987), 24:573.

110. Gouverneur Morris, 13 May 1800, *The Diary and Letters of Gouverneur Morris*, ed. Anne Cary Morris (New York: Scribner's Sons, 1888), 2:387.

111. George Washington to Jonathan Trumbull Jr., 21 July 1799, in *The Papers of George Washington: Retirement Series*, eds. Dorothy Twohig et al. (Charlottesville: University Press of Virginia, 1998–1999), 4:202.

112. AA to JA, 3 Mar. 1799, PJA–MHS.

113. Joanne B. Freeman, *Affairs of Honor: National Politics in the New Republic* (New Haven: Yale University Press, 2001), 111; JA to Lloyd, 28 Jan. 1815, *Works of JA*, 10:113.

114. TJ, "First Inaugural Address," 4 Mar. 1801, *TJ: Writings*, 494.

115. JA to John Trumbull, 10 Sept. 1800, PJA–MHS.

TEN: THE JEFFERSONIAN REVOLUTION OF 1800

1. TJ to Spencer Roane, 6 Sept. 1819, *The Writings of Thomas Jefferson*, ed. Paul Leicester Ford (New York: G. P. Putnam's Sons, 1892), 10:140.

2. TJ, "First Inaugural Address," 4 Mar. 1801, *PTJ*, 33:148–52.
3. Elbridge Gerry to TJ, 4 May 1801, *PTJ*, 34:23.
4. David Austin to TJ, 15 May 1801, *PTJ*, 34:111; JA to Thomas Boylston Adams, 9 Sept. 1801, PJA–MHS.
5. Michael A. Bellesiles, "'The Soil Will Be Soaked with Blood': Taking the Revolution Seriously," in *The Revolution of 1800: Democracy, Race, and the New Republic*, ed. James Horn, Jan Ellen Lewis, and Peter S. Horn (Charlottesville: University of Virginia Press, 2002), 59; John Ferling, *Adams vs. Jefferson: The Tumultuous Election of 1800* (New York: Oxford University Press, 2004), 136–37, 145.
6. TJ to Aaron Burr, 11 Feb. 1799, *PTJ*, 31:22; TJ to JM, 12 Feb. 1799, ibid., 31:229–30. See also Donald R. Hickey, "America's Response to the Slave Revolt in Haiti, 1791–1806," *JER* 2 (1982): 361–79.
7. TJ to BR, 16 Jan. 1811, *PTJ: RS*, 3:305–6.
8. JA to Gerry, 30 Dec. 1800, *Works of JA*, 9:578; AA to T. B. Adams, 25 Jan. 1801, PJA–MHS.
9. AA, "A Conversation Between Abigail Adams and Thomas Jefferson," Jan. 1801, PJA–MHS.
10. JA to Samuel Smith, 7 Feb. 1801, PJA–MHS.
11. TJ to John Dickinson, 6 Mar. 1801, *PTJ*, 33:196; TJ to Joseph Priestley, 21 Mar. 1801, ibid., 33:393–94.
12. TJ to Priestley, 21 Mar. 1801, *PTJ*, 33:393–94. Although in 1799 Timothy Pickering had wanted Priestley deported, JA told his secretary of state that it would not be wise to do so. "Poor Priestly . . . is as weak as water. . . . His influence is not an Atom in the World." JA had been much more eager to deport Frenchmen. JA to Timothy Pickering, 13 Aug. 1799, PJA–MHS. See also Priestley to TJ, 10 Aug. 1801, *PTJ*, 33:567, in which Priestley explained that although JA as president could not have directly opposed his deportation, he had used "circuitous" means to prevent it.
13. TJ to JM, 19 Dec. 1800, *PTJ*, 32:323.
14. TJ to JA, 17 Jan. 1801, *PTJ*, 32:476.
15. Elizabeth House Trist to TJ, 1 Mar. 1801, *PTJ*, 33:115; TJ, "First Inaugural Address," 4 Mar. 1801, ibid., 33:149.
16. Fisher Ames to Rufus King, 24 Sept. 1800, 26 Aug. 1800, Charles R. King, ed., *The Life and Correspondence of Rufus King* (New York: G. P. Putnam's Sons, 1896), 3:304, 295–97.
17. TJ to BR, 16 Jan. 1811, *PTJ: RS*, 3:305–6. See TJ, "The Anas," Ford, *Writings of TJ*, 1:313, for a somewhat different account of the meeting with JA. See also Dumas Malone, *Jefferson the President: First Term, 1801–1805* (Boston: Little, Brown, 1970), 8.
18. Malone, *Jefferson the President: First Term*, 41.
19. TJ to JA, 8 Mar. 1801, JA to TJ, 24 Mar. 1801, Cappon, 1:264.
20. Thomas Paine, *Common sense: The Rights of Man: Part Second*, in *The Complete Writings of Thomas Paine*, ed. Philip S. Foner (New York: Citadel Press, 1969), 1:4, 356.
21. James Wilson, "Lectures on Law" (1790), in *The Works of James Wilson*, ed. Robert Green McCloskey (Cambridge Mass.: Harvard University Press, 1967), 1:214.
22. TJ to Thomas Law, 13 June 1814, *PTJ: RS*, 7:414.
23. Nathaniel Chipman, *Sketches of the Principles of Government* (Rutland, Vt., 1792), 83–85.

24. TJ to Peter Carr, 10 Aug. 1787, *PTJ,* 12:15; TJ, *Notes on the State of Virginia,* ed. William Peden (Chapel Hill: University of North Carolina Press, 1955), 142–43.

25. Paine, *The Rights of Man: Part Second,* 1:373; TJ to Governor John Langdon, Mar. 5, 1810, *TJ: Writings,* 1221.

26. JA to AA, 29 Oct. 1775, *AFC,* 1:318.

27. JA to T. B. Adams, 2 Feb. 1803, PJA–MHS; JA to T. B. Adams, ? Feb. 1803, ibid.

28. JA to T. B. Adams, ? Feb. 1803, PJA–MHS.

29. Washington *National Intelligencer,* 6 Mar. 1801; Malone, *Jefferson the President: First Term,* 388.

30. Malone, *Jefferson the President: First Term,* 383, 387, 93.

31. TJ, "Circular to the Heads of Departments," 6 Nov. 1801, *PTJ,* 35:577.

32. TJ, "First Annual Message," 8 Dec. 1801, *TJ: Writings,* 504.

33. Noble E. Cunningham Jr., *The Process of Government Under Jefferson* (Princeton, N.J.: Princeton University Press, 1978), 22.

34. TJ, "First Annual Message," 504.

35. TJ to William Branch Giles, 23 Mar. 1801, *PTJ,* 33:413–14; TJ to William Findley, 24 Mar. 1801, ibid., 33:427–28; TJ to George Jefferson, 27 Mar. 1801, ibid., 33:465.

36. TJ to James Monroe, 20 June 1801, *PTJ,* 34:398–99; TJ to Thomas Mann Randolph, 18 June 1801, ibid., 34:384.

37. TJ to Samuel Adams, 26 Feb. 1800, *PTJ,* 31:395.

38. Ian W. Toll, *Six Frigates: The Epic History of the Founding of the U.S. Navy* (New York: Norton, 2006), 285.

39. TJ to Pierre-Samuel du Pont de Nemours, 18 Jan. 1802, in Ford, *Writings of TJ,* 8:127; Richard Beale Davis, ed., *Jeffersonian America: Notes on the United States of America Collected in the Years 1805–6–7 and 11–12 by Sir Augustus John Foster* (San Marino, Calif.: Huntington Library, 1954), 3.

40. TJ to Dickinson, 19 Dec. 1801, *PTJ,* 36:165–66.

41. Malone, *Jefferson the President: First Term,* 458, 462.

42. JA to William Tudor, 20 Jan. 1801, PJA–MHS.

43. JA, *Diary,* 3:253.

44. JQA to JA, 19 Nov. 1804, AFC–MHS.

45. JA to JQA, 20 Nov. 1804, AFC–MHS; JA to JQA, 6 Dec. 1804, ibid.; JA to JQA, 22 Dec. 1804, ibid.

46. JA, *Autobiography,* 3:298.

47. JA to T. B. Adams, 11 July 1801, AFC–MHS.

48. JA, "Minutes Occasioned by Remarks in the *National Intelligencer* of August 4, 1802," PJA–MHS; JA to John Trumbull, 8 July 1805, ibid.

49. JA to William Cranch, 29 June 1801, AFC–MHS.

50. JA to JQA, 6 Dec. 1804, AFC–MHS.

51. JA to T. B. Adams, 11 July 1801, AFC–MHS.

52. JA to BR, 23 Aug. 1805, *JA: Writings from the New Nation,* 432; JA to JQA, 6 Dec. 1804, AFC–MHS.

53. TJ to John Wayles Eppes, 22 Jan. 1801, *PTJ,* 31:333; TJ to Harry Innes, 23 Jan. 1806, ibid., 31:336; TJ to John Breckinridge, 20 Jan. 1800, ibid, 31:343; TJ to William Wardlaw, 28 Jan. 1800, ibid., 31:345; TJ to William Bache, 2 Feb. 1800, ibid., 31:354; TJ to T. M. Randolph, 2 Feb. 1800, ibid., 31: 358; TJ to T. M. Randolph, 4 Feb. 1800, ibid., 31:360; TJ to S. Adams, 26 Feb. 1800, ibid., 31:395.

54. TJ to Innes, 23 Jan. 1806, *PTJ*, 31:336–37.
55. TJ to Innes, 23 Jan. 1806, *PTJ*, 31:336; TJ to T. M. Randolph, 4 Feb. 1800, ibid., 31:360; TJ to Breckinbridge, 20 Jan. 1800, ibid., 31:345.
56. JA to T. B. Adams, 11 July 1801, AFC–MHS; JA, "Minutes Occasioned by Remarks in the *National Intelligencer* of August 4, 1802"; JA to Marquis de Lafayette, 6 Apr. 1801, PJA–MHS.
57. TJ to JM, 28 Aug. 1801, *Republic of Letters*, 2:1193–94.
58. JA to JQA, 6 Dec. 1804, AFC–MHS.
59. JA to BR, 25 July 1808, *JA: Writings from the New Nation*, 501–2.
60. JA to BR, 22 Dec. 1806, *JA: Writings from the New Nation*, 458–59; JA to BR, 2 Feb. 1807, ibid., 459–61; JA to BR, 11 Nov. 1807, ibid., 486; JA to BR, 21 May 1807, ibid., 467.
61. JA to William Cunningham, 16 Jan 1814, in *Correspondence Between the Hon. John Adams, Late President of the United States, and the Late William Cunningham* (Boston: E. M. Cunningham, 1823), 7–11.
62. JA to BR, 1 Sept. 1807, *JA: Writings from the New Nation*, 483; JA to BR, 2 Feb. 1807, ibid., 461.
63. TJ to JM, 28 Aug. 1789, *Republic of Letters*, 1:629.
64. JA to BR, 25 July 1808, *JA: Writings from the New Nation*, 503; JA to Joseph B. Varnum, 26 Dec. 1808, ibid., 510.
65. JA to Josiah Quincy III, 23 Dec. 1808, *JA: Writings from the New Nation*, 506–8.
66. JA to Quincy III, 23 Dec. 1808, *JA: Writings from the New Nation*, 506–8.
67. JA to BR, 8 Jan. 1812, PJA–MHS; JA to John Adams Smith, 10 Oct. 1819, AFC–MHS; JA to John T. Watson, 23 July 1818, PJA–MHS.
68. JA to BR, 29 Dec. 1812, *JA: Writings from the New Nation*, 542.
69. Benjamin Waterhouse to TJ, 1 Sept. 1815, *PTJ: RS*, 9:5.
70. JA to TJ, 19 Apr. 1817, Cappon, 2:508.
71. JA to TJ, 3 July 1813, Cappon, 2:350.
72. James Thomson Callender, Richmond *Recorder*, 1 Sept. 1802, *PTJ*, 38:323n–25n.
73. "Original Poetry," *The Port-Folio*, 30 Oct. 1802; Linda K. Kerber and Walter John Morris, "Politics and Literature: The Adams Family and the Portfolio," *WMQ* 23 (1966): 457; Linda K. Kerber, *Federalists in Dissent: Imagery and Ideology in Jeffersonian America* (Ithaca, N.Y.: Cornell University Press, 1970), 51.
74. JA to Joseph Ward, 8 Jan. 1810, *JA: Writings from the New Nation*, 517.
75. JA to George Churchman and Jacob Lindley, 24 Jan. 1801, *JA: Writings from the New Nation*, 406; JA to Thomas Crafts, 25 May 1790, PJA–MHS.
76. JA to J. Jeremy Belknap, 21 Mar. 1795, *JA: Writings from the New Nation*, 406; L. Kinvin Wroth and Hiller B. Zobel, eds., *The Legal Papers of John Adams* (Cambridge, Mass.: Belknap/Harvard University Press, 1965), 2:48–67.
77. JA to Belknap, 21 Mar. 1795, *JA: Writings from the New Nation*, 313–14.
78. JA to J. Belknap, 22 Oct. 1795, *JA: Writings from the New Nation*, 314–15.
79. JA to Churchman and Lindley, 24 Jan. 1801, *JA: Writings from the New Nation*, 406–7.
80. Annette Gordon-Reed and Peter S. Onuf, *"Most Blessed of Patriarchs": Thomas Jefferson and the Empire of the Imagination* (New York: Norton, 2016), 79–87, 153–57.
81. TJ to Angelica Schuyler Church, 27 Nov. 1793, *PTJ*, 27:449; TJ to T. M. Randolph, 23 Jan. 1801, ibid., 32:499–500; Gordon-Reed and Onuf, *"Most Blessed of*

Patriarchs," 79–87; Lucia Stanton, *"Those Who Labor for My Happiness": Slavery at Thomas Jefferson's Monticello* (Charlottesville: University of Virginia Press, 2012), 62.

82. AA to TJ, 20 May 1804, Cappon, 1:268–69; TJ to John Page, 25 June 1804, in Henry S. Randall, *The Life of Thomas Jefferson* (Philadelphia: Lippincott, 1888), 3:103.

83. TJ to AA, 13 June 1804, Cappon, 1:269–71.

84. AA to TJ, 1 July 1804, Cappon, 1:271–74.

85. TJ to AA, 22 July 1804, Cappon, 1:274–76.

86. AA to TJ, 18 Aug. 1804, Cappon, 1:276–78.

87. TJ to AA, 11 Sept. 1804, Cappon, 1:278–80.

88. AA to TJ, 25 Oct. 1804, and JA, postscript, 19 Nov. 1804, Cappon, 1:280–82. See Malone, *Jefferson the President: First Term*, 424, on TJ's notion that any reconciliation with JA would have to exclude AA.

ELEVEN: RECONCILIATION

1. George W. Corner, ed., *The Autobiography of Benjamin Rush: His "Travels Through Life" Together with His Commonplace Book for 1789–1813* (Princeton, N.J.: Princeton University Press, 1948), 103.

2. JA to BR, 6 Feb. 1805, *Old Family Letters,* 61.

3. JA to BR, 27 Feb. 1805, *Old Family Letters,* 63.

4. JA to BR, 18 Apr. 1808, *Old Family Letters,* 181.

5. JA to BR, 4 Mar. 1809, *Old Family Letters,* 219.

6. BR to JA, 17 Oct. 1809, *Letters of Rush,* 2:1021–22. See L. H. Butterfield, "The Dream of Benjamin Rush: The Reconciliation of John Adams and Thomas Jefferson," *Yale Review* 40 (1950–1951): 297–319.

7. JA to BR, 25 Oct. 1809, *Old Family Letters,* 246.

8. BR to TJ, 2 Jan. 1811, *Letters of Rush,* 2:1075.

9. TJ to BR, 16 Jan. 1811, *PTJ: RS,* 3:304–8.

10. BR to TJ, 1 Feb. 1811, *Letters of Rush,* 2:1078.

11. TJ to BR, 5 Dec. 1811, *PTJ: RS,* 4:312–14.

12. Henry S. Randall, *The Life of Thomas Jefferson* (Philadelphia: Lippincott, 1888), 3:639–40.

13. TJ to BR, 5 Dec. 1811, *PTJ: RS,* 4:312–13.

14. BR to JA, 16 Dec. 1811, *Letters of Rush,* 2:1110–11.

15. BR to TJ, 17 Dec. 1811, *Letters of Rush,* 2:1111–12.

16. JA to BR, 25 Dec. 1811, *JA: Writings from the New Nation,* 128–31.

17. JA to TJ, 1 Jan. 1812, Cappon, 2:290.

18. TJ to JA, 21 Jan. 1812, Cappon, 2:290–92.

19. TJ to BR, 21 Jan. 1812, *PTJ: RS,* 4:431.

20. TJ to JA, 23 Jan. 1812, Cappon, 2:292–93.

21. JA to TJ, 3 Feb. 1812, Cappon, 2:293–96. Roger Acherley (1665–1740) was an Englishman who wrote on law and the English constitution. Henry St. John, 1st Viscount Bolingbroke (1676–1751), was an English Tory politician and philosopher whose works were widely read by the American revolutionaries, especially by JA. Henry Neville (1626–1694), an English republican, was the author of *Plato*

Redivivus, or a Dialogue Concerning Government (1681). Marchmont Nedham (1620–1678) was an English writer whose book *The Excellency of a Free State, or the Right Constitution of Government* (1656) JA took very seriously; in fact, he spent over two hundred pages of volume 3 of his *Defence* carefully refuting it. See Zera S. Fink, *The Classical Republicans: An Essay in the Recovery of a Pattern of Thought in Seventeenth-Century England* (Evanston, Ill.: Northwestern University Press, 1945).

22. JA to TJ, 20 June 1815, Cappon, 2:446; JA to TJ, 15 July 1813, ibid., 2:357.

23. Antoine Destutt de Tracy to TJ, 12 June 1809, *PTJ: RS*, 1:260–63.

24. TJ to JA, 27 June 1822, Cappon, 2:581. Adams and Jefferson exchanged 158 letters between January 1, 1812, and their deaths in 1826, excluding the 6 letters between Jefferson and Abigail. Of these 158, Jefferson wrote only 49.

25. JA to TJ, 21 May 1819, Cappon, 2:540.

26. AA, note added to JA to TJ, 15 July 1813, Cappon, 2:358.

27. TJ to AA, 22 Aug. 1813, Cappon, 2:366–67.

28. AA to TJ, 20 Sept. 1813, Cappon, 2:377–78.

29. TJ to JA, 12 Oct. 1813, Cappon, 2:383–86.

30. AA to TJ, 15 Dec. 1816, Cappon, 2:500.

31. AA to TJ, 29 Apr. 1817, Cappon, 2:511.

32. JA to TJ, 15 July 1813, Cappon, 2:358.

33. JA to TJ, 15 Dec. 1813, Cappon, 2:413.

34. JA to TJ, 3 Mar. 1814, Cappon, 2:426.

35. JA to TJ, 9 July 1813, Cappon, 2:350.

36. JA to TJ, 3 July 1812, Cappon, 2:349.

37. JA to TJ, 19 June 1815, Cappon, 2:444; JA to TJ, 22 June 1815, ibid., 2:446–51; JA to TJ, 24 Aug. 1815, ibid., 2:454–55.

38. TJ to JA, 5 July 1814, Cappon, 2:433; JA to TJ, 3 Mar. 1814, ibid., 2:426–27; JA to TJ, 16 July 1824, ibid., 2:437; JA to TJ, 19 Dec. 1813, ibid., 2:406.

39. TJ to JA, 21 Mar. 1819, Cappon, 2:536–39; JA to TJ, 15 Dec. 1813, ibid., 2:411.

40. TJ to JA, 11 Jan. 1817, Cappon, 2:505; TJ to JA, 14 Oct. 1816, ibid., 2:491; JA to TJ, 2 Feb. 1817, ibid., 2:507.

41. TJ to JA, 10–11 Aug. 1815, Cappon, 2:453; JA to TJ, 24 Aug. 1815, ibid., 2:455.

42. JA to TJ, 10 Feb. 1812, Cappon, 2:297.

43. TJ to JA, 20 Apr. 1812, Cappon, 2:299.

44. JA to TJ, 3 May 1812, Cappon, 2:302.

45. JA to TJ, 3 May 1812, Cappon, 2:303–4.

46. JA to William Tudor Sr., 23 Sept. 1818, *JA: Writings from the New Nation*, 638–41; JA to AA, 19 Aug. 1777, *AFC*, 2:320.

47. TJ to JA, 11 June 1812, Cappon, 2:305–8.

48. JA to TJ, 28 June 1813, Cappon, 2:338–40.

49. JA to TJ, 10 June 1813, Cappon, 2:326–27; JA to TJ, 14 June 1813, ibid., 2:329–30.

50. TJ to JA, 15 June 1813, Cappon, 2:331–33; TJ to JA, 27 June 1813, ibid., 2:335–38.

51. JA to TJ, 25 June 1813, Cappon, 2:333.

52. JA to TJ, 30 June 1813, Cappon, 2:346–48.

53. JA to TJ, 3 July 1813, Cappon, 2:349; JA to TJ, 9 July 1813, ibid., 2:352; JA to TJ, 12 July 1813, ibid., 2:354.

54. JA to TJ, 13 July 1813, Cappon, 2:354–56; JA to TJ, 15 July 1813, ibid., 2:357–58.

55. JA to TJ, 4 Mar. 1816, Cappon, 2:464–65.

56. JA to TJ, 15 July 1813, Cappon, 2:257–58.

57. JA to TJ, 16 July 1813, Cappon, 2:359–60.
58. JA to TJ, 3 Mar. 1814, Cappon, 2:429.
59. TJ to JA, 22 Aug. 1813, Cappon, 2:368.
60. TJ to JA, 14 Jan. 1814, Cappon, 2:411; JA to TJ, 22 Jan. 1825, ibid., 2:607.
61. JA to TJ, 3 Dec. 1813, Cappon, 2:404; TJ to Francis Adrian Van der Kemp, 6 Aug. 1816, and TJ to James Smith, 8 Dec. 1822, in James H. Hutson, *The Founders on Religion: A Book of Quotations* (Princeton, N.J.: Princeton University Press, 2005), 217–19.
62. JA to Louisa Catherine Adams, 19 Nov. 1821, *JA: Writings from the New Nation*, 667; JA to Mordecai M. Noah, 31 Jan. 1818, ibid., 638; JA to BR, 28 Aug. 1811, ibid., 525.
63. JA to JQA, 10 May 1816, AFC–MHS; JA to TJ, 14 Sept. 1813, Cappon, 2:373–75; JA to TJ, 15 Sept. 1813, ibid., 2:375–76.
64. JA to JQA, 10 May 1816, AFC–MHS; JA to AA, 27 Oct. 1799, ibid.; JA to William White, 29 Oct. 1814, PJA–MHS; JA to JQA, 11 Mar. 1813, AFC–MHS; JA, *Diary*, 3:234; JA to Samuel Miller, 7 July 1820, *JA: Writings from the New Nation*, 658.
65. TJ to Salma Hale, 26 July 1818, in Hutson, *Founders on Religion*, 38.
66. TJ, "Bill for Establishing Religious Freedom" (1779), *TJ: Writings*, 346.
67. JA to AA, 29 Oct. 1775, *AFC*, 1:318–19.
68. JA to TJ, 25 June 1813, Cappon, 2:334; JA to BR, 1 Sept. 1809, *Old Family Letters*, 240; JA to BR, 19 June 1789, ibid., 40.
69. JA to TJ, 19 Apr. 1817, Cappon, 2:509.
70. TJ to Moses Robinson, 23 Mar. 1801, *PTJ*, 33:424.
71. TJ to Edward Dowse, 19 Apr. 1803, *PTJ*, 40:236.
72. TJ to Charles Thomson, 9 Jan. 1816, *PTJ: RS*, 9:340–41.
73. TJ to Ezra Stiles Ely, 25 June 1819, "Jefferson's Extracts from the Gospel," in Dickinson W. Adams and Ruth W. Lester, eds., *The Papers of Thomas Jefferson: Second Series* (Princeton, N.J.: Princeton University Press, 1983), 387.
74. TJ to Isaac Story, 5 Dec. 1801, *PTJ*, 36:30; JA to TJ, 3 May 1816, Cappon, 2:469–71; JA to TJ, 8 Dec. 1818, ibid., 2:530; JA to Van der Kemp, 27 Dec. 1816, *JA: Writings from the New Nation*, 619.
75. JA to TJ, 15 Sept. 1813, Cappon, 2:376; JA to TJ, 9 July 1813, ibid., 2:352.
76. TJ to JA, 27 June 1813, Cappon, 2:335–36; JA to TJ, 13 July 1813, ibid., 2:355.
77. TJ to JA, 28 Oct. 1813, Cappon, 2:388.
78. TJ to JA, 28 Oct. 1813, Cappon, 2:388–89.
79. TJ to JA, 28 Oct. 1813, Cappon, 2:389–90.
80. TJ, *Notes on the State of Virginia*, ed. William Peden (Chapel Hill: University of North Carolina Press, 1955), 146.
81. TJ, *Notes on the State of Virginia*, 146; TJ to JA, 28 Oct. 1813, Cappon, 2:389–90.
82. TJ to Nathaniel Burwell, 14 Mar. 1818, *PTJ: RS*, 12:532–33.
83. JA to Van der Kemp, 8 Apr. 1815, PJA–MHS; JA to Emma Willard, 8 Dec. 1820, *JA: Writings from the New Nation*, 650; JA to Caroline Amelia Smith De Windt, 11 Feb. 1820, PJA–MHS.
84. Zoltán Haraszti, *John Adams and the Prophets of Progress* (Cambridge, Mass.: Harvard University Press, 1955), 184–234.
85. TJ to Angelica Schuyler Church, 27 Nov. 1793, *PTJ*, 27:449.
86. Lucia Stanton, *"Those Who Labor for My Happiness": Slavery at Thomas Jefferson's Monticello* (Charlottesville: University of Virginia Press, 2012), 57–58; Annette

Gordon-Reed and Peter S. Onuf, *"Most Blessed of the Patriarchs": Thomas Jefferson and the Empire of the Imagination* (New York: Norton, 2016), 132–33; TJ to Eliza House Trist, 18 Aug. 1785, *PTJ,* 8:404; TJ to George Washington, 4 Dec. 1788, ibid., 14:330; TJ to Anne Willing Bingham, 7 Feb. 1787, ibid., 11:122–23.

87. JA to Thomas B. Adams, 17 Oct. 1799, AFC–MHS.
88. JA to TJ, 15 Nov. 1813, Cappon, 2:397–99.
89. JA to TJ, 15 Nov. 1813, Cappon, 2:398.
90. JA to TJ, 19 Dec. 1813, Cappon, 2:409; JA to TJ, 15 Nov. 1813, ibid., 2:400–402.
91. JA to TJ, 25 Dec. 1813, Cappon, 2:409.
92. TJ to JA, 14 Jan. 1814, Cappon, 2:422–25.
93. TJ to JA, 8 Apr. 1816, Cappon, 2: 467.
94. JA to TJ, 6 May 1816, Cappon 2:472–74; TJ to JA, 1 Aug. 1816, ibid., 2:483–85.
95. JA to JQA, 3 July 1816, AFC–MHS; JA to TJ, 4 Nov. 1816, Cappon, 2:493.
96. JA to TJ, 16 Dec. 1816, Cappon, 2:500–501.
97. TJ to William Duane, 16 Sept. 1810, *PTJ: RS,* 3:86; TJ to JA, 11 Jan. 1817, Cappon, 2:505–6.
98. JA to TJ, 2 Feb. 1817, Cappon, 2:506–8.

TWELVE: THE GREAT REVERSAL

1. JA to TJ, 2 Feb. 1817, Cappon, 2:508; TJ to Marquis de Lafayette, 23 Nov. 1818, in Gilbert Chinard, ed., *The Letters of Lafayette and Jefferson* (Baltimore: Johns Hopkins Press, 1929), 396.
2. JA to TJ, 30 July 1815, Cappon, 2:451.
3. TJ to William Johnson, 4 Mar. 1823, *Founders Online,* National Archives.
4. TJ to JA, 10–11 Aug. 1815, Cappon, 2:432–53; John Marshall, *The Life of George Washington . . .* (Philadelphia: C. P. Wayne, 1804–1807), 2:411n; Philip F. Detweiler, "The Changing Reputation of the Declaration of Independence: The First Fifty Years," *WMQ* 19 (1962): 566.
5. JA to TJ, 24 Aug. 1815, Cappon, 2:455; JA to Thomas McKean, 26 Nov. 1815, PJA–MHS.
6. JA to John Holmes, 10 Aug. 1815, PJA–MHS; JA to JQA, 2 Sept. 1815, AFC–MHS; JA to Hezekiah Niles, 13 Feb. 1818, *JA: Writings from the New Nation,* 629–36.
7. JA to BR, 23 July 1806, *Old Family Letters,* 104–9.
8. JA to BR, 23 July 1806, *Old Family Letters,* 104–9.
9. JA to BR, 31 Aug. 1809, *Old Family Letters,* 238–39.
10. JA to Jedidiah Morse, 4 Mar. 1815, *Works of JA,* 10:133–34.
11. JA to TJ, 18 May 1817, Cappon, 2:516.
12. Benjamin Waterhouse to TJ, 20 Feb. 1818, *PTJ: RS,* 12:493–97.
13. TJ to Waterhouse, 3 Mar., 1818, *PTJ: RS,* 12:517–19.
14. TJ to JA, 17 May 1818, Cappon, 2:523–24.
15. JA to TJ, 29 May 1818, Cappon, 2:525.
16. Thomas Ritchie to TJ, 13 Mar. 1818, *PTJ: RS,* 12:530–31.
17. TJ to Ritchie, 20 Mar. 1818, *PTJ: RS,* 12:548–49.
18. JA to William Cunningham, 15 Mar. 1804 and 24 Feb. 1804, in *Correspondence Between the Hon. John Adams, Late President of the United States, and the Late William Cunningham* (Boston: E. M. Cunningham, 1823), 18, 15.

19. *Correspondence Between Adams and Cunningham*, vi–vii.
20. TJ to JA, 12 Oct. 1823, Cappon, 2:600–601.
21. JA to TJ, 10 Nov. 1823, Cappon, 2:601.
22. TJ to William Short, 8 Jan. 1825, in *The Writings of Thomas Jefferson*, ed. Andrew A. Lipscomb and Albert Ellery Bergh (Washington, D.C.: Jefferson Memorial Association, 1903), 16:92–93.
23. TJ to JA, 21 Jan. 1812, Cappon, 2:292, 292n; TJ to JA, 17 May 1813, ibid., 2:323.
24. Detweiler, "The Changing Reputation of the Declaration of Independence," 557–74.
25. Irma B. Jaffe, *Trumbull: The Declaration of Independence* (London: Penguin, 1976), 64–66.
26. JA to John Trumbull, 1 Jan. 1817, PJA–MHS; JA to Trumbull, 18 Mar. 1817, ibid.
27. Trumbull to JA, 3 Mar. 1817, in Jaffe, *Trumbull*, 95; Gary Wills, *Inventing America: Jefferson's Declaration of Independence* (New York: Houghton Mifflin, 1978), 345–51.
28. TJ to Trumbull, 10 Jan. 1817, *PTJ: RS*, 10:655.
29. Detweiler, "The Changing Reputation of the Declaration of Independence," 569–70.
30. JA to BR, 30 Sept. 1805, *Old Family Letters*, 86; JA to BR, 21 June 1811, ibid., 287; JA to TJ, 12 Nov. 1813, Cappon, 2:393.
31. JA to Nathan Webb, 12 Oct. 1755, *PJA*, 1:4–6; JA to Cunningham, 27 Sept. 1809, in *Correspondence Between Adams and Cunningham*, 167.
32. JA to Richard Rush, 22 July 1816, PJA–MHS.
33. TJ to Joseph Delaplaine, 12 Apr. 1817, *PTJ: RS*, 11:252.
34. William Henry Hoyt, *The Mecklenburg Declaration of Independence: A Study of Evidence Showing That the Alleged Early Declaration of Independence by Mecklenburg County, North Carolina, on May 20th, 1775, Is Spurious* (New York: G. P. Putnam's Sons, 1907), 3–7.
35. JA to TJ, 22 June 1819, Cappon, 2:542; JA to William Bentley, 15 July 1819, *Works of JA*, 10:381.
36. TJ to JA, 9 July 1819, Cappon, 2:543.
37. Joseph J. Ellis, in his *Passionate Sage: The Character and Legacy of John Adams* (New York: Norton, 1993), p. 121, claimed that Adams was guilty of duplicity. He writes that JA agreed with TJ that the Mecklenburg declaration was a fiction while saying something else to friends. Ellis cited only a letter to Van der Kemp of August 21, 1819, in which JA said, "I could as Soon believe that the dozen flowers of the Hydrangia now before my Eyes were the Work of Chance, as that the Mecklenburg Resolves and Mr. Jefferson's Declaration were not derived, the one from the other." Not only does Ellis cite the wrong letter—JA made this statement in an August 21, 1819, letter to William Bentley—but, more important, all JA was saying is that the two documents were so similar that "either these Resolutions are from Mr. Jefferson's Declaration of Independence, or Mr. Jefferson's Declaration of Independence is a Plagiarism from those Resolutions." Perhaps deep down he wished the latter were true, but he never said so and in fact said the opposite. What JA meant was that the two documents were just too similar to be a matter of chance. In a subsequent August 30, 1819, letter to Bentley, he used a French idiom (*en bon train*) to bid farewell to the Mecklenburg declaration and told Bentley, "*Vive la Vérité.*" Unfortunately, Pauline Maier, in her *American Scripture: Making the Declaration of Independence* (New York:

Knopf, 1997), p. 173, cited Ellis's book to show that JA continued to believe the Mecklenburg declaration was authentic.

38. JA to TJ, 21 July 1819, Cappon, 2:545; JA to William Bentley, 20 July 1819, PJA–MHS; JA to Bentley, 28 July 1819, ibid., JA to Bentley, 27 Aug. 1819, ibid. Dr. Alexander's father had been at a meeting in Charlotte, in May 1775, at which the militia companies had issued some resolves. When these were discovered in 1838, they were very different from those Alexander claimed were the authentic resolutions. Since that original document had been burned in 1800, Alexander's father had apparently reconstructed it from memory.

39. TJ to JM, 30 Aug. 1823, *Republic of Letters*, 3:1875–76.

40. TJ to JQA, 18 July 1824, in Lipscomb and Bergh, *Writings of TJ*, 19:278.

41. TJ to Ellen W. Coolidge, 14 Nov. 1825, in Lipscomb and Bergh, *Writings of TJ*, 18:349–50; Maier, *American Scripture*, 186–87.

42. Robert E. Shalhope, "Thomas Jefferson's Republicanism and Antebellum Southern Thought," *Journal of Southern History* 42 (1976): 529–65.

43. TJ to JA, 14 Jan. 1814, Cappon, 2:424–35.

44. TJ to JA, 17 May 1818, Cappon, 2:523; TJ to Albert Gallatin, 16 Oct. 1816, *PTJ: RS*, 9:95–96.

45. TJ to Gallatin, 11 Apr. 1816, *PTJ: RS*, 9:664; TJ, "Title and Prospectus for Destutt de Tracy's *Treatise on Political Economy*," c. 6 Apr. 1816, ibid., 9:631.

46. Antoine Louis Claude Destutt de Tracy, *Treatise on Political Economy*, trans. Thomas Jefferson, ed. Jeremy Jennings (1817; repr., Indianapolis: Liberty Fund, 2011), 107, 182.

47. Destutt de Tracy, *Treatise on Political Economy*, 152, 151.

48. TJ to Gallatin, 16 Oct. 1816, *PTJ: RS*, 9:95–96.

49. JA to BR, 13 Feb. 1811, *Old Family Letters*, 281.

50. JA to TJ, 15 Nov. 1813, Cappon, 2:401–2.

51. JA to TJ, 29 Jan 1819, Cappon, 2:532.

52. JA to TJ, 29 May 1818, Cappon, 2:526.

53. JA to TJ, 16 May 1817, Cappon, 2:517–18.

54. JA to TJ, 15 July 1817, Cappon, 2:519.

55. A tragic sense of life is not the same as pessimism, as historian Maurizio Valsania seems to imply. Indeed, by becoming aware of the circumstances impinging on and limiting people's actions a sense of the tragedy of life merely clarifies what is possible; it does not deny the freedom to act. Maurizio Valsania, *The Limits of Optimism: Thomas Jefferson's Dualistic Enlightenment* (Charlottesville: University of Virginia Press, 2012), 18, 117.

56. TJ to JA, 1 Aug. 1816, Cappon, 2:485.

57. TJ to Martha Jefferson Randolph, 5 Jan. 1808, in Edwin Morris Betts and James Adam Bear Jr., eds., *The Family Letters of Thomas Jefferson* (Columbia: University of Missouri Press, 1966), 319; TJ to Mrs. Elizabeth Trist, 26 Dec. 1814, *PTJ: RS*, 8:163–64.

58. TJ to Edward Coles, 25 Aug. 1814, *PTJ: RS*, 7:603–5.

59. TJ to Thomas Humphreys, 8 Feb. 1817, *PTJ: RS*, 11: 61.

60. TJ to Waterhouse, 3 Mar. 1818, *PTJ: RS*, 12:518.

61. Gordon S. Wood, *Empire of Liberty: A History of the Early Republic, 1789–1815* (New York: Oxford University Press, 2009), 734.

62. Gordon-Reed and Onuf, in their biography of Jefferson, point out that "in the empire of this stalwart Virginian's imagination, the perfect republican society

looked a great deal like New England, and almost nothing like Virginia." An-
nette Gordon-Reed and Peter S. Onuf, *"Most Blessed of the Patriarchs": Thomas Jefferson and the Empire of the Imagination* (New York: Norton, 2016), 30.

63. Ellen Raudolph Coolidge to TJ, 1 Aug. 1825; TJ to Ellen Randolph Coolidge, 27 Aug. 1825, in Betts and Bear, *Family Letters of Thomas Jefferson*, 454–56, 457.

64. Herbert E. Sloan, *Principle and Interest: Thomas Jefferson and the Problem of Debt* (New York: Oxford University Press, 1995), 218–37; Jon Meacham, *Thomas Jefferson: The Art of Power* (New York: Random House, 2012), 485.

65. TJ, "Essay on New England Religious Intolerance," c. 16 June 1816, *PTJ: RS*, 9:380–81.

66. TJ to Ritchie, 21 Jan. 1816, *PTJ: RS*, 9:379.

67. TJ to JM, 17 Feb. 1826, *Republic of Letters*, 3:1965.

68. TJ to Joseph Cabell, 11 Jan. 1825, *Founders Online*, National Archives.

69. TJ to JA, 19 Jan. 1819, Cappon, 2:532.

70. JA to TJ, 26 May 1817, 22 Jan. 1825, Cappon, 2:518, 607.

71. TJ to Cabell, 26 Feb. 1818, *PTJ: RS*, 12:511; TJ to Thomas Cooper, 9 Mar. 1822, *Founders Online*, National Archives.

72. TJ to Samuel Kercheval, 12 July 1816, *TJ: Writings*, 1401.

73. TJ to William H. Crawford, 15 Feb. 1825, in Lipscomb and Bergh, *Writings of TJ*, 19:282–83.

74. TJ to Ritchie, 21 Dec. 1820, *TJ: Writings*, 1445–46.

75. TJ to Ritchie, 21 Dec. 1820, *TJ: Writings*, 1445–46.

76. TJ to Spencer Roane, 6 Sept. 1819, *TJ: Writings*, 1425–28.

77. TJ to John Cartwright, 5 June 1824, *Founders Online*, National Archives.

78. TJ to John Holmes, 22 Apr. 1820, *TJ: Writings*, 1434.

79. TJ to Gallatin, 26 Dec. 1820, *Founders Online*, National Archives.

80. JA to TJ, 21 Dec. 1819, Cappon, 2:551.

81. JA to TJ, 21 Feb. 1820, Cappon, 2:561.

82. JA to Louisa Catherine Adams, 13 Jan. 1820, *JA: Writings from the New Nation*, 654.

83. TJ to JA, 22 Jan. 1821, Cappon, 2:569–70.

84. JA to TJ, 3 Feb. 1821, Cappon, 2:571.

85. TJ to JM, 24 Dec. 1825, with enclosure, *Republic of Letters*, 3:1943–46.

86. JM to TJ, 28 Dec. 1825, *Republic of Letters*, 3:1947–48.

87. TJ to Claiborne W. Gooch, 9 Jan. 1826, *Founders Online*, National Archives.

88. TJ to Holmes, 22 Apr. 1820, *TJ: Writings*, 1434; TJ to Bernard Peyton, 21 Feb. 1826, *Founders Online*, National Archives; Andrew Burstein, *America's Jubilee* (New York: Knopf, 2001), 261; TJ to Thomas Jefferson Randolph, 8 Feb. 1826, in Betts and Bear, *Family Letters of TJ*, 469; TJ to Francis Adrian Van der Kemp, 11 Jan. 1825, *Founders Online*, National Archives.

89. JA to JQA, 26 July 1816, AFC–MHS; Josiah Quincy, *Figures of the Past* (1883; repr., Boston: Little, Brown, 1926), 59–60. 63–64.

90. JA to David Sewall, 22 May 1821, *JA: Writings from the New Nation*, 664.

91. Ellis, *Passionate Sage*, 80–81.

92. JA to JQA, 14 May 1815, AFC–MHS.

93. John Taylor to JA, 8 Apr. 1824, and JA to Taylor, 8 Apr. 1824, *Works of JA*, 10:411–13.

94. JA to Taylor, 15 Apr. 1814, *JA: Writings from the New Nation*, 577; JA to Matthew Carey, 9 Sept. 1820, PJA–MHS; JA to Charles Holt, 4 Sept. 1820, *JA: Writings from the New Nation*, 660–61.

95. JA to Holt, 4 Sept. 1820, *JA: Writings from the New Nation*, 660–61.
96. JA to Van der Kemp, 13 July 1815, *Works of JA*, 10:169; Ellis, *Passionate Sage*, 80–81; John Ferling, *John Adams: A Life* (1992; repr., New York: Henry Holt, 1996), 442.
97. JA to TJ, 21 May 1819, Cappon, 2:540.
98. JA to Joseph B. Varnum, 26 Dec. 1808, *JA: Writings from the New Nation*, 509–12.
99. JA to Waterhouse, 17 Sept. 1813, in Worthington Chauncey Ford, ed., *Statesman and Friend: Correspondence of John Adams with Benjamin Waterhouse, 1784–1822* (Boston: Little, Brown, 1927), 111.
100. JA to TJ, 16 May 1817, Cappon, 2:517–18.
101. TJ to JA, 8 Sept. 1817, Cappon, 2:520; JA to TJ, 10 Oct. 1817, ibid., 2:521–22.
102. JA to TJ, 15 Feb. 1825, Cappon, 2:610.
103. JA to Richard Rush, 20 Nov. 1813, *JA: Writings from the New Nation*, 576.
104. JA to L. C. Adams, 13 Jan. 1820, *JA: Writings from the New Nation*, 654.
105. Quincy, *Figures of the Past*, 64.
106. TJ to JA, 18 Dec. 1825, Cappon, 2:612; Quincy, *Figures of the Past*, 65.

Epilogue: The National Jubilee

1. JA to John Whitney, 7 June 1826, *JA: Writings from the New Nation*, 674–75.
2. TJ to Roger C. Weightman, 24 June 1826, *TJ: Writings*, 1517.
3. Andrew Burstein, *America's Jubilee* (New York: Knopf, 2001), 261.
4. Burstein, *America's Jubilee*, 266; William Cranch, *Memoir of the Life, Character, and Writings of John Adams . . .* (Washington, D.C.: S. A. Eliot, 1827), 57–58.
5. JA, *Rex v. Wemms*, 4 Dec. 1770, in *The Legal Papers of John Adams*, ed. L. Kinvin Wroth and Hiller B. Zobel (Cambridge Mass.: Belknap/Harvard University Press, 1965), 3:269.
6. JA to TJ, 2 Feb. 1816, Cappon, 2:461–63.
7. JA, "Note for an Oration on Government," Spring 1772, *JA: Revolutionary Writings, 1755–1775*, 215; JA to TJ, 25 June 1813, Cappon, 2:334; JA to TJ, 2 Feb. 1816, ibid., 2:461–63.
8. JA to William Steuben Smith, 30 May 1815, AFC–MHS; JA to TJ, 28 June 1813, Cappon, 2:339; JA to William Tudor Sr., 25 Feb. 1800, *JA: Writings from the New Nation*, 389.
9. JA to John Taylor, 19 Apr. 1814, *JA: Works*, 6:452.
10. JA to Taylor, 19 Apr. 1814, *JA: Works*, 6:453–54.
11. JA to Taylor, 5 Mar. 1814, *JA: Works*, 6:519–20.
12. JA to John Langdon, 12 Dec. 1810, PJA–MHS.
13. Hezekiah Niles to TJ and JM, 1 Nov. 1817, *PTJ: RS*, 12:160–64.
14. Abraham Lincoln to Henry L. Pierce and Others, 6 Apr. 1859, in Abraham Lincoln, *Speeches and Writings, 1832–1865*, ed. Don. E. Fehrenbacher (New York: Library of America, 1974), 2:19; Abraham Lincoln, "Speech at Chicago, Illinois," 19 July 1858, ibid., 1:456.
15. Abraham Lincoln, "Speech at Independence Hall, Philadelphia, Pennsylvania," 22 Feb. 1861, in Lincoln, *Speeches and Writings*, 2:213.

INDEX

abolitionist movement, 232, 348, 416–18

Abolition Society of Pennsylvania, 348

Acta Sanctorum (Camus), 367

Act of Settlement (1701), 84–85

Adams, Abigail "Nabby," *see* Smith, Abigail Adams "Nabby"

Adams, Abigail Smith, 13, 15, 45, 66, 99, 106, 155, 198, 202, 248–49, 253–54, 266, 268, 271, 276, 284–87, 293, 294, 370, 379, 428
  antislavery sentiment of, 53
  appearance of, 50
  as avid reader, 51–53, 159
  death of, 366, 422, 424
  in Europe, 159–66
  grievances against TJ expressed by, 352–55
  intellect and wit of, 50–53, 60–61, 135–36, 159, 382
  JA's courtship of, 49–50
  in JA's missions abroad, 63, 158–66
  letters of, *see* correspondence, between JA and Abigail; correspondence, between TJ and Abigail
  long periods of separation between JA and, 159, 248, 294
  polite, measured reconciliation between TJ and, 366
  political interest and commentary of, 53, 134, 159, 164–65, 219–20, 296, 300–301, 304–5, 307, 317, 323–24, 352–55
  strained and broken relationship between TJ and, 324, 351–55, 359, 361, 363–66
  TJ's friendship with, 159–65, 254, 261

  unique marriage of, 50–53, 56–57, 60–61, 134–36, 138–39, 150, 151, 159, 248, 294, 382, 383

Adams, Charles, 277–78
  death of, 327–28, 351, 422

Adams, Deacon, 24–25, 27–28, 31, 40–41, 51

Adams, Ebenezer, 39–40

Adams, John:
  Abigail courted by, 49–50
  acclaim for, 420–22
  as American hero, 3–4
  as amiable, 9, 36
  antislavery stance of, 19–20, 132–33, 348, 418, 424
  appearance and personal style of, 8–9
  authorship of Declaration challenged by, 398–405
  as avid reader, 10, 42, 45–46, 111, 196, 231, 366–68, 392
  birth of, 24
  contrasts between TJ and, 7–37
  cutting sense of humor of, 10, 77–78, 134, 148, 362–63, 373–74, 382, 388, 408, 423, 428
  cynicism of, 7, 122–23, 133, 203, 205–8, 214–18, 224, 228, 238, 255, 268, 299, 331–32, 409
  death of, 1, 4, 428
  diary of, 25–26, 39–40, 50, 69, 72, 75, 80–81, 84, 88, 95, 96–97, 99, 121, 134, 148, 201
  diminished legacy of, 4, 5

Adams, John *(cont.)*
  economical lifestyle of, 163–64
  eulogies for, 1–6
  evolving serenity and optimism of,
    420–25
  family background and heritage, 24–26
  growing self-confidence of, 96, 303–4
  ill health of, 426–28
  intellect of, 10, 201
  as irascible and pugnacious, 9, 10, 36–37,
    79, 105, 159, 165, 272, 283,
    366, 400
  legacy of, 390, 393–94, 420, 428–33
  letters of Abigail and, *see* correspondence,
    between JA and Abigail
  mellowing of, 420–25
  modest homes of, 77–78
  as nervous and stressed, 153–54
  northern upbringing of, 16–20
  in opposition to English oppression,
    69–76, 79
  personal temperament of, 2, 6, 154–55, 165
  personal tragedies of, 422
  as politically and socially abrasive, 252–54
  reactionary perspective of, 325–26
  religious sensibility of, 40, 374–79
  as resentful, 79, 152, 188–89, 205, 207, 228,
    256, 286, 293, 321–22, 336–37, 343,
    400–401, 404
  retirement and later years of, 389–425
  ridicule of, 8, 79, 155–56, 234, 242
  as self-critical, 25–26
  self-doubt of, 95–96
  sense of social inferiority of, 33–34, 188–89,
    199–200, 207
  sensitivity of, 50, 79
  as sensuous, 12–13
  sociability of, 420–21
  social hierarchy defined by, 31–32
  spontaneous emotionalism of, 360,
    366, 385
  unique marriage of, 50–53, 56–57, 60–61,
    134–36, 138–39, 150, 151, 159, 248, 294,
    382, 383
  unstable behavior of, 316–17
  virtue valued by, 24–25, 40–41, 48, 114,
    205–6, 231, 342
  visual memory of, 12–13
  on working and leisure classes, 208–10
  writings of, 2–3, 69–70, 79, 338; *see also*
    specific works
  writing style of, 12, 96–97, 101, 201–2,
    366–68
  see also Jefferson-Adams friendship

—CAREER:
  ambition and aspiration of, 41–44, 49, 78,
    80–81, 96, 137, 152, 155–56, 159, 195,
    227, 265, 279–81
  banks and banking eschewed by, 248–49,
    290, 408
  as cautious about enlightened reform,
    131–36
  choice of career, 40–41
  constitutional theory of, 111–120, 171–174,
    186–203, 205–7, 233–239; *see also*
    *Defence of the Constitutions of
    Government of the United States
    of America*
  criticism of, 150–51, 155–56, 234–36,
    253–54
  debating skills of, 106
  declining popularity and political
    marginalization of, 248
  farming ventures of, 22, 25, 52, 337
  as lacking in courtly protocol, 148–49
  lack of political prowess of, 280–81, 287,
    290–91, 293, 315–16
  as lawyer, 3, 41–45, 47–48, 69, 74–76, 79,
    81–84, 88, 95, 123, 137, 138, 188,
    207, 394
  in missions abroad, 3, 6, 13, 52, 138–39,
    147–52, 153–66, 167, 171, 176, 186–87,
    221, 252, 338, 375
  monarchical inclinations of, 241, 252,
    254–57, 283, 285, 315, 343, 397–98
  naïveté of, 253–54
  in patriot politics, 3, 81–85, 88–90, 94–102
  political philosophy of, 6, 79, 101, 255,
    331–32, 428–32
  as principal framer of Massachusetts
    constitution, 171, 173–81, 206
  as realist, 157–68
  retirement years of, 3, 6, 10
  as vice president, 3, 6, 8, 227–28, 240–42,
    248, 253, 258, 265, 280
—AS PRESIDENT, 3, 6, 279–319
  acclaim for, 302–4
  accomplishments of, 307, 318
  bitter aftermath of presidency, 321–24, 327,
    336–37, 397
  campaigns of, 283–86, 320–25
  censure and impeachment threat to, 315–16
  as controversial, 4, 294, 297
  election of, 286
  inauguration of, 292–93, 297
  internal conflict within, 315–16, 360
  JA's aspirations to presidency, 279–81
  lame duck period, 323, 334, 336, 352

loss of presidency, 317, 319, 322, 355, 389
in retirement, 336–37
as target of partisan press, 310
tarnished legacy of, 307–11, 333–34, 372
U.S. internal political upheaval, 279–319
Washington's cabinet retained by,
    291, 294
weakness of, 312
Adams, John Quincy, 12, 66, 137, 139, 151,
    162, 258, 271, 295, 296–97, 299, 300, 337,
    339, 347, 363–64, 366, 370, 382, 390,
    415, 420, 421
    political career of, 344, 346, 353, 397,
        404, 422
    presidency of, 424
Adams, Louisa Catherine, 382–83
Adams, Samuel, 73, 83, 105, 148, 171, 176,
    205, 393, 395
Adams, Thomas, 151, 322, 332, 338,
    383, 422
afterlife, 39, 424–25
Age of Reason, The (Paine), 293
agriculture, manufacturing vs., 243–45
Albemarle County Court, 46, 60
alcoholism, 327, 422
Alexander, Joseph McKnitt, 402
Alfred, laws of, 385
Alien and Sedition Acts (1798), 307–11,
    313–14, 342
Alien Friends Act (1789), 308–9
Ambler, Jaquelin "Jack," 53–55
American Academy of Arts and Sciences,
    266, 345
American culture:
    beauty of nature in, 166
    cynical perception of, 7
    diversity in, 429–30
    emerging and evolving national identity in,
        273–74, 389–90, 431–432–433
    evolving capitalism of, 405–6
    exceptionalism in, 7, 215, 217, 229,
        252–55, 325
    optimistic perception of, 7
    as patriarchal, 51–52, 60–61, 135,
        381–83
    patriotic role of art in, 13–14
    predictions for, 74, 245
    social hierarchy in, 20–21, 28–35
    social mobility in, 30–31
    social order in, 282–83
    TJ's and JA's divergent views on, 203–39,
        405–25
    TJ's evolving appreciation of, 231–33, 350
    TJ's skepticism about future of, 406–8

American independence:
    establishment of, 103–36
    formal declaration of, 120–21
American Philosophical Society, 266
American Revolution:
    imperial crisis as prelude to, 69–102
    Massachusetts vs. Virginia in debate over
        initiation of, 393–96
    need for historical documentation of,
        390–96
    outbreak of fighting in, 102, 103–4
    renewed interest in, 289–390
    Revolutionary War as only one part of, 391
    significance of, 6, 183, 223, 225, 321, 325,
        393–94, 427
    TJ's and JA's views of significance of,
        390–92
    warfare in, see Revolutionary War
Ames, Fisher, 53, 326
Analectic Magazine, 390
Anglicanism, 40, 71, 81, 375
Anglo-Saxon myth, utopian world of, 73, 92
Arbuthnot, John, 401
Archytas, 368
aristocracy:
    American vs. European, 192–93, 217
    in bicameral legislature, 117–18, 178,
        180–81
    as creditors, 197, 207, 219
    French, 148–50, 160–61
    ideal, 195
    JA's ambivalent obsession with, 33, 123,
        189–90, 194, 199–200, 207–10, 212–14,
        240–42, 346
    in Massachusetts, 188–89
    middling class vs., 208–10, 214–15
    natural, 212–14, 380, 414
    privileges of, 28–29, 104
    property as measure of wisdom in, 180–81
    publically eschewed by politicians, 234–35
    in the South vs. New England, 28–35,
        233–34
    in support of American independence,
        130–31
    as threat to democracy, 186–98, 212–14,
        216–17, 234, 380, 389–90
    TJ as member of, 7, 17, 22–24, 33, 59–60,
        76, 77, 104, 150, 163–64, 166, 198,
        210–12, 215, 217, 271, 382, 413
    TJ's ambivalence about, 23–24
    TJ's and JA's divergent views of, 218–20,
        379–81, 383–85
    TJ's assault on, 77, 128–29, 130–31,
        257, 261

aristocracy, governmental:
    defined, 112
    democracy vs., 119–20, 178–79, 190
Aristotle, 177
Arnold, Benedict, 143
Articles of Confederation, 220–21, 333
arts:
    JA's sensuous response to, 12–13, 15–16
    TJ's interest in, 11–15, 34
Assembly of Notables (1787), 223
Aurora, 283, 305, 332
Auteuil, JA's residence at, 159–60
autobiographies:
    of JA, 23, 25, 41, 56, 85, 337–38
    of TJ, 23, 76, 94, 128, 129, 145, 226
Autobiography (Franklin), 36

Bache, Benjamin Franklin, 305
Backus, Isaac, 175
Bacon, Francis, 124
Baltimore, Congress relocated in, 137
Bank of England, 246–47
Bank of North America, 246–47
Bank of the United States, 246–47, 283, 335
banks, banking, 298, 358, 406–8
    establishment of, 246–50
    failures of, 249
Baptists, 175
Barbary pirates, 4, 341–42
Barbé-Mabois, Marquis de, 168
Bastille, attack on, 226
Beccaria, Cesare, 129
Beckley, John, 257
Belknap, Jeremy, 348–49
Bentley, William, 403–4
Bernard, Francis, 79–80
Bernard family, 75
bicameral legislature, 109–11, 116–18, 173,
        179–81, 184–86, 188, 193, 196–97, 202,
        213, 218, 229, 380
    balance achieved by, 216
Bill for Establishing Religious Freedom
        (1786), 376
Bill of Rights, English (1689), 87–88,
        118, 310
Bill of Rights, U.S., 310
blacks:
    bias against, 322
    presumed inherent inequality of,
        125–26, 211
Blackstone, William, 85, 169
Bonaparte, Napoleon, 318, 325, 335,
        340–41, 365, 387
Boston, 139

Boston, Mass., 42, 44, 75, 77, 81
    Federalist influence in, 345
    leading patriots of, 82–83
    revolutionary dissent in, 82, 90–92, 94
    social profile of, 31, 33
Boston Commercial Gazette, 1
Boston Gazette, 70, 81, 84
Boston Massacre, JA's defense of British
        soldiers in, 82–83
Boston Patriot, 291, 338
Boston Tea Party, 90–92, 227
Botta, Carlo, 390–91
Bowdoin, James, 171
Bowdoin, James, III, 367
Boylston, Nicholas, 33
Boylston family, 24
Braintree, Mass., 24, 42, 44, 52, 74, 77, 79, 97,
        112, 137, 138
Brattle, William, 84–85
Braxton, Carter, 107, 130
breast cancer, 365
Brillon, Monsieur, 150
Brillon de Jouy, Anne-Louise de Harancourt,
        149–50
British Commonwealth, creation of, 93
Browne, Arthur, 29
Burgoyne, John, 141
Burke, Edmund, 231, 257–58
Burr, Aaron, 286, 319, 385
    treason trial of, 343–44
    as vice president, 323–24, 327
Burwell, Rebecca, TJ's courtship of, 53–57
Butler, Joseph, 330
Byrd, William, 122–23

Cabell, Joseph, 414
Callender, James Thomson, 57–58, 61, 305,
        346–48, 352–53
Calvin, John, 40, 71
Calvinism, 40, 376, 381
Camus, Armand-Gaston, 367
canon law, 70–72
Canove, Antonio, 14
capitalism, 406, 409
Carpenters' Hall, 95
Carr, Dabney, 90–91
Casanova, Francesco, 13
Catholic Church, Catholics, 70–71, 89,
        98–99, 375
Charles II, king of England, 110
Charlottesville, Va., POWs in, 141–42
charters, colonial, 89, 102, 168–69
Chastellux, Marquis de, 12, 61, 78
Cherokees, 20

Chesapeake, U.S.S., 344
childhood mortality, 61, 63, 65, 162
Chipman, Nathaniel, 122–23, 330
Church, Angelica Schuyler, 66, 164
Church of England, 72, 81, 87
Cicero, 42–43, 124
citizenship, right of, 109
Civil War, American, 144, 433
Civil War, English, 166, 168
Clarke, Richard, 80
Clinton, George, 266, 286
Clymer, George, 398
Cocke, John Hartwell, 62
Coercive Acts (Intolerable Acts; 1774), 91
Coke, Edward, 46
Coke upon Littleton (Coke), 46
Coles, Edward, 360, 410
Coles, John, 360
Collapse of a Wooden Bridge, The (Casanova), 13
College of William and Mary, TJ's education
    at, 38–39, 44
colonial constitutions, 109–36, 166, 168
Commentaries on the Laws of England
    (Blackstone), 85
*Commentary and Review of Montesquieu's Spirit
    of the Laws* (Destutt de Tracy), 386–87
commerce:
    as alternative to war, 157, 244, 275–76, 334,
        341, 344–45, 422–23
    domestic, 406
    in foreign policy toward England,
        274–77
    international, 156–58, 165, 244
Committee of Five, 120–21
common law, English, 48
Common Sense (Paine), 106, 113, 328, 403
compassionate marriage, 52
Condorcet, Marquis de, 187, 206, 224,
    228, 229
Confederation Congress, 181
    TJ's accomplishments in, 152–53
Congregationalism, 24, 40, 72
Congress, U.S., 37, 247, 265, 267, 275, 300,
    301, 305, 309, 341, 348, 404, 415, 417
    lack of documentation on proceedings
        of, 390
    powers of, 221
    Quasi-War with France sanctioned by, 306–7
    special session of, 295–96
conservatism, JA as representative of, 7
Constitution, U.S. (1787), 85, 342, 398,
    417, 419
    adoption of, 183, 220
    article I, section 10, 249

Bill of Rights of, 310
    drafting of, 167, 202–3, 220–23
    election provisions in, 286
    First Amendment, 353–54
    lack of bill of rights in, 222
    prelude to, 108–20, 167–77
    TJ's and JA's divergent responses to, 221–23,
        292, 298
Constitutional Convention (1787), 196,
    221–23
constitutional rights, development of, 109–14
constitutional theory, 103–36
    evolution of, 167–203
    fundamental vs. statutory law in, 168–71
    safeguards against corruption in, 115–16
    of TJ vs. JA, 194–96
*Constitution of England, The; or, An Account of
    the English Government* (*La Constitution de
    l'Angleterre*; De Lolme), 177–79, 228
consumerism, 238
Convention Army, 141–42
Coolidge, Ellen Randolph Wayles, 18,
    405, 412
Coolidge, Joseph, 18, 405
Cooper, Anthony Ashley, 330
Cooper, Thomas, 414, 422
corn, 22–23, 47
Cornwallis, Lord, 143
correspondence:
    between JA and Abigail, 52–53, 134–36,
        137–38, 150, 159, 248, 279–80, 317
    between TJ and Abigail, 160, 164–65,
        219–20, 223, 351–55, 359, 365–66
    between TJ and JA, 139, 164, 222, 227,
        259–61, 271–72, 288–89, 304, 327–28,
        358, 363, 364–88, 423–24
    between TJ and M. Cosway, 68
    between TJ and Monroe, 146
    TJ's and JA's personal and political
        philosophies expressed in, 373–88
    TJ's international, 365
Cosway, Maria Hadfield, 66–68
Cosway, Richard, 66–68
cotton industry, 412
council (upper house), 117–18
Cranch, Mary Smith, 49–50, 136, 163, 254
Cranch, Richard, 50, 202, 339
Cranch, William, 428
Crawford, William H., 415
criminal justice system:
    in Massachusetts, 132
    in Philadelphia, 350
    TJ's suggested reform of, 129
Cunningham, William, 396–97, 401

Cushing, Caleb, 1–4
Cushing, Charles, 41

Dana, Francis, 197
Davila, Enrico Caterino, 250–54
Deane, Silas, 147
Declaration of Independence, 112,
    174, 208, 213, 220, 277, 380, 429,
    432–33
  debated authorship of, 398–405
  drafting of, 120–22, 398
  fiftieth anniversary (golden jubilee) of, 1,
    420, 426
  JA's input in, 3, 120, 401–2, 404
  last remaining signers of, 398
  painting of the adoption of, 399–400
  preamble to, 400
  sacred character of, 405
  TJ's input in and authorship of, 3, 94, 109,
    120–22, 391, 398–405
Declaration of the Rights of the Colonies, 402
Declaration on the Necessity of Taking Up
    Arms, 105
Declaratory Act (1766), 85, 98
*Defence of the Constitutions of Government of the
    United States of America* (J. Adams), 181,
    186–88, 190–93, 200–203, 206, 215, 221,
    227, 229, 237–38, 250, 284–85, 373,
    421–22
  as influence on French Revolution, 228–29
  TJ's reaction to, 216–18, 222
Defoe, Daniel, 31
Delaware, state constitution of, 168
De Lolme, Jean Louis, 177–79, 190, 228
Démeunier, Jean Nicholas, 153
  encyclopedia of, 218
democracy:
  aristocracy vs., 119–20, 186–98, 380
  British conflict of monarchy and,
    111–14, 178
  defined, 112
  JA's fears of, 132–33, 250
  representative, 2326
Democratic-Republican Party, 264, 325, 411
Democratic-Republican societies, 267
Destutt de Tracy, Antoine, 365–66, 386–87,
    407–8
Dickinson, John, 86–87, 105–6, 325
Discourses on Davila (J. Adams), 250–54,
    256–57, 260, 373
"Dissertation on the Canon and Feudal
    Law, A" (J. Adams), 70–73, 89
DNA, 62
dominion theory of empire, 93

Don Quixote, 12
Duane, James, 96, 107
Duane, William, 305, 387
Dumas, Charles, 156
Dunmore, Lord, 143
du Pont de Nemours, Pierre-Samuel, 107, 224,
    228, 229
Dupuis, Charles François, 368

East India Company, 90
economic sanctions, 345
economy:
  evolving U.S., 405–9
  of Virginia vs. Massachusetts, 19
Edgeworth, Maria, 10
education:
  of JA, 24–25, 27–28, 31, 39–41
  as necessity for republican government,
    115, 174, 182, 206, 213, 293, 330,
    412–14, 430
  New England history of, 71–72
  in North vs. South, 18–19
  public, 129–30, 381
  restricted for slaves, 65
  restricted for women, 51
  of TJ, 38–39
  TJ's disillusionment with, 410, 413–14
  wealth and, 212–13
egalitarianism:
  as basis of reform movements, 127
  constitutional, 173, 174
  debate over, 122–27
  as expressed in Declaration of
    Independence, 122–24, 380, 400
  historical roots of, 122
  JA's evolving and changing views on, 123,
    127, 174, 187, 207–8, 213–14, 219,
    277–78, 320
  JA's faulty prediction on, 320
  moral, 277–78, 330
  in New England, 29–32
  paradoxical problem of, 216–17, 234, 237,
    277–78, 284, 380, 430–31
  popular power and, 100–101
  of republicanism, 274
  TJ's perspective on, 7, 123, 213, 217
  women in, 135–36
elections:
  of 1788, 227–28, 281
  of 1792, 264, 265–66, 281
  of 1796, 281–86
  of 1800, 6, 316–19, 320–25, 344, 355, 360,
    377, 389
  of 1804, 4

of 1824, 415
passive campaign style in, 282, 322–23
elective monarchy, 279
Elk Hill plantation, 60
Embargo Act (1807), 344–46, 423
England:
    American commercial foreign policy toward, 275–76
    America's independence from, 103–36
    commercial treaties with, 156, 276–77, 295
    constitutional theory in, 168–69, 176, 177, 225, 243
    economic theory in, 246
    governmental balance in, 111–14, 117–18, 177, 178, 235
    as hostile to U.S., 165–66
    imperial crisis of, 69–102
    influence of state constitutions on, 183–84
    JA as minister to, 3, 164–66, 252, 262, 375
    peace treaty with, 151, 152, 154–55
    TJ and JA's tour of, 165–66
    TJ's loathing of, 273
    at war with France, 269–70, 277, 297, 300, 339
    see also American Revolution; War of 1812
English constitution, 111–14, 117–18, 168–69, 256
    JA's infatuation with, 185–86, 216, 240–43, 249, 253, 274, 287, 296, 315, 358
    as model for state constitution, 177–79, 183–85, 229, 233
Enlightenment:
    Europe of, 56, 147
    evolving civility of, 35–36
    TJ's and JA's contrasting views of, 9–10
    view of human nature in, 122–27, 213
    view of war in, 275
entail, laws of, 19, 20, 381
Epicureanism, 349
Episcopal Church, 375–76
Eppes, Mary Jefferson "Polly," 63, 64, 152, 281
    death of, 351, 366
Essex Gazette, 402, 403
Essex Junto, 197, 344, 346, 379
Essex Result, 179
Ethiopian Regiment, 143
eulogies, TJ and JA compared and contrasted in, 1–6
Euripides, 55
Europe:
    aristocracy in America vs., 192–93, 218–19
    commercial treaties with, 156–58

failure of republicanism in, 276
France's incursions into other countries in, 295, 306
TJ's admiration for culture of, 14, 142, 145, 149, 150, 161
TJ's changing perspective on, 232, 331
executive:
    debate over remuneration for, 199–200
    limitations on power of, 109–10, 118–19, 142–43, 174–75
    monarchical trappings of, 232–33
    strong and independent, 179, 182, 193, 202, 213, 216, 233, 235, 236, 290, 318, 343
    term of service of, 175, 221–22, 251, 279, 286, 313, 343
    title of, 242

Farmers' Exchange Bank, 249
Fauquier, Francis, 46, 76, 122
Federalist No. 2, 273
Federalist Party, 290
Federalists:
    ascendancy of, 301
    decline of, 318, 325, 389
    division among, 317–18, 320–21
    immigration opposed by, 308
    JA's ambivalence as, 249–50, 267, 273–74, 276, 283, 290, 294, 296, 299, 315–17, 320, 344, 345
    as monarchical, 233, 397–98
    republican ideology vs., 240–78, 320–21, 326
    Republican Party vs., 279–319, 333–36, 400
    tenets of, 249
    TJ criticized by, 284
    see also High Federalists
feme covert, 51
Fenno, John, 250–51, 257, 262, 263
feudal law, 70–73
Findley, William, 208
First Continental Congress (1774), 91–92
    independence vs. reconciliation in, 97–98
    JA's service in, 3, 28, 52, 95–99, 104
    TJ's service in, 3
Flat Hat Society, 39
Fleming, William, 54
Florida, 312
Floyd, Kitty, 63
Four Books of Architecture (Palladio), 11
Fourth of July, 1826, as shared death date for TJ and JA, 1, 4, 426–28
France:
    American sentiment against, 302
    bias against, 309

France *(cont.)*
diplomatic commission sent to, 297, 299–301
Directory in, 301
immigration from, 308–9
incursions into other European countries by, 295, 306
influence of state constitutions on, 183
JA's missions to, 138–39, 147–52, 154–64, 178, 338
JA's reopening of negotiations with, 314–15, 317–18
Quasi-War with, 306–7, 318–19, 342
slavery abolished in, 64, 349
tensions between U.S. and, 292, 294–312, 314, 317–18
TJ as minister to, 164–66, 262
TJ's ambivalence about, 34, 160–61, 301
TJ's attachment to, 261–62, 283, 284, 290, 297, 301, 306
TJ's missions abroad in, 3, 34, 57, 65–66, 156–66, 223–27, 232
treaties of alliance and commerce with, 147, 157
U.S. invasion threat from, 305–9, 311–12, 314, 317–18, 322
at war with England, 269–70, 277, 297, 300, 339
Franco-American Treaty (1778), 318
Franklin, Benjamin, 10, 11, 16, 31–32, 36, 93, 120, 127–28, 148, 150, 152, 154–56, 163, 183, 187, 203, 205, 242, 255, 305, 348, 360, 425
death of, 398
JA's dislike of, 148–49, 151, 155, 338, 402
Freeman, James, 202
Freemasons, 197
French language, 381
French philosophes, 56, 206–7, 262, 306, 365, 373–74, 407
French Revolution, 223–31, 241, 369, 393, 400
American support for, 250, 268, 274, 276, 304, 306
JA's opposition to and fear of, 223, 231, 249–52, 256–57, 268, 272, 274, 277, 290, 298, 358, 373, 382, 423
onset of, 204
prelude to, 223–27
roots of, 250
stifling of, 325
TJ's and JA's divergent views of, 6, 204, 223–24, 256–57, 273, 292, 298–99, 362, 373–74, 423

TJ's optimistic enthusiasm for, 223–27, 256–57, 261–62, 267, 268–70, 273–74, 298–99, 301–2, 306, 340, 369, 373–74, 410, 423
violent outcome of, 268–69, 309, 321, 423
Freneau, Philip, 262–63

Gadsden, Christopher, 98, 395
Gage, Thomas, 91
Gallatin, Albert, 406, 407, 417
Gates, Horatio, 141
Gazette of the United States, 250–51, 257, 262–63
Genet, Edmond "Citizen," 266, 271
gentleman, defined and described, 28–31, 191–92
George III, king of England, 48, 103, 109, 141, 166
assassination attempt on, 223
TJ's direct criticism of, 93–94, 102
Gerry, Elbridge, 155, 177, 200, 206, 291, 297, 300, 307, 321
Giles, William Branch, 278, 281
Godwin, William, 328
Gordon-Reed, Annette, 62
governors:
executive authority of, 173–77, 179, 200
limitations on constitutional role of, 118–19, 174–75
terms of, 175
Gram, John, 368
Gray family, 75
Great Seal, U.S., 127–28
Gridley, Jeremiah, 42, 48
grief, JA on, 386

Hague, The, 156
Haiti, Republic of, 334, 347
"half-breeds," 21–22
Hamilton, Alexander, 66, 93, 164, 188, 234–35, 262–63, 269, 280, 282, 320, 332, 348
in compromise of 1790, 246
economic policy of, 243–49, 270, 278, 290, 314, 335
grandiose ambition and aspiration of, 312–13
JA's cabinet committed to, 291
JA's conflicts with, 253, 283, 287, 314, 316–18, 338
as secretary of the treasury, 243, 245, 248, 263–64, 267, 270
TJ attacked by, 244–46, 263

Hancock, John, 81, 82–83, 227, 393
Haraszti, Zoltán, 201
Harrington, James, 113–14, 177, 201
Harvard, 38, 345, 363
    JA's education at, 24–25, 27–28, 31, 39–41,
        48, 73, 310
Harvie, Gabriella, 63
Hemings, Betty, 59, 63
Hemings, Beverley and Harriet, 65
Hemings, Eston, 65
Hemings, James, 63–65
Hemings, Madison, 8, 64, 65
Hemings, Sally, 162
    children of, 64, 65, 347
    TJ's relationship with, 57–59, 61–65,
        346–48
Hemings family, as racially mixed, 59, 63
Henry, Patrick, 20, 76, 90–91, 131, 141, 145,
    283, 393–94
heredity:
    in monarchy, 251, 255, 267
    rights of succeeding generations in, 230,
        243, 272
Hermione, H.M.S., mutiny on, 315
High Federalists, 314, 318, 346, 369–70, 379
Historia della guerre civili de Francia
    (Davila), 250
History of the Corruption of Christianity
    (Priestley), 378
history writing, challenges of, 390–93
Hollis, Thomas Brand, 74, 185–86
Hooper, William, 113, 180
Horace, 367
Hôtel de Langeac, 64
Houdon, Jean-Antoine, 14, 165
House of Burgesses, Va.:
    dissolved, 91
    TJ elected to, 47, 76–77, 90, 91
House of Commons, 178
House of Delegates, Va., 146
House of Lords:
    House of Commons vs., 178
    senate as parallel to, 117
house of representatives:
    as representative of the common man, 180
    state constitutional powers of, 110,
        175, 176
House of Representatives, Mass., 81, 88–89,
    93, 94–95, 180–81
House of Representatives, U.S., 242, 276,
    315, 336
    election tie of 1800 decided in, 323–24, 327
Howe, Richard, 131
Hudson Valley, TJ and Madison's trip to, 262

human nature:
    desire for distinction in, 238, 250–51
    in egalitarian debate, 122–27, 187
    enlightened, liberal view of, 122–24, 127,
        224, 283–84, 299, 328–32, 387, 409–10,
        419–21, 427, 431–33
    four stages of development of, 233
    moral gyroscope of, 328–31
    nature vs. nurture in, 124, 187, 214
    negative, depraved view of, 122–23, 133,
        203, 205–8, 214–18, 224, 228, 238, 255,
        268, 299, 331–32, 401, 409, 413, 431
    rights of, 94
    TJ's and JA's divergent views of, 6, 9–10,
        204–39, 299, 303, 374, 383–84, 405–25,
        429–33
    transformative quality of, 123–24
    virtue and corruption in, 114–16
Humboldt, Alexander von, 365
Hume, David, 44, 243, 331
Hutcheson, Francis, 330
Hutchinson, Thomas, 75–76, 80–81, 88–90,
    94, 101, 198

immigrants, immigration, 432
    fear and distrust of, 306, 307–11
impeachment, of British judges, 94–95
imperium in imperio (power within a power),
    86, 89, 101
Indians, 103, 369
    Christianizing of, 72
    displacement of, 370
    Fort Stanwix conference with, 57
    hostile, 20
    as inherently equal, 125–26
    patriots disguised as, 90
    TJ's interest in, 11
inequality, paradoxical problem of, 216–17,
    234, 237, 277–78, 284, 380, 430–31
inflation, 249
Inglis, Charles, 169
Institutes of the Lawes of England (Coke), 46
internal improvements, 419
"iron law of oligarchy," 188

Jackson, Andrew, 389, 411, 415
Japanese, interned in U.S., 305
Jay, John, 152, 154, 155, 156, 224–28, 273,
    276–77, 280
Jay's Treaty (1794), 276–77, 295
Jebb, John, 199–200
Jefferson, Jane Randolph, 17, 23–24, 45, 54,
    77, 78
Jefferson, Lucy, 63

Jefferson, Martha Wayles Skelton "Patty":
  death of, 61, 64, 152
  ill health of, 128, 159
  mulatto half siblings of, 63–64
  TJ's marriage to, 58–61, 64, 76, 78, 133, 198
Jefferson, Peter, 17, 23–24, 63
Jefferson, Thomas:
  Abigail's ambivalence toward, 324
  Abigail's friendship with, 159–62, 164–65,
    254, 261
  as American hero, 3–4, 432–33
  as amiable and even tempered, 8, 25, 105,
    130, 153, 159, 160–62, 252, 256, 258,
    298, 353–54, 374, 386, 388, 395–96
  antislavery stance of, 76–77, 93–94, 129–30,
    210–12, 231–32, 350, 410–12, 416, 424
  appearance and personal style of, 8
  aristocratic lifestyle of, 7, 17, 22–24, 33,
    59–60, 76, 77, 104, 150, 163–64, 166,
    198, 210–12, 217, 245, 271, 382, 413
  arts pursued by, 11–14
  as avid reader, 10–11, 14–15, 44–46, 130
  birth of, 23
  broad intellect of, 10–12, 130, 153
  chronic headaches of, 54
  contrasts between JA and, 7–37
  controversy eschewed by, 108
  death of, 1, 4, 63, 397, 427, 428
  debts of, 45, 143–44, 163, 230–31, 267, 271,
    410, 412–13, 420, 422
  eulogies for, 1–6
  evolving disillusionment of, 405–20
  evolving religious thought of, 374–79
  family background and heritage, 23–24
  as Francophile, 261–62
  gentility of, 7, 163–64
  ill health of, 54, 161, 426–28
  intellect of, 78
  intellectual response to British
    oppression, 76
  landholdings of, 60
  legacy of, 4, 5, 390–91, 394, 405, 428–33
  library of, 44–45, 163
  marriage of, 54, 56–61, 76, 78, 133, 198
  M. Cosway and, 67–68
  as meticulous record keeper, 27, 65
  as moral idealist, 9–10
  optimistic idealism of, 7, 140–41, 157–58,
    163, 207, 220, 224, 230, 325, 326,
    328–32, 409–11, 420, 423–24, 427, 431
  personal temperament of, 2, 4–5, 6
  R. Burwell courted by, 53–57, 76
  religion eschewed by, 40, 73, 374, 413
  retirement and later years of, 389–425

  sexual passions of, 57, 61, 348
  social confidence and grace of, 34–36
  social hierarchy defined by, 21–22
  southern upbringing of, 16–20
  as tinkerer and inventor, 11, 15
  will of, 65
  on working and leisure classes, 210–12
  writing desk of, 405
  writings of, 2–3, 104; see also specific works
  writing style of, 96, 101, 366–68
 —CAREER:
  acclaim for, 153, 432–33
  agrarianism of, 244–47
  ambition and aspiration of, 271, 281
  banks and banking eschewed by, 247, 290,
    358, 406–8
  as celebrity, 365
  in compromise of 1790, 246
  constitutionalism of, 108–11, 168–71
  in despairing temporary renunciation of
    public life, 145–47
  as distrustful of the press, 311
  enlightened reformist agenda of, 128–32
  as farmer, 22–23, 47
  final retirement years of, 3, 6, 54
  first retirement of, 270–72, 277, 281, 350
  as governor of Virginia, 119, 140–47
  Hamilton vs., 244–46, 263, 290
  as lawyer, 3, 44–48, 78
  as leader of Republican Party, 264
  in missions abroad, 3, 6, 10, 12, 14, 15, 63,
    65–66, 142, 150, 156–66, 167, 187–88,
    221, 223–27, 232
  in patriot politics, 90–94
  political philosophy of, 3, 6, 108–11,
    230–31, 328–31, 432–33
  political prowess of, 9, 280–81, 291, 318
  in resignation from Washington's
    administration, 270–71
  as secretary of state, 232, 240, 257, 263, 266,
    270–71
  as vice president, 3, 6, 279–319
  in Virginia legislature, 128–32, 139
 —AS PRESIDENT: 3, 6, 85,
    311, 400
  acclaim for, 4
  domestic policies of, 342–43
  election (1800) of, 317, 319, 322, 355, 389
  governmental changes wrought by, 333–36
  inauguration of, 321, 322, 327, 332–33
  JA's criticism of, 338–44
  JA's gradual approval of, 344–45
  JA's opinion of, 396–98
  legacy of, 320, 372

reelection (1804) of, 4
in retirement, 357
Revolution of 1800, 320–44, 389
scandal and, 57–58
second term of, 357
Jefferson-Adams friendship:
affection in, 360–61
as complementary, 105
evolution of, 156–66
JA's denial of, 343
mutual benefits of, 162
onset of, 6, 104–5, 289, 297, 351–52
reconciliation in, 3, 6, 356–88
strained attempts to repair and preserve,
254, 257, 266, 271–72, 287–92, 323,
326–27, 351–52
—RIFT IN, 3, 6, 204, 223, 254
conciliatory attempts in, 254, 257, 266,
271–72, 287–92, 323, 326–27, 351–52
divergent political views in, 251–52, 254,
256–60, 264, 295–303, 305, 327, 351,
359–60, 362
duplicity in, 260–61
in election of 1796, 281–86
escalation of, 256, 257–61, 264–66, 271–74,
295–98, 303, 305, 327, 355
reconciliation of, 356–88
TJ's unsent letter in, 288–89
Jefferson Memorial, 5
Jesus Christ, 385
denial of divinity of, 16, 374–75, 377–78
Jews, bias against, 313
Johnson, William, 4, 390
Journals of Congress, 402
judiciary:
impeachment of, 336, 338
independence of, 84–85, 88, 94–95, 115,
173, 177, 338
as last stronghold of Federalists, 336
threat from, 415–16
Judiciary Act (1801), 323, 336

Kames, Lord, 330
Kant, Immanuel, 330
king-in-Parliament, 85
Knapp, Samuel L., 1–2
Knox, Henry, 227, 232, 260, 312
Knox, William, 87–88, 101
Kosciuszco, Tadeusz, 365
Kukla, Jon, 68

Lafayette, Marquis de, 144, 145, 187,
223, 224, 225, 230, 268, 341, 389
Langdon, John, 289

La Rochefoucauld-Liancourt, Duc de, 62, 183,
187, 206, 224, 268, 401
Latin America, 422
laudanum, 427
Laurens, Henry, 13, 152, 154
Lear, Tobias, 258
Lectures on Rhetoric and Oratory (J. Q. Adams),
363–64
Lee, Arthur, 148
Lee, Charles, 315
Lee, Francis Lightfoot, 90–91, 108
Lee, Henry, 58
Lee, Richard Henry, 90–91, 113
Leonard, Daniel ("Massachusettensis"),
99–101
Lespinasse, Mademoiselle de, 56
Letter from a Gentleman to his Friend
(J. Adams), 113
*Letter from Alexander Hamilton, Concerning the
Public Conduct and Character of John
Adams, Esq., President of the United States*
(Hamilton), 317, 336
Letters from a Farmer in Pennsylvania
(Dickinson), 1–5, 86–87
Lewis, Andrew, 57
Lexington and Concord, Battles of, 102,
103–4, 403
lex talionis (law of retaliation), 129
Liberty, 81
Library of Congress, 45
"Life and Morals of Jesus of Nazareth"
(T. Jefferson), 378
Life of George Washington, The (Marshall),
366–67, 391
Life of Partick Henry (Wirt), 393–94
Lincoln, Abraham, 334, 432–33
Lincoln, Benjamin, 190, 197
Lincoln, Benjamin, Jr. "The Free Republican,"
190–92, 196–97, 209
Lincoln, Mary Otis, 197
Livingston, Edward, 315
Livingston, Philip, 30
Livingston, Robert R., 120, 155, 398
Locke, John, 124, 130, 329, 361, 373,
387, 400
London, England, 63, 66, 67, 74, 165, 255, 277
Louis XVI, king of France, 157, 183, 226–27,
262, 268
execution of, 268, 369
Louis XVIII, king of France, 340
Louisiana, 312
proposed liberation from Spain of, 266
Louisiana Purchase (1803), 4, 344, 355
Lovell, James, 159

Lowndes, Rawlins, 233
Luther, Martin, 73, 99

McHenry, James, 294, 316
McKean, Thomas, 286, 311
Maclay, William, 8, 234
Macpherson, James, 16
Madison, James, 63, 172, 182–83, 227–28,
    230–31, 233, 242, 244, 247, 276, 292–93,
    300, 305, 311, 404, 414
  in compromise of 1790, 246
  constitutional theory of, 220–22
  JA disliked by, 258
  as leader of Republican Party, 264
  presidency of, 357, 401
  TJ's friendship with and dependence on,
    120, 130, 147, 154, 155–56, 159, 165, 258,
    262, 269, 272, 281–82, 285, 287–88, 290,
    313, 357, 419
  as TJ's secretary of state, 322, 326, 342
Maier, Pauline, 93
Manning, William, 208–9, 213
manufacturing:
  agriculture vs., 243–45
  American, 363–64
Marie Antoinette, queen of France, 226–27
marriage:
  of convenience, 66, 67
  traditional, patriarchal, 51–52, 60–61, 63
Marshall, John, 297, 323, 366–67, 385, 416
  TJ's dislike of, 391
Maryland, 108
  state constitution of, 168
  TJ's tour of, 34–35
Mason, George, 108, 110, 124, 256
"Massachusettensis" articles, 99–101
Massachusetts:
  aristocracy of, 188–89, 197–200
  as commonwealth, 114, 173
  in Continental Congress, 95, 97–98
  farmers' rebellion in, see Shays' Rebellion
  founding of, 395
  General Court of, 84, 88
  in initiation of American Revolution,
    393–96
  JA as cautious about reform with, 131–32
  JA as representative of, 3, 16
  JA honored in, 420
  as middle class and egalitarian, 7, 19
  parliamentary oppression of, 91
  slavery abolished in, 19, 348–49
  statistical profile of, 17–18
  Virginia culture compared to, 16–20, 132,
    381, 412

Massachusetts constitution (1780), 85, 117,
    151, 159, 167–82, 185, 189–90, 193, 206,
    233, 338
  Declaration of Rights in, 171–77, 222, 377
Massachusetts Historical Society, 348
Massachusetts Society for Promoting
    Agariculture, 345
maternal mortality, 61, 351
Mayflower, 395
Mayhew, Jonathan, 72, 395
May resolutions, 120–21
  JA's preamble to, 107–8, 402
Mazzei, Philip, 228, 296–97
mechanical arts, 15
Mecklenburg County, N.C., declaration of
    militia of, 402
Mecklenburg resolutions, 402–4
Mediterranean Sea, 341
Michaux, André, 266
middling (middle) class:
  aristocracy vs., 208–10, 214–15
  defined and described, 31–32, 191, 208–10
  JA as member of, 7, 24–25, 30–34, 51,
    188–89, 195, 197–99, 346
  as lacking in the South, 32
"midnight appointments," 323, 334, 336,
    352, 359
military, TJ's minimalization of, 334–35
Milton, John, 44, 46, 55
Mirabeau, Comte de, 218
Miranda, Francisco de, 312
Missouri crisis (1819–1820), 416–20
mixed (balanced) government theory, 117, 176,
    178, 180, 184–86, 235–36, 257
Molasses Act (1733), 87
moldboard plow, 23
monarchy:
  America's inclination toward, 232–35,
    240, 246
  British conflict of democracy and, 111–14,
    178, 190
  colonial voluntary compliance with, 93
  constitutional, 225, 232
  defined, 112
  JA's inclinations toward, 241, 252, 254–57,
    259, 283, 285, 315, 332, 343, 397–98
  proliferation of, 251
  republican, 233, 235–39, 240, 278
  republic vs., 115
  TJ's criticism and rejection of, 9–10, 93–94,
    307, 321, 328–29, 331, 332–33, 344
  trappings of, 240–42, 255, 278, 332
  twin tyrannies of religion and, 70–72, 87–89
Monroe, James, 146, 301, 414

Montesquieu, 114, 178, 244, 373, 386–87
Monticello plantation, 59, 60–65, 143, 147,
    166, 224, 410–12, 420
  building of, 77–78, 139
  farm production of, 22–23
  French decor of, 262
  TJ's first retirement at, 270–72, 277, 281,
    284, 350
  TJ's near capture at, 144
  as World Heritage Site, 5
Moreau de St. Méry, Médéric Louis Elie, 309
Morgan, John, 34
Morris, Gouverneur, 196–97
Morris, Robert, 108
Morse, Jedidiah, 392
Mortefontaine, Treaty of (1800), 318
Muhlenberg, Frederick, 278
mulattos, 59, 62–63
Murray, William, 385
music, TJ's passion for, 46, 58–59
Muslim states, 341

National Assembly, 225–26, 230
National Gazette, 262–63
Native Americans, *see* Indians
naturalization, 307–8, 333, 342
Naturalization Act (1798), 308
Navigation Acts, 86, 98
Navy Department, U.S.:
  establishment of, 307
  importance of, 340, 342, 345
  minimalization of, 335, 340
Nelson, Horatio, 318
Netherlands:
  civil war in, 222
  JA's mission in, 151–52, 154
  J. Q. Adams as minister to, 295
neutrality:
  in commerce, 157, 275
  U.S. policy of, 269–70
New England:
  as enlightened, 132
  prosperity of, 412
  religion in, 377, 381
  settlement of, 71–73
  social hierarchy in, 29–30, 383
New Hampshire, JA's trip to, 39–40
New Jersey, College of, Princeton, 262
New Orleans, Battle of, 389
New Testament, 378
New York, N.Y.:
  as temporary federal capital, 232, 240,
    248, 254
  wealth in, 33

Nicholas, Robert Carter, 124
Nicholas, William Cary, 413
Nile, Battle of the, 318
Niles, Hezekiah, 395, 431–32
Niles' Weekly Register, 395
Norman Conquest, 73, 92
North, Lord, 90
North Carolina, constitution of, 113
Notes on the State of Virginia (T. Jefferson), 21,
    125, 144, 168, 185, 210, 231, 284, 307,
    347, 350, 376
Novanglus papers (J. Adams), 100–101,
    113, 177

Observations on Government (Stevens), 228–30
*Observations on the Importance of the American
    Revolution and the Means of Making it a
    Benefit to the World* (Price), 183
octoroons, as legally white, 65
"Ode to Xanthia Phoceus" (Horace), J. Q.
    Adams's satire of, 347
Oliver, Andrew and Peter, 75, 94
On Crimes and Punishments (Beccaria), 129
Ordinance of 1784, 153
Origine de tours les cultes (Dupuis), 368
Orphan, The; or, The Unhappy Marriage
    (Otway), 55
orrery, Jefferson's fascination with, 11
Ossian, 15
Otis, James, 73, 81, 133, 197, 393, 404
Otway, Thomas, 55
"overseers," 21–22

Page, John, 34, 39, 53–54
Paine, Robert Treat, 26
Paine, Thomas, 94, 106, 113, 206, 226, 256,
    257–58, 260, 261, 271, 287, 293, 328–29,
    331–32, 347, 374, 377, 403
Paley, William, 169–70
Palladio, Andrea, 11, 78
paper money, 172, 247, 248–49, 298, 406–8
Paradise Lost (Milton), 55
Paris, France, 13, 63–64, 67, 147–50, 186–87,
    224, 225, 230, 232, 262
Paris, Treaty of (1783), 144
Parliament, British:
  colonial oppression by, 69–70, 72, 74, 76–77,
    79–80, 84–86, 90, 91, 98
  doctrine of sovereignty of, 85–90, 98, 101–2
  king as member of, 177
Parsons, Theophilus, 175, 179–80
Parton, James, 5
Patriot party (French), 224–26
patronage, 252

Pearl Harbor, attack on, 305
Pemberton, Samuel, 83
Pendleton, Edmund, 110, 124, 130, 140
Penn, John, 113
Penn, William, 405
Pennsylvania, radical state constitution of, 116–17, 173, 176, 184–85
Pentadius, 54–55
Philadelphia, Pa.:
    Continental Congress in, *see* First Continental Congress; Second Continental Congress
    French influence in, 306, 308
    as temporary capital, 248, 274, 289, 294, 304
    violent demonstrations in, 304–5
"Philosophy of Jesus, The" (T. Jefferson), 378
Pickering, Timothy, 120, 294, 309, 316, 369, 404
Pinckney, Charles Cotesworth, 295, 297, 300, 317
Pinckney, Thomas, 265, 283–86, 295
pirates, North African, *see* Barbary pirates
Pitt, William, 85
Plato, 367
Platt, Jeremiah, 33
politeness, 36
political parties:
    in elections, 282
    emergence of, 264–66, 280, 317
    factions of, 267–68, 286, 342–43
    JA's suspicion of, 250, 255, 280–81
    roots of, 263
    TJ's acceptance of, 290
    in today's world, 264–65
political science, JA's devotion to, 16
Poplar Forest plantation, 60
Port Folio (Cooper), 422
press:
    freedom of, 72, 310–11, 354
    JA targeted by, 210
    partisan, 250–51, 257, 262–63, 305, 307, 308–11, 342
    suppression of, 309
    violent attacks on, 304
    see also specific publications
"pretenders," in Virginia, 21–22
Price, Richard, 183
Priestley, Joseph, 274, 325–26, 369, 378, 409, 422
    TJ's letters to, 371–72, 374
primogeniture, 19, 20, 128–29, 381
prisoners of war, 141–42
Proclamation of Neutrality (1793), 269–70
Protestant Reformation, 70, 73, 89

"Publicola" (J. Q. Adams's pseudonym), 258–59
public schools, 18–19, 132
Puritans, Puritanism:
    in JA's sensibilities, 10, 13, 25–26, 56, 99, 149–50
    in settlement of American colonies, 71
Putnam, James, 41

Quasi-War, 306–7, 318–19, 342
Quincy, Hannah, 48–50
Quincy, Josiah, 49, 82–83, 420–21, 424
Quincy, Josiah, Jr., 82–83
Quincy, Mass., 77, 426
    JA's farm in, 248, 337, 360
Quincy, Mrs., 424
Quincy, Ned, 26
Quincy, Samuel, 26, 49, 80
Quincy family, 50–51

Raleigh Register and North Carolina Gazette, 402
Raleigh Tavern, 77, 91
Randall, Henry S., 77, 360
Randolph, Edmund, 145, 147, 263, 268
Randolph, Isham, 38
Randolph, John, 305, 419
Randolph, Martha Jefferson "Patsy," 60, 63, 64, 159, 351, 410
Randolph, Peyton, 104
Randolph, Thomas Jefferson, 23, 36, 420
Randolph, Thomas Mann, 63
Randolph family, 17, 23–24, 32, 38, 77
Recorder, 346
Reflections on the Revolution in France (Burke), 257
Reid, Thomas, 330
Reign of Terror, 309
religion:
    freedom of, 109, 129, 130, 158, 376–77
    in immigration, 308
    in Massachusetts's constitution, 175
    TJ's and JA's divergent views on, 6, 16, 98–99, 374–79, 385
    twin tyrannies of monarchy and, 70–72, 87–89
Report of a Constitution, 173–75
"Report on Commerce" (T. Jefferson), 244
Republic (Plato), 367
republic, defined, 113–14
republic, "monarchial," 233, 235–39, 279
republicanism:
    agrarian, 321
    evolving concept of, 113–20, 130, 160, 185, 389–90

Federalist ideology vs., 240–78, 320–21
informality of, 332–33
JA's skepticism of populace in,
    186, 202, 204–7, 267–68, 277–78,
    284–85
tenets of, 328–32
TJ as champion of, 261–62, 264, 321
TJ's belief in, 182–83, 232, 252
TJ's disillusionment with, 414
Republican Party, 290, 298, 302, 346
emergence of, 264–66
Federalists vs., 279–319, 326, 333–36, 400
immigrant support for, 308
JA criticized by, 284–85
policies of, 274–77
TJ as presidential choice of, 283–84
Revere, Paul, 31
Revolutionary War, 131, 218, 312, 358, 370,
    377, 391
end of, 181
federal assumption of state debts
    of, 245
French support for, 149
profiteering from, 133
TJ's idealism about, 139–44
see also American Revolution
Rex v. Corbet, 75–76
Rice, David, 211
Richmond, Va., 143
Richmond Enquirer, 395, 411
Riedesel, Baron and Baroness de, 142
Rights of Man (Paine), 257–58, 261, 328
Ritchie, Thomas, 395
Rittenhouse, David, 11, 139–40, 366
Roane, Spencer, 419
Robbins, Jonathan (Thomas Nash), extradition
    and execution of, 315–16, 372
Robertson, William, 44
Rodney, Caesar, 96
"Roman principle," 199
Rome, fall of, 73–74
Royal Academy, London, 66
Royal Society, 122
Rush, Benjamin, 37, 52, 127, 173, 238–39, 240,
    392, 400, 401
as agent of TJ and JA's reconciliation,
    6, 289, 356–64
death of, 398
dream of, 357–58
JA's friendship with, 254–55, 338, 343–46,
    356–57
TJ's relationship with, 358
Rush, Richard, 401–2, 424
Rutledge, Edward, 96

Sack of Rome, The (M. O. Warren), 252
sailors:
    impressment of, 75, 81, 315–16,
        344, 372
    seized by Barbary pirates, 341
Saint-Domingue (Haiti):
    immigration from, 308–9
    slave rebellion in, 322, 334
Sale, George, 44
Santo Domingo, 309
Saratoga, Battle of, 141–42
Sarsfield, Count, 187
science, TJ and JA's interest in, 16
Scott, John Morin, 33
Scott, Walter, 10
secession, threat of, 313, 344, 345,
    346, 417
Second Continental Congress (1775), 103–36,
    145, 246
    Board of War of, 131, 137
    JA's pivotal role in, 103–8, 127–28, 131–32,
        135, 137–39, 148, 189, 207
    as substitute for Crown, 103–4
    TJ's role in, 104–11, 120–22, 127–28
Second Great Awakening, 413
sectionalism, 282, 286
Sedition Act (1798), 309, 311, 333, 353
seditious libel, common law of, 310–11
senate:
    as representative of the propertied elite,
        117–18, 180–81, 193–94, 196, 213,
        218, 380
    state constitutional powers of, 110–11,
        175, 176
    strong, 173, 182, 183
    term of service in, 313
Senate, U.S., 336, 344
    vice president as president of, 8, 241, 248,
        276, 290
Sergeant, Jonathan Dickinson, 113
Sewall, Jonathan, 9, 42–43, 80–81, 99,
    148, 310
    as "Philanthrop," 79
Shadwell estate, 17, 23, 77
    fire at, 45, 76, 78
Shakespeare, 166
Shawnees, 20, 369
Shays' Rebellion (1786), 189, 193, 202,
    252, 278
    TJ's and JA's divergent views of,
        219–20
Sherman, Roger, 120, 176, 235–37, 398
Short, William, 68, 269, 397
Skelton, Bathurst, 59

slaveholders, 32, 122
  depravity of, 210–12, 348
  TJ as, 5, 7, 8, 17–18, 22, 23–24, 27, 47,
    59–60, 62–65, 93, 125, 143, 231–32,
    346, 382
slavery:
  abolished in France, 64
  in antiquity, 126
  JA's opposition to, 19–20, 132–33, 348,
    418, 424
  in the North, 17–19, 132, 416
  opposition to, 125, 129–30, 132, 210–12,
    407, 416–18
  paternalism in, 382
  rationale for, 417
  southern economic dependence on, 17–18,
    21, 28, 128, 130–32, 143, 245, 416
  as threat to U.S. unity, 346–51
  TJ's ambivalence about, 5, 76–77, 125–27,
    129–30, 210–12, 231–32, 410–12,
    416, 424
  in westward expansion, 153
slaves:
  breeding of, 27
  in British army, 143–44
  debate over equality of, 124–27
  manumission of, 64–65, 77
  marginalized status of, 22, 124
  moral sense possessed by, 330
  racial mixing of, 59, 62–63
  sexual involvement with, 54, 59, 62, 65,
    347–48
  TJ's freeing of, 64–65
  Virginia's population of, 17
slave trade, 19
  opposition to, 93–94
  proposed abolition of, 109, 349
Small, William, 38, 46
Smith, Abigail Adams "Nabby," 66–67,
  159, 162
  death of, 365–66
Smith, Adam, 250–51
Smith, Melancton, 234–35
Smith, Samuel, 1–3
Smith, William (Abigail's brother), 51
Smith, William (Abigail's father), 49–51
Smith, William Stephens, 66, 201
Society for Propagating the Gospel in Foreign
  Parts, 72
Society of the Cincinnati, 197, 218–19
Socrates and Jesus Compared (Priestley), 378
Sodality, 70
Sons of Liberty, 82
Southey, Robert, 423

sovereignty doctrine, 85–90, 98, 101–2
speech, freedom of, 175
Spirit of the Laws (Montesquieu), 178, 386–87
Sprague, Peleg, 4
Stamp Act (1765), opposition to, 69–70, 72,
  74, 76–77, 79–80, 85, 86, 393
Stamp Act Congress, 86
state constitutions:
  creation of individual, 108–14, 180, 203
  international interest in, 183–84
  legislative abuses of, 172
  as predecessors to federal Constitution,
    167–77
  procedures for amending of, 168, 175
states' rights, federal vs., 221, 415, 417–19
statuary, changing tastes in, 14
Statute of Westminster (1931), 93
Steuben, Baron von, 144
Stevens, John "Farmer of New Jersey," 228–30
Stiles, Ezra, 398
Stuart monarchy, 89
suffrage, right of, 109, 129, 132, 133, 136, 171,
  173, 182
Sullivan, James, 133, 136
Summary View of the Rights of British America, A
  (T. Jefferson), 1–2, 92–93, 101,
  105, 185
sumptuary laws, 115–16
Supreme Court, Mass., 180
Supreme Court, U.S., 336, 353, 391, 416, 419
Swift, Jonathan, 193, 401
"Syllabus of an Estimate on the Merit of the
  Doctrines of Jesus, compared with Those
  of Others" (T. Jefferson), 378

Tappan, Benjamin, 232
taxation:
  colonies' opposition to, 86–87
  see also specific taxes
Taylor, John, 176, 312–13, 367, 421
tea, duty on, 90–91, 227
Tea Act (1773), 90
Tecumseh, 369
Tenskwatawa "Prophet of the Wabash," 369
Theory of Moral Sentiments (A. Smith), 250
Thomson, Charles, 128
Thornton, William, 4–5
Thou, Jacques-Auguste de, 392–93
*Thoughts on Government, Applicable to the
  Present State of the American Colonies*
  (J. Adams), 113, 132, 167, 178
Ticknor, George, 411
Tillotson, John, 40
Tippecanoe, Battle of, 369

titles, JA's preoccupation with, 241–42, 255, 278
tobacco:
  production of, 17, 22, 47, 412
  use of, 40
Tories, 87, 100, 265, 302, 380
"To the Young Men of the City of
  Philadelphia" (J. Adams), 302–3,
  325–26, 371
Toussaint-Louverture, 322
Townshend, Charles, 86
Townshend Acts, opposition to, 77, 86, 90
Treatise on Political Economy, 407–8
Trinity, 374–75
tripartite government, 112–14, 118, 186, 193
  balance achieved by, 217–18
  separation of powers in, 176, 217–18, 243
  states' abuses of, 172
Trowbridge, Edmund, 197
Trumbull, John, 67–68, 318, 399
Tuckahoe plantation, 17
Tudor, William, 96, 242
Tufts, Cotton, 202
Turgot, Anne-Robert-Jacques, 183–84, 186,
  187, 208
Tyler, John, 4

unicameral government, 228–30
Unitarianism, 202, 374–75, 377, 413

Van der Kemp, Francis Adrian, 382,
  420, 422
Vergennes, Comte de, 151, 154–55
Versailles court, protocol of, 148–50
"Verses on the Death of Dr. Swift" (Swift), JA's
  parody of, 401
veto power, of executive, 118, 174–77, 200,
  235–37
Vindication of the Rights of Women
  (Wollstonecraft), 382
Virgil, 55
Virginia:
  as aristocratic and agrarian, 7, 18–19, 20–23,
    91, 122, 124, 128, 130–32
  British invasion of, 143
  constitutional history of, 168–69
  debts of, 144
  decline and desolation in, 411–12, 419
  founding of, 395
  in initiation of American Revolution,
    393–96
  Massachusetts culture compared with,
    16–20, 132, 381, 412
  revolutionary dissent in, 90–94
  social hierarchy of, 20, 28

statistical profile of, 17
  TJ as governor of, 119, 140–47
  TJ as representative of, 3, 16
  TJ's liberal and enlightened reforms for,
    128–32, 137, 139, 231
Virginia, General Court of, 47
Virginia, University of, 404
  TJ's disillusionment with, 410
  TJ's founding of, 62, 405, 413–14
Virginia constitution (1776), 108–11, 124, 146,
  167, 170–71, 173, 176, 185
  TJ's planned reform of, 181–83
virtue:
  aristocracy of, 129
  government based on, 114–15, 174, 205–6,
    331, 342
  modern vs. ancient, 330–31
Visitors of the Professorship of Natural
  History, Harvard, 345
Volney, Comte de, 62, 296, 306, 308

Walker, Elizabeth Moore "Betsy," TJ's
  advances toward, 57–58, 348
Walker, John, 57–58
Walker, Thomas, 57
Walnut Street Prison, 350
War of 1812, 345–46, 370, 379, 423
  as second American Revolution, 389–90
Warren, James, 90, 104, 107, 133, 158,
  203, 252
Warren, Joseph, 83
Warren, Mercy Otis, 107, 115, 252, 338,
  382, 421
Washington, D.C., 426
  burning of, 45
  as new capital, 327
Washington, George, 52, 198, 218, 225, 252,
  348, 392
  acclaim for, 11, 205, 256, 257, 279, 281,
    393–94
  cabinet of, 291, 294
  in charge of Continental Army, 29–30, 139,
    145, 391
  commemorative statues of, 14, 165
  commissioned as commander in chief of all
    the armies, 312, 314
  Farewell Address of, 283
  presidency of, 6, 199–200, 227–28, 232–33,
    240–42, 246, 248, 253, 257, 258, 263–64,
    265–66, 269–70, 274, 276, 279–81, 291,
    322, 334, 342
  as quintessential American hero, 3–4, 37, 391
  in retirement, 279, 282–83, 296, 297,
    312, 317

Waterhouse, Benjamin, 346, 393–95, 423
Wat Tyler (Southey), 423
Wayles, John, 59–60, 62–63, 412
wealth:
    JA awed by, 33–34
    and political power, 212–14
    as provision for election to senate, 180
    in social mobility, 30–31
Webb, Nathan, 73
Webster, Daniel, 1, 106, 428
West:
    expansion into, 20, 406
    proposed scientific expedition to, 266
    slavery issue in, 153, 416–18
whale oil, 165
wheat, 22–23
Whigs, 87–88, 92, 95, 100–101, 172, 265, 380
Whipple, Joseph, 39–40
Whiskey Rebellion (1794), 278
Wibird, Parson, 97
Willard, Emma, 382
Williamsburg, Va., 39, 44, 47, 76, 77,
    91–92, 143
Willing, Thomas, 247
Willis Creek plantation, 60
Wilson, James, 93, 279
Wilson, Woodrow, 333
Wirt, William, 20, 393–94
    TJ and JA eulogized by, 2, 3
Wolcott, Oliver, 294

Wolcott, Oliver, Jr., 283
Wollstonecraft, Mary, 382
women:
    Abigail's progressive view of, 134–36,
        159–60
    American vs. European, 56, 149
    educational restrictions on, 51, 64, 135,
        381–82
    French, 148–50, 161, 383
    Indian, 125
    TJ's and JA's divergent views on,
        381–83
    TJ's relationships with, 53–68
    in traditional, patriarchal marriage, 51–52,
        60–61, 135
    voting restrictions on, 129, 133–34,
        136, 382
work:
    denigration of, 28
    social class defined by, 31–32, 208–12
writs of assistance, 383
Wythe, George, 44, 46–47, 109, 113

XYZ Affair, 299–302

"yeomanry," 21–22, 30, 32, 244
Yorktown, Battle of, 145
Young, Thomas, 374

Zenger, John Peter, trial of, 311

ALSO AVAILABLE

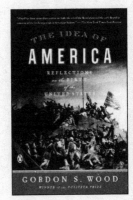 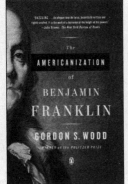 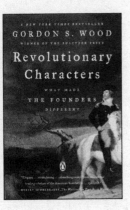

**THE AMERICANIZATION OF
BENJAMIN FRANKLIN**

THE IDEA OF AMERICA
Reflections on the Birth of the United States

THE PURPOSE OF THE PAST
Reflections on the Uses of History

REVOLUTIONARY CHARACTERS
What Made the Founders Different